Strategic Customer Management

Relationship marketing and customer relationship management (CRM) can be jointly utilised to provide a clear roadmap to excellence in customer management; this is the first textbook to demonstrate how this can be done. Written by two acclaimed experts in the field, the book shows how a holistic approach to managing relationships with customers and other key stakeholders leads to increased shareholder value. Taking a practical, step-by-step approach, the authors explain the principles of relationship marketing, apply them to the development of a CRM strategy and discuss key implementation issues. The book's up-to-date coverage includes the latest developments in digital marketing and the use of social media. Topical examples and case studies from around the world connect theory with best global practice, making this an ideal text for both students and practitioners keen to keep abreast of changes in this fast-moving field.

Dr Adrian Payne is a Professor of Marketing in the Australian School of Business at the University of New South Wales.

Dr Pennie Frow is Associate Professor of Marketing and Director of the Master of Marketing Programme at the University of Sydney Business School, Australia.

Visit the Companion Website at www.cambridge.org/payneandfrow to find valuable learning materials, including:

For lecturers

- Instructor's Manual, including recommended Harvard Business School case studies
- Full set of PowerPoint slides that can be adapted for your course
- A bank of multiple choice questions to test student learning

For Students

- Links to useful sites on the web
- Sample chapter

'Adrian Payne and Pennie Frow have written the best guide to understanding customer relationship management strategy. They have provided an excellent framework and illustrate it with a rich set of cases that both students and managers would profit from reading.'

Philip Kotler, S. C. Johnson & Son Distinguished Professor of International Marketing, Kellogg School of Management, Northwestern University

'Relationship Marketing and CRM have until now been treated as two separate processes, even though all the evidence points to the fact that most CRM systems fail because of a lack of understanding of customer needs. Adrian Payne and Pennie Frow have brought the two domains together under a title which makes sense – *Strategic Customer Management* – which from the very beginning should have been the whole purpose of CRM.'

Malcolm McDonald, Emeritus Professor, Cranfield School of Management, Cranfield University, and Chairman, Brand Finance PLC

'*Strategic Customer Management* is the most comprehensive treatise on Customer Centric Marketing. It provides insightful understanding of how to create value for customers and also for the company. I congratulate Adrian Payne and Pennie Frow for an outstanding contribution to both marketing discipline and practice.'

Jagdish N. Sheth, Charles H. Kellstadt Chair of Marketing, Goizueta Business School, Emory University

'This book is a comprehensive guide to building shareholder value through long-lasting relationships with all kinds of customers.'

James Heskett, Baker Foundation Professor Emeritus, Harvard Business School, and author of *The Culture Cycle*

'*Strategic Customer Management* takes a thorough, relational approach to the customer. By integrating relationship marketing with CRM and adding a service perspective on business, it goes far beyond conventional marketing books. It provides a comprehensive approach to how a firm can understand and manage customers in the contemporary competitive environment, where traditional marketing models are increasingly less effective.'

Christian Grönroos, Professor of Service and Relationship Marketing, Hanken School of Economics, Finland

'As Peter Drucker says, "There is only one definition of business purpose: to create a customer." If you agree with Drucker, and desire a competitive advantage, consider the strategic fundamentals and execution techniques outlined in *Strategic Customer Management: Integrating Relationship Marketing and CRM*'.

Jim Guyette, President and CEO Rolls-Royce, North America

Strategic Customer Management

Integrating Relationship Marketing and CRM

Adrian Payne

Pennie Frow

CAMBRIDGE
UNIVERSITY PRESS

CAMBRIDGE UNIVERSITY PRESS
Cambridge, New York, Melbourne, Madrid, Cape Town,
Singapore, São Paulo, Delhi, Mexico City

Cambridge University Press
The Edinburgh Building, Cambridge CB2 8RU, UK

Published in the United States of America by Cambridge University Press, New York

www.cambridge.org
Information on this title: www.cambridge.org/9781107649224

First published 2013

Printed and bound in the United Kingdom by the MPG Books Group

A catalogue record for this publication is available from the British Library

Library of Congress Cataloging-in-Publication Data
Payne, Adrian.
Strategic customer management : integrating relationship marketing and CRM /
Adrian Payne, Pennie Frow.
    pages   cm
Includes bibliographical references and index.
ISBN 978-1-107-01496-1 – ISBN 978-1-107-64922-4 (pbk.)
1. Customer relations – Management.   I. Frow, Pennie.   II. Title.
HF5415.5.P395   2013
658.8′12–dc23

2012036778

ISBN 978-1-107-01496-1 Hardback
ISBN 978-1-107-64922-4 Paperback

Additional resources for this publication at www.cambridge.org/payneandfrow

To Christopher

CONTENTS

FIGURES

ACKNOWLEDGEMENTS

The development and publication of this book would not have been possible without the help of many people. We wish to acknowledge the assistance and support of not only the organisations and people listed below, but also the numerous executives who have generously given up their time to share issues relating to relationship marketing and CRM implementation in their businesses.

In particular, we wish to thank the following organisations for their support: Accenture, BT, BroadVision, Detica, IBM, Royal Mail, Oracle, Pegasystems Inc., SAS, Salesforce.com, Teradata, TNT, Nationwide Building Society, Vectia Ltd. and Unisys.

Our very special thanks is due to David Fagan, who commented on many aspects of the book. Also many thanks to Bob Barker and Alistair Sim, who made special contributions to Chapter 9, to Heather Albrecht for her insights on digital marketing and Sue Almeida for her contribution to Chapter 5. Also, to Andrew Dickson and Jon Chidley, who helped with the development of the CRM audit in Chapter 11. We also wish to thank Kaj Storbacka of the University of Auckland and his colleagues at Vectia Ltd. (now Talent Vectia), who generously shared their insights and contributed towards some of the concepts developed in this book.

Many researchers and scholars at other institutions and practitioners have contributed to our thinking in this area. In particular, we would like to thank Martin Christopher at Cranfield School of Management, David Ballantyne at Otago University, Christian Grönroos at Hanken School of Economics, Finland, Don Shultz at Northwestern University, Evert Gummesson at Stockholm University School of Business, Jagdish Sheth at Emory University and Flemming Poulfelt at Copenhagen Business School. Also, thanks are due to Clive Humby, Don Peppers, Martha Rogers and Ron Swift – pioneers who have made great advances in the areas of relationship marketing and CRM.

Special thanks are due to Simon Knox, Lynette Ryals and Hugh Wilson of Cranfield, Reg Price of MirrorWave and Pat LaPointe of MarketingNPV for contributing case studies. All the case studies in this book remain the copyright of the authors and are used here with their permission. Anyone who wishes to use the cases should contact the authors for permission to reproduce case material. Anyone who wishes to use extracts from the text should contact the publisher for permission.

We also wish to recognise the work of our colleagues involved in relationship marketing and CRM at Cranfield University. Our journey in this area started with a rewarding and ongoing collaboration over more than two decades ago with Martin Christopher and David Ballantyne. We acknowledge the contribution of present and former colleagues at Cranfield including: Moira Clark, Hugh Davidson, Simon Knox, Malcolm McDonald, Stan

Maklan, Roger Palmer, Helen Peck, Joe Peppard, Lynette Ryals and Hugh Wilson. Parts of our co-authored works are drawn on within this book. We are also grateful for the support of our colleagues and students at the University of New South Wales and The University of Sydney. Finally, we thank Paula Parish and her colleagues at Cambridge University Press for their great support and enthusiasm.

Part I

Introduction

1 Strategic customer management

The strategic management of customer relationships is a critical activity for all enterprises. The means of effectively managing relationships with customers are typically addressed under the headings of relationship marketing and customer relationship management (CRM), to name but two terms used to describe the management of customer relationships. Resources applied to such relationship management initiatives are substantial and growing. For example, global expenditure just on CRM activity has been estimated to exceed US $100 billion when CRM-related implementation services are considered.

Since the early 1980s, relationship marketing has become the topic of great interest to both marketing scholars and marketing practitioners. In the increasingly mature and complex markets of the twenty-first century, organisations have learned that building relationships and sustaining them is usually more important than activities focusing on customer acquisition. Much of the recent interest in relationship marketing has evolved from the work undertaken in industrial marketing and services marketing in this period, although antecedents of relationship marketing can be traced back to ancient times. The importance of the topic of relationships in marketing is now undisputed.

In the early 2000s, in conjunction with the rapid rise in the use of information technology by enterprises, CRM made a high-profile entry into the corporate world as businesses saw the potential of implementing relationship marketing strategies through IT. Companies started to recognise how CRM could provide enhanced opportunities to use data and information to better understand customers and to implement relationship-based strategies. CRM built on the philosophy of relationship marketing with the objective of utilising information technology to develop a closer fit between the needs and characteristics of customers and the organisation's product and service offering.

In this chapter, we outline the development of the marketing discipline to place the concepts of relationship marketing and CRM in context. We explain the transition from transaction marketing to relationship marketing. We define both relationship marketing and CRM and explain the similarities and differences between them. Finally, we provide an overview of the structure of the book.

The domain of strategic customer management

Over the past three decades relationship marketing, CRM and other approaches for systematically managing relationships such as one-to-one marketing have developed significantly. However, there is considerable confusion in the academic and managerial literatures about how they differ and what the implications might be of using each approach for effective customer management. The terms relationship marketing and CRM have been used interchangeably[1] despite the fact that many, including us, agree with Zablah, Bellenger and Johnston,[2] who argue that relationship marketing and CRM are different phenomena and a clear distinction should be made between them.

In a recent review of the conceptual differences between the terms *CRM* and *relationship marketing* and *customer management* we define these terms and highlight key differences between them, as shown in Figure 1.1.[3] These brief definitions, developed from the academic literature and field-based research with executives, help clarify the distinction between these terms. In Chapters 2 and 6 we explore the implications of these definitions further.

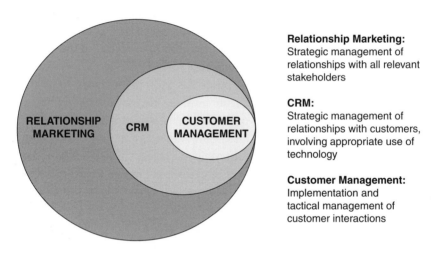

Relationship Marketing:
Strategic management of relationships with all relevant stakeholders

CRM:
Strategic management of relationships with customers, involving appropriate use of technology

Customer Management:
Implementation and tactical management of customer interactions

Figure 1.1 The domain of strategic customer management

Relationship marketing involves the strategic management of relationships with multiple stakeholders. This is a view increasingly supported within the relationship marketing literature (e.g., Christopher, Payne and Ballantyne;[4] Doyle[5] and Gummesson[6]).

Srivastava, Shervani and Fahey define CRM as an activity that addresses all aspects of identifying customers, developing customer insight and building customer relationships.[7] Boulding and his colleagues develop a similar definition emphasising the integration of processes across the many areas of the firm.[8] Thus, *CRM involves the strategic management of relationships utilising, where appropriate, technological tools.*

We also introduce a third term, *customer management, which represents that part of CRM which involves the more tactical management of customer interactions and transactions.*

These three activities *relationship marketing, CRM* and the more tactical activity of *customer management* collectively represent the domain of *strategic customer management.* We consider that the lack of clear definitions and understanding of these different, but closely related, activities has negatively impacted the successful implementation of relationship marketing and its more technological cousin CRM. In the following chapters we elaborate on these short descriptions in much more detail. As the title of this book suggests, we focus primarily on strategic aspects that relate to relationship marketing and CRM and we do not address the tactical management of customer transactions (i.e., 'customer management') in detail.

To set the development of relationship marketing and CRM in context, we now review the development of the marketing discipline.

The development of the discipline of marketing

Although marketing has its origins in the earliest forms of commerce, the widespread acceptance of the marketing concept by enterprises is relatively recent. The modern adoption of the marketing concept can be traced to the substantial period of growth following the Second World War. The adoption of marketing was especially prevalent in large US companies over this period. Little marketing literature was published prior to the 1950s.

Since the 1950s the formal study of marketing has focused on an evolving range of marketing sectors and foci, as shown in Figure 1.2. The emergence and development of these sectors do not coincide exactly with the decades show in Figure 1.2. However, these decades broadly represent the starting point of substantive research and the appearance of academic and practitioner publications relating to these sectors.

In the 1950s marketing interest was primarily focused on consumer goods, following the rise in consumer demand at the conclusion of the Second World War. The emerging consumer goods companies quickly became recognised as sophisticated marketers and were the first companies to develop formal marketing plans. Most of the academic literature on marketing around this period focused on consumer goods businesses and especially fast moving consumer goods.

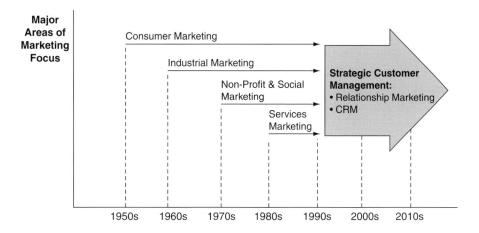

Figure 1.2 The development of the marketing discipline

In the 1960s increased attention started to be directed towards industrial markets. Books and articles on industrial marketing started to appear and make distinctions between consumer marketing and industrial marketing. Specialised marketing textbooks and journals addressing industrial markets started to appear. Much of this work focused especially on selling to business customers and later led to substantive work in the area of key account management.

In the 1970s considerable academic effort was placed on the area of non-profit or societal marketing. This required marketers operating in the not-for-profit sector to revise their thinking as such organisations did not have commercial enterprises' motive of profit. Further, they typically had more than one 'market' to serve. For example, a museum or charity had to undertake marketing activities directed at the attraction of funds from donors as well as undertaking marketing activities directed at customers.

In the 1980s attention started to be directed at the services sector, an area of marketing that had received remarkably little consideration despite its importance to the overall economy of most developed countries at that point in time. Since then, in North America and Western Europe in particular, there has been a steady and unrelenting decline in traditional manufacturing industries. Their place has been taken by numerous service-based enterprises that have been quick to spot the opportunities created by organisational needs, increased personal affluence and raised lifestyle expectations of the population.

By the 1990s a new marketing area, relationship marketing, became the subject of much attention. Relationship marketing, as a term, appears first to have been introduced in the academic literature in 1983 at an American Marketing Association conference by Leonard Berry. He described relationship marketing as 'attracting, maintaining and . . . embracing customer relationships'.[9] Shortly afterwards, two further articles addressing customer relationships were published by Theodore Levitt[10] and Barbara Bund Jackson.[11] These articles were influential in emphasising the need to understand different types of relationships and the extent to which relationship or transaction-oriented approaches are appropriate. However, it was not until the 1990s that the first book on relationship marketing appeared, published by one of the current authors and his colleagues.[12] From this period, a substantive flow of academic and practitioner articles started to appear.

In the early 2000s the term CRM or customer relationship management emerged. We use the term 'emerged', as a review of the literature on CRM does not disclose where the term was first used in a publication. CRM is increasingly found at the top of corporate agendas today. Companies large and small across a variety of sectors are embracing CRM as a major element of corporate strategy for two important reasons: new technologies now enable companies to target chosen market segments, micro-segments or individual customers more precisely, and new marketing thinking has recognised the limitations of traditional marketing and the potential of more customer-focused, process-based strategies. CRM is a business approach that seeks to create, develop and enhance relationships with carefully targeted customers in order to improve customer value and corporate profitability and thereby maximise shareholder value. CRM is often associated with utilising information technology to implement relationship marketing strategies. As such, CRM unites the potential of new technologies and new marketing thinking to deliver profitable, long-term relationships.

From the mid-2000s we have seen the rise of a new relationship-focused phenomenon – social media. Social media is a dynamic phenomenon. The rapid acceptance of social media platforms such as Facebook and Twitter – which are largely consumer-oriented platforms – and LinkedIn – which is primarily a business-oriented platform – is unparalleled in the history of marketing. Social media has important implications for strategic customer management which we consider at various points throughout this book. It is also a highly turbulent sector as characterised by the rise and fall of Myspace, which is discussed in a case study at the end of Chapter 2.

Social media has already had an important impact on relationship marketing and CRM and this will increase substantially in the next decade. However, social media, in our view, does not represent one of the major areas of marketing focus illustrated in Figure 1.2. Rather its use has significant implications for the development of relationship marketing strategies and the implementation of CRM initiatives. Collectively, relationship marketing and CRM – together with the appropriate use of social influence marketing strategies – constitute the area of strategic customer management.

The growth of the service economy

The rise of the service sector has had an important and continuing influence on both relationship marketing and CRM. As noted above, there has been a steady decline in traditional manufacturing industries over a long period. This transition is such that today more than 70 per cent of most Western economies are now in the service sector, whether measured in terms of income or numbers employed. Figure 1.3 shows estimates of the size of the service sector as a percentage of gross national product (GNP) for different countries. These statistics, published by the US Central Intelligence Agency,[13] show the dramatic transformation of the global service landscape. Hong Kong leads the world with 92 per cent of its economy in the service sector. China's economy a few decades ago was principally an agricultural economy. The service sector in China has grown by 191 per cent over the last 25 years. Today, services represent over 44 per cent of China's GNP.

Some observers refer to this shift to a services economy as the 'second industrial revolution'. As individuals spend greater proportions of their income on services including travel, entertainment and leisure, postal and communication services, restaurants, personal health and grooming and the like, the service sector responds by creating businesses and jobs. This growth in services has obvious and important implications for relationship marketing where customer relationships and service employees are especially critical.

Further, the distinction between services and manufactured products has become increasingly blurred as many manufacturing companies have seen the opportunity to

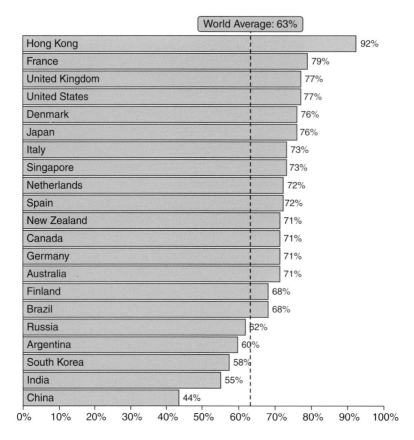

Figure 1.3 Size of the service sector as percentage of GNP for different countries

add services to their portfolios.[14] Many manufacturing organisations now have substantial service businesses with companies such as Rolls-Royce and IBM standing out as two exemplar organisations that have embraced services. Both these organisations have achieved huge growth in the services component of their businesses.

Rolls-Royce, the jet engine manufacturer, introduced their 'power by the hour' initiative which provides airline operators with a service which involves a fixed engine maintenance cost over an extended period of time. Rolls-Royce retains ownership of the engines and airline operators are assured of an accurate cost projection by buying 'power by the hour' with guaranteed performance standards. They also avoid the costs associated with unexpected engine breakdowns. Service revenue accounts for over 53 per cent of Rolls-Royce's annual revenues and it is now the world's second largest manufacturer of aircraft engines, behind General Electric.

IBM, a company once primarily involved in manufacturing large mainframe computers and later personal computers has significantly increased the share of its business derived from services. IBM has shifted its focus from commoditised hardware to higher-margin services and software. This is being achieved by both organic growth and purchase of service businesses like the consulting division of PricewaterhouseCoopers. IBM's Global Services organisation is the world's largest business and technology services provider. It is the fastest growing part of IBM, with over 190,000 workers serving customers in more than 160 countries.

Theodore Levitt, who was recognised as one of the world's leading marketing experts, commented that 'everybody is in service'. He pointed out that all industries are in services, although some have a greater or lesser service component than other industries.[15] Services scholar Evert Gummesson makes a similar point when he points out that: 'The former special case of the service sector has now become the universal case.'[16] It follows that to consider service as being confined only to service industries is no longer appropriate.

The service-dominant logic of marketing

Peter Drucker, the management guru, once said that the greatest danger in times of turbulence is not the turbulence; it is to act with yesterday's logic. Since the 1980s, the dominant logic of marketing has been increasingly challenged by newer perspectives including relationship marketing, quality management, market orientation, services marketing and brand relationships. These more recent frames of reference have challenged marketing and identified limitations in the traditional 'goods-dominant logic' of marketing. A common theme in this work is that the dominant logic of marketing is shifting from the exchange of tangible goods to the exchange of intangibles such as skills, knowledge and processes.

This view has been increasingly recognised since the publication of Stephen Vargo and Robert Lusch's award-winning research on service-dominant (S-D) logic.[17] This research provides a new perspective on service. Vargo and Lusch argue that services are more prevalent than goods and that goods need to be considered as a 'medium' for a firm's service. They consider all enterprises are in the business of providing service. Service-dominant logic makes an important distinction between 'service' (singular) and 'services' (plural). In the service-dominant logic literature, 'service' involves a process, while the plural term 'services' indicates intangible units of output.

Enterprises that produce goods only, such as an automobile manufacturer, are in fact creating a service for their customers – in this case a 'service' that enables customers to go from 'point A' to 'point B'. Many of the issues addressed by Vargo and Lusch have appeared previously within the services and relationship marketing literatures. However, what they present in their research is an important integration of many of the concepts and principles relevant to relationship marketing. They identify ten foundational premises, shown in Figure 1.4.[18]

These foundational premises are not a set of 'rules'; instead they represent a developing and collaborative effort to create a better marketing-grounded understanding of value and exchange. Central to this work is the recognition of the need for a shift from a firm perspective to a customer perspective. S-D logic emphasises that companies need to

Foundational Premise	Explanation & Comment
FP1 Service is the fundamental basis of exchange.	The application of operant resources (knowledge and skills), 'service', as defined in S-D logic, is the basis for all exchange. Service is exchanged for service.
FP2 Indirect exchange masks the fundamental basis of exchange.	Because service is provided through complex combinations of goods, money, and institutions, the service basis of exchange is not always apparent.
FP3 Goods are a distribution mechanism for service provision.	Goods (both durable and non-durable) derive their value through use – the service they provide.
FP4 Operant resources are the fundamental source of competitive advantage.	The comparative ability to cause desired change drives competition.
FP5 All economies are service economies.	Service (singular) is only now becoming more apparent with increased specialisation and outsourcing.
FP6 The customer is always a co-creator of value.	Implies value creation is interactional.
FP7 The enterprise cannot deliver value, but only offer value propositions.	Enterprises can offer their applied resources for value creation and collaboratively (interactively) create value following acceptance of value propositions, but cannot create and/or deliver value independently.
FP8 A service-centred view is inherently customer oriented and relational	Because service is defined in terms of customer-determined benefit and co-created it is inherently customer oriented and relational.
FP9 All social and economic actors are resource integrators.	Implies the context of value creation is networks of networks (resource integrators).
FP10 Value is always uniquely and phenomenologically determined by the beneficiary	Value is idiosyncratic, experiential, contextual, and meaning laden.

Figure 1.4 Service-dominant logic – key foundational premises

become continuous learning organisations working more closely with their customers and that communication with customers should be characterised by conversation and dialogue. By adopting this perspective the customer shifts from being a passive audience to an active player who is engaged more deeply in joint value creation. This idea of marketing as a facilitator and structurer of mutual creation of value with customers is gaining increased credence.

From a goods-dominant logic perspective, enterprises produce products and customers buy them.

With a service-dominant logic, customers engage in dialogue and interaction with their suppliers during product design, production, delivery and consumption. The terms co-creation or co-production are increasingly used to describe this dialogue and interaction. Service-dominant logic suggests that value starts with the supplier understanding customer value-creating processes and learning how it can support customers to co-create value.

The foundational premises of service-dominant logic have important implications for relationship marketing and CRM. In the next section we discuss the transition from transaction marketing to relationship marketing that is captured within several of these foundational premises. Later in the book we return to examine some implications of other foundational premises relating to value, co-creation and value propositions.

From transaction marketing to relationship marketing

The development of interest in relationship marketing some two decades ago was not so much the discovery but a rediscovery of an approach which has long formed the cornerstone of many successful businesses. This approach emphasises the development and enhancement of relationships over the entire customer life-cycle rather than focusing on new customer acquisition. As industries have matured, there have been changes in market demand and competitive intensity that have resulted in a shift from transaction marketing to relationship marketing. Over the past half century the way we think about marketing and the way that it is practised have altered substantially. Marketing thinking has progressed from a functionally based 'make and sell' philosophy to cross-functional orientation in which the capabilities of the enterprise focus around creating and delivering customer value to target market segments. To place relationship marketing in context, we now trace the development of the concept of the marketing mix and the transition from transaction-based marketing to current relationship-based marketing.

The 1950s represents the starting point of modern marketing. Textbooks of substance started to appear during this period and by the mid-1950s Borden published the first exposition of the concept of the marketing mix. His list consisted of 12 elements, including *product plan, price, branding, channels of distribution, personal selling, advertising, promotions, packaging, display, fact-finding and analysis, servicing,* and *physical handling.*[19] These elements represented ingredients or variables which the market could use to 'mix' into an integrated marketing plan or marketing programme.

In 1960 McCarthy developed the best-known representation of the marketing mix consisting of the '4Ps' model of marketing.[20] He simplified Borden's original list of 12 elements into just four elements:

- *Product* – the product or service being offered
- *Price* – the price charged and terms associated with its sale
- *Promotion* – the communications programme associated with marketing the product or service
- *Place* – the distribution and logistics function involved in making a firm's products and services available.

The shorthand of the '4Ps' of product, price, promotion and place was used to describe the levers that, if pulled appropriately, would lead to increased demand for the company's offer. The objective of this 'transactional' approach to marketing was to develop strategies that would optimise expenditure on the marketing mix in order to maximise sales.

Over time, the marketing mix concept gained considerable acceptance and the '4Ps' were considered to capture the key elements of marketing. However, it has been argued by some that simplifying the original list has resulted in a seductive sense of simplicity which may lead to neglect of some key relevant elements. As a result, many authors have added to the basic '4Ps' framework. Lists of additional marketing mix elements have been added which extend the '4Ps' framework to five, seven and even 11 key elements which should be considered in the marketing mix. Several authors have argued that a different marketing mix is needed for services, while others have suggested different elements for specific sectors such as professional services.

However, before considering the marketing mix and criticisms of it further, it is important to recognise that the marketing mix must not be seen in isolation. Some academics adopt a very myopic view of the marketing mix by discussing it in isolation to relationship marketing and strategic marketing perspectives.

A marketing programme not only involves the marketing mix but it also needs to consider the external market forces and is concerned with a matching process that ensures alignment of the marketing mix with these market forces. Thus the marketing process comprises three elements:

- *The marketing mix* – the important internal elements or ingredients that make up an organisation's marketing programme
- *Market forces* – external opportunities or threats in the markets in which an organisation engages
- *A matching process* – the strategic and managerial process of ensuring that the marketing mix and internal policies are appropriate to the market forces.

The market forces comprise a number of areas which need to be considered, including:

- *The customer* – buying behaviour in terms of motivation to purchase, buying habits, environment, size of market and buying power of customer segments. This includes a consideration not just of direct customers but also, where appropriate, customers' customers.
- *The industry setting* – the motivations, structure, practice and attitudes of industry participants including, retailers, intermediaries and any other members of the supply chain.
- *Competitors* – a company's position and its activities are influenced by the structure of the industry and the nature of direct and indirect competition.
- *Other key stakeholders* – there are a wide range of external stakeholders which may have an impact on an enterprise and its customers. These include the media, government and regulatory bodies and other influencers that can impact marketing activities and competitive practices. These key stakeholders are addressed in detail in Chapter 4.

The task of executives charged with developing a marketing programme is to assemble the elements of a marketing mix to ensure the best match between the internal capabilities of the enterprise and the external market environment. A key issue in the marketing programme is the recognition that the elements of the marketing mix are largely controllable by managers within the organisation, and that the market forces in the external environment are, to a large extent, uncontrollable. The success of a marketing programme depends primarily on the degree of match between the external environment and the organisation's internal capabilities and resources.

The marketing programme can thus be characterised as a matching process, and this is especially important in a relationship context. The extent to which different enterprises develop a good match or a poor match between the external market forces and their marketing mix varies greatly. This is shown in Figure 1.5. A key issue to recognise is that these external market forces are not stable. The forces can alter quickly and dramatically, as shown by the impact of deregulation, increased regulation and the emergence of new forms of competition. The escalating consumer interest in sustainability, the rise of social media, the global financial crisis, continuing wars and global conflict, and competition from unexpected sources are just some of the issues confronting organisations today. Changes in these forces create both marketing opportunities and marketing threats. Thus marketing executives need to monitor the external environment constantly and be prepared to adjust their marketing mix to create a better match with market opportunities.

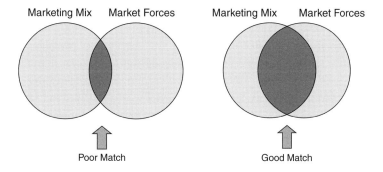

Figure 1.5 Marketing as a matching process

However, viewing the marketing mix in isolation from marketing strategy is not the only issue related to the conventional marketing mix. The marketing mix concept has been challenged by a number of academics. Amongst the criticisms, observers argue that the marketing mix: is too internally focused on what the business wants; it is more suited to fast moving consumer goods than industrial products and services; it is too functionally oriented; it does not consider repeat purchase and relationship building; it fails to take into account the mechanisms of word-of-mouth advocacy and referral marketing; and it is not sufficiently strategically oriented.

Our principal criticism is that in addition to being viewed in isolation to the marketing strategy, the marketing mix elements are heavily focused on customer acquisition and are thus not relationally oriented. The '4Ps' model oversimplifies the more complex process of winning and keeping customers. Further marketing mix elements need to be added to address issues of *keeping and growing customers*. In Figure 1.6 we identify three further marketing mix elements – people, processes and customer service – which are primarily concerned with customer retention rather than acquisition. This has similarities to a

Figure 1.6 Relationship marketing strategy

marketing mix for services developed by Booms and Bitner[21] except we highlight the criticality of customer service to a relationship marketing mix and argue that the physical evidence dimension discussed by these authors is more appropriately viewed as a sub-element of the product element of the marketing mix.

All these elements are essential in building a relationship marketing strategy. It should be emphasised that the traditional elements of product, price promotion and place are not solely concerned with 'customer winning'. Nor are the elements of people, processes and customer service only concerned with 'customer keeping'. However, it is clear that the traditional marketing mix elements are mainly concerned with 'making the offer'.

During our professional careers we have come across many businesses that execute the '4Ps' of the marketing mix very well, yet fall down in the areas of processes, people and customer service. This is especially evident in service businesses such as restaurants or the hospitality sector where a product may be excellent, the location convenient and the pricing reasonable, yet the businesses fail in terms of broken back-office processes, poor customer service and disinterested or rude staff. This is also evident in product markets. Research shows that customers purchasing a car would prefer to have a problem car with good service, than a good car and problems with service. Customers know that a car dealership with good service will pull out all the stops to ensure the problems with the car are rectified. The more enlightened car distributors recognise the relationship value of retained customers over a lifetime. If the average customer purchases a car every four years, they are likely to buy around ten cars or more over their lifetime. If a customer purchases all his or her cars, servicing of these cars, all accessories and car insurance, this may represent as much as $500,000 worth of business over that customer's lifetime. By adopting this principle Carl Sewell, a well-known US car dealer, built a chain of car dealerships which became a business with revenues of over $1 billion.

The original concept of the '4Ps' of the marketing mix was formulated with the objective of manipulating and exploiting market demand. It emerged from a period of unprecedented growth and prosperity in the US and was heavily oriented towards fast moving consumer goods. We do not agree with some extreme academics that dismiss the marketing mix as no longer relevant. Rather we endorse the more balanced view of our colleague Evert Gummesson, who points out the role of the marketing mix has changed from being one of the founding parameters of marketing to being one of the contributing parameters to relationships, networks and interaction.[22] While the marketing mix concept needs to be extended to consider the context of relationship marketing, it still has importance in developing a relationally oriented marketing strategy.

However, the dangers of failing to adopt a relationship orientation in developing the marketing mix may lead to firms becoming supplier-oriented rather than customer-oriented. As Gummesson points out:

In practice, however, the 4P approach has led to a manipulative attitude to people. If we just select the right measures in the right combination and with the right intensity, the consumer will buy; it is a matter of putting pressure on the consumer ... We often know little of what is in the mind of consumers, how they think and feel, and what their motives are. It is more of a stimulus-response model, similar to the fisherman's relationship to fish. If we improve the bait, the fish will bite and it is hooked. How the fish feels about it has been less considered.[23]

The expanded relationship marketing mix, consisting of the seven elements outlined in Figure 1.7, represents a key element in the shift from a transactional approach to a relationship approach in marketing by recognising the criticality of people, processes and customer service. This figure illustrates how each of the elements is interconnected. Each of these relationship marketing mix elements interacts with each other and they should be developed so that they are mutually supportive in obtaining the best possible match between the internal and external environments of the organisation. Essential to avoiding the manipulative approach inherent in the '4Ps' approach, as identified by Gummesson, is placing high emphasis on the relational elements of people, customer service and processes.

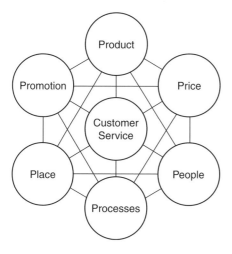

Figure 1.7 The relationship marketing mix

In developing a marketing mix strategy, marketers also need to consider the relationships *between* the elements of the mix. It has been pointed out that there are three issues to consider.[24] These include:

- *Consistency*, where there is a logical and useful fit between two or more elements of the marketing mix
- *Integration*, which involves an active harmonious interaction between the elements of the mix
- *Leverage*, which involves a more sophisticated approach and is concerned with using each element to best advantage in support of the total marketing mix.

Thus, effective relationship marketing is based on the choice and design of marketing mix elements that are mutually supportive and leveraged together so that synergy is achieved and customer value is co-created. Each of the elements of the marketing mix, and their sub-elements, needs to focus on supporting each other in terms of consistency, integration and leverage, reinforcing the positioning and delivery of the product or service required by the market segment (or segments) that is being targeted. In developing a relationally based marketing mix strategy, we also need to consider the impact of each marketing mix element on the different market segments selected. We return to consider market segmentation in Chapter 6.

Principles of relationship marketing

By the start of the twenty-first century many basic tenets of marketing were increasingly being questioned. The marketplace now is vastly different from that of the previous century. Numerous markets have matured in the sense that growth is low or non-existent, resulting in increased pressure on corporate profitability. Consumers and customers are more sophisticated and less responsive to traditional marketing pressures, particularly advertising. They are computer literate and there is a very high utilisation of the Internet as well as a high engagement in social media. Greater customer choice and convenience exists as a result of the globalisation of markets.

Some two decades ago Philip Kotler pointed to the future. He proposed a new view of organisational performance and success based on relationships, whereby the traditional marketing approach – including the marketing mix – is not replaced, but is instead 'repositioned' as the toolbox for understanding and responding to all the significant players in a company's environment. He outlines the importance of the relationship approach to stakeholders:

The consensus in . . . business is growing: if . . . companies are to compete successfully in domestic and global markets, they must engineer stronger bonds with their stakeholders, including customers, distributors, suppliers, employees, unions, governments and other critical players in the environment. Common practices such as whipsawing suppliers for better prices, dictating terms to distributors and treating employees as a cost rather than an asset, must end. Companies must move from a short-term *transaction-orientated* goal to a long-term *relationship-building* goal.[25]

Kotler's comments underscore the need for an integrated approach for understanding the different stakeholder relationships. In many large industrial enterprises, marketing is still viewed as a set of related but compartmentalised activities that are separate from the rest of the company. Relationship marketing seeks to change this perspective by managing the competing interests of customers, staff, shareholders and other stakeholders. It redefines the concept of 'a market' as one in which the competing interests are made visible and therefore more likely to be managed effectively.

The development of this broader wave of marketing thinking by marketing academics and practitioners has influenced the perceived role of marketing in business. In effect, marketing is given lead (but not sole) responsibility for strengthening the firm's market performance. In our earlier work[26] we have progressively refined our view of relationship marketing. In particular, we identify that relationship marketing:

- requires a focus on relationships rather than transactions
- represents a shift from functionally based marketing to cross-functionally based marketing
- demands full attention being placed on the creation of value to customers
- is an approach which addresses multiple 'market domains', or stakeholder groups – not just the traditional customer market
- involves a shift from marketing activities which emphasise customer acquisition to marketing activities which emphasise customer retention as well as acquisition.

We now provide a short overview of these principles of relationship marketing. In later chapters we explore these principles and their implications in greater detail.

An emphasis on relationships

The transition from traditional, 'transactional' marketing to relationship marketing is depicted in Figure 1.8. Relationship marketing emphasises two important issues. First, you can only optimise relationships with customers if you understand and manage

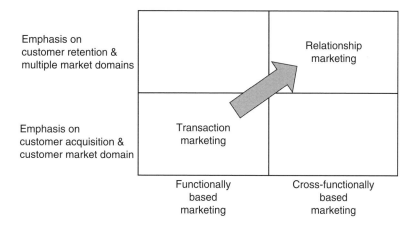

Figure 1.8 The transition to relationship marketing

relationships with other relevant stakeholders. Most businesses appreciate the critical role their employees play in delivering superior customer value, but other stakeholders may also play an important part. Second, the tools and techniques used in marketing to customers, such as marketing planning and market segmentation, can also be used equally as effectively in managing non-customer relationships. We explore the nature of this emphasis on non-customer relationships in more detail in Chapter 4.

Figure 1.8 shows some key distinguishing characteristics of relationship marketing. The first is an emphasis on customer retention and extending the 'lifetime value' of customers through strategies that focus on retaining targeted customers. The second is a recognition that companies need to develop relationships with a number of stakeholders, or 'market domains', if they are to achieve long-term success in the customer marketplace. The third feature of relationship marketing is that marketing is seen as a pan-company or cross-functional responsibility and not solely the concern of the marketing department.

An emphasis on a cross-functional approach to marketing

For a long time, marketing strategies have been developed within functionally based marketing departments. As a result, the marketing strategies developed often do not take into account their organisation-wide implications. The problem is that they are functionally focused not market-focused. They typically seek to optimise the use of inputs and hence are budget driven, rather than seeking to optimise around outputs and hence be market driven. Rarely do they consider the interrelationship of different shareholders.

To succeed in managing the multiple stakeholders effectively, marketing must be cross-functional. David Packard, co-founder of Hewlett-Packard, is reported to have said that 'marketing is too important to be left to the marketing department'. His comment could be interpreted in a number of ways, but we understand it as a call to bring marketing out of its functional silo and extend the concept and the philosophy of marketing across the business enterprise. In practice, a cross-functional approach to marketing requires an organisational culture and climate that encourages collaboration and cooperation. Everyone within the business must understand that they perform a role in serving customers, be they internal or external customers. Thus, relationship marketing involves integrating activities undertaken within a marketing department with those undertaken in other functional departments. In particular, relationship marketing requires integrating quality, customer service and marketing. We address these issues in more detail in Chapter 2.

An emphasis on creation of value for customers

Relationship marketing involves placing special attention on the creation of value for customers. There are two types of customer value. First, there is the value that customers create for the enterprise. Second, there is the value that the enterprise creates for customers. In many organisations the focus appears to be on the former type of customer value rather than the latter. Such organisations are principally concerned with extracting money from the customer, with relatively little attention paid to the value that is created for customers.

The value that an organisation can create for customers should be an early consideration in relationship marketing. If this is addressed satisfactorily, long-term profitability and future value for the enterprise will follow. In Chapter 3 we consider value creation for customers. Later, in Chapter 7, we consider value creation for the enterprise.

An emphasis on multiple markets

Relationship marketing focuses marketing action on multiple stakeholder markets. The 'six markets stakeholder model' developed by Payne, Ballantyne and Christopher[27] is one of a number of models that provide a structured approach for reviewing the role of an extended set of stakeholders. The model identifies six key groups, or market domains, that contribute to an organisation's effectiveness in the marketplace. These comprise customer markets, influencer (including shareholder) markets, recruitment markets, referral markets, internal markets and supplier/alliance markets.

Each market domain is made up of a number of key participants. Customer markets, for example, may include wholesalers, intermediaries and consumers, while influencer markets may comprise financial and investor groups, unions, industry and regulatory bodies, business press and media, user and evaluator groups, environmental groups, political and government agencies and competitors. Relationship marketing recognises that multiple market domains can directly or indirectly affect a business's ability to win and keep profitable customers. We return to explore these market domains in greater detail in Chapter 4.

An emphasis on retention of profitable customers

Maximising the lifetime value of customers is a fundamental goal of relationship marketing. In this context we define the lifetime value of a customer as the future flow of net profit, discounted back to the present, that can be attributed to a specific customer. Adopting the principle of maximising customer lifetime value forces the organisation to recognise that not all customers are equally profitable and that it must devise strategies to enhance the profitability of those customers it seeks to target.

Loyal customers are an intangible asset that adds value to the balance sheet. They represent the goodwill earned by the brand. Domino's Pizza chain in the US, for example, estimates that a customer who purchases one pizza for $5 may represent a net worth of approximately $5,000 over the ten-year life of a Domino franchise. Loyal and repeat customers not only contribute revenue by returning again and again to purchase from the same company or brand, but act as advocates, referring new customers and reducing acquisition costs. The retention of profitable and potentially profitable customers is a key consideration in the development of relation-based strategies in CRM.

Important trends in relationship marketing and CRM

Before discussing CRM and how it differs from relationship marketing, it is appropriate to reflect on some key trends which have led to both the adoption of relationship marketing and the rapid rise of CRM as a management approach in large enterprises. These trends help explain further why there has been such a sustained and increasing interest in relationship marketing and CRM. They include:

- marketing being undertaken on the basis of relationships
- the realisation that customers are a business asset and not simply a commercial audience
- the transition in structuring organisations, on a strategic basis, from functions to processes
- the recognition of the benefits of using information proactively rather than solely reactively
- the greater utilisation of technology in managing and maximising the value of information
- the acceptance of the need for trade-off between delivering and extracting customer value
- the development of one-to-one marketing approaches.

Marketing on the basis of relationships

The shift in marketing focus from increasing the number and value of transactions to growing more effective and profitable relationships with customers and other key stakeholders has had a profound impact on business enterprises. Marketing on the basis of relationships concentrates attention on building customer value in order to retain customers, a topic we examine in Chapter 7. By building on existing investments in product development and customer acquisition, firms can generate potentially higher revenue and profit at lower cost.

Marketing on the basis of transactions, by contrast, involves greater financial outlay and risk. Focusing on single sales involves winning the customer over at every sales encounter, a less efficient and effective use of investment.

Relationship marketing also produces significant intangible benefits. The prominence given to customer service encourages customer contact and customer involvement. As a result, firms can learn more about customers' needs and build this knowledge into future product and service delivery. Clearly, customer encounters that end once the transaction is completed, and with only a record of purchase details for reference, do not offer the same wealth of opportunities for service and relationship enhancement that enduring customer relationships do.

Viewing customers as business assets

This focus on the 'relationship' rather than the 'transaction' is evident in the emergent view that customer relationships represent key business assets. The implication is that relationships with customers can be selectively managed and further developed to improve customer retention and profitability. This represents a significant departure from the more traditional view that customers are simply a commercial audience that need to be 'broadcast to' by a range of advertising and other promotional activities. One aspect of a company's market value is future profit stream generated over a customer's lifetime. If customers are viewed as business assets then the company will focus on growing these business assets and their market value. CRM stresses identifying the most profitable customers and building relationships with them that increase the value of this business asset over time.

Organising in terms of processes

Over the past decade, companies have increasingly realised the advantages of organising in terms of processes rather than functions. Process-oriented firms retain their functional excellence in marketing, manufacturing and so on, but recognise that processes are what deliver value to the customer as well as to the supplier. A process is essentially any discrete activity, or set of activities, that adds value to an input. In the modern marketplace, customers rarely seek an 'isolated' product; they also want immediate delivery, guaranteed warranty and ongoing service support. The product or service offer has therefore become multifaceted; the culmination of cross-functional expertise.

Process integration and cross-functional collaboration are defining strengths of both relationship marketing and CRM. We discuss the shift from functional to cross-functional focus in greater detail in Chapter 2. The integration of key processes forms a critical part of CRM. Later in this chapter we provide an overview of the five key cross-functional processes that constitute 'The CRM Strategy Framework'. In Part III of this book, a chapter is developed devoted to each of these five CRM processes.

From reactive to proactive use of information

With an ever-expanding wealth of options on offer, customers are faced with increasingly personalised choices. The move from 'mass market' to 'mass customisation' in marketing has created a buyer's market. Empowered to choose (and to refuse), customers exert tremendous influence over the actions of supplying organisations. Their weapons are a diminished sense of loyalty and a greater propensity to switch to organisations that can promise (and deliver!) something better. This is particularly true in e-commerce, where customers can change their minds at the click of a button and savvy competitors can quickly redefine or refine their offers to gain a greater slice of customer share.

To increase customer satisfaction and reduce customer attrition, businesses must know their customers (and competitors) like never before, using this knowledge proactively. Improvements in knowledge-gathering and knowledge-sharing activities within and across organisations have greatly enhanced access to information and the insights that underpin the creation of customer value. The rapid rise of social media provides important additional opportunities for gaining insight into existing and potential customers. Customer service operations and, in particular, call centres often focus mainly on 'reactive' relationships with customers. Experience has shown, however, that carefully designed 'proactive' customer-centric initiatives can be much more effective and rewarding. For example, proactive customer support operations do not wait for complaints to be registered but actively seek to uncover and remedy customer dissatisfaction. They recognise that customers often never lodge a complaint and simply take their business elsewhere. Similarly, proactive call centres now research prospective, current and lapsed customers, feeding valuable information to cross-functional customer information and management teams.

Balancing the value trade-off

Crucially, the concept of relationship marketing highlights the trade-off between delivering and extracting customer value. Relationships are built on the creation and delivery of superior customer value on a sustained basis. There has been an increasing emphasis in companies regarding the need to create an appropriate balance between the value offered to customers and the value received in return and to recognise how this may need to be varied across different customer segments.

In a sense, optimising the value trade-off means marrying the aforementioned principles of relationship marketing with current trends implicit in CRM. For example, grocery shoppers are increasingly turning to the convenience of the Internet for their weekly shopping. More sophisticated e-shoppers are demanding online options that will allow them to compare prices among similar products, select items based on the nutritional information provided by manufacturers and check out new products.

Developing 'one-to-one' marketing

As markets become increasingly competitive and consumers and organisations seek increasingly specific solutions to their needs, markets fragment into ever smaller segments. Consultants Don Peppers and Martha Rogers have suggested that we may have to address 'segments of one' in some markets where the customer and the supplier in effect create a unique and mutually satisfactory exchange process.[28]

The increasing ubiquity of the Internet has proven to be a powerful tool for involving both business-to-consumer (B2C) and business-to-business (B2B) customers in the marketing process, enabling a one-to-one dialogue rather than relying on mass communications. The unique capabilities of the Internet allow marketers to capture the anonymous behaviour necessary to be able to answer the question, 'What does each customer want?'

CRM has a key role to play in developing such one-to-one relationships. CRM systems and processes enable a company to commit to memory each relevant customer encounter and to recall all past encounters with that customer at every future association. In effect, the capture of customer data, the interpretation of data analyses and the dissemination of resultant customer knowledge become natural and automatic functions of the organisation. How well CRM fulfils this role depends very much on how CRM is defined and adopted within the organisation concerned.

A definition of relationship marketing

The previous discussion of relationship marketing and its principles shows it covers a wide landscape of topics. In Figure 1.1 and in the accompanying discussion we gave brief definitions of the terms relationship marketing, CRM and customer management. We now provide a more formal definition of relationship marketing.

The first formal definition in the academic literature appears to have been made by Berry, who defined relationship marketing as 'attracting maintaining ... and embracing customer relationships'.[29] However, as we noted earlier and expand on in much greater detail in Chapter 2 and Chapter 4, relationship marketing is concerned with a broader set of stakeholders than just the firm–customer dyad.

Given that relationship marketing is regarded more as a general philosophy with many variations, rather than a completely unified concept,[30] it is not surprising that there are many definitions of relationship marketing. Harker[31] documents 28 definitions of relationship marketing, Dann and Dann suggest there are approximately 50 published definitions of relationship marketing[32] and Agariya and Singh consider 72 definitions associated with relationship marketing.[33] Drawing on our own and others' conceptualisations of relationship marketing, we define relationship marketing as follows:

Relationship marketing is an umbrella concept concerned with the identification of the appropriate relationships to have within a network of customers and other key stakeholders and then initiating, developing, extending, maintaining or ceasing interactions with these actors, based on the types of relationships that are desired. These relationships can be considered on a continuum ranging from an intimate partnership-type relationship, through to having no relationship at all with a given actor. The concept involves an enterprise offering value propositions which represent promises of value and maintaining relational exchanges aimed at co-creation of mutual value, long-term profitability and shareholder value.

Customer relationship management (CRM)

The trends outlined above help explain why both relationship marketing and CRM have become so important. However, the problem faced by many organisations, both in deciding whether to adopt CRM and in proceeding to implement it, stems from the fact that there remains a great deal of confusion about what constitutes CRM. As a result, organisations often view CRM from a limited perspective or adopt CRM on a fragmented basis.

This confusion surrounding CRM may be explained by:

- the lack of a widely accepted and clear definition of its role and operation within the organisation
- an emphasis on information technology aspects rather than its benefits in terms of building relationships with customers
- the wide variety of tools and services being offered by information technology vendors, which are often sold as 'CRM'.

CRM builds on the principles of relationship marketing. However, with new market demands and new technologies, the management of customer relationships has been taken to a more complex level. CRM is a response to this new and more challenging environment. The huge scale and scope of the inter- and intra-organisational changes involved in CRM led Kotorov to claim that CRM was the third most significant revolution in the organisation of business after the invention of the factory in 1718 and the introduction of the assembly line into the factory production process in 1913.[34]

Put very simply, CRM is 'information-enabled relationship marketing'. In the next section we explain the rise of CRM and provide a more detailed definition of CRM in order to help enterprises avoid confusion over the nature of what constitutes CRM.

The rise of CRM and how it differs from relationship marketing

The term CRM 'emerged' in the late 1990s although the first use of the term CRM is not identified or discussed within the academic literature. Dowling suggests the origins of the term CRM lie in two fields: first, in the US, in connection with customer-based technology solutions; and second, in Scandinavia and Northern Europe in connection with the IMP (Industrial Marketing and Purchasing) Group.[35]

In the academic and business communities the terms relationship marketing and CRM are often used interchangeably.[36] These two terms are used to reflect a range of themes and perspectives. Some of these themes offer a narrow functional marketing perspective related to database marketing while others offer a perspective that is broad and more paradigmatic in approach and orientation.[37] Zablah, Bellenger and Johnston suggest that CRM is 'a philosophically-related offspring to relationship marketing which is for the most part neglected in the literature'.[38] The use of the term CRM is further complicated with some organisations, such as the consulting firm Accenture, adopting the term *customer management* in place of CRM in response to many companies' (incorrect) association of CRM with technology solutions. As noted earlier in this chapter, we use the term 'customer management' more narrowly to represent *tactical* management of customer interactions and transactions.

Because CRM lacked early conceptual underpinnings, it is not surprising that the term has come to mean many things to many people.[39] A study by the authors found a wide range of views about what CRM means amongst practitioners: 'To some, it meant direct mail, a loyalty card scheme, or a database, whereas others envisioned it as a help desk or a call centre. Some said that it was about populating a data warehouse or undertaking data mining; others considered CRM an e-commerce solution, such as the use of a personalisation engine on the Internet or a relational database for SFA (sales force automation).'[40]

Given the scale and importance of CRM and the widely diverse and often restricted views of CRM, we contend that the lack of a clear definition has impacted negatively on its successful implementation. Gummesson is one of the few authors, to date, to distinguish between relationship marketing and CRM. He views relationship marketing as a broader, overriding concept. He defines these terms as follows: 'Relationship marketing is a form of marketing based on interaction within networks of relationships', while: 'CRM is the values and strategies of relationship marketing – with particular emphasis on customer relationships – turned into practical application'.[41] We now expand on the earlier short description of CRM and discuss the varying perspectives associated with CRM.

Varying perspectives of CRM

The lack of clarity about CRM is evident in companies today. The term CRM, or customer relationship management, is often used interchangeably with the terms 'relationship marketing', 'customer relationship marketing', 'enterprise relationship marketing', 'technology-enabled relationship marketing', 'customer managed relationships' or 'customer management'. It is also often used to refer to a specific IT solution such as a data warehouse or a specific application such as campaign management or sales force automation.

In our experience we have found that the term CRM is used very differently across different industries and within specific vertical markets. Within one large technology company, we found that the use of the term CRM even varied greatly *within that organisation.*

As part of our research we examined many definitions of CRM and explored how organisations viewed CRM. Our review identified that CRM is typically defined from one of three perspectives: *narrowly and tactically as a particular technology solution, wide-ranging technology,* and *customer centric.* These three perspectives[42] are portrayed as a continuum in Figure 1.9.

One organisation we interviewed described CRM solely in terms of its sales force automation project. At this extreme, CRM is defined narrowly and tactically as a particular technology solution. We term this 'CRM Perspective 1', shown on the left side of the continuum in Figure 1.9. In another organisation, the term CRM was used to refer to a wide range of customer-oriented IT and Internet solutions. This represented 'CRM Perspective 2', a point near the middle of the continuum in Figure 1.9. 'CRM Perspective 3', on the right side of Figure 1.9, reflects a more strategic and holistic approach to CRM that emphasises the selective management of customer relationships to create shareholder value.

The importance of how CRM is defined is not merely a question of semantics. Its definition has a significant impact on *how CRM is accepted and practised* by the entire

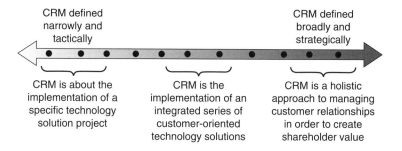

Figure 1.9 The CRM continuum

organisation. CRM is not simply an IT solution to the problem of getting the right customer base and growing it. CRM is much more. It involves a profound synthesis of strategic vision, a corporate understanding of the nature of customer value within a multi-channel environment, the utilisation of the appropriate information management and CRM applications and high-quality operations, fulfilment and service. CRM emphasises that managing customer relationships is a complex and ongoing process and a response to and reflection of a rapidly changing marketing environment. Thus we argue that CRM, in any organisation, needs to be positioned in a broad strategic context at the far right in Figure 1.9.

The dangers of not adopting this strategic perspective of CRM are made all too apparent by media coverage of CRM failures. Widespread concern regarding the performance of CRM initiatives is represented in the following statistics from Insight Technology Group, The CRM Institute, Giga and Gartner:

- '69 per cent of CRM projects have little impact on sales performance'
- 'Companies think that their CRM projects are significantly less successful than their consultants or suppliers'
- '70 per cent of CRM initiatives will fail over the next 18 months'
- '60 per cent of CRM projects end in failure'.

CRM, viewed from this strategic perspective, is concerned with how the organisation can create increased shareholder value through developing superior customer relationships. However, rejecting CRM and the potential benefits that it can deliver in terms of shareholder value because of specific past failures of IT implementation in other companies is short-sighted to say the least! At the same time, organisations should be aware of the risks of specific IT project failures and their associated cost. We return to discuss this issue in Chapter 11, which considers implementation issues.

A definition of CRM and types of CRM

Any organisation will benefit from adopting a definition of what CRM means in strategic terms for their business and ensuring that this definition is used in a consistent manner throughout their organisation. We define CRM as follows:

CRM is a cross-functional strategic approach concerned with creating improved shareholder value through the development of appropriate relationships with key customers and customer segments. It typically involves identifying appropriate business and customer strategies, the acquisition and diffusion of customer knowledge, deciding appropriate segment granularity, managing the co-creation of customer value, developing integrated channel strategies and the intelligent use of data and technology solutions to create superior customer experiences.

This definition highlights CRM's emphasis on integration of processes across different functions and how it is distinctive from the definition of relationship marketing proposed above. Hopefully, over time, clear definitions of CRM and associated terms will develop into common usage. Until that time organisations need to be clear about what they mean when they discuss CRM.

Types of CRM

Analyst firms such as Gartner classify CRM into several types:

- *Operational CRM* This is the area that is concerned with the automation of business processes involving front-office customer contact points. These areas include sales automation, marketing automation and customer service automation. Historically, operational CRM has been a major area of enterprise expenditure as companies develop call centres or adopt sales force automation systems. CRM vendors focus on offering an increasingly wide range of operational CRM solutions.
- *Analytical CRM* This involves the capture, storage, organisation, analysis, interpretation and use of data created from the operational side of the business. Integration of analytical CRM solutions with operational CRM solutions is an important consideration.
- *Collaborative CRM* This involves the use of collaborative services and infrastructure to make interaction between a company and its multiple channels possible. This enables interaction between customers, the enterprise and its employees.

Together, these three components of CRM support and feed into each other. Successful CRM, which results in a superior customer experience, requires integration of all three of these component parts. Collaborative CRM enables customers to contact the enterprise through a range of different channels and undergo a common experience across these channels. Operational CRM facilitates the customer contacts with the organisation and subsequent processing and fulfilment of their requirements. Analytical CRM enables the right customers to be targeted with appropriate offers and permits personalisation and one-to one-marketing to be undertaken through superior customer knowledge. While historically operational and collaborative CRM had the greatest emphasis, enterprises are now more cognisant of the need for analytical CRM to enable better optimisation of their customer-facing activities and the creation of value for the customer and the enterprise. We discuss these forms of CRM in more detail in Chapter 9.

Other terminology used in discussing CRM includes:

- *Strategic CRM* This involves the development of an approach to CRM that starts with the business strategy of the enterprise and is concerned with development of customer relationships that result in long-term shareholder value creation. This is the approach emphasised throughout the book. It should be noted some authors use the term strategic CRM in a more restrictive sense to refer to analytical CRM.
- *E-CRM* The term e-CRM refers to the use of e-commerce tools or electronic channels in CRM. (We do not make a distinction between CRM and e-CRM in this book; nor, as noted below, do we use the term Social CRM. E-CRM and Social CRM, if the terms are used, are simply part of CRM.) Confusingly, e-CRM is sometimes used to refer to 'enterprise CRM' – that is having an enterprise-wide view of the customer across different channels.
- *Partner Relationship Marketing or PRM* This term is used to refer to CRM activities that involve the enterprise's activities with its alliance partners or value-added resellers (VARs). The majority of IT business is done through indirect channels, so PRM

activities with intermediaries are an essential element of a vendor's CRM programme. For example, Siebel, part of Oracle Corporation, identifies five types of partner: consulting partners, platform partners, technical partners, content partners and software partners.

- *Social CRM* This involves an organisation using social media and social influence marketing techniques to engage with their customers. It involves engaging customers in collaborative two-way conversations. We discuss social media and social influence marketing in some detail in Chapter 5 and in later chapters in Part III. As with e-CRM, we avoid making too much of a distinction between CRM and Social CRM, but rather consider CRM's use of social media and social influence marketing.

CRM and software vendors

The need for increasingly sophisticated and scalable options means almost infinite scope for providers of CRM products and services. However, despite the popular claim to be 'complete CRM solution providers', relatively few software vendors can claim to provide the full range of functionality that a complex company's CRM business strategy requires. The IT challenge is that the requirements for sales, marketing and customer service and support are complex. The increasing number, variety and combination of applications and services to choose from stresses the highly customised nature of CRM, as well as the burgeoning sector of CRM providers.

Analysts have pointed out that companies seeking to adopt or improve their CRM and customer-facing activities need to appreciate that when they are being offered a CRM solution by a particular vendor, its nature will vary according to the category of vendor. The Gartner Group, for instance, identifies the key vendor groups as marketing, selling, servicing and e-commerce. This variation derives not only from the differences in the products and services sold, but from the differences in the way the vendors define CRM. For example, Gartner have segmented CRM application architecture types as follows.[43]

The key segments for CRM applications architecture types include:

- CRM Suite (e.g., Microsoft, salesforce.com, Siebel – owned by Oracle)
- Enterprise Suite (e.g., Oracle, Sage, SAP)
- CRM Best of Breed (e.g., SAS, Teradata)
- Model-driven Application (e.g., Oracle, SAP/Netweaver)
- Model-driven Framework (e.g., Chordiant, Pegasystems).

The wide variety of CRM service providers and consultants that offer implementation support include:

- Corporate strategy (e.g., McKinsey & Co., Bain & Co.)
- CRM strategy (e.g., Peppers & Rogers)
- Change management, organisation design, training, HR, etc. (e.g., Accenture)
- Business transformation (e.g., IBM, PwC)

- Infrastructure build, systems integrators (e.g., Logica, Unisys)
- Infrastructure outsourcing (e.g., EDS, CSC)
- Business insight, analytics, research, etc. (e.g., SAS, Dunnhumby)
- Business process outsourcing (e.g., Acxiom).

A number of these companies operate in more than one of these sectors. We return to discuss CRM vendors and their selection in Chapter 11.

It is important for those vendors supplying CRM solutions to position CRM in its strategic context so that their propositions and business benefits to potential customers are represented strongly. Sales of CRM technology solutions conducted in the absence of such a perspective should be a source of great concern to both companies and their vendors. Establishing this strategic context involves more than simply understanding the overall business strategy of an organisation and where a CRM solution fits in. It also entails getting closer to customers and gaining an in-depth understanding of their situations, motivations and behaviours. While sophisticated technological tools and techniques have made this task easier, the secret of success in using them lies in their specification, integration and careful implementation. In essence, this means determining the key CRM processes relevant to that organisation and asking the right questions about them. This task should guide the actions of both providers and users of CRM.

Key CRM processes and a strategy framework for CRM

Earlier in the chapter we emphasised the importance of a cross-functional approach, involving not only the marketing function, but the entire enterprise. Developing a cross-functional approach to CRM requires first identifying the key processes that need to be addressed and second identifying the key issues or questions that need to be addressed by the organisation for each of these processes. From our research we have identified that there are five key CRM processes that need to be considered by most organisations.[44] These are:

- a *strategy development* process
- an *enterprise value creation* process
- a *multi-channel integration* process
- an *information management* process
- a *performance assessment* process.

The identification of these key CRM processes is the result of considerable research, which included detailed discussions with business executives from a wide range of industries. These processes should not be surprising, given our earlier detailed definition of CRM.

CRM should be viewed as a strategic set of processes or activities that commences with a detailed review of an organisation's strategy (*the strategy development process*) and concludes with an improvement in business results and increased shareholder value (*the performance assessment process*). The notion that competitive advantage stems from the creation of value for the customer *and* for the company (*the value creation process*) is key to the success of any relationship. CRM activities for all substantial companies will involve collecting and intelligently utilising customer and other relevant data (*the information management process*) to build a superior customer experience at each touch point where the customer and supplier interact (*the multi-channel integration process*).

While these CRM processes appear to have universal application, the extent to which they are adopted will need to vary according to the unique situation of the organisation concerned. Some organisations may wish to add to the key CRM processes identified here. For example, one telecommunications company we interviewed pointed out that its billing process (involving every telephone interaction that customers had with the company) was so pervasive, complicated and pivotal that the billing process itself needed to be considered as an additional key CRM process.

Because CRM is a cross-functional activity and one that, in large companies, seeks to focus on potentially millions of individual customer relationships simultaneously, it can be unwieldy to implement and impossible to get right without a purposeful and systematic framework. The purpose of Part III of this book is to present in considerable detail a framework which shows CRM as a strategic set of processes that can be creatively managed to achieve an improvement in shareholder value.

The *CRM Strategy Framework* shown in Figure 1.10 is based on the interaction of the five business processes outlined above that deal with strategy formulation, enterprise value creation, information management, multi-channel integration and performance assessment. These processes make a greater contribution to organisational prosperity collectively than they can individually and they should therefore be treated as an integrated and iterative set of activities. It is also important to point out that the framework is not intended to include all the aspects of implementation, for CRM implementation issues will vary greatly from one organisation to another. However, CRM should begin with

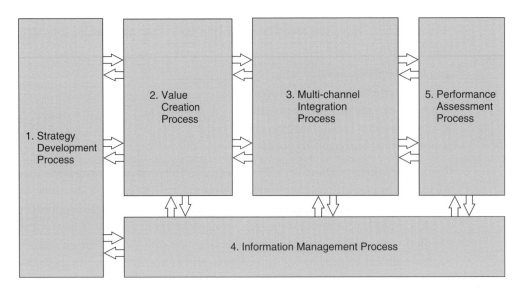

Figure 1.10 The CRM Strategy Framework

strategic planning and end, ultimately, with performance improvement. We consider implementation issues in the last chapter of this book.

Figure 1.10 provides a diagrammatic overview of these five key processes. At the start of each of the five chapters in Part III of this book (Chapters 6 to 10), we provide a more detailed diagrammatic representation of the building blocks in Figure 1.10.

The structure of the book

We have now provided an overview of the strategic customer management domain including a review of its relationship marketing and CRM, its key constituent elements. The final section of this introductory chapter now provides a roadmap of the contents of the book.

This book is divided into four parts. Part I consists of one chapter which provides an introduction to strategic customer management. Part II includes four chapters on relationship marketing which deal, in turn, with: the origins and development of relationship marketing; creating value for customers; building relationships with multiple stakeholders; and relationships and technology, including a discussion of digital marketing and social media. Part III comprises five chapters which each address one of the key CRM processes outlined above: strategy development; enterprise value creation; multi-channel integration; information and technology management and performance assessment. Part IV concludes the book with a chapter highlighting crucial organisational issues involved in implementation of strategic customer management. Two real-life case studies are included at the end of each of Chapters 2 to 11 to highlight key issues in strategic customer management.

The following overview of the content of chapters should provide a useful summary for first-time readers as well as a reference for those returning to the book.

Part I: Introduction

Chapter 1: Strategic customer management

Chapter 1 provides an overview of the domain of strategic customer management. It explains the development of the discipline of marketing through an examination of the major areas of marketing focus over the last six decades. It discusses how relationship marketing and CRM have developed out of this prior work, especially in response to the growth of the service economy. The principles of relationship marketing are outlined as well as key trends influencing the adoption of relationship marketing and CRM. The chapter then considers how relationship marketing differs from CRM. Three broad perspectives of CRM are explained and the importance of adopting a customer-centric strategic perspective is highlighted. The three main types of CRM – operational CRM, analytical CRM and collaborative CRM – are explained. An overview is then provided of the five key strategic processes that comprise 'The CRM Strategy Framework' and that form the basis for Part III of the book.

Part II: Relationship marketing

Chapter 2: Relationship marketing: Development and key concepts

Chapter 2 discusses the origin and development of relationship marketing. It discusses early precursor work undertaken in the area of industrial marketing and services marketing. The chapter then traces the emergence of relationship marketing as a field of academic study. Several alternative approaches to relationship marketing are reviewed. This chapter explores in greater detail a number of key relationship marketing concepts and themes that were briefly considered in Chapter 1. These include: the shift from transaction-based marketing to relationship marketing; the shift from a functional to a cross-functional orientation; the emphasis on business processes; the integration of quality, customer service and marketing; the drivers of customer relationships; trust, commitment and satisfaction as building blocks of relationships; customer loyalty; the scope of relationships; relationship marketing and multiple markets; networks and relationship marketing; and the planning of market relationships.

Chapter 3: Customer value creation

Chapter 3 first explains how the term 'value creation' has two meanings – *the value the company provides its customers* and *the value the enterprise receives from its customers*. This chapter focuses on the first of these meanings – the creation of value for customers. Later, Chapter 7 explores the creation of value for the enterprise, especially in the context of CRM. Chapter 3 examines in detail the nature of the value that the customer receives. The concepts of the core product, the expected product, the augmented product and the potential product are reviewed as background to an explanation of the supplementary services framework which helps identify how additional value can be developed for customers. How relationships add value and the customer relationship ladder of loyalty (which identifies different stages of relationship development) are then discussed. The chapter then considers how brands can help build relationships before exploring the nature of value propositions and concluding with a discussion of value assessment and an example of applying trade-off analysis.

Chapter 4: Building relationships with multiple stakeholders

Chapter 4 considers the building of relationships with both customers and other stakeholder groups. Traditional marketing approaches have not placed sufficient emphasis on management of all relevant stakeholders. This chapter outlines the 'six markets relationship marketing framework'. This framework identifies six key stakeholder groups or market domains. These include the customer market, the referral market, the supplier and alliance market, the influence market, the recruitment market domain and the internal market. Each of these market domains is comprised of a series of stakeholder subgroups. The nature and importance of each of these market domains is considered. A process of assessing activity in each of these market domains is also explored using a tool termed 'the relationship marketing radar chart'. This stakeholder approach emphasises that while marketing activities directed at customers are essential, they do not in themselves constitute relationship marketing. Successful relationship marketing involves adopting an integrated approach to managing relationships with all relevant market domains.

Chapter 5: Relationships and technology: Digital marketing and social media

Chapter 5 examines how technology has had an increasingly important role to play in building customer relationships over the past two decades. In particular, during the current decade, social media has now assumed high significance. This chapter reviews the changing technological landscape and focuses on the closely related areas of digital, mobile and social media. It explores the digital Internet infrastructure, the evolution of the World Wide Web – including its three stages of development: Web 1.0, Web 2.0 and Web 3.0 – and the key elements of digital marketing. It then proceeds to examine social media and to review the development of social media networks and the social media ecosystem. The chapter examines the growing area of social influence marketing, including the social behaviour of consumers and social media segmentation. We then provide a framework for developing a social media strategy. Key developments in this fast-changing area are reviewed.

Part III: Customer relationship management: Key processes

Chapter 6: Strategy development

Chapter 6 commences with a more detailed review of the CRM Strategy Framework and the component processes which were briefly discussed in Chapter 1. These CRM processes include strategy development, value creation, information management, multi-channel integration and performance assessment, which form the topic of this chapter and the next four chapters. Chapter 6 highlights the importance of grounding any CRM initiative in a well thought-out strategy which demands a dual focus on the organisation's business strategy and its customer strategy. The topics of business vision, industry and competitive characteristics, customer choice and market segmentation are reviewed. The CRM strategy matrix is introduced. This framework is based on two dimensions, the completeness of customer information and the degree of customer individualisation. It is used to explain four broad strategic positions which relate to alternative approaches to managing customer relationships.

Chapter 7: Enterprise value creation

Chapter 7 is concerned with transforming the outputs of the strategy development process into programmes that both *extract and deliver* value. The three key elements of the value creation process are: determining what value the company can provide for its customers (the 'value the customer receives'); determining what value the company can extract from its customers (the 'value the organisation receives') and, by successfully managing this value exchange, maximising the lifetime value of desirable customer segments. Co-creation of value forms an important part of this process. Creating value for customers has already been discussed in Chapter 3. This chapter focuses on the creation of value for the enterprise and how the process of co-creation can assist this process. The aim is to create a value proposition which is superior to and more profitable than those of competitors and which delivers a seamless customer experience. The proven link between customer retention and profitability is examined. The chapter also explains the ACURA framework – an integrated series of activities aimed at acquisition, cross-selling, up-selling, retention and advocacy. The economics of customer acquisition and customer retention is examined.

Chapter 8: Multi-channel integration

Chapter 8 focuses on decisions about what is the most appropriate combination of channels to use; how to ensure the customer experiences highly positive interactions within those channels; and, where customers interact with more than one channel, how to create and present a 'single unified view' of the customer. This chapter also addresses the nature of industry structure and channel participants. To determine the best customer interface it is necessary to consider: the key issues underlying channel selection; the purpose of multi-channel integration; the channel options available and, the importance of integrated channel management for maintaining the same high standards *across* multiple, different channels. An effective multi-channel service must match the individual (and changing) needs of customers who may belong to a number of different customer segments simultaneously.

Chapter 9: Information and technology management

Chapter 9 focuses on the information management process, which involves the collection, collation and usage of customer data and information from all customer contact points. This is the process that enables the enterprise to construct complete and current customer profiles, which can be used to enhance the quality of the customer experience. The key material elements of the information management process discussed in this chapter are: the data repository, potentially consisting of databases, data marts and a data warehouse. The data repository provides a powerful corporate memory of customers that is capable of analysis; IT systems comprising the organisation's computer hardware (and related software and middle-ware); analytical tools to undertake tasks such as data mining and front-office and back-office applications which support the many activities involved in interfacing directly with customers and managing internal administration and supplier relationships. These front-office and back-office applications cover a wide range of organisational tasks such as sales force automation, call centre management, human resources, procurement, warehouse management, logistics software and financial processes.

Chapter 10: Performance assessment

Chapter 10 covers the essential task of ensuring the organisation's strategic aims, in terms of CRM, are being delivered to an appropriate and acceptable standard and that the basis for future improvement is established. This chapter focuses on the two main components of this process: *shareholder results*, which provide a 'macro' view of the overall relationships that drive performance; and *performance monitoring*, which gives a more detailed 'micro' view of metrics and key performance indicators (KPIs). As traditional performance measurement and monitoring systems, which tend to be functionally driven, are inappropriate for the cross-functional approach of CRM, care must be taken in defining the drivers and indicators of good performance across the five key CRM processes. The key drivers of shareholder results are highlighted: building employee value; building customer value; building shareholder value and reducing end-to-end supply chain costs. More detailed standards, measures and KPIs are needed to ensure CRM activities are planned and practised effectively and that a feedback loop exists to maximise performance improvement and organisational learning.

Part IV: Strategic customer management implementation

Chapter 11: Organising for implementation

This final chapter considers the all-important task of organising for implementation. Numerous reports of disappointment with CRM have caused many to question the value and implications of investing in customer relationship management activities and technologies. While some failures are inevitable, most of them can be prevented by paying more attention to the organisational issues involved in: assessing the organisation's readiness for strategic customer management; fully addressing the project management and change management requirements; understanding the role of employee engagement and planning and carefully executing and evaluating relationship marketing and CRM programmes. Experience has shown that successful implementation is preceded by the development of a clear, relevant and well-communicated business strategy. Short-term wins have more chance of securing enterprise-wide commitment than do drawn out projects with over-ambitious goals. Moreover, a business strategy designed to deliver incremental returns provides the flexibility and scope for progressive improvement. The adoption of best practice, underscored by strong leadership, is the key to positive outcomes. No amount of IT can compensate for the requirement of human investment. This is evident in the aim of strategic customer management: to create a seamless personalised customer experience that is consistently and continually enhanced.

Part II

Relationship marketing

2 | Relationship marketing: Development and key concepts

Relationship Marketing: Development and Key Concepts (Ch. 2)
- Origins and alternative approaches to relationship marketing
- Characteristics and key concepts in relationship marketing

Creating Customer Value (Ch. 3)
- The value the customer receives
- How relationships add value
- How brands add value
- The value proposition
- Value assessment

Relationship Marketing

Building Relationships with Multiple Stakeholders (Ch. 4)
- Customer markets
- Supplier/alliance markets
- Internal markets
- Recruitment markets
- Influence markets
- Referral markets

Relationships and Technology (Ch. 5)
- Digital marketing
- Social media and social influence marketing

This chapter is the first of four chapters that examine the field of relationship marketing in more detail and that build on the introductory discussion of relationship marketing in Chapter 1. The figure provides a navigation diagram outlining the main content of these four chapters.

As shown in the top box in the navigation diagram, in this chapter we trace the origins and historical development of relationship marketing, examine several broad alternative approaches to relationship marketing and then review key foundational concepts of relationship marketing. The following three chapters then consider further aspects of relationship marketing, including: *creating customer value* (Chapter 3); *building relationships with multiple stakeholders* (Chapter 4); and, *relationships and technology*, including a discussion of the considerable influence that digital marketing and social media are now playing in relationship marketing (Chapter 5).

As we explain below, the field of relationship marketing has developed into maturity with a great deal of literature now published on this topic. In the notes to this chapter we provide a substantial number of further references for those wishing to explore specialised themes within the large and growing relationship marketing literature in greater detail.

Origins of relationship marketing and alternative approaches

The emergence of relationship marketing in the 1980s was not so much a discovery as a rediscovery of an approach that has long proved to be the cornerstone of many successful enterprises. Relationship marketing has been described as a 'new-old concept'[1] and there are many historical antecedents of modern relationship marketing. For example, Grönroos[2] describes ancient Chinese and Middle Eastern stories that demonstrate relational approaches, and other authors have pointed to earlier works that emphasise the need to market to existing customers.[3] Many of the ideas behind relationship marketing have been addressed previously but not under the more contemporary heading of relationship marketing. Moller and Halinen trace academic roots of relationship marketing in earlier literature.[4] However, the topic of relationships has been greatly underemphasised in the pre-1990s marketing literature. It has also been disregarded by the many business enterprises that focus their marketing activities on customer acquisition.

Relationship marketing – its origins

The academic study of relationship marketing has its more recent origins in the areas of industrial and services marketing.

In the *industrial marketing* area, the early work of Levitt focused on the idea that the real value of a relationship between a customer and a supplier occurs *after the sale*.[5] Levitt argued that the supplier's emphasis needs to shift from closing a sale to delivering superior customer satisfaction throughout the lifetime of the supplier–customer relationship. Work by Jackson was among the early literature to differentiate between transaction marketing and relationship marketing.[6] Jackson outlined the importance of relationships and how the context of the industrial sale set the scene for the type of relationship that is possible. She argued that building and enhancing long-term customer relationships involves concentrating on issues that have to be executed over long periods and in a consistent manner. Her work was based on organisations operating in the shipping, communications and computer industries.

In the *services marketing* area, researchers at Texas A&M University started to study the applicability of relationship marketing to services. Berry's 1983 landmark paper was one of the earliest to draw attention to the importance of internal marketing's role in creating an organisational climate that supports external marketing activities.[7] He also drew attention to a number of relationship-building strategies that an organisation could use.

Although work on relationship marketing in the US continued to develop over the balance of the 1980s, intensive research in this area did not commence until early in the following decade. In the early 1990s several specialist university research centres were established. These included: the *Center for Relationship Marketing* at Emory University in the US led by Jagdish Sheth and Atul Parvatiyar; the *Centre for Relationship Marketing and Service Management* at Cranfield University led by Martin Christopher and Adrian Payne and the *Centre for Relationship Marketing and Service Management* at the Hanken School of Economics in Finland led by Christian Grönroos. Several major international research conferences were held at Emory University in the US, Monash University in Australia, Cranfield University in the UK and the Hanken School of Economics in Finland between 1982 and 1986. By the mid-1990s relationship marketing had moved to the forefront of marketing practice and academic marketing research, after being 'on marketing's back burner for so many years'.[8]

Alternative approaches to relationship marketing

In an effort to categorise the alternative approaches that were developing, Coote identified three broad approaches to relationship marketing, all of which have different emphases and scope.[9] He termed these alternative perspectives of relationship marketing the 'Nordic approach', the 'North American approach' and the 'Anglo-Australian approach', and he outlined the foundational theories associated with each. These approaches are shown in Figure 2.1.

Although Coote's review of alternative approaches to relationship marketing is not complete, it illustrates some key differences in approach to the domain of relationship marketing. The first approach, the Anglo-Australian school, is based on the work of

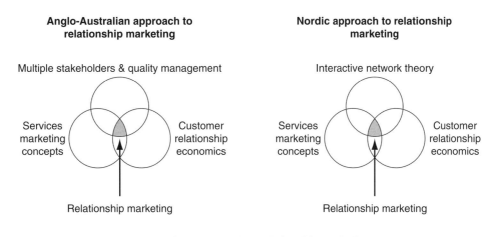

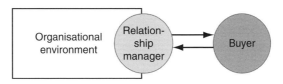

Figure 2.1 Alternative approaches to relationship marketing.
Source: Adapted from Coote (1994)

Christopher, Payne and Ballantyne and emphasises the integration of quality manage-ment, services marketing concepts and customer relationship economics.[10] It also adopts a multi-stakeholder perspective. The second approach is based on the work of Scandinavian academics such as Grönroos[11] and Gummesson.[12] Coote suggests that the foundations of the Nordic approach include the interactive network theory of industrial marketing, services marketing concepts and customer relationship economics. The North American approach emphasises the relationship between the buyer and seller in the context of the organisational environment; it is characterised by the works of Berry,[13] Levitt,[14] Perrien, Filiatrault and Ricard[15] and Sheth and Parvatiyar.[16]

The review of alternative approaches undertaken by Coote does not capture an influ-ential body of work undertaken by the IMP Group. The IMP Group, which originally consisted of 12 researchers from Germany, France, Italy, Sweden and the United Kingdom, is concerned with researching networks, interactions and relationships in the setting of industrial markets. Since the 1980s, the IMP Group has made a considerable contribution to the literature on industrial markets. A number of books have summarised this work.[17] The IMP Group work has attracted special attention because of its equal emphasis on the characteristics of the buyer and the seller. While the coverage of its work is wide-ranging, it is most closely associated with the North American approach shown in Figure 2.1.

As Egan points out, relationship marketing's rise to prominence was rapid.[18] By the 1990s interest had heightened amongst academics, practitioners, management consul-tants as well as customers. Enterprises started to adopt relationship marketing principles and create new positions in companies. Volvo was one of the earliest companies to appoint executives to positions such as 'customer retention manager' and 'lifetime care manager'.[19] Most major airlines started to build relationship marketing programmes, some with well over one million members. Companies as diverse as Italian pasta manu-facturer Buitoni and motorcycle manufacturer Harley-Davidson formed customer 'clubs' such as Casa Buitoni and the Harley Owners' Group. Management consulting firms such as McKinsey & Co. and Bain & Co. started to provide specialised advice to large corpo-rations seeking to build relationships. The latter firm in particular built a substantial business based on customer relationships and the economics of customer retention (see Chapter 7).

Following the first academic textbook on relationship marketing by Christopher, Payne and Ballantyne,[20] other academic and practitioner books started to appear. In the years that followed, specialist relationship-oriented management journals were published, including the *Journal of Relationship Marketing* and the *International Journal of Customer Relationship Management*. Some years later, two further journals – the *International Journal of Customer Relationship Marketing and Management* and the *International Journal of Electronic Customer Relationship Management* – were established.

By the start of the 2000s it had become recognised that the scope of relationship marketing was broad enough to cover the entire spectrum of marketing sub-disciplines, including channels, business-to-business marketing, services marketing, marketing research, marketing communication, marketing strategy, international marketing and direct marketing. The broadened scope of relationship marketing was recognised in 2000 in an influential edited book by Sheth and Parvatiyar, the *Handbook of Relationship Marketing*.[21] Following this period of vigorous research activity, it was recognised that relationship marketing had shifted beyond the introduction stage and had become a mature concept.[22] If further verification is needed that relationship marketing is now an important and mature discipline, this can be confirmed by viewing *Relationship Marketing*, a substantive three-volume scholarly work edited by Egan and Harker that was published in 2005,[23] and Palmatier's authoritative monograph *Relationship Marketing*, published by the Marketing Science Institute in 2008.[24]

Key concepts in relationship marketing

As relationship marketing matured, a number of key characteristics emerged which distinguished relationship marketing from transactional marketing. These are shown in Figure 2.2. Firms undertaking relationship marketing recognised that it was important to balance the benefits to the firm with the benefits to the customer. For high-involvement products and services, it started to be recognised that many customers may wish to become 'relationship customers' and build close relationships with their suppliers.[25]

Several of these characteristics require further explanation and are discussed both here and in later chapters. First, we examine the shift in marketing from a functionally based approach to a cross-functionally based approach. Second, we discuss the relationship between quality, customer service and marketing. Third, we consider the drivers of customer relationships. Fourth, we describe some of the building blocks of relationships, and especially the important role of trust and commitment and customer satisfaction. Fifth, we discuss the scope of customer relationships. Sixth, we review the shift in marketing emphasis from a sole focus on customer markets to considering a much wider range of stakeholders. Seventh, we consider marketing relationships and networks, including both

Characteristics	Transactions Focus	Relationships Focus
Marketing emphasis	Obtaining new customers	Customer retention
Market emphasis	Customer markets	Multiple stakeholder markets
Focus	Functional (marketing)	Cross-functional (all functions)
Orientation	Service features	Customer value
Timescale	Short	Long
Customer Service	Little emphasis	High emphasis
Customer Commitment	Limited	High
Customer Contact	Limited	High
Quality	An operations concern	The concern of all

Figure 2.2 Transaction marketing and relationship marketing

business and social networks. Finally, we discuss some key issues related to the planning of marketing relationships.

Shifting from a functional to cross-functional orientation

The discussion above suggests that it is imperative for customers to be viewed as a set of interrelated interactions comprising a relationship, rather than being viewed as a series of individual transactions carried out by different functions within the enterprise. For an enterprise to develop a unified view of its customers it needs to engage in collaboration with its customers that extends beyond the enterprise's functional boundaries.

Traditionally, sales, marketing and customer service and support have operated from disparate functional silos with little or limited interaction. The traditional functionally oriented 'command and control' organisational structure tends to focus too heavily on the operations of the company and too little on customers. This structure is shown in Figure 2.3. The danger of such a structure is that customers may be undervalued by the firm and effectively put to one side – as shown in this figure. As a result, opportunities for building relationships which maximise customer value and corporate profitability are often lost.

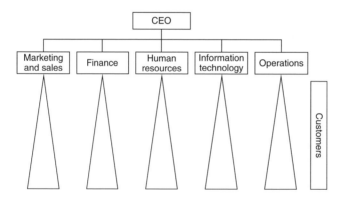

Figure 2.3 Marketing as a functional activity – the command and control organisational structure

To elaborate, the concept of relationship marketing involves shifting from a narrow, transactional, one-sale-at-a-time view of marketing depicted on the left-hand side of Figure 2.4. This outdated view has a *vertical organisational focus* around functions and is input focused and budget driven. Relationship marketing has a much stronger and more continuous relationship between the firm and its markets. This is shown on the right-hand side of Figure 2.4. Relationship marketing adopts a cross-functional or *horizontal organisational focus* which is market driven and output focused. However, it is not just the transaction orientation of traditional marketing which can limit the development of customer relationships. In many instances the way the organisation is structured may also limit its ability to serve customers well and develop long-term relationships with them.

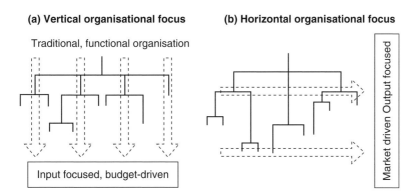

(a) Vertical organisational focus

(b) Horizontal organisational focus

Figure 2.4 The shift from a vertical organisational focus to a horizontal focus

The emphasis on processes

In recent years, companies have started to realise the advantages of organising in terms of cross-functional *processes* rather than functions. Process-oriented firms retain their functional excellence in marketing, manufacturing and so on, but recognise that it is their *processes* that deliver value to the customer and the enterprise. A process is essentially any discrete activity, or set of activities, that adds value to an input. In the modern marketplace, customers rarely seek an 'isolated' product; they also want immediate delivery, guaranteed warranty and ongoing service support. The product or service offer has therefore become multifaceted; the culmination of cross-functional expertise. Process integration and cross-functional collaboration are defining strengths of a relationship-oriented enterprise.

In an influential article, Srivastava, Shervani and Fahey identify three high-level *business processes*: new product development, customer relationship management and supply chain management. Each of these macro-level business processes, shown in Figure 2.5, makes a major contribution to customer value creation. As these authors point out, customer value creation necessitates accomplishing three key organisational tasks:

- The development of new customer solutions and/or the reinvigoration of existing solutions;
- Continual enhancement of the acquisition of inputs and their transformation into desired customer outputs; and
- The creation and leveraging of linkages and relationships to external marketplace entities, especially channels and end users.[26]

All three macro processes are relevant to marketing and business strategy. Each of these three processes includes a number of more specific processes. The customer relationship management macro process is the subject of Part III of this book. As outlined in Chapter 1, we identify five key processes that comprise customer relationship management when viewed from a strategic perspective: the strategy development process; the enterprise value creation process; the multi-channel integration process; information management process and the performance assessment process.

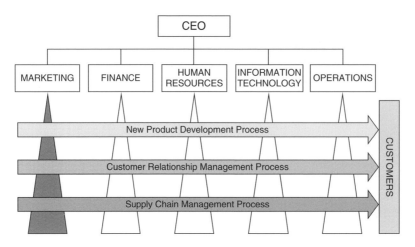

Figure 2.5 The shift from functions to processes

These business processes – new product development, customer relationship management and supply chain management – cannot be the sole preserve of an individual function. Leading companies who have adopted a cross-functional approach typically form multidisciplinary teams to bring together a wide range of appropriate skills and knowledge. Teams such as this benefit from interaction with colleagues from different functional disciplines and can often move very fast with implementation activities.

However, most organisations are still hierarchically structured and functionally oriented. This approach seeks to optimise the individual functions of the enterprise such as marketing, operations or manufacturing, finance and human resources at the expense of a coordinated approach to the customer and the whole business. Despite discussions of developing a cross-functional orientation in organisations, which extends back at least two decades, the reality is most organisations today are still stuck in functional silos. Given the difficulties of achieving cross-functional integration, this topic is one receiving considerable current academic interest, with recent work focusing on marketing and operations cross-functional relationships,[27] supply chain management and marketing to integration,[28] and cross-functional integration of R&D, marketing and manufacturing.[29]

Integrating marketing, customer service and quality

The cross-functional approach emphasises the coordination of activities across functional departments. While this is important across all areas of the company's operations, it is possibly at its most critical in the linkages between customer service, quality and marketing. Relationship marketing, at least as emphasised by the Anglo-Australian 'school' of relationship marketing, places special emphasis on the integration of marketing, customer service and quality. Too often these activities are managed by separate functions with inadequate coordination between them.

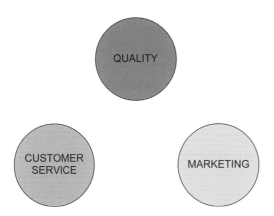

Figure 2.6 The transaction marketing 'stage'

In transactionally oriented marketing, these three functional activities are like spotlights on the stage in a theatre, as shown in Figure 2.6. All of these activities are under the 'spotlight' within the individual functions, but in seeking to optimise one of these activities it may interfere with another. The key challenge in relationship marketing is to bring these three spotlights or circles into much closer alignment.

In enterprises there is generally insufficient collaboration between these three functional activities and a lack of understanding about the important relationships between them. There are clear connections between these three activities (see Figure 2.7):

- Quality should be determined from the perspective of the customer, not the supplier. Determination of quality should be based on reviewer research and monitoring.
- Customer service levels should not be determined on an ad hoc basis. They should be based on an understanding of the needs of different customer segments and should be identified by research.
- The concept of total quality should influence the process areas such as managing the moment of truth in the service encounter.[30]

A coherent relationship marketing strategy assists an enterprise in increasing its level of customer focus. Integrating these three functional activities is at the heart of developing the customer focus inherent in relationship marketing. However, it seems that many organisations have difficulty in adopting a focus on customers.

Over the past decade and a half we have asked over 2,000 senior and middle-level executives, from large and medium-sized companies, two questions. The first question is: 'Does your chief executive claim your organisation is marketing driven, customer centric, marketing oriented or customer focused?' Approximately 90 per cent of managers claim that these or similar terms are used by their chief executives in describing their organisations. We then asked the second question: 'What percentage of the top 200 organisations, in your home country, is really customer focused?' We asked these executives to consider all the organisations that they come into contact with in the course of their employer's business activities and all the organisations they come into contact with

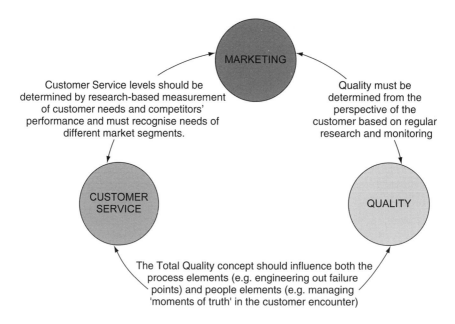

Figure 2.7 The connection between quality, customer service and marketing

as a consumer – such as their bank, mobile phone company, insurance company, electricity supply, travel agent etc. The individual responses varied, but on average these executives concluded that only about 10 per cent of organisations are truly customer focused. It seems that there is an enormous gap between the number of organisations that claim to be customer focused and those which actually are.

Just as enterprises may not have been successful in achieving a customer focus, success has also evaded many of them in their quality and customer service initiatives. Despite the introduction of total quality management initiatives, formal quality standards and application for quality awards – such as the Malcolm Baldrige National Quality Awards in the US, the EFQM (European Foundation for Quality Management) Quality Award in Europe and the Deming Quality Prize in Asia – organisations are continuing to address quality primarily on the basis of an operations perspective concerned with *conformance to specifications*, rather than from a *customer-perceived quality* perspective. In many companies there is a continuing frustration with their quality initiatives.

Over the past two decades there has been a huge effort directed at the area of customer service and service quality. Customer service programmes have been embraced widely, especially within the financial services, telecommunications, airlines, public utilities and the hospitality sector. However, although there has been considerable effort and expenditure, the results have been slow to materialise despite the widespread use of service quality measurement tools such as SERQUAL.[31] Customer service initiatives *should* be closely related to quality initiatives but this is not always the case. Our view is that this failure is attributable to a lack of company-wide alignment of purpose towards meeting customers' requirements. The traditional transactional approach towards marketing must bear much of the responsibility for this.

Research supports the argument that *customer-focused quality* is a highly important strategic dimension. The PIMS (Profit Impact of Market Strategies) research studies undertaken by the Strategic Planning Institute show that relative customer-perceived quality is a critical variable in profitability. One PIMS study concluded that, long term, the single most important factor affecting the performance of a business unit is the quality of its products or services relative to those of its competitors. The findings from such studies suggest that relative perceived quality is more positively related to a company's financial performance than such things as relative market share. While a combination of high relative market share and superior relative quality yield the highest return on investment (ROI) it is possible to obtain good profitability with a low relative market share through high relative quality. Buzzell, in a retrospective appraisal of this work, concluded:

PIMS-based research has consistently shown a strong, positive association between quality and profitability ... studies using more complex models have confirmed the basic results. One study ... [showed] that quality improvements lead to gains in market share as well as higher selling prices ... Similar relationships were observed in another study ... Still another confirmation of the impact of relative quality on profitability ... revealed that quality improvement is the single most important source of gains in market share, which in turn favourably affect prices and various costs and, ultimately, profitability.[32]

Given the importance of quality, it is important to re-emphasise the importance of *customer-perceived quality* as opposed to *enterprise-perceived quality*. Quality can be viewed from two perspectives: internal and external. Internal quality, or enterprise-perceived quality, is based on conformance to specifications. External quality is based on relative customer-perceived quality. The important point is that it is essential that quality is measured from the customer's perspective, not from what managers within a company think their customers' views are!

Several reasons have been identified as to why it is unsafe to rely on managerial opinions of customer perceptions. These include:

- Management may not know what specific purchase criteria users consider important. For example, customers frequently identify key purchase criteria not identified by management. Even when the criteria are correctly identified, management may misjudge the relative importance of individual criteria.
- Management may misjudge how users perceive the performance of competitive products on specific performance criteria. These differences in perception of performance may exist for the most basic of criteria.
- Management may fail to recognise that user needs have evolved in response to competitive product developments, technological advances, or other market or environmental influences.[33]

The metaphor of a theatre stage was used earlier to depict three separate spotlights on a stage, suggesting quality, customer service and marketing may receive a substantial level

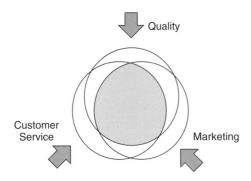

Figure 2.8 The relationship marketing 'stage'

of attention in the organisation but on a separate individual basis. Figure 2.8 shows the relationship marketing 'stage' where the three spotlights fall on the same area. As shown, relationship marketing is concerned with bringing all three elements much closer together.

The drivers of customer relationships

A key question for supplier organisations is to understand the motivations as to why customers engage in marketing relationships. Researchers have investigated this important issue from several different perspectives.

One approach includes identifying those ingredients of a relationship that a customer cannot find more efficiently elsewhere. These ingredients include three types: *economic* (the financial benefits exceed the costs involved in engagement), *social* (recognition, identity and shared values) and *resource* (confidence, preferential treatment, brand reputation).[34] A relationship develops when customers perceive greater advantages in developing bonds across these broad categories than in obtaining them elsewhere. The quality of the relationship depends not only on shared trust and commitment between the two parties, but also on the intensity of interaction between them.

A second approach to understanding the drivers of relationships considers the psychological aspects involved in a customer transaction. These subjective aspects include the level of risk in engaging in the relationship, the level of importance associated with the relationship and the emotions that result from the engagement. Generally, in situations where a purchase is very important to a customer, there is greater risk in engaging in the relationship and more intense cognitive dissonance results. These relationships are likely to benefit from marketing strategies where frequent, customised and personalised interactions reassure the customer of his or her risky decision. Alternatively, when a purchase is of relatively low importance to the customer, risk is lower and the emotional impact is diminished. In these situations, relationship marketing strategies are less likely to prosper.[35]

A third approach investigates the relational drivers and links these to the outcome of the relationship, especially in terms of customer value. Trust, commitment and relationship quality are all linked to the outcome of the relationship.[36] More recently, researchers have investigated other factors that may impact these relational drivers. For example, in business-to-business (B2B) relationships the development of multiple contacts with customers is important, especially where relationships are characterised by high employee turnover rates.[37] Also, forging relationships with key decision makers within customer firms is important, especially where a customer is difficult to forge relationships with.

A fourth approach emphasises the importance of relational interactions as a means for co-creating value. Recent interest in co-creation suggests that relational exchanges allow sharing of resources including knowledge between partners. This approach, which represents one of the foundational premises of service-dominant logic discussed in Chapter 1, switches the emphasis of marketing from the supplier and customer exchanging value that is embedded in products, to sharing of valuable resources through their relationships.[38] We consider co-creation in greater detail in Chapter 7.

The building blocks of relationships – trust, commitment, satisfaction and loyalty

A question that intrigues marketers is: What are the ingredients of successful long-term relationships? Many researchers have investigated this important question and tried to identify those key factors that make the difference between short-term and long-term relationships. Four key ingredients that are consistently identified include commitment, trust, satisfaction and loyalty. In this section, we first explore the various phases of relationship development and next discuss commitment, trust and customer satisfaction as important building blocks of relationships. We describe the significance of these vital ingredients to lasting relationships and identify why these ingredients are especially important.

Stages of relationship development

Relationships tend to develop over time, typically moving through several stages of development. Dwyer and his colleagues identified five distinct phases through which relationships evolve, each phase representing a distinct way in which each party regards the other.[39] These phases include *awareness*, *exploration*, *expansion*, *commitment* and *dissolution*.

Awareness occurs when one party recognises that another offers potential as an attractive exchange party. Although at this stage direct interaction has not yet started, each party may try to position themselves advantageously, making themselves more attractive as a relationship partner to the other party.

During *exploration*, relationship partners test the benefits and costs of the exchange. Here partners may trial the relationship, testing products and seeking information that will give greater confidence in making a firmer commitment to each other.

The *expansion* phase is characterised by the growing interdependence between the exchange partners. Here, partners expand the basis of their relationship, exchanging a wider range of products and embarking on greater risk-taking. As the partners interact in multiple exchanges, the beginnings of trust and commitment emerge.

During the *commitment* phase, partners agree to continue the relationship. The certainty of future benefits in the relationship allows higher degrees of risk-taking, greater efficiency due to long term mutual goals and increased effectiveness through mutual trust. Below, we explore commitment and trust in greater detail, as these ingredients are fundamental to long-term relationships.

The final phase occurs with the *dissolution* of the relationship. Although this phase may occur at any stage in the relationship, the impact of dissolution is likely to be greater when a relationship is well established and the termination decision is initiated by one partner. When both parties cease to benefit from the relationship, the dissolution may create less impact. Ideally, a supplier can have a migration process to ensure a smooth termination of partner relationships that have ceased to be attractive. For example, a mobile phone operator developed a process to migrate unprofitable customers to an alternative supplier who offered a service package suited to this segment of low volume users. Of course, all relationships do not end in dissolution!

On the other hand, if customers are not getting what they want, or an alternative supplier makes a better offer, customers may leave a company in large numbers. The first case study at the end of this chapter, 'Myspace – the rise and fall', provides a sobering case of relationship dissolution on the part of customers. Launched in 2003, Myspace was acquired by News Corporation in 2005 for $580 million and became the most visited social networking site in the world, in June 2006 surpassing Google as the most visited website in the US. Since then, with the rise of Facebook, the number of Myspace users has massively declined. It was sold in mid-2011 for just $35 million.

Commitment and trust

As we have indicated, commitment and trust are essential building blocks of lasting relationships. These two ingredients are important as they lead directly to cooperative behaviours that are vital for long-lasting, mutually beneficial relationships. In contrast to this relational perspective, traditional marketing emphasises the power and coerciveness of one party over the other, compelling parties to stay in a relationship. However, without commitment and trust parties may seek to take advantage of each other and look for short-term opportunism.

Commitment is characterised by distinctive attitudes and resulting behaviours, sometimes described as 'have to', 'ought to' and 'want to'.[40] Parties can feel they must stay in a relationship, because the alternative is likely to result in a greater downside. Parties may remain in a relationship because of a sense of duty and responsibility to the other party. However, the most beneficial attitude is when a party wants to remain in a relationship and actively endeavours to make the relationship successful. It is this affective commitment that organisations should strive to achieve with those partners who offer the greatest long-term potential. However, the commitment of one party can be significantly influenced by perceptions of the commitment of other parties. This 'cycle of commitment' means that it is important that there is reciprocity in commitment behaviours.[41]

Morgan and Hunt, the authors of a seminal paper that investigates the central role of trust and commitment in relationships, describe trust as the confidence in a partner's reliability and integrity.[42] Parties feel 'trusting' of each other when they are confident of specific types of behaviour in the relationship. Trust is a behaviour that helps build relationships, reducing perceptions of the risks involved in the partnership. Without trust, opportunism between parties can often result, leading to the termination of the relationship.

Establishing trust in a relationship has become increasingly significant in the digital age, where virtual relationships may not establish the confidence and mutual respect that stabilise a partnership. We consider these types of virtual relationships in greater detail in Chapter 5, where we discuss new channels for developing relationships and especially the important social media channel.

Customer satisfaction

Customer satisfaction is a measure of how the products and services of an enterprise meet or exceed customer expectations. Customer satisfaction has been defined as 'the number of customers, or percentage of total customers, whose reported experience with a firm, its products, or its services (ratings) exceeds specified satisfaction goals'.[43] Customer satisfaction represents an indicator of likely customer purchase intentions and loyalty. The measurement of customer satisfaction is widely used throughout virtually all industries, as well is in the not-for-profit sector. The enterprise that develops a reputation for delivering superior levels of customer satisfaction clearly has an advantage over its competitors.

As Gitman and McDaniel observe:

Within organisations, customer satisfaction ratings can have powerful effects. They focus employees on the importance of fulfilling customers' expectations. Furthermore, when these ratings dip, they warn of problems that can affect sales and profitability ... These metrics quantify an important dynamic. When a brand has loyal customers, it gains positive word-of-mouth marketing, which is both free and highly effective.[44]

The usual way of measuring customer satisfaction is to make a comparison of the customer's actual perception of a product or service with their expectations. Jones and Sasser identified that it is the *degree* of satisfaction that is important to the levels of repeat purchase. They point out that the difference between repeat purchase behaviour from those customers who score 4 out of 5 on a customer satisfaction survey and those customers who score 5 out of 5 on a customer satisfaction survey is *six times*. They concluded that it is not enough to have high satisfaction (4 out of 5 on a satisfaction survey), but it is essential to delight the customers (5 out of 5 on a satisfaction survey) in order to achieve high levels of repeat purchase.[45] However, research by Mittal and Lassar found that even satisfied customers may leave if a competitor's offer is sufficiently attractive. They found that even when customers have extremely high levels of satisfaction (5 out of 5 on a satisfaction survey) a significant proportion of customers – approximately 20 per cent of customers in the healthcare sector and 30 per cent in automotive repair – are willing to switch to another supplier. For those customers who scored one point further down on the satisfaction scale (4 out of 5 on a satisfaction survey) the potential defection levels increased to 32 per cent for healthcare and 78 per cent for automotive repair.[46]

Research by Parasuraman, Zeithaml and Berry provides the basis for customer satisfaction measurement in service organisations by identifying the gap between the customer's expectation of performance and their perceived experience of performance. This provides a measure of an objective and quantitative 'gap'. Later work by Cronin and Taylor develops a 'confirmation/disconfirmation' theory of satisfaction.[47] This theory suggests that if customers perceive their expectations are being met, then they are satisfied. However, if their expectations are not met then they will be dissatisfied. This is termed negative disconfirmation. Positive disconfirmation, on the other hand, results when a customer's expectations are exceeded.

As Egan points out, great claims are often made regarding high customer satisfaction levels – including that customer satisfaction increases customer loyalty and insulates an enterprise's market share from competitors.[48] However, customer satisfaction does not necessarily imply loyalty, as existing dissatisfied customers may continue patronage through inertia or other reasons and satisfied customers may be interested in patronising other suppliers in the hope of getting an even better offer and resulting satisfaction.[49] Although customer satisfaction measures have been used as measures of loyalty in the past, research suggests that satisfied customers are not necessarily loyal. As Reichheld points out, satisfaction measures have proven to be ineffective measures of loyalty.[50]

There are many commercial and academic measures and standards for customer satisfaction. The American Customer Satisfaction Index and the J.D. Power and Associates measures of customer satisfaction are amongst the two best known of these. A scholarly monograph by Oliver provides what is probably the best exploration of satisfaction.[51]

Customer loyalty

A further aspect of relationships is customer loyalty. Historically, customer loyalty has been considered mainly in terms of purchasing behaviour. Customer loyalty was measured on a range of variables that included purchasing patterns such as frequency of visits to a store or share of wallet. However, past purchasing behaviour does not necessarily mean a preference for a given organisation's products or services. An enterprise, such as a supermarket, department store or an airline, may consider its customers are loyal if they take out a store card or frequent flyer card. However, the customer may purchase much more from another competitor. Research by Dowling and Uncles suggests that customers may be more loyal to a loyalty scheme than to the company that initiated the loyalty scheme.[52] A further important dimension of loyalty, in addition to behavioural loyalty, is attitudinal loyalty. Attitudes involve strong internal dispositions which lead to customer purchase. They can be conceptualised in terms of a continuum of favourability towards a brand. If a customer has a strong preference for a particular brand, compared to a competitor's brand, they are attitudinally more loyal.

Dick and Basu have developed a model that brings together both behavioural and attitudinal loyalty.[53] They produce a typology of loyalty that distinguishes between four categories, as shown in Figure 2.9, including:

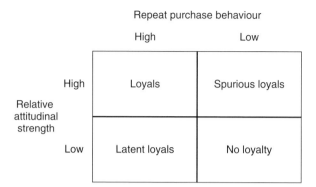

Figure 2.9 Four categories of customer loyalty.
Source: Adapted from Dick and Basu (1994)

- Loyals – customers on this category have high repeat purchase and their relative attitude towards the organisation is high. This is a desirable situation and the organisation should focus on retaining these customers.
- Latent loyals – this category represents customers that have low repeat purchase but have a high level of attitudinal strength. Customers in this category are favourably disposed towards the organisation and would like to purchase its products or services. However, customers may be inhibited in making a purchase because of access to a store location, inconvenient opening hours, or other factors. Research should be directed at understanding why these customers have difficulty accessing the organisation's products.
- Spurious loyals – here the customer repeat purchase rate is high but the relative attitudinal strength is low. Customers may be purchasing solely for convenience reasons or because of special promotions and deals.
- No loyalty – this category represents customers who have low repeat purchase and the relative attitude to a given organisation is low.

Further segmentation of loyal customers has been undertaken by researchers such as Rowley, who categorises customers into contented, convenience seekers, committed and captive customers.[54] There is now a substantial amount of research that has been conducted into customer loyalty and customer satisfaction. Baron and his colleagues provide a concise discussion on this topic from a consumer experience perspective.[55] The international supermarket Tesco, which is headquartered in the UK, represents an enterprise which has amongst the deepest insight into customer loyalty of any organisation. The case study on Tesco at the end of Chapter 6 explains how this company has developed a CRM system that rewards loyalty based on deep customer insight.

The scope of customer relationships

Up to this point, we have discussed customer relationships generally. However, there are several types of customer relationships which have important implications for how best to manage them. One frequently used categorisation is distinguishing business-to-consumer (B2C) and business-to-business (B2B) relationships. In the former, the supplier typically forms a relationship with an individual, often grouped within a segment of consumers that share common characteristics. In the latter, the supplier and the customer form a relationship that involves a group of individuals within the company and a group of individuals within the customer.

Recent trends in B2C marketing encourage individual customers to develop a relationship with the suppler organisations. For example, Procter & Gamble (P&G) displays customer service contact details on every product they manufacture, allowing customers to feed back to them suggestions, complaints and information. P&G recognises that developing a relationship with an individual person encourages greater customer loyalty and retention than impersonal relationships. These insights have evolved from inter-personal research studies[56] as well as the concept of one-to-one marketing popularised by Peppers and Rogers.[57]

In B2B marketing, relationships are typically more complex than those in B2C, because multiple persons may play key roles in decision making. Interpersonal relationships are again important, with individuals in the supplier organisation developing bonds with those in the customer organisation. However, when individuals change or move within either organisation, research indicates that the relationship between organisations often continues. There are two explanations. First, where there are multiple individual relationships between the two organisations, the dislocation of one or two of these may not significantly impact the overall relationship. Second, a bonding occurs that is independent of individual company employees. Gummesson suggests this is the 'embedded knowledge' that exists between the two organisations and is independent of individual relationships.[58] The second case study at the end of this chapter 'PlaceMakers – success factors in the building supplies sector' provides a good illustration of a company building interpersonal relationships in the B2B sector. PlaceMakers is the retail trading arm of Fletcher Building Limited. It is the largest nationwide building materials business in New Zealand. The company introduced a unique feedback management method which uses longitudinal research to follow individual customer relationships. PlaceMakers uses this feedback to enhance the relationship between its branches and their customers.

Despite the distinction between B2C and B2B relationships, the two types have much in common, as both essentially involve relationships with individual people. Companies that consider purchasing behaviour without the emotional and relational context of individuals may overlook important aspects of the relationship. As leading researchers Fournier and Avery point out, companies that do not acknowledge the different ways of relating to people can fail in their efforts to forge strong relationships with them.[59] Essential knowledge includes information about how individuals feel, what they value and their daily practices. Suppliers can use these insights to their advantage in developing strong bonds with their customers.

When relationships become deeply trusting and mutually committed, they are referred to as partnerships. These partnership relationships are more common in B2B associations, but they are possible in B2C as well. Fournier describes these partnership relationships in her discussion of consumers' relationships with brands, characterising them as: 'a long term, voluntarily imposed, socially supported union high in trust and a commitment to stay together despite adverse circumstances'.[60] Trust contributes to the level of commitment within a relationship and impacts the willingness between partners to cooperate more closely together.[61] Partner relationships in B2B contexts are especially important as the trust between parties encourages intensive knowledge sharing that further strengthens the relational bonds.

A widely used metaphor in relationship marketing is that of marriage. This is often contrasted with 'the affair'. The metaphor is used to illustrate alternative orientations to managing business relations.[62] However, Tynan points out that marriage has become such a widely used a metaphor in marketing that it has lost its relevance.[63] Other relationship metaphors do exist, although they are not so widely used. These include the metaphors of business dancing and business mating.[64] However, these metaphors are concerned with business relationships and do not sufficiently highlight the issues associated with consumer relationships.

Recently, Fournier and Avery identified a comprehensive categorisation of different types of relationship that consumers have with brands and companies. They develop a map of 18 different types of relationships, as shown in Figure 2.10. Some relationships are deep and long-lasting; others are superficial and fleeting. As

Figure 2.10 Types of relationships.
Source: S. Fournier and J. Avery (2011), Putting the 'Relationship' Back into CRM, *MIT Sloan Management Review*, Vol. 52, No. 3, pp. 63–72

Figure 2.10 illustrates, some of these relationships focus on emotional or social needs while others are more utilitarian and functionally oriented. Relationships may be hierarchical or equal in terms of power and they can be positive or negative. Fournier and Avery conclude:

Although the range of brand relationships is quite varied, most companies focus on loyal 'brand marriages,' despite the fact that there are several other types of emotionally vested loyal relationships, including 'best friendships,' 'addictions' and 'flings.' Rather than focusing narrowly on marriages, companies have significant opportunities to build incremental value by focusing on and adapting their strategies to the relationship types that are best suited to their brands. We have found that there is profit potential in many different types of relationships; the trick is to understand the specific relationship contract. Relationship contracts establish both the norms and the terms for the relationship, and they also signal what companies must do (and must not do) to keep the relationship sound.[65]

Emerging from work exploring aspects of relationship marketing in the B2B sector are studies investigating key account management (KAM). KAM emphasises a key concept of relationship marketing, specifically how to build appropriate, long-term relationships with chosen customers. McDonald and Woodburn, experts in KAM, identify specific characteristics associated with each stage of KAM as relationships deepen and the bonds become increasingly important to both parties.[66] Partnership between two organisations operates when there is sufficient interdependence and integration between the parties that if the relationship were to break down it would be costly to both. The selling company is seen by the buying company as a strategic external resource. Partnership relationships are characterised by a willingness to share sensitive information, agreeing long-term strategies including pricing policies that ensure both sides achieve a profit.

Relationship marketing and multiple markets

Much of the initial work in relationship marketing focused on the traditional supplier–customer relationship. At the start of this chapter we described different 'schools' or perspectives of relationship marketing. The Nordic approach and the Anglo-Australian approach shared common ground and viewed relationship marketing from a broader and more holistic perspective. The North American school, in its initial days, argued strongly for narrowly restricting the focus of relationship marketing to the supplier–customer dyad. The Anglo-Australian approach recognised the importance of relationships in six key stakeholder groupings, or market domains. The Nordic approach also recognised the importance of other stakeholders beyond the supplier–customer dyad and this aspect is emphasised in the work of Gummesson and Grönroos.[67]

The origins of stakeholder theory lie in the strategic management literature.[68] This literature is important as it addresses those stakeholder groups that are central to the success of a firm. However, despite an extensive strategic management literature on stakeholders, there is little agreement in this literature regarding which constituent groups an organisation should consider as stakeholders.[69] Insights from the strategic management literature have been influential in the development of multiple stakeholder approaches to relationship marketing. However, in contrast to the strategic management literature, the relationship marketing literature on stakeholders has developed stakeholder classification schemes of specific relevance to the application of marketing. This concept of addressing a wide range of markets is not new to marketing. Four decades ago, in 1972, Kotler argued for a broadening of the perspective of marketing to take account of the relationships between an organisation and what he termed 'its publics'.[70] This broader perspective of markets, or what we term 'market domains', is now widely accepted in the relationship marketing literature.

Stakeholder models in relationship marketing

A number of authors have developed different but related models and frameworks for describing and classifying stakeholders within the relationship marketing literature. First, Christopher, Payne and Ballantyne identify six key stakeholder 'markets' or market domains, which they further subdivided into constituent categories.[71] Second, Kotler identifies ten stakeholder groupings in the immediate macro environment.[72] Third, Morgan and Hunt outline ten stakeholder groups containing buyer, supplier, lateral and internal groups.[73] Fourth, Gummesson describes 30 relationships, of which 17 are market-based relationships and 13 non-market relationships.[74] Fifth, Doyle reviews four types of networks including supplier, external, internal and customer partnerships.[75] Sixth, Buttle suggests five stakeholder groupings including customers, suppliers, owners/investors, employees and other partners.[76] Seventh, Laczniak and Murphy propose six stakeholder groups, which are divided into primary stakeholders and secondary stakeholders.[77] Finally, Ross and Robertson, categorise relationships into four basic types of stakeholder and consider the increasing complexity of contemporary 'compound relationships'.[78] We are certainly not short of stakeholder models in relationship marketing!

However, while scholars working in the field of relationship marketing will place considerable emphasis on building relationships with multiple stakeholders, this is not true of the general marketing literature. For a long time, publications in the mainstream marketing literature neglected the important issue of understanding and building long-term relationships with customers *and* other stakeholder groups. More recently this has changed. Marketing scholars are now increasingly interested in this broader stakeholder context. This shift has partly been influenced by the growing relationship marketing literature and partly by other initiatives such as work by the *Stakeholder Marketing Consortium* – a Marketing Science Institute collaborative project aimed at identifying the need to better understand relationships within an enterprise's network of stakeholders. Bhattacharya and Korschun provide a summary of this work.[79]

Each of the eight relationship marketing models and frameworks for classifying stakeholders referenced above has merit and helps clarify and categorise stakeholder relationships in different contexts. Of all these frameworks, Gummesson's description of 30 relationships, or '30 Rs', is the widest ranging. In a substantive monograph, Gummesson catalogues 17 'market-based relationships' and '13 non-market relationships'.[80] His detailed analysis goes beyond the consideration of more classical stakeholder groupings. He discusses non-customer stakeholders that include suppliers, competitors and internal markets, but he also catalogues many other forms of relationship. These include: close versus distant relationships; relationships with dissatisfied customers; monopoly relationships; electronic relationships; social relationships and relationships within criminal networks. The broad coverage of this monograph includes 'mega relationships' and 'nano relationships' – two types of what Gummesson terms 'non-market relationships'. This discussion extends well beyond the stakeholder classification coverage in this book. However, it will be of special interest to those wishing to examine broader relationships that concern the economy and society in general.

From this brief description, it is clear that relationship marketing offers a reformist stakeholder agenda with an emphasis on collaboration with stakeholders beyond the immediacy of customer-firm transactions.[81] Given the similarities between the remaining seven relationship marketing models and frameworks outlined above, any one could be selected for detailed examination.

In this book we adopt the 'six markets' stakeholder model developed by Christopher, Payne and Ballantyne. The six markets, or market domains, in this model are shown in Figure 2.11 and comprise: *customer markets* (including existing and prospective customers, as well as intermediaries); *referral markets* (including two main categories: existing customers who recommend their suppliers to others and referral sources); *influence markets* (including financial analysts, shareholders, the business press, the government and consumer groups); *recruitment markets* (which are concerned with attracting the right employees to the organisation); *supplier/alliance markets* (including traditional suppliers as well as organisations with which the firm has some form of strategic alliance); and *internal markets* (including internal organisational departments and staff).[82] Chapter 4 discusses this model in much greater detail.

Before concluding this section, a comment should be made on the distinction between the term 'publics', used in public relations, and the term 'relationship markets' or 'market

Figure 2.11 The six markets framework

domains' as it is employed in relationship marketing. In relationship marketing there is a *marketing management* orientation placed on interacting with these stakeholder groups, with the use of tools such as segmentation, positioning, and the development of marketing strategies and plans aimed at achieving specific strategic objectives. We suggest this marketing management orientation is fundamentally different in its rigour when compared with the 'influencing' or 'communicating' associated with much of public relations activities aimed at 'publics'.

Relationship marketing and networks

As discussed in Chapter 1, relationship marketing is typically defined in terms of developing long-term relationships with customers. However, Gummesson develops a more generic definition: 'relationship marketing is interaction in networks and relationships'.[83] Gummesson's definition highlights the increasing importance of networks, of which there are many forms – both business and social.

Business networks

The business network is a relatively recent organisational form that is now receiving substantial attention. The growth in network or 'virtual organisations' has important implications for relationship marketing, as it involves an extensive 'value net' of relationships. This potentially involves a much broader set of stakeholders than exists for the traditional enterprise.

As Christopher, Payne and Ballantyne point out:

But today a different model is emerging, based on the idea of the firm as an element in a network that competes through the way it leverages the resources and capabilities of its individual members. Each member of the network specialises in that aspect of the value creation process where it has the greatest differential advantage. This model of business activity sees the network, not the individual firm, as the value delivery system.... In the past organisations were typically structured and managed to optimise their own operations with little regard to the way they interfaced with suppliers and customers. The business model was essentially 'transactional' – that is, products and services were bought and sold on an arm's length basis and there was little enthusiasm for the concept of longer-term, mutually dependent relationships ... Today's emerging competitive paradigm is a stark contrast to the conventional model. It suggests that sustainable advantage lies in managing the complex web of relationships that link highly focused providers of specific elements of the final offer in a cost-effective, value-adding network.[84]

A couple of examples can best demonstrate the concept of the network organisation.

The Smart Car

The last two decades in particular have seen enterprises increasingly becoming engaged in network activities. The 'Smart Car' venture originally involved collaboration between Daimler-Benz (now Daimler) and SMH (the company that manufactures

Swatch watches). This idea was initiated by SMH chief executive Nicolas Hayek, who developed the idea for a new car that used the same personalisation strategies used with Swatch watches. During the design phase, the concept, known internally as the 'Swatchmobile', was shown to several automotive manufacturers and an agreement was reached with Volkswagen to jointly develop the new project. However, the new Volkswagen Chief Executive Officer (CEO) terminated the agreement leading to a new agreement being reached with Daimler-Benz. The new Smart car was assembled using modules from seven strategic partners who operated their own facilities in parallel with the assembly-line operations. Unfortunately, this network organisation ran into financial problems and disagreement about the type of drivetrain, with SMH wanting a hybrid drivetrain but Daimler-Benz insisting on a conventional gasoline engine. As a result, Daimler-Benz purchased SMH's remaining stake in the company and the company became a wholly owned subsidiary of Daimler-Benz. This example illustrates the difficulties inherent in network organisations where members have different objectives.

Gant USA and Pyramid Sportswear

Gant is a highly successful casual clothing brand that was owned by Swedish company Pyramid Sportswear. It is an outstanding example of a network or virtual organisation. Figure 2.12 depicts the Pyramid Sportswear value web.[85] This figure shows the relationship between Pyramid Sportswear and a network of designers, contract manufacturers and retailers and external agencies who manage the brand and marketing communications. In

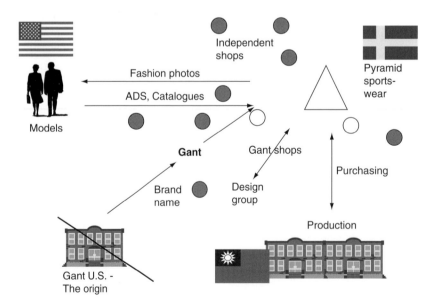

Figure 2.12 The Gant USA brand – the Pyramid Sportswear value web.
Source: B. Hedberg, G. Dahlgren, J. Hansson and N. Olve (1997), *Virtual Organisations and Beyond*, Chichester: Wiley

the early 1990s, when this diagram was produced, Pyramid Sportswear had developed a substantial business, yet employed only eight people.

The business started in 1980 when three Swedish entrepreneurs obtained the licensing rights to design and distribute the American brand Gant in the Swedish market. In less than three decades the Swedish entrepreneurs purchased the brand from the US owners and built a global business, based on a network organisation, with annual retail brand sales of approximately $1.5 billion and over 4,000 points of sale in 70 countries. IT has a central role in running the network together. Pyramid's Internet-based system permits retailers to see what is in stock for their specific geographic markets and place their orders on a 24/7 basis. The IT system is linked to a central warehouse, which makes it possible for franchisees and their retailers to place orders. Members of the network, the Gant country franchisees, typically place three or four bulk orders per season. Gant outsources much of its business activities including design. However, as the company grew, it built its own design staff. Gant was sold by its Swedish owners to a private Swiss company, Maus Frères S.A., in 2008 and today has around 600 stores worldwide.[86]

Social networks

Social networks have existed since the start of civilisation. However, with the rise of communications and transportation, the extent of individuals' social networks has expanded greatly. More recently, the rise of customer communities and social media has led to much greater proliferation and size of social networks. In less than a decade, social media has created huge networks where people separated by vast geographic distances can communicate readily. We address social media in more detail in Chapter 5.

Social networks represent the very fabric of our society. They are important for many reasons. However, for marketing they are especially important because they are the mechanism by which we often learn about goods and services. While we can learn about goods and services as a result of direct promotional activity on the part of the enterprise, word-of-mouth communication represents a much more credible form of information.

Godson categorises social networks into three broad categories: formal networks, informal networks and cultural networks.[87] Some examples are shown in Figure 2.13.

Formal networks	Informal networks	Cultural networks
sports clubs professional associations hobby clubs learned societies alumni groups church groups	friends family neighbours work colleagues acquaintances electronic relationships	nationality social class religion ethnic background language

Figure 2.13 Some examples of social networks.
Source: Based on Godson (2009)

Formal networks represent a good way for organisations to connect with a large number of potential customers. For example, many countries have motoring associations which provide a wide range of benefits to their members, including breakdown assistance, insurance and travel services – to name but a few. Such motoring associations may recommend the products of particular companies, thus giving these companies access to a large number of customers. Usually, there is a prescribed mechanism by which customers join a formal organisation. This often involves payment of a fee (in the case of a professional association or learned society) or agreeing to a certain level of commitment (attending church regularly or agreeing to play a certain number of football matches each season).

We are all involved in many types of *informal networks*. These informal networks often have a profound impact on purchasing behaviour and they are an important source of recommendation. Informal networks include friends, family, neighbours and work colleagues. Increasingly, electronic relationships represent important informal networks. The high market penetration of personal computers and mobile devices in most countries has created a huge number of informal networks. A large amount of business is conducted through informal networks such as groups of people who went to the same school or university.

Cultural networks are typically based on characteristics such as the country of birth, religion, ethnic background and social class. Certain ethnic or religious groups who do not live in their home country develop especially strong bonds and do a large amount of business with each other. Social class can also represent an important consideration in certain industries. For example, a British investment bank found that many of its upper-middle-class, privately educated account directors did not mix easily with wealthy young entrepreneurs who came from more modest social backgrounds. As a result, the bank segmented its private clients and recruited additional staff with the objective of minimising the social differences between account directors and the bank's important clients.

Planning marketing relationships

Although building deep customer relationships through relationship marketing may appear attractive to marketers, this strategy is appropriate only for customers in specific contexts. One of the great misunderstandings about relationship marketing is that it is concerned with developing deep relationships with all customers. On the contrary, relationship marketing is concerned with determining the appropriate type of relationship to have with particular customers or customer segments. This could range from having a deep 'partnership' relationship with certain customers, through to having no relationships with particular customers or customer segments. Indeed, an important part of relationship marketing is determining which customers *not to have relationships with* and identifying where initiating dissolution is appropriate – provided it is legally and ethically appropriate to undertake the 'firing' of customers. Figure 2.10 above highlights the many possible types of relationship.

Furthermore, some customers may be more willing to enter into a relational engagement with a firm, while others may wish to have a less intense, transactional relationship. For marketers, a key task is identifying which customers fit within each category, avoiding wasting time and other resources in unwanted contact. Grönroos adds a further distinction for customers in a relational mode, identifying customers who actively seek contact and distinguishing them from passive customers who are confident that the supplier will support them if they need assistance.[88] We discuss the different levels of customer relationships in the next chapter when we discuss the customer relationship ladder of loyalty.

Encouraging good customers and avoiding bad customers is just one aspect of relationship marketing; as Fournier and Avery point out, a more problematic issue involves improving relationships when they are strained: 'In our experience, a high proportion of commercial relationships today are conflict-ridden, and when relationships become troubled, most companies are quick to blame the customer. Effective CRM systems should help companies understand their own roles in shaping relationships, for good or for bad.'[89] Some companies may deliberately or un-deliberately encourage bad customer behaviour. Relationship marketing activity should be directed at encouraging good customer behaviour through an appropriate planning process. We now consider how the marketing planning process can assist in building relationships.

Relationship marketing planning

Despite a substantial amount that has been written on marketing planning more generally, in both academic and managerial publications, there is remarkably little discussion of planning in the context of relationship marketing. This is surprising as there is now a large relationship marketing literature that includes well over 20 books on relationship marketing. Scholarly articles rarely consider relationship marketing planning and the few books on relationship marketing that discuss marketing planning at all tend to rely on generic planning models, rather than considering the full context of relationship marketing, including managing relationships with multiple stakeholders.

Grönroos argues that the traditional approach to marketing planning is inappropriate for relationship marketing practice. One of his propositions is that relationship marketing cannot be planned in traditional marketing plans. Instead, he suggests that a market orientation has to be instilled in all plans and these have to be integrated through 'a market-oriented corporate plan as a governing relationship plan'.[90] We have some sympathy with this view as we consider traditional marketing planning is often approached in organisations as a functional activity and is usually managed by the marketing department who give limited consideration to the effect of marketing actions on other functions. This form of marketing planning involves marketers completing a marketing audit, summarising the output in SWOT (strengths, weaknesses, opportunities and threats) analyses, setting marketing objectives, designing marketing strategies and developing budgets and detailed implementation plans. However, it is important that in addition to planning for customer relationships, the broader context of relationship marketing is considered.

As we continually emphasise in this book, relationship marketing requires a cross-functional approach to marketing, aimed at breaking down the traditional functional divisions that exist in most enterprises. Developing marketing plans that involve relationship marketing strategies requires a cross-functional approach to customers and a consideration of the multiple markets with which the enterprise interacts. These markets include the key stakeholder groups outlined above in the section – 'relationship marketing and multiple markets'. These 'markets' are discussed in much greater detail in Chapter 4. Relationship marketing also requires additional information and analysis aimed at identifying those customers and customer segments most likely to benefit from intense interaction and relationship investment – as well as activities that need to be directed at these other stakeholder groups or market domains.

Planning for multiple stakeholder markets

As noted above, there are a number of alternative stakeholder models in relationship marketing that are used to classify different stakeholder groups or market domains. In this book we use the 'six markets' stakeholder model. In Chapter 4 we explain the reasons for using this particular model, which include its acknowledgement of the multiple roles that stakeholders can play and the model's previous successful use in projects within many organisations.

An organisation needs to successfully engage with all these six market domains, but it is important to recognise that it is not the primary role or function of the marketing department to prepare plans for the other five non-customer market domains. However, the tools and methodologies of marketing planning can be used to develop market plans for these other market domains, and the expertise of the marketing department can play an important role in assisting in their development.

Clearly, managing these other markets is the ultimate responsibility of the Board of Directors, through both the functional heads who manage each area and the management of cross-functional activities within the organisation. For example, the recruitment and internal market domains are typically managed by the human resources function, the shareholders and external analysts within the influence market domain are managed by the corporate affairs function, and the supplier market domain is managed by the purchasing or procurement function. All these non-customer market domains need to be managed with a view to achieving success within the customer market domain.

Figure 2.14 shows how, in complex enterprises, formal plans may need to be developed for each market domain. However, as McDonald, Frow and Payne point out, not all of these market domains are going to be of equal importance to companies.[91] Therefore, each enterprise will need to make decisions regarding what levels of attention and resources they will devote to developing plans for each market domain.

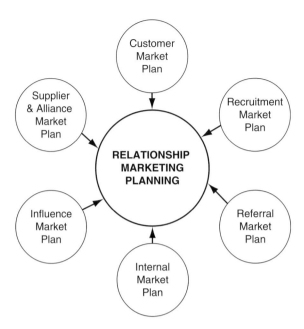

Figure 2.14 Relationship marketing planning

The planning process needs to be overseen at a corporate level and should consider the following steps:

- Which of these market domains will have the greatest impact on our future success?
- Who are the key participants in these markets?
- What are the expectations and requirements of these participants?
- To what extent is the enterprise currently meeting these expectations and requirements?
- What strategy needs to be formulated to bring these relationships to the desired level?
- Are any of the strategies in these non-customer market domains sufficiently complex or resource intensive to justify the need for a formal written plan?

A consideration of these issues will help determine the extent to which formal plans need to be developed for each market domain.

The 'relationship management chain'

Christopher and his colleagues propose a planning template for relationship marketing known as the 'relationship management chain', which operationalises the six markets model.[92] This framework aims at ensuring the whole enterprise is focused on delivering the enterprise's value proposition and managing key relationships. There are four distinct – but linked – central elements in the chain, as shown in Figure 2.15: define the value proposition; identify customer value segments; design product/service offer; and deliver offer and manage relationships. These central activities form the basis for managing the

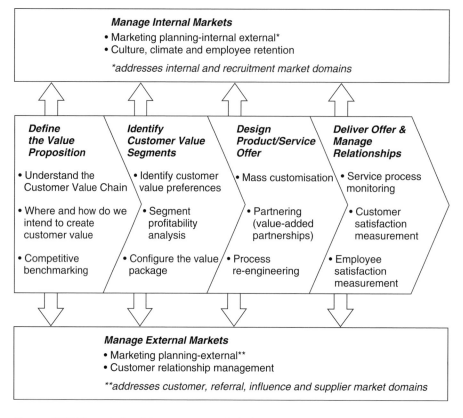

Figure 2.15 The relationship management chain

six market domains. The 'manage internal markets' box at the top of Figure 2.15 is concerned with managing the internal market and recruitment market domains. The 'manage external markets' box at the bottom of Figure 2.15 is concerned with managing the customer market, the referral market, the influence market and supply market domains.

Define the value proposition

Every customer may have a different idea of what represents value. What is valuable to one customer may be less valuable to another. At its most fundamental level, 'value' represents customers' perceptions of the benefits they believe they will receive from owning or consuming a product relative to the total costs of owning it. Customer value, which is discussed in more detail in Chapter 7, is best defined as 'the impact the enterprise's offer has on the customer's own value chain'. If the offer enhances performance, increases perceived benefits or reduces the customer's costs, then customers will see it as clearly adding value to them. Accordingly, the starting point of any relationship marketing programme should be to define and specify the precise nature of the value to be offered, market segment by market segment – or even customer by customer. This is the basis of the 'value proposition' concept, which, put simply, involves answering the question 'how do we intend to create value for our customers?' This step involves understanding the customer's value chain, determining how the organisation aims at creating a value offering, and undertaking competitive benchmarking of other companies' offerings – in order to ensure that the enterprise has a completely differentiated offer. We examine the development of value propositions in Chapter 3.

Identify customer value segments

Customers' different perceptions and requirements of value give marketers an important means of segmenting their markets. In-depth customer research will help reveal the salient dimensions of value, and techniques such as 'trade-off analysis' (discussed in Chapter 3) can identify groups of customers who share common value preferences. In other words, companies can segment markets on the basis of groups of customers who share common *value preferences*. The resulting segments might well cut across the more traditional bases for segmentation such as demographic or socioeconomic variables, but marketing strategies based on customer value preferences are more likely to succeed. We examine market segmentation in more detail in Chapter 6. An analysis of the potential profitability of customer segments is used to help identify and configure the specific value offering to be made to the customer segments.

Design product/service offer

The means by which the enterprise designs and produces the product or service offer is, in itself, a key element of the relationship. This includes not just the design of products or services, but also the co-creation aspects discussed in Chapter 7, the multiple marketing channels a company uses, the flexibility of its response to customers, the way it links buyer and supplier logistics and information systems, and so on. In other words, we view design as a critical way of forging stronger linkages between the customer's value chain and the supplier's value chain. Increasing fragmentation of many industries' markets has led customers to demand greater variety in products or services, which means enterprises need to make their delivery systems more flexible – i.e. to tailor products and services to the precise needs of individual customers or segments – this is the area of mass customisation.

To build such flexibility into its systems, the enterprise will frequently have to radically review the conventional wisdom on manufacturing and distribution. In the light of customer needs and competitive pressures, the enterprise needs to consider the extent to which it should re-engineer its processes. The enterprise also needs to assess its approach to the development of the offer and consider whether it could create more value for customers by developing value-added partnerships. These value-added partnerships may be motivated by enabling greater value to be experienced by customers and/or by reducing costs.

Deliver offer and manage relationships

This step involves delivery of the offer and managing customer satisfaction. The quality and strength of customer relationships is critical to the survival and profitability of any enterprise, so companies must regularly monitor the processes that deliver satisfaction, as well as the customers' perceptions of performance. In the same way that the quality of physical products depends on how well companies control the process that manufactures them, so too the quality of customer service depends on how well companies control the way services are delivered. We consider the relationship between employee satisfaction and customer satisfaction when we consider the service profit chain concept in Chapter 10.

Manage internal and external markets

The upper and lower boxes in Figure 2.14 show the important processes of managing external markets and managing internal markets. Much of the previous emphasis in marketing has appropriately been directed at external customers. However, the other market domains outlined in the six markets model also need to be considered. As we explained above, the extent to which formal marketing plans need to be developed for the other non-customer market domains – including the referral, influence, internal, recruitment and supplier markets – will depend on the specific circumstances of the enterprise.

The management of external markets involves developing marketing plans for each relevant external market and ensuring the implementation of a CRM programme. The techniques for external marketing planning are well established and effective frameworks have been established for developing marketing plans for customer markets.[93] We consider the key processes in CRM in Chapters 6 to 10 and then address its implementation in Chapter 11.

A relationship-based approach to *external markets* will only be successful if the strategy is supported by management of the organisation's *internal markets*. Internal marketing planning involves not only the existing members of the enterprise's internal market domain but also a consideration of the recruitment market domain. Managing relationships with recruitment markets is essential to ensuring high-quality staff are recruited in order to ensure high quality is maintained on an ongoing basis within the internal market. The principles of internal and external marketing are basically the same. In planning for internal marketing activities, the enterprise seeks to establish the needs of internal customers and to develop systems and procedures that meet the goals of internal customers as cost effectively as possible.

The internal marketing plan is a means of bringing these issues to the surface and ensuring that a focus is placed on undertaking the necessary actions to improve the performance of internal relationships. Here the development of a customer-oriented culture and climate is essential in order to maximise employee retention. It is the organisation's culture – which consists of deep-seated shared values and norms – which has the greatest impact on employee behaviour, attitudes and morale. The culture of the organisation in turn dictates its climate, which includes the policies and practices which characterise the organisation and reflect its cultural beliefs.[94]

SUMMARY

This chapter is the first of four chapters in Part II of the book that considers the field of relationship marketing. In this chapter we considered the origins of relationship marketing and its development and then outlined key concepts that underpin the relationship marketing discipline. In particular, the discipline has evolved through advances in the areas of industrial marketing and services marketing. We outlined a number of alternative approaches to relationship marketing that included the Anglo-Australian approach, the Nordic approach, the North American approach and the IMP Group approach. All these approaches have led to substantial insights into different aspects of relationship marketing. The early approaches and definitions of relationship marketing focused largely on the supplier–customer dyadic relationship. However, the focus of the discipline of relationship marketing shifted quickly to incorporate other stakeholders or 'market relationships', as exemplified by the Anglo-Australian and Nordic approaches to relationship marketing.

Research in the discipline of relationship marketing has grown to include many aspects. In this chapter we highlighted the key concepts which have contributed to the development of the discipline. Amongst the most important of these, especially when contrasting relationship marketing with traditional transactional marketing, are: the shift from a functional to a cross-functional orientation; the emphasis on business processes; the integration of customer service and quality, with marketing, trust, commitment, satisfaction and loyalty as building blocks of relationships; the drivers and scope of relationships; the focus on multiple markets or market domains beyond the supplier–customer dyad; the rise of the network organisation and relationship marketing planning. Many of these themes are elaborated on in the next three chapters of the book. Some other important concepts such as customer retention are mentioned more briefly, as they are examined in detail in Part III of the book.

At the heart of relationship marketing is the creation of value for customers so that strong and enduring bonds are built between the enterprise and the customer. This involves understanding the nature of the total value offer that can be made to customers and how this might be enhanced. The enterprise also needs to understand the different levels of relationship that constitute the relationship ladder of loyalty and why it is important to selectively move the right customers to higher levels of loyalty. Brands, in particular, can play an important role in communicating customer value. The development of a clear value proposition and the assessment of the value offered to customers form critical components of relationship marketing. These topics are discussed in the next chapter on customer value creation.

CASE 2.1: Myspace – the rise and fall

The company

Over the last decade, the phenomenal popularity of social networking has changed the face of establishing and managing customer relationships. However, the sudden growth of this new communication channel has witnessed both the rapid rise and spectacular fall of some key players. Myspace is an example of one of these enterprises. Within seven years, from 2003–2010, Myspace experienced a huge growth followed by a rapid demise, illustrating the pace of change in this volatile channel. Its turbulent short history is replete with examples of mismanagement, which illustrate how a great idea can go horribly wrong.

The fluctuations in the value of Myspace tell a story of swift change in fortunes. Launched in 2003, Myspace was acquired by News Corporation in 2005 for $580 million and the social networking site quickly became the most visited in the world. However, since then the growth of user-friendly Facebook has caused a massive decline, leading to the sale in mid-2011 for just $35 million. What went wrong and why has Facebook managed to succeed where Myspace did not?

Like many companies operating in the turbulent technology sector, Myspace grew from small beginnings. In August 2003, several eUniverse employees in Beverly Hills, California designed the original Myspace site. Their idea was to copy and combine popular features from other existing social networking sites and make it the most frequented site amongst those entering rapidly into this space. To attract new users, the company held contests to see who could sign up the most users. They kick-started a user community, contacting 20 million users and subscribers of eUniverse to provide an initial customer base.

Swiftly, popularity of the site grew and in July 2005 Myspace was purchased by Rupert Murdoch's News Corporation for $580 million. Murdoch saw the potential contribution of Myspace to his Fox Broadcasting media empire. In January 2006, Fox signalled its desire to move into the UK music scene with a launch of a UK version of Myspace. This announcement was quickly followed by release of a version in China and in several other countries. By August 2006, Myspace had signed up 100 million accounts, a phenomenal success and one that outstripped any of its current rivals. Until the end of 2007, Myspace was considered the leading social networking site, outstripping the growing competition of Facebook. At this time, the company was valued at around $12 billion.

The challenges and problems

However, from early 2008, the tide turned. Myspace suffered a rapid loss of membership as people flocked to the rival Facebook. Over the next three years, News Corporation tried to reinvent Myspace, redefining it as a social entertainment website, with a focus on music, movies, celebrities and TV, but these attempts failed. Recognising the strong competition, Myspace developed a link with Facebook that allowed musicians and bands to manage their Facebook profiles. However, Facebook continued to outstrip their flagging rival. As Myspace accounts fell, advertisers became increasingly unwilling to commit to long-term deals with the site, destabilising the financial security of the company. In late February 2011, News Corporation put the site up for sale with a reserve price of $100 million. However, this figure was not achieved and, in June 2011, Myspace was acquired by Specific Media and the actor

Justin Timberlake for just $35 million. The new owners hope to give Myspace new life, but the task of recapturing users is a massive challenge that will require inspiration, creativity and rapid action.

Many suggestions have been given explaining the turbulent rise and fall of Myspace and an examination of these provide insights into some of the challenges facing relationship marketing and CRM. Understanding changes in how people use social media has implications for the development of relationship marketing strategies and the implementation of CRM initiatives. We now examine some of the reasons that help explain the fate of Myspace and discuss the broader implications for relationship marketing.

Site design

From the start, Myspace was poorly designed, lacking innovative features and especially those that made the experience hassle-free and easily managed. Myspace made the fatal mistake of not listening to what users wanted, but was driven by technology and financial greed. Myspace failed to understand the features that were important to users and from the start did not offer an easy-to-use means of connecting with friends and family. Users did not enjoy the ugly and unintuitive profile pages and did not want to control and design their own profiles. Instead, they simply wanted to communicate with their network of social contacts. It was only a small segment of users, mainly high school children and technology geeks, who enjoyed customising their own pages, but for many this feature was highly undesirable. By contrast, Facebook started in the social networking field by offering a simple-to-use, standardised solution that was immediately accessible to the masses. People flocked to the alternative site, experiencing low switching costs (these included entering contacts and circulating account details to friends) and in return received an easy-to-use, pleasurable experience. Myspace could do little to stop this exodus other than attempt to play catch up, but too late.

Data security

Myspace failed to recognise the importance of data security to users of social networking sites. During its short history, the site was plagued with viruses, child predators and spammers, which gave it a poor reputation. In 2006, the Connecticut Attorney General, Richard Blumenthal, launched an investigation that set in motion a viral spread of negative word-of-mouth. It was alleged that minors were exposed to pornography on Myspace and quickly the site gained a reputation as a 'vortex of perversion'. Sadly, Myspace acted slowly, unable to build an effective spam filter, and so competitors stepped in. Around this time, Twitter was formed and quickly began targeting Myspace users. Meanwhile Facebook rolled out communication tools which were seen as safe in comparison to Myspace. The situation was made worse as Myspace suffered problems with vandalism, phishing and spam, which it failed to curtail, making the site seem unfriendly and risky.

Poor management

Myspace was poorly managed within the Murdoch empire. Driven by profits, Murdoch was constantly frustrated that Myspace did not perform as strongly as he anticipated, placing unrealistic financial objectives on the site. Managers at Myspace were forced to focus on short-term goals rather than building a solid foundation to grow the site. For example, Myspace entered into a three-year advertising deal with Google, which offered short-term cash, but restricted some key design features of the site. This deal required Myspace to place additional ads on the site, which was already crowded with promotions. As a result, the site was slow, even more difficult to use and less flexible. The deal meant that Myspace could not experiment with the site without loss of revenue, while Facebook offered a new clean site design.

User experience

Myspace considered how they could extract revenue with less thought about the implications to user experience. Myspace did not recognise the importance of providing an uninterrupted user experience, uncluttered by ads and pop-ups. As the business model of the company relied on advertising revenue, the company's ambitious financial goals meant there was a huge pressure to attract advertisers. Myspace offered increasingly prominent ad placements, which were disruptive to site users and conflicted with their desired site-user experience. The result was that users looked for alternative sites that offered a less cluttered experience, and they migrated to Facebook in droves.

Key segment needs ignored

When Myspace first launched, users were required to customise their own pages and this was attractive to teenagers. Facebook, with its standardised pages, was attractive to the 18–24 age group (especially college students), who were a much more desirable audience for advertisers. Gradually, Facebook attracted a much wider audience of customer segments. It has been especially successful at winning older users, who have greater disposable income. Facebook has continued to increase its powerful reach. Myspace failed to engage with more mature audiences, especially as it tried hard to redesign the site, making changes that users did not want and did not like. Facebook, in contrast, avoided making major site redesigns, recognising that users disliked too many tweaks to the design of the site.

Lack of clear strategy

Myspace lacked direction and it was unclear how the company wanted to grow. The company experienced several management shakeups as Murdoch attempted to save the failing company. His expectations of using Myspace as a distribution outlet for Fox studio content failed, even though he attempted to redefine the site as a social entertainment website. For example, Myspace developed a linkup with Facebook allowing musicians and bands to manage their Facebook profiles. But these attempts to build bridges with the fast-growing competitor failed and the fortunes of Myspace continued to dwindle.

Myspace, once one of the biggest social networks on the Web, had its sharpest decline in the month of February 2011. Monthly traffic had fallen from 44 to 37 million unique US visitors. As a result, advertisers became unwilling to commit to long-term deals with Myspace. From the one-time valuation of $12 billion in mid-2011, Myspace was acquired for $35 million by Specific Media – a digital media company – and award-winning artist Justin Timberlake. It was reported that Timberlake would play a major role in developing the creative direction and strategy for the company moving forward.

The future

Under new ownership, it remains to be seen if Myspace can rebuild its strength and popularity. In late 2011, Justin Timberlake told MTV News: 'I don't have anything on my plate other than think-tanking a lot of different ideas for Myspace.' Timberlake elaborated further: 'There's a need for a place where fans can go to interact with their favorite entertainers, listen to music, watch videos, share and discover cool stuff and just connect. Myspace has the potential to be that place.' Specific Media and Timberlake together plan to develop Myspace into the top digital destination for original shows, video content and music. 'We're thrilled about the opportunity to rebuild and reinvigorate Myspace', said Tim Vanderhook, CEO of Specific Media.

Early in 2012, the company announced their next step involving the introduction of Myspace TV together with TV manufacturer Panasonic. This involves the planning of a new service that makes 'the television experience social'. Using the new generation of Panasonic VIERA Web-enabled HDTVs, Myspace TV's ambition is to put viewers in control by allowing them to discover, share and comment on the programmes they're viewing in a social context. Myspace TV plans to extend its activities beyond music to include movies, news, sports and reality channels. Replicating the same TV content that existing TV service providers offer, Myspace TV will permit users to chat about what they're viewing while they're viewing it and invite friends to watch TV with them virtually. The platform aims at fully integrating social media and television in new ways, which will add a new dimension to content discovery and evolve the traditional TV experience. Companion applications are planned on tablets, iPads and smartphones.

Can Myspace develop a clear direction and build its empire amidst the increasingly turbulent media space? What lessons can be learned from the previous mistakes that Myspace has made? Will similar mistakes be repeated in the future? How can Myspace, as a relatively small company, defend its position amongst huge players, including Facebook, Google, Apple, as well as the traditional large players in the television market. A range of large and well-funded industry players may view this new initiative of 'social entertainment' as an attractive new business opportunity. The answers to these questions are at the heart of planning a company's future strategic customer management initiatives.

CASE 2.2: PlaceMakers – success factors in the building supplies sector

The company

PlaceMakers is the trading name of Fletcher Distribution Limited, the retail trading arm of Fletcher Building Limited in New Zealand. Fletcher Building Limited is the largest listed company in New Zealand, with a market capitalisation of over NZ $4.5 billion. The company was spun off from Fletcher Challenge in 2001, which was formerly New Zealand's largest multinational business. Fletcher Building has five separate divisions – building products, steel, laminates and panels, infra-structure and distribution. The company manufactures building materials, such as plasterboard, 'Pink Batts' insulation and steel roof tiles. Many of these products are sold through Fletcher's retail division, PlaceMakers, which is the leading tools and building supplies retail store chain in New Zealand. In 1981, the first PlaceMakers superstore opened and by 1984 PlaceMakers had 55 branches throughout

New Zealand. Following various acquisitions, a merger in 1988 with Winstone Trading Limited produced the largest nationwide building materials business in New Zealand.

In 1990, PlaceMakers introduced an owner-operator programme. Under this initiative, selected branch managers were able to become owner-operators. The company currently employs over 2,500 people, has 63 branches and depots, sells 74,000 product lines and serves over 300,000 customers. By 2012, most of these branches are now operated in a partnership with local owners/operators.

The challenge

In the period following the global financial crisis (GFC), PlaceMakers and their trade account clients were faced with difficult trading conditions as the number of building consents issued plunged. The imperative quickly changed from simply getting sufficient supply to clients in the pre-GFC building boom to ensuring they had the best possible relationships with their trade customers. Ensuring customer retention and maximising share of wallet were especially important considerations. The challenge for PlaceMakers was to help their owner-operator partners to get a regular 'temperature reading' of their trade clients so that they could take fast, decisive action to fix emerging issues and to flush out opportunities. Traditional survey research just didn't fit these tough and turbulent times and would be met with scepticism from 'tradies'. What was needed was an approach that was a positive experience for clients and that engaged rather than annoyed them. For owner-operators, a solution was needed to put the feedback right in their hands so that it was easy to get on with recovering vulnerable relationships and strengthening and leveraging strong ones. Among the wide choice of differing research offerings, which consulting firm should PlaceMakers choose?

The solution

The solution came through the adoption of a unique feedback management methodology named 'MirrorWave', which was developed by a team of innovative New Zealand-based customer management consultants. MirrorWave utilises a longitudinal research method that follows individual relationships or experiences by regularly re-contacting customers for feedback, using the same three questions. This feedback is obtained in pulses or 'waves', hence the name of the company. By identifying the changes from one wave to another, a company's management can identify opportunities to detect and respond rapidly to changes in relationships – both bad changes and good changes. The objective of this methodology is to understand the reason for any change and initiate improvement actions aimed at improving individual relationships. Consulting practices embedded in the MirrorWave programme process ensure that insights are converted to action.

The MirrorWave feedback management process is focused on delivering more profitable relationships with customers, with a particular focus on: better retention; boosting share of wallet; reducing the cost to serve and encouraging stronger word-of-mouth.

A fundamental insight underpinning the MirrorWave methodology is that most people hate surveys but like being listened to. The first step is the establishment of the 'feedback family' – the customers, partners or employees who will assist performance improvement over a period of time are courteously and personally invited in. Participants feel encouraged to participate because: instead of a battery of questions, they will be asked only three questions; respondents get to say what they think, rather than answer questions the companies think should be asked; a rapid response is received to issues raised and respondents are kept in the loop about priorities the company is working on. This is part of a conscious strategy to do things differently to the much-maligned traditional customer satisfaction survey.

Changes in individual relationships are then followed across a number of 'waves'. The re-contact method shows how an individual's score is changing from one wave to another and why. This illuminates individual issues and dynamics that cross-sectional averages and statistics often fail to uncover. That is another key insight – stories are better than snapshots. For example, achieving the same average score from one wave to another might tempt a manager to conclude that not much has changed. In reality, though, a longitudinal method often shows that the scores from many individual customers have gone up and many have gone down – giving plenty to work on despite no movement in the average relationship stories – and score change scenarios can be amalgamated to map out sentiment across a key national account or a region. This relationship orientated flow of feedback lends itself to PlaceMakers' trade account based business-to-business setting.

Built into the MirrorWave process are feedback loops. According to the scores customers have given over the previous two waves, response rules are pre-configured with suggestions as to what actions should happen and who should undertake them. An inbuilt task management system sends action items directly to the relationship manager responsible – in the PlaceMakers' case, this is the owner-operator – who can then act themselves or pass on the action item to the Trade Sales Manager responsible. Action items might include, for example, initiating an immediate call from an owner-operator to a customer with problems or a contact from a Trade Sales Manager to recognise an ongoing strong relationship and to talk about possible referrals. An interactive, hosted online console reporting system is used to show managers and leaders in PlaceMakers the key things they need to know about their relationships with trade customers.

The success factors

PlaceMakers' MirrorWave programme followed managed trade account relationships over two waves a year for all owner-operators. In the first two waves, endangered accounts were identified and appropriate relationship-building initiatives were put in place. Many of the accounts that were under threat were saved, resulting in several millions of dollars of revenue being retained. By matching changes in relationships with share of wallet variations, there was a substantial improvement in category management and resulting profitability.

Some of the key success factors in this initiative include:

- A great deal of effort being placed on working with PlaceMakers' account managers to get buy-in prior to receiving the 'wave 1' results. One concern was that they might react adversely to some of the feedback, so the need to not take the feedback personally was emphasised.
- Decisive and individual responses being made by the owner-operator. One owner-operator immediately rang low-scoring key customers the day after the customer submitted his or her feedback and apologised. He said that he was making it his personal goal to make sure things would be turned around by the time of the next MirrorWave in six months. It was also agreed that the account management team would 'get out there' and talk to their customers, whether the feedback was good or not.
- Many owner-operators chose the top 'lift factors' that applied across the branch and worked out how they could strengthen them. They also chose the bottom 'drag factors' and worked out what

they were going to do to fix these issues. By setting an average score target to evaluate progress, they could see in the next wave what impact they had had.

- MirrorWave also formed part of monthly communications to trade customers and teams at the branch. The branch also received a 'Friday Flash' which talked about MirrorWave priorities and progress.
- MirrorWave participation level and scores are also included in the mix of performance metrics which are used to assess performance between the owner-operator and the master franchise holder, Fletcher Distribution.

The results

In 2011, the building industry in New Zealand experience resulted in the worst trading conditions since the beginning of the global financial crisis. These adverse conditions included a 12 per cent decline in residential building consents over the prior year, as both residential and commercial activity declined dramatically. Despite the adverse economic conditions, the relationship-building activities undertaken by PlaceMakers have had a significant role in helping them withstand these difficult operating conditions. The 2011 annual report shows how, despite a 3 per cent sales decline, the operating profit at PlaceMakers rose by 3 per cent. The company performed much better than many rival firms in the building industry and achieved an annualised return of 27 per cent.

The framework was used to assess the return from the MirrorWave programme and focused on:

- better retention – saving vulnerable relationships and strengthening strong ones. Many owner-operators saved valuable but threatened trade relationships. For example, one owner-operator discovered that four key clients, who had been 'funny', were on the verge of leaving. A quick and personal response from the owner-operator and some hard work on resolving issues saved three of them and with it hundreds of thousands of dollars of revenue;
- boosting share of wallet – from better dialogue and relationships with customers. A change of account manager, as a result of feedback, improved the relationship chemistry and three house lots of business were gained;
- reducing the cost to serve – especially focusing on the time spent on service recovery. Although time and cost were not quantified, the trade teams across many owner-operators felt they were less tied up with responding to escalated problems, because they could more easily nip in the bud emerging issues identified from the feedback; and
- encouraging stronger word-of-mouth – the process makes listening and caring more tangible. It is aimed at stimulating positive word-of-mouth and, as a result, new customer acquisition. Owner-operators gave examples of several frustrated trade customers turning into active advocates, which, in turn, led to significant new business.

This case study was written by Reg Price of MirrorWave and is used with his permission.

3 Customer value creation

Relationship Marketing: Development and Key Concepts (Ch. 2)
- Origins and alternative approaches to relationship marketing
- Characteristics and key concepts in relationship marketing

Creating Customer Value (Ch. 3)
- The value the customer receives
- How relationships add value
- How brands add value
- The value proposition
- Value assessment

Relationship Marketing

Building Relationships with Multiple Stakeholders (Ch. 4)
- Customer markets
- Supplier/alliance markets
- Internal markets
- Recruitment markets
- Influence markets
- Referral markets

Relationships and Technology (Ch. 5)
- Digital marketing
- Social media and social influence marketing

The creation of customer value is a key component in relationship marketing and it is increasingly seen as the primary source of competitive advantage. Yet, despite growing attention on this topic, there is remarkably little by way of agreement among managers and commentators on what constitutes 'customer value'. Further, companies typically do not specify in sufficient detail *what* value they seek to deliver to clearly identified customer segments and *how* they propose to deliver this value.

The term 'value creation' has two meanings – the value the company can provide its customers (the 'value the customer receives') and the value the enterprise receives from its customers (the 'value the enterprise receives'). In this chapter we focus on how the enterprise can create and deliver value to its customers. Later, as part of our discussion of CRM in Chapter 8, we discuss how the enterprise can successfully manage relationships to maximise the value it receives from its customers.

Unfortunately, the emphasis in many companies is on this latter element of value. To these companies, customer value means:

- How much money can we extract from the customer?
- How can we sell them more of the existing products and services they are buying?
- How can we cross-sell them new products and services?

Yet in today's competitive arena, where a growing number of businesses vie for a greater share of a finite customer pool, it has become imperative to *first* consider customer value in terms of customer benefit and how we can ensure the customer value proposition is relevant and attractive and that the customer experience is consistently positive. This is at the heart of building relationships.

The value the customer receives

The value the customer receives from the supplier organisation is the total package of benefits, or added values, that enhance the core product. As pointed out by Theodore Levitt, competition exists not between what companies produce in their factories but between 'what they add to their factory output in the form of packaging, services, advertising, customer advice, financing, delivery arrangements, warehousing, and other things that people value'.[1] The value the customer attributes to these benefits is in proportion to the perceived ability of the offer to solve whatever customer problem prompted the purchase.

In this section of the chapter we first review the nature of what the customer buys by explaining how the core and augmented product, relationships and brands all contribute to an enterprise's value proposition. In the next section we then examine the nature of the value proposition and the value assessment.

The nature of value – what the customer buys

Customers do not really buy products or services – when they buy they expect benefits and value from the *total offer* the company provides. This is not just a semantic point; it is an important distinction which can be strategically vital for the long-term survival of a firm. There are many examples of companies who have taken a narrow view and considered their business purely in terms of the traditional products or services. As a result they were forced out of business when a competitor or competitors effectively reshaped the market by not only getting customers, but by keeping them!

How the core and augmented offer add value

For an effective CRM strategy to be realised an understanding of exactly what the customer is buying is critical. Customers derive benefits from the purchase of either goods or services. This is called 'the offer'. An offer can be visualised as a central core surrounded by a series of tangible and intangible attributes, features and benefits. If you think of the core as offering the customer essential solutions, then the surrounding elements are about services and support of various kinds. These may include packaging, information, finance, delivery, warehousing, advice, quality of the website, warranty, reliability, styling and so on.

The offer can be viewed at several levels. These include:[2]

- *Core or generic.* For consumer or industrial products this consists of the basic physical product. The core elements for a camera, for example, consist of the camera body, the viewer, the winding mechanism, the lens and the other core basic physical components which make up the camera. For a banking service, the core elements might be safety and transactional utility in the form of deposits and withdrawals.
- *Expected.* This consists of the generic product together with the minimal purchase conditions which need to be met. When a customer buys a videocassette recorder they expect an instruction book which explains how to programme it, a warranty for a reasonable period should it break down and a service network so that it can be repaired.
- *Augmented.* This is the area that enables one offer to be differentiated from another. For example, IBM's hardware has a reputation for excellent after-sales service. Because of this high-quality service it may be preferred by customers even though the core product – the hardware – may not be the most technologically advanced. They differentiate by 'adding value' to the core, in terms of service, reliability and responsiveness.
- *Potential.* This consists of all potential added features and benefits that are or may be of utility to some buyers. The potential for redefinition of the product gives advantages in attracting new users or enhancing relationships with existing customers. This could make it difficult or expensive for customers to switch to another supplier.

Thus a firm's offer is a complex set of value-based promises and the offer that is developed by the enterprise often needs to be varied according to the target market being considered. People buy to solve problems and they attach value to any offer in proportion to this perception of its ability to achieve their particular ends. In other words, value is assigned by buyers in relationship to the perceived benefits they receive matched against their expectations.

This approach reconciles the company's traditional view of the *product*, seen in the terms of various inputs and processes needed to produce it and the consumer's view of the offer, as being a set of solutions and supporting benefits. Together these elements comprise the total value offer. An example of this is shown in Figure 3.1 based on the personal computer.[3]

The *core product* for a computer is a device that permits input, processing, storage and retrieval of data. This is the minimum requirement. The *expected product* consists of not just the above but also service support, warranty, a recognisable brand name and attractive packaging. The *augmented product* may include the supply of free diagnostic software, a generous trade-in allowance, use of the 'Apple Genius Bar' (for Apple computer users), where you can get friendly and expert advice at the Genius Bar, and other augmentations which are valuable to personal computer buyers. The *potential product* may consist of future applications including a systems controller, a music composer and a host of future 'apps'.

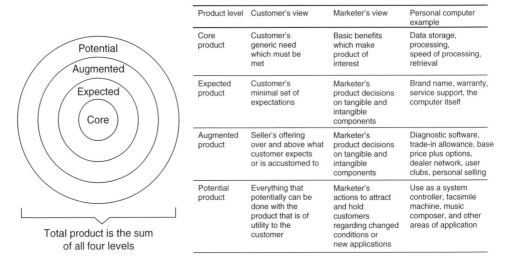

Product level	Customer's view	Marketer's view	Personal computer example
Core product	Customer's generic need which must be met	Basic benefits which make product of interest	Data storage, processing, speed of processing, retrieval
Expected product	Customer's minimal set of expectations	Marketer's product decisions on tangible and intangible components	Brand name, warranty, service support, the computer itself
Augmented product	Seller's offering over and above what customer expects or is accustomed to	Marketer's product decisions on tangible and intangible components	Diagnostic software, trade-in allowance, base price plus options, dealer network, user clubs, personal selling
Potential product	Everything that potentially can be done with the product that is of utility to the customer	Marketer's actions to attract and hold customers regarding changed conditions or new applications	Use as a system controller, facsimile machine, music composer, and other areas of application

Figure 3.1 The total value offer.
Source: Adapted from Collins (1995)

This total value offer concept has had a significant impact on the thinking of managers. Its special contribution lies in a recognition that additional elements, beyond that of the product itself, have a profound impact on the value that can be added for customers. Its limitation has been that there has been no structured approach available for managers to use to identify which elements could be added to the core product. Thus the 'total value offer' highlights the importance of extending the core offer but does not provide much guidance on how to do it.

The supplementary services model

The 'supplementary services' model, developed by former Harvard professor Christopher Lovelock, operationalises the total value offer by providing specific guidelines on where to seek value enhancement for customers. His model identifies eight key elements of supplementary services that can be used to add value to the core product or service. This provides a far more structured approach for considering the expected, augmented and potential elements of a product or service. He suggests there are potentially dozens of different supplementary services, but most can be classified into the following eight clusters: information, consultation, order taking, hospitality services, safe-keeping, exceptions, billing and payment.

Lovelock views these eight supplementary service elements as 'a flower of service', as shown at the top of Figure 3.2. A brief description of these eight clusters and the elements within them follows, based on his pioneering work.[4]

Information

To obtain full value from any service or good, customers need relevant information about it, especially if they are first-time users. Information elements include directions to the

1. Information element
- Easy recognisible phone number
- 24 hour service
- Clear pricing policy
- 'Plain English' wording
- Simple claims handling
- Brochure with full details of product range and features
- Clear details of who we are and where we are
- Easy methods of contact (phone reply paid form, letter, Internet)
- Contact name(s) / team
- Train staff and have systems (e.g. CTI) to deliver
- Members' magazine
- Service guarantee

2. Consultation element
- Information database & computer telephony integration (CTI)
- Quick response
- Technically competent
- 'Customer-friendly' help desk and call centre
- Inventory pro-forma
- Exploit cross-selling opportunities
- Internet advice (detailed)
- Add on benefits (for specific segments or customers)
- Security advice
- Simplified calculations of sum assured
- Legal advice services

3. Order taking element
- Make it easy for different customer segments
    - mail
    - phone
    - fax
    - internet
    - partially pre-completed forms
- Offer alternative payment mechanism
    - credit card
    - instalment
    - payment timings
- Cooling down period
- Add on benefits
- Use of clubs and special programmes
- Generate additional customer information for event-driven marketing

4. Hospitality element
- Toll free claims number
- Telephone manner
- Empathy
- Fast replacement system
- Immediate assistance
- Empowered claims staff
- Dedicated client team
- Free gifts (on 2nd anniversary)
- Add on benefits (car hire, towing)

5. Safekeeping element
- Data security/protection
- Security advice
- Photocopying items
- Anti-theft devices at free or heavily discounted prices
- Help line for emergencies
- Personal alarms

6. Exceptions element
- Specialist help desks for
    - high sums assured
    - high risk items
    - high risk areas
- Bad claims record
- Antiques special cover
- Complaints hot line
- Unconditional service guarantee
- Quality control on repairers
- Customer feedback surveys
- Publicise advocacy

7. Billing element
- No claim discount structure
- Offer of other insurance at discounted rates
- Bonus on second anniversary of policy
- Tips of value/other product offers
- Offers at highly attractive terms for customer

8. Payment element
- Loyalty discount
- Continuous collection
- Monthly payments
- Credit card only
- Use as cross-sale opportunity
- No renewals

Figure 3.2 Using the supplementary services checklist – a personal lines insurance example

site, hours of opening, pricing and instructions for use. The enterprise may be able to attract and keep many more customers if everybody knows about your product, its capabilities, where to get it and how to obtain maximum value from it.

Consultation

Providing information suggests a simple response to customers' questions. Consultation, by contrast, involves a dialogue to probe customer requirements and then develop a tailored solution. In business-to-business markets, 'solution selling', used with expensive industrial equipment and services, is a good example of more complex consultation. Here the sales engineer researches the customer's situation and offers objective advice about the particular package of equipment and systems and service which will yield the best results for the customer.

Order taking

Once customers are ready to buy, a key supplementary service element – order taking – comes into play, which involves accepting applications, orders and reservations. Clear and accurate order taking is essential. Some companies, like banks and insurance companies and utilities, establish a formal relationship with customers and screen out those who do not meet basic enrolment criteria. However, is this policing function excessively bureaucratic involving lengthy forms and delays? There is a risk that the effort to get rid of poor prospects will turn off good ones.

Hospitality services

Hospitality involves taking care of the customer. It finds its full expression in face-to-face encounters with the customer. The enterprise should show pleasure at meeting new customers and recognising existing ones when they return. It may include elements such as offer of transport to and from the service site, availability of drinks and other amenities, customer recognition systems, etc. Here there is a need to adopt the Disney philosophy and treat all customers as 'guests'.

Safe-keeping

The list of potential safe-keeping supplementary services is a long one, but many of these will only be relevant to a given enterprise. For example, customers who purchase computers, motor cars or cameras will be greatly interested in supplementary services such as repair and maintenance services and if they can purchase contracts as a form of insurance against breakdown or damage. Some safe-keeping services add value to physical products and may include packaging, pick-up and delivery, assembly, installation, cleaning and inspection.

Exceptions

Exceptions involve a group of supplementary services that fall outside the routine of normal service delivery. Exceptions include special requests for customised treatment that require a departure from normal operating procedures, problem solving when normal service delivery fails to run smoothly as a result of accidents or delays, equipment failures, or customers experiencing a difficulty using the product. Complaints, suggestions or compliments should be developed through well-defined procedures that make it easy for employees to respond. Restitution in compensating customers for performance failures may involve refunds; compensation or free repair should also be addressed.

Billing

Billing is common to most transactions. Inaccurate, illegible or incomplete bills are very likely to disappoint customers who, up to that point, may have been quite satisfied with the service. Billing should be timely because it will probably result in faster payment. Customers value well-presented billing information. American Express is excellent at doing this. Some companies help customers view their bills at their convenience at an earlier stage than normal. For example, by having billing information provided on an Extranet site.

Payment

In most cases billing and payment are still separate activities. A bill usually requires the customer to take action on payment which may take a lot of time. A challenge is to balance the needs of the organisation for security and efficiency with the customer's own preference for convenience and credit. One element within payment is verification and control. Here organisations need to ensure appropriate controls are in place to ensure correct payment is made without alienating customers through unduly intrusive processes.

The eight supplementary services act as a checklist in a search for new ways to augment existing core products as well as to help design new offerings. Companies wishing to use this framework can usefully start with a workshop with relevant managers to undertake the following tasks:

1. Review generic elements for each of the eight areas of supplementary service and determine which elements are relevant to your business. Service blueprints or flowcharts[5] are useful here to identify the current service activities which will consist of a combination of elements of the core product and supplementary services.
2. Determine if all eight areas are important for your team/business. (Not all products have eight clusters and the nature of the product helps determine which of the supplementary services must be offered and which might be used to enhance customer value.) Identify any new areas and delete those which are not relevant.
3. For each of the important areas selected, identify the key elements that:
   (a) exist at present;
   (b) should be improved or enhanced;
   (c) should be added to enhance customer value.
4. Design an improved offer, subgrouping elements where appropriate.

The example of attributes under each heading in Figure 3.2 is taken from an exercise undertaken for a major European insurance company for their 'personal lines' business. This is a disguised summary of the output of several workshops held to identify a new enhanced insurance product.

Lovelock points out that over time core products become commoditised, so competition shifts to the supplementary services. It is these supplementary services that differentiate successful firms from the less than successful ones and create value for customers. Major new product/service development often takes years to implement and is very costly. Improvements to supplementary services can be more modest in cost and scope but can have a dramatic impact on customer value.

However, creating a superior offer is not enough. It needs to be leveraged by building lasting relationships with those customer groups with whom the enterprise has chosen to do business and also by building greater brand value for customers.

How relationships add value

Once a superior offer has been developed, the enterprise needs to focus on building enduring relationships with customers. Customers value relationships with trusted suppliers who make a superior offer. As relationships are an important dimension of value, considerable effort needs to be expended on building and enhancing these relationships over time.

However, experience suggests that most companies direct the greater part of their marketing activity at winning new customers. But while businesses need new customers, they must also ensure that they are directing enough of their efforts at existing customers. Those companies that focus too much on marketing to new customers often experience the 'leaking bucket' effect, where they lose customers because they are directing insufficient marketing activity generally – and customer service specifically – at them.

Author William Davidow has highlighted this problem: 'It has always been incredible to me how insensitive companies can be to their customers. Most of them don't seem to understand that their future business depends on having the same customer come back again and again.'[6] Too many companies, having secured a customer's order, then turn their attention to seeking new customers without understanding the importance of maintaining and enhancing the relationships with their existing customers.

Customer relationship ladder of loyalty

The customer relationship ladder of loyalty, illustrated in Figure 3.3, identifies the different stages of relationship development. Sales management and charity marketing have used such ladders for many years. We have shown the ladder steps but have depicted the ladder as a rock-face in this figure. This suggests that the transition of customers from one level to another is not necessarily an effortless one but may require considerable energy on the company's part to effect the change. The ladder is relevant for all groups within the channel chain referred to above – direct buyers, intermediaries as well as final consumers.

The first task is to move a new 'Prospect' up to the first rung to a 'Buyer'. The next objective is to turn the new purchaser into a 'Client' who purchases regularly and then a 'Supporter' of the company and its products. The next step is to create 'Advocates' who provide powerful word-of-mouth endorsement for a company. In a business-to-business context an advocate may ultimately develop into a 'Partner' who is closely linked in a trusting and strategic relationship with the supplier.

General Electric's (GE) Appliance Division in the US is a good example of an organisation which has created value by building a closer relationship with its final consumers through an innovative call centre and moving customers from a 'buyer' or 'client' level to a 'supporter' or 'advocate' level on the ladder. The GE Answer Center is widely regarded as one of the best in the world. In setting up this call centre in the 1980s, GE sought to 'personalise GE to consumer and to personalise the consumer to GE'. Unlike most manufacturers, who avoided any contact with the final consumer, GE did an unusual thing at

Figure 3.3 The customer relationship ladder of loyalty

this time and gave its phone number to customers. The Answer Center has now evolved over three decades into an increasingly important relationship-building capability where the current call centres receive millions of calls each year.

Management consultants Robert Wayland and Paul Cole have outlined how GE's Answer Center has contributed to increased customer relationship value in three key areas:

First, resolving immediate problems results in a probability-of-repurchase rate of 80 per cent for the previously dissatisfied customer, as compared to 10 per cent for the dissatisfied but uncomplaining customer and 27 per cent for an average customer. In other words, by making it easier to reach the company and by responding effectively, GE gets more opportunities to convert dissatisfied customers and to strengthen relationships. Second, contact with the centre significantly increases customers' awareness of the GE appliance line and their consideration level. Finally, the knowledge that is generated through customer interactions provides valuable input to the sales, marketing, and new product development processes.[7]

GE's Appliance Division has progressively built capability over the years to make it easy for customers to contact them in a whole variety of ways that extends well beyond its original concept of a telephone-based answer centre. Figure 3.4 provides an image of GE's current appliance website. It provides details of not only the GE Answer Center but also how to contact them for genuine GE parts, warranty management and servicing of appliances. It provides the opportunity to search electronically the GE Appliance Knowledge Base and also provides Facebook, Twitter and YouTube links.

Customers post blogs which are accessible to other customers and potential customers, thus enhancing advocacy. A recent post on bricksandbouquets.blogspot.com stated:

Figure 3.4 General Electric's appliance contact centre website

Bouquet to GE Answer Center (for General Electric appliance)

Our GE microwave/oven combo got into a strange condition this weekend, with a 'Door Locked' status showing while the oven door was open. A call by Karen to the GE Answer Center (on a weekend evening) got an immediate answer; a representative looked up the model and condition immediately; advised us on the immediate remedy. Very cool!

Social media is having an increasingly important role in building relationships with customers and advancing customers to high levels on the relationship ladder. Research shows that customers' and potential customers' commentary placed on social media regarding a company's products by their peers are more trusted than communications directly from the companies themselves.

Positions on the ladder, once reached, are not necessarily stable over time. Different patterns occur in different industries. Research in industries such as retailing suggests that advocacy may reach a peak at the time of purchase but may drop off after that. Thus relationship-based efforts may need to be put in place to build on earlier transactions and interactions with customers. On the other hand, the advancement to a higher level on the ladder may occur slowly over time, as a result of continued product use or experience with a company. For example, one of the authors only became an advocate of Hewlett-Packard printers after a number of years of faultless printer operation, during which time all his other pieces of office equipment developed faults or broke down.

It is not always desirable to progress a relationship with every customer. Some customers or customer segments may not justify the investment needed to develop a 'Supporter' or 'Advocate' relationship, as it may prove too costly to do so. Some customers at the 'Client' level may be 'mercenaries' who exhibit little loyalty and are often expensive to acquire and quick to defect; others may be 'hostages' who are dissatisfied but are locked in by switching costs or monopolistic supplier behaviour. Managers therefore need to consider the existing and potential lifetime value of customers and determine whether it is appropriate to make this commitment. We address this later in the chapter.

The role of advocates

The 'advocate' level on the customer ladder of loyalty is worthy of special emphasis. Referrals from customers are among the most relevant, effective and believable sources of information for other customers. A number of researchers have argued that word-of-mouth is the most effective source of information for consumers. While commercial sources normally inform the buyer, personal sources legitimise or evaluate products for them. Legitimisation makes the step of converting prospects into customers on the ladder of loyalty that much easier.

As noted in Chapter 3, Jones and Sasser of Harvard Business School found that, except in rare cases, total or complete customer satisfaction is key to securing customer loyalty and that there is a tremendous difference between the loyalty of merely satisfied and the loyalty of completely satisfied customers. They cite Xerox research that found totally satisfied customers were six times more likely than satisfied customers to repurchase Xerox products and services over the next 18 months.

These authors concluded that customer referrals, endorsements and spreading the word are extremely important forms of consumer behaviour for a company. In many product and service categories, word-of-mouth is one of the most important factors in acquiring new customers. Frequently, it is easier for a customer to respond honestly to a question about whether he or she would recommend the product or service to others than to a question about whether he or she intended to repurchase the product or service. Such indications of loyalty, obtained through customer surveys, are frequently ignored because they are soft measures of behaviour that are difficult to link to eventual purchasing behaviour.[8]

Which companies have a high proportion of customers who make such referrals and endorsement and exhibit advocacy? Discussions with consumers and executives suggest the following as examples:

- Airlines: Singapore Airlines, Virgin Atlantic, Southwest Airlines
- Banking: First Direct – a UK bank
- Computers and mobile devices: Apple Computers
- Healthcare: Shouldice – a Canadian hospital
- Industrial services: Service Master – a US cleaning services company
- Motor cars: Mercedes-Benz, Lexus

- Retailing: Nordstroms in the US, Marks & Spencer in the UK, Lane Crawford in Hong Kong, Woolworths in South Africa
- Trucks: Scania, Volvo
- Watches: Rolex.

However, neither company practice nor academic researchers pay sufficient attention to the important area of advocacy and referral marketing. Few organisations have any formal processes that utilise referrals from existing customers. Though many organisations recognise that customers can be the most legitimate source of referrals to their prospective customers, most tend simply to let referrals happen rather than proactively developing marketing activities to leverage the power of advocacy.

The role of terrorists

The Jones and Sasser research identifies a similar set of customer types to those in the ladder above. They point out that customers behave in one of four basic ways: as loyalists, as defectors, as mercenaries or as hostages. 'Turning as many customers as possible into the most valuable type of loyalist, the apostle, and eliminating the most dangerous type of defector or hostage, the terrorist, should be every company's ultimate objective.'[9] In particular, this latter category 'the terrorist', not mentioned earlier, is of special interest.

Terrorists represent the most dangerous group of defectors. These are customers who have had a bad experience and make it a crusade to tell others about their anger and frustration. Unfortunately, terrorists are typically far more committed and effective at creating negative word-of-mouth than advocates are at demonstrating positive word-of-mouth.

Consumer 'terrorism' and militancy are on the increase and as customer expectations appear to increase at a faster rate than organisations' capacity to improve customer service, we can expect increased activity in this arena in the years ahead. Television programmes such as *Watchdog* in the UK (www.bbc.co.uk/watchdog), consumer advocate columns in Sunday newspapers and many sites on the Internet provide enormous opportunities for 'terrorist' activity. Websites such as www.Grumbletext.com shown in Figure 3.5 provide a structured environment for individuals to vent their displeasure.

The low cost and pervasive nature of the Internet make it an ideal channel for aggrieved customers to communicate their dissatisfaction, frustration or anger to a wide range of existing or prospective customers. The following selection represents a very small number of the many websites aimed at such communications:

www.insurancejustice.com

www.screwedbyinsurance.com

www.allstateinsurancesucks.com

www.amexsux.com

www.untied.co

www.notgoodenough.org

www.shamscam.com

Figure 3.5 grumbletext.com website home page

As part of their value creation activities, organisations should consider not just the task of building customer satisfaction and advocacy but also how to deal with negative reactions to their products or services. A content review of the websites listed above suggests that in many cases it was not so much the issue that there was a problem experienced by customers, but rather little or nothing was done to address the problem.

Leading relationship-oriented companies take the view 'the customer who complains is your friend'. They create customer value by building mechanisms to surface problems and to react accordingly. For example:

- Procter & Gamble publish 0800 telephone numbers and Internet addresses on all their products to encourage customer feedback. Johnson and Johnson responded immediately and with total integrity to the Tylenol incident. (Compare their reaction to that of BP in the Gulf of Mexico oil spill!)
- Marriott Hotels put enormous emphasis on encouraging all guests to complete customer satisfaction forms on completion of a visit to their hotels.
- Many companies are now offering unconditional service guarantees that signal a customer promise to both external customers and internal employees.
- Intuit's listening posts.

Such initiatives may not represent a high level of sophistication but are as important to building customer value as moving customers to higher levels of loyalty.

How brands add value

The brand is also an important element in contributing to the value proposition. Originally the role of a brand was to enable a customer to identify the manufacturer of a product. Over time the concept of a brand broadened to include further meaning: symbols, images, feelings and relationships. Brands add value to the company because they add value to the customer. Thus a product is something that is made by a company; a brand is something that is bought by a customer. A product can be imitated by competitors, while a brand is different from that of its competitors. A strong brand is unique.

David Aaker, a professor of Marketing Strategy at the University of California at Berkeley, has neatly summed up the role of the brand in value creation for the customer:

Brand-equity assets generally add or subtract value for customers. They can help them interpret, process and store huge quantities of information about products and brands. They also can affect customer confidence in the purchase decision (due to either past-use experience, familiarity with the brand and its characteristics). Potentially more important is the fact that both perceived quality and brand associations can enhance customers' satisfaction with the use experience. Knowing that a piece of jewellery came from Tiffany can affect the experience of wearing it: the user can actually feel different.[10]

We discussed above how the core and augmented product offer adds to customer value. A brand adds to this offer in ways that differentiate it from other similar products, in ways that are important and of *value* to the customer. What distinguishes a brand from an unbranded product and gives it value to the customer is the sum total of customers' perceptions about both product performance and their complete experience with the brand. Brands have become a major determining factor in repeat purchase and an important way of adding differentiation. Branding also has an important role in helping customers be assured of high and consistent quality.

Perceived quality is as dependent on factors such as reliability, responsiveness, assurance and empathy as it is on tangibles. This means that managers should give increased attention to these factors, which increase customer value as a means of brand building. The American Express card is a good example of a strong brand that is valued highly by customers as a result of association with these factors. Historically, in strict product terms, it has compared unfavourably with Visa or Mastercard:

- For many years American Express offered no card with a convenient option to pay off its bill monthly. The entire balance had to be paid upon receipt of the statement. Only around a quarter or less of the number of merchants worldwide that take Visa/Mastercard accept American Express.
- Emergency cash is available to American Express holders at more limited locations than for the Visa or Mastercard holder.
- The American Express yearly fee is typically more than any Visa or Mastercard – some of the competitive offerings do not charge any annual fees.

Despite these shortcomings, the American Express card is a highly successful brand. Many consumers are willing to pay more for a less useful, less convenient credit card.

By positioning their card as a 'travel and entertainment card' and themselves as a customer-focused organisation, American Express has created a distinctive set of perceived benefits that no other card has achieved. Among these is a high degree of responsiveness when the cardholder has a real problem such as a lost card. One of the authors recently reflected on how, over 20 years ago, the American Express office in New York could replace a stolen card within two hours, while in the late 2000s it took a major British bank over 15 days to accomplish the same task. As a result of such experiences, the brand image is further enhanced or diminished in the eyes of the customer.

The importance of brand image

Examples of the value of brand image are apparent in all industries. One of the best illustrations of this is the taste test for diet Coke and diet Pepsi, shown in Figure 3.6. The column titled 'open' shows the results of a survey of an open taste where the two products were placed in front of the respondents. Apparently using their most discriminating taste sensitivities, 65 per cent of those surveyed preferred Coke, while 23 per cent preferred Pepsi and 12 per cent of them ranked them equally.

When a matched sample was subjected to a blind taste test (where the identity of the two colas was concealed – see column titled 'blind'), there was a very different result. The blind taste test showed 44 per cent preferred Coke and 51 per cent preferred Pepsi, an increase in preference for Pepsi of over 120 per cent. Significantly different results were obtained from the consumers in the two different controlled tests.

	Open	Blind
Prefer Pepsi	23%	51%
Prefer Coke	65%	44%
Equal/Can't Say	12%	5%

Figure 3.6 Brand image study: Coke versus Pepsi

How can this great difference be explained? The answer is that customers 'taste' both the drink and its brand image. This brand image adds value to the consumer when they see the familiar Coke packaging and logo. While these 'added values' may relate to an emotional level they are, nevertheless, real for the customer perceiving them. The subsequent well-known 'New Coke debacle' when Coca-Cola introduced a new product that tasted better in blind taste tests but was not acceptable to customers, taught them a painful lesson about their brand. Coke is not only seen as a drink by its consumers, but also in the light of what it represents in terms of Americana, its heritage and its past relationship with them.

In the business-to-business sector, a similar form of trust and loyalty can be built with the brand. Many executives who have purchased from companies such as IBM and McKinsey & Co. have heard such quotes as: 'No purchasing manager in recorded history has ever been fired for buying IBM'; and 'McKinsey is the safe option'. Brands such as these have historically been able to create customer value by positioning themselves as highly trusted partners.

Value for the customer is added through the creation of brand image. As a result, the owners of strong brand names can command higher prices for their offerings as they are valued more by customers. The value embedded in brands can be profound, as Kevin Lane Keller, a professor at Amos Tuck School, has pointed out: 'the relationship between brand and the consumer can be seen as a type of bond or pact. Consumers offer their trust and loyalty with the implicit understanding that the brand will behave in certain ways and provide them utility through consistent product performance and appropriate pricing, promotion and distribution programs and actions.'[11]

Building brand value through relationships

Don Peppers and Martha Rogers have noted that business is about persuading consumers to participate in a dialogue by establishing a relationship that helps bond the consumer to the brand. By building a relationship with customers, the organisation can create real and tangible value for them. A good example of this value creation can be seen in motorcycle manufacturer Harley-Davidson's successful turnaround. Harley's success is closely tied to needs, aspirations and relationships with its customer base and they have played to that strength (see box).

Harley-Davidson: building a relationship brand

The Harley-Davidson story is one that shows how a world-famous brand used customer relationships to emerge from near extinction and reclaim its pre-eminent position in the market. It delivered double-digit growth in both turnover and profits for many years. In 1903, Harley-Davidson produced a total of three motorcycles. In 2003, they built more than 250,000 and shipped them with extensive lines of branded clothing, parts and accessories and collectibles to more than 60 countries worldwide. Sales were over $4 billion. Gross profit over $1 billion and net income more than $0.5 billion. By 2008, Harley built over 300,000 motorcycles, nearly double the number it assembled in 2000.

A well-established Harley Owners Group (HOG) holds regular rallies around the world. These are often attended by company executives so that they can meet customers and talk about the company's vision and values. Anyone who buys a Harley-Davidson motorcycle becomes a member of the Harley-Davidson Club. The clubs meet at the dealerships, where they can ride together and also buy the company's branded clothing.

HOG is a sub-brand that represents a relationship to a community of people, an affinity group of motorcycle owners. With HOG clubhouses strategically located in the dealerships, owners consume their product as part of a Harley-Davidson community. They have not only bought a Harley motorcycle, they have formed a relationship with other members of the owners club and identify with the group through wearing branded merchandise. Harley-Davidson owners place great value on the brand and are extremely loyal with a 95 per cent repurchase rate.[1] A good number of them demonstrate their relationship to the brand by having a Harley-Davidson tattoo on their arms – a unique and permanent symbol of loyalty to the brand!

[1] Gummesson, E. (2008), *Total Relationship Marketing*, 3rd edn., Oxford: Butterworth-Heinemann, p. 134.

Despite excellent relationships with existing customers, more recently Harley-Davidson has had problems. This is partly a result of unrealistic projections of future demand which resulted in substantial increase in production capacity and resulting increased costs, and partly because of the global financial crisis in 2008. In addition to the global financial crisis, a key problem has been the profile of its core customer, the middle-aged white American male. This group will contract in the coming decade. As analysts point out, Harley-Davidson survived earlier economic downturns because their motorcycles were in short supply. With increased capacity, Harley became just another manufacturer, vulnerable to a cyclical economy. In the fourth quarter of 2009, it suffered its first quarterly loss in 16 years

By the end of 2011, there were signs of improvement in Harley-Davidson's position. The company experienced over 5 per cent increase in growth in the third quarter of the year and a substantial increase in profitability over the previous period. It still commands roughly 50 per cent of the US market and is one of the most recognised brands in the world, providing scale advantages over many of its competitors with the exception of Japanese companies such as Honda. The company is highly focused on improving its cost structure and restructuring its business to be more profitable in the future. Harley-Davidson has a substantial opportunity to leverage its brand to penetrate international markets. The company reported that, in 2010, three new dealerships were opened in India and a subsidiary operation in China. It has plans to introduce more dealerships in China and new dealerships in Brazil over the next two years. Despite its over-capacity problems created by unrealistic projections of demand, Harley-Davidson remains a stellar example of building a relationship-based brand.

The behaviour of employees also contributes greatly to the brand, whether it is Harley-Davidson executives meeting with customers, outstanding customer service in the first class suite in the Singapore Airlines A380, or exemplary service recovery at Marriot hotel.

Singapore Airlines is known as one of the most successful airlines in the world and one of the best for customer service. It is a good example of an enterprise putting considerable emphasis on building a brand relationship through moments of truth. Through its 'Singapore Girl' campaign, the brand is closely associated with high-quality service. It delivers this outstanding service by having a ratio of one flight attendant to every 22 passengers, the highest in the world and well above the industry average. Singapore Airlines' branding places great emphasis on its staff. In a very real sense *its staff is its brand*. High-quality service is not just confined to the first class and business class offerings of major airlines. Regional US carrier Southwest Airlines provides a no-frills service to its customers, yet it has an outstanding reputation for encouraging its employees to contribute to the brand experience. Southwest has many initiatives in place to encourage its employees to behave in an authentic and caring manner towards its customer base.

Branding the Internet and social media

Two brand experts, Martin Lindstrom and Tim Andersen, use Procter & Gamble (P&G) as an illustration of the increasing importance of branding on the Internet and in social media.[12] In 1930 Procter & Gamble did not spend any media dollars on radio. All money was dedicated to the print media. By 1935, some 50 per cent of the total Procter & Gamble media budget was devoted to radio. In 1950, three per cent of Procter's media spending went to television. By 1955, 80 per cent of their total media budget was devoted to television. In 1998 Procter & Gamble established their first worldwide online centre. The purpose: to ensure that Procter & Gamble would be ready to move their television budget onto the Internet at the right time.

By 1999, P&G Interactive was named Marketer of the Year by *Advertising Age*. They have led the way in gaining online consumer acceptance, standardising measurement, defining advertising models and making online media easier to buy. They have also demonstrated considerable ingenuity in their Internet branding campaigns. For example, in an online campaign for Bounty paper towels, P&G created a new advertising format called 'sequential messaging' in which it broke down the message into four units and delivered them to the user at different areas of the site, based on their level of involvement with the company. P&G found that sequential messaging significantly increased purchase intent.[13]

By 2011, digital media has 'become very integrated with how we operate, it's become part of the way we do marketing,' stated P&G marketing chief Marc Pritchard. 'It's kind of the oldest form of marketing – word-of-mouth – with the newest form of technology.' P&G currently spends over $9 billion per year to advertise its products. The company is finding social media sites such as Twitter, Facebook and YouTube to be more effective channels for reaching women and has spent much of 2010 experimenting with campaigns in these arenas. A number of smaller P&G brands, including Pepto-Bismol, Braun and Aussie, now have digital media as the biggest piece of their marketing plans.

Bob McDonald, the new Chairman and CEO of P&G, clearly has made digital marketing a high priority. 'We're going to be the most digitized company in the world,' he said in 2011. 'The eventuality of the world,' he said, 'is a one-on-one relationship with every consumer [which] results in trust, loyalty, all the things that a brand wants. So the first company in the world that's able to create that one-on-one relationship with the consumer by definition will win.' In 2010, P&G invested heavily in Facebook marketing to build relationship marketing programmes. It now has at least 15 brands with six-figure Facebook followings, and two – Pringles and Old Spice – with 9 million and 1.3 million respectively. P&G also has been using its Facebook pages for e-commerce.

According to *eMarketer* statistics, spending in the US online advertising market will increase 20.2 per cent to $31.1 billion in 2011, driven in large part by growth among consumer packaged goods companies, with this number increasing by 14 per cent to 29 per cent each year through 2015.[14] We return to examine digital marketing and social influence marketing in detail later in Chapter 5.

Value and branding in context

Three decades ago branding was mainly the domain of consumer goods. Now we see efforts to establish and sustain distinctive brands in every sector. In the past, many companies have emphasised the brand name rather than brand equity. Brand equity represents the set of brand assets and liabilities that collectively add to or subtract from customer value and this has recently become a key area of focus for all enterprises. With a widespread acceptance of the importance of brands, there has been increasing recognition that the consumer's choice depends less on evaluation of the functional benefits of a product or service and more on their assessment of the company and the people behind it.

In an offline environment, the relationship that customers have with a brand is frequently the result of their interactions with the staff of that organisation and their perceptions of service quality. The brand relationship is the outcome of a series of brand contacts that the customer has with the organisation. Over time these customer contacts or 'moments of truth' result in increased or decreased customer value.

In an online environment, the Internet and social media creates major opportunities and threats for brands. The greatest opportunities relate to speed, cost and ubiquity. The great advantage the Internet has over more traditional media is its ability to manage customer relationships from awareness to buying action. It also potentially enables customer contact 24 hours per day at much lower cost. However, as noted above, it is a much less trusted medium. The power of social media, whereby existing customers support and endorse products, adds a new and exciting dimension to relationship building. Overall, there are probably more similarities than differences when building a traditional versus an online brand. The key issue is to ensure that where customers use offline and online channels there is brand consistency and they have superior customer experiences. We will return to this issue when we discuss multi-channel integration in Chapter 8.

The value proposition

Having examined how product and service offers, relationships and brands can be utilised in order to create customer value, we now turn our attention to how these components of customer value can be utilised in a formal statement of value, or *value proposition*.

In recent years managers have started to use the term value proposition increasingly frequently. This term is employed in two ways by organisations. First, in general terms it is used to describe the notion of creating value in a very broad sense. Second, in more specific terms, it is used to describe a detailed analytical approach to value creation. However, the term is most frequently used in the general sense without any analytical underpinnings. Discussions with many organisations suggest that relatively few attempts have been made by them to develop a structured approach to formulating value propositions. Where they do have a formal statement of their value proposition this is often not based on any analysis.

A value proposition defines the relationship between what a supplier offers and what a customer purchases by identifying how the supplier satisfies the customers' needs across different customer activities (e.g., acquiring, using and disposing of a product). Specifically, it defines the relationship between the performance attributes of a product or service, the fulfilment of needs and the total cost. The aim of all businesses is to create a value proposition for customers, be it implicit or explicit, which is superior to and more profitable than those of their competitors.

Value propositions explain the relationship between the performance of the product, the fulfilment of the customer's needs and the total cost to the customer over the customer relationship life-cycle (from acquisition of the product through to usage and ownership and eventual disposal). As every customer is different and has changing needs, it is crucial that the value proposition for each customer is clearly and individually articulated and cognisant of the customer's lifetime value. Thus the economic value of customer segments to the organisation informs decisions about the value proposition.

A structured method for developing value propositions, originated by consulting firm McKinsey & Co. and further developed by others,[15] is comprised of two main parts: *formulation of the value proposition* and profitable delivery of this value proposition by means of a *value delivery system.*

Formulating the value proposition

Formulating the value proposition forms the first part of the value proposition concept. Some examples of value propositions, based on work by consultants Michael Lanning and Lynn Phillips,[16] are shown in Figure 3.7. The approach followed in developing these value propositions involves determining:

- the target customers,
- the benefits offered to these customers,
- the price charged relative to the competition, and
- a formal statement of the value proposition.

The value proposition approach suggests companies should adopt a three-step sequence of:

Company/ Product	Target Customers	Benefits	Price	Value Proposition
Perdue (chicken)	Quality-conscious consumers of chicken	Tenderness	10 per cent premium	More tender, golden chicken at a moderate price premium
Volvo (station wagon)	Safety-conscious 'upscale' families	Durability and safety	20 per cent premium	The safest, most durable station wagon your family can travel in at a significant price premium
Domino's (pizza)	Convenience– minded pizza lovers	Delivery speed and good quality	15 per cent premium	A good pizza, delivered hot to your door within 30 minutes of ordering, at a moderate price premium

Figure 3.7 Examples of value propositions for various industries

- analysing and segmenting markets by the values customers desire;
- rigorously assessing opportunities in each segment to deliver superior value;
- explicitly choosing the value proposition that optimises these opportunities.

Step 1: Analysing markets based on value

This first step involves understanding the price/benefit opportunities that exist within the market and here the value map can prove a useful tool. Value maps provide a graphical presentation of the relative positions of different competitors in terms of the benefits and price attributes that relate to customer value.

Figure 3.8 shows a value map for the airline industry past and present following a study undertaken by a group of New York University researchers.[17] The map depicts a value frontier that incorporates the price/benefit positions of the major carriers. If all competitors are in a similar position on such a map, commoditisation and reduced profitability would probably result. This situation is apparent with many players in the airline industry. On the other hand, highly successful companies tend to establish differentiated positions on the value frontier. If companies fall consistently in the underperformer region of the map their future survival is questionable.

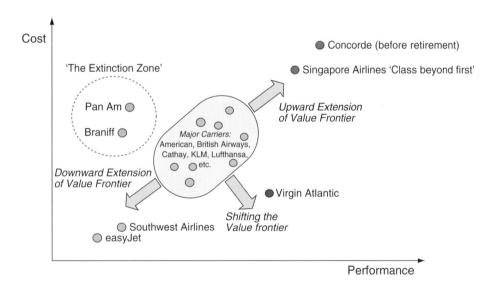

Figure 3.8 Value map for the airline industry – past and present.
Source: Developed from Kambil, Ginsberg and Bloch (1996)

The researchers suggest three generic strategies for developing differentiated value propositions on the value map:[18]

1. *Extend the value frontier towards the low end of the value map* – the strategy adopted by Southwest Airlines in the US and by easyJet airlines in Europe.
2. *Extend the value frontier towards the high end of the value map* – this strategy was adopted by British Airways and Air France with their Concorde fleets before they were retired.

Pursuit of this strategy is often based on technological innovation. Singapore Airlines now offer a first class suite with their 'class beyond first' offering.

3 *Shift the value frontier* – the strategy adopted by Virgin Atlantic with its 'upper class' service, first class facilities and a highly distinctive personality based on a business class fare structure.

High-performance companies characteristically focus on the development of superior value propositions in order to take advantage of new growth opportunities and identifiable, attractive customer groups.

Step 2: Assessing opportunities in each segment to deliver superior value

When a critical review of any market is undertaken it soon becomes obvious that the idea of a single market for a given product or service is a highly restrictive viewpoint. As we discussed in the previous chapter, all markets are made up of market segments, or groups of customers with the same or similar needs. Reaching the most profitable and suitable market segments is a matter of evaluating the opportunities and limitations in each segment for delivering superior customer value. Even where the offer made to customers is technically identical to competitors' offers, efforts to differentiate the total or 'package' offer in terms of relationships and branding can reap significant rewards.

Many companies that have adopted a market aggregation or macro-segmentation strategy in the past are now actively addressing new ways of appealing to customers at lower levels of segment granularity. In considering new attributes that may form part of an enhanced offer made to more specific customer segments, companies will find it useful to use the 'supplementary services' approach illustrated in Figure 3.2 as a creativity tool.

Value maps may also be constructed at the market segment level to enable very specific price/benefit opportunities to be evaluated within them, thus highlighting the most promising ones and the most appropriate propositions for these segments. Assessments of potential opportunities for delivering superlative value should involve a rigorous analysis of cost, competitive offers and, importantly, organisational 'fit' on both strategic and operational levels. Part of this exercise should include a formal assessment of the market attractiveness and business strengths within each segment. Frameworks such as the directional policy matrix[19] can be used to undertake this analysis.

Step 3: Explicitly choosing the value proposition

Having identified the target market segments, the next priority is to create a value proposition of winning relevance. The characteristics of the segments that form some markets may vary so radically that different value propositions will be required for different segments. For example, in the automotive industry, the needs and preferences of customers in the luxury segment who buy Rolls-Royce cars are clearly distinct from those of customers in the trendy youth segment who buy Smart cars or VW Beetles. Businesses that justifiably exhibit fewer marked differences between their product and service offers may benefit from approaching the value proposition issue by developing a generic value proposition for the market as a whole and then developing more specific variants for each specific segment.

Once formulated, value propositions should be carefully reviewed to confirm that they are truly distinctive and appropriate. The checklist in Figure 3.9 can be used to determine whether a superior value proposition has really been developed.

1. Is the target customer clearly identified?
2. Are the customer benefits explicit, specific, measurable and distinctive?
3. Is the price, relative to competition, explicitly stated?
4. Is the value proposition clearly superior for the target customer (superior benefits, lower price or both)?
5. Do we have, or can we build, the skills to deliver it?
6. Can we deliver it at a cost that permits an adequate profit?
7. Is it viable and sustainable in the light of competitors and their capabilities?
8. Is it the best of several value propositions we considered?
9. Are there any impending discontinuities (in technology, customer habits, regulation, market growth, etc.) that could change our position?
10. Is the value proposition clear and simple?

Figure 3.9 Value proposition checklist.
Source: Adapted from M. Lanning and E. Michaels (1988), A Business Is a Value Delivery System, McKinsey Staff Paper, and Lanning and Phillips (1991)

The value delivery system

The means by which the value proposition is delivered represents the other half of the value proposition concept. The importance of having a system or framework for value delivery stems from the realisation that focusing on the traditional physical sequence of 'make the product/service and sell the product/service' is suboptimal. The value delivery system emphasises that companies need to shift from a traditional view of seeing their business as a set of functional activities to an externally oriented view that sees their business as a vehicle for value delivery. The value delivery system consists of three parts as portrayed in Figure 3.10: choose the value, provide the value and communicate the value.

Choose the value. Choosing the most appropriate value proposition involves understanding the forces driving demand, customer economics, the buying process and how well the competition serves customer needs, particularly in terms of their products, service and prices charged.

Provide the value. Developing a product and service package that provides clear and superior value involves focusing on product quality and performance, service cost and responsiveness, manufacturing cost and flexibility, channel structure and performance and price structure.

Communicate the value. Engaging in promotional activity to persuade customers that the value offered is better than that of competitors not only involves sales promotion, advertising and the sales force, but also the provision of outstanding service in a way that is recognised and remembered by the target audience.

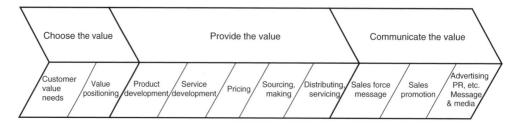

Figure 3.10 The value delivery system.
Source: Adapted from Bower and Garda (1998)

Building the value proposition

Correct formulation of the proposition and building a value delivery system to ensure it has an impact on the customer base represent the two main elements of the value proposition. Much of the success of a value delivery system depends on the thoroughness and innovation with which value is both generated and reinforced throughout the supplier organisation. 'Differentiating the winners is the extent to which this value proposition is echoed in the business system, through changes in branch service delivery, new products, systems that provide integrated information to customers and those serving them, relationship pricing, etc. Executing these changes is more difficult than choosing the value but also provides formidable obstacles to imitation.'[20]

In the case studies at the end of this chapter we provide two examples of companies that have developed formal approaches to value proposition development. The case studies show how British Telecommunications plc, one of the world's leading telecommunications providers and one of the largest private sector companies in Europe, has developed a sophisticated approach to the development of value propositions with its business-to-business customers, and how Zurich Financial Services, a leading provider of financial protection and wealth accumulation products and solutions has developed an approach for developing value propositions for its consumer markets.

Value assessment

To determine if the value proposition is likely to result in a superior customer experience, it is necessary to quantify the relative importance that customers place upon the various attributes of a product. A value assessment based on subjective judgments about the attributes and benefits that are important to the customer can fall prey to the assumption that the supplier and customer attach the same importance to the various product attributes – rarely do they.

Managers seeking to build customer-oriented offers need to know what specific combination of product and service features, relationships and brands are most important to the organisation's key customer segments. This is the domain of value assessment. Value assessment can be undertaken by a company using its managers' perceptions of what customers view as important or by seeking this information directly from customers.

Experienced and informed managers may have a reasonably accurate perspective regarding the product and service features and benefits that are most important to their customers, especially where these views are supported by other evidence. We have seen good examples of companies successfully using their managers' experience to identify key attributes by which customers make choices.

However, a frequent mistake made by companies is assuming customers attach the same importance to these attributes as do the company's own managers. Experience suggests that even when an organisation correctly identifies most of those attributes which are most relevant to the customer, frequently the relative ranking of these by the customer and the supplier vary substantially. A much better way is to assess the offer from the customer's perspective and to take into account differences in customer perception across market segments.

Traditional means of customers' assessment of value

The most common means of discovering the perceived value of product attributes is to ask a representative sample of customers to rank them in terms of importance on a five, seven or ten point scale. Most managers are very familiar with this approach, which requests respondents to rank particular features or service attributes on, for instance, a four or five-point scale from 'very satisfied' to 'very dissatisfied' or 'very important' to 'very unimportant'.

However, where a large number of attributes are concerned, this method is impractical and offers little real insight. An alternative approach is to ask respondents to place a weight from one to ten against each attribute while ranking them on a scale of, say, 'very satisfied' to 'very dissatisfied'. This approach is also prone to problems, particularly where respondents do not know the importance of some features, may be unwilling to disclose their opinions, may rate too many attributes as being very high in importance, or may be influenced by peer pressure, causing some features to be overrated.

Another approach is to request respondents to allocate a total of 100 points among all the elements identified. However, this can be a daunting task and can result in an arbitrary allocation of points. Dissatisfaction with such methods led researchers to develop a research technique called 'trade-off analysis'. This tool is a much more robust method for identifying the implicit importance that customers attach to key attributes.

Improving value assessment using trade-off analysis

A more realistic evaluation of customer value can be obtained by asking a representative sample of customers to rank the product's attributes and then, using an analytical tool such as conjoint analysis, or trade-off analysis, to apply a weighting system to discover the weight given to different levels of each attribute. Here advanced computer analysis is used to calibrate the importance 'weights', which can then be aggregated to provide an objective measure of the 'utility' that customers prescribe to each element of customer value.

This technique is based on the simple concept of trading off one attribute against another. For example, the purchaser of a new car is likely to trade-off a number of specific product attributes in agreeing the purchase price and specifications. Vehicle performance, petrol economy, number of seats, safety features, boot capacity, low price and so on will have factored in his or her decision. Trade-off analysis can also be used to identify customers who share common preferences in terms of product attributes and may reveal substantial market segments with service needs that are not fully catered for by existing offers.

Trade-off analysis possesses several advantages over more traditional forms of value assessment, as it:

1. employs measures of attribute importance that do not rely on direct rating by respondents;
2. forces a trade-off among very important attributes to determine which are the most important; and
3. achieves this for each customer separately.

There are two forms of trade-off analysis. The 'full profile' approach presents respondents with a full profile description of an offer and asks them to rate the offer's constituent elements. The 'pairwise' trade-off approach asks respondents to rank combinations of variants of two attributes, from the least preferred to the most preferred, and then repeats this for a series of other pairs of attributes.[21]

The 'full profile' form of trade-off analysis is a more commonly used approach and is often deemed more realistic by researchers as all the product's aspects are considered at the same time. However, if the number of attributes is large then the judging process used for each individual profile in the 'full profile' approach can become very complex and demanding. For that reason other researchers prefer the 'pairwise' trade-off approach. The Robotic Components example (see box) demonstrates the use of the pairwise trade-off analysis. Specialist market research texts provide more detailed discussion of these trade-off approaches including the full profile form.[22]

Robotic Components Inc.

Robotic Components Inc. is a manufacturer of components for the growing industrial robot market. As part of a new relationship marketing initiative they are examining various alternative value propositions in order to improve their logistics to customers. For example, they believe that buyers might be prepared to sacrifice some decrease in stock availability for an improvement in delivery reliability of a day or two. They decided to undertake a value assessment, using the pairwise trade-off approach, based on the following options of stock availability, order cycle time and delivery reliability:

Stock availability:	75%
	85%
	95%
Order cycle time:	2 days
	3 days
	4 days
Delivery reliability	± 1 day
	± 3 days

With this pairwise form of conjoint analysis, the various trade-offs are placed before the respondent as a series of matrices. The respondent then completes each matrix to illustrate his/her preference for service alternatives. Thus, with the first trade-off matrix between order cycle time and stock availability, shown below, the most preferred combination would be an order cycle time of 2 days with a stock availability of 95 per cent (where the number 1 in the matrix represents the first preferred option). The last preferred combination is an order cycle time of 5 days with a stock availability of 75 per cent (where the number 9 in the matrix represents the ninth and least preferred option). For the other combinations the respondents complete the matrix to show their own preferences. An example of a typical response is given below for each of the three trade-off matrices:

Distribution service trade-off matrices

		Order cycle time		
		2 days	*3 days*	*4 days*
Stock availability:	75%	6	8	9
	85%	3	5	7
	95%	1	2	4

		Order cycle time		
		2 days	*3 days*	*4 days*
Delivery reliability:	±1 day	1	3	5
	±3 days	2	4	6

		Stock availability		
		75%	*85%*	*95%*
Delivery reliability:	±1 day	4	2	1
	±3 days	6	5	3

Once these trade-off matrices are completed, computer analysis is used to determine the implicit 'importance weights' that underlie the initial preference rankings. For the data in the above example the following weights are identified for a given respondent:

Service element		Importance weight
1. Stock availability:	75%	−0.480
	85%	0
	95%	+0.480

2. Delivery time:	2 days	+0.456
	3 days	0
	4 days	−0.456
3. Delivery reliability:	±1 day	+0.239
	±3 days	−0.239

Thus, for this respondent, stock availability appears to be marginally more important than delivery time and both were in the region of twice as important as delivery reliability. Information such as this can be most useful. For example, in this case, a stock availability of 85 per cent with 2 days' delivery and a reliability of ±1 day is seen as being almost equally acceptable as 95 per cent with 2 days' delivery and a reliability of ±3 day (a combined weight of 0.695 [0 + 0.456 + 0.239] compared with 0.697 [0.480 + 0.456 −0.239]). This suggests that a tightening up on delivery reliability might reduce stockholding and still provide an acceptable level of customer service.

Robotic Components then repeated this for different customers, identified key customer segments and used this information to create appropriate offers to different customer segments.

Source: Adapted from an example by Professor Martin Christopher and used with his permission

Trade-off analysis can be used to identify customers who share common preferences in terms of attributes. Experience of researchers and consultants working in this area suggests that this form of analysis may often reveal substantial market segments with service needs that are not fully catered for by existing product or service offers. Numerous studies using this approach have now been carried out by both consultants and market researchers. As a result its commercial acceptance as a means of value assessment has grown greatly.

Having completed our discussion of 'the value the customer receives', including its two main components – we conclude this chapter by very briefly considering 'the value the enterprise receives'.

The value the enterprise receives

The value the enterprise receives from the customer also has a strong association with the term 'customer value'. Customer value from this perspective is the *outcome* of providing and delivering superior value for the customer, deploying improved acquisition and retention strategies and utilising effective channel management. Fundamental to this view of customer value are two key elements. First, determining how existing and potential customer profitability varies across different customers and customer segments. Second, understanding the economics of customer acquisition and customer retention and capitalising on opportunities for cross-selling, up-selling and building customer advocacy. How these elements contribute to increasing customer lifetime value is integral to this perspective of value creation. These topics are examined in Chapter 7.

SUMMARY

Customer value creation is a critical part of both relationship marketing and CRM. An insufficient focus on the value provided for all customers, and key customer segments, can seriously diminish the impact of the perceived value of the enterprise's offer.

To anticipate and satisfy the needs of current and potential customers, the enterprise must be able to target specific customers and demonstrate real added value through differentiated value propositions and superior service delivery. This means adopting an analytical approach to value creation, supported by a dynamic, detailed knowledge of customers, competitors, opportunities and the company's own performance capabilities.

In mature markets, and as competition intensifies, it becomes imperative for the enterprise to recognise that existing customers are easier to sell to and are frequently more profitable. But although managers may agree intellectually with this view, the practices within their organisations often tell a different story. They may take existing customers for granted and focus too much of their attention and resources at attracting new customers. More sophisticated approaches to value proposition development will help companies better understand how value should be created for the customer.

CASE 3.1: British Telecommunications (BT) – creating new customer value propositions

The company

BT Group plc (British Telecommunications) is one of the world's leading telecommunications providers and one of the largest private sector companies in Europe. BT has four customer-facing lines of business: BT Retail (serving business and residential customers); BT Global Services (global managed services and solutions serving multi-site organisations worldwide); BT Wholesale (BT's networks and network services and solutions to other communication companies) and Openreach (the UK access network and roll-out of superfast broadband). These are supported by two internal service units, BT Innovate & Design and BT Operate.

Based in London, with offices throughout the UK and ventures in many countries, BT services customers in more than 170 countries. BT is the UK's main telecommunications provider. Its core activities include local, long distance and international telecommunications services, Internet and broadband services and IT solutions. It also provides network services to other licensed operators. In 2012, the company employed over 90,000 people and had an annual turnover of £20 billion.

BT Retail has 5.7 million broadband customers, 1 million SME (small and medium enterprise) customers and nearly £8 billion annual revenue. BT Retail serves UK and Republic of Ireland consumers and SMEs through four customer-facing divisions: BT Consumer, BT Business, BT Enterprises and BT Ireland. BT Enterprises also serves global customers. BT Retail delivers tailored information technology solutions for small and medium enterprises and larger organisations in the public and private sectors. BT Retail strives to enable its business and residential customers to communicate easily with the world around them, using an extensive product and service portfolio covering voice, data, Internet and multi-media, as well as managed and packaged communications solutions.

The challenge

From the start of the first decade of the 2000s, competition in the telecommunications market has accelerated. Under these conditions of increased competition it has become increasingly important for BT to develop a greater focus on delivering value to its customers. BT Retail has for many years been concerned with delivering value to its business and residential customers. It has done this by focusing on helping its customers communicate easily with the world around them, using an extensive product and service portfolio covering voice, data, Internet and multi-media, as well as managed and packaged communications solutions. However, what is needed is a more formal approach to ensure that customers are receiving tailored offers of direct relevance that deliver real and sustained value to them.

The solution

BT Retail took up this challenge by implementing a customer-centric strategy with the intention of becoming recognised as the telecommunication industry's customer service champion. BT Retail is integrating traditional products and services with new wave technologies to provide carefully developed customer value propositions.

To address this challenge, a project on proposition development was initiated. This initially focused on the major corporate customers. The former Managing Director of this area of the business stated the objective as follows: 'I want Corporate Clients to be judged by the value we bring to the customer, not just as a supplier of telecoms. What we have to offer is a value proposition. We have to use our understanding of the customer to create a compelling value proposition.'

BT regards a customer proposition as the combination of products and services offered to a customer based on an accurately identified set of customer needs. It recognises that becoming totally customer focused depends on first defining customer needs and then allowing them to drive the development of winning value propositions and world-class communications and e-business solutions which fulfil the proposition and deliver the value promise. BT shares the view that business today revolves around the needs being served, not the products being offered.

Through this concentration on proposition development, BT focused on improving the quality of its service delivery and enhancing customer satisfaction while, at the same time, reducing costs by cementing efficiencies and driving greater productivity. This commitment to customer value marked a change in BT's business approach from one which is product and technology-led to one which focuses on understanding customer needs and building value-based revenue streams.

BT's propositions project works at unifying the value system, integrating three core elements of the organisation: the Customer (*Sell-side*); the Enterprise itself (*In-side*) and Suppliers and Partners (*Buy-side*). BT sees the following activities as key to providing this integration and delivering an excellent value proposition:

- having an excellent understanding of the customer's industry
- having an excellent understanding of BT's own industry
- building excellent relationships with clients
- being excellent at what BT does with its industry and global partners.

These aims are reflected in six proposition areas developed by BT Retail:

1. *Customer relationship management*
   CRM solutions are those that provide BT's clients with the ability intelligently to handle their customer contacts, resulting in more efficient management of resource and enhanced customer relationships. Example: a system to improve call handling (e.g., call centre).
2. *Supply chain management*
   Allows seamless interaction between suppliers, internal functions and customers to promote efficiency and flexibility. Example: electronic procurement/catalogues.
3. *Knowledge management*
   Gaining commercial advantage through the active management of Intellectual Capital: the way we develop, share and exploit our knowledge. Example: website which allows knowledge sharing across departments. Example: an intranet used internally within BT.
4. *Organisational effectiveness*
   Improves work processes and styles. Example: remote working, HR outsourcing.
5. *Flexible working*
   Work anytime and anywhere solutions, from mobility to conferencing and including ancillary support devices and services which maximise the benefits of moving customers towards the vision of a virtual organisation.

6. *e-Business*

e-Business is fundamental to each theme area, both at a strategic level and in terms of proposition development, solutions delivery and how BT communicates its capability.

Creating value

BT's approach to customer value creation comprised two main components: the *value statement* and the *value proposition*.

The value statement describes the impact that BT can have on the market or on an industry segment. It is a general statement of intent that is applicable to the customer's business sector. The value statement is used to position BT and generate interest and takes the following form:

(*Name of customer*) will be able to (*improve what*) through the ability to (*do what*) as a result of (*BT enabler, technology and/or service*).

The value proposition is a customer-specific proposal, usually using a value statement as a starting point, that is quantifiable in both value returned to the customer and revenue to BT. It is a clear statement of the value BT brings to a particular client and answers the questions:

- How much value (financial benefit to the customer)?
- How soon can the value be realised (timing)?
- How sure is the value (risk)?
- How will the value be measured (value return)?

The value proposition builds on the value statement and takes the following form:

(*Name of customer*) will be able to (*improve what*) by (*how much and/or what percentage*) through the ability to (*do what*) as a result of (*what BT enabler, technology, and/or service*) for (*what total cost – tangible and intangible*). By (*time factor*) BT will be able to demonstrate the delivery of value by (*a specific, quantifiable measure*).

The strongest value propositions should therefore have at their core a financial linkage from an initiative to a measurable improvement in the business, especially around critical issues.

BT Retail understood that it could no longer rely on perceived value to win contracts. If BT Retail could quantify the value they offered, they would be better positioned to command premium margins based on the value offered, rather than being based on their cost or the competitors' prices.

BT Retail management emphasised that throughout the sales cycle the value of the business issue and the offering must be continually quantified so that the customer believes in and owns the value proposition: 'It is important to get the customer to understand the financial impact of their problem. The customer is more likely to quantify pain early in the sales cycle. If we can keep our customers focused on a clear statement of BT's net value, the higher our success rate and revenue will be.'

BT Retail ensured that the company's propositions, products and services were supported by economic value equations which provided examples of the value that BT Retail could add to its major business customers. These sources of value include quality levels, customer satisfaction levels, productivity of assets, people and capital, employee satisfaction – turnover; headcount reduction, financial measures – ROI (return on investment), new revenue streams, expense reduction, market share, reducing risk, timeliness of getting products to market and variety and quality of products. These value formulas need to be based on sources of value relevant to individual customers, as defined by detailed analyses and customer profiling.

The results

BT's proposition approach was enthusiastically supported by their marketing community. The value proposition themes meant that the focus of both the marketing and the sales function was on the customer need, which resulted in a better understanding of customer requirements and their reasons to purchase. In addition, product development was now driven by this understanding of customer need, moving BT Retail towards a market-led rather than product driven approach. Propositions can now be developed against a specific set of customers and therefore messages are not only more relevant, but only customers who have the need are communicated with, resulting in better customer satisfaction and less confusion. The learning from the programme led to more customer-focused value proposition themes – for instance 'interacting with customers' – rather than the more technology orientated emphasis often associated with the term customer relationship management.

BT's emphasis on creating customer value is strongly echoed in BT Group's current strategy. A cornerstone of their strategy is customer service and customer experience and BT aims to be highly customer-focused in the markets in which it operates. In discussing BT's business strategy, the 2011 BT Annual Report states: 'Our strategy starts with customer service and we continually work to improve the level of customer experience. In practice this means keeping our promises, being easy to contact and straightforward to deal with; it means keeping our customers informed and taking prompt action to put things right if they have cause to complain; above all it means trying to do things right first time.' Total shareholder return, reflecting share price movement and dividends, for the financial year period to March 2011 was 57 per cent compared with the European Telco Index of 16 per cent and the FTSE100 Index of 7 per cent.

This strategy of focusing on customer service and customer experience responds to the growing challenge of maintaining competitive advantage in an ever-changing marketplace. With traditional business models of 'buy and sell' being replaced by value-based negotiations, companies such as BT are looking to new and innovative ways of convincing customers to choose their products over those of competitors. The development and use of carefully constructed value propositions, such as those outlined above, will enable companies both to deliver superior value to their customers and to achieve competitive advantage.

CASE 3.2: Zurich Financial Services – building value propositions

The company

The Zurich Financial Services Group (Zurich) is a leading provider of financial protection and wealth accumulation products and solutions. Zurich is one of the world's largest insurance groups, and one of the few to operate on a truly global basis. Their mission is to help their customers understand and protect themselves from risk. Zurich has over 60,000 employees serving customers in more than 170 countries. With this global strength, Zurich has a deep local understanding of markets across Europe, North America, Latin America, Southern Africa, Asia-Pacific and the Middle East.

Based in Zurich, Switzerland, the company has three main business segments. These are (1) *General Insurance*, which provides property and casualty products and services to individuals, businesses and major multinational corporations around the world. Zurich reaches these customers through a range of divisions – including Europe General Insurance, North America Commercial and Global Corporate – and a mix of distribution channels; (2) *Global Life*, which offers a broad range of life insurance, investments, savings and pension propositions to individuals and companies across the world. Global Life's business is managed globally while remaining focused on local customer and distributor needs; and (3) *Farmers*, which manages the personal lines and small business insurance sold in the US by the Farmers Exchanges, which the company does not own. These three business segments are united by Zurich's ambition to be the leading insurance provider in their chosen markets, and to deliver to their customers when and where it matters. Zurich reaches the majority of its retail customers through three main distribution channels: Zurich agents, independent financial advisers/brokers and banks.

The challenge

Zurich's strategy for creating sustainable shareholder value is built on six cornerstones designed to promote customer and employee retention, drive profitability and capture synergies within its global business. Central to this approach is delivering on the company's brand promise, developing an agile organisation, maintaining financial discipline and staying true to their core values of integrity, customer centricity, excellence, teamwork and sustainable value creation.

Managing customer relationships effectively across this diverse customer base and comprehensive product/service portfolio is a demanding and ongoing challenge for Zurich. Competitive performance demands continuous innovation and dedicated attention to the ever-changing requirements of customers. In order to retain its high market-responsiveness, entrepreneurialism and expertise, Zurich addressed this challenge through an initiative that focused on the design and delivery of superior customer value propositions. This case study reviews the formal process that Zurich created for value proposition development.

The solution

To ensure a profitable customer base and high-quality outcomes, Zurich devised a methodology for developing value propositions. The inputs to proposition development constitute a description of the business opportunity and a detailed outline of the needs of the selected customer segments concerned. The outputs comprise all the components required to deliver the new value proposition, such as product literature, IT systems, business processes, training and licensing, and sales support tools. The value proposition framework, given in Figure 1, consists of a series of five processes.

1. *Core proposition development function*
   The initial process is concerned with the detailed specification of the proposition to be developed. It normally involves cross-functional collaboration with staff involved in some or all of the constituent sub-processes. For example, a major new product development may require several iterations of all three sub-processes, whereas a simple re-pricing is unlikely to require any testing.

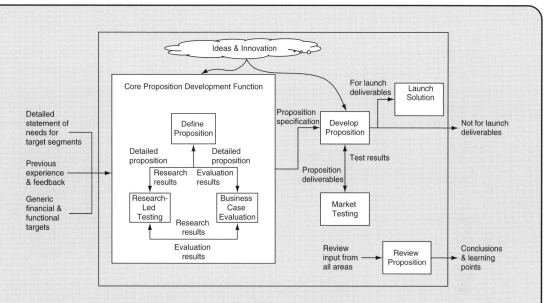

Figure 1 Zurich Financial Services value proposition framework

(a) *Define proposition* – turning the outlined business opportunity into an articulated specification, covering (as appropriate): product, service, distribution, communication and pricing. The amount of work entailed depends on the nature of the customer requirement. Clearly, creating a new proposition is more involved than modifying an existing one.

(b) *Business case evaluation* – determining the business rationale for the defined proposition, incorporating a financial evaluation. This activity is carried out alongside other processes and several iterations may be necessary before a viable proposition is reached.

(c) *Research-led testing* – using various test methods, such as focus groups and customer surveys, to examine one or more aspect of a prospective value proposition. For example, testing the demand for specific benefits or investigating the degree of price sensitivity. This process is invoked as and when necessary and is usually conducted in partnership with third-party specialists.

2. *Develop proposition*

The next process encompasses the cross-functional activities involved in actually creating the deliverables of the planned value proposition. It will vary in scope and content, depending on the proposition, but may include developing or amending business processes, IT systems, training material, marketing material and product literature. The process may be carried out in stages over a significant period of time. For example, a new product may have deliverables that are not required for launch but are needed in time for the first anniversary of the policy.

3. *Market testing*

This process involves offering the developed value proposition to a representative selection of target customers in a controlled way, in order to test specific aspects of it. The process is applied where necessary and is generally more relevant in the context of a service-based proposition than a product-based proposition. As with step 1(c), third-party specialists are usually involved.

4. *Launch solution*

   This is the process of making the value proposition available to customers on a full-scale basis. Again, it covers a range of activities, not all of which will be relevant in every instance. These include: training and licensing distributors; producing and distributing literature; implementing IT systems and equipping and managing administrators.

5. *Review proposition*

   This review process is carried out once for each proposition at an agreed period of time after launch. All aspects of proposition development are examined and performance is compared to forecasts. Resultant learning acquired from the insights and analyses generated is then fed back into management and decision-making processes to inform future activity in the areas of client acquisition, customer segmentation and proposition development.

Zurich started testing value propositions developed on this basis in the early 2000s. As such, it was an innovator in value proposition development. Most companies, if they used the term at all, only use the term in a general sense to describe their thinking about delivery of value to customers. Arvind Malhotra, previously Zurich's UK Marketing Director, explained: 'For each target segment we seek to define a single value proposition which encompasses our offering to them over the lifetime of our relationship with them. We then deliver this proposition through the solutions we build to meet their needs.'

As an example, within the 'small business' segment, the company identified the customer need to manage their personal finances and business pressures concurrently as a key area of development. By centralising expertise, Zurich was able to offer an integrated solution that jointly addressed both concerns in a simple, straightforward manner. Similarly, for the 'family' segment, recognising that moving home is a key event in the customer's life stage and a very stressful one, Zurich started to develop a readily available solution which offers customised flexibility. The proposition to this customer segment is one of 'convenience and choice'.

The key feature of this methodology is its emphasis on customer focus. Zurich proactively asks its customers what they want. Customer feedback is intended to be used to inform all decision making. Prior to the introduction of the framework, value propositions were organised on product lines and the company delivered several individual products. The catalyst for Zurich's refocus was learning that customers do not just want a whole range of products, but require solutions that are pertinent to their lives and needs. Furthermore, this customer intelligence is not self-contained within 'proposition development', but is actively channelled to sales advisers, customer communications managers and other functions. 'Traditionally, we operated product silos. Now we work across these silos to create solutions', commented Malhotra.

The results

Zurich's approach to developing value propositions illustrates significant sophistication. First, the framework recognises the imperative of specificity – the need to target the specific requirements of specific customers. Experience has shown that a casual or broad-brushed attitude to market segmentation and problem definition is inadequate. Secondly, the framework emphasises the iterative nature of value – value can be tailored, augmented and improved. Feedback points are evident at the top and sides of the framework, enabling valuable ideas, learning and market intelligence to be integrated into future proposition development activity. Thirdly, the framework considers time – a fundamental prerequisite and critical success factor of any strategic process. For the right value propositions to be created for the right customers, decisions must be based on meaningful information and tested and refined in a real environment. The investment of time is one of the most important resource allocations, as inept or inaccurate decisions can be costly in both the short and the long term.

Zurich's focus on building value propositions in a more formalised and strategic manner is an effective means of tackling some of the competitive challenges that lie ahead in the retail financial services sector. Zurich's move to elicit customer feedback and inject customer perspective into proposition development provided a powerful launch pad for that process.

Since its introduction in the first decade of the 2000s, Zurich has extended its use of the value proposition concept throughout the organisation. A review of publicly available materials shows the value proposition approach is being used in many Zurich divisions and in many of their country operations around the world. The original concept has been developed further to undertake value proposition benchmarking exercises where Zurich is compared with its main competitors across key proposition dimensions. Its use has also been extended to the company's financial advisers. For example, in 2011, Zurich's Australian operation published a value proposition resource titled 'Uncover the Value in your Advice' as part of Zurich's 'HelpPoint' initiative. This is aimed at helping Zurich's financial advisers identify more clearly the value they add to their clients.

The value proposition approach adopted by Zurich Financial Services helps keep the company's products and services customer focused – a central plank of the company's strategy. As a recent Zurich Annual Report stated: 'Our customers are at the heart of all we do. This means we understand our personal, commercial and corporate customers' needs, and are entirely focused on meeting those needs.' This commitment to an unrelenting focus on the customer has helped position Zurich as one of the world's top 100 global brands, with brand consultancy Interbrand recently estimating their brand value at $3.5 billion.

4 Building relationships with multiple stakeholders

Relationship Marketing: Development and Key Concepts *(Ch. 2)*
- Origins and alternative approaches to relationship marketing
- Characteristics and key concepts in relationship marketing

Creating Customer Value *(Ch. 3)*
- The value the customer receives
- How relationships add value
- How brands add value
- The value proposition
- Value assessment

Relationship Marketing

Building Relationships with Multiple Stakeholders *(Ch. 4)*
- Customer markets
- Supplier/alliance markets
- Internal markets
- Recruitment markets
- Influence markets
- Referral markets

Relationships and Technology *(Ch. 5)*
- Digital marketing
- Social media and social influence marketing

In Chapter 2 we examined some key concepts in relationship marketing including the need to address multiple stakeholders *beyond the customer–firm dyad*. We pointed out that the mainstream marketing literature has neglected this important issue of understanding and building long-term relationships with both customers *and* other stakeholder groups. The value the enterprise creates for the customer, discussed in Chapter 3, is impacted by the enterprise's relationships with these other key stakeholders 'markets' or what we term 'market domains'. Managing the organisation's internal and external relationships with key stakeholders is now acknowledged as critical to economic profitability and, as such, needs to become a more central activity. Traditional marketing approaches have not placed sufficient emphasis on careful stakeholder management. In this chapter we consider, in detail, six key stakeholder markets or market domains which are shown in the chapter navigation diagram. This emphasis is well overdue. An IBM survey of some 1,500 global CEOs published in 2010 found that the biggest challenges CEOs faced was the ability of their organisations to relate to diverse corporate stakeholders; the ability to foster 'dexterous' organisations that could act quickly, change as needed and be self-correcting in a bottom-up rather than top-down approach; and the ability to generate creativity throughout all aspects of a company's business.[1]

The role of multiple stakeholders

All organisations have a large and diverse range of stakeholders. These include suppliers, the financial community, employees, customers, the government, trade unions, environmentalists, alliance partners and so on. The top managers of the organisation play a key role in managing these relationships in order to maximise customer and shareholder value. But all too often management do not manage these stakeholders in an integrated manner.

Stakeholder management is frequently not integrated because, in practice, stakeholders are typically managed on a day-to-day basis within different parts of the organisation. For example, the marketing department is responsible for managing relationships with customers, the purchasing department with suppliers and the finance department with the financial community. The human resources department, together with line management, manages relationships with internal staff, potential recruits, unions and so on, and it falls to the public relations and corporate affairs departments to manage many of the other external stakeholders such as the media. As so many different parts of the organisation are involved, the various stakeholder groups are frequently managed in an uncoordinated, disparate manner.

As discussed in Chapter 2, enlightened companies are using the stakeholder philosophy of relationship marketing in managing their stakeholder relationships. Two key concepts underpin the use of relationship marketing in this context. First, an organisation can only optimise relationships with customers if it understands and successfully manages relationships with other relevant stakeholders. Most enterprises recognise the critical role their employees play in delivering superior customer value and the importance of internal marketing, but other stakeholders can also play a key role. Second, the tools and techniques used in marketing to customers, such as marketing planning and market segmentation, can also be used effectively to plan and manage non-customer relationships.

Implementing relationship marketing strategies requires managers to go beyond their traditional functional roles. They need to take a broader perspective of the role of stakeholders in order to develop much closer relationships between suppliers, internal staff, customers and other relevant markets. Reorienting thinking and actions towards building a more customer-focused organisation through addressing multiple stakeholders represents a significant challenge for senior managers. While some companies adopt a strong integrated relationship approach to managing their stakeholders, they are still in the minority.

A stakeholder model for relationship marketing

In Chapter 2 we briefly outlined seven relationship marketing models and frameworks that have been developed by different scholars. Six of these models and frameworks focus on stakeholder classification, while the work by Gummesson addresses a much broader range of types of relationship.[2] Managers seeking to classify stakeholders for the purposes of developing a relationship marketing strategy could use any of the six approaches to stakeholder classification. Readers wishing to explore the nuances of these different models in detail should consult the references given in Chapter 2.

In this chapter we use the Christopher, Payne and Ballantyne 'six markets model',[3] which classifies stakeholders into the six broad market groups or market domains. While this model is the one that we are most familiar with, there are some further reasons for its use. First, Malhotra and Agarwal suggest that it is the most comprehensive of the approaches concerned with traditional enterprise stakeholders, in that each of the six market domains can be subdivided in a manner that includes all major stakeholder groups.[4] Second, as Tzokas and Saren point out, this model acknowledges the *multiple roles* that stakeholders can play.[5] Third, it is a well-tested model. It has stood the test of time and been used on projects with many organisations,[6] including organisations in both the business sector[7] and the not-for-profit sector.[8] We have not identified reported use of the other frameworks within enterprises. This model has been used in relationship marketing projects with many organisations.

One of the current authors developed the first version of this model in a Cranfield University working paper; it was published in the book by Christopher, Payne and Ballantyne[9] and in various articles. The original model has undergone some minor amendments over time, following experience in using it with a substantial number of organisations. The most recent version is shown in Figure 4.1.

The six markets model is a useful tool for reviewing the role of an extended set of stakeholders. It is applicable to business-to-consumer (B2C) and business-to-business (B2B) markets, as well as the not-for-profit sector. It has also been used to identify stakeholders for a European country in the context of that country's brand building activities.[10]

This model identifies six key market domains, representing stakeholder groups that can contribute to an organisation's marketplace effectiveness.[11] While customers are viewed in this framework as a major central stakeholder, five other stakeholder groups, or market domains, are also identified: influence (including shareholders) markets; recruitment

Figure 4.1 The six markets model

markets; referral markets; internal markets and supplier/alliance markets. Relationship marketing focuses on building stronger relationships between the enterprise and the whole gambit of relevant stakeholder markets. The enterprise needs to give greater attention to issues such as understanding how these markets are changing and how this impacts its position in the marketplace.

The model identifies the key stakeholder market groupings or market domains where managers need to assess their enterprises' performance. Not all market domains are of equal importance. However, for many enterprises three key stakeholders – customers, employees (internal markets) and shareholders (usually a dominant category within the influence market) – are particularly important. The enterprise needs to make an assessment of which market domains are the most important to them. An important point that differentiates this model from others is that it recognises that a given stakeholder may play a role in more than one market domain. The most obvious example is the customer who clearly plays a role within the customer market domain (where the interaction is between a firm and its customers) but can also have a role to play in the referral market (where the interaction is between an existing customer and a prospective customer).

Coutts & Co., the private bank, now owned by the Royal Bank of Scotland Group, is just one example of an organisation applying this model to its key stakeholders (see box).

Relationship marketing at Coutts & Co.: It's not just about clients

Relationship management is not only about clients. Coutts is looking long and hard at the way it services five distinct markets, in addition to its traditional client market, to make sure it maintains consistent, high-quality relationships with them.

Coutts Group's additional relationship markets

Internal markets: Coutts involves and communicates with all staff – relationship managers, product managers and support staff – in and about its relationship management priorities. As such it is seeking to ensure there is no weak link in the chain that makes up the whole Coutts service offering.

Referral markets: Referral markets are a critical area of focus for Coutts. Lawyers, consultants and financial advisers are a significant source of new business for the bank. These people meet prospective clients every day and advise them on how best to invest their wealth, be it the gains from recently selling a company or a newly acquired inheritance. Coutts calls these sources of referral regularly and delivers regular tailored information to them so that Coutts is at the front of their minds when they are advising their clients who to place their wealth with.

Suppliers: Suppliers are equally important to Coutts. Although the bank is a service provider, it needs to ensure that every tangible offering – from brochures to events, its premises to its lapel badges – matches the quality image it tries to portray through its staff. It works very closely with just a few suppliers who, over time, get to know its ways and the standards it sets.

Potential employees: Coutts knows how it important it is that employees and prospective employees perceive the organisation as one they can relate to and want to work for. In banking, a new client relationship manager can often bring a new portfolio of business with them so Coutts is at pains to sustain its quality image among its peers in order to attract the best recruits.

Influencers: Influence markets are important to Coutts in the broad review of relationship management and marketing. One of its key influence markets is the governments and financial authorities of the jurisdictions in which it works. These authorities actively seek the bank's views on legislative changes to safeguard their jurisdiction's status, and on the kind of new product opportunities that might attract investment to their countries in the future.[1]

[1] N. Shaw (1997), Unification Theory, *Customer Service Management*, June, pp. 26–29.

The objective of the six markets model is to enable the enterprise to undertake a structured review of the key market domains that are of importance to them. The extent to which an organisation needs to place substantial focus on a given market domain will vary from enterprise to enterprise. In the following sections, we consider each of these market domains in turn.

Customer market domain

At the centre of the model is the customer market domain. It is clear that customers should be the main focus of marketing activity. In focusing on the customer market domain, companies need to adopt the relationship marketing approach, which has been outlined in previous chapters. Success in the marketplace is closely tied to building deep relationships with appropriate customer segments. The customer market domain, shown in Figure 4.2, includes three broad groupings: direct buyers, intermediaries and final consumers.

To consider these groups, consider a manufacturer of LCD TVs. This manufacturer sells to a number of approved wholesalers, who in turn sell the products to retail outlets, who in turn sell the appliances to individual consumers. In this example the wholesaler is the *buyer*, the retailer the *intermediary* and the individual who purchases the appliance from the retailer is the *consumer*. The term 'customer' generally applies to all these three groups.

A large number of markets today are what are known as intermediated markets and conform to the type of network outlined in Figure 4.2. In the case of the manufacturer of LCD TVs, the three groupings in the 'customer' market domain are the:

- *Buyer* – the direct customer of the manufacturing enterprise, that is, the wholesaler
- *Intermediary* – the retailer to whom the wholesaler sells the TVs
- *Consumer* – the individual customers who purchases TVs from the retail outlet.

Of course, in some industries and countries there may be an even longer chain of intermediaries, which creates additional steps within the channel chain. We discuss the role of intermediation in further detail when we discuss multi-channel integration in Chapter 8. Many enterprises use multiple channels to serve the final consumer, while

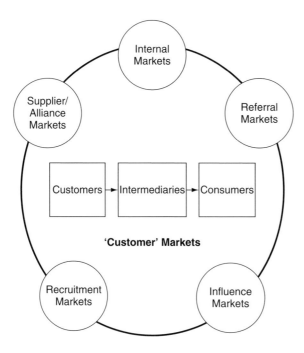

Figure 4.2 The customer market domain

some use only one channel. For example, restaurants create a product – the meal – and sell this directly to the final consumer without going through any intermediaries.

Some enterprises are limited in terms of the channel choice that they have. Other companies can select from a wide range of different channels, in some cases using multiple channels to serve the final consumer. All enterprises should regularly review their channel options, as circumstances change and new opportunities present themselves. It is increasingly acknowledged that a firm needs to create a supply chain that is more effective than that of its competitors if it is to be successful. So it is supply chains, or market networks (discussed in Chapter 3), that compete rather than just companies.

Developments in information technology and computing have spawned new channels to market, including electronic commerce, mobile commerce and social media. We discuss these channels in more detail in Chapter 5 and Chapter 8.

Companies adopting a relationship marketing programme should undertake a detailed market analysis at each level in their value delivery network and identify the type of marketing activity they need to direct at each of the various channel members including direct buyers, intermediaries and final consumers. They then need to do further analysis by segmenting and understanding the decision-making units of different levels. This should be completed before determining the marketing expenditure and effort that should be directed at each level. Developing a market structure map (see Chapter 8, Figure 8.2) will help the company analyse its value delivery network. As Chapter 8 provides a detailed review of channels and multi-channel integration, the discussion of this topic at this point is hence fairly brief.

The amount of marketing effort a company directs at different channel members needs to be regularly evaluated and, when appropriate, changed. In certain industries intermediaries may be a valuable channel member, while in others the value of intermediaries is being challenged. Unless an intermediary is adding value to the customer relationship, it may prove to be an unnecessary cost and may be bypassed. Many organisations are now finding that in order to build stronger relationships with final consumers they need to change the emphasis and expenditure at different channel levels or, alternatively, refocus the existing expenditure in ways that build deeper and more sustained relationships. We will illustrate this point with an example.

Let us consider a manufacturer of domestic dishwashing machines. This company may have traditionally spent a large proportion of its marketing efforts and marketing budget on trade marketing aimed at getting the dishwashers into large retail outlets such as department stores. It may have directed much of its marketing expenditure at: developing strong key account management; undertaking in-store point-of-sale merchandising; creating a discount structure based on volume; and establishing training programmes for sales staff in the retailers. It may have supplemented this with a considerable amount of trade advertising and trade promotion, aiming only a limited amount of advertising at final individual consumers.

This manufacturer may, however, decide to review its marketing approach and implement an alternative marketing strategy that focuses more closely on the final consumer. It may seek to identify the needs of final consumers through completed warranty cards or some other form of direct promotional activity: by sending them a questionnaire to help identify their interest in particular products and services; by monitoring social media; by setting up a major telephone call centre to answer consumers' enquiries; by creating a 'club' for customers; and so on. The manufacturer could consider these and other options as a means of building relationships with the final consumers.

Some manufacturers fail to develop direct relationships with their final consumers. Most readers will no doubt have had disappointing experiences when purchasing a range of consumer durable products, including motor cars. They might have been motivated to buy a car as a result of promotional activity by the car manufacturer, only to be highly disappointed by the subsequent lack of interest by the dealer in maintaining the car and satisfactorily rectifying faults that occur within the warranty period. The consumer may be further upset when they seek to obtain redress directly from the manufacturer and find the manufacturer is totally uninterested in having any dialogue with them.

However, within the motor car sector, radical changes in both distribution and other marketing practices are now being adopted by car manufacturers seeking to find ways of developing closer relationships with their final consumers. (For an example, see the Mercedes-Benz case study at the end of Chapter 11.) Companies in the fast moving consumer goods sector are also rethinking their marketing strategy and are developing more direct relationships with consumers. Procter & Gamble, for instance, is now focused on developing direct relationships with consumers through many activities including direct response promotion and social media campaigns.

Customer markets: a summary

In the past, the marketing function has traditionally focused on winning customers and emphasised the value of the individual sale. But this transactional approach is gradually being replaced by a relationship marketing approach that emphasises the value of long-term relationships and repeat purchases. In Chapter 1 we briefly outlined the importance of customer retention. However, despite managers' growing awareness of the need to strike the right balance between acquiring and retaining customers, few companies have achieved that in practice. Focusing too heavily on marketing activities directed at new customers is dangerous. A company may spend too much on acquiring them, only to lose them later because it puts too little effort into keeping them. If customer service does not meet customer expectations, customers are likely to defect and damage the company's reputation by adverse word-of-mouth publicity.

Marketing programmes aimed at retaining customers can be expensive as they often involve increasing customer service levels and tailoring the product or service to suit individual customers or customer groups. Successful retention programmes segment customers according to their potential lifetime profitability and then determine the type and frequency of marketing activity relevant for each group to exploit and increase this potential. We explore these issues in greater detail in Chapter 7.

Referral market domain

Within the referral market domain there are two main categories – *customer referral* and *non-customer referral* sources. An organisation's current customers are frequently its best marketers, which is why creating positive word-of-mouth referral, through delivering outstanding service quality, is so important. A variety of non-customer groups can recommend organisations to prospective customers. These groups are known by various terms within different industry settings, including networks, multipliers, connectors, third-party introducers and agencies.

Existing and former customers constitute the first broad category within this domain. Over the past two decades customer referrals have become even more important with the rise of Internet-based ranking sites and commentary by customers in social media. The importance of the second broad category, non-customer referral sources, depends on the organisation involved.

Enterprises can significantly increase their revenue and profits by using the principles of relationship marketing to systematically manage relationships with both these sources of referral. The main categories of the referral market domain are shown in Figure 4.3.

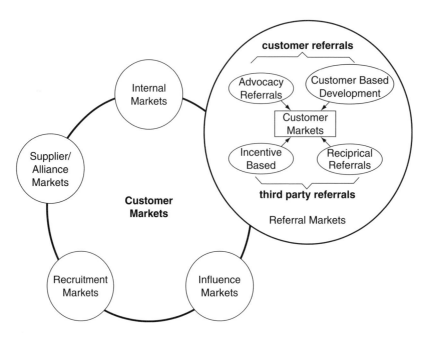

Figure 4.3 The referral market domain

Customer referrals

Within the 'customer referrals' category there are two sub-categories: *advocacy referrals* (or advocate-initiated customer referrals) and *customer-base development* (or company-initiated customer referrals). We discussed the first sub-category of advocacy referrals in Chapter 3, when explaining the customer relationship ladder of loyalty and outlining the role of advocates in assisting a company's marketing efforts. The second sub-category of customer-base development relates to an organisation's explicit attempts to use its existing customers as part of its marketing activities in order to gain new customers.

Advocacy referrals – advocate-initiated customer referrals

Customers become advocates when they are totally satisfied with a company's products or services. A relatively small number of organisations benefit greatly from their proactive efforts to turn their customers into advocates, getting them to refer other customers to them. Advocacy referrals have contributed greatly to the success of Amazon, Apple, Nordstrom, Virgin Atlantic, Southwest Airlines and UK bank First Direct.

First Direct was the world's first all-telephone bank and later became an Internet bank. By 2012, the company had attracted 1.16 million high net worth or potentially high net worth customers. Some 950,000 customers use Internet banking and 420,000 of them use SMS (Short Message Service) banking. A significant part of First Direct's growth has been through referral from its very satisfied customers. Research conducted by First Direct showed that around 85 per cent of its customers have referred new customers to the bank, compared to an average of 15 per cent for the other five major UK banks.

Customer-base development – company-initiated customer referrals

With *advocacy referrals*, described above, the customers initiate the referral. With *company-initiated customer referrals* the company directs activities or initiatives aimed at persuading existing customers to make referrals. The enterprise may simply ask customers to refer other potential customers to them, or it may offer them some form of inducement to do so.

'Advocates' on the relationship marketing ladder (see Chapter 3) often actively initiate referrals, but 'Supporters' – the next rung down the ladder, although typically positive about the enterprise, tend to be more passive. Asking supporters for a referral can be a very good way of generating business from them. For example, a study into referrals by lawyers' clients,[12] found that only 49 per cent of the clients said that law firms had asked them for a referral. But of those who were asked to make a referral 95 per cent provided at least one, compared with just 8 per cent amongst those who were not asked. Few of the organisations we have discussed this issue with have any formal process for requesting referrals.

Membership organisations represent a sector that is placing considerable effort in using their membership base to reach further members. American Express, professional societies, wine clubs and many other such organisations regularly run promotions aimed at generating new customers through their existing customer base. These 'member get a member' marketing efforts are frequently accompanied by some form of incentive, inducement or reward.

Non-customer or third-party referrals

Other parties, in addition to an organisation's customers, can be a great source of referrals for a business. Referrals may be made informally when an individual's experiences of an organisation and its general reputation cause them to recommend that organisation to others. But some companies have more formal systems of referrals. Non-customer third-party referrals can be divided into the following groups:

- general referrals
- reciprocal referrals
- incentive-based referrals
- staff referrals.

General referrals

This grouping covers a broad range of referrals that result in business being generated for an organisation. These can be further divided into four sub-categories.

Professional referrals are those where one professional recommends the services of another. For example, a medical general practitioner may refer a patient to a specialist consultant, or a solicitor may refer a client to a barrister.

Customers may seek *expertise referrals* because of the referrer's specialist expertise or knowledge. These referrals are typically made on an irregular or ad hoc basis.

Specification referrals are those where an organisation or person specifies or strongly recommends that a particular product or service is used. For example, architects may mandate within their architectural plans that a specific brand of electrical appliances, such as washing machines and ovens, must be installed by the builder.

Substitute and complementary referrals occur in circumstances where organisations which are at over-capacity, have long lead times to undertake work, or cannot fulfil a specific need, may refer a customer to one of their competitors.

Reciprocal referrals

Some referrals, especially those between professional firms, are interdependent and under this referral system, referrals may be made backwards and forwards between firms in different professions. For example an accounting firm may recommend a law firm or bank, and vice versa. Historically, professional ethics in professions such as law and accounting have precluded advertising and aggressive competition. Before the relaxation of these restrictions, most of the professional firms in these sectors had to rely extensively on referrals from third parties. As a consequence, referrals were often the main source of work for professional services firms. Now restrictions on advertising and promotional activity have been removed in almost all countries and most professions – although restrictions on advertising and promotional activity do still remain in place in some instances. However, reciprocal referrals remain very important, especially in the professions.

Incentive-based referrals

Incentive-based referrals are appropriate in a number of circumstances. First, where members of the referral channel are highly dependent on each other, it may be to their advantage to create a formal arrangement that helps reinforce this interdependence. Second, if a business is receiving many referrals but is giving back relatively few referrals – and there is little potential to change this – it may seek to redress the balance by providing some incentive-based method of compensating its source of referrals.

The potential for using incentives varies considerably across industries. A company that uses financial incentives as part of its referral system must ensure its referral processes are managed ethically. Indeed, in some industry sectors, incentives are considered unethical or may even be prohibited under the rules of a professional body or industry regulator.

Staff referrals

Existing staff are an important source of referrals within many industry sectors. Staff referrals are especially common within service businesses, but there are also examples of organisations where referrals can be generated between a number of different divisions or products aimed at similar customer segments.

Former staff may be a useful source of business referral in certain types of organisation. Again, professional service firms provide a good example. Consultants like McKinsey & Co. and the 'Big 4' accounting firms place considerable emphasis on their 'alumni' and run regular activities to keep them involved with their old firm, with the aim of maintaining relationships and hopefully getting new business referred by their former employees.

Referral markets: a summary

Organisations often fail to exploit the opportunity to maximise referrals from their own customers, from third parties, and, where appropriate, from their own staff. What is more, many organisations still do not realise the power of customer delight and the benefits that accrue from significantly exceeding customer expectations. However, there are a small, but increasing, number of companies that do significantly exceed customer expectations. These organisations have been able to grow faster through word-of-mouth referrals from highly satisfied customers.

Most organisations need to consider both existing customers and intermediaries as sources of future business. Therefore, they should identify both present and prospective referral sources and develop a plan for allocating marketing resources to them. They also need to make efforts to monitor the cost-benefit, while recognising that the benefits of increased referral marketing may take some time to come to fruition.

Supplier and alliance market domain

Supplier and alliance relationships can both be viewed as partnerships. However, there is a subtle distinction between the contributions each can make to a successful relationship marketing strategy. We define supplier and alliance markets as follows:

Supplier markets: Suppliers represent vendors that usually provide physical resources to the business. Sometimes these resources are augmented by services but typically suppliers are characterised as the upstream source of raw materials, components, products or other tangible items that flow on a continuing basis into and through the customer's business.

Alliance markets: Alliance partners are suppliers too. The difference is that typically they supply competencies and capabilities that are knowledge-based rather than product-based. Alliance partners may well provide services too, and alliances are often created in response to the company's perceived need to outsource an activity within its value chain.

There has been a dramatic reduction in the supplier base of many large companies over the past 25 years. Over this period, one European motor manufacturer reduced its supplier base from over 1,000 suppliers to a few hundred preferred partners. With this reduction there has been a shift from arm's-length and often adversarial relationships to a greater number of close alliances. Over a period of a decade, one UK high street retailer, which used to buy clothing products from over 1,000 suppliers, reduced its supplier base to around 50 strategic suppliers. These two examples reflect a significant change in the way companies view their supplier base.

Other organisations have engaged in alliances to import resources, capabilities and expertise into the business instead of trying to keep everything 'in-house' as they used to. These new style relationships are a radical departure from companies' traditional focus on vertical integration, whereby they sought to bring as much as possible of the value-added in the final product under the same legal ownership. In its early days in North America, Ford used to own the steel mills that made the steel for its cars, as well as most of the factories that made the components.

Now there is an emphasis on 'virtual' integration – that is, a confederation of organisations combining their capabilities and competencies in a closely integrated network with shared goals and objectives. Figure 4.4 brings together the concept of vertical supply relationships and horizontal alliance partnerships as a closely coupled network within the six markets model.

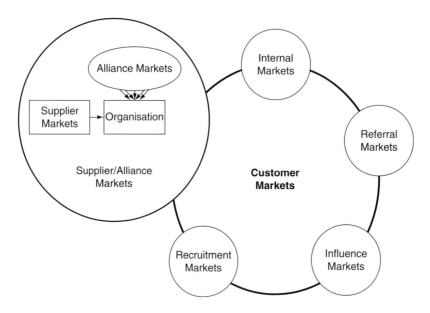

Figure 4.4 The supplier/alliance market domain

It is useful to think of alliances as 'horizontal' partnerships – in the sense that an alliance partner plays a value-creating role within the firm's value chain – and suppliers as 'vertical' partnerships – in the sense that suppliers are an extension of the firm. In this approach – sometimes termed 'the extended enterprise' – suppliers and alliance partners link with the core organisation to help present more cost-effective, timely and innovative offers to customers. Virtual integration seeks to reap the benefits that accrue to companies which focus on core competencies, while at the same time delivering the advantages of coordination and integration that can flow from vertical integration.

It is now recognised that managing such interlocking networks of organisations – and, in particular, the relationships between them – is vital to competitive success. We consider that the way supplier and alliance 'markets' are proactively managed forms a central element of relationship marketing strategy.

Supplier and alliance markets: a summary

Alliances bring new skills or competencies into the business, or they may strengthen existing skills and competencies. The move to outsource activities that are considered 'non-core' to the business has gathered pace in recent years, giving further impetus to the search for appropriate alliance partners. Increasingly value creation is no longer confined to a single firm, but instead is rooted in a confederation of firms that contribute specialist skill and capabilities. The value chain, in effect, now spans several organisations that work as partners in creating and bringing products to market. Such relationships need to be managed quite differently from more traditional 'sub-contract' relationships. Top management in these 'network' or virtual' organisations needs to create a 'boundaryless' business with joint decision-making, complete transparency on costs and the sharing of risks and rewards.

Influence market domain

The influence market domain has the most diverse range of constituent groups. Among these are shareholders, financial analysts, stockbrokers, and media of all forms (the business press, the daily press, magazines, radio, television, social media, etc.), user and consumer groups, environmentalists and unions. Each of these constituent groups can potentially impact or exert influence over the organisation.

The importance of specific groups within the influence market will vary considerably according to industry sector. For example, companies selling infrastructure services such as telecommunications or utilities will place governments and regulatory bodies high on their list of important constituents within their influence market domain. Highly visible public listed companies are likely to focus a great deal of attention on shareholders, financial analysts and the financial and business press. Manufacturing companies and the petrochemical sector may be especially concerned with environmentalists and government. Figure 4.5 illustrates several of the major groups within the influence market domain.

The importance of different groups within the influence market domain will also vary at different points in time for the enterprise. For example, a bank faced with fraud or insider trading may suddenly find the press, regulatory bodies and the central bank at the top of its influence market agenda. Similarly, actions by environmentalists, Greenpeace and other parties over BP's oil spill in the Gulf of Mexico in 2010 brought the media, government and environmentalists to the top of BP's agenda.

BP's oil spill flowed unabated for three months and caused extensive damage to marine and wildlife habitats and to the Gulf's fishing and tourism industries. BP CEO Tony Hayward paid for this with the loss of his job in 2010. There was a series of mistakes that demonstrated how *not* to interact with stakeholders. It started with denial, followed by claims that just a trickle of oil was leaking and the impact on the environment would be modest. At that time up to 1.5 million gallons poured into

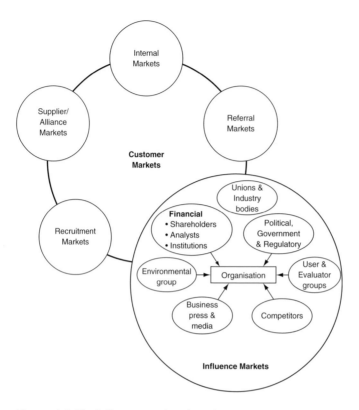

Figure 4.5 The influence market domain

the Gulf every day. BP later described those affected by the disaster as 'small people'. The eventual begrudging establishment of a £20 billion compensation fund by BP was also handled badly.

While the influence market domain may comprise a considerable number of potential groups, a firm may only need to address a relatively few important ones at any given point. Several categories are of special interest because they are common to many organisations. These include:

- Financial and investor influence markets
- Environmental influence markets
- Competitor influence markets
- Government, political and regulatory influence markets

Financial and investor influence markets

Many organisations need to win the support and loyalty of a quite wide range of financial market participants or 'actors'. Financial and investor influence markets are especially critical for organisations listed or planning to list on a stock market. But they are also important to other organisations, including 'mutuals' (organisations owned by subscribers, depositors or customers) such as non-listed insurance companies and building societies.

Investor loyalty is very important in the financial and investor influence market. Reichheld highlighted this in his early work that showed that investor churn in the average public company in the US is more than 50 per cent a year.[13] He concluded that managers find it nearly impossible to pursue long-term value-creating strategies without the support of loyal, knowledgeable investors. Reichheld's work is among a body of research that has begun to focus on financial and investor influence markets, recognising their importance in relationship marketing.

Environmental influence markets

Environmental influence markets are a key group for organisations involved in industries such as petrochemicals, mining and manufacturing. Environmental bodies and pressure groups are becoming increasingly active and even militant, and can wreak serious damage on organisations that they target as being environmentally unfriendly.

The events following Shell's decision to dispose of its Brent Spar platform in the North Sea back in the 1990s remains a vivid illustration of the importance of this market domain. Greenpeace occupied the Brent Spar platform, activists in Germany and other countries fire-bombed Shell's petrol stations, and these and other events – including behind-the-scenes activity by the British Government – led Shell to reverse its decision regarding the disposal of the Brent Spar platform. Shell clearly failed both to develop appropriate relational strategies and to communicate effectively with these key environmental groups. A decade and a half later, following BP's oil spill in the Gulf of Mexico, BP's executives seemed to have learned little from Shell's earlier experiences.

By contrast, The Body Shop, now part of the L'Oreal group, is an excellent example of an organisation which has managed its relationships with environmentalists and other influence market groups very well. For example, it has formed alliances with Greenpeace and Friends of the Earth and developed close relationships with other influence market groups, such as local communities, by ensuring every one of its shops develops local community projects.

Competitor influence markets

Large organisations, especially those that are high profile or dominate their industry sector, need to consider carefully the relationships they have with their competitors. Adopting the stance of industry statesman can be a good strategy. Jorgen Knudstorp, CEO of the Danish-based children's company LEGO, is a good example of an industry statesman when he says that what the company really cares about is inspiring young people who will build our tomorrow.[14]

By contrast British Airways' industry statesmanship was eroded during the 1990s when it attracted negative publicity over its so-called 'dirty tricks' campaign against Virgin Atlantic. As a consequence, Virgin's position in the marketplace was strengthened. Virgin got lots of free positive publicity and its popularity and familiarity grew among the public at large. In the era of the Internet and social media these things are remembered for a long period. In 2012 the search-term 'British Airways dirty tricks campaign' brings up over 240,000 results on Google!

Government, political and regulatory influence markets

The political category covers a number of groups including members of parliament, government ministers, central and local government departments and other government and quasi-government bodies. These groups may affect organisations within a given country, within an economic region such as the European Union or on a global basis.

Companies may need to direct marketing activity at government and/or regulatory bodies. Professor Evert Gummesson has pointed out that these two groups are particularly relevant for companies that sell infrastructure equipment such as nuclear reactors, telephone systems and defence products. Such products may affect the country's economic performance, employment levels or financial status, or may be politically important in other ways.

Influence markets: a summary

The penalties for failing to manage influence markets properly are illustrated by the UK jewellery retailer Ratners. In the 1990s, chief executive Gerald Ratner made a speech at the Institute of Directors in which he described his jewellery products as 'total crap'. The general press picked up the story, which was reported widely. Following the speech, the value of the Ratners' group plummeted by around £500 million, the company nearly collapsed and Ratner resigned. A year after Gerald Ratner's resignation, the company was forced to change its name because of the adverse image that had been created. Two decades later, Ratner's mistake is well-remembered. His gaffe has been immortalised in the UK corporate world and today such mistakes are known as 'Doing a Ratner'. Similar mistakes have been made more recently by Barclays Bank ex-CEO Matt Barrett, who suggested that consumers should avoid his company's product, the Barclaycard, because it was so expensive, and by Brand Director David Shepherd of UK clothing chain Topman, who, when asked to clarify his firm's target market, replied: 'Hooligans or whatever ... Very few of our customers have to wear suits for work. They'll be for his first interview or first court case.' Top management clearly needs to avoid such stupid mistakes which damage their company's relationships.

Recruitment market domain

Organisations now recognise that people are the most important resource in business. To attract and retain the highest quality recruits – those who share the organisation's values and will contribute significantly to its future success – firms have to market themselves to potential employees, or the recruitment market. This involves creating an appropriate organisational climate and then communicating the benefits of that organisation to potential employees. Marketing to recruitment markets is particularly important for companies where staff is a key element of competitive advantage, for example in service businesses, in order to secure a constant supply of high-quality recruits.

The scarcest resource for most organisations is no longer capital or raw materials, but skilled people. A trained and experienced workforce is perhaps the most vital element in delivering customer service. Global economics and the changing nature of employment have not helped to enlarge the recruitment pool, even though unemployment has climbed to historic levels. If attracting the best quality recruits is important to business success then the recruitment market has become a priority for most companies.

The recruitment market comprises all potential employees together with the third parties that serve as access channels to potential employees. Figure 4.6 shows the main access channels for the recruitment market domain.

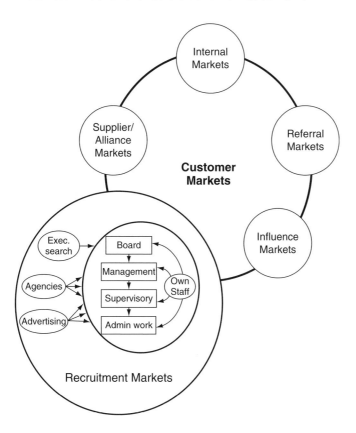

Figure 4.6 The recruitment market domain

Potential employees may join a business through a number of these channels. They may respond to advertisements placed by the employer or their recruitment agency. For senior appointments, they may be approached by executive search consultants. Where there is a dearth of high calibre recruits, some firms are turning to their own staff to suggest potential applicants, offering substantial payments as inducements. Accenture, the consulting firm, and Cisco Systems Inc., the networking equipment multinational, both successfully use staff recommendations as part of their recruitment process. Such 'bounty schemes' are increasingly common in the IT area. Companies may also recruit staff via placement departments in universities and colleges, direct approaches and, increasingly, through the Internet.

Large companies competing in a competitive job market need to manage a wide range of recruitment market channels. A department within human resources (HR) frequently manages this complex marketing task, but HR does not typically have the marketing skills and competencies to manage this complex set of relationships in a sophisticated way. The following example demonstrates how a professional service firm improved their recruitment process.

A large and well-known accountancy practice was having difficulty attracting newly qualified recruits. It was not difficult to find out why. The firm's recruitment literature was old-fashioned and lacked visual impact. On visits to university campuses – a traditional source of recruits – the firm was represented by an old and uninspiring partner and disinterested administrative staff. After a review and the identification of the problem, the firm then developed a marketing plan to improve the situation. This involved redesigning recruitment literature (with the help of recent graduates), sending the brightest young partners on university visits, accompanied by managers who had interesting experiences to recount, and sponsoring awards and prizes at target universities. As a result of the recruitment marketing campaign, the firm dramatically increased its 'offers to acceptances' ratio.

A number of studies have highlighted the impact of recruitment practices on company performance. Organisations need to market themselves in a way that attracts the calibre of person that matches the image of the firm they want to project to customers. More companies are now identifying a psychometric profile of the type of employee most likely to be successful in achieving customer-driven goals. The recruitment process itself is also an opportunity for the company to build a positive image with new recruits.

The value employees add to business success is tied closely to the way they are selected, trained, motivated and led. Examples abound of businesses failing or succeeding as a consequence of the way they manage their people. The expression 'our employees are our greatest asset' is increasingly common – but, more often than not, it is a platitude. If CEOs and their boards were more proactive in recognising employees' contributions in winning and keeping customers, they would substantially enhance their firms' competitive performance. In the rest of this section we discuss issues relating to recruiting and selecting employees within the recruitment market.

Recruiting the best employees

Annual employee turnover is as high as 150 per cent or more in some service businesses. This represents a significant cost to the company in terms of advertising, interviewing time, administration, training and possibly relocation expenses. There are also other costs because of reduced productivity during the handover from an experienced employee to a new recruit, or when a situation is vacant for a period of time. Some estimates suggest that the cost of replacing an employee may be around 50 per cent of their annual salary.

With the costs of recruitment so high, it is becoming increasingly important to find employees who not only have the necessary skills and competencies and match the profile that the company wants to portray to its customers, but who are keen and likely to stay.

Potential employees need to be given realistic expectations of the job from the outset. Unless press advertisements, brochures and information supplied by third parties accurately reflect the job requirements and the company environment, the result will be disillusioned employees, low employee retention and poor word-of-mouth referrals.

McKinsey & Co. argues that there is a 'war for talent' and that demographic and social changes are playing a growing role in this trend. In the US and in most other developed countries the supply of workers in the 35 to 44 age group is shrinking. Further, many of the best-trained people entering the workforce do not join traditional companies. Beechler and Woodward provide a contemporary account of the 'global' war for talent.[15] They conclude that despite the aftermath of the global financial crisis talent remains a critical agenda in organisations.

Selecting employees

Enterprises must choose their recruits carefully if they are to be successful and gain competitive advantage. The values and motivations of potential employees must be in keeping with the organisation's service ethic, so companies should not necessarily base candidates' suitability on their technical skills, which can be taught later, but on their psychological characteristics.

Techniques for selection range from the traditional interview, through self-assessment, group methods and assessment centres, to the increasingly popular psychometric tests. Psychometric testing is an effective way of identifying the personality profile of people who are likely to be successful in delivering service quality and developing relationships with customers. Traditionally used more for management and graduate jobs, organisations are now using these techniques for a wider range of positions, including administrative, secretarial and manual. This reflects the importance that companies are now placing on the 'emotional content' of front-line positions.

A good example of an organisation that understands the importance of emotional content among front-line employees is Southwest Airlines. Southwest's selection strategy is based on finding individuals with a sense of humour and who genuinely enjoying serving people.[16] Southwest's hiring process is unconventional. The process they use to screen prospective flight attendants is similar to a Hollywood casting call. Candidates are evaluated by a panel that includes flight attendants, ground personnel, managers and customers. Among other things, they are asked to recount the most embarrassing experience in their life in front of other potential staff. Southwest's customers hold the airline in such high regard that they willingly give up their time to help the airline select the best flight attendants. Following the interview, the panel compares notes on each of the candidates. The process is also competitive and highly selective. In one year the company received some 85,000 job applications and hired only 3 per cent of the applicants. Southwest uses a psychometric profile that it has developed as a result of studying its most successful and least successful employees in different job roles, to help it recruit, for example, flight attendants. It uses this to supplement the panel interviews and help find the people who best fit the profile for each job role within Southwest.

Recruitment markets: a summary

Research has shown that employees who are unclear about the role they are supposed to perform become demotivated, which in turn can lead to customer dissatisfaction and defection. So new employees must be carefully prepared for the work ahead of them, as their early days in a company colour their attitudes and perceptions towards it. Those organisations lacking a strong service ethos may need to implement a major change management programme aimed at all employees. Development programmes aimed at instilling a customer consciousness and service orientation in employees are referred to as 'internal marketing'.

Internal market domain

Organisations typically underestimate the important collaborative role marketing can play, in conjunction with the operations and HR functions, in getting the internal market exchange processes working better. Internal marketing encompasses many management issues, but has two main aspects.

First, every employee and every department in an organisation is both an internal customer and/or an internal supplier. So organisations need to work as effectively as possible to ensure that every department and individual provides and receives high standards of internal service. Second, all staff must work together in a way that is aligned to the organisation's mission, strategy and goals. Here internal marketing should ensure that all staff 'live the brand' by representing the organisation as well as possible, whether face-to-face, over the phone, by mail or electronically.

In Chapter 2 we explained how the structure of the organisation can severely impede the development of customer relationships. Traditional vertical organisations with a hierarchical structure and functional orientation often favour individual functions at the expense of the whole business and the customer. Relationship marketing, with its emphasis on cross-functional marketing, focuses on the processes that deliver value for the customer. Building an organisation that is focused on the customer requires a strong emphasis on internal marketing.

The fundamental aims of internal marketing are to develop awareness among employees of both internal and external customers, and to remove functional barriers to organisational effectiveness. Figure 4.7 illustrates the structure of the internal market based on the organisational chart. However, this particular version of the organisational chart is inverted, following one used by Jan Carlzon, the former CEO of SAS (formerly Scandinavian Airline System).

Segmenting the internal market on the basis of organisation levels is obvious. However, not so obvious is this inversion of the organisational chart to reflect the critical role of

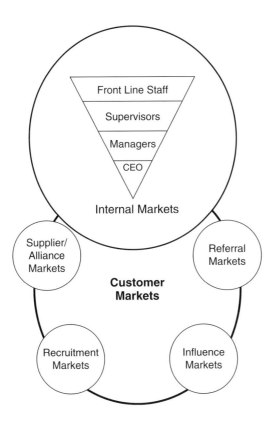

Figure 4.7 The internal market domain

front-line employees. This inverted chart reflects Carlzon's view that the primary purpose of the whole organisation is to support all front-line employees and ensure all their interactions with customers, or 'moments of truth', result in a superior experience for the customer. Other leading organisations have adopted a similar approach in their internal marketing activities.

For example, Nordstrom, the leading US retailer that we referred to earlier in this chapter, adheres to the philosophy that the staff on the sales floor are the major contributors in the organisation. In Nordstrom's version of the 'upside down' organisational chart, the customer is included at the top of the chart and salespeople occupy *the* highest internal rung on the chart. Next are buyers, merchandisers and department and store managers. At the very bottom of the organisation chart are the joint presidents of the organisation. Richard Pascale, a leading US consultant and academic, considers Nordstrom 'has a particular genius at defining a unique relationship with its internal customer – the salesperson'.[17] Anyone wanting to join the organisation and progress to a managerial position must start in the sales role on the floor regardless of the seniority of the position they may have occupied in another organisation. Nordstrom believes everybody must demonstrate the ability to respond to customers and to sell effectively and it has developed a unique culture where everybody is promoted from within. Pascale quotes a senior executive as saying that it is 'almost impossible' to overstate the importance of this common career track to Nordstrom's ability to communicate within the company.

'It's like we all speak a common language from top to bottom. It helps us avoid the "we" versus "them" mentality.'

If an organisation is to segment its internal market based on organisational hierarchy, it must understand the most important levels of hierarchy and the type of staff at which internal marketing effort needs to be directed. For most organisations this will be front-line employees. In the case of an airline it is all staff that have any sort of interaction with the customer. That means everyone from telephone sales to check-in staff, cabin crew and even baggage handlers.

But in other organisations the main target for internal marketing activities may be different. In a large telecommunications company in Australia, for example, the principal focus of an internal marketing programme was middle management. Top management had decided the company must become more customer focused, but middle managers were very technically oriented and were inhibiting the company's progress towards a customer orientation.

Segmentation of the internal market based on job role

Just as there are different ways of segmenting the customer market, there are alternative ways of segmenting the internal market. An essential aspect of internal market segmentation is to recognise the different marketing and customer contact roles within the business. Judd has developed a categorisation scheme based on the frequency of customer contact and the extent to which staff are involved with conventional marketing activities. This categorisation results in four groups: *contactors*, *modifiers*, *influencers* and *isolateds*.[18]

Contactors have frequent or regular customer contact and are typically heavily involved with conventional marketing activities. They hold a range of positions in service firms including selling and customer service roles. Whether they are involved in planning or executing marketing strategy they need to be well versed in the firm's marketing strategies. They should be well trained, prepared and motivated to serve customers on a day-to-day basis in a responsive manner. They should be recruited, evaluated and rewarded based on their potential and actual responsiveness to customer needs.

Modifiers are people such as receptionists, the credit department and switchboard personnel who, though not directly involved with conventional marketing activities, nevertheless have frequent contact with customers. These people need a clear view of the organisation's marketing strategy and the role they can play in being responsive to customers' needs. They play a vital role particularly, but not exclusively, in service businesses. Modifiers need to develop high levels of customer relationship skills, and it is important to train them and monitor their performance.

Influencers are involved with the traditional elements of the marketing mix but have little or no customer contact. (Note that Judd uses the word 'influencer' in a different context from the term 'influence market', used in the six markets model.) But these people play a big part in implementing the organisation's marketing strategy. Influencers work in roles such as product development, market research and so on. Companies recruiting influencers should seek people with the potential to develop a sense of customer responsiveness. They should evaluate and reward influencers according to customer-oriented performance standards, and programme opportunities to enhance the level of customer contact into their activities.

Isolateds are employees in the various support functions that have neither frequent customer contact nor a great deal to do with conventional marketing activities. However, as support staff, their activities critically affect the organisation's performance. Staff functions falling within this category include the purchasing department, personnel and data processing. Staff in such functions need to be sensitive to the fact that internal customers as well as external customers have needs which must be satisfied. They need to understand the company's overall marketing strategy and how their functions contribute to the quality of delivered value to the customer.

The adoption of internal marketing approaches by companies

Virgin Atlantic has long recognised the critical role internal marketing plays in its success. One of the secrets of the airline's success has been enthusiastic, empowered and motivated employees. Sir Richard Branson has said: 'I want employees in the airline to feel that it is *they* who can make the difference, and influence what passengers get ... We aren't interested in having just happy employees. We want employees who feel involved and prepared to express dissatisfaction when necessary. In fact, we think that the constructively dissatisfied employee is an asset we should encourage and we need an organisation that allows us to do this – and that encourages employees to take responsibility, since I don't believe it is enough for us simply to give it.' Virgin Atlantic's philosophy aims at stimulating the individual, encouraging staff to take initiatives and empowering them to do so.

The Walt Disney Company has practised sophisticated internal marketing since its inception. Employees are rigorously trained to understand that their job is to satisfy customers. Employees are part of the 'cast' at Disney and must at all times ensure that all visitors to their theme parks (known as 'Guests') have a highly enjoyable experience. Strict dress and conduct rules are maintained in order that employees conform to standards.

Internal markets: a summary

The current interest in internal marketing has been prompted by the renewed acknowledgement by organisations of the importance of their people. Internal marketing strategies involve recognising the importance of attracting, motivating, training and retaining quality employees through developing jobs to satisfy individual needs. Internal marketing aims to encourage staff to behave in a way that will attract customers to the firm. Further, the most talented people will want to work in those companies they regard as good employers.

People now recognise internal marketing as an important component of a customer-focused organisation, and it is starting to be treated as an important management topic. Many companies are taking a more formal approach to internal marketing. A number of books on internal marketing have now been published providing commentary on research and managerial insights.[19]

Assessing performance in the six markets

Any enterprise should aim to build a strong position in each of the six markets described above, but the precise emphasis they give to each market domain and groups within them needs to reflect their relative importance. Companies can determine the appropriate level of attention and resources that should be directed at each through the following steps:

- Identify key participants, or 'market' segments, in each of the market domains (and sub-categories);
- Undertake research to identify the expectations and requirements of key groups;
- Review the current and proposed level of emphasis in each market overall and for major participants in each market;
- Formulate a desired relationship strategy and determine whether a formal marketing plan is necessary.

Identifying key groups or segments in each market domain is the first step in applying the six markets model to an organisation. For example, Figure 4.8 lists the key markets and market segments for the property division of BAA (formerly the British Airports Authority).

The next step is to identify the expectations and requirements of the key participants in each market. In some cases there will be sufficient information within the company; in others market research will be needed to gather information from outside.

Two case studies at the end of this chapter provide illustrations of how particular market domains become especially important for the effective operation of the enterprise. For AirAsia, in addition to the customer and internal market, getting political buy-in from the

Customer markets
Existing
- airlines
- utility services
- freight forwarders
- cargo handlers
- hotels

New
- off market airlines
- new airlines
- international airports
- logistics/integrators
- development around airports

Internal markets
- marketing 'property' to BAA group

Referral markets
- existing satisfied BAA customers
- other airport people
- business advisers/surveyors
- property consultants/surveyors

Supplier markets
- framework suppliers
- consultants
- contractors
- international suppliers

Recruitment markets
- employment agencies
- headhunters/search firms
- graduates
- internal transfers

Influence markets
- shareholders
- city analysts/stockbrokers
- business press
- general press and media
- regulator
- government
- local authorities

Figure 4.8 BAA – a review of key market participants in the six market domains

government was critical to making the airline viable. For the City Car Club of Helsinki, the enterprise has to manage stakeholders within a wide range of market domains – including partners and influencers such as the Helsinki City and Regional Public Transport Authority, a range of new technology suppliers and potential customers – both businesses and the general public need to be convinced of the benefits of using car sharing.

Identifying emphasis on the six markets

Once the company has identified the broad groups and the segments within them for each market domain, it can assess what level of marketing emphasis it gives to each market domain currently, and what level it needs to give. It can use a relationship marketing radar chart or network diagram (also known as a 'spidergram'), such as that shown in Figure 4.9, to identify the appropriate level of emphasis.

The diagram in Figure 4.9 has seven axes – two for customers (existing and new) and one for each of the other five relationship markets discussed above. The scale of 1 (low) to 10 (high) reflects the degree of emphasis (cost and effort) placed on each relationship market. Dividing customers into 'new' and 'existing' reflects the two critical tasks within the customer market domain – customer attraction and customer retention. A group of managers within a firm can assess their current and desired levels of emphasis on each market domain by means of a jury of executive opinion and plot the results on the relationship marketing network diagram.

We illustrate this approach to reviewing the six markets by reference to the illustrative relationship marketing radar chart for The Royal Society for the Protection of Birds (RSPB), a leading British conservation charity, shown in Figure 4.10. This diagram was based on

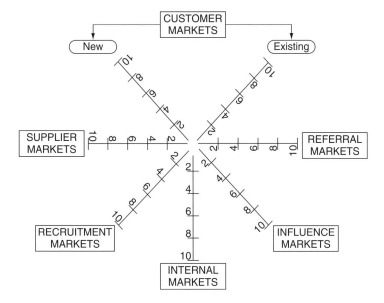

Figure 4.9 The six markets radar chart

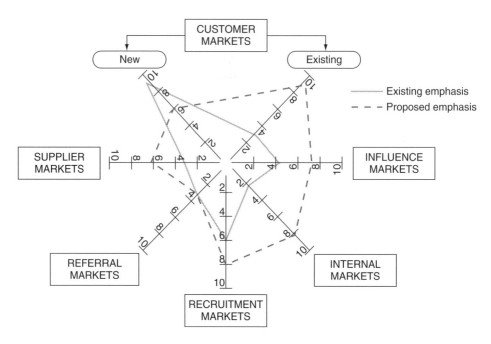

Figure 4.10 RSPB relationship marketing radar chart

the views of a number of people, including former executives at RSPB, and represents an external assessment of developments in that organisation a number of years ago.

The RSPB at this point in time might have considered a number of issues regarding the six markets, as shown in Figure 4.10, including:

- reducing its emphasis on acquiring members and increasing emphasis on retaining existing members;
- focusing more strongly on influence markets;
- reinforcing customer care and service quality issues with internal staff.

This analysis represents the first stage of the diagnostic process. The second stage examines the groups or segments within each market domain in terms of present and desired marketing emphasis. Further radar charts can then be developed for *each* market domain. For example, Figure 4.11 shows a network diagram for the referral markets of an accounting firm.

Figure 4.11 illustrates five key referral markets identified by the firm: existing satisfied clients, the firm's audit practice, banks, joint venture candidates and the offices of its international practice overseas. The firm concluded that though it was doing a satisfactory job for its audit practice and banks, it could improve referrals by putting more emphasis on the other three areas.

The two levels of analysis described above identify the key groups or segments in each market domain and provide an initial view of the existing and potential levels of marketing emphasis directed at them. The final step involves determining the appropriate relationship strategies for each market including which of them requires a detailed marketing plan to be developed.[20]

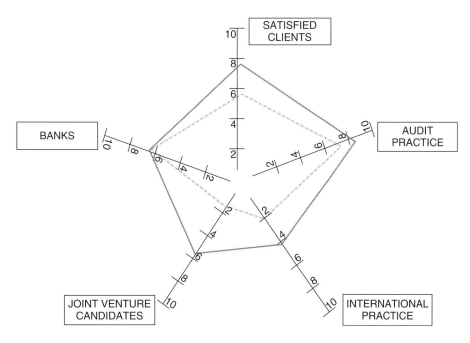

Figure 4.11 Referral market audit for an accounting firm

SUMMARY

In this chapter we have shown that relationship-based marketing activities directed at customers are necessary, but do not in themselves fully constitute relationship marketing. Organisations must also address the other relevant market domains and the key segments within them. Successful relationship marketing involves an informed and integrated approach to all these market domains in order to achieve competitive advantage. This stakeholder approach to relationship marketing recognises a diversity of key markets or market domains that organisations need to consider. It identifies where organisations should direct their marketing activity and where they may need to develop more detailed marketing plans and strategies. The six markets model has been successfully applied in many organisations including those in the business-to-business, business-to-consumer and not-for-profit sectors. The model has proved to be a robust tool to help organisations recognise and respond to their network of stakeholder markets.

This chapter has focused on the stakeholder relationships a company must develop with its customers, partners and other entities markets. In a world of rapid technological change, information is available to and shared with these stakeholders to an extent never experienced before. Customers, in particular, can rapidly find out what other consumers think about an enterprise's products or services via the Internet and social media. In the next chapter we examine relationships and technology and more specifically the role of digital marketing and social influence marketing.

CASE 4.1: AirAsia spreads its wings

The company

AirAsia Bhd started life in 1993 as a subsidiary of the Malaysian Government-owned conglomerate Hicom Bhd. It commenced operations in 1996. The then Prime Minister, Dr Mahathir Mohamad, was a prime mover behind the new airline and he continued to take an interest in its operations after its launch. Although the government sold a majority stake to a local entrepreneur, Yahya Ismail, it continued to exert managerial direction over the company.

The airline was dogged with problems over the next five years. Malaysia Airlines, the country's national carrier, resisted sharing its regional routes with AirAsia. Further, despite its desire to add additional international operations to China none of these were granted. The airline was also interested in flying rights to Japan but these did not eventuate either. For a number of years the Malaysian Government frustrated AirAsia's plans to develop into a strong regional carrier. Behind the government's actions were worries that providing further routes to AirAsia would adversely impact Malaysia Airlines, the poorly performing national carrier. However, by 2000 the company did achieve rights to land at several regional destinations including ones in Taiwan, Indonesia, Hong Kong and Thailand. The airline also suffered from bad luck in terms of timing, with the onset of the Asian crisis at the end of the 1990s. As a result of this crisis, passenger loads decreased, staff were laid off and services to Taiwan, Indonesia and parts of Malaysia were suspended.

The challenge

By 2001, AirAsia was in dire straits. It had large accumulated losses of $11 million and its strategy, based on competing with Malaysia Airlines as a full cost carrier, was flawed. The Malaysian entrepreneur, Yahya Ismail, had died some years before in a helicopter explosion. There was no evidence of a clear strategy to address the competitive and political imperatives and the parlous financial situation. However, despite its uncertain future, the airline had several positive factors. It had a good safety record together with good pilots and staff. Importantly, it also had a well-recognised brand.

The challenge of addressing these problems involved several key constituencies. The key to success was to successfully manage relationships with stakeholder groups, or 'market domains', that included the government, customers and employees. Getting political buy-in to AirAsia's plan for the future would be critical in gaining sufficient routes to make the airline viable. Large numbers of potential customers needed to be motivated to fly with the airline. Further, the management team was frustrated and front-line staff were concerned about job security and their future – these employees needed to be motivated and engaged. With rumours of a possible sale of AirAsia, the question remained – how could the airline be successfully turned around?

The solution

AirAsia's salvation came at the hands of the consortium led by Dr Tony Fernandes. Fernandes, a British trained accountant and former Time Warner executive, was investigating the opportunity of starting up an airline from scratch based on the low-cost model used in North America and Europe by airlines such as Southwest Airlines, easyJet and Ryanair. Previously Fernandes had worked for Sir Richard Branson's Virgin Records. With his partners, he started putting plans together. However, there were problems associated with obtaining a licence. One of his partners, Datuk Pahamin, a civil servant, arranged a meeting with Dr Mahathir Mohamad who was Prime Minister at the time.

The meeting clearly went well. Dr Mahathir Mohamad indicated a preference for the consortium purchasing an existing airline, rather than starting one up from scratch, potentially in competition with AirAsia. Fernandes was successful in selling his vision of a low-cost airline to Dr Mahathir. In December 2001, Tune Air Sdn Bhd, a holding company founded by Fernandes, purchased AirAsia from HICOM (then renamed DRB-Hicom) for a token RM 1 (1 Malaysian Ringot = US 26 cents). The transaction included two Boeing jets and a mountain of debt.

With airline analysts sceptical about the possibility of turning the airline around, Fernandes and his team started to evolve a new strategy based on the low-cost airline business model. The operating principles and business model of AirAsia were to parallel very closely those of Southwest Airlines, arguably the most successful long-term low-cost carrier in the world. In common with Southwest Airlines and other low-cost airlines, AirAsia's new strategy was to be driven by several key fundamental strategic imperatives including high aircraft utilisation, low fares and no frills, and operations in short-haul non-stop flights in a point-to-point network. The challenges facing Fernandes were substantial. Shortly after acquiring AirAsia, the attack on the Twin Towers in New York occurred in September 2001. This tragedy damaged the airline industry globally for some time.

At the time of the acquisition, AirAsia had flights from Kuala Lumpur to four other destinations, as well as a charter arrangement with part of the Malaysian Government which involved flying pilgrims to Mecca. Acquiring a third Boeing 737–300 in 2002, the airline implemented its low-cost business model, targeting the huge Asian population, many of whom had not flown in aircraft before.

Following the successful Southwest Airlines/Ryanair business model, fares were set at a low cost, a one type of aircraft policy was adopted, online ticketing was promoted to avoid paying travel agents commission, meals were charged for, turnaround time was reduced to around 25 minutes and flight frequency was increased. This strategy worked quickly. By the end of 2002, further destinations were added and the number of aircraft increased to five. Some 600,000 passengers travelled with AirAsia in 2002, over double the number that had flown in the previous year. The growth continued in 2003, as AirAsia began flights from a second hub at Senai International Airport, one hour's drive from Singapore.

By 2003 Fernandes was considering how to undertake greater expansion in Asia. The Asian arena was attracting the attention of other players in the airline industry who saw the potential for a low-cost

Asian airline. For example Ryanair, one of Europe's largest low-cost airlines, had already entered into a partnership with Singapore Airlines to launch a new low-cost airline.

Fernandes proved remarkably successful in dealing with the political and government stakeholder groups. This was not easy, as the Malaysian chief airline regulator, who could approve airline routes, sat on the Board of Malaysia Airlines. When Malaysia Airlines started massive discounting aimed at damaging AirAsia, Fernandes adopted a more confrontational approach in the media by criticising the government.

Ultimately Fernandes needed to lobby a range of government officials, including the Transport Minister Ling Liong Sik and Prime Minister Mohamad. During 2003, Fernandes persuaded Dr Mohamed to approach leaders of Singapore, Indonesia and Thailand with the objective of moving towards an 'open skies' agreement. This resulted in AirAsia eventually gaining landing rights in these countries. In 2003 AirAsia partnered with domestic entrepreneurs in Thailand to establish AirAsia Thailand. Fernandes was ultimately victorious in winning over government bureaucrats who were intent on protecting national carriers.

In 2004 a decision was made to replace the ageing fleet of Boeing 737s with Airbus A320s. The Airbus A320 is a more fuel-efficient and cost-efficient type of aircraft. In common with Southwest Airlines, AirAsia's philosophy is based on running one type of aircraft, which minimises a wide range of activities from pilot training to repairs, spare parts and maintenance. In 2005 AirAsia commenced flights to Cambodia and, through its sister company, AirAsia Indonesia, commenced services between Jakarta and Singapore. The business continued to grow and in 2007 AirAsia placed the world's largest Airbus A320 order involving a total of 225 aircraft.

In 2008 the airline reached a major milestone when it reached a total of 50 million passengers who had flown with it – a remarkable success to achieve within six years of operation. The airline also introduced the *AirAsia On-Time Guarantee*, which gave passengers who were delayed for more than two hours an *e-gift voucher* to be used on future flights. The airline also eliminated fuel surcharges.

The following year, in 2009, AirAsia introduced *Web check-in* and a *self check-in* facility within the entire AirAsia Group network. New routes were introduced, including travel to Brunei, Macau, Ho Chi Minh City and Perth. In 2010 AirAsia, and new sister company AirAsia X, launched direct flights to six new locations in India. In October 2010, AirAsia celebrated having flown a total of 100 million passengers. An agreement was made to form a new low-cost airline in the Philippines, AirAsia Philippines. In 2010 AirAsia introduced a new IT booking system in the form of *New Skies*, which allows customers to manage their online bookings more easily. Further, with the advent of social media, platforms such as Facebook, Twitter and blogs have become integral to the Group's customer relationship initiatives. AirAsia is recognised as the most popular airline in the region on Facebook in terms of fan base.

Figure 1 provides a summary of the key aspects of AirAsia's strategy, which is based on four key elements of low fares, service, safety and simplicity. Collectively, these strategies have established AirAsia as the lowest-cost airline in the world.

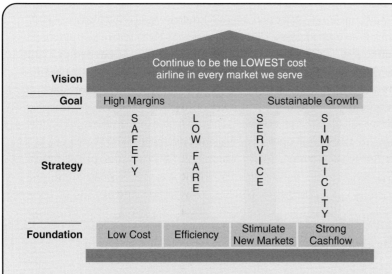

Figure 1 AirAsia – summary of its strategy

Despite a host of rivals, including Singapore's Tiger Airways, Qantas' Jetstar and many others, AirAsia has continued to grow from strength to strength. From being an airline with only two aircraft covering six routes in Malaysia in 2002, AirAsia has grown dramatically over the past ten years. Today, it has around 140 routes, with 40 of them not being offered by any other airline. It flies to some 80 destinations in 18 countries, employs more than 8,000 staff and has a market capitalisation of over RM 7 billion. It has established subsidiaries in Thailand, Indonesia, Vietnam, the Philippines and Japan. Through its associate company, AirAsia X, it offers long-haul services from Kuala Lumpur to Australia, China, France, India, Japan, New Zealand and the UK. In 2011 AirAsia built a strategic relationship with Malaysia Airlines through a share swap.

The results

Fernandes' clear strategy, his unwavering commitment to its implementation and his superb relationship building with disparate stakeholder groups has paid off handsomely. AirAsia has evolved from a bankrupt government-owned airline to being the region's most successful low-cost carrier. AirAsia's strategic success is undoubtedly largely due to the attention paid to managing key stakeholder groups. Fernandes has had a major role in moving the Asian region towards an open skies policy and he has been masterful at lobbying the Malaysian Government and other Asian governments to permit AirAsia, and its sister companies, to fly to a large number of new destinations. The 2010 annual report highlights the importance AirAsia places on relationships with its staff and its customers, and reflects a strong emphasis on corporate responsibility. By offering an excellent value proposition to passengers, strong relationships with the customer stakeholder group have been formed. This has resulted in outstanding growth. The number of customers carried each year increased from 8.7 million to 16 million between 2007 and 2011. As Peter Harbison, Managing Director of consultancy The Centre for Asia Pacific Aviation, observed: 'Fernandes has had a remarkable influence in shaping government and airline thinking in South-East Asia and beyond. The Asia-Pacific airline industry will never be the same again.'

The financial results have been equally impressive: over a three and a half year period from June 2007 to December 2010, revenue increased from Malaysian RM 1,600 million to RM 3,950 million and profit increased from RM 498 million to RM 1,060 million. AirAsia's success has been recognised by many industry awards including the 2011 Best Asian Low-Cost Carrier by TTG Travel. Other recent awards include: the World's Best Low-Cost Airline and the Best Low-Cost Airline – Asia by Skytrax; the Best Company for Investor Relations – Mid Cap; and the Best Investor Relations Website – Mid Cap by Malaysian Investor Relations Association; the Fastest Growing Foreign Airline for Cargo by Guangzhou Baiyun International Airport; and the 2010 Asiamoney Best Managed Company Award.

CASE 4.2: The City Car Club, Helsinki – driving sustainable car use

The company

Car sharing schemes, such as the City Car Club (CCC) in Helsinki, Finland, are becoming a popular alternative to car ownership in many cities around the world. CCC, which commenced operations in March 2000, was the first car sharing scheme of its kind in Finland. CCC provides its services both to individuals and to businesses. Companies such as CCC are interesting, as their success depends on building and managing successful relationships with a diverse group of constituencies in both the private and public sectors. CCC is a company that has developed relationships with a complex web of multiple stakeholders or 'market domains' within the private and public sectors. These stakeholders include not only customers (individual and corporate) but also government agencies (municipal authorities and legislators), suppliers (of innovative technology solutions and vehicles), partners (advertisers), influencers (environmental groups and environmentally conscious individuals) and, of course, CCC's employees.

There are a number of approaches that have been developed that categorise stakeholder groups, including the 'six markets model', developed by a group of scholars working in the area of relationship marketing at the Cranfield School of Management. This model demonstrates that identifying key stakeholders at an early stage and ensuring that appropriate relationship marketing plans are developed for each stakeholder group, or market domain, are critical steps in complex businesses where success is dependent on the ability to simultaneously manage a multiplicity of relationships. In this case study, we consider several key stakeholder groups that have been critical to the success of CCC, explain why they are important to the company and outline the benefits that successful management of these relationships brings to the company.

The challenge

Helsinki is a small, compact city of almost 600,000 people. At the start of the new millennium, in the crowded city centre, traffic volume and insufficient parking space were causing increasing concern to the public, businesses and city authorities. Pollution by traffic is a high priority for political activists in Finland, a country that is renowned for its environmental conscience. Although public transport in

Helsinki is efficient, commuters and shoppers enjoy the convenience of car travel, especially during the freezing winter. Standing in a bus queue in a blizzard is not an attractive alternative to travel in a car.

The challenge for CCC was to convince the general public and businesses of the benefits of using a car sharing scheme. Market research was undertaken and the results suggested that car sharing was attractive to specific groups of customers, especially those who make occasional use of a vehicle or wish to access a vehicle that differs in size or features to the type they own. For companies, such a scheme was attractive for occasional out-of-town business and the scheme offered companies a favourable option to maintaining an expensive fleet. It was also attractive for consumers who could benefit from the convenience of private cars without the costs and responsibility of ownership. The market research also showed that the scheme appealed to younger, environmentally conscious people and especially males. There were several hurdles for CCC to overcome in making the scheme effective. First, CCC needed to prove that the scheme was cost-effective and offered a cost advantage over car ownership. Second, car drop pick-up and drop-off points had to be conveniently located. These locations included the heart of the city where parking spaces were expensive. Third, the car sharing service needed to be easy to use and efficient so that users could quickly learn and operate vehicles with minimal problems. Finally, in order to make the scheme cost-effective, CCC needed to partner with other key stakeholders who would benefit from the scheme as well as assist in making the scheme viable.

The solution

CCC recognised that managing a network of stakeholders was critical to successfully developing the business. The company developed its business plan and value proposition for customers with careful thought given as to what was required in order to launch the venture successfully. It researched customer needs and placed great effort on understanding how they should communicate their offer to customers, who would be unfamiliar with the offering and how it could be used. They worked very closely with suppliers and technology partners to develop a convenient and streamlined service offering. Finally, they successfully engaged with municipal authorities who were critical to the venture's success.

Customers

Attracting customers was a key priority for the company. CCC designed the business to offer a cost-effective, flexible, convenient and environmentally friendly way of driving. From the start, CCC promoted 'membership', providing differentiation from car rental services. Membership details could be stored and accessed, making each rental process fast and efficient. Being 'members' encouraged the customers to feel an emotional bond with each other and to feel champions of an environmentally conscious 'club'.

The scheme offers members convenience, providing cars at any time, and members can book and collect a car online or by telephoning a 24 hour booking centre. The booking system uses GSM (Global System for Mobile Communications) and SMS messages, without the necessity of a costly call centre. A short video, accessed online, teaches new members how to use the car rental system, making the process easy to use and minimising problems for customers. Cars can be booked for a time period that extends from just one hour to several weeks. Billing is based upon time and kilometres driven, with special discounts applied to night hours and single journeys. Discounts are also applied to monthly totals, ensuring that the price of the car rental is highly competitive with alternative transport options. The transparency and ease of billing is especially appealing to corporate members who can readily access details and compile records of corporate expenses.

Suppliers

CCC recognised that customers likely to use a car sharing scheme would look for cost savings, compared with car ownership, as well as a convenient and efficient system. The company forged strong supplier relationships so that the entire customer rental experience is accessed through innovative technology solutions. Technology is used throughout the rental process to reduce costs and enhance the car club experience. For example, customers can use their mobile phone to book a car, access the vehicle, complete the rental and pay for usage. Customers enjoy the convenience and reduced costs of self-service, which especially suits busy city workers. Car keys are left inside the car, instead of operating expensive lockers for the keys outside the car. At the beginning of a rental period, the customer gains access to the car using a mobile phone by calling and keying a unique pin number and the car registration, which releases the locked car doors. A similar system operates at the end of the car rental period. Customers return the car to an agreed CCC reserved space and call a number and enter their pin. The doors lock using a central locking system and the car is now waiting for the next customer.

CCC's business model includes revenue from advertisers, who form another important group. Cars provide effective mobile advertising, especially for products that complement the environmentally friendly image of CCC. Cars driven around the city centre and parked in collection points promote not only car sharing but also the products displayed on the body of each car. In 2008 CCC launched its first 'Media Cars' and the revenue from advertising enhances the profitability of the company.

Partners and influencers

Managing relationships with municipal authorities was critical to the success of CCC. Both business and individual customers require convenient pick-up and drop-off zones. CCC has forged strong relationships with the City of Helsinki, securing reserved special residential car parking spaces that are located at prime positions around the city. As a favourable customer experience depends on the ambience of these collection and drop-off points, CCC maintains them for the benefit not only of the customers but also for the general public.

Transport authorities, including Helsinki City and Regional Public Transport, are important partners for CCC. The company found that collaborating with public transport authorities was important in winning customers to the car sharing scheme. Customer surveys suggested that such schemes are more appealing to users of public transport than those who value the convenience of cars. Partnership arrangements include providing the public with a package deal, combining public transport with car sharing. Both parties profit from such a combined arrangement, which enhances customer usage – and the customer benefits from cost savings without compromising convenience. For example, season ticket holders of Helsinki City Transport secure free access to CCC (saving the cost of membership of CCC – currently about 60 euros) and pay a discounted monthly membership fee. Ticket holders for Helsinki Metropolitan Council get a voucher for some CCC charges.

One of the greatest attractions of membership to CCC is the environmental benefits of car sharing schemes. CCC has promoted 'green' issues and developed strong links with environmental groups in Finland, a country known for its interest in sustainability and environmental concerns. These links endorse the image of CCC and provide emotional appeal to its members. CCC communicates the environmental benefits of sharing a car over car ownership through its website and blogs endorsing efforts to reduce pollution. Club members share their ideas on green issues, enhancing the 'green' image of CCC. As the success of the company has grown, CCC has partnered with other service organisations, offering complimentary services to its members. These include holiday and hotel offers, often with those organisations that reflect the environment-friendly image of the club.

The results

CCC is a profitable company with a steady growth of over 10 per cent per annum. Critically, customers are very enthusiastic about the service and the car sharing experience. CCC has encouraged club members to blog online and there is now a 'brand community' of enthusiastic CCC bloggers, keen to share their stories. Interestingly, acting in an environmentally responsible manner encourages members to discuss not only their car usage experiences but also other topics related to sustainability and environmental concerns. For CCC, this 'green' image helps widen the appeal of club membership.

Recent trends suggest that car sharing in busy city centres is becoming more and more popular as people look for new sustainable options to car ownership. CCC has pioneered this movement and looks set to continue its healthy growth. In 2012 CCC had over 2,500 customers, including more than 2,000 private users and over 450 company users. From a modest start, the company now has a fleet of over 100 cars and vans available for collection and drop-off at over 110 locations around Helsinki. The company has plans to extend coverage beyond its original base in Helsinki and its operations in other cities in Finland.

5 Relationships and technology: Digital marketing and social media

Relationship Marketing: Development and Key Concepts *(Ch. 2)*
- Origins and alternative approaches to relationship marketing
- Characteristics and key concepts in relationship marketing

Creating Customer Value *(Ch. 3)*
- The value the customer receives
- How relationships add value
- How brands add value
- The value proposition
- Value assessment

Relationship Marketing

Building Relationships with Multiple Stakeholders *(Ch. 4)*
- Customer markets
- Supplier/alliance markets
- Internal markets
- Recruitment markets
- Influence markets
- Referral markets

Relationships and Technology *(Ch. 5)*
- Digital marketing
- Social media and social influence marketing

In this chapter we explore the greatly enhanced role of technology in customer relationships management and in particular the closely related areas of digital, mobile and social media. In Chapter 1, we described the importance of organisations adapting their customer relationship management programmes to the changing environment. These environmental forces fall into four broad categories: changes driven by the customer; market forces – such as the industry setting and competitors; external forces unfolding in the broader environment and technology. In this chapter we focus on technology, but within the context of the changing environment for relationships. Later, in Chapter 9, we examine specific aspects of technology that relate to information management and CRM.

Over the past three decades these forces have interacted as never before and at various points in time they have created major periods of transformational change. The times when these forces converge set the stage for periods of rapid technological advancement and adoption. An early example when such forces converged was the period of global telecommunications deregulation and trade liberalisation in the early 1990s. These changes coincided with the expansion of venture capital available for innovative start-ups. This combination triggered the development of the broadband and mobile Internet infrastructure that exists to this day. A more recent example is the interaction of technology with competitive forces. Digital, mobile and social technologies have triggered a fast adoption by end users and changes in the competitive environment have resulted in a rush of new entrants with new business models. Technological innovation has influenced what the relationship manager can do in response to these changes.

These environmental forces can and do change the market environment dramatically. During the last 20 years we have seen the most fundamental, rapid, and dramatic changes in the marketplace since the advent of modern marketing. This acceleration is being driven by two key principles that were first articulated in the 1980s in the context of networking and computing, but have since proven to be more fundamental principles driving digital, mobile and social innovation. The first principle, Metcalfe's law, also known as the law of network effects, is popularly credited to 3Com founder and Ethernet co-inventor Robert Metcalfe. This states that the value of a network is proportional to the square of the number of connected users. The second principle, Moore's law, proposed by Intel co-founder Gordon E. Moore in 1965, was first applied to predict a doubling of the number of transistors on a chip every 18 to 24 months. This exponential pace of performance improvement has been observed in almost every area of digital technology.

These principles point to the substantial impact that technology can have on relationship marketing. As each evolving technological generation unfolds, it impacts the behaviour of people and market forces and enables advances in relationship marketing practices. Each transformational wave seems to advance at shorter and shorter intervals. This pace of change presents substantial opportunities and threats for enterprises seeking to enhance customer relationships.

This chapter is divided into the following nine main sections:

- First, we briefly review *the rise of technology* over the last half century and how both enterprises and their customers have gained from technological developments.
- Second, we summarise *the impact of digital, mobile and social technologies* on the customer and the enterprise.
- Third, we explore *digital Internet infrastructure* by discussing digital networks and the nature and uptake of the digital devices that facilitate the use of digital networks.
- Fourth, we review the *evolution of the World Wide Web* including its three stages of development – Web 1.0, Web 2.0 and Web 3.0.
- Fifth, we consider the key elements of *digital marketing* and define key terms used in contemporary digital marketing.
- Sixth, we consider *social media* and review the development of social media networks and the social media ecosystem.
- Seventh, we examine the growing area of *social influence marketing*, including the social behaviour of consumers and social media segmentation.
- Eighth, we provide a framework for developing *social media strategy*, including a discussion of social media campaigns, social media analytics and measuring social media returns.

- Finally, we discuss the *integration of marketing*, including how both digital and non-digital marketing activities in paid, owned and earned media need to be balanced in order to maximise the effectiveness of relationship marketing activities.

The domain of digital marketing, social media and social influence marketing has evolved into a huge, complex and fast changing arena. To address this domain fully would require, at the very least, a large book on its own. However, to date, we have not identified any one volume that covers this domain in detail and is fully up to date – this latter point is important as the area is so dynamic and fast changing. This chapter focuses on major developments in these areas and especially aims at giving the reader an understanding of the progression of digital technology, how this is likely to change in the future and the impact on customer relationships. Fortunately, even though this area is changing rapidly there are many frequent reports and updates produced by analysts and industry observers that are charting new developments. Online searches will provide the reader with a substantial amount of contemporary material in the areas of digital marketing, social media and social influence marketing.

The rise of technology

Rapid changes in technology over the last half century have sparked new thinking and practice in virtually all enterprises. Many of the key marketing and customer management breakthroughs over this period were inspired, enabled or amplified by technological advancements.

The early days: 1960s to 1970s

The end of the Second World War triggered a period of dramatic change. Television was the exciting new media that caused families to change their behaviour. A new pastime for a family at this time included watching TV shows together, rather than the previous shared activity of listening to radio broadcasts. The 1960s and 1970s marked the full permeation of television into the lives of consumers and also ushered in the trends of increased transparency, declining trust and the rise of activism among the media, citizens and consumers. This period marked the start of the decline in trust of formal institutions, including corporations and their brand messages, that continues to this day.

The information age: the 1980s

In the 1980s, the focus on product quality expanded beyond the assembly line to the whole supply chain. It coincided with the globalisation of production and operations, with a focus on cutting costs. This led to low cost production and ultimately oversupply of quality products in many sectors. The concept of relationship marketing extended the boundaries of traditional marketing by recognising the strategic importance of cross-functional interactions in enterprises, the relationship between customer satisfaction and retention, and ultimately, customer lifetime value and profit. Developments in services marketing also made visible the notion of listening to the 'voice of the customer', a concept with roots in optimising call centre channels, where technologies such as speech analytics attempted to discover critical patterns buried in recorded customer calls.

The Internet age: from the 1990s

The business environment from the 1990s onwards has been driven by rapid advancements in the digital, mobile and social technologies discussed in this chapter. Managerial and academic attention moved from considering brand essence and brand associations to interest in the brand ecosystem. These developments raised the question of how relationships should be managed in the social age – including the idea that conversations do not only occur in the form of a firm-customer 'dyad', but rather they take the form of a 'triad' where customers talk about a brand with each other, as well as with the firm. These digital, mobile and social fields are constantly changing, increasingly overlapping and will continue to expand in the years ahead. It is important to recognise that these technologies will change more rapidly in the future.

Figure 5.1 provides an overview of the projected growth of digital marketing in the US between 2011 and 2016. The figure compares search marketing, display advertising, mobile marketing e-mail marketing and social media. The figure shows that while e-mail marketing and search marketing are growing at a relatively modest rate over this period, social media is anticipated to grow at an impressive compound annual growth rate

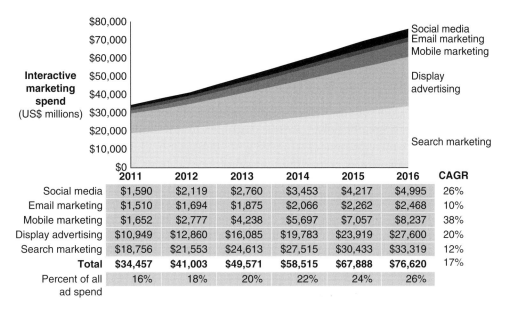

	2011	2012	2013	2014	2015	2016	CAGR
Social media	$1,590	$2,119	$2,760	$3,453	$4,217	$4,995	26%
Email marketing	$1,510	$1,694	$1,875	$2,066	$2,262	$2,468	10%
Mobile marketing	$1,652	$2,777	$4,238	$5,697	$7,057	$8,237	38%
Display advertising	$10,949	$12,860	$16,085	$19,783	$23,919	$27,600	20%
Search marketing	$18,756	$21,553	$24,613	$27,515	$30,433	$33,319	12%
Total	**$34,457**	**$41,003**	**$49,571**	**$58,515**	**$67,888**	**$76,620**	17%
Percent of all ad spend	16%	18%	20%	22%	24%	26%	

Figure 5.1 Projected growth of digital marketing in the US to 2016.
Source: Forrester Research Inc., US Interactive Marketing Forecast, 2011 to 2016, 24 August 2011, updated: 7 September 2011

of 26 per cent and mobile marketing at a compound annual growth rate of 38 per cent. This represents expenditure on 'paid' media. However, as discussed later in this chapter, one of the big shifts is that significant digital marketing spend is in 'owned' media – including the content that populates all the websites and social channels.

As Forrester Research points out, the digital decade has arrived. They forecast that by 2016 advertisers will spend as much on interactive marketing as they do on television advertising today. This research concludes that investment in search marketing, display marketing, e-mail marketing, mobile marketing and social media will grow to nearly $80 billion by 2016. This represents 35 per cent of all advertising, an indication of how interactive channels are gaining legitimacy in the marketing mix.[1]

In the current business environment, strategic customer management needs to embrace the three technology-driven areas of digital, mobile and social and identify opportunities to improve relationships with customers. However, the lines between these technologies are increasingly blurred as social applications are run over digital and mobile platforms and traditional non-social digital tools and platforms are extended to include social concepts and features. We now consider the impact of these digital, mobile and social technologies on relationships with customers. While our focus in this chapter is on customers, as we discuss in this chapter, the principles apply more broadly to the other key stakeholders discussed in Chapter 4.

The impact of digital, mobile and social technologies

Before considering the nature of digital, mobile and social technologies in more detail, we first consider how several key shifts have impacted relationships between enterprises and their customers.

The power shift to consumers and the rise of low-price producers

The adoption of digital, mobile and social technologies has resulted in customers assuming much greater power in the customer–firm relationship. The proliferation of the Internet and e-commerce, coupled with globalisation, has resulted in much wider choice and greater accessibility. These changes have shifted price points in many industries, reduced barriers to entry and lowered cost structures – enabling an influx of new players, many of them utilising lower prices as the basis of competition. The shift in power to consumers and the disruptive marketplace force of low-price competitors provided the impetus for firms to change and seek new ways of delivering value innovation and developing long-term relationships with customers.

From passive customer to active co-creator

The voices and opinions that play a key role in shaping the perceptions about the firm and its brand meaning have moved irrevocably from the firm's locus of control into the hands, minds and hearts of customers and other stakeholders. Information is no longer a one-way communication that is packaged and transmitted from the firm and received and internalised by its customers. A key aspect of the impact of social and mobile technology is the enhanced ability of customers to co-create value. The role of the customer has moved from passive audience to active player. There is now increasing recognition that the best form of marketing is to perform in such a way that customers, and other intermediaries, undertake the marketing for the enterprise, especially through word-of-mouth.

The rise of viral word-of-mouth

Firms now operate in an environment where anyone can publicly post their opinion, anywhere and at any time. Each opinion that is posted has the potential to spontaneously spread virally around the globe and for existing and potential customers, as well as other stakeholders, to read, internalise, and reshape their opinions about the firm – all in real time. Largely unfiltered, this running real time commentary spans the full spectrum of positive and negative opinions, messages and images, collectively defining the perceptions of the good, the bad and the ugly about a firm.

Good experiences result in positive word-of-mouth; bad experiences negative word-of-mouth – both outcomes can have dramatic effects on the company's bottom line and long-term profitability. Positive word-of-mouth can launch new products, services or businesses. For example, new music stars like Justin Bieber have spawned number one hits from YouTube videos. Conversely, bad customer experiences can escalate into public relations disasters – destroying brand equity that has taken years to accumulate. For example, several years ago when Canadian musician Dave Carroll published a song on YouTube and iTunes that recounted his negative experience of United Airlines dealing with the breaking of his guitar, the airline's stock price fell 10 per cent within four days, costing shareholders around $180 million. Carroll published a series of three videos on YouTube describing the poor response of United Airlines to his complaint. These attracted over 10 million hits over a six month period.

Increased engagement with stakeholders

Advancements in digital, mobile and social technology impact not only the dynamics of the customer–firm relationship, but also the firms' relationship with all its stakeholders. Opinions about the firm, its brands, product and service offers, delivery, and customer experience are now instantly accessible not only to customers but to the widest range of stakeholders whose relationships are critical to a firm's ongoing success. We discuss these stakeholder groups, or market domains, more fully in Chapter 4. In particular, referral networks, internal staff, the recruitment pool of potential future employees, suppliers and alliance partners, and influencers – including government agencies, regulatory bodies, media, labour unions, social activists and investors – all have an increasingly important role to play. These stakeholders have real-time access to the many and varied communication flows about the firm emanating from anyone, anywhere. The traditional model of creating carefully crafted centrally controlled positive messages and images for stakeholders and communicating these at regular and strategic intervals has gone. Instead, there is organic and spontaneous commentary – and even activism – unfolding in real time.

Digital, mobile and social – implications for the firm

The ascendance of customers and their purchasing power, along with the unprecedented public visibility of the collective voices of the firms' customers, staff, suppliers, investors and other influential stakeholders has important implications for the firm, particularly impacting the ways in which it manages its strategic relationships. For example, the initial response by many companies to social technologies has been to appoint relatively inexperienced and low-level staff to undertake, for instance, creation of Facebook and Twitter accounts and to commence blogging on a few key topics thought to be of some purchasing influence in the minds of prospective customers.

However, the rapid onslaught and uptake of social technologies has quickly necessitated moving this function well beyond early experimental side projects. These technologies must be harnessed in a much more strategic way so that they can take their place within the firm's overall mix of marketing and customer relationship management activities. The success of firms today depends on rapid and iterative responses to these new technological advancements and cultural values. This agility requires: understanding the consequences of the new cultural values; understanding the consequences of each innovation; the ability to leverage the new values and innovations for customer benefit and acquiring the processes and tools to seamlessly execute these strategies across the functions of the enterprise and its brand and social media ecosystem.

The era of mass production and its associated organisational structures and marketing practices brought tremendous efficiency, quality and choice. However, these benefits came at a price, distancing organisations from the human element of relationships. As a result, much of the personal touch in relationships was lost. Today, digital, mobile and particularly social technologies are providing firms with the opportunity to re-inject that humanity and to evolve into more relationship-focused enterprises. When applied collectively and intelligently, technology provides the opportunity for firms to practise better and more personalised relationship marketing.

The digital Internet infrastructure

It is important for readers, whether they are top executives, managers or students, to have a broad understanding of the technological infrastructure – including digital, mobile and social – that can lead to enterprises developing improved relationship marketing. In this section and the next section we provide an overview of developments in the Internet and World Wide Web. In this section we consider digital Internet infrastructure under two headings: *digital networks* and *digital devices*. In the following section we discuss the evolution of the World Wide Web from its Web 1.0, the first stage of development, to Web 3.0, the new emerging developments in the Web.

The building blocks of the Internet infrastructure had its roots in the 1980s, but grew rapidly in the early 1990s with the commercialisation of the Internet and some break-through technological innovations. This progress continues, with ever faster speeds, bigger data, more intelligent multi-purpose devices and further coverage. However, before going further, it is important to distinguish between the Internet and the Web (or World Wide Web). These terms are often used interchangeably, but this overlooks the distinction between them.[2]

The *Internet* (the interconnection of computer networks) is essentially a huge network of networks, or a networking infrastructure. It connects together hundreds of millions of computers globally and forms a network in which any computer can communicate with any other computer while they are both connected to the Internet. The information that is transmitted over the Internet is communicated in different digital languages known as Internet protocols.

The *World Wide Web* (or in short form, 'the Web'), is a means of accessing information over the medium of the Internet. It is an information-sharing framework that exists on top of the Internet. The World Wide Web uses the protocol known as HTTP (Hypertext Transfer Protocol), which is a language used on the Internet to transmit data. Web services, which use HTTP to allow applications to communicate in order to exchange business logic, use the Web to share information. The Web utilises Internet browsers, such as Internet Explorer, Google Chrome, Safari or Firefox, to access Web documents – which are called Web pages. Web pages are linked to each other by hyperlinks.

Digital networks

Advancements in technological infrastructure gained momentum in the 1980s with the introduction of the personal computer (PC) and the explosion of cheap, pervasive computing and storage predicted by Moore's law. The 1980s saw the introduction of networked computing, and, with it, the foundational architecture and associated technologies of the Internet. These technologies have evolved to the current infrastructure that now underpins broadband and mobile networks.

In the 1990s, major events were: the commercialisation of the Internet, previously the domain of government agencies and universities; the global deregulation of telecommunications allowing competition; and innovation in fibre optic, broadband, mobile and Internet infrastructure technologies. Global coverage and reach, ease of use, coupled with the free use that characterised the Internet, started the shift away from proprietary 'islands' of networks. This open and interconnected Internet provided the foundation for future evolution. By the end of the 1990s, secure variants of public Internet services, such as Intranets and Extranets, gained serious impetus as replacements for closed private networks for businesses.

Advances in data centre technologies set the stage, in the 2000s, for moving applications and data centre infrastructure to the Cloud. Initially called Application Service Providers, or ASPs, Cloud-provided services are currently in the midst of a mainstream diffusion curve. We discuss 'the Cloud' later in Chapter 9, in the context of the information management process. Over this period, the Internet infrastructure also became a viable platform for traditional forms of media. Telephone/video calls, television and radio, traditionally delivered in analogue format over separate networks, now operate in digital formats, increasingly via the Internet (as in Skype or Internet downloaded movies viewed on a TV set or computer).

The evolution of mobile technology and mobile networks took a similar path: moving from early generation analogue, closed proprietary systems in the 1980s, to today's nearly globally standardised broadband 2G, 3G, 4G cellular wireless and Wi-Fi. '4G' is the fourth generation standard which provides high-speed mobile broadband Internet access to computers, smartphones and other mobile devices for services like hi-definition mobile TV, videoconferencing, multi-media streaming and gaming. Today, some version of 4G services is available in over 30 countries, mobile 2G has reached 90 per cent of the world's population and 3G, 45 per cent of the world's population across 159 countries. Available speeds are also growing exponentially. A form of mobile access is Wi-Fi, a form of wireless Local Area Network. Wi-Fi offers additional flexibility; for example Wi-Fi hotspots now provide Internet access in many public places and coffee shops around the world.

Digital devices

Digital devices are a combination of hardware and software that facilitate the use of the digital networks described above. Digital media devices can be categorised into four main categories: television, computers, tablets and smartphones. An increasingly common way to refer to these devices is with regard to the 'screen' they represent. Marketers are now using a terminology where television is described as the first screen; the computer the second screen; tablet devices the third screen and the mobile smartphones the fourth screen. The importance of referring to these 'four screens' is in the potential interplay of different media across different screens. Users now wish to access a wide range of data, store data and interact through each screen, often using more than one screen simultaneously, creating a challenge for marketers attempting to manage customer interactions within and across devices.

The *first screen*, television, began as a social experience, with family and friends gathered to watch a TV show; later, people started having televisions in multiple rooms and solo watching was also common. As different countries are progressively converted to digital TV, there will be new opportunities, including innovative forms of video-on-demand and TV e-commerce – purchasing through the television. The *second screen*, the computer screen, started as the classic desktop personal computer in the 1980s. This trend was followed by the laptop/netbook/notebook era from the 1990s. The *third screen* is media tablets, including the iPad and e-readers such as the Kindle. The *fourth screen*, current mobile phones, which evolved from initial generations of mobile feature phones to PDAs (personal digital assistant or palmtop computer) and ultimately to today's smartphones. Computer tablets and mobile phones are mainly used as solo experiences, though games are encouraging shared experiences between gamers.

We can expect both content providers and device manufacturers to make considerable efforts to create integration across the four screens. For example, in the content space, the UK's BBC (British Broadcasting Corporation) is adopting a four screens strategy, with the objective of creating a mobile news site that embraces devices of all sizes and specification. This initiative aims at determining the specific requirements of a particular customer's phone or tablet and then delivering a touch-screen optimised site suited to that device's particular profile.[3] Among device manufacturers, Lenovo, the Chinese laptop, PC and tablet manufacturer, plans to make the Cloud integral to what it also calls its four screens strategy. Lenovo has two objectives: first, to share content between the four different types of device; second, to use different devices to control each other – for example, playing content on a smart TV from a laptop while controlling playback with a smart phone or tablet.[4] This type of sharing and controlling is typically done over a local network, but Lenovo's Cloud system means that the devices do not have to be on the same network so long as they are all connected to the Internet.

The digital media landscape is shifting rapidly and any statistics can change dramatically within a few months. For example, the user penetration of tablets doubled from 4.2 per cent in 2010 to 10.8 per cent in 2011 and is estimated to grow to 27.7 per cent in 2014.[5] It is interesting that there are indications of a decline in television penetration with the shift to digital broadcasts that can be received on the other screens. We can expect rapid evolution and enhancements in both tablets and smartphones in the years ahead. As increased functionality is added to tablets and smartphones, the take up of these devices will be dramatic. Figure 5.2 shows the estimated sales of personal computers, smart phones and tablets to 2016.

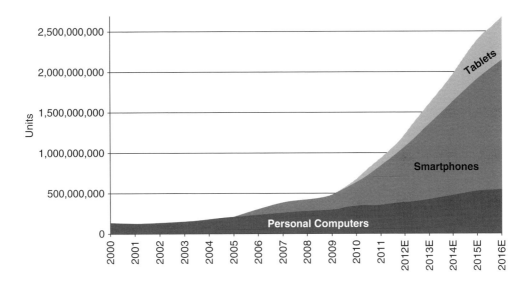

Figure 5.2 Estimates of sales of personal computers, smartphones and tablets to 2016.
Source: Business Insider Intelligence

By 2011 the number of smart phones sold exceeded the number of PCs sold. Tablet sales, including e-readers, are estimated to exceed 500 million units a year in 2016. The growth will be driven by lower prices combined with wider tablet penetration in the enterprise and education markets. The take up in emerging markets will also bolster sales. As BI Intelligence analyst Alex Cocotas points out: 'We really are in a post-PC era. Smartphone unit sales passed PC sales last year. Tablet sales will follow in a few years.' As Steve Jobs said, 'PCs will become like "trucks" and tablets like "cars": PCs will still be around, and they'll still be a big market, but they won't become the most common way people do their computing anymore.'[6]

There is now an increase in demand for smartphones and a decline of basic feature phones, except in developing countries. This trend was accelerated by the introduction of low-end mass market smartphones and the addition of smartphone features to standard mobile phones. By 2016, as shown in Figure 5.2, sales of smartphones, with substantially increased functionality, will exceed sales of PCs and tablets combined.

A further important technology trend in the digital Internet infrastructure is the take up of embedded devices, a concept initially described as pervasive computing. While industry initially struggled with marrying the capability of embedded technology with commercially viable applications, by the early 2010s much of the focus was on smart vehicles, smart meters, smart roads and other functional areas. It appears that the original vision of smart devices embedded everywhere is now gaining momentum.

Growth of the Internet economy

The main outcome of this technological advancement is: faster speed and greater connectivity, simplicity, openness and amplification effects. The impact of the digital Internet infrastructure is that relationship marketing executives can now develop strategic and tactical marketing plans with the knowledge that the people they seek to interact with are armed with smart, multi-purpose devices connected via broadband anywhere, anytime.

A recent study by The Boston Consulting Group (BCG) highlights the dramatic growth of the Internet on a global basis.[7] This study investigates the uptake of the Internet in the G20 countries. BCG forecasts that by 2016 there will be 3 billion Internet users globally – which represents nearly half the world's population. By this time the Internet economy is expected to reach $4.2 trillion within the G20 economies. Figure 5.3, which is taken from this study, shows several key trends, including:

- Growth in Internet users in G20 countries: more than a 275 per cent growth in users between 2005 and 2015. A substantial shift towards a much greater percentage of use within developing markets when compared with developed markets.
- The shift from fixed to mobile broadband connections: consumer broadband connections will increase almost exponentially from 167 million to 2.7 billion between 2005 and 2015. Consumer *mobile* broadband connections will represent more than 75 per cent of all broadband connections.
- An explosion in global Internet traffic by a factor of more than 30 between 2005 and 2015.

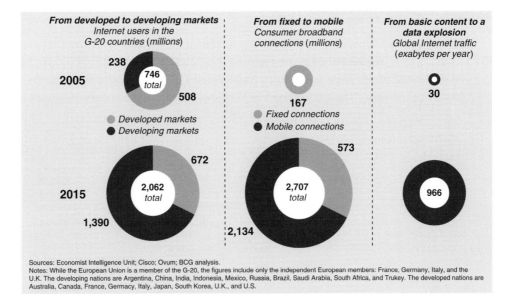

Figure 5.3 Projected growth of the Internet 2005–2015.
Source: The Internet Economy in the G-20: The $4.2 Trillion Growth Opportunity, © 2012, The Boston Consulting Group. This data is based on: Economic Intelligence Unit, Cisco; Ovum, BCG analysis.

The 'Internet economy' includes all financial transactions undertaken through the medium of the Internet. The BCG study points out that if the Internet economy was a national economy it would rank in the world's top five economies behind only the US, China, Japan and India. It concludes that the Internet economy will represent an average of 5.3 per cent of GDP in the G20 countries in 2016. However, the percentage of the Internet economy, as a proportion of GDP, will vary substantially. For example, in the UK it will represent 12.4 per cent, or around one eighth of the total economy, by 2016 – this represents a compound annual growth rate of 10.9 per cent between 2010 and 2016. There will be even higher compound annual growth rates for the Internet economies in China (17.4 per cent) and India (23.0 per cent) between 2010 and 2016. The study also underlines the growing predominance of mobile devices such as smartphones and tablets, which will account for four out of five broadband connections by 2016. These findings suggest how customers interact with firms will change in the future and we will see much greater expenditure via the Internet and especially through connections with mobile devices.

The evolution of the World Wide Web

Having described the Internet infrastructure and its dramatic growth, we now review the development and evolution of the World Wide Web in terms of its main stages of development. Knowing how the Web has evolved helps our understanding of how relationship marketing practices have changed and will need to evolve in the future.

Development of the World Wide Web

The Web is a browsing and searching system that operates over the Internet much the same way as e-mail does. The first generation of the Web started in the early 1990s. By the late 1990s, many large companies had started to recognise the importance of having a website presence. The main stages of Web development are shown in Figure 5.4.

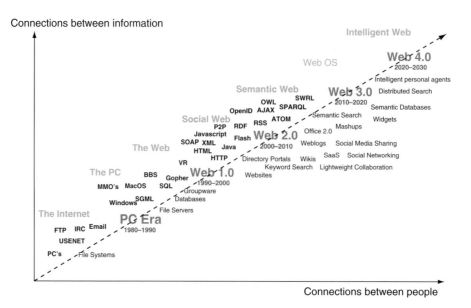

Figure 5.4 Evolution of the World Wide Web.
Source: Nova Spivack: http://novaspivack.com

Web 1.0

Web 1.0 is a term used to describe the first substantive stage of the evolution of the World Wide Web. Usage of the Internet spread rapidly, as users of early generations of closed proprietary services like CompuServe and AOL migrated to the public Internet and new users came onboard. The volume of users became compelling and firms responded with an explosion of websites, a rush of new Web-based business models and online services, and companion communication services like e-mail, IM (instant messaging), chat, conferencing and mobile SMS.

Most of the breakthrough innovations in this generation occurred during the 1990s. These included Web and search advertising and permission-based e-campaigns, widespread e-commerce and the beginnings of m-commerce. The uniting feature of this generation was its common purpose: to publish content. The Web 1.0 generation is distinct from later generations that support much greater interactivity. The technologies, platforms and new channels made widely available over this period enabled users to perform functions that included: browse, search and subscribe to e-letters for information, entertainment, products and services; download and consume content and entertainment posted and broadcast by firms; play games; send e-mails; and buy products and services and provide location maps – as provided initially by Mapquest.com and later dominated by Google Maps.

Web 2.0

Although the term Web 2.0 is described in various ways, there is a common set of key themes, which include: social networking; users shifting from single interactions to social interactions and structures, and enterprises' engagement with customers changing from individuals to networks of consumers. Whereas Web 1.0 gave users content, e-commerce and one-to-one communications, Web 2.0 expanded the user experience in a number of ways, including: providing and consuming commentary, word-of-mouth and interactive conversations; participating in communities of shared interests or activities; co-creating content or products, not just passively receiving firm-created content or products; participating in visible many-to-many communications not just one-to-one or one-to-many communications; and shopping and buying with others, not just as a solo shopping experience. Web 2.0 applications also involve much greater interaction with the end user. Here the end user becomes not only a user but also a participant in a range of activities such as blogs, podcasts, tagging, RSS feeds (real simple syndication), social networking and voting on Web content.

Web 3.0

The term Web 3.0 was introduced in 2006 and represents a third generation of Internet-based services, what Nova Spivak, a leading digital commentator, calls 'the intelligent Web'.[8] As Figure 5.4 suggests, it is at an embryonic stage of development. Spivak argues that as several major technology trends start to reach a new maturity they become mutually reinforcing and are collectively driving this third generation of the Web. He highlights the following technology trends that are converging or that will converge in the future:[9]

Ubiquitous Connectivity:	Broadband adoption; mobile Internet access; mobile devices;
Network Computing:	software-as-a-service business models; Web services interoperability; distributed computing;
Open Technologies:	open APIs (application program interfaces) and protocols; open data formats; open-source software platforms; open data (Creative Commons, etc.);
Open Identity:	open identity (OpenID); open reputation; portable identity and personal data;
The Intelligent Web:	Semantic Web technologies; distributed databases – 'The World Wide Database' (wide-area distributed database interoperability enabled by Semantic Web technologies); intelligent applications (natural language processing, machine learning, machine reasoning, autonomous agents).

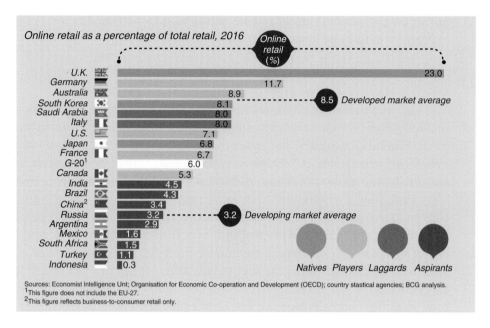

Figure 5.5 Estimated online retail sales as a percentage of total retail sales in 2016.
Source: The Internet Economy in the G-20: The $4.2 Trillion Growth Opportunity, © 2012, The Boston Consulting Group. This data is based on: Economist Intelligence Unit; Organisation for Economic Co-operation and Development (OECD); country statistical agencies; BCG analysis.
Notes: [1] This figure does not include the EU-27. [2] This figure reflects business-to-consumer retail only.

These trends show that Web 3.0 will become more connected, open and intelligent. Spivak suggests this involves moving beyond social networks that just connect people, to a semantic network which connects a much wider range of elements. Thus, the role of the Web 3.0 is to develop the current version of the Web so that users can identify, share and utilise information more easily. In sum, its aim is to interpret and categorise information, so humans have less work to undertake. Spivak has also forecast a further more intelligent evolution of the Web – Web 4.0 – beyond 2020.

Relationship implications of Web evolution

Web 1.0 transformed the information available to consumers, increasing their power and ability to move between suppliers who offered more desirable offers. Enterprises adopted new online business models that reduced their costs and added to their flexibility. For traditional businesses, this meant competitive intensity increased, triggering a search for a strategic response. The result was an increase in product innovation, service differentiation and offering superior customer experience as a basis for competition. Marketers and relationship managers leveraged this new Web technology, especially in the areas of advertising, communications and promotion. However, customer service, loyalty and referral programmes also benefited. These were implemented as websites, display and search advertising, digital campaigns, self-service Web support and multiple channels integrated mainly around call centres, Web presence, e-mail and text messaging.

The progression to Web 2.0 filled many of the gaps needed for today's relationship marketing requirements, but there are still limitations. The proliferation of information unleashed by the network effects of the Internet and social sharing has led to increasingly chaotic and exhausting online experiences for users. For relationship managers, ploughing through the massive flow of real-time customer and competitor information became a problem. As Magnify.net CEO Steve Rosenbaum observes, 'The volume of raw data coming at us has increased more than 50% this past year. As more digital devices and software services proliferate, the volume of data and speed of increase will grow exponentially. This simply isn't sustainable ... People have reached their capacity to manage data.'[10]

It is still too early to tell the exact shape Web 3.0 will ultimately take. With the experience from Web 2.0, the initial focus is on the following areas: improving richness of profiles, analytics, analysis, segmentation and the overall customer experience; taking the end-to-end customer experience and online experiences to the next level of engagement; recognising that context, not content, conversation or even community, is critical; and mechanisms such as social curation for managing the overwhelming floods of information being created.

The concept of 'social curation' requires some explanation. Social curation is a term loosely used to describe the process of making sense of content created by a group on the Internet, above and beyond that provided by search engines. This includes RSS feeds and feed readers such as those provided by Feedburner.com. It also includes social bookmarking, as exemplified by early entrants such as Digg and Delicious. As social technologies encourage co-creation, posting and sharing, the previous data bank on the Internet is being dwarfed by massive amounts of new information originating from multiple sources. This means that social curation is set to become one of the critical areas addressed in Web 3.0.

In the previous two sections we have discussed the digital Internet infrastructure, including both the nature of digital networks and the digital devices that provide access to these networks, and the evolution of the World Wide Web. In the next three sections we discuss digital marketing, social media and social influence marketing. Although we view digital as including social media, many industry observers, authors and practitioners consider them separately. However, given that traditional digital marketing, as represented by Web 1.0, has largely been concerned with content – and social media, as characterised by Web 2.0, is associated with much greater interaction with and between end users – we discuss digital marketing and social media, and then social influence marketing, in consecutive sections.

Digital marketing

We view digital marketing as an umbrella term encompassing digital, mobile and social. Technically, digital also includes use of digital media channels such as digital outdoor (billboards and street furniture), digital kiosks, etc. However, most practitioners consider 'digital marketing' to be website and e-mail and associated marketing, sales and advertising activities. This suggests that digital marketing can be viewed in a broad or narrow sense. To make a distinction between these different views of digital marketing, we refer to digital marketing in the broad sense as *contemporary digital marketing* and the narrow sense as *traditional digital marketing*.

The execution of advertising, communications and promotional campaigns evolved from traditional media (such as print, television, radio and outdoor billboards, and street furniture) to include digital media in the marketing mix, creating what is often referred to as integrated marketing communications. This early use of digital media has since given way to a broader concept of digital marketing – whereby virtually all aspects of campaigns can be automated and executed in the context of consumers' online experiences. Thus, the digital marketing revolution covers many aspects, including:

- Websites, microsites, mobile sites and apps;
- Content for consumption created by the firm and distributed via their websites and apps in the form of information and entertainment packaged as downloadable files, or broadcast via Webinars, podcasts and Internet radio;
- As websites and other online initiatives grew, Internet advertising, in the form of display advertisements (such as banner ads) and search-term relevant advertising supplemented traditional forms of media delivery such as print, television and radio. Affiliate networks sprung up to enable click-through advertising. Search Engine Optimisation (SEO) and Search Engine Marketing (SEM) became common practices;
- Where appropriate, marketers used game advertising or advertising placement in the game environment, while others developed games specifically to advertise their product, sometimes referred to as 'advertgaming'. This is an area where the line between entertainment and advertising starts to blur;
- Direct response marketing recognised the need for permission-based marketing. Here, the audience are invited to opt-in to receive automated e-letters and e-campaigns. Similar techniques are applied in mobile marketing via SMS text and MMS (multi-media messaging).

As a result of these developments, a proliferation of terms has developed within the digital arena over the last two decades. We now consider some of the more commonly used terms.[11]

Digital marketing terminology

Digital Marketing is an umbrella term that encompasses all forms of marketing activity undertaken with the support of digital channels. It utilises the Internet as well as other digital channels including mobile phones and digital TV. Social media now represents a key channel for digital marketing. As noted above, we make a distinction between *traditional digital marketing*, which is mainly associated with use of the Internet and e-mail, and *contemporary digital marketing*, which encompasses a broader range of digital channels, including social media. Digital marketing is also sometimes referred to as *e-marketing*.

E-business (electronic business) involves the use of information and communication technology within a range of business activities. E-business tools have existed for a considerable time. Before the introduction of the Internet they included such things as barcoding, electronic data interchange, electronic funds transfers and local area networks (LANs). Since the advent of the Internet, e-business encompasses the use of digital networks for sharing business information, maintaining relationships and undertaking business transactions.

E-commerce (electronic commerce) usually refers to the sales activities associated with e-business. This includes buying and selling products or services through electronic channels such as the Internet.

M-commerce (mobile commerce) refers to sales activities, including products and services, conducted via mobile services and through mobile devices. M-commerce is a subset of e-commerce.

Social networks consist of communities of people that join websites such as Facebook or Twitter as well as traditional brand communities. Many brand communities, such as car clubs, hobby groups and professional institutions, are social networks which may have no digital connection.

Social media includes Web-based and mobile-based technologies which are used to share content, commentary and media and to turn information into interactive dialogue between individuals, communities and organisations.

Social commerce is a subset of electronic commerce that involves firms engaging with customers using social media, leading to online purchase of products and services.

Social influence marketing involves the use of social media to undertake marketing activity. It has been defined as marketing to the network of peers that surround and influence the customer across social platforms and on brand websites.[12] It can be used in combination with other forms of traditional digital marketing as well as with non-digital marketing.

In practice, such terms are often used interchangeably and there is little rigour in the way these terms are applied across industry. We propose that all enterprises should adopt a common terminology so, in this complex field, it is clear what they are referring to. Given that social media and social influence marketing are still relatively recent developments, we first consider the traditional areas of digital marketing.

Forms of e-commerce

The Internet has created a range of new opportunities for e-commerce. Hollensen distinguishes between four forms of e-commerce:[13]

Business-to-business e-commerce relationships

There are a great number of business-to-business electronic relationships. They are characterised by electronic data interchange, especially within the supply chain management arena. Walmart's electronic relationship with its suppliers, such as Procter & Gamble, is a well-known example of this form of relationship.

Consumer-to-business e-commerce relationships

This form of relationship has become more popular with the introduction of the Internet. Here customers form a group, sometimes setting a price, and enterprises can then bid for the business. This is a form of reverse auction. Priceline.com was originally focused on this form of relationship but they have since changed this focus. Many e-commerce websites of this type have come and gone. A Google search of 'consumer Internet auctions' will provide the reader with details of current ones that are operating.

Consumer-to-consumer e-commerce relationships

Consumer-to-consumer relationships have moved from a cottage setting to a mainstream industry. Historically, consumers traded with each other in town markets and later through newspaper advertising and specialist magazines that offered products for sale – typically with titles such as *Exchange & Mart* or *Trading Post*. The advent of the Internet transformed this type of activity to a totally new level. eBay would be the best known of these e-commerce websites. eBay also provides for business-to-consumer relationships.

Business-to-consumer e-commerce relationships

This is the area where there has been the greatest attention. Businesses of all sizes and geographic locations have been able to offer their products to customers in all geographies. E-commerce retail sales have experienced amazing growth, impacting virtually every sector from book sales (e.g., Amazon) to online supermarket shopping (e.g., Tesco), cinema ticket purchases and equipment purchases – to name just a few examples. As we explain in the next section, even when customers purchase through traditional channels, the purchasing behaviour is often highly influenced by consumers researching the products online before purchasing offline.

The growth of e-commerce

Two of the most visible outcomes of the digital era have been the growth in online marketing and advertising and the growth in online e-commerce sales. With the rise of digital marketing, advertising expenditure has shifted to digital channels. In the US market, generally regarded as the lead market, online marketing expenditure is growing rapidly. Figure 5.1, near the start of this chapter, shows the predicted rapid growth of digital marketing expenditure in the US to 2016.

Research by emarketer.com shows that total print advertising is expected to continue to decline in the years ahead, while online advertising expenditure will grow at a rapid rate. In 2012, a watershed point was reached in the US when online advertising expenditure exceeded total print expenditure for the first time. This reflected the growing amount of time that consumers are spending on digital platforms and the view that the Internet is a more measurable medium. Since the start of the 2010s, more firms, especially retailers, are reaching a point where digital marketing is a bigger budget item than traditional media. Within the broader definition of contemporary digital marketing, developments in mobile marketing are also included.

A recent report by The Boston Consulting Group demonstrates the increasing importance of retail e-commerce sales. Figure 5.5 shows that by 2016 retail e-commerce sales will represent 8.5 per cent of the total retail sales within developed countries. However, this will vary substantially across different countries. As this study points out, all retail sales represent almost one-third of total GDP in the G20 countries, and e-commerce retail sales contribute a significant and increasing share of total retail sales in many countries. This impact is especially pronounced in the UK, where, because of high Internet penetration, an efficient delivery infrastructure, a competitive retail market, and high credit card usage by consumers, the UK has become a nation of digital shopkeepers.[14]

However, actual retail sales via the Internet represent only part of the impact of online searches by consumers. The BCG report points out that many consumers *research online* and then *purchase offline* – this is known as 'ROPO'. For example, a large proportion of consumers research consumer durables such as motor vehicles and white goods online, but actually purchase these at the retailer. ROPO spending is higher than online retail sales in virtually all the countries studied by BCG. For example, in 2010 direct US online retail sales rose to $252 billion, but ROPO sales added a further $482 billion. In the UK, online retail sales in US$ were $89 billion with ROPO sales of a further $139 billion. In China, online retail sales were the equivalent of $10 billion, with ROPO sales a further $96 billion.[15]

E-commerce, to most people, means buying and/or selling products through the Internet and is usually associated with online shopping. Although business-to-consumer sales are the most obvious side of e-commerce, the 2010 US Census data (the most recent Census figures at the time of publishing) show estimates for US business-to-business revenue transacted online to be approximately $300 billion. When compared to online retail sales in the US, the importance of business-to-business e-commerce also becomes apparent.[16]

Traditional digital marketing

We now briefly review traditional digital marketing – which does not include a substantial social media component – and, later in the chapter, we discuss contemporary digital marketing, which includes mainstream social media. There are two main forms of digital marketing, pull digital marketing and push digital marketing. *Pull digital marketing* involves the customer actively seeking marketing content via the Web, or alternatively where the recipient has given permission to receive content sent by e-mail, text message and Web feed. Other forms of pull digital marketing include websites, blogs and audio and video-streaming media. *Push digital marketing* involves the enterprise sending a message, typically without the consent of the recipient. Examples include display advertising on websites and e-mail and text messages sent to recipients, often in the form of spam, where recipients have not given permission to receive the message.[17]

In the early days, much of digital marketing focused on reducing costs. At that point, strengthening customer relationships through improved customer service was not a high priority in most enterprises. Customer service and support was considered a cost centre rather than a strategic customer-facing touch point. As customers started to make much more extensive use of e-mail and texting, there was interest in adding new additional channels for customers. However, many of the initiatives centred on adding self-service mechanisms, such as making information readily available to customers online and posting FAQs (Frequently Asked Questions) on websites. Integration was mostly in the form of ensuring support e-mails were directed at the call centre staff or adding text messaging notifications when problems were resolved.

Firms that had utilised call centre support staff for up-selling and cross-selling, or those that ran outbound telemarketing in support of new customer acquisition, also then added Live Chat to their websites. Visitors were offered the opportunity to chat with staff at various points in their journey through the site, for example, pre-sales, while browsing for product information or comparing product options on a site, and post-sales, as part of the support process. Support options were generally packaged and presented in order of cost-to-provide, as in FAQ, then e-mail or text, then chat, and finally via a phone call, with different levels of support often carrying different price tags. While this expanded the number of touch points, it still fell way short of the fully integrated multi-channel integration demanded by strategic CRM – a topic we discuss in Chapter 8.

Firms' marketing activities during Web 1.0 transformed the reach, coverage and cost structure delivered by the Internet. Firms made substantial progress, but it was largely limited to: achieving unprecedented coverage and reach; lowering marketing, delivery and support costs by automating traditional marketing; implementing cross-sell/up-sell, retention and loyalty elements of relationship marketing through permission-based e-mail campaigns and e-letter subscriptions; and expanded channels and touch points (e-mail, messaging and chat). Digital marketing programmes adopted existing marketing practices and were centred mainly on new customer acquisition.

This phase made the Internet and mobile phones an integral part of everyday life. It enabled marketers to automate and scale campaigns and communications and support teams to become more cost-effective and responsive, and enabled relationship managers to leverage CRM systems. This functionality continues with the next stage of development – Web 2.0 and the rise of social media. However, some features started to be replaced by their social counterparts, as in the use of social media platforms and trends such as the shift of e-mail users to Facebook for their interpersonal messaging.

Social media

This contemporary form of digital marketing is continuing to have a profound impact on how enterprises develop relationships with customers. In this section we consider social networks, the social media ecosystem, key players in social media, the classification of social media, enterprise use of social media and gaining value from social media.

Social networks

Social networks of one form or another have existed throughout mankind's history. People are social animals and have constantly built group affiliations through common interests. Clubs and societies of people with common interests existed well before the introduction of technologies such as telecommunications, the Internet and social media. In the context of business enterprises, social networks built around brands or products became known as 'brand communities'. A brand community is a self-selecting group of people sharing a system of values, standards and representations, creating bonds of membership with each other and with the community of which they are part.

Brand communities have formed around a great number of enterprises in many industry sectors, as well as in other social institutions. More recently, social networks have expanded hugely as social technologies have provided individuals with much greater opportunity and motivation to interact with each other.

Social media and social networking platforms

The evolution of social media and social networking has followed the typical, though accelerated, diffusion model. The dynamic nature of the social networking space is characterised by rapid shifts in the relative popularity of different social network sites.

It is useful to make a distinction between *social media* and *social networking platforms*. Again, people use such terms interchangeably, but for us, while they are closely related, social media is a somewhat broader term than the social networking platform, or social networking site.

Social media consists of websites that allow users to view and share content, commentary and media of many forms. Typical examples include not only the popular social networking platforms for sites such as Facebook, Google, etc., but also YouTube, Flickr, Pinterest and Instagram and other sites aimed at photograph, image and video sharing. Web-based reference sources such as Wikipedia and news aggregators are also counted in the social media bucket. Micro-blogging sites such as Twitter are also included as social media.

A *social networking platform*, or *social networking site*, focuses on facilitating the building of social networks or social relations among people who share interests, activities, backgrounds or other forms of connection. Most social network platforms are Web-based and enable customers, users and other stakeholders to interact using the Internet.

A further term used by some in the social media arena is *Social CRM*. In Chapter 1 we pointed out that we do not make a distinction between e-CRM and CRM or 'Social CRM' and 'CRM'. Rather, we suggest viewing those social media aspects that relate to customer relationship management under the general heading of CRM – and marketing activities relating to social media, as *social influence marketing*. In a recent article titled 'Social CRM is Dead', Bob Thompson, a digital marketing expert, points out that no executives really seem to know what the term Social CRM means and business leaders do not associate social media closely with CRM. Thompson provides many examples of enterprises that have moved away from using this term.[18] Nevertheless, this term is still used widely within the social media arena.

The complex social media ecosystem

Before discussing some of the most commonly used social networking platforms, it is important to understand fully the vast scope of the broader *social media ecosystem*. There are a number of different representations of the social media ecosystem. Some of these focus just on social media networking platforms and some address the social media ecosystem more broadly – including linkages with non-digital media, as well as other forms of digital media.

Figure 5.6 shows an overview of the social software and media ecosystem developed in 2007 by Internet industry veteran Deborah Schultz.[19] She identifies the dynamic collection of tools and channels that both individuals and enterprises have at their disposal in the emerging world of social media. She argues that it is important for enterprises to learn to 'weave' through this complex ecosystem. Her representation of the social media ecosystem includes both digital and non-digital social media. As well as using social media networks, social media tools such as the blogosphere and Wikis, it also points to the integration with social events and mass media.

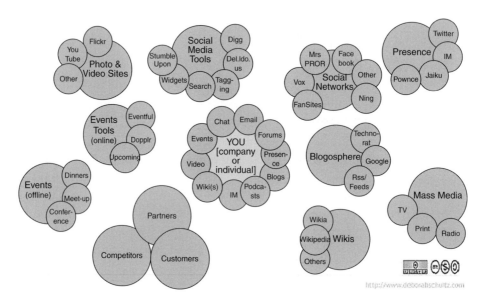

Figure 5.6 The social media ecosystem.
Source: Deborah Schultz: www.deborahschultz.com

Fred Cavazza, a leading French social media commentator, has developed a more digitally focused representation of what he terms the *social media landscape*. This version of the social media ecosystem is shown in Figure 5.7.[20] The objective of this figure is to make it easier to comprehend the complex nature of social media in all its complexity, rather than to provide a full list of available social networking platforms.

Figure 5.7 shows the conversations and social interactions that can occur on the 'four screens' discussed earlier in this chapter – on computers, smartphones, tablets and connected television screens. Three major players, Facebook, Twitter and Google+, are shown in the central circle, as they provide users with a large set of

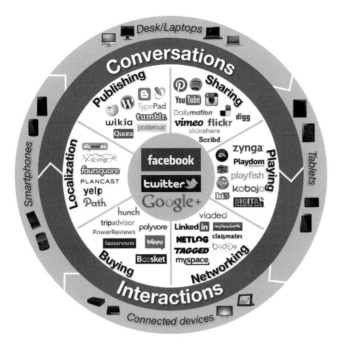

Figure 5.7 The social media landscape 2012.
Source: Fred Cavazza: www.FredCavazza.net

functionalities. Each of these three players has a somewhat different orientation: Twitter for content discovery, Google+ to manage your online identity and Facebook to interact with your friends. The social media platforms are broken down into six major use categories:

- *Publishing*, with blog engines (e.g., Wordpress), wiki platforms (e.g., Wikipedia), lifeblog services (e.g., Tumblr) and social Q&A (e.g., Quora)
- *Sharing*, with dedicated online services for videos (e.g., YouTube), photographs (e.g., Flickr), links (e.g., Delicious), products (e.g., Pinterest), music (e.g., Spotify) and documents (e.g., Slideshare)
- *Playing*, with major editors (e.g., Zynga), dedicated platforms (e.g., Hi) and smaller but innovative editors (e.g., Digital Chocolate)
- *Networking*, professional (e.g., LinkedIn), personal (e.g., Facebook) or for former acquaintances (e.g., MyYearBook)
- *Buying*, with customer intelligence platforms (e.g., Bazaarvoice), purchase sharing (e.g., Polyvore) or recommendation (e.g., Hunch)
- *Localisation*, with mobile applications (e.g., Foursquare), socialised city guides (e.g., Yelp) or upcoming events or venues (e.g., Plancast).

The social media landscape will continue to evolve quickly with new players emerging at frequent intervals. This is in response to new innovations in social media and to the increasing sophistication of users whose expectations rise the more they use social media. As Cavazza points out, it is important for enterprises not to focus on choosing the right platform, but to build a consistent social architecture: 'Installing your brand on social media is not about choosing one or several social platforms and opening profiles, it is about defining objectives and allocating resources. The platform choice is only the tactical declaration of your strategy. Furthermore, the only truly viable social platforms on the long run are the ones you host and manage.'[21]

The emergence and growth of social media and the major players

Having provided an overview of the broader social media ecosystem, we now consider the emergence and growth of social media and some key current players within it. Given the high level of social media penetration amongst key players such as Facebook, Twitter, Myspace and LinkedIn, most readers will be familiar with these social media platforms and a significant proportion will have experience using them.

The emergence of social media networks

Boyd and Ellison have documented the early growth of social media platforms. They state the first recognisable social network site was launched in 1997 by SixDegrees.com.[22] This platform permitted users to create profiles, list their friends and, by the start of 1998, surf the friends lists. Many of these individual features existed, in some form, in other platforms before the advent of SixDegrees. For example, profiles existed on most major matchmaking and dating sites as well as community sites. Classmates.com permitted people to affiliate with their high school or college and use the network to look for other students who were also affiliated with the school or college, but these users could not create profiles or list friends until some years later. SixDegrees was the first platform to have fairly full functionality; however, it failed to become a viable business and the platform closed in 2000.

Classmates.com then rose into prominence in 2004 followed by Myspace in 2005. By 2006, Myspace's popularity soared, Facebook's popularity was rising and Classmates.com's was dropping off. The year 2007 was a watershed year in the evolution of social media, marked by a rush of new entrants and social media sites breaking into the 'top five' websites. By 2010, another important year, Facebook.com reached a top five position; a shakeout of early entrants occurred and social sites like Wordpress, Linked In, Yelp and Twitter moved to positions in the top 50. In 2012 the IPO (initial public offering) of Facebook occurred amidst considerable controversy. It valued Facebook at over $100 billion and was the largest Internet IPO in the US and the third largest IPO ever.

There are now a large number of social media sites and these are increasing daily. It is beyond the scope of this book to attempt to review these in detail. We now provide a brief overview of three of the main social networking sites – Facebook, Twitter and LinkedIn. Given the rapidly changing dynamics of social media sites, any statistics will become rapidly out of date.

Facebook

Facebook, founded in 2004, started as a niche site providing a platform for Harvard University students to keep in touch with each other. The site has since expanded globally to provide a universal platform aimed at all demographic segments. As is often the case in technological businesses, Facebook leveraged its second mover position to dominate and by 2010 was the leading social platform. By 2012, Facebook's scope and size has reached impressive levels including:

- 70 languages; 80 per cent of users outside the US; with 300,000 user volunteers crowd-sourcing translation through the Translation App
- Over one billion active users; 50 per cent log-in on any given day; over 900 million objects, that include pages, groups, events and community pages
- Average user has 130 friends and connections to 80 objects
- Approximately half the users access Facebook via mobile; over 475 mobile operators globally deploy and promote Facebook mobile products
- Over 7 million applications and websites are integrated with Facebook; 500 million people per month use an application in Facebook or experience the Facebook platform on other sites; on average more than 20 million 'apps' are installed per day.

These impressive statistics demonstrate the rapid growth and dominance of Facebook in the social media space to date.

Twitter

Twitter, was launched in July 2006. Twitter emulated the SMS of the mobile world on the Internet through the use of its 140-character tweets. Encouraging participation through the question 'What's Happening' and the tagline 'The best way to discover what's new', Twitter reached widespread usage in a short time period, as captured by the company's posts on its official blog:

- 21 languages: 400,000 users volunteer crowd source translation through the Translation Center[23]
- By 2012: 140 million active monthly users and over 1 billion tweets every three days
- 1 million registered apps (up from 150,000 in previous year); 750,000 developers; new app is published every 1.5 seconds.[24]

Twitter fulfils a different social purpose to Facebook and other social networking sites. The messaging platform provides easy, fast and brief connection between friends, contrasting with much richer, holistic approaches to social relationship building provided by Facebook.

LinkedIn

LinkedIn positions itself as '… the world's largest professional network on the Internet with more than 150 million members in over 200 countries and territories'. LinkedIn members can create, manage and share their professional identity online, allowing them to build and engage with their professional network, sharing knowledge and experiences and identifying business opportunities with network partners. Launched in May 2003, within one month LinkedIn reached 4,500 members, growing swiftly to surpass other business-oriented social platforms. By 2012, LinkedIn had reached:

- 14 languages, 200 countries
- Membership of over 150 million; growth of two new members per second
- 2 billion people searches, projected to reach 4 billion by end of 2011
- 1 million LinkedIn Groups
- 400,000 developers using LinkedIn APIs, 2 billion API calls/month; 180,000 unique domains using the LinkedIn Share button to send content to the site; and referrals up 75 per cent on the previous quarter
- Total revenue reached $139m, a 126 per cent increase year-on-year and the fifth straight quarter of more than 100 per cent growth.

By the start of the second decade of the 2000s, the importance of the social networking platforms was clear: many marketers had all but replaced mentions of their own websites in their TV and Internet advertising, instead inviting customers to 'Find us on Facebook' and 'Follow us on Twitter'.

Classification of social media

There are a number of alternative approaches to classifying social media developed by different consultants, academics and analyst firms. For example, Cavazza's social media landscape in Figure 5.7 classifies social media into publishing, sharing, playing, networking, buying and localisation, which is a classification based on activity. Kaplan and Haenlein develop an alternative approach and classify social media based on the relative degree of social presence/media richness and the extent of self-preservation/self-disclosure. Their analysis results in a managerial framework that consists of six types of social media including: collaborative projects; blogs; content communities; social networking sites; virtual game worlds and virtual social worlds.[25]

Collaborative projects

This form of social media enables the joint and simultaneous creation of content by many end users. Possibly the best example of this is the online encyclopaedia Wikipedia, which is available in more than 230 languages. A further example is Delicious, which permits storage and sharing of Web bookmarks. We can expect many new forms of collaborative projects to emerge in the future.

Blogs

Blogs, short for Web logs, and forums are among the oldest of social applications. Blogs are essentially a running conversation thread generally led by the blog owner and commented on by anyone. One can easily create a blog on sites such as Wordpress, or easily add one on many websites. The power of blogs comes from their social nature, where people tag and link to other blogs, comment on each other's blog entries and so on. Micro-blogging, also referred to as activity streaming, is the term used to describe Twitter and similar types of services, where people create accounts, follow others and develop followers, and post and participate in mini-posts that form some level of conversation stream. The case study on Indian consumer goods brand Hippo at the end of this chapter, is an excellent example of how Twitter can be used in imaginative ways to enhance the company's marketing activity – in this case creating presence for the brand and also managing the company's distribution chain.

Content communities

The purpose of content communities is to share media content between users. There are a wide range of content communities which cover different media types. Here the focus is on content creation, which usually does not require contributors to provide a great deal, if any, personal information. The best-known types of content community are those that share videos (e.g., YouTube), presentations (e.g., Slideshare) and photographs (e.g., Flickr). Content communities have become hugely popular with consumers and have a high market penetration amongst users of social media. There are also business-to-business examples of marketing success using content communities. The case study on Blendtec at the end of this chapter is a good example of how a small company can achieve a worldwide following through carefully placed media in a content community.

Social networking sites

Social networking sites are a fast transforming area. One can classify these sites as: *horizontal platforms* such as Facebook, LinkedIn, Google+ and Foursquare; *function-specific platforms*, which focus on particular functions, like YouTube (videos) or Flickr (photographs); *domain-specific platforms*, which focus on specific topics such as TripAdvisor (travel), Yelp (local restaurants) or MyCozi (family calendar); and *enabling platforms*, which are platforms that operate behind the scenes, often in a white-label fashion supporting functions on another company's site. There are now a huge number of these platforms, covering areas such as social commerce, social support and social analytics.

Virtual game worlds

There are two main arenas of social gaming. First, is the game industry itself; second, is the application of augmented reality techniques and game mechanics theory to make the customer experience more fun and engaging. There is now widespread usage of game consoles that plug into a home entertainment system and also games that can be downloaded and played on a computer or smartphone. Games are an important feature in many social networking platforms, for example, social games are consistently the most popular applications on Facebook. In the past, widespread usage of these social gaming sites had been restricted by broadband speed and this has negatively impacted the user experience – but as speeds keep improving, more people participate in this form of social interaction.

Virtual social worlds

Virtual worlds, such as Second Life, where a player creates and participates in a fully simulated virtual world, complete with characters, environments and virtual items that can be purchased with real or virtual currency, could also be classed as a form of social gaming. Augmented reality bridges the real and virtual worlds by applying computer-generated objects that include images, sounds and videos to a real world environment. This technique is not unlike the use of computer-generated imagery in professional movie production. While revenues from social gaming are small compared to social advertising overall, it is a fast-growing area of social media – actually virtual goods represent 60 per cent of the revenue from social games, advertising accounts for 20 per cent, and the remaining 20 per cent of the revenue comes from other sources.[26]

Enterprise use of social media

As social media continues its substantial growth, more and more enterprises will start to recognise the opportunities inherent in social media and capitalise on these opportunities to augment their existing relationship marketing activities. Enterprises operating both within the business-to-business and business-to-consumer sectors will start to recognise the power of benchmarking the activities of successful early innovators in social media. However, this will require a shift in attitude on the part of laggard companies that are slow to grasp the opportunities inherent in social media. The case studies at the end of this chapter – Hippo in India and Blendtec in the US – provide excellent examples of how the use of social media platforms, in these examples using Twitter and YouTube respectively, have led to relationship marketing success. There is now a great deal of activity in each of the six different types of social media described above. Many innovative enterprises have been quick to see the possibility of social media and have successfully launched social commerce initiatives.

Social commerce

Social commerce involves firms engaging with customers, using social media, leading to online purchase of products and services. The term social commerce has been attributed to Yahoo! who, in 2005, used the term to represent places where consumers can share experiences, get advice from each other, identify goods and services, and purchase them.[27]

Social commerce and social shopping add capabilities to the core e-commerce/ m-commerce capabilities that have existed for years in some enterprises. Arguably, Amazon was one of the first to provide social commerce and social networking in its early use of user ratings and reviews, which have now become a fairly standard feature. Competitions and contests, sweepstakes and promotions have always been a major part of mobile marketing and Web and e-campaigns. Early incarnations were coupons down-loaded from websites, emailed to users as part of opt-in e-campaigns, or mobile coupons downloaded or texted to a user's smartphone. With the entrance of social commerce, additional dimensions were added, for example, including features that enabled the crowdsourcing of discounts (the more users who register for a deal, the deeper the promotional discount). Essentially, social commerce involves the monetisation of social media with e-commerce. Digital marketing expert Paul Marsden has summarised some good examples of social commerce:

- 1–800-Flowers, setting up the first online retail store embedded into Facebook
- US fashion chain The Limited creating a newsfeed store on Facebook allowing users to buy directly from within newsfeeds
- Toy manufacturer, Mattel, adding a 'social shopping' toolbar to its e-commerce site, allowing friends to shop and chat together while browsing
- Burberry curating a user-generated 'Art of the Trench' discussion gallery of customers modelling Burberry trench coats
- Dell offering a 'deal feed' on popular micro-blogging service Twitter, netting it over $7 million in sales. Dell offering Dell Swarm, a group-buy tool linked to social networks – the more people who buy, the cheaper the price
- Amazon and Best Buy extending their reach beyond their sites with social media services such as social bookmarking and 'universal wishlists'
- The mainstreaming of Facebook Connect, a service that adds Facebook functionality to e-commerce, allowing people to shop with their social networks
- Carrefour, the world's second largest retail group, selling on Facebook with 'Faceshopping' flash deals, a deal feed for Facebook members only.[28]

These examples of successful monetisation show how enterprises in many different sectors are successfully implementing social commerce initiatives.

Gaining value from social media

A recent study on 'putting social media to work' by strategy consultants Bain & Co. concludes that, despite the attention social networking services such as Facebook and Twitter have evoked, many businesses remain on the sidelines. This study suggests that there are substantial gaps between the early adopters and those who are still considering what to do. They point out that while the average billion-dollar company spends around $750,000 on social media each year, some advanced companies are spending tens of millions of dollars each year on social media.[29]

The Bain & Co. study found that early adopters have captured real economic value from their investments in social media. This study, of over 3,000 consumers, identified that customers who engage with companies over social media spend 20 to 40 per cent more money with those companies than other companies. Further, these consumers show a deeper emotional commitment to those enterprises, resulting in a higher Net Promoter Score (the Net Promoter Score concept is discussed in Chapter 7). Since well over 85 per cent of Internet-connected individuals in the US now engage with one or more social media platforms, enterprises cannot neglect the opportunity to connect with a huge base of existing and potential customers and engage in social influence marketing. The study points out that 'the leading firms invest significantly more. They pursue integrated social media strategies, with more holistic assessment of the value that social media can create across businesses, and with efforts directly tied to strategic business objectives.'

To gain higher levels of economic value from social media, Bain & Co. concludes that enterprises will need to focus on five key principles:

- link social media efforts to concrete business objectives;
- focus on tailoring your efforts to engage your key customers;
- build a social media organisation to deliver results;
- monitor and measure the results;
- be flexible and adaptive, recognising that it is still early days in the era of social media.

Bain & Co. expect the gap between social media leaders and others to continue to grow. The successes of the early innovators in social media should motivate those who have not yet engaged in substantive social media initiatives to understand the role of social influence marketing and start to develop a planned approach to developing a social media strategy.

Social influence marketing

The previous discussion suggests that enterprises are split into two broad categories in terms of their social media engagement. There are those that see the potential of social media and those that still do not see a relevant connection to their businesses. However, this latter group is now starting to awaken to the potential of social media. As Muniz and Schau point out: 'Marketing is evolving into true participatory conversations. Once-tidy, controlled marketing communications with distinct, identifiable corporate spokespeople are giving way to a messy tangle of market-based communications consisting of multiple authors including customers, competitors, observers, employees and interested collectives ... Unmoored from the calculated, coordinated pristine corporate-driven communications, these sometimes riotous market-oriented conversations create, re-create and disseminate multi-vocal marketing messages and meanings.'[30]

Social influence marketing involves the use of social media to undertake marketing activity. As an embryonic form of marketing, there is not yet a definitive framework to captures its key components. From our research in this area we conclude that the following building blocks are critical to the development of a social influence marketing programme: understanding the *social behaviour of consumers*; *social media segmentation*; *developing social media strategies* – including individual campaigns within the strategy; social media analysis; and *measurement of social media returns*.

Social behaviour of consumers

There are many aspects relating to the social behaviour of customers. Although significant progress is being made, this is an area that is still developing and in the years ahead we will see increased sophistication in understanding how customers interact with social media and how this influences their purchasing decisions. The Altimeter Group has developed an approach called Socialgraphics, which is aimed at helping businesses understand the social behaviour of consumers. The approach involves addressing several key questions and helping the enterprise focus and tailor resources to specific customer groups, including:[31]

- Where are your customers online?
- What is your customers' social behaviour online?
- What social information or people do your customers rely on?
- What is your customers' social influence? Who trusts them?
- How do your customers use social technologies in the context of your products?

Altimeter has developed an 'Engagement Pyramid' which focuses and ranks social behaviour based on the following five roles for consumers:

- *Curating* – Heavily involved in online communities such as discussion boards, fan pages, and Wikipedia through moderation, contribution, editing, etc. These Curators contribute their time, energy, and perspective to improve the foundation for available information on a given subject.
- *Producing* – Creates and publishes original content and social objects as a way of expressing expertise, positions, as well as contributing to the ecosystem of information to share thoughts and also make decisions.
- *Commenting* – Responds to the content created by producers. Even though they do not actively create and distribute original social objects, their activity is still influential to those around them.
- *Sharing* – Individuals who actively update their status on social sites and upload/forward photos, videos, articles, etc. This behaviour earns relevance and also demonstrates knowledge and awareness.
- *Watching* – Content consumers who are seeking information in order to make decisions or learn from peers, or purely seeking entertainment.

Increasingly there is a substantial amount of data available to companies seeking to understand the social behaviour of consumers. Many social media research agencies and analyst firms are undertaking research. In some cases this information is freely available in the public domain and in other cases it is proprietary and only available on a subscription basis.

In seeking to understand information on consumer behaviour, it is important to ensure any third-party research is relevant to the specific enterprise or brand being investigated and the geographic jurisdiction of interest. For example, there are marked differences between the business-to-business and business-to-consumer sectors, and substantial variation between different geographies.

A digital marketing study of over 500 marketing professionals in the US, conducted by Webmarketing123, highlights the difference between the business-to-business and business-to-consumer sectors in terms of the primary social networks that are being used. The results of this part of the study are shown in Figure 5.8.

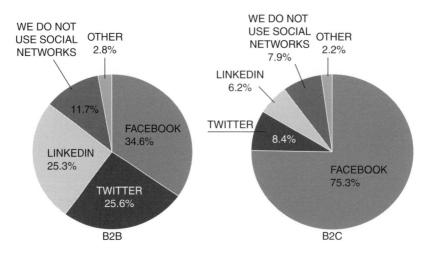

Figure 5.8 Social networks where B2B and B2C brands are most active in US.
Source: Webmarketing123 (2011), State of Digital Marketing Survey

In the business-to-business sector, the study showed a broadly equal balance between use of the three primary social networks of Facebook, Twitter and LinkedIn, with use of other networks only representing 2.8 per cent. In the business-to-consumer sector, Facebook represented by far the most dominant social network – 75.3 per cent of users – representing more than three times the use of all other social media combined in this sector.

Understanding the social behaviour of consumers leads to a consideration of social media segments and the need to understand the proportion of consumers within different segments for a given brand. Once initial data have been collected and a social media strategy has been implemented there needs to be ongoing monitoring of social media activity. This involves analytics and setting up social media listening posts and measuring return on investment, which we address shortly.

Social media segmentation

Later in Chapter 6, in our discussion of customer strategy, we examine the concept of market segmentation in some detail and we review alternative bases for segmentation of consumers including geographic segmentation, demographic and socio-economic segmentation, psychographic segmentation, benefit segmentation and other forms of segmentation. However, some discussion should be undertaken at this point on social media segmentation.

In the age of social media, consumers are more socially mobile and transient than when demographic and socio-economic segmentation approaches were first introduced – as a result of Web 2.0 and social media, consumers are also much better informed. As a consequence, conventional ways of segmenting can be less relevant in the social media space. Within social media, forms of psychographic segmentation appear to be the most favoured approaches. Psychographic segmentation involves analysing lifestyle characteristics, attitudes and personality, and classifying customers based on these dimensions.

One of the best-known forms of social media segmentation is that undertaken by analyst firm Forrester Research Inc. with their 'Social Technographics' segmentation. Forrester developed Technographic segmentation as a research tool to identify and profile the characteristics of consumers. As Forrester Research points out:

Many companies approach social computing as a list of technologies to be deployed as needed – a blog here, a podcast there – to achieve a marketing goal. But a more coherent approach is to start with your target audience and determine what kind of relationship you want to build with them, based on what they are ready for. Forrester categorises social computing behaviours into a ladder with six levels of participation; we use the term 'Social Technographics' to describe analysing a population according to its participation in these levels. Brands, websites, and any other company pursuing social technologies should analyse their customers' Social Technographics first, and then create a social strategy based on that profile.[32]

Forrester identifies the following seven groups of consumers, which have strong similarities to the groups in Altimeter's Engagement Pyramid:

- *Creators*: At the top of the ladder are Creators. These are online consumers who create social content that is consumed by others. They publish blogs, maintain Web pages, or upload videos to sites like YouTube.
- *Conversationalists*: This group voices opinions to other consumers and to enterprises usually using social media. They regularly update their statuses on social networking sites.
- *Critics*: This group responds to content from others – commenting on blogs or posting ratings and reviews on sites. This level of participation is not nearly as intense as being a Creator as Critics are selective where they offer their expertise.
- *Collectors*: This group organises content for themselves or others using a service like delicious.com or using RSS feeds, tags and voting sites like Digg.com.
- *Joiners*: This group participates in social networks such as Facebook and Twitter. They create and maintain profiles on social networking sites.
- *Spectators*: This group is more passive and consumes social content such as blogs, user-generated video forums and reviews.
- *Inactives*: This Social Technographic group does not participate at all in social computing activities, either as a creator or consumer.[33]

Figure 5.9 shows the levels in the Social Technographics ladder together with data on consumer segments from the US and Europe. Consumers are segmented into the seven groups above based on their online activities. In considering these segments it is important to recognise that consumers can fall into more than one group, with the exception of 'Inactives'. The goal of Social Technographics is not just to classify individual participation in social media, but also to encourage the design of specific marketing, branding and engagement programmes that appeal to these respective groups.

Using the Social Technographics ladder, Forrester has collected data over a number of years. These data show the ways in which consumers' engagement with social media is changing over time. With the rapid uptake of social media, usage patterns have changed

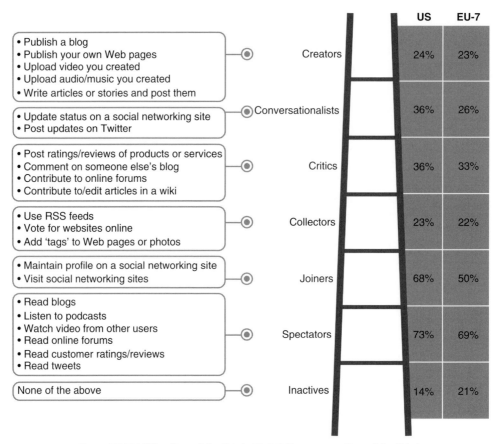

Base: 57,924 US online adults (18+); 16,473 European online adults (18+)

Figure 5.9 Forrester Research Technographics® segmentation.
Source: Forrester Research, Inc., Global Social Media Adoption in 2011, 4 January 2012

markedly. For example, between 2007 and 2011 there was an approximate doubling of 'Creators', a doubling of 'Critics', a tripling of 'Joiners' and a threefold reduction in the number of 'Inactives'.[34]

Forrester has identified that, in 2012, 86 per cent of online US adults and 79 per cent of European online adults already engaged with social media.[35] Further, consumers in emerging markets are also engaging in social media at a rapid rate. Figure 5.9 shows that the majority of US and European online consumers are 'Spectators'. That means that they use the social media content but do not necessarily create it. This figure also shows that less than 25 per cent of consumers in the US and Europe are 'Creators' – consumers who are actively involved in generating social content. Interestingly, while in US and European markets there is a comparatively passive approach to engagement in social media, in some emerging markets there is much greater involvement as 'Creators' of social media content. For example, in the metropolitan areas of China and India more than two-thirds of online consumers are 'Creators'.[36]

Data such as these are available to clients of Forrester Research for different countries and different groups of users of social media. As just one example, Forrester has undertaken a detailed analysis of US and European business technology buyers and has identified, using the social demographics framework, variations in six different age ranges for each of the Technographic groupings.[37] This highlights the power of being able to use the segmentation approach at a highly refined level and to apply it to plan a firm's relationship marketing activities in social media for a given target audience. These Technographic groupings can be cross tabulated with more conventional customer segments.

Developing social media strategies

A study by McKinsey & Co. points out that it no longer makes sense to treat social media as an experiment.[38] Enterprises need a framework to think about their overall social media strategy as well as the more specific activity of developing a social media campaign. In this section we review two frameworks for undertaking these two activities.

The social media strategy framework

Social media expert Ross Dawson has developed an integrated framework for developing a social media strategy. The framework, shown in Figure 5.10, outlines the key steps involved

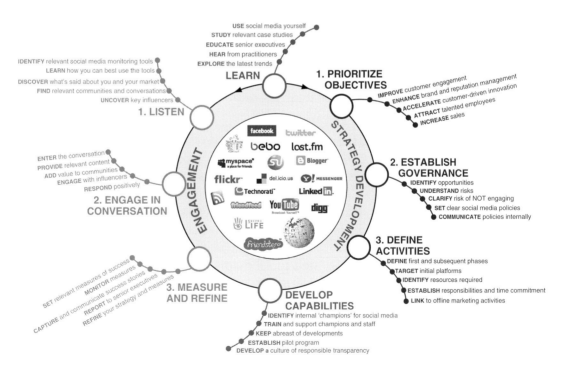

Figure 5.10 Social media strategy framework.
Source: Ross Dawson, Chairman, Advanced Human Technologies

in developing social media strategies. It begins with a 'learn' activity, followed by a further two streams of activity, shown on the left and right side of this figure – 'engagement' and 'strategy development'. These elements then come together in the ongoing activity of 'develop capabilities'.

The *learn activity* includes the following components: use social media yourself; study relevant case studies; educate senior executives; hear from practitioners and explore the latest trends.

The *engagement stream* involves three steps:

- *Listen*: identify relevant social media monitoring tools; learn how you can best use the tools; discover what's said about you and your market; find relevant communities and conversations; and uncover key influencers.
- *Engage in conversation*: enter the conversation; provide relevant content; add value to communities; engage with influencers; and respond positively.
- *Measure and refine*: set relevant measures of success; monitor measures; capture and communicate success stories; report to senior executives and refine your strategy and measures.

The *strategy development* stream involves three steps:

- *Prioritise objectives*: improve customer engagement; enhance brand and reputation management; accelerate customer-driven innovation; attract talented employees; and increase sales. Selecting priority objectives will help dictate how you develop your social media strategy.
- *Establish governance*: identify opportunities; understand risks; clarify risk of not engaging; set clear social media policies; and communicate policies internally.
- *Define activities*: define first and subsequent phases; target initial platforms; identify resources required; establish responsibilities and time commitment; and link to offline marketing activities.

The components for the final activity, *develop capabilities*, include: identify internal 'champions' for social media; train and support champions and staff; keep abreast of developments; establish pilot programmes; and develop a culture of responsible transparency.

This framework represents a clear set of steps to help enterprises engage in constructive communications with customers in the fast changing and complex world of social media.

Developing an integrated social media campaign

Within an overall social media strategy, more discrete social media campaigns will need to be developed. This may involve addressing one of several objectives identified as part of the overall social media strategy, or it may involve addressing one specific defined activity. Thus specific social media campaigns will represent an ongoing set of activities within the overall social media strategy.

Connie Benson, a social media strategist, formerly at Alterian and now with Dell, has outlined the key steps for developing an integrated social media campaign. She identifies the following steps which echo similar thoughts to those within the social media strategy framework above:

Listen

It is imperative to understand the online presence of your target market and your brand. Listening first and devising a plan based on that intelligence will provide the greatest ROI for your online efforts.

Plan the strategy and establish metrics

Here are some questions that need answering: What are the campaign objectives? What will resonate with consumers? What will inspire and motivate them to participate? How can you make it easy for them to share the campaign with others? Social media monitoring tools help you identify a baseline for setting expectations. After the campaign is over, these benchmarks will provide comparatives that make it easy to measure success.

Online engagement

One of the overarching goals for your social media strategy should include building community around your brand. This is the premise of every social engagement. Every campaign requires metrics and reporting in order to determine the extent to which it has met the business objectives. A social media monitoring tool aggregates the conversations from all of the social channels in one place and makes it easy to create high-level reports for management depicting things such as the increase of volume of conversations about your brand compared to the benchmark, the sentiment around the campaign and your brand, and main topics of discussion around the campaign, etc.

Evaluate and revise

Reviewing the success of a campaign is essential for planning future ones. Here are some questions to consider: What worked and what could have been executed better? Did the campaign increase customer satisfaction? Was the effort worth the investment of resources – i.e., was ROI realised both in value (increased brand visibility through word-of-mouth) and bottom line (increased sales or decreased demand on services)?[39]

As Benson points out social media marketing is not only about campaigns – it is also about utilising social channels to build customer relationships which augment enterprises' objectives. 'One must remember that a social media campaign is a small part of a larger social media strategy that needs to be an ongoing effort ... A social monitoring tool is essential for measuring progress and overall success.'[40]

Social media analysis, listening and measurement

There are now a number of free and an increasing number of proprietary social monitoring tools. Proper monitoring of social media activity is essential for developing meaningful performance metrics for the enterprise and gauging customer sentiment with respect to the enterprise's brand.

Social analytics

Analytics have become increasingly sophisticated over recent years. During the Web 1.0 period much of the analysis and market research undertaken used fairly traditional methods. Marketers relied on user needs studies, using both qualitative and quantitative methods. These studies were typically expensive, took weeks or months to complete and the relevance and reliability of the results were sometimes questionable. In particular, research that measured a respondent's intentions to purchase did not necessarily reflect their subsequent purchasing actions.

However, with the rise of Web 2.0, the field of social media analysis or social analytics has become an important part of social influence marketing. It is important because social media involves word-of-mouth communication between consumers. Word-of-mouth is a powerful influence on actual purchase decisions as well as perceptions of service experiences.

Analyst firm Gartner defines social analytics as follows: 'Social analytics described the process of measuring analysing and interpreting the results and interactions of associations among people, topics and ideas.'[41] There are many interpretations of what constitutes analytics in social media, with many vendors offering services in this area. One relatively simple, yet fairly complete, representation has been developed by Tata Consulting Services. They propose focusing on three specific elements: customer sentiment analysis, brand reputation and customer experience. These elements use inputs from social media – including social networking sites, blogs, forums, news and other websites, CRM data, and data from different traditional channels such as television, print and radio. The elements include:

- *Customer sentiment analysis*: Outputs include analysis of social networks in terms of features such as pricing, flexibility and service as well as detailed analysis of major social media platforms
- *Brand reputation*: Outcomes include information on overall brand reputation as well as customers' positive negative or neutral attitudes towards the brand
- *Customer experience*: Measures of customer experience attracted, with details of analysis of satisfaction and dissatisfaction.[42]

A joint report, by Altimeter Group and Web Analytics Demystified, points out that no perfect solution exists for the analysis of social media and that there is no single vendor that can effectively provide measurement of all aspects of social media: 'While many vendors in the space offer capable tools with usable interfaces, the reality is that businesses turn to multiple solutions for capturing, analysing and interpreting their social media activities. Most use an amalgamation of commercial solutions geared for capturing social buzz, free tools offering limited information and a whole lot of managerial intervention for aggregating and analysing social media data. Don't expect this to change in the near term.'[43]

Although specific business objectives for social media will vary from enterprise to enterprise, the joint report identifies four broad objectives, together with a series of associated key performance indicators:

- *Foster dialogue*: share of voice; audience engagement; conversation rate
- *Promote advocacy*: active advocates; advocate influence; advocacy impact
- *Facilitate support*: resolution rate; resolution time; satisfaction score
- *Spur innovation*: topic trends; sentiment ratio; idea impact.

For the reader wishing to learn how to measure these performance indicators, Altimeter/ Web Analytics provide specific equations for measuring each of these 12 metrics together with a list of vendors which provide measurement services for each of these metrics. As this reports shows there are a growing number of vendors providing platforms that enable firms to listen, analyse and respond to social media in real time.

Actual behaviour can now be observed in real time, not predicted after months of analysis. Marketers can now engage with the right message to the right people at the right time and react in real time to any complaints or groundswells of negativity before these get out of hand. User expectations for real-time accountability from enterprises are high and tolerance for waiting for responses is low. Gone are the days where a firm can hold rounds of internal meetings to carefully craft responses. Reacting in real time will soon become a necessary institutionalised behaviour, and having appropriate social media analytics to monitor engagement with the brand is critical.

Mission control listening centres

With the huge increase in social media usage, some enterprises are taking a more active role in seeking to monitor engagement with their brand. A number of leading companies have now created a social media intelligence centre that resembles a war room. One example of this is the 'mission control' centre. These command centres started at the end of the first decade of the twenty-first century. Some of the best-known proponents of such centres include Gatorade's 'Mission Control', Intel's 'Social Media Center of Excellence' and Dell's 'Social Media Listening Command Center'.

Gatorade, a division of PepsiCo, is possibly the most reported social media command centre. Gatorade's 'Mission Control' has a dedicated glass room with many huge monitors and five seats for Gatorade's marketing team. This marketing team can now monitor and react to, in real time, what is happening in the social media space. Gatorade's objective is to take the largest sports drink brand in the world and turn it into the largest participatory brand in the world.[44] To that end, the company is not only monitoring its brand on social media, but is giving its fans increased access to its athletes and scientists. On a day-to-day basis, Gatorade's tools are also being used for more conventional marketing tactics – like optimising landing pages and making sure followers are being sent to the top performing pages.

Intel launched its Social Media Center of Excellence in 2009. It seeks to provide early warning signals about problems in the brand such as malfunctioning computer chips or negative responses following a product launch. It has seven employees, organised by business function, to listen to and engage in online discussion. It aims to identify problems and respond before the issue goes viral. Its future plans include more proactive outbound social media campaigns.

Dell's Social Media Listening Command Center was launched in late 2010. Around 70 people are involved – 11 people monitor and respond to online conversations and over 50 people working at @Dellcares are involved in monitoring conversations in a dozen languages around the world – helping, engaging, mitigating and offering meaningful support to customers online. Dell uses Radian6 as a monitoring and management tool. This company tracks some 25,000 social media events for the company each day.

Listening centres for social media are not restricted to the for-profit sector. The Red Cross launched its social media command centre in early 2012. Formerly named the 'American Red Cross Digital Operations Center', the command centre tracks Twitter, YouTube and Facebook to help communicate with disaster victims, for example, by helping to find emergency victims and pass on information to rescuers to help get aid to disaster victims. A further not-for-profit organisation, Clemson University in the US, has also created a social media command centre. This centre provides hands-on experience to students, facilitates graduate students' research, and enables monitoring of the university's social media interactions.

Measuring social media returns

Bain & Co. endorse the view that it is critical to link social media efforts to concrete business objectives. They point out that companies using social media that have business objectives aimed at serving the needs of customers can achieve real returns at every touch point. They provide the following examples of where companies have achieved returns on social media at different touch points from awareness to retention:

- *Awareness*: Ford achieved the same level of brand recognition with the Fiesta social media campaign at 10 per cent of the traditional TV advertising cost.
- *Purchase*: WetSeal.com reports social shoppers at 2.5 times greater conversion rate than the average customer.
- *Use*: Nike+ product and social community is credited with increasing Nike running shoes market share from 48 to 61 per cent.
- *Service*: Intuit's own QuickBook customers answer 70 per cent of fellow customers' service questions online.
- *Feedback*: LEGO credits customer idea sourcing with its decision to launch more expensive and customer-innovated sets, such as the 500 piece Star Wars product.
- *Retention*: eBay community users spend 54 per cent more than other customers.[45]

However, as Bain & Co. point out, the most beneficial results are achieved by companies that aim at unlocking value at every touch point from awareness to retention.

To unlock value, enterprises need to understand and incorporate relevant approaches to measuring social marketing ROI. Developing appropriate ROI measures is critical if enterprises are to engage in substantial marketing expenditure on social media. Social media strategist Heather Albrecht has produced a useful summary of four approaches to social influence marketing ROI:[46]

- *Direct ROI measurement*: This measure is appropriate where the content distributed by social media places the customer just one trackable click away from measurable revenue.
- *Correlated ROI measurement*: Correlated ROI is a function of tracking measurable social media activities over a given time (e.g. focused blogging effort, a community site, Facebook page, etc.) and relating it to the performance of key business or marketing metrics such as sales volume or volume of leads over the same period.
- *Proxy ROI measurement*: Proxy ROI is closely related to the concept of return on marketing investment (ROMI) attempts to determine the long term impact of marketing investments using metrics such as an unaided brand awareness, purchase intent, customer satisfaction, Net Promoter Scores, etc.
- *Relative ROI measurement*: Relative ROI involves comparing the impact and cost-effectiveness of your social media efforts against the measurable impact of other marketing channels such as TV, print, online display, direct marketing, etc.

There is considerable current debate regarding measuring the results of social media and identifying social media ROI. There is much controversy related to this topic and no shortage of discussion – a Google search of 'social media ROI' produces 2.8 million hits! A more detailed exposition of return on investment in social media is beyond the scope of this chapter. However, for the reader wishing to investigate social media ROI further, at this reference we provide a list of books that examine this topic in greater detail.[47]

Integrating Marketing

Before concluding this chapter, some comments should be made regarding the integration of different forms of marketing media. Corcoran identifies three media types: *paid or bought media, owned media* and *earned media*.[48] These forms of media are sometimes thought about only in terms of digital marketing but they also include non-digital marketing. Figure 5.11 summarises the interrelationship between these three forms of media, illustrative examples of the specific media for each media type, and the main target audience to which each media type is directed.

Paid or bought media: This involves all media that is purchased by the marketer. It includes non-digital media such as print, television, magazines, direct mail, cinema, sponsorship, etc., as well as digital media such as banner advertisements, display advertising, search, pay per click and renting third-party e-mail lists. This form of media is primarily targeted at future customers or 'strangers'.

Owned media: This form of media is owned or controlled by the marketer. It includes retail store locations, brochures, company website, Facebook pages, mobile applications developed by the company, etc. However, in the case of social media such as Facebook pages and Twitter accounts, an enterprise has limited control over the companies that own these media. Further, control of content in social media is limited, as external people can post content on these social media platforms. This form of media is targeted at both existing and prospective customers.

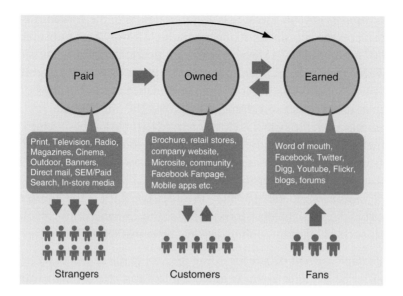

Figure 5.11 Paid, owned and bought media.
Source: Sofus Midtgaard: Leaderlab.com, with inspiration from MEC, Starbucks and Forrester

Earned media: This form of media includes media which is not controlled or purchased by the marketer. Historically, verbal word-of-mouth marketing has been the main form of earned media. With the rise of social media, digital word-of-mouth and viral marketing have increasingly important roles to play. Earned media includes content on media such as blogs, forums, Facebook, Twitter and YouTube. This form of media is directed not just at prospective and existing customers, but a much wider range of potential influencers – which are considered in our discussion of the influence market domain in Chapter 4. This form of media aims at developing fans and advocates for the enterprise.

Enterprises need to recognise the extent to which they have control over these three forms of media and their potential reach. The relative control and reach of these media types is illustrated in Figure 5.12.

Enterprises need to develop an appropriate balance between owned, paid or bought media and earned media. Owned, bought/paid and earned media need to be developed together. Earned media, in particular, has a key role in greatly increasing reach to customers and other stakeholders. Owned media and bought media are necessary to create greater awareness and motivate people to engage with your brand – thus impacting the earned media space.

The relationship between these media types should be clearly understood if relationship marketing activities are to be successful. Owned media provides continuous messages about the enterprise's brand. Paid media usually tends to be episodic and is often delivered in short bursts or spikes – however, large organisations will often have a continuous stream of paid media activity. As media expert Greg Shove points out, bought/paid media provides campaigns that provide intensity, 100 per cent message control, and

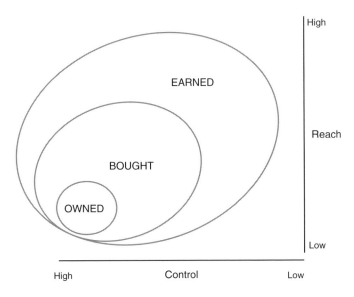

Figure 5.12 Reach and control of the three media types.
Source: Daniel Goodall: danielgoodall.com

potentially good demographic and geographic targeting. However, earned media is potentially more scalable, sustainable and influential.[49] Collectively, this represents a new model for integrating non-digital and digital relationship marketing activities. Leverage of owned, paid media and earned media is essential if enterprises' relationship marketing activities are to be successful.

SUMMARY

This chapter has explored the dramatic shifts enabled and, in some cases, forced by the rise of digital, mobile and social technologies. Each technology wave presents a significant set of opportunities to exploit, threats against which to defend, and challenges to overcome. The digital Internet infrastructure has grown rapidly and continues to advance in terms of pervasiveness, speed and intelligence. The implication for relationship marketing is that enterprise executives can expect customers and other stakeholders to be digitally connected anytime, anywhere.

The Web 1.0 phase started in the 1990s and brought with it: Web browsing and searching; the ability to download content and play games; the ability to shop and purchase online via e-commerce and m-commerce; the ability to send/receive one-to-one and one-to-many messages online and via mobile access; and the ability to find locations using global positioning. The impact for strategic customer management was primarily the automation of front-end marketing functions.

The Web 2.0 phase started in the 2000s and expanded to worldwide adoption. It heralded the rise of social networking platforms such as Facebook, Twitter and

LinkedIn. It then expanded to a much wider range of activities including social commerce and social gaming, and provided the opportunity to better understand customer behaviour via social analytics. It has the potential to close many of the gaps in achieving strategic customer management.

The opportunities and challenges for relationship marketers are broad and far-reaching. The social dimensions of Web 2.0 enable and ultimately demand firms to: move from scheduled campaigns to continuous engagement punctuated by campaigns; move integrated and self-service support to real-time social support and response systems and processes; move from traditional marketing, which aims to build awareness and brand equity, to social influence marketing that is more about invitation and engagement rather than interrupt and push; and to utilise the power of social analysis and analytics-derived insights. In the future, the development of Web 3.0 represents new opportunities and challenges as the Web becomes more open and intelligent.

Many companies have adopted aspects of digital, mobile and social technology as part of their marketing and CRM strategy. However, this has often resulted in a piecemeal approach, with enterprises not having a clear strategic framework for their CRM activities and, as a consequence, not achieving the potential benefit from their customer-oriented initiatives. (We return to discuss how social media fits into CRM later and especially in Chapter 9.)

Enterprises that wish to build capabilities to sustain lasting relationships with the most desirable customer segments need to adopt a strategic approach to CRM that integrates those aspects of relationship marketing and technology that we have described so far in this book. The next five chapters provide a strategic framework for developing a customer relationship management strategy, with the aim of creating the type of authentic and mutually profitable customer relationship that the corner shop proprietor of old would routinely offer.

CASE 5.1: Hippo in India – using Twitter to manage the supply chain

The company

Social media is still at an early stage of evolution, with marketers only beginning to understand the vast opportunities offered by this new communication channel. Some commentators suggest that for business there are limited applications for Twitter, Facebook and other new interactive sites. However, this is not the case. Hippo, an Indian brand of snacking chip, has proved that Twitter can be a powerful force to augment the traditional marketing mix, providing a valuable and low-cost solution to improving sales and distribution.

Parle Products was founded in 1921 and over the last 90 years this family-owned company has enjoyed outstanding success. Starting with a small factory set up in the suburbs of Mumbai to manufacture confectionery products, a decade later the company expanded its product line to manufacture biscuits. Since then, Parle has expanded continually and today the company has the largest biscuit and confectionery plants in India. The original Parle company was later split into three separate companies, owned by the different members of the original Chauhan family.

Parle Agro Pvt Ltd. is one of these companies. Commencing operations in 1984, the company quickly grew, manufacturing India's best-selling mango drink, the best-selling biscuit, Parle-G, along with many other highly popular brands. The company has a massive 40 per cent share of the biscuit market and 15 per cent share of the confectionery market in India, making it one of the fastest growing enterprises in the country. In 2010 Parle Agro launched 'Hippo Baked Munchies' into the Indian snack food market. Apart from the appeal of the taste and texture of the snack, an important aspect of the rapid consumer uptake of Hippo was the creative communication message using the appealing 'Hippo' character. From the outset, this lovable anthropomorphic character assured that the brand stood apart in this crowded market sector. Hippo communicated with consumers as a friend, offering a humorous opinion on many topics. Consumers flocked to Twitter, Facebook, Blogspot and the friendly website www.hippofighthunger.com to chat with Hippo and share amusing stories.

Integrated communications

Hippo's successful products launch was backed by clever positioning and a highly creative integrated communications strategy created by leading Indian agency Creativeland Asia. The key to this ongoing campaign is the use of Hippo as a brand mascot and brand identity. The integrated communications strategy incorporated multi-channels including radio, TV, print, a website, point-of sale materials and social media. Hippo used a simple message which reflected common sense, especially within the diverse Indian market that ranges from the poorest to those with extreme wealth: 'Hunger is the root of all evil. So, don't go hungry.' The Hippo brand stood for a cause, which was engaging to consumers who willingly participated as 'hunger fighters'.

Figure 1 presents some key themes from 'the Hippo story'. The promotional material on the website explains the brand personality of Hippo:

Figure 1 The Hippo story

He cares. He cooks. He is Hippo. Hippo is very disappointed with superheroes, intelligence agencies and world leaders. He thinks none care about fighting the world's biggest enemy, hunger. So, Hippo has taken matters into his own hands and kitchen. To fight hunger, Hippo has made delicious baked munchies in flavours from around the world like Italian Pizza, Yoghurt Mint Chutney, Chinese Manchurian, Hot-n-Sweet Tomato, Thai Chilli, Indian Chatpatta and Arabian Salted.

Hippo speaks to his customers more like a friend rather than as a typical FMCG (fast moving consumer goods) brand talking to its consumers.

A memorable series of TV commercials were made and these can be viewed on YouTube. These advertisements featured groups such as terrorists and hostile rioters who were rendered docile, friendly and happy as a result of eating Hippos. The TV campaign was following by a radio campaign, which builds on its positioning of 'Fight Hunger, Fight Evil'. The radio campaigns used famous speeches from evil dictators including Adolf Hitler, Saddam Hussein and Joseph Stalin. These speeches were 'translated' into English as a voiceover on top of the speeches, in a light hearted way, in 'Hippo speak'. In these voiceovers, Hippo reinterprets the speeches to tell the world how hungry the dictators are – suggesting that hunger is the cause of the dictators' evil dispositions and intentions. At the end of each speech, the voiceover continues: 'Hunger is the root of all evil, don't go hungry'. As Sajan Raj Kurup, Chairman and Chief Creative Officer of Creativeland Asia, notes: 'The challenge was to stay true to the positioning of fighting hunger, even on radio. The idea behind the radio campaign was to do a satire on famous war speeches by famous dictators from history.' However, the innovative integrated communications programme and resulting strong market acceptance of the product created a major supply chain challenge.

The challenge

Hippo was launched onto the snack food market and quickly became a huge success. Stock sold rapidly as consumers rushed to try this innovative brand. However, the brilliant communication strategy was plagued by a poor distribution network. The popularity of the Hippo brand meant that stock was quickly used and several valuable selling days could pass before shelves were replenished. In India, almost 94 per cent of retailing occurs through small kiosks, market stalls and unorganised sales outlets. Snack foods, especially, are sold across the nation in a wide range of outlets and these small vendors are essential to the success of a brand. Larger shops and hypermarkets are also important and here stock control is an easier task than monitoring the supplies of small vendors.

A key challenge for any food manufacturer in India is keeping track of stock through this diverse distribution network and identifying across over 400,000 outlets nationwide where there are empty shelves. After the initial success of the launch, Hippo did not want to lose the impressive sales momentum. The company recognised that consumers could interpret empty shelves either as evidence of the brand's popularity or that the product was a failure and stores were not bothering to restock. The traditional stock-taking process involved sales representatives visiting each outlet within their territory and sending their report back to the company. This process took several days and meant that valuable sales time was lost to competitors.

The solution

The company launched 'Plan-T' (Plan Twitter), with the comical Hippo character urging consumers to use the Twitter social media site to identify stock outs and 'Tweet' him whenever they found empty shelves. Tweets not only gave information about locations but even specific stores where Hippo packs were unavailable. These stores included those already sold out of Hippo, as well as outlets that previously had not stocked the snack. Tweets arrived from throughout the country, with consumers tweeting on their cellphones from kiosks, grocery stores and hypermarkets. Some typical examples of Hippo tweets are shown in Figure 2.

Figure 2 Examples of Hippo 'Tweets'

As some 92 per cent of the snack market in India is unorganised and in the hands of small outlets, inventory tracking is usually a huge logistical challenge for retailers. To solve this, Hippo turned to its customers on Twitter and asked them to tweet whenever they couldn't find the snack in a store or other outlet. Tweets poured in from over 50 cities. A Hippo team was set up in Parle Agro. The Hippo team collected and analysed this information, allowing the company to inform local distributors as they attempted to quickly restock outlets. Loyal customers who 'Tweet' very frequently with advice on where Hippo was out of stock were rewarded with special 'excellence in hunger fighting' certificates (see Figure 3) and large 'Hunger Fighter' hampers of Hippos.

Figure 3 Hippo 'Excellence in Hunger Fighting' certificate

The results

When Hippo launched this social media initiative, there were 800 people on Twitter following the brand. This figure rose during the campaign, with the number of people tracking Hippo chips inventory equalling over 50 per cent of the sales and distribution network itself – and with very little cost to the company. Sales figures rose dramatically, increasing by 76 per cent in a very short time.

Hippo consumers learned that a tweet from them could effectively ensure that their favourite snack was restocked in their neighbourhood store. This knowledge was fulfilling and gave consumers a feeling of power and pride in the brand. They could play an active role in ensuring the success of the brand and added to the enjoyment of their own personal consumption experience. This consumer-led means of tracking inventory was faster and more convenient than any of Hippo's competitors, who had million-dollar marketing and sales budgets.

Hippo's biggest competitors keenly watched the results of the campaign and tried to copy it by setting up a Twitter account and following Hippo's fans. However, Hippo had a first mover advantage and successfully fought off these competitive actions. The popularity of the Hippo character and the recognition of the brand itself ensure that the sales trend continues, with the snack remaining highly successful within the Indian market.

This campaign broke new ground in several ways. It appears to be the first consumer brand in the history of marketing that has been able to get its consumers to track inventory and to help a company make a very substantial increase in sales volume. It is also the first time a consumer brand has used the Twitter social media platform as a means of addressing complex sales and distribution challenges. Finally, the Hippo brand has become a 'best-in-class exemplar' of the use of an integrated marketing communications and sales programme using social media that incorporates both distribution and sales activities. The Hippo Twitter Trackers team at the company's headquarters still check every tweet and replenish the supply in each store accordingly. Each hour, each day, and week after week. All this has been achieved by the Hippo team and its consumers at a surprisingly low cost.

CASE 5.2: Blendtec – the 'will it blend' viral marketing initiative

The company

Blendtec is an Orem, Utah-based, division of K-Tec Inc. with sales of over $40 million. It sells professional and home food blenders, serving both business and consumer markets. K-Tec Inc. is a small company with an excellent reputation for quality and reliability. Established in the mid-1970s, the company initially manufactured a 'micronising' grain mill that could be used in the home. Since then, they developed a range of kitchen appliances, with their key current product being blenders. The company initially developed blenders for commercial use and these were later adapted for consumer use in the home.

The company was founded by CEO Tom Dickson. His innovative foray into food appliances drove him to revolutionise the home wheat milling industry, shifting it from stone grinding to his patented stainless steel milling heads. Like most inventors, he continued to innovate. Dickson developed a mixer that would make wholesome bread in minutes. Later he decided to add a blender with a square pitcher, rather than the conventional round shaped pitcher. He then began developing commercial blending machines, just as the era of the 'smoothie' began. Over the next decade, as the smoothie revolution grew, retail food outlets turned to Blendtec to adapt blender technology for commercial use. Blendtec was the first blender to use a microprocessor to govern the motor and later development of the blender included a sound enclosure (containing the noise of the motor), programmability (allowing users to input a specific programme), auto-start and stop, and safety-interlock features.

The challenge

As a small enterprise, Blendtec had a small marketing budget and preferred to spend its money on engineering and design. As the majority of sales were in the commercial B2B market, Blendtec relied on demonstrations at trade shows and word-of-mouth referrals. In 2006 George Wright joined Blendtec as the Director of Marketing and Sales, a new position for the company. Wright, with previous experience in strategy, brand building and advertising, came with fresh ideas and his arrival marked a shift in strategic thinking in the way Blendtec wanted the marketplace to view the brand. Wright pointed out that Blendtec was subject to the following equation: *Great products + Weak branding = Weak sales*. Although Blendtec manufactured very high-quality blenders and other products which were sold globally, they had very low brand awareness. Wright's challenge was to substantially increase brand awareness with a minimal marketing budget.

The solution

The inspiration for the solution came in late 2006 when Wright was walking through Blendtec's demonstration room and he noticed a pile of wood chips and sawdust on the floor next to one of the blenders. He learned that Tom Dickson, the CEO, had been chopping up 2" x 2" pieces of timber and other objects in order to check the robustness and durability of the drive components of the home use blender. Out of this explanation a new marketing programme evolved. Wright felt consumers would enjoy watching the test and witness a demonstration of the quality and strength of the appliance by viewing strange things going into a blender.

While discussing plans for advertising, the idea of using viral videos to launch Blendtec to a wide audience was developed. After obtaining management agreement, Kels Goodman, the staff video producer, was asked to produce five videos of CEO Dickson destroying various items in a Blendtec blender. Wright and his team purchased a white laboratory coat and a number of items including marbles, a garden rake, a McDonald's Meal, a chicken and a Coke, and made the five videos. The video series was called 'Will It Blend?' The initial campaign was reported to have cost $50.

CEO Tom Dickson is an unlikely video star. A chubby middle-aged Mormon with 11 children, he has little by way of acting skills. Yet Dickson, wearing the white coat and safety glasses, is the star of the series. In these infomercials, Dickson blends a number of unusual items in order to show off the power of his blender. At the end of each 'Will It Blend?' video, the contents of the blender are tipped out onto the bench top, at which stage a subtitle 'Yes, it blends!' appears on the screen.

In late 2006, when the initial five videos were released, Marketing Director Wright reported to Dickson that the initial video series had gone viral: 'We just hit a homerun on "YouTube" with 6 million views in 5 days.' More and more videos were posted over the next six years including the 'blending' of golf balls, matches, a Rubik's cube, TV remote controls, an iPhone and more recently an iPad. The iPhone 'Will It Blend?' video, see screenshot in Figure 1, had astonishing popularity, with over ten million views on YouTube. A total of over 80 'Will It Blend?' videos have been produced so far.

Establishing a social media presence across all the social media channels as well as the existing legacy channels requires an integrated approach to channel management. Blendtec is an early adopter of social media and a perfect example of integration across all digital channels, as shown in Figure 2. The 'Will It Blend?' concept is integrated into all Blendtec's marketing. Blendtec is on Twitter, on Facebook, on a 'Will It Blend?' microsite, on Blendtec websites and a corporate blog. Blendtec have two main websites, a B2C website for their domestic products and a B2B website for their commercial products. The 'Will it Blend?' (www.willitblend.com/) channel is a novel and irreverent way of promoting their products to consumers.

The 'Will it Blend?' website is Blendtec's central digital media hub. From this website it's possible to view the 'Will it Blend?' videos via streaming. Also, from this website are simple links to visit their other digital channels. These include the:

- B2C corporate website: Blendtec home blenders (http://blendtec.com/)
- B2B corporate website: Blendtec commercial blenders (http://commercial.blendtec.com/)
- 'Will it Blend?' corporate BLOG: 'Will it Blend?' (http://blog.blendtec.com/)
- YouTube channel: (www.youtube.com/blendtec)
- Twitter tweets: (http://twitter.com/blendtec)
- Facebook page: (www.facebook.com/willitblend).

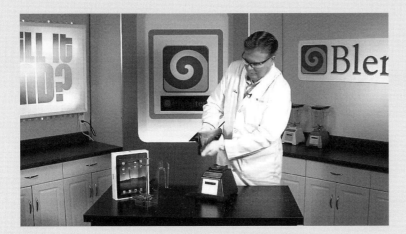

Figure 1 Screenshot of CEO Dickson about to 'blend' an iPhone

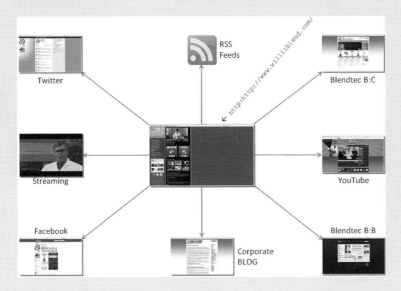

Figure 2 Blendtec's integration across digital channels

All of these channels have a consistent look and feel, but each exploits the strengths unique to that channel. All channels are consistently cross-linked, enabling free and easy mobility across the channels. Blendtec also interacts with its customers, permitting them to propose items for Dickson to blend, which in turn may become future videos. The Blendtec social media strategy can be summarised under the headings of *identify*, *create and edit* and *publish and syndicate*, as shown in Figure 3, with each published source drawing on the same creative content.

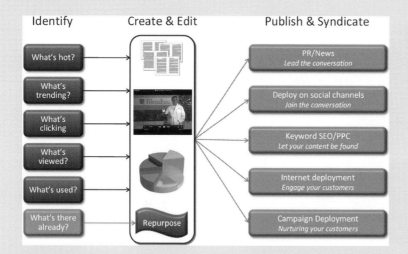

Figure 3 The Blendtec social media strategy

The results

BlendTec's viral marketing campaign has given the brand worldwide recognition. Today, Blendtec blenders are used in restaurants, coffee shops, juice bars, health clubs and consumers' homes in 70 countries around the world. The 'Will it Blend?' campaign has been a remarkably successful social media campaign, with impressive statistics that demonstrate the power of viral marketing. By 2012, the 'Will it Blend?' videos had achieved a total of 180 million views on YouTube and 'Will it Blend' brings up over 12 million hits on Google. Described by some commentators as the 'best viral marketing campaign ever', the videos have won or been nominated for many industry awards. CEO Dickson has become a popular radio and television celebrity, with appearances on many US TV programmes such as *The Tonight Show* and *Today*. Dickson has also become a sought-after conference speaker. More importantly, there has been a huge return on investment in terms of both brand equity and sales. Despite the premium pricing strategy (the consumer blender is around $400 and the commercial blender is more than $1,000), sales have grown substantially. In 2011 Blendtec reported a 1,000 per cent increase in retail sales and a 1,000 per cent increase in online sales as a result of the campaign.

Part III

Customer relationship management: Key processes

6 | Strategy development

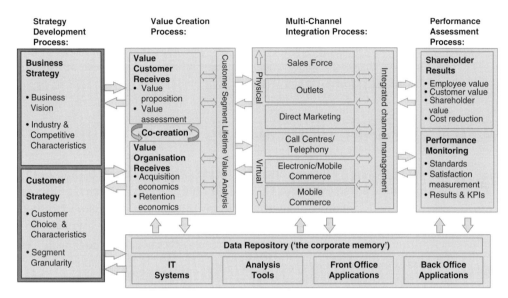

The CRM Strategy Framework

In the previous chapters of this book we explored the key concepts and themes that constitute relationship marketing. We pointed out that while relationship marketing involves the development of relationships with *multiple stakeholders*, CRM involves the strategic management of *customers* utilising appropriate technology. As Gummesson points out, CRM is about the values of relationship marketing, with a special emphasis on customer relationships and practical application.[1]

In Chapter 1 we discussed a CRM continuum. At one end of this continuum, CRM is defined narrowly and tactically and has a focus on implementation of a specific technology solution project. At the other end of the continuum, CRM is viewed as a strategic approach to managing customer relationships in order to create shareholder value. We explained in Chapter 1 why it was important to adopt this latter perspective and we provided a definition of CRM viewed from this strategic perspective, which we restate below:

CRM is a cross-functional strategic approach concerned with creating improved shareholder value through the development of appropriate relationships with key customers and customer segments. It typically involves identifying appropriate business and customer strategies, the acquisition and diffusion of customer knowledge, deciding appropriate segment granularity, managing the co-creation of customer value, developing integrated channel strategies and the intelligent use of data and technology solutions to create superior customer experiences.

This strategic perspective, serves as the basis for the detailed discussion of CRM over the next five chapters that comprise Part III of this book. In Chapter 1, we provided an overview of the CRM Strategy Framework and its five key component processes. Figure 1.10 in Chapter 1 showed a high-level representation of these processes. At the start of this and each of the following four chapters we provide a more detailed diagrammatic representation of the elements contained within each process.

This chapter is structured as follows. First, we briefly review alternative CRM models and frameworks. Second, we explain the rationale and development of the CRM Strategy Framework used in the next five chapters. We then focus on the first key process – the strategy development process, exploring its two major interrelated components: the formulation of business strategy and customer strategy.

Alternative CRM models and frameworks

The earliest CRM models we identified were developed in 2001. For example, Sue and Morin outline a framework for CRM based on initiatives, expected results and contributions, but this is not process based, and 'many initiatives are not explicitly identified in the framework'.[2]

Another early model developed by Winer involves a 'basic model, which contains a set of seven basic components: a database of customer activity; analyses of the database; given the analyses, decisions about which customers to target; tools for targeting the customers; how to build relationships with the targeted customers; privacy issues; and metrics for measuring the success of the CRM program'.[3] This model, though useful, is not a cross-functional process-based conceptualisation.

Peppers and Rogers develop a pragmatic approach to the implementation of their one-to-one marketing approach with their IDIC process. This four step process includes: identify your customers – recognising that you can only have a relationship with an individual; differentiate your customers – reflecting the need to treat different customers differently; interact with customers – maximising interaction and dialogue with customers; and, customise treatment – using customer insights to treat individual customers differently.[4]

Buttle[5] develops a CRM value chain model based on the concept of Porter's value chain concept.[6] He identifies five primary stages and four supporting conditions in his model. The primary stages include the: customer portfolio analysis; customer intimacy; network development; value proposition development and management of customer life-cycle. The supporting conditions include leadership and culture, data and IT, people and processes – which enable effective functioning of the CRM strategy.

Analyst firm Gartner Inc. developed a CRM competency framework – the 'Eight Building Blocks of CRM' model.[7] These eight building blocks include: CRM vision; CRM strategy; valued customer experience; organisational collaboration; CRM processes; CRM information; CRM technology and CRM metrics. This model is used by Gartner to assess enterprises' current and required CRM capabilities and to help them understand their current position and future strategies.

A further framework was developed by QCi, a company purchased by OgilvyOne Worldwide and which is part of the WPP group of companies. Their CMAT customer management assessment tool is based on the following elements: analysis and planning; the proposition; people and organisation; information technology; process management; customer management activity and measuring the effect.[8] As its name suggests, this framework is a tool for assessing CRM performance. The CMAT model is discussed further in this context in Chapter 10.

These models were developed from different viewpoints and for different purposes. Readers wishing to explore these particular models in more detail should refer to the references to this chapter. Some of these models are concerned with CRM strategy formulation, others with CRM implementation. Some of the models are normative managerial frameworks without clear theoretical underpinnings. Others, such as CMAT, are proprietary consulting tools concerned with CRM assessment. In Chapter 2, we pointed out that process integration and cross-functional collaboration are defining strengths of a relationship orientation, as highlighted in Srivastava, Shervani and Fahey's important work on defining businesses processes.[9] Although a cross-functional and processes emphasis is implicit in some of these models, we consider these important elements insufficiently emphasised within them.

The CRM Strategy Framework

We concluded that there was a need for a new process-based CRM strategy framework. Our reasoning was that synthesis of the diverse concepts in the literature on CRM and relationship marketing into a single, process-based framework should provide practical insights to help companies achieve greater success with CRM strategy development and implementation. This conclusion resulted in the development of the CRM Strategy Framework used in this book.

Development of the framework

In our research, we integrated an extensive review of the literature with learning from field-based interactions with highly experienced CRM executives to develop the CRM Strategy Framework. The research process we used is what Gummesson terms 'interaction research'.[10] The field-based research was undertaken with executives from large enterprises in the business-to-business and business-to-consumer sectors and included:

- an expert panel of 34 executives highly experienced in CRM;
- interviews with 20 executives working in CRM, marketing and IT roles in companies in the financial services sector;
- interviews with six executives from large CRM vendors and with five executives from three CRM and strategy consultancies;

- individual and group discussions with CRM, marketing and IT managers at workshops with 18 CRM vendors, analysts and their clients, including Accenture, Baan, BroadVision, Chordiant, EDS, E.piphany, Hewlett-Packard, IBM, Gartner, NCR Teradata, Peoplesoft, Oracle, SAP, SAS Institute, Siebel, Sybase and Unisys;
- piloting the framework as a planning tool in the financial services and automotive sectors;
- using the framework as a planning tool in six workshops with a global telecommunications company and a global logistics firm.

The development of the CRM Strategy Framework is described fully in an article in the *Journal of Marketing*.[11] We started by identifying possible generic CRM processes from the CRM and related business literature. We then discussed these potential processes with the groups of executives outlined above. The outcome of this work was a short list of seven processes. We then used the expert panel of highly experienced CRM executives to nominate the CRM processes that they considered important and to agree on those that were the most relevant and generic. As a result of this interactive method, five key CRM processes were identified that met the selection criteria. These five key generic CRM processes were incorporated into a preliminary version of the framework. Using this interaction approach with executives, the structure within each process was developed. The framework went through a number of major iterations and minor revisions. The framework has since been validated by use in 32 organisations in many different industry sectors. Figure 6.1 shows the latest version of the framework.

The arrows in Figure 6.1 show interaction and feedback loops between the different processes, emphasising the iterative nature of CRM. For example, shifts in disintermediation within a given industry, considered within the strategy development process, may have an impact on channel choices within the multi-channel integration process. Likewise, changes within the multi-channel integration process may have a direct impact on decisions taken within the value creation process. Further, decisions on choice of customer segments taken as part of the strategy development process may be changed as a result of economic modelling undertaken as part of the value creation process.

In considering each of the five CRM processes in Figure 6.1, enterprises need to ask themselves some fundamental questions.

Process 1: the strategy development process
- Where are we and what do we want to achieve?
- Who are the customers that we want and how should we segment them?

Process 2: the value creation process
- How should we offer value to our customers?
- How should we maximise the lifetime value of the customers we want?

Process 3: the multi-channel integration process
- What are the best ways for us to get to customers and for customers to get to us?
- What does an outstanding customer experience, deliverable at an affordable cost, look like?

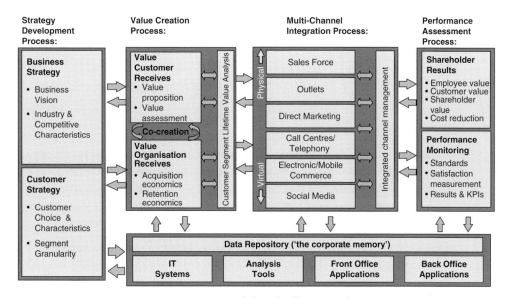

Figure 6.1 The CRM Strategy Framework

Process 4: the information management process
- How should we organise information on customers?
- How can we 'replicate' the mind of customers and use this to improve our CRM activities?

Process 5: the performance assessment process
- How can we create increased profits and shareholder value?
- How should we set standards, develop metrics, measure our results and improve our performance?

While these five CRM processes have universal application, the extent to which they are emphasised will vary according to each organisation's unique situation. Large customer-facing businesses will certainly need to review all these CRM processes and all the key questions underpinning them. However, small and medium-sized enterprises and other organisations, such as those in the public sector, may need to modify some of the questions above to ensure they are of utmost relevance. Having discussed the CRM strategy model, we now turn our attention to the main focus of this chapter – the strategy development process.

The strategy development process

The strategy development process is deservedly the first process to be considered in the CRM Strategy Framework. It not only shapes the nature of the other four key CRM processes but, more importantly, it defines the overall objectives and parameters for the organisation's CRM activities. As highlighted in the figure above, the strategy development process involves determining the *business strategy* and the *customer strategy* and ensuring that they are integrated.

There are numerous definitions of strategy, but the one developed by Norman and Ramirez remains, in our view, the best definition. It is one that highlights the criticality of customer relationships:

Strategy is the art of creating value. It provides the intellectual frameworks, conceptual models and governing ideas that allow a company's managers to identify opportunities for bringing value to customers and for delivering that value at a profit. In this respect, strategy is the way a company defines its business and links together the only two resources that really matter in today's economy: knowledge and relationships or an organization's competencies and customers.[12]

This definition emphasises that it is not sufficient just to have a strategy – it is the art of creating value. To be successful at strategy, the enterprise needs to develop *strategic capability*. As Ian McDonald Wood, director of the FutureValue Strategic Value Research Programme and a leading digital business observer, points out:

Strategic capability is quite simply the capacity of a business to survive, prosper and deliver future value. It comprises a number of distinct components. Clarity of thinking and action in objectives and strategy; evidence of strategy in action and strategic progress in operational achievement; sensitivity to the future and to the impact of controllable and uncontrollable trends and factors upon future performance; investment in resources, strengths and less tangible drivers of value; and, an approach to social ethical and environmental matters that is integral to the strategy of the business.[13]

While most companies recognise the importance of having clearly defined business and customer strategies, relatively few actively develop a formal CRM strategy with a focus on building appropriate customer relationships. Yet, central to the concept of strategy is the delivery of value to the customer. This implies knowing who the customers are, what they want and whether and how the organisation can satisfy this known demand on a sustainable basis.

With much attention being directed at CRM, some managers advocate the quick introduction of a particular IT solution to solve their strategic challenges. However, many organisations' experiences with IT are mixed. Some are hostages to out-of-date legacy systems, some to a legacy culture where IT is inappropriately viewed as an ever-escalating cost rather than a source of competitive advantage. The result is either inappropriate investment in new technology (which may fail to break free of the legacy 'bonds') or an organisation focused solely on the technology challenge instead of on the underlying critical business issues. Alternatively, the organisation may adopt one particular technology too rapidly; focus insufficiently on building customer relationships or resist the use of new technologies for improved CRM.

Rather than concentrate immediately on a technology solution, managers should first consider CRM in the context of their organisation's overall strategy development. In other words, what are the goals of the organisation given the opportunities and constraints within which it operates? In the following sections of this chapter we address the following issues:

Business strategy
- The role of business strategy
- Business vision
- Industry and competitive characteristics
- Analysing industry structure and the competitive environment
- Focusing on business strategy

Customer strategy
- The role of customer strategy
- Customer choice and customer characteristics
- Segment granularity

CRM strategy development
- CRM strategies
- Transition paths for CRM.

Business strategy

The first part of the CRM strategy development process is to review the organisation's *business strategy*. A detailed understanding of the business strategy is essential if an appropriate *customer strategy* is to be implemented. We should emphasise from the outset that CRM is not primarily about developing a business strategy. Rather it is about fully understanding the business strategy in order to determine how the appropriate customer strategy should be developed and how it should evolve over time. CRM should not seek responsibility for business strategy development. However, it should intervene and ensure top management's attention is directed at business strategy when a thorough review of it clearly shows that it is wrongly directed or it is not taking account of a changing competitive landscape. This is because it is crucial for the CRM activities to be aligned with and supportive of an appropriate business strategy.

We do not attempt a fully comprehensive coverage of all aspects of business strategy here. Rather we examine the key issues that need to be considered and some frameworks that can be used to make an assessment of the organisation's business strategy in order that the CRM strategy is appropriately focused.

The role of business strategy

Business strategy is a top management responsibility that involves identifying the future direction of the enterprise as well as managing the creative interaction of the functional disciplines of operations, marketing, finance and human resource management. It is both a process and a way of thinking which leads to the development of a set of strategies that assist the business in achieving its corporate objectives.

All companies have a business strategy; however, this may be implicit or explicit. While some companies, often smaller ones, are successful with only an implicit strategy guiding the chief executive and the management team, it is our experience that companies developing an explicit strategy through a planned approach have a greater chance of long-term success. Almost all large companies that have introduced CRM will have developed an explicit business strategy. However, the daily financial newspapers, research studies, Internet blogs and business journals provide us with a frequent reminder that such strategies are often not well formulated or well implemented, or neither, and do not automatically result in success.

Corporate success can be the result of an implicit strategy being evolved based on creative entrepreneurial insights on the part of a company; or it may be the result of opportunistic effectiveness. That is, effective intuitive responses to short-term opportunities in the marketplace. A further factor that can influence corporate success is luck, which often plays an important role in success. However, these factors cannot be relied upon to produce long-term results. While they may result in initial success for a company, a further factor, *developing a formal business strategy*, provides an opportunity to influence sustained success over the longer term. Companies wishing to adopt such an approach need to start by clearly defining their business vision and then formulating a business strategy that takes full account of the competitive characteristics within the areas in which they have chosen to operate.

Business vision

The process of business strategy formulation should commence with a review or articulation of an enterprise's vision. The business vision should explicitly reflect the basic beliefs, values and aspirations of the organisation. It should be noted, however, that many companies' statements of their vision display a great deal of similarity to each other and read like public relations releases rather than reflecting the commitment to values that they are intended to be.

A *business vision* should be an enduring statement of purpose that distinguishes the organisation from its competitors, and it should act as an important device for coordinating activity in an organisation. A company's business vision should reflect the shared value systems which are held within the organisation. It can provide a framework to enable the diverse staff of an organisation to work together in a coordinated manner towards the achievement of the overall objectives and philosophy of the enterprise. Unfortunately, many companies' vision statements do not conform to these requirements.

Vision statements need not be long and platitudinous. Tom Watson, the founder of IBM, articulated his company's philosophy in the phrase 'IBM means service'. The business vision described by Watson was simple: not just to be a *good* service company, but to be the *best* service company. Tom Watson argued the vision of the organisation had a great deal more to do with its performance on this dimension than did technological or economic resources, organisational structure, innovation or timing. Over most of the company's history it has maintained this strong customer service focus.

In other work we have argued that research by Hugh Davidson represents the most authoritative work on business vision and identifying and communicating values.[14] Davidson's research was prompted by the fact that most of the written material on vision and values discusses how important they are and provides guidance on how to design statements, but there is little published about how to make vision and values work in practice.[15] He undertook a two-year research study on how to make vision and values really work in organisations. His research involved interviewing top management (chairmen and chief executives) in 125 well-run companies and non-profit organisations in the US and UK – companies which included BP, FedEx, DuPont, Tesco, Nestlé, Johnson & Johnson and IBM, as well as many non-profit organisations.

Organisations use a variety of terms to describe their business vision. These include mission statements or 'missions', business definition, statement of business philosophy, belief statement, credo, vision statement, statement of purpose and so on. Davidson found the term 'mission', which has been widely used over the last 30 years, has become less popular in recent years as managers feel the use of the term has been abused. He concluded that it did not matter which words were used to describe the business vision; what was important were three fundamental questions. The questions and terms he uses to describe them are:

- *Purpose* – What are we here for?
- *Vision* – What is our long-term destination?
- *Values* – What beliefs and behaviours will guide us on the journey?

The business vision and its associated values form an important element of a company's strategy. Put simply, without a clear, concise and well-communicated vision the company is less likely to be highly successful in achieving its goals. Organisations are now realising that developing a vision and a set of values associated with it may be difficult but it is a very worthwhile activity. A business vision is typically developed as part of an enterprise-wide consultative process which involves input from different functional areas and management levels.

Experience has shown that vision and values are often developed the wrong way. Inventing slogans like: 'the customer is king' or 'let's be customer focused' are exactly the wrong way to develop vision and values. You have got to start off by identifying what are the key future factors for success in your marketplace and then build the values around achieving those key factors for success. In that way, if you make your values work they build competitive advantage. Otherwise, as Davidson points out, they are quite irrelevant.

To assist in the development of business vision and values, Davidson identified seven best practices for making vision and values work (Figure 6.2). He applied these best practices to the 125 organisations he studied, defining 'excellence' as the achievement of all seven of them. Only 6 per cent of the organisations, including Johnson & Johnson and the Mayo Clinic, attained an excellence rating. The average company addressed only four of the seven practices. Davidson concluded that 'the seven best practices are

---

1. *Building foundations*: Needs of key stakeholders understood and linked through vision and values
2. *Strong vision*: Vision is memorable, clear, motivating, ambitious, customer related and translated into measurable strategies
3. *Strong values*: Values support the vision, are based on key factors for success and turned into measurable practices
4. *Communication*: Consistent communication by action, signals, words
5. *Embedding*: Recruitment, training, appraisal, rewards, promotion and succession, all reflect values
6. *Branding*: Organisation's branding expresses vision and values
7. *Measurement* : Rigorous measurement of how effectively vision and values are implemented

---

Figure 6.2 Best practices in making vision and values work.
Source: Based on Davidson (2002)

synergistic and work together: Four out of seven is not 55 per cent, it's about 33 per cent in terms of performance.' His research findings show most organisations still had a long way to go in making their vision and values deliver demonstrable returns.

Developing a strong business vision represents an important first stage in establishing a successful business strategy. We will revisit this topic when change management is discussed in Chapter 11.

Industry and competitive characteristics

Having determined the business vision, the next step in business strategy formulation is to undertake a review of the industry and competitive environment, including an assessment of both existing and potential competition. This addresses the question raised above of 'where are we?'

The competitive landscape

The last couple of decades have seen a new competitive landscape emerge which has profound competitive and technological implications for most businesses. All companies need to understand how this new environment impacts on their ability to create value and attract and retain customers, at present and in the future. The means of value creation they use and in what combination will depend on each company's specific circumstances. However, what is imperative to all enterprises is the need to be continually learning about their customers and innovating new ways in which to provide their customers with ever-greater value.

We are at a disruptive phase in terms of the current competitive environment. In addition to profound changes in customer-related issues, which we reviewed in Chapter 1, there have also been substantial technological changes, which we discussed in Chapter 5. A balanced review needs to be undertaken of the opportunities and threats presented by the current competitive landscape. An awareness of these significant changes and their implications will assist the development of the enterprise's business and customer strategies.

It is important not to be overly influenced by specific trends without fully understanding them in the broader industry and business context. A case in point is the current attention being directed at social media. As discussed in Chapter 5, there is a huge groundswell of interest in the topic of social media. In many organisations the topic dominates discussion almost to the exclusion of other communication and relationship-building issues. Special terms such as 'Social CRM' are being parlayed around as a new panacea for relationship building. However, as noted previously we prefer to see social media in the broader context of CRM. It is simply one tool that can be used to build or enhance relationships. Social media has a role, but is not *the* role in CRM. The current emphasis, some would say hype, on Social CRM is akin to the emphasis placed on e-CRM and e-business strategies around a decade ago. While the growth of the digital economy and social media has implications for strategy, it is important that the online world and social electronic interactions are seen in context. As Harvard Business School's Michael Porter commented:

We need to move away from the rhetoric about 'Internet Industries', 'e-business strategies', and a 'new economy' and see the Internet for what it is: an enabling technology – a powerful set of tools that can be used, wisely or unwisely in almost any industry, and as part of almost any strategy ... In our quest to see how the Internet is different, we failed to see how the Internet is the same.[16]

The same applies to social media. It is an enabling technology. Companies need to understand the implications of the new digital and social media worlds, but ensure the integration of strategies developed for the new economy with their existing business activities.

Changes in industry structure and evolution

The characteristics of the industry need to be assessed not only in terms of the existing structure, but also in terms of future possible structural changes. The technological developments over the past two decades, as well as new strategic insights have led to greater competitive activity on the part of both new entrants and existing competitors. This has created increasing challenges to traditional business models. In many industries, ranging from bookselling to automotive suppliers and software developers, the fundamental industry structure and dynamics are being reconfigured

Especially over the last 15 years, the traditional channel structures of many industries have been dismantled and reconfigured in response to new technologies that have opened new paths to market. Managers responsible for business strategy need to understand both the nature of their industry structure now and how it is likely to alter in the future. Valuable insights into emerging trends within industry structures can be gained from examining the experiences of other sectors or other industries on a global basis.

Two types of structural behaviour are important: *disintermediation* – where a company ceases to need to use one or more intermediaries or channel members; and *reintermediation* – where changes in the current business model result in the emergence of additional new intermediaries. In particular, the Internet has had a role in both these forms of structural change. These changes in industry structure need to be first considered at a macro-level as part of the strategy development process. Once macro-level decisions have been made regarding the most appropriate paths to market, the extent to which intermediaries are to be used and how these may change over time, the organisation then needs to consider multi-channel options and their combination in greater detail at a micro-level. We will address disintermediation and reintermediation in greater detail later when we consider the multi-channel integration process in Chapter 8.

Analysing industry structure and the competitive environment

A number of frameworks and conceptual models are especially helpful in both developing business strategy and assessing whether it has been formulated with sufficient clarity and detail in the context of the competition. We now review four of the more important and enduring frameworks for assessing the industry and competitive environment in order to develop an improved business strategy, including:

- the industry analysis model;
- the generic strategies framework;
- the Market Leaders framework;
- 'Blue Ocean' strategy.

The first two of these frameworks were developed by Michael Porter, who is recognised as the pre-eminent strategic management scholar. He has provided much of the modern theory in strategic management and made the discipline accessible to practising executives. His important work has been acknowledged by Accenture's Institute for Strategic Change which, in 2003, ranked Porter as the most influential business intellectual in the world.

Industry analysis model

The industry dynamics in which the firm operates are commonly analysed using a framework such as Porter's five forces model,[17] so that all known forces and not so well understood contingencies are brought into consideration. Porter's model is an important aid to understanding the competitive characteristics, identifying the key factors for success and determining the profit potential in an industry. In undertaking an analysis of any industry, he proposed that its characteristics and long-term prospects should be analysed in terms of five dimensions: the nature and degree of competition; the barriers to entry to that business; the competitive power of substitute products; the degree of buyer power; and the degree of supplier power.

However, a consideration of these 'forces' should be augmented by a more contemporary perspective that includes other forces. As Slater and Olson observe, industry dynamics have changed in subtle and not so subtle ways since the publication of Porter's original article: 'We have moved closer to a global marketplace in many industries; technology has advanced rapidly and in unforeseen ways; deregulation has opened the door for aggressive forms of entrepreneurship; and the Internet has created an entirely new way to do business.'[18] Slater and Olson suggest augmenting Porter's five forces model to reflect these and related developments. Newer thinking suggests we should supplement Porter's analysis with a consideration of: co-opetition and networks; deeper environmental analysis; and the impact of disruptive technologies. The five forces concept has also been criticised on the basis that the unit of analysis is the industry rather than the individual firm.[19] These changes in the environment suggest that a broader framework needs to be considered. A revised industry framework, based on an expanded set of forces, is shown in Figure 6.3.

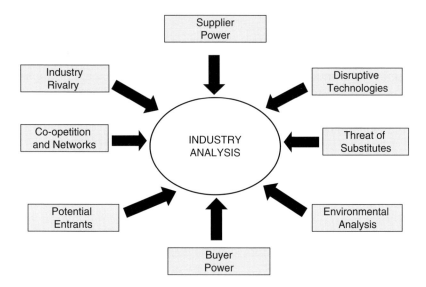

Figure 6.3 A framework for industry analysis

Through analysis of these eight dimensions, which include Porter's original five forces, insights can be gained into opportunities and threats as well as the key factors for competitive success in the industry under consideration.

Potential entrants
Two factors determine how strong this force will be: the existing barriers to entry and the likelihood of a strong competitive reaction from established competitors. The threat of entry tends to be low if barriers to entry are high and/or aspiring new entrants can expect extremely hostile retaliation from the established firms within the industry. If the threat of entry is low, profitability of the industry tends to be high. The threat of potential new entrants has been enhanced in many sectors with the advent of the Internet, which provides new entrants with the opportunity to access large markets at low cost.

Buyer power
The bargaining power of buyers is high if a number of factors are present. These include: if the products that a company purchases form a large proportion, in terms of cost, of its own product; if the buyer group is operating in an industry of low profitability; if the products supplied are undifferentiated and it is easy for the buyer to switch between suppliers at little cost; if the products are purchased in large volumes; or if the buyers have the potential to integrate backwards. Further, buyer power can be increased through

proactive engagement by customers in customer communities. Social media can permit a huge number of customers to be potentially mobilised and express their views on a company's brand and product or service performance. Conditions of high buyer power will result in lower industry profitability.

Supplier power

Similarly, the bargaining power of suppliers can be high if there are relatively few suppliers; if the industry is not an important customer of the supplier group; if the supplier has the potential to integrate forward into the customer's business; if there are few or no direct substitutes for the product; if the industry is dominated by only a few suppliers; or if the supplier's products are sufficiently differentiated so that the firm being supplied with the goods cannot easily switch to another supplier. Conditions of high supplier power lead to reduced industry profitability.

Threat of substitutes

In many product areas it is possible to identify products which can serve as substitutes. In industries ranging from telecommunications to car making, the threat of substitution is present. The higher the threat of substitution, the lower the profitability is likely to be within the industry because threat of substitution generally sets a limit on the prices that can be charged. The factors which influence the threat of substitution include the substitute product price-performance trade-off and the extent of switching costs associated with changing from one supplier to the supplier of the substitute. If the threat of substitution is low, industry profitability will tend to be high.

Industry rivalry and competition

The degree of industry competition is characterised by the amount of rivalry between existing firms. This can vary considerably and is not related necessarily to whether or not the industry is highly profitable. Intense rivalry can exist if there is slow growth within the industry; if competitors are evenly balanced in size and capability; where switching costs are low; where there is a high fixed cost structure and companies need to keep volumes high; where exit barriers are high such that unprofitable companies may still remain within the industry; and where competitors have different strategies, the result of which is that some firms may be willing to pursue a strategy that results in considerable conflict within the industry. A common outcome of this is price wars. A high degree of rivalry depresses industry profitability.

Environmental analysis

This analysis, known as a PESTE analysis, involves a review of political, economic, social, technological and environmental issues. Managers should develop a detailed list of major factors under each of these headings. PESTE analysis encourages managers to review broad environmental influences on the enterprise. A PESTE analysis helps understanding of the competitive dynamics of the industry and should lead to the identification of opportunities and threats facing the business.

Disruptive technologies

The environmental analysis should help consideration of evolutionary technological factors impacting on the business. Successful companies are usually good at responding to such evolutionary changes in their markets but have problems initiating revolutionary changes, or dealing with *disruptive innovation*. As Harvard academic Clayton Christensen and his colleagues point out, such innovations are disruptive in that they do not address the next-generation needs of leading customers in existing markets. Rather they have attributes that enable new market applications to emerge – and the disruptive innovations improve so rapidly that they ultimately can address the needs of customers in the mainstream of the market as well. Such disruptive technologies or innovations should be closely studied as they can create an entirely new market. Christensen's concept of disruptive innovation has been applied across many sectors including healthcare[20] and education.[21]

Co-opetition and networks

Increasingly, networks of companies are being developed that simultaneously combine cooperation and competition. Such 'co-opetition' is widely present in the information technology and CRM industries. Although competition has been increasing among these firms, so too has the nature of their collaborative activities. The concept of co-opetition, developed by Professors Brandenburger and Nalebuff,[22] illustrates how in an increasingly networked economy, companies cooperate and compete at the same time to maximise customer and firm value creation within their markets. As Julie Bowser, of IBM's Strategy and Change Consulting Group, has pointed out, changing business dynamics make the collaborative value inherent in co-opetition more necessary. Companies need to challenge themselves to develop their business by initiating, leveraging and redefining relationships with other players to create and capture value.

The aim of this analysis is for managers to identify a position in their industry where their company can best take advantage of, or defend itself against, these forces. This analysis can be performed by different groups of managers within the organisation to help gain additional insights regarding competitive characteristics. As the strategy evolves, it can also be undertaken at a more specific level by applying it to particular customer segments. A complete and balanced analysis of the competitive environment in which a firm is operating should lead to a good understanding of the key factors for success within that industry and the key tasks to be addressed in the firm.

The generic strategies framework

Once the industry structure has been analysed, an enterprise can consider the appropriate strategy to compete within it. A number of natural or generic strategies that can be adopted by an enterprise have been proposed by various writers. One approach, also developed by Porter,[23] suggests that a choice of one of three generic strategies is appropriate for a given business. These include a cost leadership strategy, a differentiation strategy, or a focus strategy. Figure 6.4 illustrates a revised view of the generic strategies based on differentiation and cost. The alternative strategies in this figure illustrate that companies must avoid

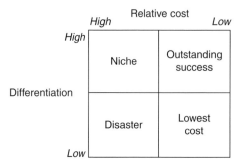

Figure 6.4 Alternative strategies based on differentiation and cost

having a high cost structure and low differentiation – a recipe for disaster. They should adopt a strategy of low cost or differentiation. These three strategies include:

Cost leadership strategy

A cost leadership strategy requires a company to set out with the objective of being the lowest-cost producer in the industry. Companies must seek economies of scale, proprietary technology not available to other firms, preferential access to raw materials and cost minimisation over a wide range of areas.

Differentiation

With a differentiation strategy, a firm seeks to be different within the industry it is operating in by being unique on some dimension or set of dimensions of value to buyers. The company seeks one or more dimensions by which to differentiate itself and, as a result, hopes to earn a premium price for its products or services.

Focus strategy

A focus strategy involves concentrating on a particular buyer group, geographic area or product/market segment. By selecting a particular segment or group of segments the company attempts to tailor its strategy to serving the needs of its segment better than the competition. It is essentially a strategy of gaining competitive advantage in the target segment because the company is not likely to enjoy competitive advantage across the market as a whole. A focus strategy may emphasise differentiation or cost advantage.

Cost leadership is often pursued by businesses with a low-cost position that wish to create shareholder value by gaining market share through very competitive pricing. Texas Instruments has historically adopted a cost leadership strategy by seeking high market share through low pricing and thus benefiting from the cost effects of the experience curve.

An industry-wide *differentiation* strategy seeks to create differentiation that is perceived as different and unique across that industry. The appropriate means of differentiation vary considerably across different industries. Differentiation could be in terms of technology, features, customer service, dealer network used, styling and product positioning.

Mercedes-Benz has, for example, differentiated itself from its competition by adopting a strategy on the basis of design, image, styling and engineering.

The approach adopted for a *focus* strategy can take many forms. The focus strategy is concerned with a specific market segment and is more concentrated than the differentiation approach, which appeals to a wider market. While Japanese motor car manufacturers typically adopt a cost leadership approach, manufacturers such as Mercedes and BMW typically adopt a differentiation approach. Other marques, such as Ferrari and Lamborghini, now owned by larger automotive groups, focus on very tightly defined market segments. The focus strategy is concerned with servicing a particular target segment better than other competitors within the industry who adopt either focus strategies aimed at other segments or broader strategies of differentiation or cost leadership.

The dilemma facing managers is to choose the best strategy and consider if all these strategies are relevant in a digital context. Regarding the latter point, Kim, Nam and Stimpert[24] have argued that generic strategies of differentiation and cost leadership are broadly applicable to e-business firms. However, the focus strategy may not be as viable for e-business firms, compared to their more traditional counterparts.

Regarding the choice of the best strategy, do organisations have to choose between cost leadership and differentiation? Conventional strategists have suggested that attempting to follow more than one generic strategy at the same time is inappropriate as firms which attempt to do this become 'stuck in the middle', a situation where they fail to achieve a strong competitive position on any dimension. However, as Parnell has pointed out, the stuck in the middle concept has been challenged by both scholars and practitioners.[25]

There are a number of companies which have successfully adopted more than one of Porter's generic strategies and great success can result from an enterprise achieving both differentiation and cost leadership together. For example, IKEA and Toyota's Lexus product range have both been successful by creatively combining both a differentiation strategy and cost leadership strategy that results in prices lower than those of major competitors.

The Market Leaders framework

A further framework of generic strategies has been developed by US consultants Treacy and Wiersema.[26] Their 'Disciplines of Market Leaders' framework suggests three broad business strategies:

- operational excellence;
- product leadership;
- customer intimacy.

Treacy and Wiersema called these three routes to success 'value disciplines' (Figure 6.5). Based upon their research, they suggest that marketplace success is usually based upon what kind of value proposition the companies pursued – best total cost, best product or best total solution. Their work is especially useful as it is supported by many examples.

Treacy and Wiersema state: 'by operational excellence, we mean providing customers with reliable products or services at competitive prices, delivered with minimal difficulty

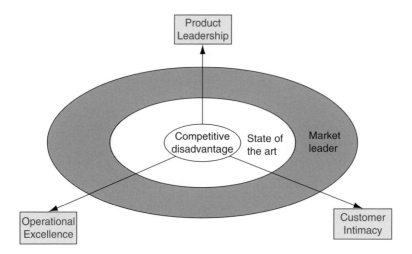

Figure 6.5 Value disciplines for market leaders

or inconvenience. By product leadership, we mean providing products that continually redefine the state of the art. And by customer intimacy, we mean selling the customer a total solution not just a product or service.'[27]

While these three 'disciplines' or 'generic' strategies should not be assumed to be mutually exclusive, it will more often be the case that companies have different strengths – or weaknesses – in each of the three. While a strong position in each of these markets should be the aim of any business, it is suggested that the activities within the business should reflect the chosen underlying generic strategy. Thus choosing one discipline to emphasise does not imply ignoring the others. As suggested by Figure 6.5, the business chooses one dimension of value upon which to base its *market reputation*.

Organisations seeking to follow the discipline of *operational excellence* need to have an internal culture that is based on 'lean thinking'. This involves focusing on continuing improvement, multi-skilling and all those CRM activities that lead to greater internal efficiency. Equally, significant emphasis must be placed upon developing superior supplier relationships since, for many organisations, the costs of materials and supplies are a major proportion of total cost. By working more closely with suppliers many opportunities for cost reduction and quality improvements can usually be identified. In the same way, it can be argued, the interface with downstream intermediaries such as distributors and retailers will need to be managed closely. For example, through the use of electronic data interchange and other forms of electronic commerce, it will often be possible to significantly enhance the responsiveness and cost-effectiveness of the supply chain.

Companies that seek to place the emphasis in their strategic focus on *product leadership* will need to invest in creating an internal culture that encourages innovation, risk-taking and entrepreneurship. Here recruitment practices need to focus on attracting and retaining people who will be able to contribute to the innovation process – perhaps with a skills profile and experience that indicate their creativity or their in-depth knowledge of technologies or markets. It is interesting to reflect that Microsoft, an acknowledged world leader in its field, has declared that its sole criterion in recruitment is 'intelligence'. Businesses that seek product leadership also need to concentrate on supplier relationships as today a significant proportion of innovation is supplier driven. Closely related to the focus on suppliers for those companies seeking product leadership is the leverage that can be gained through developing alliances with other organisations in order to capitalise on their specific skills, knowledge bases and market understanding. This is especially true of the relationships that CRM vendors have with their alliance partners.

The third 'discipline' is *customer intimacy*. This requires a continuing focus on the means whereby the relationship with customers can be made more personalised and customised. As such it is the 'internal' market that becomes of critical importance. A large amount of research confirms the impact of employee motivation and commitment on customer satisfaction. Customer intimacy emphasises building relationships with existing customers with the greatest potential for growth and profitability.

There are clear similarities between Porter's generic strategies and Treacy and Wiersema's value disciplines. As Bowman points out, operational excellence is very similar to Porter's low-cost strategy, product leadership is a strategy of differentiation through innovation and customer intimacy is a strategy of differentiation with a high degree of emphasis on service and customer relationships.[28] In terms of CRM, customer intimacy strategies are especially appropriate. Here emphasis is placed on understanding customer segments, micro-segments and determining where one-to-one strategies are appropriate – a topic which we discuss shortly.

Blue Ocean strategy

'Blue Ocean' strategy offers a fourth contrasting alternative framework for developing corporate strategy. Devised by INSEAD professors Kim and Mauborgne, this approach challenges traditional 'Red Ocean' strategies that involve considering how to compete with industry incumbents and dividing up the existing market.[29] By contrast, strategists should consider creating a Blue Ocean strategy, by identifying and defining unexplored market spaces. This involves creating new demand through offering attractive value propositions in these uncontested areas of the market.

In devising their approach, Kim and Mauborgne studied the business launches of over 150 companies. They analysed which of these were incremental changes to existing industry offerings (competing in Red Oceans, containing industries in existence today) and which of them created entirely new markets or Blue Oceans (industries not yet in existence). Unsurprisingly, they found that the majority of companies adopted a Red Ocean approach. In such instances, they calculated that revenues improved significantly, but profit gains were more sluggish. In contrast, those few companies adopting a Blue Ocean strategic approach, developing new market spaces without competitors, enjoyed high profits but with lower total revenue. They concluded that creating Blue Oceans offered a new approach for corporate strategists, with exciting opportunities for significant performance improvement.

A key characteristic common to Blue Ocean strategies is that they do not consider other industry players as a competitive benchmark. The traditional strategic approaches outlined above suggest a company chooses between offering either greater value to customers at a higher cost or creating acceptable value at a lower cost, i.e., differentiating or lowering costs. Kim and Mauborgne challenged these assumptions and suggested strategists should focus on creating new demand in untapped market spaces, driving cost down while providing greater value for customers. These authors developed a series of tools and frameworks to help managers create Blue Ocean strategies that we now describe.

The strategy canvas

This diagnostic tool allows a firm to identify the current product and service features. These factors are inherent in the industry, clarifying where current players are investing and which of these impact customer value. These factors are mapped, with a horizontal axis identifying each factor and a vertical axis depicting the value customers receive across them. The resulting value curve graphically shows a company's relative performance within its industry for each of these factors. This process identifies how companies are different, frequently illustrating that competitors choose to differentiate in similar ways – attempting to offer customers a little more for a little less. Next, the strategist considers reconstructing elements that buyers value and shifting the focus from current competition to alternative offerings for 'non-customers'. Often this may involve redefining inherent problems in an industry and coming up with new solutions that are attractive to those who are not currently customers.

The four actions framework

Once the strategy canvas is drawn up, the next task consists of reconstructing the buyer value elements identified in the strategy canvas and adding new ones, creating a new value curve. Here, four key questions force strategists to question the strategic logic of the industry and their existing business model. These questions include: which factors could be eliminated as they offer little value to customers but add cost; how factors might change if existing products and services are simplified without significant loss of value to customers; what additional factors could be added that are of high value to customers, yet currently are not offered; and, are there new sources of value, as yet inexperienced and unknown by customers, that could be added? Together, these questions allow a company to identify where to invest in offering customers a new experience that is of high value, yet with an appropriate cost structure.

The eliminate-reduce-raise-create grid

This tool supplements the frameworks described above, forcing strategists to act on the outcome of completing the strategy canvas and the four actions framework. Kim and Mauborgne suggest that by compiling a grid depicting those factors that are eliminated, reduced, raised or created, managers engage with the process of constructing a new value curve and quickly realise the benefits of this new strategic focus.

Kim and Mauborgne provide a useful approach to finding uncontested market space. In their work, these authors describe how Cirque du Soleil used Blue Ocean to devise a whole new approach within a declining industry. Cirque du Soleil recognised that many of the elements of a circus that the industry considered essential were unnecessary and often costly. Circuses traditionally tried to attract a shrinking audience through offering more of the same entertainment yet at increased costs. For example, including expensive animal acts added cost yet was often not valued, especially as public opinion challenged how circuses provided for the welfare of these creatures.

Cirque du Soleil identified that three key traditional features of the circus were highly valued by audiences: the Big Top, acrobatic acts and the clowns. The company used these three elements and added some aspects of theatre entertainment, devising a totally new form of spectacle that offered excitement and was different from other circus experiences. For example, each show has a theme and a story, providing an additional level of interest for the audience beyond the series of unrelated acts performed by a traditional circus. Similar to the theatre, the themes and stories of each performance build on each other, encouraging audiences to return again for another visit. Cirque du Soleil combines some key features of the traditional circus with those of the theatre, offering the best of both experiences while driving down costs.

Despite this example and others described in their work, critics suggest that there are few examples of success stories of companies that have applied a Blue Ocean approach to their strategy. Kim and Mauborgne describe successful innovations that can be explained from their Blue Ocean perspective, but these examples interpret the strategic approach, rather than provide evidence of companies setting out to identify new market spaces. Regardless of these criticisms, the Blue Ocean metaphor is appealing and managers can usefully apply the ideas to assist them in 'thinking out of the box'.

Focusing on business strategy

Business strategy involves development of an effective strategy or set of strategies that help the business achieve its corporate objectives. It involves undertaking an in-depth analysis of the external environment of the company and undertaking an analysis of the internal competencies of the company. The external analysis should review issues in the political, social and technological environments as well as providing an in-depth examination of markets, customers and competitors. The internal analysis consists of a review of a wide range of factors that can ultimately affect the company's success or failure. The output of these analyses should enable a thorough assessment to be made of the overall attractiveness of the business and the firm's competitive position within that business. The fundamental objective of this analysis is to identify those trends, forces and conditions that have a potential impact on the formulation and implementation of the company's strategies.

A variety of techniques can be used to help determine the business strategy. The industry analysis framework described above enables a complete and balanced analysis of the competitive environment in which a firm is operating and should lead to a good understanding of the key factors for success within that industry. Such an analysis can make a major impact on managers' understanding of their strengths and weaknesses and the opportunities and threats within their industry. The other techniques described above can also be used to support the review of business strategy.

One of the most important aspects of this analysis is the identification of the key factors for success in that business. If these key factors are not correctly identified this could have a disastrous effect on the business because it could result in an inappropriate strategy being adopted. Consequently, the identification of the key factors for success should be a high priority area when using the analytical frameworks discussed above. It should be noted that these key factors can change over time. For example, in the motor car industry the key factors for success have changed considerably in recent years. Demand has changed to smaller cars, SUVs (sports utility vehicles), four-wheel-drive vehicles and hybrid petrol/electric cars. Factors such as quality of styling, reliability, sustainability, fuel efficiency, safety and after-sales service have also become more important.

The two case studies at the end of this chapter provide excellent examples of how companies have identified the key factors for success in their respective businesses. Tesco, one of the largest retailers in the world, has built a global business based on utilising customer insight to build customer relationships. Samsung has identified the key factors for success in shifting from a marginal low-cost producer to the role of global product leadership.

The objective of addressing business strategy, as part of the strategy development process in CRM, is to determine how the enterprise's customer strategy should be developed or extended and how it will evolve in the future. For companies with a clear and appropriate business strategy, a review of it will help ensure the resulting customer strategy is properly focused. For those companies where an examination of the business strategy shows it is unclear, inappropriate or has inconsistencies, a more detailed review, using appropriate analytical techniques, needs to be carried out. The resulting analysis should lead to a carefully chosen and well-argued case for pursuing a particular business strategy. While a company can pursue any of the strategies we have outlined in this section, we consider a business strategy based on customer intimacy is particularly appropriate to the underlying principles and ethos of CRM.

Customer strategy

The second major component of the strategy development process within the CRM Strategy Framework involves deciding which customers the business wants to attract and to keep most, and which customers it would prefer to be without. In an environment of increasing competition, few firms can successfully be 'all things to all people'. Thus determining a distinctive *customer strategy* and directing all efforts to maintaining and developing it is a key means for enterprises not only to survive but also thrive.

The role of customer strategy

While business strategy is usually the responsibility of the CEO, along with the Board and strategy director, in contrast, customer strategy is typically the responsibility of the marketing department. However, as we have pointed out, both relationship marketing and CRM require a cross-functional, or 'pan-company', approach if they are to be fully effective. In reality, in most organisations, marketing is still represented by a functionally based marketing department. Responsibility for CRM is also often vested in functionally based roles, including IT and marketing, although an increasing number of enterprises are now starting to adopt a pan-company approach.

While alignment and integration of business strategy and customer strategy is a high priority for all organisations, special attention should be placed on alignment where different departments are involved in these two areas of strategy development. The prior review of business strategy will be instrumental in reaching a view on broad customer focus. However, organisations need to determine more specifically their choice of customers and their characteristics. This is the role of customer strategy.

Customer strategy involves examining the firm's existing and potential customers and identifying which forms of segmentation are most appropriate. The organisation needs to identify the characteristics of their customers and customer segments. This may require analysis of a considerable amount of customer data, which has significant implications regarding the collection and organisation of these data in appropriate data repositories, such as a data warehouse. We examine this topic in Chapter 9. As part of this process, the organisation also needs to consider 'segment granularity', which involves considering the appropriate level of sub-division of customer segments. This involves making decisions about whether a macro-, micro- or one-to-one segmentation approach is appropriate.

Customer choice and characteristics: the role of market segmentation

It is important to recognise that because customers differ significantly, the relationships developed with customers will have to be managed differently if they are to be successful. This is a key principle of CRM. The aim of CRM is to build relationship strategies that refine and redefine relationships and in this way increase their value. Creating competitive advantage through the skilful management of customer relationships will normally require a reappraisal of the way in which customers are approached and segmented and the way in which resources are allocated and used. To achieve this level of refinement requires a careful choice of the levels at which segmentation is undertaken. However, first we need to consider the nature of the 'customer'.

Who is the customer?

For businesses that sell directly to final consumers, the answer to the question 'who is the customer?' may seem straightforward. However, many companies, in at least parts of their business, sell their products and services through some form of intermediary. In such cases the issue 'who is the customer?' becomes more complicated. The 'customer' may include three broad groups: direct buyers, intermediaries and final consumers such as those shown in Figure 6.6. We discussed this issue briefly in Chapter 4 in the context of the customer market domain.

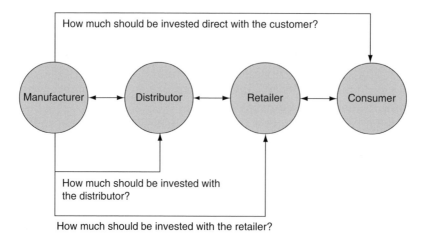

Figure 6.6 Balance marketing effort directed at the 'customer'

Where companies operate in an intermediated market they need to consider carefully 'who is the customer?' The answer is, of course, *all of them* are customers and the company needs to balance the amount of time, money and effort that should be directed at each group.

We have found many businesses where this is poorly balanced. Examples include:

- a fast moving consumer goods (FMCG) company which placed most of its emphasis on an advertising programme aimed at final consumers; in doing so it failed to build strong enough relationships with its retailers;
- a consumer durables company that placed most of its emphasis on trade marketing to the retailer; as a result it failed to invest enough resources to build the brand franchise with its final consumers;
- a 'captive' finance company of a major car manufacturer that historically had placed virtually all of its effort on the motor dealers; more recently it has recognised the importance of the retention of final customers and has readdressed this balance.

Further, advances in information technology are changing the nature and importance of different groups. Many organisations are now finding that in order to build stronger relationships with final consumers they need to change the emphasis and expenditure at different channel levels or, alternatively, refocus the existing expenditure in ways that build deeper and more sustained relationships. This may mean monitoring, or engaging in new areas, where and how customers interact in social media and in brand communities. In some industries, intermediaries are becoming increasingly valuable channel members, while in others the value of intermediaries is being challenged. We will examine the role of intermediaries in more detail in Chapter 8.

Market segmentation

In both business-to-business and business-to-consumer markets, market segmentation is essential for the successful development of a customer strategy. Once companies understand the distinctive characteristics of their segments they can adopt a much more targeted approach to their customers. As the previous section suggests, in intermediated businesses segmentation may need to be undertaken at the distributor, intermediary and final consumer levels.

Market segmentation involves dividing a total market up into a series of sub-markets (or market segments) based on customer characteristics. A market segmentation exercise involves the following steps:

- defining the relevant market to be addressed;
- determining the criteria for market segment viability;
- considering the alternative bases for segmentation;
- choosing specific segments to focus on.

As part of this process, the degree of disaggregation of segments, or segment granularity, needs to be determined.

Definition of the relevant market

The definition of the relevant market to be addressed involves specifying the broad customer group at which the company is seeking to market its products or services. In undertaking this task, the organisation needs to consider its strengths and weaknesses and review the resources which are available to it. The choice of the market to be addressed or 'served market' will be based around decisions relating to:

- the breadth of the service line;
- the types of customers;
- the geographic scope;
- the areas of 'value-added' in which the service firm decides to operate.

Successful market segmentation means satisfying the needs of existing and potential customers in a clearly defined market. This involves understanding customer attitudes and customer preferences as well as the benefits which are sought. Definition of the target market and its requirements is the first essential step in the segmentation process.

Criteria for market segment viability

The identification and selection of particular market segments for targeting with a distinctive offering may depend on many factors, but particularly on the size of the segment; their special needs; the extent to which these needs are already being met by the company or by competitors; and whether the company has the resources available to meet the service requirements.

There are various widely accepted criteria for determining if a market segment is viable:

- the segment must be measurable in size and characteristics;
- the segment must be meaningful. It must be capable of generating sufficient long-run profit to merit separate marketing attention;
- the segment must be reachable within budget confines;

- the segment must be durable over time; if the distinction between segments is likely to diminish as the product or service matures, then it is not suitable for a segmented marketing approach.

Companies may wish to develop their own criteria according to their specific circumstances.

Considering the alternative bases for segmentation

Markets may be segmented in many ways, but the following categories are the most important in business-to-business (B2B) and business-to-consumer (B2C) segmentation. These categories include both traditional forms of segmentation, such as demographics, and more contemporary value, or needs-based, segmentation.

Business-to-business market segmentation

Segmentation by industry type: The segmentation of markets on the basis of Standard Industrial Classification (SIC) is quite widespread, but only partially useful. Sometimes these segments are thought of as 'vertical' markets and defined around business sectors such as the construction industry or the telecoms industry. The problem with this type of segmentation is that it provides no guide as to how the behaviour of buyers might differ simply because they happen to be in different industries.

Segmentation by service: This approach is concerned with how customers respond to service offerings. Companies can offer a range of different service options and provide different service levels within those options, giving them considerable scope to design service packages appropriate to different market segments. If a supplier measures the perceived importance of different customer service elements across market segments, they can respond to that segment's identified needs and allocate an appropriate service offering to it.

Segmentation by value sought: Different customers may respond differently to the seller's 'value offering'. Knowing what customers value and what weight they put on the different elements of a value proposition can help a company develop more targeted solutions. It is critical to have a deep understanding of the motivations behind the purchase decision.

Business-to-consumer market segmentation

Geographic segmentation: This approach differentiates customers on the basis of where they are located. So customers may be segmented into urban, suburban or rural groups, for example. Customers are commonly segmented by postcodes, which might also represent different groups in terms of relative wealth and socio-economic and other factors.

Demographic and socio-economic segmentation: This is based on a wide range of factors including age, sex, family size, income, education, social class and ethnic origins. So it is helpful in indicating the profile of people who buy a company's products or services.

Psychographic segmentation: This involves analysing lifestyle characteristics, attitudes and personality. Recent research in several countries suggests that the population can be divided into between 10 and 15 groups, each of which has an identifiable set of lifestyle, attitude and personality characteristics.

Benefit segmentation: This groups customers together on the basis of the benefits they are seeking from a product. For example, car buyers seek widely varying benefits, from fuel economy, size and boot space, to performance, reliability or prestige.

Usage segmentation: This is a very important variable for many products. It usually divides consumers into heavy users, medium users, occasional users and non-users of the product or service in question. Marketers are often concerned with the heavy user segment.

Loyalty segmentation: This involves identifying customers' loyalty to a brand or product. Customers tend to be very loyal, moderately loyal or disloyal. These groups are then examined to try to identify any common characteristics so the product can be targeted at prospectively loyal customers.

Occasion segmentation: This recognises that customers may use a product or brand in different ways depending on the situation. For example, a beer drinker may drink light beer with his colleagues after work, a conventional beer in his home and a premium or imported beer at a special dinner in a licensed restaurant.

Both B2C and B2B companies, at least initially, need to categorise markets according to value preferences or benefits sought when undertaking market segmentation. If organisations understand what different customers value and how this influences their purchase decisions, then they can subsequently see if those value preferences correlate with other segmentation criteria.

Choosing specific segments

Organisations are now taking a more rigorous approach to segment choice. For example, one bank examined the number and percentage of heads of households in each lifestyle category in terms of:

- *demographic profile*: including age of household head, occupation, education, home ownership, number of full time wage earners in household, annual household income and net worth and average balances;
- *service penetration*: by transaction accounts, regular savings accounts and time deposits. Details of credit services, credit cards used, trust-related services and electronic funds transfer services were included;
- *average dollars balance*: by transactions accounts, savings accounts, time deposits, instalment credit and revolving lines of credit.

The bank then measured the dollars profit produced after each dollar of delivery cost required to service that segment before deciding on which segments it wished to concentrate on. Further segmentation followed and predictive modelling was used to explore the likelihood that customers might take a particular course of future action. Predictive modelling is used in areas including product cross-sell, product up-sell, churn management and lifetime value analysis.

Choice of the resulting target markets segments should be based on detailed review of existing and potential value and profitability of the segments. Identification of the economic value of customer segments to the enterprise is critical. This is where there is a high degree of interactivity between the strategy development process and the enterprise value creation process. The strategy development process leads to an initial view being taken on the present and future economic desirability of different segments. The enterprise value creation process refines this view by identifying segment variables such as expected acquisition costs, profit per customer, retention rates and customer acquisition targets. These variables can then be used to identify economic value of different segments including estimates of annual contribution and profitability and lifetime value expressed in terms of net present value.

We have now reviewed the four steps involved in the market segmentation process. However, choice of customer segments has an additional layer of complexity – segment granularity. Added to this is the possibility that some customers may fit into more than one segment. This can result in the need for a more detailed analysis of economic value at a more stratified level before final choice of segments can be made.

Segment granularity: from mass marketing to 'one-to-one' marketing

In addition to considering the relevant segmentation base for its business, the company also needs to consider the *level of segmentation*. Segment granularity refers to the decision of whether a macro-segmentation, micro-segmentation or a 'one-to-one' approach to segmentation should be adopted. We can also call this one-to-one approach 'individualisation' or 'personalisation'.

Decisions regarding level of segmentation need to be taken in the context of a number of considerations including: the existing and potential profitability of different customer types; the available information on customers; the opportunity to 'reach' customers in terms of both communication and physical delivery; and the cost of doing it. Figure 6.7

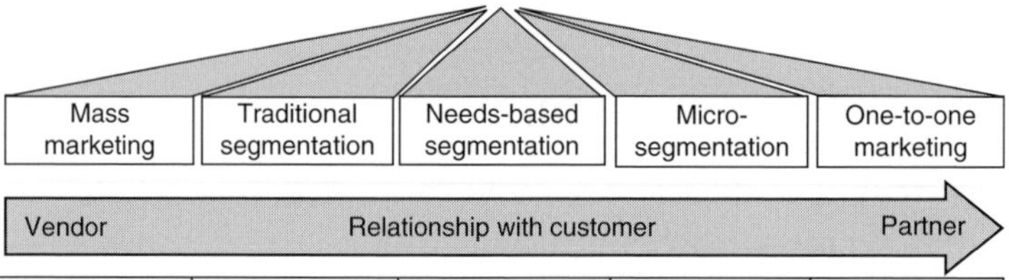

	Mass marketing	Traditional segmentation	Needs-based segmentation	Micro-segmentation	One-to-one marketing
Vendor ——— Relationship with customer ——— Partner					
Key focus:	Product	Segment	Segment	Micro-Segment	Customer
Market segment:	One segment-homogeneous market	Segments based on demographics, etc.	Segments based on psychographics, lifestyles, etc.	Narrowly defined, high value segments	Segment of one
Product/service offering:	One standard offering	Offerings modified to segment	Integrated offerings to segment needs	Integrated offerings to micro-segment needs	Mass-customisation
Communication:	Broadcast marketing	Tallored messages	Tallored messages	Highly tallored messages	Dialogue marketing
Measure of success:	Market share	Segment share	Segment share	Segment share	Share of customer

Figure 6.7 Levels of segmentation emphasis

provides an overview of the options in terms of levels of segmentation, together with the tailoring of the product or service offer; the style of communication needed and suggested means of measuring success.[30]

'One-to-one' markets and permission marketing

We are now seeing markets fragment into ever smaller segments. Customers – consumers and organisations – are now increasingly seeking specific solutions to their buying 'problems'. Organisations cannot just offer a choice these days; they have to be able to meet their customers' precise requirements. Relationships will increasingly need to be built on the platform of individualised marketing, where the customer and the supplier in effect create a unique and mutually satisfactory exchange process. The Internet now provides a powerful means of involving customers much more closely in the marketing process through enabling dialogue rather than one-way communication.

As we discussed briefly in Chapter 1, much attention has been directed at the leading edge work by consultants Don Peppers and Martha Rogers.[31] Their work has excited many managers with respect to the potential for shifting from a mass market to an individualised or *one-to-one marketing* environment. Exploiting e-commerce opportunities and the fundamental economic characteristics of the Internet can enable a much deeper level of segmentation granularity than is affordable in most other channels.

However, segment granularity needs to be examined in the company and industry context in which it is being considered. In some cases, especially in an e-commerce environment, a migration to a 'one-to-one' or a 'one-to-few' may be undertaken relatively easily. However, in more traditional businesses, more 'macro' forms of segmentation may be relevant. Of course, many companies in the B2B sector have for a long time adopted one-to-one marketing through a key account management system, although it has not been referred to as such.

An obvious but important point is that 'one-to-one' marketing does not imply adopting a 'one-to-one' approach with every single customer. Rather, it suggests understanding customers in terms of their economic importance and then adjusting the marketing approach to reflect the importance of different customer groups according to their existing and potential profitability. Peppers and Rogers emphasise this in their work; however, it is sometimes disregarded when a discussion of one-to-one marketing is underway.

Permission marketing is especially relevant in the context of one-to-one relationships. Seth Godin introduced the concept of permission marketing, which involves consumers giving marketers permission to send them certain types of promotional messages.[32] Proponents of permission marketing argue that the biggest problem with mass marketing is that it fights for people's attention by interrupting them. Potential customers are often annoyed when their most coveted commodity – time – is interrupted. Permission marketing involves offering consumers incentives to accept information and promotional activity voluntarily. By reaching out only to those individuals who have signalled an interest in learning more about a product, permission marketing enables companies to develop long-term relationships with customers, create trust, build brand awareness and greatly improve the chances of making a sale. However, most individuals are unlikely to join a permission marketing programme just to make some monetary benefit. The main attraction is to receive promotional offers consistent with their needs.

Interactive technology means that marketers can now inexpensively engage consumers in one-to-one relationships fuelled by two-way 'conversations' played out with mouse clicks on a computer, or touch-tone buttons on a telephone pushed to signal to an interactive voice response application, or surveys completed by mail or at a kiosk. Although permission marketing can be implemented in any direct medium, it has emerged as a serious idea only with the advent of the Internet due to the low cost of marketer-to-consumer communication and the rapid feedback mechanisms due to instantaneous two-way interactions.

Reflecting on the development and use of permission marketing, Godin points out that its major measurable impact is the growth of truly opt-in marketing 'from close to zero to a number big enough that we've all seen it and are part of it'.[33] Permission-based, ethical e-mail marketing has become a $1 billion industry with a substantial number of companies being built on the simple concept. The growth and potential of this sector was demonstrated by US cable company Comcast's purchase of DailyCandy.com, an e-mail newsletter on style and beauty based in New York. DailyCandy expanded to publish editions specific to a dozen other cities. It is essentially a permission marketing engine but was sold for $125 million! Permission marketing is having an increasingly important role to play in personalising communications in a one-to-one context.

Mass customisation

Closely related to one-to-one marketing is the concept of mass customisation. One-to-one marketing requires individual solutions for individual buying problems. Customers may not want the physical product to be differentiated, although many do, but require the accompanying service package to be tailored. Today, efforts are being directed at developing cost-effective strategies to achieve what is termed 'mass customisation'.[34] Mass customisation is the ability to take standard components, elements or modules and, through customer-specific combinations or configurations, produce a tailored solution.

In a manufacturing sector, the aim would be to produce generic semi-finished products in volume to achieve economies of scale and then finish the product later to meet individual customers' requirements. An oft-quoted example of mass customisation is the Japanese National Bicycle Company, which offers customers the opportunity to configure their own bicycle from different style, colour, size and components options. Within two weeks the company delivers the tailored bike to the customer. The company has become the market leader in Japan as a result of this marketing and logistics innovation.

However, as Kaplan and Haenlein point out it is only through recent advances in manufacturing technology and information technology, including the Internet, that mass customisation has become a viable option for a broader range of products.[35] In an online environment, mass customisation is made possible because it enables information about an individual's particular interests and needs to be captured, stored and processed each time the individual interacts with the company. The company can then use this knowledge to guide the specific offers made to customers in the future.

With each successive interaction, the company can learn more about that specific customer and adapt their offer to be even more suited to the customer's particular needs and circumstances. In a sense, the customer is progressively teaching the company about him or herself in order to receive a product or service that is ever more tailored to his or her needs and that is thus of greater value. The understanding the firm gains of its customers can then be used not only to drive the offers made to the customers in the immediate term but also to drive the longer-term strategic development of the organisation, the alliances it forms with other organisations and the products and services it offers in the future.

Peppers and Rogers, working with consultant Joseph Pine, distinguish between the production process of mass customisation and the parallel marketing approach of 'one-to-one' strategy:

A company that aspires to give customers exactly what they want must ... use technology to become two things: a mass customizer that efficiently provides individually customized goods and services, and a one-to-one marketer that elicits information from each customer about his or her specific needs and preferences. The twin logic of mass customization and one-to-one marketing binds producer and consumer together in what we call a learning relationship – an ongoing connection that becomes smarter as the two interact with each other, collaborating to meet the consumer's needs over time.[36]

As well as ensuring that the organisation develops in line with the needs of its most valuable customers, mass customisation helps retain customers. The tailored service customers receive is a result of them 'teaching' the company about themselves over the lifetime of their relationship. To receive the same service from a competitor would involve that organisation having to learn about the customers from 'scratch', which will of course take time. Thus, if a company practises mass customisation effectively, its customers are presented with a significant switching cost if they defect to a competitor organisation.

Under mass customisation, the value proposition the organisation offers its customers ceases simply to reside in the individual products it offers them. Rather it lies in the company becoming a trusted partner who can be relied upon to meet the customer's ongoing individual needs over time, helping customers live their lives. As a result it becomes more difficult for customers to make simple direct comparisons between one company and another on a product-by-product basis, helping to alleviate downward price pressure and commoditisation.

Achieving mass customisation involves attending to three areas. First, the company needs to set up the technological infrastructure to enable it to have a dialogue with its customers individually and capture their responses. Second, it needs to have the means of processing those data if this dialogue is to enable the firm to gain an ever better understanding of its customers as individuals. Finally, it needs to be able to structure its processes such that the organisation's manufacturing of products or services is customised to the needs of individual customers. These areas represent fundamental changes for most organisations but, in the emerging network economy, their implementation not only offers high rewards; in many cases it will also be imperative for survival.

Communities or segments?

One of the problems inherent in segmentation is that customers may not conform to the neat market segments that companies allocate them to. Consider the dilemma faced by an airline in allocating a specific individual customer to a market segment and understanding his or her purchasing behaviour.

Initially, the airline has only a limited amount of information on this particular customer's travel with that airline based on details of frequent flyer or executive club activity. If the airline has records of three business class and three economy tickets for this customer – what are they to make of this?

The airline may then develop a data warehouse that captures all that passenger's travel with their airline, including travel not registered on the frequent flyer card database (by, for example, requesting details of the passport number each time the customer takes a flight). As a result, they identify that the passenger has made five business class trips and three economy trips over a two-year period – but what are they to make of this limited data?

If they seek more complete data by incentivising this customer to keep a complete diary of all airline travel, or if they can collect the information through market research, the picture for this frequently travelling executive may be very different. Suppose the full diary for all airlines shows the following return trips: two first class; eight business class; and 12 economy – but what are they to make of this more complete data?

Making sense of this is difficult until you understand that the customer is a member of a number of different *communities*. His travel type may depend on whether he is acting as a business executive, a member of a sports club or a family member. Even within a given community he may purchase different types of travel. A brief interview with this customer elicited the following 'rules' for his travel purchase behaviour within each community (see box).

Business executive community member: always travels business class (exceptions: his director sent him first class when he had to travel on his birthday and he had just sold a huge project to a client; when he is on overseas business trips he may be accompanied by family members and travel economy class provided the costs to the company of both tickets does not exceed one business class fare).

Family community member: always travels on cheapest economy fare on vacations as he prefers to spend money on quality accommodation; but only on flights up to 12 hours (exceptions: for trips of over 12 hours to Asia and Australasia the family travel on the cheapest business class tickets available; for his tenth wedding anniversary he travelled on first class with his wife to the US).

Sports club community member: always travels on cheapest economy fare with his football club (exceptions: none – the club never chooses a location to which cheap tickets cannot be purchased).

The airline, armed with this knowledge as well as share of wallet information on the relative use of their airline and competitive airlines can then mould their CRM programme on an individual basis to such clients. The challenge is to identify if this information can be collected and acted upon in a cost-effective manner. Acquiring such customer knowledge on *all* customers, even the highest value ones, is not likely to be cost-effective in most businesses. However, the insights gained from selective market research can be used to identify customers who are members of such communities.

Focusing on customer strategy

Customer strategy involves taking the business strategy and identifying which customer the enterprise needs to focus on. It starts with a definition of the target market to be served and how it plans to serve this market. In an intermediated market, the enterprise recognises that it may have a number of customer groups and each of these needs to be fully considered. Regardless of whether the customer group comprises distributors, intermediaries or final consumers, an effective customer strategy requires each group to be segmented in an appropriate manner.

The market segmentation process involves consideration of the alternative bases for segmenting the market and determining the appropriate level of segmentation – macro-, micro- or one-to-one. In the Chapter 7 we provide an example of a UK electricity supplier that historically treated all residential customers in the same way. About six mailings per annum were sent to every customer and no attempt was made at segmentation. The review of customer economics outlined in Chapter 7 illustrates how macro-, micro- and one-to-one segmentation approaches were all applicable depending on the segment or sub-segment economics.

The identification of segmentation bases and the appropriate level of segment granularity should involve a high degree of creativity. Companies should constantly be considering alternative ways of segmenting the market and seeking ways in which they can create differential advantage over their competitors. Readers needing a more detailed discussion on market segmentation should consult a standard text on market segmentation such as McDonald and Dunbar's work.[37]

Once the organisation has identified and chosen the appropriate customer segments to target and the level of segment granularity, the enterprise needs to focus on the customer relationships within them. Here permission marketing, mass customisation and whether a customer fits into more than one segment or community need to be considered.

Customer strategy is not only concerned with which customer segments to serve but also what products and services to sell to them. Although the latter is primarily a concern of product policy and marketing planning some brief discussion should be made here.

Product and service options for a company can be conveniently divided into existing products and services and new products and services. When these options are placed in a matrix with present and new products on one axis and present and new markets or customer segments on the other this gives rise to the following four broad product/market options:

- concentrating on marketing existing products or services to existing markets;
- developing new products or services for existing markets;
- developing new markets or customer segments for existing products or services;
- diversifying into new products for new markets or customer segments.

Each of these broad customer strategies represents a number of specific opportunities. These are shown in Figure 6.8.

PRODUCTS

	Present	New
Present	**Market penetration** 1. Increasing number of users 　(a) attracting competitor's users 　(b) converting non-users into users 2. Increasing purchasing frequency 3. Increasing average quantity 　purchased per transaction 4. Increasing lifetime value 　(customer retention)	**Product development** 1. Product improvement 2. Product quality extensions 3. Product line extension 4. New product development
New	**Market development** 1. Increasing number of users 　in new market segments in 　present geographic market 2. Increasing number of users in 　new market segments 　(a) Regional 　(b) National 　(c) International expansion	**Diversification** 1. Concentric 2. Conglomerate

MARKET

Figure 6.8 Review of product/service and market/customer segment options

A final issue to consider under the heading of customer strategy is the need for creativity and innovation. In an era of unparalleled change and 'hyper-competition' managers need to pay special attention to this aspect, as the traditional approach of identifying and responding to new customers' needs is not enough. Figure 6.9 illustrates the dangers of an approach that is highly dependent on traditional market research as a source of new initiatives. By just considering present ideas from market research, the value opportunities are greatly restricted. Companies such as 3M and Sony rely just as heavily on their own creativity and intuition with respect to new market developments as they do on customer research. Customers often cannot clearly articulate their future needs. Companies who do not think outside their traditional mindset will find their customers going to those competitors who do.

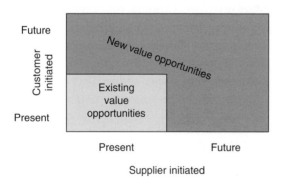

Figure 6.9 The danger of 'current focus'

A great example of such creativity is the initiative launched by Starbucks when they introduced their mobile Internet service in the early 2000s. This service enabled customers to have wireless Internet connection in Starbucks' coffee outlets (see Figure 6.10). The initiative resulted in a significantly increased revenue stream through an initial subscription service as well as increased revenue in its core business. An added benefit was that many customers used this service outside peak times. The revenue model changed over time. As wireless networks became more widespread, Starbucks reduced its pricing and had a set fee for two hours of Internet use. From 2010, the service in the US became free for customers. Customers with a registered Starbucks loyalty card can now get two hours of free wireless Internet access. Although wireless networks have now been replicated by other companies such as McDonald's, Starbucks benefited from a 'first mover advantage' and customers have formed a 'Starbucks habit'.

Starbucks' wireless Internet initiative

- Starbucks' 'T-Mobile Hot Spot service' offered wireless Internet connectivity in about 2,000 initial locations in the US and Europe in early 2000s

- Used technology to enhance its core offer–the Starbvcks experience.

- $5 for a cup of coffee and initially $49.99 per month for a wireless connection. Later they charged for two hour blocks of usage. From mid 2010 the service became free.

- The average network customer is in the store 45 minutes, which exceeds average, 90% outside peak times; they buy more products and created revenue from the wireless network subscriptions

- Starbucks aims at becoming the 'other place' in people's lives where they can be connected to the Internet.

- Wireless access replicated by others, but customers had formed a 'Starbucks habit'.

Figure 6.10 Starbucks' wireless Internet initiative

Aligning business strategy and customer strategy

As noted earlier, alignment and integration of business strategy and customer strategy should be a high priority, especially where they are developed within different functions of the business. This lack of alignment between business strategies may be more common than expected. One of the authors ran a CRM workshop as part of a ten-day senior management development programme for a group of country heads and senior executives for a well-known consumer durables brand. One of the country heads reported that the contents of a workshop on business strategy held on the previous day, given by the Group Strategic Planning Director, 'had absolutely no connection to the real-life customer strategy issues and problems in his country'. His colleagues from other countries unanimously agreed with him. Subsequent discussion showed major gaps in alignment between the business strategy and customer strategy and the specific needs of the customers in many of their country markets.

Experienced observers of industry, be they managers, consultants or academics, will have their own examples of instances where business strategy and customer strategy are not clearly aligned or where they come into conflict (see box for an example).

The Leisure Group

The Leisure Group was formed by two young MBAs who had recently left a leading firm of US strategy consultants. Over a number of years they purchased some 13 companies operating in the leisure industry. These were organised into three divisions – lawn and garden, youth recreation and sporting goods. A further acquisition, Himalayan Industries – a manufacturer of backpacks based in Monterey, California – was considered for purchase. Despite a clear business strategy and a set of acquisition criteria at group level, which indicated that the candidate was a poor strategic fit and far too small in terms of turnover, this business was acquired.

Prior to the acquisition, Himalayan's progress had been restricted by a poor choice of distribution partner, inadequate marketing and restrictions in capacity in the company's operations. Following the acquisition of Himalayan, an extremely expensive marketing campaign was introduced. A completely new range of backpacking equipment was designed. The marketing programme was complex in terms of different quality levels being introduced and a significant number of new product lines being developed.

Expensive design and marketing consultants were involved and a considerable amount of time was spent on the programme by the parent company's top management. Although the company's existing sales were very small in relation to other companies within the group, a disproportionate amount of resources and effort was placed on the customer strategy and marketing activity.

However, from a group perspective, the company should not have been acquired in the first place as it was not a good fit with the existing product lines and placed additional stress on the already heavily extended group sales force. In terms of the company's business strategy, the amount of resources and money spent on the customer strategy was not justified by the future business prospects of the new subsidiary.

This lack of fit between business strategy and customer strategy resulted in the subsidiary's subsequent sale 'because it resulted in the diversion of working capital that would be better placed in more profitable businesses'. Not long afterwards, the parent company experienced huge losses and collapsed. The clear conclusion was that business strategy and customer strategy were not aligned and that the business leaders were better at acquiring companies than effectively running them.

CRM strategy development

Business strategy and customer strategy form the major components of the strategy development process. From our earlier discussion it is clear that a given organisation needs to consider its current position within its industry and the future role it realistically can play within it. Central to this will be making decisions about customer choice, customer characteristics and segment granularity. This includes determining the extent to which an individualised customer, or one-to-one, approach is appropriate and affordable for the enterprise and determining the completeness of customer information that exists and is potentially available. Such decisions should be based on both the present situation and the possible situation in the future. In this section we discuss how a consideration of business and customer strategies leads to CRM strategy development.

Researchers investigating reasons for success and failure of CRM identify that frequently a company has insufficient and inaccurate customer information on which to build a robust CRM platform.[38] A fundamental decision for a company when considering a CRM strategy is determining the type of relationship that is appropriate and possible for different customers, from both the customer and the organisation's perspectives. Deck points out that for CRM strategy to be truly effective, the firm must decide what kind of customer information it is looking for and what it intends to do with that information.[39] The CRM strategy matrix, shown in Figure 6.11, provides a tool for considering a company's present and future circumstances.

The vertical axis of the framework in this figure shows *completeness of customer information*. This dimension includes determining how much information is held on customers and the level of sophistication in the analysis of that information. This involves a

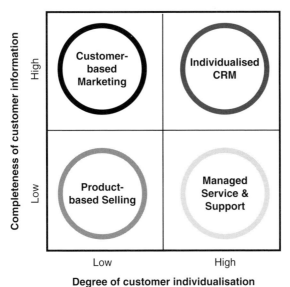

Figure 6.11 The CRM strategy matrix

consideration not only of what information we have internally within the organisation, but also what information we can get access to. The rise of social media together with recent capabilities for the capture and analysis of information derived from the social media provides a new important source of data. This includes information about what customers think about the brand, their experiences with customer service and support and other aspects, such as product features and pricing. It also provides competitive information; for example, how does a new iPhone stack up against the Google android phone?

The horizontal axis shows the *degree of customer individualisation* – the extent to which the organisation can use whatever information it has on customers to give them individualised or customised service. The matrix shows four broad strategic positions and forms of CRM which may be appropriate for an organisation. Adoption of a given form of CRM will depend on the strategic issues identified above and the organisation's specific circumstances.

CRM strategies

The matrix identifies four alternative strategic approaches towards customer relationships.[40] Some organisations may consider that an optimal customer strategy involves immediately migrating customer relationships towards greater customer individualisation using more complete customer information. However, consideration of this approach should be undertaken with caution. A decision about the migration strategy should only be taken after careful assessment of the trade-off of cost and benefits of developing these individualised relationships. Relationships that are tailored to a specific customer require significant knowledge about all aspects of customer buying behaviour. Acquiring and maintaining accurate and complete data on a customer is time consuming and expensive and is only appropriate when customers or customer segments have sufficient profit potential. Equally important is an assessment of the extent to which a customer wishes to engage in an individualised relationship with an organisation.

Different industry sectors are moving at varying rates towards individualised customer relationships. Some sectors that are suited to online channels have advanced very quickly and have taken advantage of cost efficient data collection and data mining opportunities. For example, Amazon.com has developed a business model around individualised customer relationships, quickly realising that using knowledge willingly supplied by customers helps provide a level of customisation that sets Amazon apart from many other booksellers. Other industries that have been slower to adopt online channels face a greater challenge in acquiring and maintaining robust customer data. For example, the financial services industry has struggled with legacy systems, inaccurate customer data and product-focused processes, forming a significant barrier to developing individualised customer relationships. Four strategy options suggested by the matrix are now examined.

Product-based selling

Where there is little collection and use of customer information and a low level of customisation to the specific requirements of an individual customer, then marketing efforts tend to focus on products. In such cases data analysis involves understanding profitability by product and channel, with little attention given to understanding the characteristics of customer segments. Often there are insufficient data to analyse individual customer buying behaviour. *Product-based selling*, represented on the lower left quadrant of the CRM strategy matrix, dominates much of the FMCG industry. Only relatively recently have some FMCG companies started gathering data on individual consumers. Typically, companies in this sector have organised themselves around products and brands, measuring brand performance and relying on intermediaries to develop relationships with customers. However, in recent years, there has been renewed attention on engaging consumers. Even with a relatively unsophisticated database, overlaying data from external sources can improve the depth of market analysis. For example, operational data can be combined with purchased mailing lists to give a more detailed picture of customers. Customer profiling tools such as Mosaic, a geo-demographic analytical tool, can be used in this way.

Product-based selling may be entirely appropriate to certain industries and organisations. For example, a small retailer may have excellent information about the sales and profitability for specific products, but may have little information that links individual purchases to a customer. Customers make frequent purchases in such stores and the personal contact between store owner and customer maintains a strong relationship. However, larger retailers and supermarkets recognise the value of developing detailed profiles of their customers and have used methods such as loyalty cards to gather vast amounts of data on their customers. Using these data, they can develop customised approaches and enhance customer loyalty.

Managed service and support

On the lower right-hand position of the CRM strategy matrix is *managed service and support*. This quadrant represents business situations where there is a limited amount of customer data but relatively high levels of customer individualisation. From our research, we have learned that most companies tend to move from product-based selling to managed service and support as the first development of their CRM capabilities, often by setting up call centres and help desks. An inbound call centre may provide excellent customer service and assistance as a means of retaining and building customer relationships, yet collection and use of customer data are not extensive. This form of CRM often utilises a limited amount of customer information, as the interaction is typically between a customer and the customer service staff who respond directly to customer queries. In some cases, relevant information is captured. When such data are available and readily accessible to customer service staff, customer relationships can become more individualised.

Technology can be very useful in managing customer service with this form of CRM. For example, a sales force automation system can link a salesperson in the field to their office base via a laptop, smart phone or other smart device. The system allows rapid order processing and order status enquiring, which is beneficial during the sales process. This form of CRM has led to substantial improvements in the productivity of field-based sales forces.

Utilities, such as companies providing electricity, gas and water, are good examples of organisations adopting the managed service and support form of CRM. Here much of the communication with customers is through a call centre where a customer may be channelled into broad segments such as 'business' and 'residential'. The services provided are product focused with individual customer service tailored only through the person-to-person dialogue. Customer data are used primarily for product management, for example to enhance sales forecasting, and are used only to a limited extent to enhance the customer relationship by organisations adopting this form of CRM.

Customer-based marketing

In the top left-hand quadrant of the framework is *customer-based marketing*. Organisations adopting this form of CRM focus more on the customer and move away from just tracking individual product sales. In this form of CRM, the customers become the number one focus of a CRM strategy. Here the organisation seeks to gain a detailed understanding of customers and use this knowledge to tailor relationships with them. An organisation may use data to understand aspects of customer behaviour including profitability, competitor responses, churn management, customer loyalty, risk management and causes of defection. Data from individual customers are grouped into customer segments, profiling those with similar characteristics that require similar types of relationships with their supplier. For example, the amount a supplier may choose to invest in developing relationships with a group of customers may be calculated by the profit potential and propensity to churn of that segment. The segment characteristics may determine the offer made to these customers and the opportunities to maximise customer profitability by individual cross-selling and up-selling activities. Although companies adopting customer-based CRM have a more customised approach to relationships with their customers than those adopting a product focus, they still do not provide highly individualised customer service.

Tesco, the highly successful UK supermarket chain, has focused on customer-based marketing. The company owes much of its success to the intelligent use of customer data. Tesco has gathered vast amounts of data on individual customers, largely through the Tesco Clubcard. This loyalty card, which accumulates transaction data on customer purchases, allows the supermarket to refine aspects of the store layout, product positioning and presentation to enhance the customer buying experience. Tesco uses customer information to alter the mix of products carried by a store based on demographic profiling and customer profitability analysis. The retailer has developed 'own-label' products that exactly match the needs and aspirations of customer segments with high net lifetime values. Based on detailed knowledge of segments, Tesco develops new products and promotes them more effectively to carefully selected customer segments. In the grocery industry, data ownership has caused a shift in the balance of power, so companies like Tesco are able to sell customer data to manufacturers. These suppliers are increasingly dependent upon Tesco as they require the customer data to help refine their offer. Tesco has now progressed towards more individualised interactions with their customers.

Individualised CRM

The fourth form of CRM, *individualised CRM*, is characterised by full customer data with technology being used to provide a high degree of customisation. Success is dependent upon accurate and complete customer data with technology utilised to assemble, store and mine this source of customer knowledge. Data platforms and applications are used to intelligently exploit data. For example, these applications may include advanced computer-telephony integration, which allows a call centre operator to interrogate customer data and respond with individualised service to the customer. Channels may be closely integrated with data assembled, analysed and accessed across channels permitting individualised customer relationships.

Individualised CRM (or personalised CRM) is particularly relevant to companies using multiple channels.[41] Here, integrating customer data across channels is especially important when delivering a consistent customer experience. Sophisticated systems allow customer information to instantly feed back into the main operational systems so that it is readily accessible regardless of channel. Tesco's huge resource of customer data has allowed the supermarket recently to move from customised CRM, in the form of customer-based marketing, towards individualised CRM.

Individualised CRM operates through any channel and does not necessarily involve face-to-face contact. A considerable challenge for companies adopting this form of CRM is managing, within their organisation, the distinct internal sub-cultures associated with different channels. For example, there may be resistance between direct sales channels and online channels, resulting in a reluctance to share information. Salespeople may see their power eroded if valuable customer data are passed to central operating systems.

Sophisticated CRM applications require integration of different channels, including e-commerce systems, with a customer-orientated data warehouse that is able to use customer intelligence from the Internet. An essential feature of this approach is an enterprise data warehouse which captures data and is the memory for the system, enabling the customer to be given a totally individualised and coordinated service across all CRM interfaces. Several components are typically needed. These include a specially designed Web front-end for interacting with the customer; sophisticated application software for the capture, navigation, processing and matching of customers to products and services; a link to other customer systems such as the call centre and field sales support systems; and links to the main operational systems. We discuss these issues further in Chapter 9.

Transition paths for CRM

The CRM Strategy Framework outlined above also provides a migration path for companies to follow in the progressive development of their CRM activities. A product-based selling approach is appropriate in the very early stages of CRM, where there is little use of data with which to develop individual customer relationships. Despite massive investment in CRM systems, remarkably few companies appear to have achieved successful individualised CRM. Increasingly companies have successfully implemented managed service and support or customer-based marketing, but have not made the further transition to individualised CRM. Many companies are still product focused and restricted by a culture and processes that form a barrier for them becoming more customer-focused.

Before embarking on an attempt to develop a more advanced form of CRM, a company needs to assess the benefits of the required financial and organisational investment and to make certain that any migration in terms of CRM activities is congruent with the business strategy.

Once a decision is made to migrate towards more sophisticated relationship with customers, then an appropriate transition can be mapped out. Some organisations have already successfully implemented 'managed service and support' or 'customer-based' marketing. A few, such as the most developed Internet booksellers, have already adopted advanced forms of individualised relationship marketing. However, many companies still need to develop from the position of product-based selling. Organisations starting with product-based selling should initially be concerned with integrating their key existing customer-facing activities. They need to look forward in time to see what business benefits would be realisable through a more advanced form of CRM. A range of possible transitions is shown in Figure 6.12.

A company wishing to move from product-based selling has two usual choices of migration path. Such a decision should be based on an analysis of the factors discussed earlier, which identify how the industry is changing and the competitive positioning of the company now and in the future. Path 1 identifies migration to managed service and support, when a call centre, help desk and person-to-person customer service may be used to increase customer intimacy. Alternatively, Path 2 may involve acquiring and analysing additional customer data to refine an approach to segmenting customers. Migrating directly to an individualised CRM approach will not be desirable for most

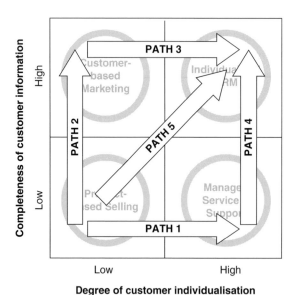

Figure 6.12 Transition paths for CRM

organisations. There are several reasons that may restrict achieving this most sophisticated form of CRM.

First, customers in a particular industry may not wish to have individualised customer relationships. This situation is typical with transactional purchases in industry sectors such as commodities and utilities.

Second, the investment costs may outweigh the benefits of individualised CRM. The investment in technology can be large, but this is only a starting point to the massive resources required in implementing CRM. In interviews conducted as part of our field-based research, we identified several companies that had unsuccessfully sought to implement expensive CRM technology solutions aimed at individualised CRM. Each of them had discontinued the use of the CRM software and reverted back to less developed forms of CRM.

Third, some companies do not have direct interaction with customers and sell through an intermediary in the supply chain. In these instances, a company must weigh up the advantages of reconfiguring the supply chain and developing relationships directly with customers.

Migration to individualised CRM can involve migration Path 3 – from customer-based marketing – Path 4 – from managed service and support – or Path 5 – directly from product-based selling. Migration Path 3 is probably the most common transition route, where an organisation is culturally orientated to the customer and yet requires additional sophistication in collecting, storing and using data to develop individualised relationships. Migration Path 4 is more difficult to achieve as the organisation may still, culturally, be product focused, even though it may provide responsive customer service. Path 5, which involves moving directly from product-based selling to individualised CRM, is the most problematic migration path. Companies may achieve this route more easily when there is no entrenched culture and where legacy systems do not inhibit the development of an integrated technology platform.

Highly differentiated segments and intermediated markets

Businesses which deal directly with a relatively homogeneous set of final customers are likely to adopt, or consider migration from, one of the four strategy quadrants shown in Figure 6.12. However, for companies dealing with substantially different market segments, there needs to be a deeper consideration of the appropriate strategies. In some instances, as noted above, a company may have little information that links individual purchases to a customer – or the required financial and organisational investment does not justify a different or more sophisticated strategy being adopted. In a case such as this, the same strategy approach will usually be adopted for these different segments. In other cases, a different strategy may be adopted for different customer segments. For example, a utilities company may have markedly different segments to serve, including large business customers and residential household consumers. Here, it may be appropriate to adopt a *product-based selling* approach for individual consumers and *customer-based marketing* or *individualised CRM* approach for large corporate customers.

The route to market also needs to be considered. For a manufacturer selling directly to final customers, as is the case with many business-to-business organisations, choice of one of the four strategic approaches shown in Figure 6.11 will be based upon the considerations outlined above. However, for organisations operating in an intermediated market, the relevant approach for the direct customers of a manufacturer (e.g., distributors) and for final customers both need to be considered. In some instances the same approach as that adopted for the end user may be relevant for the direct customer. Alternatively, a different approach may be appropriate for a distributor. A firm operating in an intermediated market will need to consider their own specific circumstances in order to arrive at the appropriate strategy for the reseller and the final customer.

SUMMARY

This chapter has examined the strategy development process in CRM. The process of CRM strategy development includes a detailed exploration of both the business strategy and the customer strategy of the enterprise. If the existing business strategy is comprehensive, thorough and forward looking the task then is to ensure that the subsequent customer strategy is clearly aligned and integrated with it. If the existing business strategy is incomplete, unclear or fails to consider the future business environment, then the role of CRM is to ensure that top management's attention is directed towards addressing this.

Once an appropriate business strategy is determined and agreed, the customer strategy needs to be addressed. The customer strategy involves examining the existing and potential customer base and making choices about which customers the company wishes to serve. This involves undertaking a detailed analysis of customer characteristics and determining the most appropriate customer segments to serve. It also involves decisions about segment granularity and whether a macro-, micro- or one-to-one approach to segmentation is needed. Additionally, decisions need to be made about the products and services to be offered to these segments.

CRM strategy development involves considering the present and potential future position that the enterprise has within its industry and determining how it needs to address its customer base. Depending on the industry and competitive issues, each organisation needs to consider the CRM strategy that is appropriate to it now and in the future. We have described four broad strategic options: product-based selling, customer-based marketing, managed service and support and individualised CRM. The choice of strategy will depend on a number of factors including the completeness of customer information and the extent to which the company can and wishes to use this information to provide customised service. Of these options, individualised CRM is the most sophisticated – it requires collection and analysis of extensive information about customers, the ability and desire to give customers individualised service, and it needs to be economically viable. However, the CRM strategy option adopted should not be a static one. Most companies should consider a suitable migration path over time from one option to a more advanced one in terms of CRM sophistication.

Once an appropriate business and customer strategy has been agreed, a consideration of enterprise value creation forms the next important process in the CRM Strategy Framework – the topic of the next chapter.

CASE 6.1: Tesco – the relationship strategy superstar

The company

Tesco plc is today one of the largest retailers in the world. Globally it operates more than 5,300 supermarkets and convenience stores and employs some 500,000 people. Tesco's core business is in the UK, where the company ranks as the largest private sector employer and the largest food retailer, operating nearly 2,700 stores. The company also operates in the Czech Republic, Hungary, Poland, the Republic of Ireland, Slovakia, Turkey, Malaysia, South Korea, Taiwan and Thailand. Its Tesco.com Internet business is the largest online supermarket in the world.

The company opened its first store in 1929 and was listed on the London stock exchange in 1947. Over the next four and a half decades the company grew substantially through both organic growth and by purchase of other stores and supermarkets. Its market positioning was based on the founder Jack Cohen's positioning of 'pile it high and sell it cheap'. However, the company, which had been previously unresponsive to the changing market needs, started to recognise the importance of quality rather than quantity. The more recent history of Tesco offers a remarkable story of the transition to a best-in-class CRM enterprise. Tesco changed its business strategy to a focus on the customer. This case study traces Tesco's successful relationship-based strategy from the early 1990s to the present.

The challenge

In the early 1990s, Tesco suffered from declining customer satisfaction, poor customer retention and unclear positioning in the highly competitive UK grocery market. The company found itself in an increasingly competitive grocery market. At this time, the business strategy was to grow the business through offering customers low prices. However, the entry of discount grocery chains left Tesco without clear market differentiation. As a result, the retailer witnessed declining profits which threatened the returns to investors. Critically, Tesco experienced a flow of customers who defected to the competitors, as they were unimpressed by the quality of the shopping experience.

The solution

The solution to this competitive challenge started with the identification of clear strategic objectives. Based on their research, Tesco developed a new set of strategic objectives: 'Tesco should aim to be positively classless, the best value, offering the best shopping trip. This will be achieved by having a contemporary business and therefore one that remains relevant by responding to changing needs. We should aim to be ... customer focused.' To achieve these objectives, Tesco developed a wide range of strategic initiatives. These initiatives can be considered under two broad headings: improving the shopping experience and utilising customer insight to build customer relationships.

As Tesco evolved a clear *business strategy*, it was clear that its *customer strategy* was not well developed. In fact, the company did not know its customers and did not have a profile of the typical customer who wanted to shop in a Tesco store. Further, Tesco did not have a close relationship with its customers. Market research revealed that Tesco lacked a clear position in the crowded grocery market. Tesco customers covered a broad range of demographic profiles and wanted better value products, innovative ideas and great customer service. In fact, customers wanted a grocery store that was focused on their needs – one that was truly customer-focused. Tesco management considered how they could acquire in-depth knowledge about their customers. Not only were they interested in gaining, by means of market research, a detailed picture of their customers, they also wanted to have real-time, accurate data on each individual customer – including the contents of each shopping basket – every time a Tesco customer visited the store. What they needed was to build a comprehensive, 360 degree view of each customer.

Improving the shopping experience

To stave off the threat from the new price discounters such as Aldi, Tesco launched the 'Tesco Value' range, initially spanning 70 core products. In their distinctive blue and white striped packaging, they were designed to communicate value for money, hopefully negating the need for cross-shopping at discount stores. Customers responded positively and trading improved. This was followed by a reduction in the price of key popular branded items. The company went on to launch 600 new own-label products in 1993. Tesco wanted to offer its shoppers cheap prices, yet avoid alienating its more up-market customers.

Under the guidance of Marketing Director Terry Leahy, a series of new customer-focused initiatives was introduced, aimed at providing the best shopping experience for the customers. Shoppers were recruited to sit on Customer Panels for half-day sessions, providing an opportunity for local managers and head office staff to find out exactly what customers really wanted. Signage was improved and a 'New Look' programme of store extensions and refurbishment was launched. In-store bakeries and meat counters were installed in some of the larger stores, as were pharmacies, fresh fish counters and cafés. Other improvements included fully equipped baby changing rooms and customer service desks installed and positioned to be the first thing customers saw as they entered a store.

A total of £15 million was spent in ensuring that Tesco could pledge to open more tills immediately if at any time there was more than one person in front of a customer – the very successful 'one-in-front' initiative which is still operational today. Tesco addressed the issue of service improvement with the 'First Class Service' training programme, a radical shift from the company's centralised 'command and control' style of management. Each member of the then 130,000-strong staff was given responsibility to look after customers in the way they thought best. At the same time, staff were made aware that the average potential lifetime spend of a customer at Tesco was £90,000. Some £20 million was spent in hiring and developing Customer Assistants whose only responsibility was to help customers within the store.

Tesco's ongoing strategic initiatives continued to reinforce this new market positioning throughout the first decade of the 2000s. Engagement of the substantial workforce and exceptionally clear communication of their strategic intent to all stakeholders is a key feature of Tesco's successful strategy. The Tesco Strategy Wheel, shown in the Tesco 2009 annual report (Figure 1), exemplifies Tesco's ability to distil its relationship-based strategy and make it exceptional for its customers, its employees and the community at large.

Figure 1 Tesco strategy wheel.
Source: © 2012 Tesco Stores Limited

Gaining and utilising deep customer insight

In February 1995, in parallel with these other developments, the concept of the Tesco Clubcard was born. Working closely with data mining experts Dunnhumby Associates, a special Customer-Insights team within Tesco set about launching the UK's first national loyalty card. Senior management envisaged the Clubcard as providing multiple benefits, not only to Tesco but also to the customer. Tesco would have detailed information about what, when and how customers buy. Micro-marketing to identified segments or individuals would now be possible. As a result, Tesco could anticipate and address precisely defined customer needs. Tesco would also be able to use this customer insight to improve its operational efficiency, implement better inventory control and provide immediate feedback on product offerings, for example, with new product launches. In addition, Clubcard membership offered Tesco a new channel for communicating with customers where messages could be carefully tailored to a specific market segment, helping build customer relationships and loyalty.

For the customer, Clubcard membership included a compelling financial benefit of 1 per cent discount on every purchase. Customers accumulated discounts on their Clubcard account and regularly received cash vouchers, dispatched through the mail along with a carefully personalised Club magazine and other purchasing offers.

Before the launch of Clubcard, market analysts were not impressed. They considered the concept a 'me too' loyalty scheme, with the administration costs and discounts offered by the card as unnecessary expenses. However, they were proved incorrect. The response to the launch of Clubcard was overwhelming as customers rushed to enjoy the benefits of membership. By the end of March 1995, over 5 million customers had signed up to the Clubcard and Tesco reported 7 per cent increase in sales. For the first time, Tesco outstripped its main competitor, Sainsbury, to become the leading grocery retailer in the UK.

Overnight, Tesco had access to massive amounts of detailed information about their customers. Every customer transaction revealed what, how and when customers purchased goods at Tesco. Club membership involved completing a form giving name, contact details and some basic lifestyle information. Using this information, Tesco could now identify the precise purchasing habits of individuals. Tesco senior management was amazed that data mining experts at Dunnhumby could reveal so much about their customers – valuable, detailed knowledge that allowed precise segmentation on many different variables. Using this detailed analysis of each customer's shopping patterns Tesco could now develop and implement marketing and retailing programmes that tackled issues of declining customer satisfaction and loyalty.

Tesco now focused on offering customers a tailored shopping experience that matched their lifestyle and life stage. For example, in 1997 Tesco launched Baby Club, focusing on high spending young mothers with babies. A signed-up mother-to-be received a gift pack on the birth of her baby along with a quarterly magazine that offered relevant and useful content and special offers. The success of this first club led to the launch of other interest clubs during the early 2000s. These clubs included Toddlers Club (providing a migration pathway for mothers following the Baby Club); World of Wine Club; a Healthy Living Club; a Christmas Savers Club and a Kids Club. Each of these clubs offered Tesco an opportunity to participate in the special interests of customer groupings, forging relationships based on life stage and lifestyle.

Tesco recognised that armed with these new customer insights it could begin to shape the business around customers. In May 1998, Tesco launched 'TIE' – the Tesco Information Exchange system, which allowed electronic data exchange across the supply chain. Tesco and its suppliers could plan promotions, assess instantly the effectiveness of new products, manage inventory and work together to improve every aspect of the customer's shopping experience. Tesco became a valued partner to suppliers, as the retailer could provide suppliers with more precise and detailed information.

Further initiatives

The next step in Tesco's growth was to enter new product categories – again using customer insights to ensure these market extensions were in line with customer needs. Home shopping was introduced in the mid-1990s and quickly became an outstanding success. Tesco.com is now the largest and most profitable e-grocer in the world. Financial services have also proved highly successful, with many products linked to Clubcard points on purchases. Financial and insurance products were launched at a similar time, each becoming an instant hit with customers. Tesco's bank, now independent of the troubled Royal Bank of Scotland, is enjoying steady growth despite the troubled UK financial market. In the early 2000s, Tesco partnered with mobile phone company O2 and launched into telecoms. In 2003 Tesco entered the clothing market, launching new brands, including its Cherokee range and Florence and Fred. Within two years, Tesco's clothing brands were the fastest growing in the UK and, by 2011, revenues exceed £1 billion. Product categories quickly extended across a very wide range, with Tesco becoming a significant player, if not the market leader, in each category. Tesco has also invested in growing new retail service businesses. Entry into mobile telephony was followed by a move into broadband and other related IT services. Each of these businesses offers another source of customer data which can help Tesco build a more comprehensive picture of each customer's purchasing behaviour and lifestyle.

The results

In 1997 Tesco set out on an ambitious strategy to grow the core grocery business and diversify with new products and services into new markets. Over the last 15 years, these goals have been achieved through building the business around customer relationships. Today there are over 15 million UK Clubcard customers who have a relationship with Tesco in the UK. The Clubcard is operational in 7 of the 14 countries in which Tesco operates. Tesco's core purpose is to earn the loyalty of its customers through creating exceptional value for them, and the retail giant has succeeded by truly understanding and providing what each customer wants. Tesco has substantially outperformed competing supermarkets such as Sainsbury and Walmart/Asda. Figure 2 illustrates how Tesco outperforms these competing super-market chains, using the 'Market Leaders framework' in the critical areas of customer intimacy and product leadership. Unlike most retailers, Tesco has managed to appeal to a wide range of market segments.

Tesco is recognised as the world expert in company loyalty schemes. However, Clubcard is not just another loyalty scheme. As Martin Glen, President of PepsiCo, recently remarked: 'Customer loyalty schemes are not a new idea ... but what Tesco has done is to develop a contemporary version of the original concept which goes much further in developing an active relationship with its customers.'

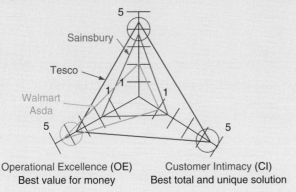

Figure 2 The Market Leaders framework for UK supermarkets

International growth is a priority within Tesco's business plan. To date Tesco has enjoyed incredible success in each new international market in which it operates, with one exception – the US. By late 2012, Tesco was planning to withdraw from the US. China and India represent the biggest challenge for Tesco, yet between them these two markets offer huge potential. Tesco is penetrating these markets, using the same formula it has used elsewhere – to gain and use a comprehensive understanding of customers and potential customers. At the heart of this CRM strategy lies Clubcard, the source of customer insights about each of these diverse markets.

In 2011 the new Chief Executive, Philip Clarke, set out a vision for the future of the business, to become the most highly valued business in the world – valued by customers, communities, staff and shareholders. He recognises that to achieve this ambitious goal, Tesco needs to understand customers locally in each market. Despite the wealth of experience the retailer has gained though successfully growing its business over the last decade, applying this knowledge elsewhere in new markets is insufficient. Tesco must remain true to its strategy of seeking detailed knowledge of each customer's purchasing needs and earning his or her loyalty. This formula has worked for the company in the past and the same dedication to customers is likely to work into the future.

Tesco provides a fascinating example of how a retail giant has grown through adopting a carefully focused relationship strategy, aligning both business and customer goals. From a weak position in the competitive UK grocery market, over the last two decades Tesco has more than doubled sales and profit in its UK business, spread operations into 13 international markets, grown sales to £67.6 billion with £3.8 billion profit before tax. However, Tesco cannot rest on its laurels. In 2012, it was reported that UK sales had weakened – partly as a consequence of the lingering financial pressure on consumers in the aftermath of the global financial crisis. In the presence of increased competition from low-cost competitors such as Aldi, and competitors which are perceived as more exclusive such as Marks & Spencer, Tesco will need to continue to focus on building and sustaining relationships with its customers.

This case study is based on an earlier case study and research by Professor Simon Knox of Cranfield School of Management. It was updated and summarised in 2012 by Professors Simon Knox and Pennie Frow.

CASE 6.2: Samsung – from low-cost producer to product leadership

The company

Samsung Group, the Korean multinational conglomerate, illustrates how dedication to a carefully designed business strategy can deliver spectacular results. The strategy development process in CRM consists of two components, the business strategy and the customer strategy. This case study focuses on the *business strategy* and examines how Samsung moved from a focus on low-cost product leadership to a winning strategy of delivering high-value products to appreciative global customers.

Samsung was founded in 1938 as a small export business, but quickly diversified into several large domestic manufacturing companies, focusing from the late 1960s on the growing consumer electronics industry. From the 1990s, Samsung Electronics, one of four businesses in the group, began to compete heavily in the world market and the fortunes of the company grew rapidly. Today, Samsung Electronics has sales of over US$15 billion, achieving a growth of over 6 per cent in 2010–2011 despite the adverse global trading conditions.

Samsung is a world leader in innovation and marketing, with a brand that is more valuable than Pepsi, Nike or American Express and is the envy of its global competitors. The company is best known as a producer of semiconductors, cell phones, TVs and LCD panels. However, the group is diverse, operating across a wide range of industries, including financial services, information technology, machinery, ship building and chemicals.

Samsung operates in very fast moving product markets, and retaining its position of global leader across several products requires relentless investment in innovation. Samsung recognises that the challenges of leading in the digital age mean developing new technologies, introducing competitive products and innovating through every aspect of its business. For a company that grew up with a traditional Japanese manufacturing culture, Samsung has had to change radically to succeed with its ambitious growth strategy.

The challenge

In the early years, Samsung's strategy depended on manufacturing a wide range of products at lower cost than its competitors. The size and scale of production meant that the company could successfully occupy a cost leadership position, especially in the home market. The strategic focus on the local market offered significant opportunities during the rapid development of South Korea during the late 1980s and Samsung was well placed to dominate here. When, in 1987, Lee Kun-Hee was appointed as chairman, Samsung enjoyed a leadership position in most electronic markets in South Korea, but cheap Japanese goods posed a significant threat to the company's overseas expansion plans. The Japanese were seizing upon the opportunity provided by lower wages in South-East Asia, building new factories in these emerging economies. In South Korea, the economic boom was causing the domestic wage bill to rise rapidly and Samsung needed to look at offshore manufacturing as well as entering global export markets.

Lee recognised that the company could not sustain its position of low-cost provider to OEMs (original equipment manufacturers) in either the traditional domestic market or through expanding into the fiercely competitive global market. His new vision was for Samsung to move strategically to become a global provider of high value-added products, a position that required a totally different business model. This new position could only be achieved through a new marketing strategy that emphasised customer excellence and that grew the value of the Samsung brand.

In the early 1990s, Lee identified an opportunity in the digital technology market where he could transform his new vision into action. Even though the Japanese led in the lucrative analogue market, they failed to move quickly enough into this new part of the electronics market. Consumer demand was high for digital technology in cameras, audio equipment and other electronic products. However, Lee recognised that for Samsung there was the significant challenge of redesigning the business into an agile and innovative organisation that could capture this new, high-value and profitable market.

The solution

The opportunity to move into digital technology was a huge risk for Samsung. The investment in innovation cost the company over $2.45 billion annually, but resulted in a steady flow of new digital products which flooded onto the premium product market. Samsung's R&D centres employed over 17,000 scientists and designers who ensured that the company stayed at the forefront of research in this lucrative new product area. Each year, four or five new products were selected to receive special marketing support. Scientists competed for the accolade of developing one of these chosen products, ensuring that Samsung achieved new standards in quality, design and performance. The breadth of technology ensured that Samsung could turn a product concept into a commercial product in less than five months, outstripping Japanese rivals by many weeks.

Lee recognised that his new business strategy required a significant change in the culture and management practices of Samsung. For a company that was built on rigid Japanese management principles and was focused on product leadership, the shift in mindset was significant if the organisation was to become flexible and focused on the customer. In 1993, Lee launched a 'new management initiative', which aimed at redesigning the company. This initiative included importing Western best practices in strategy formulation and people management, and incorporating these practices into the successful Samsung business model. These business practices focused on changing the culture of the company, making it more flexible and more open to new initiatives and change, while retaining the company's strength in manufacturing and operations. Lee's strategy focused on three key principles: investment in innovation; producing premium products; and building brand value.

Samsung adopted Western business practices, especially in restructuring its reward and talent management strategies, introducing a merit-based system which was a huge shift from pay structured on seniority. Lee encouraged new ideas to infiltrate the company, bringing in new talent from abroad and sending senior management overseas in order to experience foreign business cultures.

In 1999 Lee appointed a new Vice President of Global Marketing, Eric Kim. Kim was Korean born but had worked very successfully in the US software market. On joining the company, his challenge was to build a strong brand image for Samsung globally and move the company away from product-focused businesses to a truly customer-focused enterprise. Kim viewed the Samsung brand as a core strategic asset that required investment and over time could gain global recognition. However, he encountered strong opposition from managers who had grown up in a culture which espoused the idea that good products sell themselves. Marketing was undervalued and core marketing processes, such as marketing planning and budgeting, were non-existent. Kim had a hard task ahead to educate his colleagues on the value of marketing. He realised that his first hurdle was to overcome the resistance and lack of customer focus internally. Kim set about the task of changing the internal marketing culture. He embarked on a programme of marketing education, which he captured in three words: 'wow' (innovations that were compelling to consumers); 'simple' (products that were easy to use) and 'inclusive' (products that were affordable and readily available to the consumer).

Establishing a consistent brand message was critical to Kim's plans. He consolidated advertising within a single agency, terminating contracts with over 55 agencies globally. Kim implemented strict guidelines for usage of the company logo and a consistent style for all brand communications, putting an end to many company sub-brands. He also changed the apportioning of marketing budgets, allocating marketing funds to those products that were projected to produce the highest returns. This practice was a major break from traditional budgeting that used current sales data to determine future investment. For example, regions such as China were receiving a small marketing allocation even though they offered huge growth potential for Samsung. Inevitably, regional and product managers resisted these changes, but over time improvement in market share and operating profit proved that the reallocation made good sense.

Kim's new drive towards becoming marketing focused was referred to internally as market-driven change (MDC). Marketing moved from a tactical communication campaign to become an important business function. MDC involved using customer insights to identify attractive customer segments for Samsung's high-value, innovative products. To improve brand visibility, Kim launched 'DigitAll – Everyone's Invited'. The aim of this campaign was to position the brand as offering high-value digital convergence through innovative products.

Over the past decade the company has worked hard to understand the image of its brand in different markets. Samsung uses a 'relationship monitor' model which identifies 13 relational dimensions that connect the consumer with the brand and seven relationship styles that describe different levels of brand loyalty. Using this model, Samsung can identify the extent to which different segments of consumers are loyal to the brand.

Samsung understands that its brand is in different stages of development across global markets. Country markets are grouped into three categories: accelerator, turning point and advanced. These groupings allow the company to develop and implement appropriate brand strategies that reflect consumer awareness and loyalty to the brand.

Samsung seeks sponsorship programmes that could complement the brand and extend the reach to new audiences. In 2003 Kim partnered with Warner Brothers, and a Samsung phone played a significant role in the successful movie *The Matrix Reloaded*. This sponsorship aimed to appeal especially to the 20 to 30 age segment, who were important consumers of Samsung products and tended to shift between brands. Samsung invested heavily in sports sponsorship and this strategy has made a huge impact on customer awareness of the brand. In 1997 Samsung secured worldwide Olympic sponsorship in the wireless equipment category. Success with this arrangement has continued through subsequent games and the company was a partner in the London 2012 Olympics. Sponsorship of these events has led to significant improvement in brand perceptions in global markets.

The results

Samsung's vision for 2020 is simple: 'Inspire the World, Create the Future'. To achieve this vision, the company looks to three key strengths: new technology, innovative products and creative solutions. The company recognises that engaging more closely with customers and their changing needs will provide new value throughout its network and with three key stakeholders – customers, partners and employees.

Product quality is a priority, as Samsung knows that building consumer loyalty depends on it. Products are tested in a reliability lab and new products are developed incorporating customer insights on ease of use and reliability in real-life situations. Excellence in customer service and after-sales care is also central to Samsung's strategy. The company excels in customer care and has processes that provide swift action to respond to and rectify product defects and repairs. The Samsung brand is now synonymous with value, quality and reliability.

Samsung today is committed to being the world's best in key products. Samsung's mission over the last two decades is to make life better for consumers around the world. Using this lofty goal, the company has achieved No.1 global market share for 13 products. Through investing heavily in research and development Samsung aims to sustain and build on its market leadership in key product areas. As part of the new vision, Samsung's strategic plan involves challenging targets of reaching revenues in excess of $400 billion and becoming one of the world's top five brands by 2020. To achieve these goals, Samsung is exploring new market areas, including health, medicine and biotechnology, where it can use its unique capabilities to innovate creatively. The company is now positioned to dominate even more markets globally and build on its successful history.

7 Enterprise value creation

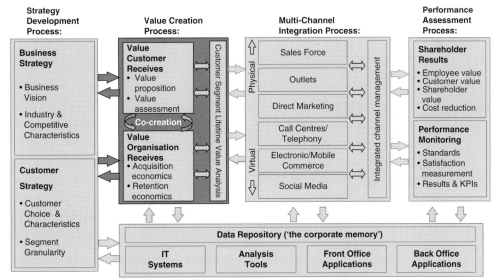

The CRM Strategy Framework

This chapter is the second of two chapters addressing value creation. In Chapter 3 we explained that the term value creation has two broad meanings: the value the company can provide its customers – *customer value creation* – and the value the organisation receives from its customers – *enterprise value creation*. As the navigation diagram above shows, these two components of value creation are closely linked.

The *value creation process* consists of four key elements: determining what value the company can provide its customers with (the value the customer receives); determining the value the organisation receives from its customers (the value the enterprise receives); engaging more actively in *co-creation*; and, by successfully managing this value exchange, maximising the lifetime value of desirable customer segments. The overall value creation process addresses two key questions: how can we create value with our customers and how can we maximise the lifetime value of the customers that we want?

In Chapter 3 we reviewed the nature of what the customer buys and explained how the core and augmented product, relationships and brands all contribute to the enterprise's offering. We also discussed the concept of the value proposition and how the value the customer receives can be assessed. In Chapter 2 we also explained the key concepts and philosophy of relationship marketing, which aims at increasing customer focus and ensuring customers receive appropriate value through a carefully designed and augmented offer.

As this book, somewhat uniquely, examines both relationship marketing and CRM, fittingly, customer value creation is addressed in the earlier section of the book dealing with relationship marketing. Nevertheless, it is essential to recognise how customer value creation forms a critical component of the overall value creation process as a precursor to considering how the enterprise can maximise the lifetime value of desirable customer segments

This chapter focuses on enterprise value creation with the aim of maximising customer lifetime value through co-creating value with customers. The value creation process is a critical component of CRM as it translates business and customer strategies into specific statements of what value is to be delivered to customers and, consequently, what value is to be delivered to the supplier organisation.[1]

Enterprise value creation

The value the enterprise receives from the customer probably has the greatest association with the term 'customer value'. Customer value from this perspective is the *outcome* of providing superior value propositions to the customer, deploying improved acquisition and retention strategies and utilising effective channel management. Fundamental to the concept of enterprise value creation are the key elements that we explore in the following six sections of this chapter:

- determining existing and potential customer profitability across customer segments;
- understanding the economics of customer acquisition and customer retention;
- a framework for customer retention improvement;
- building profit improvement including opportunities for cross-selling, up-selling and advocacy;
- maximising customer lifetime value as a key part of the value creation process;
- increasing the level of co-creation activity undertaken by the enterprise, its customers and its partners.

Customer profitability

In Chapter 6 we emphasised the importance of market segmentation. Carefully segmenting the market and developing an approach that maximises the value of the most desirable customer segments, and the corresponding lifetime value that these customer groups produce for the enterprise, lie at the heart of the value creation process. Companies need to understand the existing profitability of their key customer segments (and, where appropriate, the profitability of individual customers) and initiate action to realise the potential profitability of those segments and consequently improve customer lifetime value.

It is somewhat surprising that many companies focus on identifying the profitability of products rather than customers, when it is customers who generate profits, not products.[2] Products create costs but customers create profits. This distinction is not just semantic. We find that the difference between profit and loss is typically determined *after* a product is manufactured. The costs of storing, moving and supporting products are significant. Customers differ widely in their requirements for delivery service, in their ordering patterns and, indeed, in the products they purchase. Each product has its own unique profile of margin, value/density, volume and handling requirements. Similarly, customers will order different product mixes, will have their own unique requirements as to the number of delivery points and, of course, the number of times they order and the complexity of their orders will differ. Putting all these factors together can produce widely differing cost implications for the supplier.

The 80/20 rule, or the 'Pareto Law', suggests that 80 per cent of the total sales volume of a business is typically generated by just 20 per cent of its customers and that 80 per cent of the total costs of servicing all the customers will probably be incurred by only 20 per cent of the customers (but probably not the same 20 per cent).

The profitability of customers varies considerably whether we are examining profitability at the customer segment or individual, or one-to-one, customer level. Figure 7.1 shows the shape of the profit distribution resulting from the uneven spread of profits across an illustrative customer base. From this example, it can be seen that there is a 'tail' of customers who are actually unprofitable and who therefore reduce total profit contribution. It is essential to understand into which segment these customers fit. The analysis in this figure, which is based on large corporate customers, applies equally at the customer segment level.

A key aim of CRM is to develop close relationships with customers in segments that are, or have the potential to become, highly profitable. So the ability to create customer segment profit and loss accounts at the appropriate level – segment, micro-segment or individual customer – is fundamental to a successful CRM strategy.

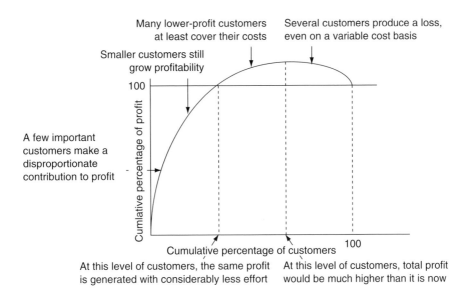

Figure 7.1 Customer profitability analysis.
Source: Adapted from Christopher and Peck (2003)

The problem is that traditional accounting systems make it difficult, if not impossible, to identify the true costs of serving individual customers. Companies often assume that there is an 'average' cost of serving a customer, thus forgoing the opportunity to target those customers or segments that have real potential for transforming their own bottom line.

Why customers differ in their real profitability

Customers' profitability may vary because different customers often buy a different mix of products with different gross margins. Also, there will usually be substantial differences in the costs of servicing individual customers. As noted above, profitability is frequently determined by what happens *after* the point of production.

The costs of service begin with initiation of contact with the customer or the order itself: how much time does the sales person spend with the customer; is there a key account manager who spends their time wholly or in part working with that customer; what commissions do we pay on these sales, and so forth? Also, there are the order processing costs which themselves differ according to the number of product lines on the order, the number of orders and their complexity.

For physical products there are also transportation costs, materials handling costs and often – particularly if goods are held on a dedicated basis for customers, such as with own-label products – inventory and warehousing costs. Further, for large corporate customers, suppliers often allocate specific funds for customer promotions, advertising support, additional discounts and the like. Promotions – a special pack for a particular retailer, for instance – will often carry additional hidden costs to the supplier. For example, the disruption to production schedules and the additional inventory holding cost is rarely accounted for or assigned to customers.

The basic principle of customer profitability analysis is that the company should seek to assign all costs that are specific to individual accounts. A useful test to apply when looking at these costs is to ask: 'What costs would I *avoid* if I didn't do business with this customer?' The benefit of using the principle of 'avoidability' is that many costs of servicing customers are actually shared among several or many customers. The warehouse is a good example: unless the supplier could release warehousing space for other purposes then it would be incorrect to allocate a proportion of the total warehousing costs to a particular customer.

Though it may be impracticable to undertake such analysis for individual accounts, organisations should be able to select a sample of representative customers in order to gain a view of the relative costs associated with different types of accounts, distribution channels and market segments. What often emerges from customer profitability studies is that the largest customers in terms of volume, or even revenue, may not be the most profitable because they cost so much to service. So though these larger customers may gain bigger volume-based discounts, they may require more frequent deliveries to more dispersed locations and they may insist on other requirements such as non-standard packaging.

Understanding future profit potential

Once the enterprise has a clear view on existing profitability of its major customers or customer segments it then needs to consider their *future* profitability. Hence, we need to identify the potential to build and extend customer segment profitability further.

Peppers and Rogers have developed a customer typology that helps businesses rank their customers and identify relevant strategies. They suggest ranking customers into five groups in terms of their potential lifetime value and they propose that special emphasis is placed on three groups:[3]

- 'MVCs' or *most valuable customers* are those customers which have the highest actual lifetime values. They represent the core of a company's current business and the CRM objective with regard to them is *customer retention*.
- 'STCs' or *second tier customers* represent those customers with the highest unrealised potential. They could be a source of greater profitability for the company than they currently are and the CRM objective with regard to them is *customer growth*.
- 'BZs' or *below zero customers* are those customers who will probably never earn sufficient profit to justify the expense involved in serving them. The CRM objective with regard to them is *customer divestment*.

A customer value typology such as this is useful in helping an organisation reach appropriate decisions as to how it can best utilise its resources. Because of the high value that they already represent for a business, the focus for MVCs is developing appropriate customer retention strategies. STCs may be similar to MVCs in terms of their potential profitability and lifetime value. Here the opportunity is to obtain a larger size of their wallet as they may be purchasing products from competitors. BZs represent customers who usually cost more to serve than they are ever likely to return in profit to the company. If there is no potential for profit improvement, the company needs to consider how to divest itself of these customers *provided it is ethically responsible to do this*. Ideally, the company should persuade the customers to shift to one of its competitors where they can be equally unprofitable for that company. This suggests the company needs to be careful to acquire only those customers that have the potential to be profitable for the enterprise.

Ideally the organisation should seek to develop financial systems that routinely collect and analyse customer profitability data. Essential to such analysis is the need for organisational understanding of how customer acquisition, customer retention and opportunities for cross-selling, up-selling and building customer advocacy contribute to profitability across different customer segments.

Customer acquisition and customer retention economics

In this section of the chapter we consider the economics of customer acquisition and customer retention and then review acquisition and retention activities in practice. Given the great impact customer retention can have on profitability, in the following section we provide a framework and detailed discussion that addresses how to improve customer retention activities.

Customer acquisition and its economics

The role and relative importance of customer acquisition varies considerably according to a company's specific situation. For example, a new market entrant will mainly be focused on customer acquisition, while an established enterprise will be concerned more with customer retention.

The customer acquisition process is typically concerned with issues such as:

- acquiring customers at a lower cost,
- acquiring more customers,
- acquiring more attractive customers, and
- acquiring customers utilising new channels.

The starting point in understanding customer value from the perspective of the supplier organisation is to determine the existing customer acquisition costs within the major channels used by the company and to identify how these costs vary within different customer segments.

Customer acquisition at 'United Electricity plc'

We can illustrate the economics of both customer acquisition and customer retention by using the example of a large UK electricity supplier.

Since the end of the 1990s, the residential sector of the electricity market has gone through substantial changes as electricity companies, for the first time, could sell electricity outside their traditional geographic boundaries. The full opening up of the retail electricity market occurred in the majority of OECD countries between 2000 and 2011, although a small number of OECD countries have not yet fully deregulated.[4] Following full deregulation of the retail electricity market in the UK, United Electricity, the disguised name of the electricity supplier, faced competition within its own territory from other electricity providers; but United Electricity could now also market its services outside its traditional geographic territory.

A market segmentation of United Electricity's customer base identified four key market segments, each of which displayed different characteristics in terms of socio-economic grouping, expected switching behaviour and customer profiles.[5] The data needed to undertake an analysis of customer acquisition and customer retention economics at United Electricity, at the segment level, were collected. The data included the number of existing customers within each segment, annual customer acquisition targets with reference to the total UK customer base, the cost of acquisition (per customer) and estimates of gross profit per customer per annum for each segment. The likely annual retention rates in the new competitive environment were considered. Different levels of retention for each segment were estimated; one scenario of the broad characteristics of these segments is shown in Figure 7.2. Some figures have been changed to protect proprietary information.

	Segment	No. existing customers (S)	Acquisition target (N)	Cost of acquisition (C)	Annual retention rate (α)	Profit per customer per year (K)
Group 1	Struggling empty nest super-loyals	421,300	500	£110	99%	£6
Group 2	Older settled marrieds	618,000	66,000	£70	97%	£9
Group 3	Switchable middles	497,900	110,000	£55	94%	£18
Group 4	Promiscuous averages	459,600	220,000	£30	90%	£22

Figure 7.2 Customer segment data template for 'United Electricity plc'

United Electricity estimated the acquisition costs (in £) per customer at the customer segment level shown in Figure 7.2 as follows:

- Segment 1 – 'struggling empty nest super-loyals' £110
- Segment 2 – 'older settled marrieds' £70
- Segment 3 – 'switchable middles' £55
- Segment 4 – 'promiscuous averages' £30.

To enable a comparison of acquisition costs, the expected profitability of the average customer in each segment and the overall profit potential of each segment were also considered. When the customer acquisition cost is divided by the profit per customer per annum, the number of years required to break even is identified (making the simplifying assumption that profit levels remain the same). The annual profit per customer in Segment 1 (the 'struggling empty nest super-loyals') was £6, making a break-even of 18.3 years. As this segment comprises elderly people, any newly acquired customers in this segment may well die before they break even! In the case of Segment 4 (the 'promiscuous averages'), the annual profit per customer was £22, making a break-even of 1.36 years. This segment appears highly attractive in terms of acquisition economics, especially if CRM strategies to successfully retain these customers are put in place.

We have observed that many B2C organisations do not differentiate their CRM activities at the segment level. They contact each prospect with the same frequency (as United Electricity had done since its establishment) instead of applying a level of effort consistent with the cost of acquisition and profit potential. Such unrefined use of resources not only leads to wasted investment but can cause annoyance among customers who may have too much or too little attention and customer service directed at them. This situation highlights the importance of understanding acquisition economics at the segment level.

Acquisition within different channels

Having determined the acquisition costs for different segments, the enterprise then needs to review how acquisition costs vary across different channels. For example, as we discuss in the next chapter, electronic communication channels enable companies to acquire customers at a fraction of the cost of using more traditional channels such as direct mail.

Companies need to understand the relative costs of customer acquisition in different channels including direct mail, television advertising, a direct sales force, e-commerce and social media. The apparent high cost of certain channels does not mean that they should be disregarded. For example certain companies have found a direct sales approach to households an effective way to generate sales despite its higher sales costs as a channel.

Further, customers acquired in different channels may be different or may behave differently. For example, one frozen food retailer supplemented its traditional retail sales channel with an Internet site. As a result it acquired customers from a more affluent segment – one that was not well represented within its existing lower socio-economic customer base. Further, the average order size of these Internet customers was higher and more profitable than for traditional customers who physically shopped in its retail branches.

Improving acquisition activities

Even companies with high retention rates lose customers, so they also continually need to acquire new ones. When customer acquisition costs (and how they vary at the segment and channel levels) are properly understood, companies can then consider how to improve their acquisition activities. This may involve acquiring a greater number of customers or more attractive customers, or getting them at a lower cost. In many instances customer acquisition can be improved through acting on insights from the value assessment described in Chapter 3. Well-targeted promotional campaigns, thoughtful use of social media and the encouragement of customer referrals can also attract customers who meet the company's acquisition criteria.

Customer retention and its economics

Although many companies recognise that customer retention is important, relatively few fully understand the economics of customer retention within their own firm. Research has identified the financial benefits of customer acquisition versus customer retention. For example, Fred Reichheld, a partner at consulting firm Bain & Co., and Earl Sasser, a professor at the Harvard Business School, published revealing research which demonstrated the financial impact of customer retention. They found even a small increase in customer retention produced a dramatic and positive effect on profitability: a five percentage points increase in customer retention yielded a very high improvement in profitability in net present value (NPV) terms. If the customer retention rate was increased from, say, 85 to 90 per cent this represented an average NPV profit increase of around 40 per cent. Figure 7.3 shows this NPV varied from 35 to 95 per cent among the businesses studied.[6]

These results have had a significant impact in drawing attention to the critical role customer retention has to play within CRM strategy. However, as Reichheld has observed,

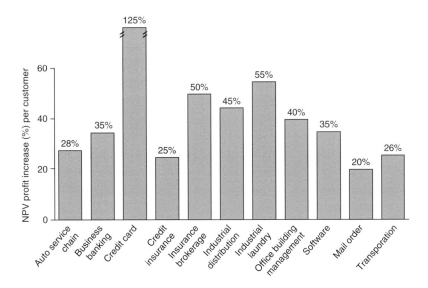

Figure 7.3 Profit impact of a 5 percentage point increase in customer retention for selected businesses.
Source: Adapted from Reichheld and Sasser (1990)

the economics of retention are often lost in the shadows of traditional accounting. This is because changes in defection rates may have little effect on this year's profits, but the resulting effect on long-term profit and growth can be enormous.

Customer retention at 'United Electricity plc'

Using the United Electricity plc example above, we now consider the impact of improvement in customer retention. Experienced executives in United Electricity estimated the potential improvement in customer retention that could be achieved through a CRM strategy based on improved service, given the relative attractiveness of the four segments. These resulted in the following customer retention percentage improvement targets: Segment 1 – 1 per cent, Segment 2 – 2 per cent, Segment 3 – 5 per cent and Segment 4 – 9 per cent, based on a service strategy. Using these increases in retention rates for each segment we modelled the increase in 'gross' profit in five and ten years' time and compared it with the base case.

The results in Figure 7.4 show a significant increase in overall gross profit, before costs of improved service, of 48 per cent at year 5 (from £21.7m to £32.2m) and 71 per cent at year 10 (from £23.8m to £40.6m). The results within each of the four different segments varied significantly because of differences in improvement in retention rates and other inputs to the model. We have found relatively few organisations who undertake evaluation of segment profitability in this way. However, the broad approach is straightforward – understand the profit potential in each segment (gross profit less costs) and selectively manage the segments to maximise profits.

Segment	Existing retention rate		Retention rate with improved service	
	Profit in 5 years (£m)	Profit in 10 years (£m)	Profit in 5 years (£m)	Profit in 10 years (£m)
1	2.697	2.089	2.848	2.331
2	4.477	5.112	5.347	6.692
3	6.377	7.586	9.343	12.704
4	8.167	8.989	14.663	18.828
Total	21.718	23.776	32.201	40.555

Figure 7.4 Profit projections for improved retention at 'United Electricity plc'

Of course any costs incurred as a result of customer retention activities need to be subtracted from gross profit improvement to identify the net profit improvement. However, when considering CRM initiatives, it should be emphasised that the costs of improving customer retention are not necessarily substantial. The most attractive CRM initiatives are those that are of high value to the customer but are of low cost to the supplier. Organisations should first consider a reallocation of the existing expenditure such that greater emphasis is placed on those segments that have the greatest potential for increasing profitability. This may involve no significant increase in costs. For example, if United Electricity was mailing each of its customers seven times per year it may wish to reduce the expenditure greatly on the one million plus customers in Segments 1 and 2 and apply these savings to customers in Segments 3 and 4.

The organisation can next identify where additional incremental expenditure should selectively be placed on the most relevant market segments. The objective of this activity is to ensure the overall cost-benefit of the increased expenditure significantly enhances profitability.

Why retention improvement impacts profitability

The reasons why retention has such a significant effect on profitability have been highlighted by Reichheld and Sasser:

- Acquiring new customers involves costs that can be significant and it may take some years to turn a new customer into a profitable customer.
- As customers become more satisfied and confident in their relationship with a supplier, they are more likely to give the supplier a larger proportion of their business, or share of wallet.
- As the relationship with a customer develops, there is greater mutual understanding and collaboration, which produces efficiencies that lower operating costs. Sometimes customers are willing to integrate their IT systems, including planning, ordering and scheduling, with those of their suppliers and this further reduces costs.
- Satisfied customers are more likely to refer others, which promotes profit generation as the cost of acquisition of these new customers is dramatically reduced. In some

industries, customer advocacy can play a very important role in acquiring new customers, particularly when there is a high risk involved in choosing a supplier.

- Loyal customers can be less price sensitive and may be less likely to defect due to price increases. This is especially true in business-to-business (B2B) markets where the relationship with the supplier becomes more valued and switching costs increase.[7]

However, despite these findings, our experience suggests that companies have been slow to implement changes in marketing activities to emphasise customer retention.

Acquisition and retention activities in practice

A number of previous studies have pointed out that many companies are still more strongly focused on the acquisition of new customers than on the development of their existing customer base.[8] For example, one survey of the financial services carried out by Berry Consulting and AT&T showed that expenditure on customer acquisition (48 per cent) was more than double that spent on customer retention (22 per cent).

In a survey we carried out of the marketing practices of 225 organisations, in a wide range of industries, there were similar results. We found the greatest proportion of marketing budgets – 41 per cent – was spent on customer acquisition, while only 23 per cent was spent on customer retention. Given that the majority of firms surveyed in this sample were in mature industries, the research suggests to us that economics of customer retention and customer acquisition are poorly understood and hugely under-exploited.

Figure 7.5 presents data from a study by KPMG that show results for a range of different industries. This figure shows that the marketing budgets in most sectors emphasise

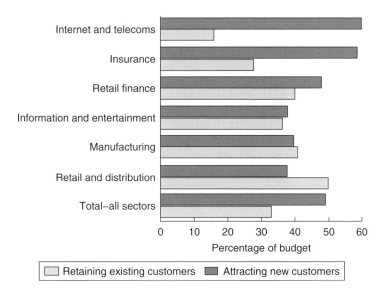

Figure 7.5 Expenditure on customer acquisition and customer retention.
Source: Adapted from KPMG (1997), The Hidden Advantage: A Research Report into Data Warehousing

acquisition more than retention. Marketing expenditure is particularly heavily slanted towards the acquisition of new customers in the insurance and Internet and telecoms sectors. The bias towards acquiring new customers in the latter sector is less surprising given the continuing emergence of new companies in this sector.

Different companies will need to place different emphasis on customer retention and customer acquisition. So a conclusion regarding the relative amounts being spent in both these areas needs to be drawn based on the individual circumstances of that enterprise. Research by the authors has found that many organisations are not placing the optimal balance of expenditure on acquisition and retention activities. In one study we found a significant misallocation in the amount of money spent on customer acquisition and customer retention. Our study identified three categories of organisation – 'acquirers', 'retainers' and 'profit maximisers through CRM'. Acquirers spent too much on customer acquisition activities at the expense of customer retention activities. The majority of firms, 80 per cent of them, were in this category. Retainers, by contrast, spent too much on customer retention activities at the expense of customer acquisition – this group represented 10 per cent of firms. The 'profit maximisers through CRM' represented only 10 per cent of firms in the survey. Only this last category considered they had identified the appropriate balance in spend between acquisition and retention activities.

Taken together, these studies suggest a significant under-emphasis on customer retention by companies. We are not suggesting that new customers are unimportant, indeed, they are essential for sustained success. However, a balance is needed between the marketing efforts directed towards existing and new customers. CRM activities need to emphasise customer retention improvement more strongly.

A framework for customer retention improvement

Given the dramatic impact that improved customer retention can have on business profitability and the fact that many organisations continue to place too much emphasis on customer acquisition at the expense of customer retention, we now outline in some detail a structured approach which organisations can follow to enhance their retention and profitability levels. The three major steps involved in such an approach include: the measurement of customer retention; the identification of root causes of defection and key service issues; and the development of corrective action to improve retention. This framework is shown in Figure 7.6.[9]

Step 1: Measurement of customer retention

The measurement of retention rates for existing customers is the first step in improving customer loyalty and profitability. It involves two major tasks – measurement of customer retention rates and profitability analysis by segment.

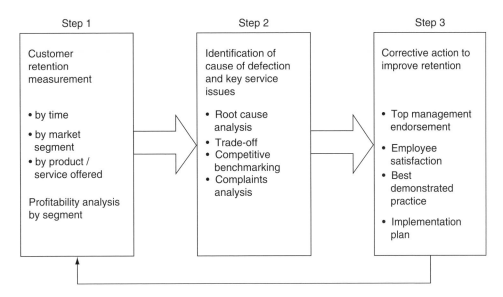

Figure 7.6 Customer retention improvement framework

Dimensions of customer retention measurement

To measure customer retention and identify changes in it, a number of dimensions need to be analysed in detail. These include measurement of customer retention rates – over time, by market segment and by product/service offered.

As some customers will buy all their products or services from one company whereas other customers will be serviced by many suppliers, it is necessary to weight customers by the amount they spend. Otherwise high apparent customer retention rates can hide a serious problem. For example, there are many banks who boast high levels of customer retention but which, in fact, have high levels of account dormancy, where customers have defected to other banks but have not closed their accounts. If customers buy from a number of suppliers, share of wallet should also be identified.

Segment profitability analysis

The next task within this initial step is to ensure that relevant segmentation analysis is undertaken. It must not be assumed that companies will wish to retain all their customers. Some customers may actually cost too much money to service, and may never prove to be worthwhile and profitable. Clearly, it would be inappropriate to invest further in these customers. Market segmentation is discussed in greater detail in the previous chapter.

As discussed earlier in this chapter, different customer segments need to be considered on the basis of both present and future profitability, especially MVCs – most valued customers – and STCs – second tier customers. Increasing customer retention of the most attractive segments should become a critical element of an enterprise's strategy. This will assist in identifying the type and frequency of the marketing activity that should be directed towards the different segments. We term this activity 'developing a segmented service strategy'. To assist with this task, an index can be developed and used to grade the customer base according to profitability so that appropriate strategies can be devised to manage customer relationships most effectively.

Adopting such an approach may present some surprises. For example, a large insurance company discovered that it was not high net worth individuals that were providing the largest future profit streams, although this group had been the focus of much of the company's customer retention activity. Instead, segment profitability analysis showed that schoolteachers were actually the most profitable market segment. Previously, the company had never considered schoolteachers a worthwhile market segment and had directed little marketing activity towards them.

Measurement systems are needed which allow managers to analyse their customer base, identify the profit potential within each segment and then develop strategies to retain the most profitable prospects. An important part of this evaluation process is establishing both the existing and potential customer lifetime value (CLV). We address the calculation of CLV shortly.

The stage reached in customers' life-cycles can also impact profit potential. This will influence the pattern as well as the extent of customer profitability. For example, early in customers' life-cycles, profitability may be low. Marketing activity may be directed at relationship building and gaining a greater share of wallet. However, later in the life-cycle, when there is greater understanding and trust in customer relationships, profitability may increase. During the advanced stages of customers' life-cycles marketing activity may decline, especially if the customers' needs change and other suppliers are able to provide greater value or a more appropriate offering.

The outcome of this first step should be a clear definition of customer retention, a measurement of present customer retention rates and an understanding of the existing and future profit potential for each market segment.

Step 2: Identification of causes of defection and key service issues

When the customer retention and profit improvement potential has been measured, the second step in Figure 7.6 can be taken. This involves the identification of the underlying causes of customer defection. Four analytical approaches are useful in undertaking this task. These include root cause of defection analysis, trade-off analysis, competitive benchmarking, and customer complaint analysis.

Root cause of defection analysis

Traditional marketing research into customer satisfaction does not typically provide accurate answers as to why customers abandon one supplier for another. All too often customer satisfaction questionnaires are poorly designed, superficial and fail to address the key issues, forcing respondents to tick predetermined response choices. For example, a questionnaire for a major retail bank asked departing customers why they were closing their accounts. Among the available multiple-choice answers was 'the account is no longer required'. Not surprisingly, the vast majority of respondents ticked this box because it represented a safe and easy answer and none of the alternative answers addressed the real reasons for defection.

The root causes of customer defections should be clearly identified, for it is only by understanding these causes that the company can begin to implement a successful customer retention programme. It is imperative that root cause of defection analysis be undertaken by properly trained researchers. For example, customers may say that they no longer frequent a particular supermarket because the prices are too high, while in reality customers have been put off by factors such as unhelpful staff, long queues and difficulty in finding products on the shelves.

Trade-off analysis

It is also important to undertake research to identify the key customer service dimensions that result in customers being retained. This can be accomplished through trade-off analysis, which allows the different service features identified by the customer to be 'traded off' against each other in order to establish the customer's service priorities. The supplier can then use this information to develop service strategies that match customer needs and priorities. Trade-off analysis is described in more detail in Chapter 3, where we discussed customer value assessment.

Competitive benchmarking

Competitive benchmarking enables companies to compare their performance and that of their competitors on critical elements of customer service and retention performance. It is then possible to establish service standards that match or exceed those of competitors. The search for best practice may involve questions such as: What is the maximum length of time a customer should be left waiting in a queue? Should employees be expected to answer the telephone within three rings? What level of product knowledge should employees be expected to have about the products and services that they sell? Service standards should also consider how competitors perform and focus on the service dimensions that are most important to customers. We discuss general standards for CRM in Chapter 10.

Customer complaint analysis

A further useful way of identifying key service issues is to analyse customers' complaints. Customer complaint analysis not only highlights possible causes of customer defection, but also acts as an early warning system, enabling the company to resolve problems with customers early on and to implement preventive action to avoid the same problems recurring. Some companies use customer recovery teams which immediately move into action when a high-value defector is identified. The recovery team is charged with finding out the real reasons for the customer's dissatisfaction and is empowered to come up with solutions and develop a customer rescue plan (where appropriate) which forms part of the final step.

Step 3: Corrective action to improve retention

The third and final step involves undertaking corrective action aimed at generating improved customer loyalty. At this point, plans to improve retention become highly specific to the organisation concerned and any actions taken will be particular to its context. We can, however, identify some broad guidelines that should form part of any plan to improve retention. These include ensuring visible top management endorsement, generating employee satisfaction and commitment to building long-term customer relationships, utilising best demonstrated practice techniques to improve performance and the development of an implementation plan. Many of these factors are also relevant to the broader task of implementation of CRM, which is addressed in Chapter 11.

Top management endorsement

Visible top management endorsement is vital to the success of customer retention programmes. If employees see that management are genuinely enthusiastic, supportive and involved in a new retention initiative, it is more likely that employees will be inspired to follow management's example and take the retention programme seriously. However, if the employees see that this is just another management fad they will not adopt the practices necessary to implement an effective retention programme. They will make the superficial changes essential for survival, but underneath the facade nothing will have fundamentally changed. Employees will just wait for the novelty to wear off and revert to their old routines. The level of enthusiasm, involvement, effort and visibility that top management put behind such programmes is, therefore, often seen by employees as indicative of the amount of support that they should give such programmes.

Employee satisfaction and customer retention

A major key to customer retention improvement, it can be argued, is the extent to which an appropriate climate can be established whereby employees see, as their main priority, the satisfaction and retention of customers. There is certainly a strong link between the internal customer service climate and its impact upon employee satisfaction and customer retention. Happy employees will make for happy customers. The happier the customers, the more likely it is that the employees will find their work satisfying and rewarding and wish to stay with the company for a long time. This improved employee retention is likely to deliver improved internal and external service quality. We discuss this relationship further in Chapter 10 when we consider the service profit chain concept and linkage models.

Selection and recruitment of customer contact staff that have the appropriate interpersonal skills to build relationships with customers is also necessary. These people must then be trained by the company so they acquire the knowledge and skills necessary to identify and meet customer needs and expectations and exceed the service standards already specified. Staff performance must then be monitored against these standards. Finally, it is also important to develop the company's reward and recognition systems to ensure that staff who perform are appropriately rewarded by the organisation.

Utilising best demonstrated practice

Best demonstrated practice is a useful technique for disseminating superior practices throughout a company.[10] In this context best demonstrated practice involves identifying the best retention performers in the industry (and also within departments or regions of the enterprise's own organisation). Executives can then examine these entities to see how they are managed and then develop new approaches to raise customer satisfaction and increase retention in their own businesses. Sometimes it is worthwhile looking outside the company's own industry for best practice. There may well be more likelihood of achieving competitive advantage if practices are borrowed from other industries.

Implementation plan for customer retention

In addition to the usual procedural steps that form the basis of any implementation plan, several additional opportunities to create customer loyalty are now considered.

A good retention strategy should try to identify and build barriers that stop 'good' customers from switching to the competition no matter what inducements the competition is offering. Strategic bundling of products is an example of building a barrier to customer defections. Groups of associated products or services are offered to the customer with the advantage of convenience and/or cost savings. Bank accounts are a good example of this, where customers often use their bank for mortgages, insurance policies, as well as the more usual cheque accounts and deposit accounts. Bain & Co.'s research in financial services suggests retention rates are significantly greater where customers use two or more of the organisation's services, than where they use only one service. However, if customers feel that the company is taking advantage of past loyalty, attempts to offer them bundled products and cross-selling will be resented.

In a business-to-business context, team-based relationship management can create a very effective barrier to customer defections. The relationship with the customer is managed by an account manager who manages a team-based approach to relationship building. The aim is to make the relationship more enduring by building as many links as possible between the customer and supplier. Figure 7.7(a) illustrates the establishment of multiple contacts between, for example, the supplier's production team and the customer's operations team; and with the supplier's marketing team and the customer's business development team; and so on. This is in contrast to Figure 7.7(b), which shows a traditional buyer–seller relationship dependent on the sometimes fragile and fairly limited connection between a supplier's key account executive and a retailer's buyer.[11]

Electronic data interchange (EDI) can also be a 'tie that binds'. Getting customers to invest in sharing information about sales and inventories can provide a powerful disincentive to switch supplier. The benefits can be reduced system costs, improved efficiency and increased customer and consumer satisfaction.

In many industries switching barriers should only be built if they are in the best interests of both customer and supplier. This suggestion is not based on philanthropy or morality. Bad publicity, generated by disgruntled customers locked into unsatisfactory supplier relationships, can significantly reduce profits. This is especially true in consumer markets where, if things go wrong, switching barriers mean that customers find

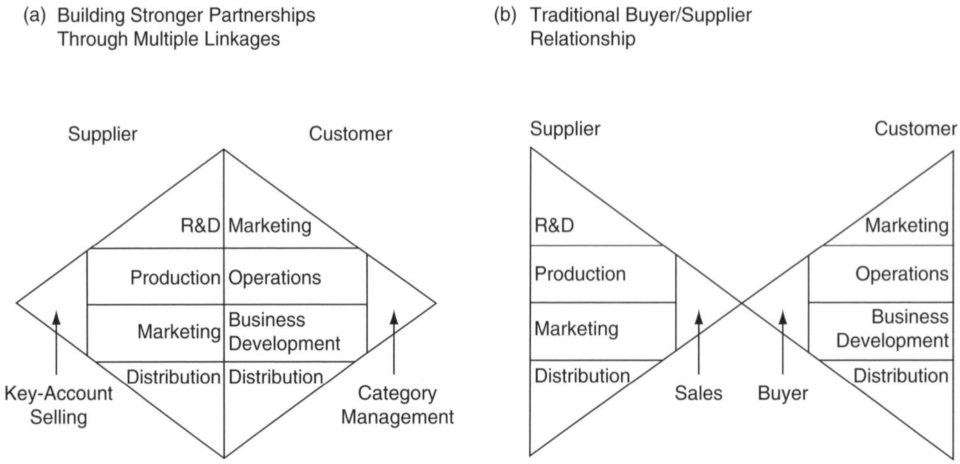

Figure 7.7 Team-based relationship management.
Source: Martin Christopher, Cranfield School of Management

themselves in a system from which it is difficult to leave. Customers may feel trapped, helpless and even cheated. For example, bank customers who feel dissatisfied with the service they receive often find the task of moving their account too onerous to carry out. The result is very unhappy customers who go out of their way to tell others of their negative experiences and who warn others of the pitfalls that await them should they deal with these organisations.

Many organisations now aim to boost their customer acquisition and retention rates as a means of improving their business performance. However, the more enlightened enterprises are also thinking about building profit improvement more systematically through a consideration of three other sources of potential profitability – up-selling, cross-selling and advocacy.

Building profit improvement

In seeking to build future profitability, companies need to develop a systematic and integrated programme that addresses customer acquisition, customer retention and other related activities that can improve CLV. One framework for reviewing such profit opportunities is the ACURA model, shown in Figure 7.8.[12]

The acronym ACURA stands for: acquisition, cross-sell, up-sell, retention and advocacy. Only rarely do companies *systematically* build CRM strategies that focus on all the elements within this ACURA framework. While companies may seek to improve customer acquisition and customer retention, they also need to exploit cross-selling, up-selling and advocacy opportunities.

When organisations model their potential future profit, they need to take into account the fact that individual consumers may be persuaded to buy other products – cross-

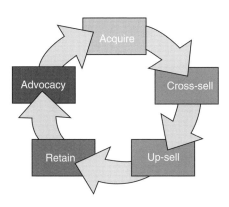

Figure 7.8 The ACURA framework.
Source: Based on A. Payne and P. Frow (2013)

selling – or to buy more of an existing product over time – up-selling. Also, corporate customers tend to buy from a range of suppliers. By improving its service, a supplier may be able to increase share of wallet as well as market share, especially through exploiting alternative channel structures. Companies such as McDonald's and American Express are excellent at cross-selling and up-selling and Apple and Virgin Atlantic excel at creating advocacy within their customer bases.

In the previous sections of this chapter we emphasised how companies should manage customer acquisition and retention to improve their profitability. To become even more profitable, they need to develop integrated programmes that also address related activities that can improve customer lifetime value. As we have already discussed customer acquisition and customer retention, we now focus on cross-selling, up-selling and advocacy.

For each element of ACURA, companies should review potential strategies to improve profitability by market segment and then identify their potential profit impact. The main steps involved in applying the ACURA framework are as follows:

- Identify key segments and their characteristics – typically selecting three or four key customer segments with the greatest long-term profit potential;
- Determine generic ACURA strategies;
- Decide which ACURA strategies relate to which segments and make a rough estimate of profit potential;
- Identify key metrics for each segment and overall profit potential;
- Determine critical factors for success in CRM implementation, investment required and strategy for selling internally.

Cross-selling and up-selling

An overview of an exercise for strategies to improve cross-selling in a supermarket is shown in Figure 7.9. The same approach will be undertaken for up-selling as well as for the other ACURA elements.

Cross-sell	Segment			
	1	2	3	4
Wider product range		$$$		
Linked offers				
Special offers		$$		$
Loyalty cards		$		
Train staff to link products	$			
Shelf design	$		$$	
In store promotions		$	$	
Buy in bulk		$$$		$
Oven ready convenience foods			$	

Figure 7.9 ACURA model cross-selling template for a supermarket

The supermarket first identifies generic strategies to improve each element in the ACURA model. In the example in Figure 7.9, the generic cross-sell strategies that may be relevant to a number of segments include developing a wider product range, making linked or special offers, introducing loyalty cards, etc. The profit potential of applying each of these strategies for each customer segment is then considered. An estimate of this is represented by the number of $ signs for each segment strategy. Appropriate metrics which measure the impact of cross-sell strategies are then identified. Finally, each relevant strategy is considered in more detail including the investment required to implement each strategy and the likely return in each segment. The same approach is taken for the other elements in the ACURA framework.

The potential of up-selling and cross-selling as elements of the ACURA framework can be appreciated when McDonald's Corporation is considered. McDonald's have a systematic approach to up-selling and cross-selling that typically results in a customer having a 'Big Mac' rather than a standard hamburger; being asked if they want fries to go with the hamburger; then 'will that be a large fries?' and 'would you like a drink to go with that?' and 'will that be a large Coke?'. The combination of successful up-selling and cross-selling, if carried out where it is relevant to customer needs and on a consistent basis by all employees, has the potential to make a huge improvement in profitability when compared with an organisation that does not emphasise these key elements of enterprise customer value.

Advocacy

In Chapter 3 we discussed the role of advocates and gave a number of examples of outstanding companies that had created a large number of advocates within their customer bases. We also discussed the many sources of potential advocacy and positive word-of-mouth when we considered the referral market domain in Chapter 4. Whilst the power of advocacy is obvious – you get marketing effort for free – companies have typically struggled to quantify the financial benefits of advocacy.

One fairly recent measurement tool, the 'Net Promoter Score' (NPS) has helped a number of companies in this regard. This tool, developed by Reichheld and his colleagues, involves asking just one question: 'How likely is it that you would recommend our company to a friend or colleague?' The NPS is calculated by taking the share of customer 'promoters' – respondents highly likely to recommend your organisation to others (scoring 9 to 10 on a 10-point scale), and subtracting the share of customers who are detractors (scoring 0 to 6 on a 10-point scale). The NPS represents a calculation of advocacy. If the company has a substantially higher NPS than the competition, it is likely to grow at a much faster rate than its competitors.

Reichheld provides an illustration of the economics of advocacy and word-of-mouth with a case study on Dell Computers. The following is a summary of some key statistics from this case study:

- 25 per cent of new customers are word-of-mouth referrals.
- 60 per cent of Dell's customers are promoters and 15 per cent are detractors, yielding an NPS score of 45 per cent.
- Each promoter is worth $328 to Dell through purchases and referrals.
- Each detractor costs the company $57 through higher customer service costs and negative referrals.
- Converting half of the 15 per cent of customers who are detractors into regular customers could add $160 million to Dell's bottom line.[13]

This research, conducted by Bain & Co. in conjunction with Satmetrix, represents one of the first efforts to quantify the financial benefits of advocacy. Measures such as the Net Promoter Score can, despite some limitations,[14] help companies make a judgment as to how far they have progressed in terms of delivering an outstanding or perfect customer experience – a topic we return to in Chapter 8. Measures such as Net Promoter Score or other customer satisfaction metrics reflect the summation of a customer's previous (and present) encounters and experiences with the product or brand.

We have described a process of enterprise value creation and the substantial benefits of placing emphasis on acquisition, cross-selling, up-selling, retention and advocacy. The two case studies at the end of this chapter provide very different examples of enterprise value creation. The Coca-Cola in China case study shows how Coca-Cola developed a new value creation strategy, based on customer acquisition, for the fast-growing Chinese market. The Sydney Opera House case study illustrates how the ACURA framework can be applied to identify opportunities to create enterprise value in the performing arts sector. In the next section we turn our attention to considering customer lifetime value in more detail.

Customer lifetime value

Customer lifetime value is defined in many ways. In some instances companies use sales revenues, in others they use contribution, gross profit or net profit. Some consider lifetime value in terms of what the customer will contribute in the future, others in terms of what the customer has contributed in the past, while some think about the value of all purchases – past and future.

Let us start by considering a simple description of lifetime value in terms of revenue. In Chapter 1, we gave an example of a person who has purchased a car every four years. Over a customer lifetime of say 40 years and at an average price of $50,000 paid for each car, this represents $500,000 in revenues – just for the vehicles purchased. However, this future lifetime revenue does not represent the real value to the dealer. The profit margin needs to be applied to the sales revenue in order to calculate an expected lifetime profit from car sales for a customer. Then a discount rate needs to be applied to all future profits (including those from other sources which we now identify) to reflect the time value of money.

The profit from car sales needs to be readjusted to account for a number of other issues that can increase lifetime value. Other purchases such as servicing the car may need to be taken into account. Also, opportunities to cross-sell the customer other related products such as insurance, extended warranties and leasing need to be considered. Next, opportunities to up-sell the customer into more expensive models in the future need to be taken into account. Further, the customer may purchase vehicles for members of his family. Finally, if the dealer delivers outstanding service, the customer may become an advocate of that dealership and recommend many friends and business colleagues to it. It is easy to see that such a customer lifetime value may not be $500,000, but could be double that – or more! Car dealerships like Fletcher Jones Mercedes-Benz dealers in Southern California, reputedly the best Mercedes dealer in the world, have developed a legendary reputation for exceptional customer service and, as a result, have developed an outstanding asset in terms of the lifetime value of their customers.

In B2B relationships there is a further source of relationship value – reference value. It is not enough for an enterprise to have profitable and well-regarded customers; they should also benefit from being able to use them as reference sites. Efforts need to be directed at identifying and motivating business customers to act as these reference sites. Ryals identifies four sources of relational value including reference value, referral value, learning value and innovation value.[15]

Defining the role of customer lifetime value

Today, many organisations are creating strategies around the concept of customer lifetime value and loyalty. To calculate a customer's real lifetime value an enterprise needs to look at the projected future profit over the life of the account. We define customer lifetime value as follows:

CLV is the net present value of the future profit flows over the lifetime of the customer relationship. This represents the entire expected profit flow, adjusted by an appropriate discount rate, over a customer's lifetime including the elements outlined above such as cross-selling, up-selling, advocacy and, where relevant, reference effects. The CLV should be calculated at the level of segmentation granularity appropriate to that business. Care should be taken to be sensibly conservative when making future estimates.

Customer lifetime value is difficult to measure because of the difficulties in putting quantification on future events. However, although there are a number of different ways of calculating lifetime value and difficulties in measurement this does not mean the concept should be rejected. Peppers and Rogers point out that:

Statistical models of individual customer lifetime values are only as good as the data and analysis that go into them ... and even with perfect data they can never provide perfect predictions. With a reasonable amount of care, nevertheless, such a model will serve your purpose. You don't need an exact figure. What you need is a means of comparing the advantage of one marketing program or selling strategy with another. You need figures that can provide usable information.[16]

It should not be assumed that companies will wish to retain all their customers into the future. Some customers may cost too much money to service, or have such high acquisition costs in relation to their profitability, that they will never prove to be worthwhile and profitable in terms of CLV. Clearly, it would be inadvisable to invest further in such customer segments. It is likely that within a given portfolio of customers, there may be some segments that are profitable, some that are at break-even point and some that are unprofitable in terms of their CLV. Thus, increasing customer retention does not always yield positive increases in CLV. In some instances, increasing the retention of such unprofitable customers will create negative CLV. It should be recognised, however, that some 'unprofitable customers' may be valuable in their contribution towards fixed costs and overheads and considerable caution needs to be placed in the allocation of fixed and variable costs to ensure that customers who make a contribution are not simply discarded.

Calculating customer lifetime value

A simple example of the calculation of customer lifetime value is given in Figure 7.10. This customer has no revenues or profit in the first year and then generates a profit of $1,000,000 in year 1, increasing steadily to a profit of $5,000,000 in year 5.

In the figure we use a discount rate of 10 per cent, as profit made in the future is not as valuable as profit made today. The discount rate is used to reduce these future profits down

Year	Future profit ($000s)	Discount factor Based on (10%)	NPV ($ 000s)
Year 1	1,000	0.91	910
Year 2	2,000	0.83	1,660
Year 3	3,000	0.75	2,250
Year 4	4,000	0.68	2,720
Year 5	5,000	0.62	3,100
CLV			10,670

Figure 7.10 Calculation of customer lifetime value

to their NPV to make future profits values comparable to any current profits or costs. The formula used for the discount rate is:

$$D = (1 + i)^n$$

Where:

  i = the market rate of interest including risk, and
  n = the number of years.

The discount rates may be calculated from this formula or are readily accessible in the discount tables published in most financial textbooks. Here we use discount factors relevant to an annual interest rate of 10 per cent. By multiplying the expected future profit for each year by the relevant discount factor we calculate an NPV profit for each year. Added together, these give a customer lifetime value of $10,670,000 over a 5-year lifetime. More detailed mathematical formulations can be used to show the calculation of customer lifetime value for more complex examples. Those wishing to look into such mathematical formulations should see the work of Northwestern Professor Robert Blattberg and his colleagues[17] or Cranfield Professor Lynette Ryals.[18]

We have shown the need for managers to develop a stronger emphasis on customer retention and identify its impact on CLV. Some companies are now starting to build comprehensive models that enable them to measure CLV at the segment level. Such models can be used to depict the trade-off between acquisition and retention strategies in specific businesses. They enable the CLV profit impact of changes in customer retention, customer acquisition and other variables to be measured at the aggregate, segment, micro-segment and individual customer levels.

However, few organisations have reached the stage of fully understanding their business acquisition economics and retention economics, let alone gone beyond it to calculate the financial benefits of cross-selling, up-selling and advocacy. Modelling of future profit potential takes into account the potential benefits from each element in the ACURA framework. By enhancing their predictive modelling capability, enterprises can identify ways to increase share of wallet as well as market share, especially through exploitation of new channel structures, a topic discussed in the next chapter.

Co-creation

The fourth and final element that forms part of the value creation process on the CRM Strategy Framework is the co-creation of value. In Chapter 1 we introduced the concept of service-dominant logic and discussed its foundational premises, one of which is: 'The customer is always a co-creator of value'.[19] Traditionally, suppliers produced goods and services, and customers purchased goods and services. Today, customers engage in dia-logue with suppliers much more readily during each stage of product design and product delivery. Together, supplier and customer have the opportunity to create value through customised, co-produced offerings. The co-creation of value is a desirable goal as it can assist firms in highlighting the customer's point of view and in improving the process of identifying customers' needs and wants.[20]

A framework for co-creation of value

In Chapter 2 we introduced the importance of processes in relationship management. In Figure 7.11 we show a framework for co-creation of value where these processes include the procedures, activities and interactions which support the co-creation of value.[21] This process highlights the need to see the relationship between the enterprise and the customer as a longitudinal, dynamic, interactive set of experiences and activities. The framework consists of three elements:

- *Customer value-creating processes* – in a business-to-consumer relationship, the processes, resources and practices which customers use to manage their activities. In a business-to-business relationship, the processes are ones which the customer organisation uses to manage its business and its relationships with suppliers.
- *Supplier value-creating processes* – the processes, resources and practices which the supplier uses to manage its business and its relationships with customer and other relevant stakeholders.
- *Encounter processes* – the processes and practices of interaction and exchange that take place within customer and supplier relationships and which need to be managed in order to develop successful co-creation opportunities.

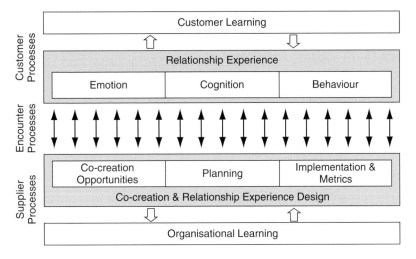

Figure 7.11 A conceptual framework for value co-creation.
Source: Based on Payne, Storbacka and Frow (2008)

Customer value-creating processes and customer learning

The customer's value creation processes include activities performed by the customer to achieve a particular goal. One key aspect of the customer's ability to create value is the amount of information, knowledge and skills that customers can access and use. The importance of recognising customer processes rests with the need to develop a full understanding of where a supplier's offering fits within the customer's overall activities.

For example, a leading international airline 'mapped' how the travel experience on their aircraft fitted within the total consumption system of their first class and business class passengers. The airline used a 'shadowing' technique where, with the customer's prior permission, highly personable employees of the airline arrived at the customer's home as they were preparing to travel. The airline employee then accompanied the business customer to the airport, travelled with them to their destination, remained with them throughout the day, flew back with them and returned with them to their home. The insights gained were used to inform future service development.

The customer's experience of a supplier and its products is a culmination of the customer's cognitions, emotions and behaviour during the relationship. These elements are interdependent and involve the customer in thinking, feeling and doing as an integral part of their role in value co-creation. Importantly, the relationship experience leads to customer learning. Customer satisfaction and the degree of customer involvement help determine whether the relationship is ongoing. The supplier's role is, therefore, one of providing experiential interactions and encounters which customers perceive as helping them utilise their resources. By understanding the customer cognition, emotion and behaviour in this broader experiential sense, the supplier can shift the focus of marketing communications from attention seeking to dialogue with customers in support of their experiences and learning processes.

Supplier value-creating processes

From the supplier's perspective, creating value for the customer begins with an understanding of the customer's value-creating processes. Customers produce value independently, but with the support of the supplier.[22] We suggest that suppliers consider at least three significant types of value co-creation opportunity:

Opportunities provided by technological breakthroughs: As new technology solutions develop they create new ways for suppliers to engage with customers to co-create innovative goods, services and experiences.

Opportunities provided by changes in industry logics: The transformation of industries is partly driven by the development of new channels for reaching customers.

Opportunities provided by changes in customer preferences and lifestyles: Based on their learning and knowledge of the customer, suppliers should be constantly looking for opportunities based on changes in customers' preferences and lifestyles.

Value co-creation demands a change in planning processes from 'making, selling and servicing' to 'listening, customising and co-creating'. Improved ways of measuring the delivery of customer value are required. Marketing metrics and measures should mean-ingfully assess the value co-creation potential of customer relationships. The develop-ment of appropriate metrics is another key issue for the supplier.

Knowledge about customers' value-creating processes should not be based solely on hard data such as customer satisfaction measures and Net Promoter Scores, but should incorporate a deep understanding of customer experiences and processes. The use of anthropological research methods can assist with this dimension of organisational learn-ing. A key issue is how to ensure the diverse elements of customer knowledge are captured and utilised effectively to improve knowledge management and its impact on co-creation.

Encounter processes

The encounter process involves a series of two-way interactions and transactions occur-ring between the customer and the supplier. Encounters, sometimes referred to as 'touch points' and 'contacts', can occur either on the initiative of the company (e.g., through direct mailings, telephone calls, and invoicing); on the initiative of the customer (e.g., via enquiries, orders and complaints); or on the initiative of both (e.g., meeting at a trade fair).

We suggest that three broad forms of encounter facilitate value co-creation: *communi-cation encounters, usage encounters* and *service encounters*. By communication encounters we mean activities which are primarily carried out in order to connect with customers and promote and enact dialogue (e.g., through advertisements, brochures, Internet home-pages and manuals). Usage encounters refer to customer practices in using a product or service and include the services which support such usage (e.g., using an Internet banking service). Service encounters comprise customer interactions with customer service person-nel or service applications (e.g., via a contact centre). Managing encounter value-creating processes includes setting goals for both customer and supplier, and evaluating whether current encounters are achieving these goals.

We conclude that while enterprises may be interested in the potential of co-creation, many of them do not yet appear engaged in substantive co-creation activity. This con-clusion is supported by a recent study of 500 European companies.[23] The study showed that although 70 per cent of the respondents expected revenues from co-creation to increase in future years, only 25 per cent indicated that they involved customers in the design and development of new products or services. We conclude that addressing co-creation as a general concept creates a barrier to achieving the full potential of co-creation.

SUMMARY

The value creation process is crucial to transforming the outputs of the strategy develop-ment process in CRM into programmes that both *extract* and *deliver* value. An insufficient focus on the value provided for key customers, as opposed to the income derived from them, can seriously diminish the impact of the offer in terms of its perceived value. Only a balanced value exchange will ensure that both parties enjoy a good return on investment, leading to a good (long-term and profitable) relationship.

Achieving the ideal equilibrium between giving value to customers and getting value from customers is a critical component of CRM and requires competence in managing the perception and projection of value within the reality of acquisition and retention economics. To anticipate and satisfy the needs of current and potential customers, the enterprise must be able to target specific customers and to demonstrate added value through differentiated value propositions and service delivery. This means adopting an analytical approach to value creation, supported by a dynamic, detailed knowledge of customers, competitors, opportunities and the company's own performance capabilities.

In mature markets, and as competition intensifies, it becomes imperative for organisations to recognise that existing customers are easier to sell to and are frequently more profitable. But, although managers may agree intellectually with this view, the practices within their organisations often tell a different story. They can take existing customers for granted, while focusing too much of their attention and resources on attracting new customers. There are many examples of organisations that have invested too heavily in unselective customer acquisition only to find that a significant proportion of the customer base they have attracted is marginal or unprofitable.

Increasingly sophisticated approaches to customer segmentation, value propositions development and lifetime value calculation will help companies better understand how value should be created for the customer and the enterprise. However, this will only be realised by ensuring a superior customer experience within and across all the channels in which the company interacts with its customers – the topic of the next chapter.

CASE 7.1: Coca-Cola in China – bringing fizz to the Chinese beverages market

The company

Coca-Cola is sold in over 200 countries in a wide range of supermarkets, department stores, restaurants and other retail outlets. In 2011 brand consultancy Interbrand identified Coca-Cola as the world's most valuable brand. The company's core product is Coca-Cola concentrate, which is sold to licensed Coca-Cola bottlers around the world. These bottlers have territorial franchises and produce the product in the familiar cans and bottles. Less well known is the extent of the company's foray into other beverage markets. The Coca-Cola Company has more than 500 brands and 3,500 beverage products, which include: sparkling sodas, such as Coca-Cola, Diet Coke, Fanta and Sprite and still beverages, such as waters, juices and juice drinks, teas, coffees, energy drinks and sports drinks. As a huge global public company with sales of over $35 billion, Coca-Cola places great emphasis on enterprise value creation. To achieve sustained value creation Coca-Cola has a relentless focus on maximising revenues and profits from key geographic market segments. It has four key value creation metrics: market share gains, consistent revenue growth, expanding operating margins and healthy cash flows. This case study reviews key elements of Coca-Cola's product strategy aimed at creating value by capitalising on the huge market opportunity in China.

Coca-Cola has long recognised the value creation opportunities offered by China. Despite the difficulties of a tightly controlled Chinese beverage market, which is highly regulated and subject to government approval, Coca-Cola has progressively developed a substantial position in this fast-growing market, which is now the fourth largest soft drink market in the world. In the early 1980s, the company built bottling plants in several regions, giving ownership of the plants to the Chinese government in exchange for sales and distribution rights. Initially its sales were restricted to designated retail outlets including hotels and 'Friendship Stores'. However, by 1985 the government allowed Coca-Cola to sell its products directly to the Chinese people. Since that time Coca-Cola has expanded its operations, bottling facilities and distribution to many regions in China. During the last three decades the company has established some 29 bottling plants and 33 production locations and employs 15,000 local staff in China.

The challenge

As large corporations expanded internationally in the 1980s and 1990s they increasingly sought to standardise their operations and marketing. This approach is epitomised by Coca-Cola's CEO Robert Goizueta, who, in 1996, stated: 'The labels "international" and "domestic" ... no longer apply.' This approach was captured in the slogan 'Think global, act global', which was advocated by many, including Harvard Business School Professor Theodore Levitt, who cited Coca-Cola Corporation as a par excellence example of his 'globalisation of markets' thesis. However, by 1999 Goizueta's globalisation strategy had run into problems, corporate earnings had dropped and the company had lost $70 billion from its peak market value. The challenge was to adopt a new value creation strategy for fast-growing international markets.

The solution

By this time it was clear that Coca-Cola's 'one size fits all' globalisation strategy was not consistent with a value creation strategy. The solution for Coca-Cola involved a new approach to its global markets and, in particular, in the increasingly important Chinese market. Recognising the need for a change in strategy, Douglas Daft, who became the new Coca-Cola Chairman and CEO in 2000, introduced an entirely new approach to marketing which focused on addressing the needs of consumers in each individual market. He summed this up as: 'Think local, act local'. This represented a substantial shift from the previous strategy of 'Think global, act global'. Daft highlighted the need to understand and respond to local needs: 'Understanding comes from recognising, respecting and celebrating the diversity of local needs and wants.' Coca-Cola started to develop a much deeper insight into local markets and introduced new ranges of product especially for them. In some cases this involved a purely local strategy and in others a more regional approach. The new strategy for value creation was product-based and recognised the need to identify and respond to the requirements of local markets. Through careful market analysis and product development, Coca-Cola developed a product-based value creation strategy, focusing on a wide range of carbonated and non-carbonated drinks and beverages.

Carbonated drinks

The customer base for drinks and beverages in China is diversified, with differing levels of education, income, lifestyle, beliefs and knowledge about US products. The language can also pose difficulties for US products. Coca-Cola picked its local name for its core product with great care: 'Ke Kou Ke Le'. This sounds quite similar to the product's English name, but translates as: 'really tasty, really fun'.

To break into and grow the carbonated drinks market segment, Coca-Cola targeted young urban consumers in major cities such as Beijing and Shanghai. The product was initially relatively expensive for Chinese consumers, although recently competition has increased and Coke's prices have fallen. Coca-Cola has also expanded its brand reach through its availability in McDonald's, Subway Sandwiches and Domino's Pizza. Coca-Cola has even had some success in penetrating the traditional Chinese fast food stalls, which are now as likely to offer their customers Coke as tea to go with their noodles. Coke is also available alongside its competitors in 7-Eleven convenience stores. The main Coke drinkers are people in their teens, 20s and 30s. However, this is the very consumer group where health concerns have arisen most strongly, with the result that this segment has been losing market share to herbal drinks and teas. In fact, these consumers perceive the clear colour and citrus flavour of Sprite as 'healthier' and this segment now consumes more of Coca-Cola Company's drink Sprite than Coke. China is Coca-Cola's largest market for Sprite, where it slightly outsells Coke.

Non-carbonated drinks

The non-carbonated drinks category includes sports and energy drinks, flavoured milk, juices, bottled water and bottled tea. *Sports drinks* are designed with nutrition in mind, whereas *energy drinks* are heavily caffeinated. Recently, sports and energy drinks such as Red Bull and Maidong have gained rapidly in popularity. The Chinese sports drink market is growing very rapidly, although Chinese per capita sports drink consumption is just 7 per cent of that in developed countries. Sports and energy drinks are aimed at young, active, well-off consumers. Although Coca-Cola's Powerade sports drink is successful in Hong Kong, its presence in China needs substantial development activity.

The *milk drinks* market is also growing strongly in China, and, in October 2009, Coca-Cola launched its first diary product in China. 'Minute Maid Pulpy Super Milky' launched in Shanghai, supported by considerable publicity. The Shanghai launch was followed by launches in Beijing, Guangdong and Zhejiang, with the objective of reaching 300 Chinese cities by the end of 2009.

At 14 million tons, China is the largest market for *bottled water* in Asia and one of the ten largest markets in the world. The bottled water market is currently growing about 20 per cent per annum as consumers become more health conscious and more companies purchase bottled water for their offices. Local producers provide 70 per cent of the market, with the largest including Wahaha (16 per cent) and Nongfu Spring (10 per cent). Coca-Cola now has 7 per cent of the market.

A striking aspect of Coca-Cola's 'Think local, act local' strategy has, however, not been in carbonated drinks at all but in the *bottled tea market*. Tea drinking is increasing worldwide. Growing health consciousness is leading to a resurgence in green tea drinking at the expense of carbonated soft drinks. In 2008 bottled tea accounted for 20 per cent of the overall soft drinks market and is forecast to grow at an average rate of 9 per cent per annum. Initially, Coca-Cola launched Coca-Cola Lan Feng (a bottled honey-flavoured tea product) and Tian Yu Di (Oolong tea, jasmine tea and lemon tea). However, these products failed because neither was tailored properly to Chinese tastes. Coca-Cola rethought its strategy and launched Cha Yan Gong Fang, a green tea product tailored to local tastes. In 2010 this was followed with Spritea (a carbonated blend of local green tea flavours). Recent reports say that this product range is now proving a success for Coca-Cola.

Like tea, the *juice market* is dominated by local Taiwanese or Chinese manufacturers. Coca-Cola is the fifth player in the juice market with Qoo, an orange, apple or mixed fruit flavour juice drink enriched with calcium and vitamin C which is aimed mainly at children. The name is based on a translation of 'Cool Kid'. However, the step change for Coca-Cola in the juice market was the introduction of its US Minute Maid brand into China. This led to the development of Pulpy, a fruit drink developed by Coca-Cola's Chinese subsidiary for the local market which has been a runaway success both in China and in other emerging markets such as Indonesia and Latin America. In 2011 growth in sales of Pulpy was up 27 per cent, and, in June 2011, Pulpy became the first $1 billion dollar brand developed in the East rather than in the US.

The value creation strategies that focused on these product categories have been supported by a communications strategy that again adheres to principles of 'Think local, act local'. Coca-Cola's communications strategy is largely aimed at young, affluent Chinese consumers. The beverage giant has localised its TV advertising strategies for over a decade in response to changing consumer attitudes in China toward foreign products. In 2007 Coca-Cola launched *Sprite Yard* in China, a mobile interactive music platform that allows users to download music and celebrity images, and to read entertainment news and receive coupons. Coca-Cola was a lead sponsor for the 2008 Beijing Olympics. Coca-Cola recognises the potential benefits of celebrity endorsement. Its current line-up of celebrities, used in its offline and online marketing activities, includes celebrity music groups, track superstars and characters based on the World of Warcraft.

The results

Coca-Cola sees the Chinese market as a major opportunity for enterprise value creation. On average, each Chinese consumer drank 39 soft drinks in 2008, compared to 760 in the US, 674 in Mexico, 315 in Brazil and 149 in Russia – this represents a large potential uplift in consumption. In 2011, commenting on the potential of the Chinese market, Coca-Cola Company Chairman and CEO Muhtar Kent announced that the company will be spending $4 billion in China over the next three years, bringing the company's investments in China between 2009 and 2014 to a total of $7 billion. Doug Jackson, President of Coca-Cola's Greater China and Korea Business Unit comments: 'We believe that China could become the largest market for Coca-Cola, however, it is hard to predict when it will happen, but it certainly will. Our long-term vision is to make China our largest market.'

In its latest reported quarter, Coca-Cola's worldwide volume was up 3 per cent, but North America and Europe grew just 1 per cent. China was 'up double digits in the quarter and for the full-year, making this nine out of the last 10 years that our business in China has delivered double-digit growth', commented Chief Executive Kent. He is confident that Coca-Cola has 'the right strategies and the right capabilities in place in China to deliver sustainable double-digit growth over the long-term'.

Coca-Cola's new product-centred value creation strategy is its most aggressive ever, and it is investing heavily in advertising that supports this strategy. But there are still risks to this strategy. China is fiercely competitive for Coca-Cola, and much of this competition comes not from arch rival Pepsi but from local brands. In 2011 Coca-Cola was in its seventh year of double-digit growth in China. Coca-Cola will need to continue to innovate in order to sustain this performance.

This case study is based on a 2011 case study written by Professor Lynette Ryals of Cranfield University School of Management and is adapted with her permission. This version was developed by Pennie Frow and Adrian Payne in 2012 from publicly available documents.

CASE 7.2: Sydney Opera House – exploring value creation strategies

The organisation

Sydney Opera House is a world-class performing arts centre and has become a symbol of Sydney and the Australian nation. It is perhaps the best-known building of the twentieth century. Sydney Opera House received UNESCO World Heritage recognition in 2007. The expert evaluation report stated: '...it stands by itself as one of the indisputable masterpieces of human creativity, not only in the 20th century but in the history of humankind'. Sydney Opera House offers a broad diversity of challenging and dynamic performing arts events which engage and entertain audiences. Sydney Opera House's Vision is to be the most distinguished and prominent performing arts centre that hosts performances. It strives to offer its patrons excellence in customer experience and enjoyment by being a perfect host in one of the world's most astounding buildings. Over 8 million people visit Sydney Opera House each year.

The challenge

Funding for the performing arts is a key challenge within all of its sectors – especially in times of adverse financial economic conditions. Despite the recent global financial crisis and its aftermath, Sydney Opera House has achieved an operating profit over the last five years. In the 2010/11 financial year, operations profit was A$3.2m on revenues of A$93.5m. However, an ongoing challenge for Sydney Opera House is to achieve its goals and maintain financial stability by increasing the financial contribution from customers, donors and the government. In this case study we consider potential value creation strategies relating to Sydney Opera House's *customers*.

Exploring customer value creation strategies

This case study differs from others that typically document what an organisation is actually doing. Instead, four experienced marketing executives, with no association with Sydney Opera House and working in other industry sectors, undertook a project that considered potential customer value creation strategies for this organisation. This approach was adopted for the case study because of the general unwillingness of organisations to permit publication of details of their highly specific initiatives with respect to customer acquisition, up-selling, customer retention and loyalty activities. The executives used the ACURA value creation framework in this project. This framework involves examining opportunities to grow customer revenue through a combination of activities aimed at increasing acquisition, cross-selling, up-selling, retention and advocacy (See Payne and Frow, *Strategic Customer Management* Cambridge University Press, 2013, Chapter 7). These executives first considered how patrons of Sydney Opera House might be segmented. They then addressed the issue of how additional value might be obtained from customers using the ACURA framework.

Customer segments

There are many ways to segment the Opera House customers as they can have different lifestyles, demographics, price sensitivities, tastes, gender, purposes for the visit, etc. After considering various options, the segmentation shown in Table 1 was used in this project.

Table 1 Illustrative segmentation of Sydney Opera House patrons

Segment	Characteristics
Retired:	Aged 60 years or older, go to the opera alone or in groups, have lots of free time, pay concession tickets, go to shows like opera, ballet, classical music, old time favourites. Could go to the opera anytime during the week. Mildly price sensitive.
Mature Sophisticated	Age group 45–60, are still working, have decent disposable income since any children are adolescent or have left home, can be single or married, and have other hobbies besides going to the opera. Most likely will go to the opera on a weekend at night (or gala night). Not price sensitive. Enjoys activities that they can do with office friends and reflects well on their taste/social status, willing to pay to eliminate hassles for a good experience.
Gen X	Arty Bohemian, between 30–35, most likely single, passionate about arts and culture, has a good job and money to spend for themselves. Also interested in other cultural activities like theatre, museums, film festivals, etc. Will go to the opera anytime in the week at night or Sunday afternoon. Not price sensitive. Influenced by peer pressure.
Families	Age group 35–45, married with children, have little time for them, but will take the children to family shows. Probably have less disposable income due to high family expenditures; their interest is seasonal with increased interest on school vacation time, public holidays or weekends. Very price sensitive. They look for convenience and for good deals (or packages) as a family.
Students	Age group 20–30, local or international, going to the opera is aspirational, always looking for cheap tickets. Will wait in line before the show to fill in the empty spaces. No problems with the timing of the shows and most likely will prefer trendy shows rather than classic. Very price sensitive. Look for the best value, open minded to new things.

Table 1 (cont.)

Segment	Characteristics
Tourist	Of all ages and group sizes, International and Australians from other states. Going to the opera is part of coming to Sydney, being inside the building is an experience in itself, will probably go to any show and at any time – they are on vacation. Not price sensitive except for Backpackers. Trust recommendations on websites and other travellers, seeking the 'complete' Australian experience.

Investigation into the number of customers that visit Sydney Opera House, combined with statistics in the Australian Bureau of Statistics *Arts and Culture in Australia: A Statistical Overview, 2008*, permitted an estimate to be made of the composition of Sydney Opera House patrons in each segment, as shown in Table 2.

Table 2 Estimated patrons – composition of segments

Code	Segments	% of Audience	No. of Customers
R	Retired	11%	135,779
MS	Mature Sophisticated	34%	436,383
GX	Gen X	27%	342,470
F	Family	13%	165,099
S	Students	5%	63,500
T	Tourist	10%	127,000
Total			1,270,231

In order to select the most profitable segments, customer lifetime value was estimated for each segment. To analyse the frequency of purchase per segment, an average value was obtained using information from the Australian Bureau of Statistics. This analysis suggested that for all segments close to 46 per cent of patrons go once a year and 41 per cent of customers visit selected entertainment events two to four times a year. This is consistent with a recent Sydney Opera House Annual Report which stated 45 per cent of their patrons are new to their events. The analysis of the customer lifetime value of the six segments suggested that the segments 'Mature Sophisticated', 'Gen X' and 'Families' provide Sydney Opera House with the highest long-term profitability and customer lifetime value. These segments provide the best opportunities for value creation initiatives. Segments 'Mature Sophisticated' and 'Gen X' form the two biggest customer groups and provide highest short-term profitability. The 'Families' segment has the greatest potential customer lifetime value, despite its smaller size, due to potential extended patronage years starting with children and teenagers who will hopefully turn into loyal long-term customers. An additional factor supporting a decision to focus on the 'Mature Sophisticated', 'Gen X' and 'Families' segments lies in the fact that they account for an estimated 75 per cent of the total Opera House audience, suggesting that marketing and CRM investments should mainly focus on these segments.

Generic ACURA strategies

In developing an ACURA strategy it is usual to focus, at least initially, on a relatively small number of customer segments. For Sydney Opera House the above three segments are considered here. Once the most attractive segments are selected, the first step is to consider *generic* ACURA strategies in terms of their potential impact on profitability and improving customer lifetime value. Typically, all key customer segments will be examined for potential acquisition, cross- and up-selling, retention and advocacy initiatives. The second step is to explore *specific* ACURA strategies *for each key segment*. The discussion on ACURA strategies below is a summary from the project report, which provides details of the analysis and key assumptions made. This case study focuses on the first step of identifying generic ACURA strategies.

Acquisition: The role and relative importance of customer acquisition varies significantly according to an organisation's specific situation and objectives. Established enterprises like Sydney Opera House will typically have a greater emphasis on growing customer revenue and focusing on customer retention; nevertheless, since the average used capacity of its halls is 80 per cent, there is still some room for acquiring new customers. The acquisition element of the ACURA framework addresses the need to acquire new customers to combat customer defection rates. Table 3 identifies some generic acquisition strategies aimed at increasing the number of new customers. In identifying the impact of each acquisition strategy in each key segment, a subjective evaluation of the potential profit is typically made by experienced executives in the organisation. This estimate of potential profitability is shown in the table by the number of dollar signs ($), ranging from nought to three.

Table 3 Acquisition strategies

Acquire Element / Channels	MS	GX	F
Develop segmented sales teams to target: associations, executives, sports and yacht clubs, etc.	$$$	$$	$
Advertising: interstate and tourism boards, Direct mail/e-mail	$	$$	$$
Package of tickets (price)	$	$	$$$
Family friendly facilities (specific)	$		$$$
Transport included in ticket price		$	$$
Partnership with other cultural institutions	$$$	$$$	$
Road shows and events	$$	$$	$

Cross-selling: Cross-selling strategies represent an important part in building profitability as many opportunities exist for patrons to purchase complementary products and services. For Sydney Opera House, revenue sources such as food and beverage, merchandising and guided tours, represent an important part of increasing sales. Cross-selling options that can be considered include bundling popular events with less popular ones as an incentive to attract audiences to a broad range of events, and additional development of events/activities that can be sold as a package with the main event and are presented prior to and after attending. The main purpose of cross-selling activities should be to encourage customers to buy more from the organisation by improving the customer experience and the value received. Improving the quality and variety of the beverage and food selection offered will also provide an incentive to increase customers' spend in 'outside ticketing' products. Channels also play a key role in the success of cross-selling strategies since product cross-selling can be promoted across appropriate customer touch points. Internet booking, social media and face-to-face interaction represent good opportunities to suggest other products to customers. Table 4 shows a list of potential generic cross-selling activities.

Table 4 Cross-selling strategies

Cross-selling	MS	GX	F
Beverage, Food and Merchandising variety	$$$	$$	$$
Implement purchase recommendation online and with Box office staff	$$	$$	$
Food and beverage included with the ticket (when buying from bar)	$	$$	$$$
Dinner and show package	$$$	$	

Table 4 (cont.)

Cross-selling	MS	GX	F
Cross-sell with the Backstage Tour		$	$
Flexible Show package (Theatre + Opera; Classic + Dance; etc.)	$	$$	
Gift Cards	$$	$$	

Up-Selling: The purpose of up-selling is for an organisation to persuade customers to purchase higher-priced products/services or upgrade to a better offer from their planned purchase. The up-selling strategies that Sydney Opera House can consider include exclusive offers for patrons and enhancement of the customer experience. Activities to promote more exclusive treatment of patrons could include access to private lounges during intervals with free refreshments, bar counter and exclusive restrooms/cloakrooms with an assortment of utilities for patrons to use such as toiletries. Other means of providing exclusive services would be to provide back-stage passes or invitations to a reception for patrons, enabling them to get close to the stars of the performance. Sydney Opera House could offer returning patrons upgraded tickets, e.g., with an integrated system that recognised a returning customer and offered enhanced (reserved) seats through online bookings, or, an early-bird private booking. Special dining packages could also be an option to up-sell the Sydney Opera House experience including special menus, select wines and restricted seats as part of an exclusive treat. Some potential general strategies are shown in Table 5.

Table 5 Up-selling strategies

Up-selling	MS	GX	F
First class, private lounge, canapés and exclusive treatment	$$$		
Meet the stars, backstage passes, after-performance reception		$$$	
Buy autographed merchandise i.e. photos/limited edition CD music, programmes, posters, postcards, etc.	$$	$$$	$$
Early bird better seats/communication	$$	$$$	$
Higher quality food, dining packages before performances.	$$$	$$	

Retention: One of the most important ACURA elements is the retention of current customers. An increase in customer retention can produce a tremendous effect on long-term profitability and growth by significantly increasing customer lifetime value. Also, customer retention strategies should place the greatest emphasis on those customers that have the greatest profit potential. In order to improve customer satisfaction and retention, a CRM database needs to ensure that repeat customers will be recognised and treated attentively. In order to provide existing customers with more value, a loyalty programme that rewards customers for repeat patronage is recommended. Value-added promotions for loyal customers might include offers for special occasions like birthdays, Mother's Day, etc., using personalised direct or e-mail. Finally, the value gained by being a loyal customer needs to be communicated effectively via frequent personalised communication. Table 6 suggests potential generic retention strategies for each segment and their profit potential.

Table 6 Retention strategies

Retention	MS	GX	F
Implementation of CRM databases	$$$	$$	$$
Improve customer satisfaction/customer experience	$$$	$$$	$$

Table 6 (cont.)

Retention	MS	GX	F
Improve customer buying experience	$$$	$$	$$
Loyalty programme	$$$	$$	$$
Special intimate shows exclusive for loyal customers	$$	$	
Special offers for personal special occasions		$	$
Adding value through free pre- and post-show events	$$	$$	
Implementation of feedback channels	$$	$$	$
Communicate value gained via direct mail	$	$$	$

Advocacy: Advocacy is extremely important to Sydney Opera House. Advocacy results from positive word-of-mouth from satisfied patrons, who will later make recommendations which attract new customers. In order to have high customer satisfaction, the quality of the events and services provided must meet, and ideally exceed, expectations. One means of increasing advocacy is to continue presenting events that offer a great experience. Great quality shows will generate advocates who enjoy the experience so much that they will spread positive word-of-mouth/buzz. Australia has many stars that have Hollywood status; therefore generating advocacy through star endorsement is likely to impact revenue positively. Consumers often aspire to frequent the same place as their favourite movie star. For example, if Nicole Kidman recommended/endorsed a ballet she has seen recently, the sales for that event are likely to increase. Table 7 identifies potential advocacy strategies.

Table 7 Advocacy strategies

Advocacy	MS	GX	F
Quality of the show/Show experience	$$$	$$	$$
International recommendations	$$$	$$	$
Follow up/After-show Pictures giveaway		$	$
Referral promotions	$$$	$$$	
Star endorsement (invite them to the event)	$$	$	
Autographed photos	$	$	$
Movie premieres and other outside events	$$$	$$$	$$

Specific ACURA strategies

The executives identified possible ACURA strategies, as outlined above. This analysis was accompanied by their subjective estimation of the potential profit impact of each strategy for each key segment. As outlined above, the second step involves an in-depth examination in each key segment and explores the potential profit impact in much greater detail. A consideration of each segment starts with a review of the generic ACURA strategies. These are then augmented by identification of further strategies which are *segment-specific* – under the heading of acquisition, cross-selling, up-selling, retention and advocacy. The profit potential is then considered with much greater precision. The overall estimated investment needed to implement each proposed strategy is analysed together with estimated revenues and costs. The return on investment and payback period is calculated using an appropriate discount rate in order to justify the investment. Careful analysis is required to determine how any recommended incremental investment should be distributed among competing opportunities such as customer database management, building a loyalty programme, advertising and improving employee performance in order to provide superior customer experience and promoting cross- and up-selling of existing products. This analysis clearly involves considerable detail so is not included in this case study.

Sydney Opera House's overall strategy needs to consider key marketing goals including customer satisfaction, behavioural loyalty and the use of customer feedback as an input into new product development. Metrics should then be put in place and monitored for the key marketing and financial indicators that will determine the overall success of the implementation process. A further factor for success is the deep understanding of customer's experience from the patron's point of view.

The future

Sydney Opera House makes a substantial contribution to the Australian economy. A report to the Commonwealth Government, *The Economic Activity of Australia's World Heritage Areas*, in 2008 estimated Sydney Opera House contributes A$758m in direct and indirect household income and over 12,000 direct and indirect jobs to the economy. In the financial year to 2011, 318,000 people attended 1,800 performances, an increase of 3.6 per cent in attendance over the previous year. Sydney Opera House Presents staged a total of 849 performances to audiences of 384,000, an increase of 17 per cent on the prior year. The most successful of the Vivid LIVE programmes was held with 33 performances and 59 per cent of the 40,258 attendees were first-time patrons to Sydney Opera House. During 2010/11 the profit from general operations was A$3.2m. Operational revenues increased by 16 per cent to A$13.1m due to increased activity levels, patronage, funding and interest.

Sydney Opera House's first membership programme, *Insiders*, was launched in September 2010 and gained its two thousandth member in mid-2011. The *Insiders* programme provides members with priority booking, ticket and parking discounts, dining offers and other benefits with partners on-site and around Sydney. Sydney Opera House now has robust measures of service quality in place. Overall patron satisfaction for 2011 was 83 per cent – an increase of 5 per cent from four years ago. Artistic quality/excellence, a new measure, was a high 90 per cent. Sydney Opera House has continually evolved its marketing and CRM activities. These initiatives have contributed substantially to the organisation's success. However, the challenges of obtaining increased revenue flow in the performing arts sector will remain. Strategies that are successful in achieving improvement in customer acquisition, cross-selling, up-selling, retention and advocacy will have an important role to play in sustaining the organisation's future success. Sydney Opera House, as a public not-for-profit institution, has to balance its social objectives that include community outreach and participation with its commercial imperatives.

This case study is based on an Advanced Marketing Strategy project undertaken at the University of New South Wales by Inka Schrader, Lindsay Tan, Nakamol Bongkojkerd and Veronica Figarella. It was developed from publicly available information. The purpose of this case study is to demonstrate how the ACURA framework can be applied to identify strategies which lead to an increase in enterprise value creation. As the case study has been undertaken without the involvement of Sydney Opera House, it is meant for illustrative purposes only. Some of the strategies outlined above may not be appropriate, and others, such as the *Insiders* membership loyalty programme, have recently been introduced by Sydney Opera House.

8 | Multi-channel integration

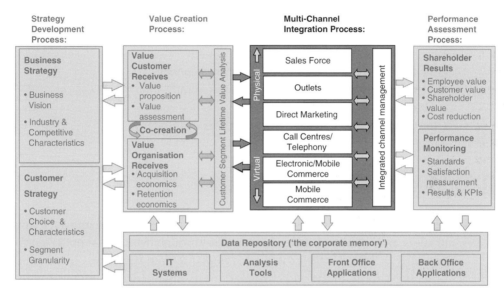

Strategy Development Process:	Value Creation Process:	Multi-Channel Integration Process:		Performance Assessment Process:

The CRM Strategy Framework

The multi-channel integration process has a pivotal role to play in CRM as it takes the outputs of the business strategy and value creation processes and translates them into value-adding interactions with customers. These include all pre-sales communications, the sales interaction, post-sales service and support with the customer.

This process involves making decisions about the most appropriate combination of channel participants and channel options through which to interact with your customer base, how to ensure the customer experience is highly positive within those channels and, where the customer interacts with more than one channel, how to obtain and present a 'single unified view of the customer'. Put simply, the multi-channel integration process is concerned with two key questions:

1. What are the best ways for us to get to customers and for customers to get to us?
2. What does a perfect or outstanding customer experience, deliverable at an affordable cost, look like?

Multi-channel integration involves all the direct contacts and interfaces between the customer and the organisation supplying them, as well as indirect contacts via social media. There are now a large number of channels through which customers and suppliers may interact in a variety of communications, sales and service situations. Integrating these channel participants and channel options is the key to success. Many large organisations are now starting to think about implementing a multi-channel delivery capability in an integrated way.

This chapter reviews the *multi-channel integration process* with the objective of providing an understanding of integrated channel management and the role of the six channel categories in the CRM Strategy Framework. In order to consider the optimal nature of the enterprise's customer interface in a multi-channel environment the following issues are addressed in this chapter:

- the nature of channel participants and channel options;
- the structure of industry channels;
- the types of channel options and channel categories;
- the channel strategies a business can select from;
- the nature of the customer experience;
- the development of an integrated multi-channel strategy.

Channel participants and channel options

Channel participants (or *channel members*) refer to the intermediaries such as wholesalers, retailers and value-added resellers (VARs) through which a supplier reaches its final customers. *Channel options* (or *channel media*) refer to the means by which the supplier (if selling directly to the end customer), or its intermediaries, interacts with customers. Sales forces, retail branches, call centres and the Internet are examples of channel options. Collectively the term channel is used here to include both channel participants and channel options. This multitude of channels creates enormous opportunities for improving the scope and strength of customer relationships but considerable challenges in managing the complexity of channels in a successful and cost-effective manner. With the rise of social media, the enterprise is confronted with a further challenge: how to capitalise on a channel where they have very limited control.

To establish a strong customer relationship, both supplier and customer must have ready and reliable communications, interactions and access to each other. Thus, ensuring that effective and efficient two-way (and where appropriate, one-way) contact exists with the customer is a priority issue for successful CRM.

The development of electronic channels

Of particular importance is the recent development of electronic channels. In today's environment, costs within many traditional channels, such as in sales forces and branch networks, are increasing at an alarming rate. As a result, there is continuing pressure on organisations to move to electronic channels and seek to develop customer self-service strategies in order to reduce cost.

Many customers in both business-to-consumer (B2C) and business-to-business (B2B) sectors are now embracing self-service. Self-service enables customers to order products or services, seek information and solve problems at the time and place their needs dictate. This is made possible through a combination of personalised websites, contact centres and social media platforms. Benefits to the customer can be identified through regular customer satisfaction tracking surveys. In B2C markets there are an increasing number of companies such as Amazon, Book Depository, Expedia and lastminute.com that have successfully developed self-service models. Consumer markets, with relatively simple product offers, especially lend themselves to the use of Internet self-service. However, not all companies should or will move to full self-service models.

In B2B markets, for example, important interactions such as major sales are likely to be encouraged in face-to-face encounters while various more routine transactions are handled via e-channels. By channelling low value and less complex transactions through electronic routes, scarce resources, such as an account manager's time, can be much better deployed. In B2B markets, rarely does an electronic channel fully support its own business case – it needs to be seen in the overall context of the full channel mix. For example, in online purchasing, business customers will generally want to speak to someone to purchase the services they require so the integration of call centre and Web becomes essential. Also, the overall economics of individual channels needs be considered in the context of the economics of the overarching full channel mix. For example, reductions in headcount for face-to-face sales support the investment in desk-based teams and the electronic channels.

However, as companies seek to introduce such cost savings, it is essential that there is no significant reduction in customer value as the result of the introduction of a new channel. The dramatic decline of the technology stocks listed on stock exchanges at the start of the 2000s caused an increased focus on electronic channel solutions that address real customer needs and create significant customer value and that are based on sound business models. Thus, a more sophisticated approach to using electronic channels is emerging – one that seeks increases in customer satisfaction and increases in sales and profits, as well as reducing the cost of sale.

Reviewing industry channel structures

A review of the existing industry structure and its channel participants, as well as likely future shifts in it, needs to be undertaken prior to addressing how multiple channels should best work together. While this review is typically undertaken as part of the strategy development process discussed in Chapter 6, it needs to now be considered at a much more detailed level within the multi-channel integration process.

Channel participants

The existing industry channel structure needs to be reviewed and documented. This involves a study of the current channel participants and their roles. There are a number of channel participants through which a company may seek to serve the final customer,

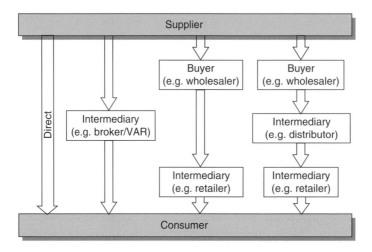

Figure 8.1 Alternative industry structures in terms of channel participants

some of which are illustrated in Figure 8.1. The channel structure that will be appropriate for any given organisation will depend upon which approach can best attract the final customers in the target segment, which, in turn, will depend upon the organisation's and intermediaries' ability to create value relevant to those customers' needs.

Of increasing importance in B2B markets is one type of intermediary – 'business partners'. In the IT sector, for example, such business partners range from being small niche operators or VARs to large system integrators. A number of IT software suppliers have found their competencies lie more in software development than customer relationships and, for this reason or because of capacity problems and implementation weaknesses, businesses have turned to this type of partner.

The choice regarding channel alternatives should be made following a determination of the value proposition relevant to the final customer in the desired segments that a company wishes to serve and may involve a combination of those shown above. Central to these decisions will be an analysis of the value of these customer segments to the organisation, based on the economics of segments. This topic is discussed in Chapter 7.

Reviewing channel alternatives

In the context of rapid technological change, the role of channel participants should be subject to regular scrutiny as circumstances change and new opportunities present themselves. There is now an increasing recognition that for a firm to be successful it needs to create a demand chain that is more effective than that of its competitors. Therefore, it is demand chains or market networks that compete, rather than just companies. Thus, the task that needs to be addressed is how to create superiority in what has been termed the *value delivery network*.[1]

As well as considering target customers' current buying behaviours and motivations, it is important for a company also to consider how these might change over time, particularly with respect to the impact of developing technology. Over the last decade, the traditional channel structures of many industries have been dismantled and reconfigured in response to new electronic technologies that have opened new paths to market.

Organisations are now developing new channel management teams who map channel coverage for new propositions and products as they come to market. Such teams will manage changes in the channel mix, based on consequent shifts in margins, as products move through their life-cycle.

Understanding structural change – the role of intermediaries

Managers responsible for channel strategy need to understand both the nature of their industry channel structure now and how it is likely to alter in the future. Valuable insights into emerging trends within channel structures can be gained from understanding the previous evolution of the industry channel structure as well as examining the experiences of other sectors or other industries on a global basis. Of particular relevance are the opportunities and threats that result from two forms of structural change amongst 'middlemen' or intermediaries: disintermediation and reintermediation. Three different types of intermediaries can be involved in the transactions:[2]

- traditional intermediaries,
- electronic commerce-able intermediaries, and
- electronic commerce-only intermediaries.

Disintermediation
Disintermediation is where changes in the current business model or advances in technology mean that a company ceases to need to use intermediaries to create the value sought by end customers.

Numerous examples of disintermediation can be found in businesses that have utilised e-commerce channels or have adopted call centre technology and computer-telephony integration (CTI), rather than utilising more traditional branch-based intermediaries. These include computer companies such as Dell, insurance companies such as Direct Line in the UK, and low-cost airlines such as easyJet and Ryanair.

Disintermediation in the computer industry
Dell Computers provides a well-known example of successful disintermediation. Michael Dell realised he could purchase computer components, assemble them and sell them directly to the final customer. This strategy enabled him to bypass the traditional channels of distribution favoured by the established computer manufacturers and to offer them at a significant discount. The Internet channel played an increasingly important role for Dell and the $1 million per day in sales achieved in 1997 has multiplied greatly since then as

the Internet's use as a sales and service channel has increased. Starting in 2007, Dell recognised the importance of adopting further channels and developed a multi-channel approach. Dell has now formed partnerships with large retailers across the US, Europe and Asia. Among these are Walmart stores, Best Buy, Costco Wholesale, Staples, Carrefour, and Suning and Gome, China's largest electronics store. By 2012 Dell was selling over $60 billion of computers and related services annually.

Disintermediation in the insurance industry

UK insurance company Direct Line, now part of the RBS Insurance Division of the Royal Bank of Scotland, initially utilised call centre technology and IT, and later the Internet, to create additional value for their target market compared to the channel structure consisting mainly of retail insurance brokers that had dominated the insurance industry until then.

By focusing on individuals with low insurance risk, the company was able to offer them even lower premiums by enabling customers to deal directly with the company, so eliminating the need to factor costly brokerage commissions (and the overheads associated with supporting a broker network) into the prices of policies. Moreover, by dealing with their customers directly, the company was able to develop a fuller understanding of them, enabling Direct Line to develop new products tailored to their needs and proactively pursue cross-selling opportunities. The division has now expanded into Spain, Japan (in partnership with Yasuda Life), Germany and Italy.

Reintermediation

Reintermediation is where changes in the current business model or advances in technology result in the emergence of new types of intermediary that can create more value than was possible in the previous channel structure.

A good example of reintermediation exists on the Web in the form of so-called 'infomediaries', or Web-enabled information agents. Rather than the customer having to spend considerable time researching the possible alternatives when considering purchasing a type of product, the infomediary performs activities on their behalf. These activities may take the form of simple so-called buying engines where the customer enters their specific purchase criteria and the agent searches the offers available from different suppliers that meet those criteria. The buying engine then provides the consumer with details of products meeting the criteria they entered along with comparative prices, where they can be purchased, etc.

There are many examples of reintermediation in the travel industry, both with general players (Travelocity, Expedia) and those targeting specific niches such as surfing (Wavehunters.com), and in the automotive sector (Autobytel and CarsDirect.com). Infomediaries also exist as 'buyer collectives' where consumers wishing to purchase a particular product are able to combine their purchasing power to secure volume discounts from suppliers of that product.

Reintermediation in the automobile industry

Some infomediaries have developed successful additional services, such as the supply of general information about a particular product category or products meeting a series of different needs based around general life events. In the world of online new and used car sales, electronic intermediaries assist buyers and/or sellers. These are new reintermediaries, intermediaries that have restructured their role in the purchase process.

For example, Autobytel.com, a Web-based car sales intermediary, started by offering customers general information about cars which helped them in identifying their search criteria and gave them the ability to research dealers from whom they could purchase the specified vehicle. The company assists customers with financing, insurance and service scheduling, increasingly performing many of the functions previously undertaken by dealers and taking ownership of the long-term relationship with the customer. Autobytel offers automotive dealers information, tools and products to help them manage their businesses. Their products include: the Rapid Response programme that connects dealers to online customers via phone; an E-mail Manager programme, which manages long-term e-mail campaigns on behalf of the dealership; and LeadCall, a live call programme, which arranges in-dealership appointments and develops a score of customer readiness to buy from auto dealers. A further initiative is the AutoReach Ad Network. This is an automotive advertising network of third-party Web publishers that is visited by millions of consumers. Autobytel's focus provides the opportunity to reach the new Web 2.0 age of automotive consumers.

Benchmarking structural change

Benchmarking structural changes in analogous industry sectors may be especially useful in understanding opportunities and threats within your own industry. In considering experiences in other sectors, the role of mediation warrants careful examination. In some industries, intermediaries are becoming more valuable channel members, while in others the value of intermediaries is being challenged. Unless the intermediary is adding value to the customer relationship, it may prove to be an unnecessary cost and the intermediary may be bypassed. Many organisations are now finding that in order to build stronger relationships with final customers they need to change the emphasis and expenditure at different channel levels or, alternatively, refocus the existing expenditure in ways that build deeper and more sustained relationships. The example of Amazon.com (see box) illustrates some of the issues of mediation in an industry where there has been profound structural change.

Amazon.com: disintermediation or reintermediation in the bookselling industry?

By providing their bookselling service on the Web, Amazon.com avoided the need for expensive high street outlets and was able to pass on the cost savings to customers in lower prices. Added value was offered in terms of customer convenience, for customers could order a book at any time of the day or night from their own home or office computer. The use of sophisticated Web and database technologies greatly enhanced the company's customer intelligence, enabling them also to recommend books to individual customers and notify them of forthcoming releases within their areas of interest.

However, unlike major retail book chains that order direct from the book publisher, Amazon used book wholesalers extensively. Some observers cite this as an example of disintermediation; however, in this context it can be considered an example of reintermediation, as an extra channel layer has been added when compared with a situation where customers deal directly with book publishers. Amazon are also potentially well placed to deal directly with book authors and sell their books, possibly in electronic form, thus organisations like Amazon could possibly disintermediate the book publisher and book wholesaler out of the channel chain at some point in the future.

In 2012 MarketWatch named Amazon's leader Jeff Bezos its CEO of the Year, highlighting his ability to lead Amazon through a period of growth despite general economic turbulence. Amazon's stock price rose 40 per cent between January and October of 2011. Amazon dismisses the conventional wisdom that says businesses should excel primarily at one service. Amazon has progressively moved into a range of different businesses. Amazon is an outstanding company applying strategic customer management. CEO Bezos stated, at a recent shareholder's meeting, that when he was in the process of developing new business ideas, unlike leaders of many other companies, he tries to start with customer needs and work backward, even if it means that industry observers have doubts about his company's plans.[1]

---

[1] S. Langlois (2012), CEO of the Year: Cloud, Fire lifted Amazon's Bezos, MarketWatch. Available at: www.marketwatch.com/story/ceo-of-the-year-cloud-fire-lifted-amazons-bezos-2012-01-17.

Orientation of intermediaries

In addressing structural change, the orientation of existing and future intermediaries needs to be considered. One can categorise intermediaries according to their 'allegiance'. Some are clearly allied to selling a specific company's products. In contrast, buying engines have no such allegiance. Their role is not to sell a particular company's products; it is simply to provide consumers with information on those products that best meet their needs, regardless of who supplies them, and to secure for consumers the lowest price. In between these two extremes, one can identify channel members that are neutral in their orientation. Thus a traditional retailer stocks a range of goods. While it has an interest in selling goods and supporting the most profitable price possible, it typically does not have any vested interest in selling one company's products more than another's.

The difference in allegiance clearly comes from who controls the channel member. Thus seller-oriented members will typically be owned by the seller or rely on the seller for most of their income. Here, the seller enjoys a high degree of direct control. In contrast, buyer-oriented ones rely on the buyer for their income (e.g., through subscriptions or the volumes of buyers they are able to attract and thus the advertising revenue or commissions they can secure). Hence their allegiance is with the buyer. Neutral channel members rely on both buyers and sellers and thus their allegiance is on neither one side nor the other.

These differences in the relative degree of control of intermediaries require the company to understand their orientation and motives fully and to adopt different strategies to engage with the different types of channel member.

Buyer-oriented intermediaries

The Internet has given rise to a large increase in new buyer-oriented intermediaries, so these are worthy of some further discussion. There are two major categories of buyer-oriented intermediaries: buying engines and communities.[3]

Buying engines simply offer users the means of reviewing different companies' offers on the basis of cost. They are typically only relevant to buyers with a thorough understanding of the product area in which they are purchasing and a clear specification of what they require. The clear threat is that such intermediaries may lead to downward pressure on prices to buyers and hence commoditisation. Except for companies that can enjoy cost leadership in their industries, the only response open to companies facing the emergence of such intermediaries is CRM – extending individualised relationships to customers and creating value so that it is hard for such commodity-based intermediaries to compete.

Communities, on the other hand, serve buyers with greater information and support needs. Those that prove popular will impact strongly on customers' buying decisions. They will potentially have considerable control over the relationship with the end customer. Faced with the emergence of such an intermediary, enterprises need to examine how they can create partnerships with them to add to the value created for their users.

Developing market structure maps

The existing industry structure and the role of channel participants can be better understood by means of a market structure map that shows how products or services flow from the producer through various intermediaries to the final customer. The market map identifies the volumes of product and services sold and the sales values associated with them. An example of a market map is shown in Figure 8.2.

A market map is constructed by plotting the various stages in the channel structure. It identifies all stages from the production of goods or services by the enterprise (and its competitors), through the various channel members to the final users. Quantification of the volumes or values at each of these stages is a key element in the process. Where possible, changes in volumes and values over time should be identified on the market map

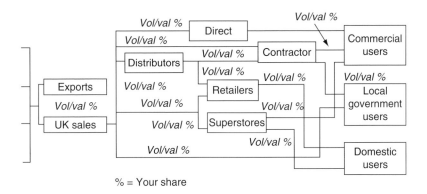

Figure 8.2 Market structure map.
Source: Based on McDonald and Dunbar (2010)

so the dynamics of channels can be better understood. Ideally, margins retained by each channel member at each stage of the market map should be identified, as well as how these may have changed over time. As the market map is developed further, refinements are made to it including the addition of information about specific market segments and different purchasing procedures encountered by channel members.[4]

Market maps help evaluate the success of existing channel participants, the amount of CRM effort directed at different groups and the consideration of alternative future channel structures. The analysis of the industry and competitive environment, discussed as part of the strategy development process in Chapter 6, will provide very useful input into a consideration of what structural changes may occur. In particular, the eight forces industry analysis, discussed in Chapter 6, can be used to help identify future likely structural changes. The company starts by reviewing whether removing one of the intermediaries or adding a new type of intermediary would result in better optimisation of information flows and physical flows, as well as volumes, values and profits. If so, then the company may have grounds for expecting such a change may happen in the future, or it may consider introducing such changes for its organisation – if its role within the industry structure enables it to make these changes.

For example, the current structure of the car industry is such that manufacturers supply myriad dealers who in turn supply product information, test drives, servicing, sales and financing to the customer. However, such an approach has tremendous inefficiencies and costs built in, such as having huge numbers of cars sitting on dealer forecourts throughout the country. Many changes and structural shifts are occurring in this industry. In Europe, some changes were driven by the 'block exemption' regulatory environment, some by the rise of competitors such as car supermarkets and others by changes in customer purchasing behaviour, with an increasing number of customers shopping on the Internet. Further changes may occur, such as the use of more centralised distribution from which cars are delivered direct to the end consumer, reducing the high levels of stock carried in the dealer network.

Channel options and categories

Equipped with a sound understanding of the key issues underlying selection of the appropriate channel participants, managers can then examine and evaluate the channel options (or channel media) available.

Channel categories

These options fall into six main channel categories, as shown in the CRM Strategy Framework. Although there are many individual channel options, we have found it convenient to group them into these six categories. Thus options such as retail branches and kiosks are included within 'outlets' and the Internet and digital TV within 'electronic/mobile commerce'. Current mobile commerce technology and new smart devices (like the iPhone and iPad) can access and use all business services. Mobile commerce also adds 'location based services' and 'apps' to the technology mix. Because of device convergence and the factors above, electronic commerce and mobile commerce (e-commerce and m-commerce), which were addressed separately in our earlier work,[5] are now grouped together under the electronic/mobile commerce category. Social media, which came of age in the latter part of the 2000s, represents a relatively new channel. The six channel categories are:

- *Sales force*: including field account management, service and personal representation;
- *Outlets*: including retail branches, stores, depots and kiosks;
- *Call centres/telephony*: including traditional telephone, facsimile, telex and call centre contact;
- *Direct marketing*: including direct mail, radio, traditional TV, etc., but excluding e-commerce;
- *Electronic/mobile commerce*: including e-mail, the Internet, digital TV, smart mobile devices, location based services and apps for mobile devices;
- *Social media*: including collaborative projects (e.g., Wikipedia), blogs/microblogs (e.g., Twitter), content sharing communities (e.g., YouTube), social networking sites (e.g., Facebook), virtual game worlds (e.g., World of Warcraft) and virtual social worlds (e.g., Second Life).

Figure 8.3 summarises the general characteristics and functionality of these different channel types and indicates the kinds of customer needs they can satisfy.[6]

In the following section, for simplicity we use the term 'e-commerce' to include both electronic commerce and mobile commerce, unless we need to refer to the latter more specifically. We use the term 'digital' more generally to include electronic commerce, mobile commerce and the use of social media.

Integration and the channel categories

Faced with the necessity of offering consumers different channel options to meet their changing needs, there are two integration imperatives that must be addressed if a company is to deliver a consistent individualised relationship to customers, create the maximum value for them and provide an outstanding customer experience. These imperatives are to integrate the activities *within* a given channel and to integrate the activities performed *across* the different channels during different stages of the customer's relationship with the enterprise.

We now look at examples of the use of different channel types, contrasting an integrated solution with a non-integrated solution. Insight into the impact that can be achieved through such effective integration of channel activity can be gained by contrasting the experience of customers using a channel option of a company whose activities are not integrated (too often the reality) with that of a customer using a channel where the company has achieved integration.

Channel Option	General characteristics and functionality
Sales force	The interactive nature of face-to-face communication with customers means that sales staff can deal effectively with complex non-standard queries. They are also well placed to determine an individual's specific needs and to make purchase recommendations. Sales force automation systems (SFAs) can be used to individualise customer service further by ensuring that those handling sales enquiries have the necessary knowledge and skills to respond to customers' individual information needs. Using printed materials or product samples, sales representatives can also convey large amounts of information and demonstrate product features. However, sales staff offer limited customer access, partly because they generally only work during office hours and partly because they are limited in the number of customers they can serve at any one time. Personal selling via sales representatives therefore tends to be an extremely expensive form of marketing channel.
Outlets	The physical presence of stores and other outlets offers a number of benefits. As well as being reassuringly visible, they allow for the physical inspection of products and the return of unwanted sales. Customers can browse among products at liberty and can gain large amounts of information, both via product displays and through conversation with sales assistants. Moreover, assuming staff are well-trained, in-store conversations can be used to resolve complex non-standard queries. However, accessibility is limited by restricted opening hours and the requirement that customers make the journey to and from the store. Further, the level of individual attention the customer receives in the store (according to their specific needs and value to the organisation) can be difficult to achieve on a mass scale. To provide further scope for individualising service, some retailers are installing kiosks to provide a Web-based service channel in-store. Online search and service facilities can also be tailored to the customer according to the customer's contact history and purchase profile. Also, the capture of purchase information in-store via electronic point of sale (EPOS) and loyalty cards can also be used to develop individual customer profiles to drive tailored activity in other channels, such as direct mail.
Direct Marketing	When based on full and accurate database records of the customer, including their contact and purchase histories and customer profile, direct marketing can offer a reasonable degree of service customisation. E.g., direct mail can be tailored to the customer's individual interests and life events. The advent of digital printing has made small print runs far cheaper than was previously possible under lithographic printing, enabling far more mail pieces to be targeted at far smaller segments. Large amounts of information can be relayed through text and graphics, allowing many products to be featured, such as in a product catalogue. Customers are offered the opportunity to browse through the company's products and perhaps also to place an order via post. Direct marketing does not generally represent a fast and flexible medium in terms of its customer responsiveness. Information sent via telephone or Internet can be more easily and quickly adapted to customer feedback – with mailings one has to send a mail piece, wait a number of days for the customer's response (if there is one) and then dispatch another progressively updated item. Moreover, direct mail offers the customer little access to a company and limited opportunity for the company to deal with customer queries – again requiring the recipient to complete a response device, mail it to the company, have it processed and so on (unless of course a company integrates another channel to handle the response, such as allowing customers to respond by phone or email). Mail offers no means of physically inspecting a product (unless a sample of the product is enclosed). While the tangible quality of the mail piece can provide a degree of customer reassurance, there is the potential for customer mistrust if the customer is not already familiar with the company through using other channels.
Call Centres/ Telephony	In principle, call centres can offer access to a company 24 hours, 7 days. The service provided to a customer via this channel can be tailored cost-effectively to their particular interests and their value to the organisation by using company records to guide the script brought up on the operative's screen and by directing their call to suitably skilled personnel via automated call routing systems. By affording human dialogue, the telephone channel is well suited for dealing with complex, vague or unclear questions from customers. It also enables the information conveyed to be adapted in real time according to the customer's earlier responses during the interaction. However, the amount of information that can be exchanged is limited by the extent to which it can be conveyed verbally and can be retained by a listener. The telephone is best suited to providing responses to specific queries from a customer, i.e., it does not readily offer the customer an opportunity to 'browse' or the call centre representative to easily 'sell' a complex proposition. Nor does it enable the physical inspection of a product. By its 'virtual' nature this channel is more subject to engendering customer mistrust, unless the customer has a familiar and comfortable relationship with the company built through other channels.

Figure 8.3 General characteristics of the different channel options.
Source: Based on Payne and Frow (2012)

Channel Option	General characteristics and functionality
Electronic/ Mobile Commerce	The Web truly offers customers 24/7 access to the company and the company unique access to its users. Clever website design can enable the company to recognise individual users through log-in procedures or 'cookie' technology. The information conveyed to users via the site can be tailored or personalised to their particular interests, purchase history and value to the organisation, in real time, based on a 'memory' of their previous visits to the site. Trading over the Internet supports the development of 1:1 relationships with customers on a mass scale. Moreover, the volume of information that can be conveyed is potentially infinite, considering the sophisticated facilities of multimedia and hyperlinks to other sites. The customer can readily browse the company's products online and can revisit the information by saving it on a computer or printing it out for later reference.
	However, while the medium deals well with simple standard queries via tables of FAQs, many non-standard or more complex queries will need to be dealt with by a human operative (via e-mail in the case of the former or telephone in the case of the latter). In addition, physical inspection of the actual product is again impossible. The 'virtual' nature of e-commerce can generate customer mistrust unless the customer is already familiar with the company via other channels.
	In the mobile commerce arena technology is evolving rapidly. Over the last few years there has been a phenomenal increase in mobile network access speeds as well as coverage. The promise of wider implementations of 4G networks is eagerly anticipated. In parallel with this we have seen the rise of the smart device from Apple, Blackberry, and Samsung amongst others. This intersection of emerging technologies has created the possibility of customers that are always on-line, wherever they are. By using a global positioning system (GPS), most smart devices also know where they are, so it's now possible to develop location-based services that can target customers based on 'where' they are as well as all the other attributes marketers have used in the past.
Social Media	One way for business to look at social media is as consumer-generated media (CGM) that is a blending of technology and social interaction for the co-creation of value. It has long been possible for people obtain information, education, news, and other data from electronic media and print media. Social media is different from industrial or traditional media, such as newspapers, television, and film. Compared to industrial media, social media is relatively inexpensive and is accessible to anyone to publish what they want, when they want. One characteristic shared by both social media and industrial media is the capability to reach small or large audiences; for example, either a blog post or a television show may reach few people or millions of people.
	Some of the properties that help describe the differences between social media and industrial media are:
	Reach: both industrial and social media technologies provide scale and are capable of reaching a global audience. Industrial media, however, typically use a centralised framework for organisation, production, and dissemination, whereas social media are by their very nature more decentralised, less hierarchical, and distinguished by multiple points of production and utility.
	Accessibility: the means of production for industrial media are typically government and/or privately owned; social media tools are generally available to the public at little or no cost.
	Usability: industrial media production typically requires specialised skills and training. Conversely, most social media production does not require specialized skills and training, or requires only modest reinterpretation of existing skills; in theory, anyone with access can operate the means of social media production.
	Immediacy: the time lag between communications produced by industrial media can be long (days, weeks, or even months) compared to social media (which can be capable of virtually instantaneous responses; only the participants determine any delay in response). However, as industrial media begin adopting aspects of production normally associated with social media tools, this feature may not prove distinctive over time.
	Permanence: industrial media, once created, cannot be altered (once a magazine article is printed and distributed changes cannot be made to that same article) whereas social media can be altered almost instantaneously by comments or editing.
	Community media constitute an interesting hybrid of industrial and social media. Though community-owned, some community radios, TV and newspapers are run by professionals and some by amateurs. They use both social and industrial media frameworks. As well as understanding the difference between industrial and social media it is also crucial to be aware of the mind-set and drive social media advocates. Social media is all about sharing. Sharing opinions, experiences, data, and knowledge. This philosophy of sharing can also lead to brushes with the law by also sharing music, videos, other content types that are protected by intellectual property and copyright. Typical social media applications for business are: (1) brand monitoring; (2) communication; (3) collaboration/authority building; (4) entertainment; (5) multi-media; and (6) reviews & opinions.

Figure 8.3 (cont.)

Sales force

Non-integrated

An international bank in Hong Kong responded to a tender for a large piece of business from a major corporation. The customer was visited by two senior managers from different departments in the bank on the same day, each with a response to the tender. Unfortunately, each manager was unaware that the other was seeing the client. Although both presented similar proposals with respect to content, the fees they quoted for the work differed by 25 per cent. This resulted in considerable embarrassment at the bank and considerable amusement amongst the local financial community – neither bid won the business.

Integrated

In a company that has integrated its channels with its customers, there is an IT system that enables the company to identify previous contact with the customer. This is typically achieved with a sales force automation (SFA) system. Moreover, not only does this hold relevant and up-to-date information about the individual customer, but processes are in place to use it to ensure their staff tailor their activities by taking into account any previous contacts the customer has had with the organisation. Any contact with the customer is logged on the system regardless of whether the channel is personal contact, a letter, a telephone call or an e-mail.

Outlets

Non-integrated

A customer learns of a new product their bank has launched through receiving a direct mail piece. His interest was particularly aroused because the mail piece said the product was in line with the bank's mission to provide outstanding service and make life easier for its customers. However, on visiting their local branch during lunchtime, the customer finds he has to queue because most counter staff are on their lunch break. When he does finally reach a representative, he finds the representative has received no training in the product and is not familiar with it. Moreover, the representative seems disinterested and unhappy in his work. And, of course, the computer system is down.

Integrated

McDonald's ensures its restaurants consistently deliver the customer service promised in its advertising through rigorous training of its staff in a prescribed mode for customer interaction. The staff member first smiles, establishes eye contact and greets the customer. Then, after taking the order, she makes suggestions of additional items the customer may want to accompany his meal. As well as ensuring all of its customers are consistently made to feel welcome, this approach maximises the cross-selling and up-selling opportunities for the company without complex and expensive CRM systems.

Direct marketing
Non-integrated

Many of us are familiar with receiving a constant barrage of unsolicited materials that have little relevance to us. Indeed, we may even be bombarded by solicitations from a company to take up a product that we have already purchased from them. However, to add insult to injury, this time there may be a special offer that was unavailable when we attempted to purchase it. Moreover, the barrage of direct mail may consist of offers from different departments in the organisation with no apparent guiding logic. In addition, they may be completely incompatible with information we have already supplied to the organisation via other channels (e.g., via a conversation with a call centre or a staff member in the branch).

Integrated

If customers receive information that is highly relevant to their interests, they do not perceive it as junk mail but as a valued communication. Rover Cars was among the first automotive companies to understand this. Many years ago, it produced *Catalyst*, a unique magazine that allowed customers to choose a significant part of the content based on their individual lifestyle interests including gardening, cooking and sports. Many different versions of the magazine reflected the customer's profile. This programme was carefully integrated with other points of channel contact. Each issue contained a questionnaire to update the customer's details and identify where the customer was in her 'purchase window', in order to integrate with the company's campaign management.

Call centres/telephony
Non-integrated

Consider the most recent calls you have made to a call centre. How many have been positive experiences for you? You are not alone in being disappointed. All too often even major business clients find themselves having to wait for long periods of time while ironically being repeatedly told that 'Your call is important to us' by a pre-recorded voice. Frequently the person eventually answering the call does not have the skills to deal with the query and the caller again finds herself put 'on hold' while she is passed to yet another department. Interestingly, many large organisations with advanced call centre technology fail to exploit its full functionality.

Integrated

A corporate customer calls a company's call centre. Call Line Identification (CLI) helps identify the customer by recognising the telephone number of the incoming call (or if the customer is calling from someone else's phone, he is recognised by the PIN (personal identification number) he is invited to enter, with the same effect). Upon recognition, the customer is automatically shifted from call 120 to number five in the queue and is answered within 30 seconds. In addition, the customer's records are brought up onto the operator's screen and, depending upon the time or the day of the week, rules-based procedures may configure the screen with the items most likely to be of relevance to that customer's call on the basis of the caller's history of contact with the organisation. Some call centres are using rules-based prioritisation based on location whereby landline calls from more socially affluent areas are prioritised in the queue. However, there are obvious concerns if customers call from different landline locations and receive different service levels.

Electronic/mobile commerce

Non-integrated

Any regular user of the Internet will be only too familiar with the exasperating experience of using badly thought out and poorly constructed websites. In spite of company's positioning their e-commerce presence as a means of giving customers added convenience, many of our encounters with these sites are frustrating. In particular, registration processes and purchasing procedures seem designed to deter usage, with many organisations requiring so much information that the customer is put off and never completes the process. Alternatively, if a mistake is made in completing fields, it can be impossible to identify where that mistake is and how to correct it. Moreover, there is frequently no phone number or e-mail address through which one might sort out problems. Customers who have to contact their mobile service provider also have widely different experiences depending on the identity of their service provider. Some companies' skills seem to be in sales and branding, rather than customer service. In the mobile sector, mobile operators seem especially prone to poor customer service and complaints.[7] 'Vodafone complaints' gets approximately 2 million hits on Google! Customers experience great frustration when they have to wait exceptionally long times in a queue or, if they are prepaid customers who are topping up their balance, find their credit card not authorised through a fault in the system. Poor communication to customers has contributed to these problems as much as bad design of systems and limitations in the bandwidth and coverage.

Integrated

By contrast, Internet users of Amazon.com have a far more positive experience. When they use the site, it is personalised to them using collaborative filtering organisation to provide recommendations of other books likely to be of interest to them, based on what previous purchasers of that book have also bought. Moreover, the fulfilment process is integrated with the ordering channel and the brand identity is highly uniform across the different points of contact. Items purchased not only arrive in a timely manner; they are well packaged and have a range of useful enclosures, for example, bookmarks. The effect is to reinforce the customer's positive impressions of the company formed through their previous interactions with it. In mobile commerce, as experience grows and new generations of mobile technology emerge, there are great opportunities to deliver positive customer experiences, provided that the limitations of this channel are effectively communicated to the customer. This is true both for business customers, whose time is scarce and who often are very mobile, and for individual consumers who wish to be updated frequently on the news, weather and activities of their football team.

Social media
Non-integrated

Adopting social media gives marketers another opportunity to revisit all their classic non-integrated marketing mistakes that they have previously made when implementing other channels. These include: establishing a presence without knowing 'why' (not having a social media strategy); using social media as just another channel to 'broadcast' to potential customers; when ignored by potential customers, 'shouting' even louder; moving to social media before the organisation can competently handle a customer via other channels (e.g., via a visit, phone call or e-mail); and taking a purely aggregated view of markets and completely ignoring individuals. A further factor also influences companies having a non-integrated approach to social media marketing – the appointment of junior staff to positions with responsibility for social media and social influence marketing. We have experienced instances in many companies where relatively junior staff, with knowledge of social media, are appointed to look after this area. Although they may be highly familiar with all digital media, including Facebook, Twitter and LinkedIn etc., they typically do not have sufficiently broad experience to develop initiatives in these media that are integrated with the overall marketing and CRM strategies of the business. Also, they often do not have the attention of the more senior colleagues. Fortunately, this situation is now starting to change.

Integrated

Most successful adoptions of the social media channel start by 'listening' rather than 'broadcasting'. Typical 'listening' applications begin with monitoring and analysing brand-focused conversations. This provides marketers with new insights into brand-focused perceptions, based on the customers' own words and value analysis. Further analysis can highlight recurring conversations that should be addressed. The first steps in integration are to identify key influencers that can be exploited during future campaigns and product launches.

The next steps in integration are to use the analysis of brand-focused conversations to map social keywords and to use these to drive content for marketing output through all channels. These keywords can explicitly be used to maximise search engine optimisation of the organisation's website, which should drive more hits through organic searches. If the organisation is paying for 'clicks' through advertising on search engines, then these keywords can be used to increase the cost-effectiveness of this advertising by more focused targeting. For success, an integrated approach is also needed to establishing a social media presence across all the social media channels as well as the existing legacy channels. A good example of this is Blendtec – a manufacturer of domestic and commercial food blenders that was the topic of a case study in Chapter 5 (Case 5.2).

Combining channels

The six main channel categories in the CRM Strategy Framework can be represented as a continuum of forms of customer contact ranging from the physical (such as a face-to-face encounter with a company sales representative) to the virtual (such as e-commerce or social media). Clearly, employing a combination of the channels most appropriate to the target customer base and company structure will provide the greatest commercial exposure and return. In many instances, different types of channels can be used concurrently. Thus there will be an increasing convergence of channel options into what has become known as a 'contact centre'. These contact centres can integrate, for example, telephone, e-mail and Web contact. Developments such as 'VOIP' (voice over Internet protocol) integrate both telephony and the Internet in a more interactive way.

In B2C markets, the evaluation and choice may be relatively simple. However, in B2B markets, where there are complex account management issues and large product portfolios, there will inevitably be the need for a more detailed evaluation and for a wider range of channels to be utilised. An extra layer of complexity can occur here because of the channel hand-off required as the product or proposition moves through the sales cycle from demand generation to fulfilment.

Channel integration at Lands' End

The website of US fashion retailer Lands' End (Landsend.com) provides a good example of a B2C organisation that has integrated different channels to increase the value created for the customer. Online models can be dressed in your chosen garment and choice of colour, in part creating the means of 'trying on' the clothing that one can perform in a physical shop. In 2002 US retailer Sears purchased Lands' End so, in addition to operating a mail order, online business and Lands' End Outlet stores, Sears has since offered a Lands' End clothing line in a large selection of its retail stores.

However, what is difficult to replicate on a site is the function of a sales assistant with the inherent ability of human conversation to deal with complex or unfocused non-standard queries. To deal with this, the site is integrated with the company's call centre. By clicking the 'Land's End Live' button, users can opt to be phoned by a company representative or interact with them in an audio or video chatroom using IRC (Internet Relay Chat). Areas in which they might seek such assistance include how to find a particular item, how to use the site, or simply to discuss possible outfits with another person. Moreover, the call centre staff can tailor their advice to the individual's situation both by being able to view the same pages as the individual or by examining the individual's past purchase history to suggest items that might be of interest to that user or that might match items the user can see are already in his wardrobe. By bringing these channels together in this way, a greater range of the customer's needs can be met, and more value created for the customer in the interaction than would be possible were the customer to deal with either channel separately.

Channel integration at Schiphol Airport

Mobile commerce has particular challenges when enterprises wish to make the same information that is available on their websites also available on small mobile devices. Although incredibly powerful in computing terms, most smartphones do not have large enough screens for easy access to normal e-commerce websites. So enterprises wishing to

Figure 8.4 The Schiphol Airport website: www.schiphol.com

make it easier for highly mobile customers to use their smartphones to do e-commerce need to build special websites designed for the smaller screen sizes of these devices and provide easier access to e-commerce systems by developing specific 'apps' for these smartphones.

A good example of this is the e-commerce strategy of Schiphol Airport at Amsterdam in The Netherlands. For normal e-commerce, via a computer screen, customers can visit the full website www.schiphol.com (see screenshot in Figure 8.4) – here customers can find a complete set of information about Schiphol Airport (including arrivals, departures, flight timetables, public transport to and from Schiphol, parking, shops, restaurants, etc.).

For all smart devices, similar information is available through the Schiphol Airport 'mobile' website: www.schiphol.mobi – focused on making it incredibly easy to check flight arrivals and departures – see Figure 8.5.

Since the introduction of the iPhone and similar devices, mobile commerce has to some extent shifted from SMS to applications that sit on the mobile device. For users of certain smartphones (currently Apple's iPhone and Android phones) Schiphol Airport offers a free 'app'. This app is specifically designed to take full advantage of the available technology in these smart device to make browsing intuitive and easy – see Figure 8.6. The smartphone app

Figure 8.5 The Schiphol Airport 'mobile' website: www.schiphol.mobi

developed by Schiphol Airport is by far the quickest and easiest way to check flight arrivals and departures.

Many organisations are now looking to exploit the GPS functionality of smart devices for business advantage. Google Maps are a great example of exploiting the user's location for information centricity. It is possible to ask Google Maps to show what businesses are nearby and who they are. It is then possible to click on each identified business to drill down to further information. For example it is possible to ask 'What pharmacies are in the neighbourhood?', or 'What restaurants are in the vicinity?'

In the retail environment, many companies now take advantage of mobile commerce by utilising mobile capabilities such as location based services, barcode scanning and push notifications to enhance the customer experience of shopping in physical stores. By developing a multi-channel, 'bricks & clicks' approach, companies enable customers to access the benefits of shopping online (such as reading product reviews and studying product specifications and other information) while still shopping in the physical store.

Figure 8.6 The Schiphol Airport iPhone app

Channel strategies

The basic decisions relating to a firm's strategic channel decisions have been identified by researchers such as Professor Burt Rosenbloom of Drexel University, who identifies six key areas for decisions:

- What role should channels play in a firm's overall objectives and strategies?
- What role should channels play in the marketing mix?
- How should the firm's marketing channels be designed to achieve its distribution objectives?
- What kinds of channel members should be selected to meet the firm's distribution objectives?
- How can the external marketing channel and partners be managed to implement the firm's channel design effectively and efficiently on a continuing basis?
- How can channel member performance be evaluated?[8]

These six areas represent important issues for a firm to take into account as it considers its channel strategy options.

Channel strategy options

The starting point in addressing channel strategy options is to consider objectively who should dictate channel strategy – the customer or the supplier. In general, the customer's needs are the ones that should be considered. If customers in the firm's target segments have demands that can be satisfied best through a particular channel strategy, this should be emphasised in the firm's CRM strategy. However, circumstances including capacity, competencies and capabilities and business ambitions, may dictate a more supplier-oriented and less customer-oriented, approach.

Companies usually select from one of the following broad channel strategy options:

A *mono-channel provider strategy* is based on customer interactions through one main channel. UK companies Direct Line and First Direct both started as telephone operations, while in the online environment companies such as Amazon and Expedia adopted single channel Internet strategies referred to as 'pure play'.

A *customer segment channel strategy* recognises that different customer groups may wish to interact with different channel types. Zurich Financial Services has used different channels and brands to appeal to particular market segments. Thus, Zurich's brands, such as Allied Dunbar and Zurich, can utilise different routes to market, including a direct sales force, independent financial advisers (IFAs) and a telephone contact centre, in order to serve numerous customer groups with differing needs and attitudes.

A *graduated account management strategy* is based on the existing and future potential value of customers. Many B2B companies have implemented a graduated approach where important commercial customers are served by key account managers; medium-sized businesses through telephone-based account managers; and small customers through a call centre.

A *channel migrator strategy* is concerned with migrating customers from one channel to another. This strategy may be driven by the potential within a new channel to serve more lucrative customer segments or the opportunities to reduce cost or increase customer value. Low-cost airline easyJet commenced selling tickets solely through a call centre, but now almost all their customers purchase their tickets through the Internet. EasyJet used a combination of financial incentives and reduced levels of service in the call centre successfully to encourage its customers to buy online.

An *activity-based channel strategy* recognises that customers may wish to use different channels in combination to undertake different tasks. Thus, a customer purchasing a computer may visit a branch physically to inspect it; use the Internet to select the exact specification of the computer; telephone a call centre to confirm this specification will meet the customer's specific needs; and then use the Internet to order it.

An *integrated multi-channel strategy* involves utilising the full range of commercially viable channels to serve customers and integrate them without attempting to influence the channel that the customer wishes to use. Banks such as Intelligent Finance in the UK (now a division of the Bank of Scotland) and Merita Bank in Scandinavia (now part of Nordea), which developed the first mobile phone-based banking service, are examples of successful implementation of multi-channel approaches. In the telecoms industry, BT plc in the UK responded to its corporate market demands by deploying a sophisticated integrated multi-channel strategy. A business adopting such a strategy should seek to capture all customer information across all channels and integrate it within a single data repository so the business can recognise previous interactions with the customer, regardless of the channel in which the interactions took place, and use this to enhance the customer experience.

The role of a multi-channel strategy

Given the range of channel strategies outlined above, why are more and more businesses adopting multi-channel integration? Is not the appropriate strategy for some companies to create and build businesses based on only one channel?

While some businesses may choose a single channel strategy, many more will benefit from a strategy based on the integration of multiple channels. For example, firms trading solely on the Internet may have much to gain from adopting a multi-channel approach. Around a decade ago, McKinsey & Co. pointed to the future: 'To be successful, online retailers need to exploit other marketing channels simultaneously, such as in-store and catalogue sales, as well as private labels ... multi-channel players can increase their share of wallet, as many customers are already browsing on the Web before buying in the store.'[9]

A multi-channel strategy offers greater scope for respecting customers' channel preferences and propensities of use, therefore enhancing the company's attractiveness and, ultimately, responsiveness to customers. In today's business arena, customer service is regarded not only as the key to differential advantage but also as a baseline requirement to compete. Excellent customer service sees customer choice as a right, not a privilege and this extends to allowing customers to use whatever channel they wish (such as mail, phone, fax, Internet, mobile, social media or face-to-face, etc.) for whatever reason motivates them to contact the company (such as to place an order, ask a query, register a complaint, track a fault, request a service or respond to a promotion, etc.). Likewise, it also respects how customers wish to be contacted by the company to receive notifications, such as payment reminders or special offers, or to contribute to value enhancement, such as participating in market surveys or enabling after-sales service fulfilment.

Understanding the customer relationship life-cycle

Discussions about channel options are often dominated by considerations relating to making the sale. However, for *strategic CRM* the channels need to be considered in the context of the whole interaction over the life-cycle of the customer relationship, not just in terms of the sales activity. Customer understanding needs to go beyond traditional market research, which tends to be descriptive and aggregate results together, and drill down at a micro-level into the characteristics of the customer value chain for key customer types or segments. In other words, we need to understand the processes that a business engages in – running an assembly line, an airline, or a professional services firm – and then identify the opportunities to create value within those processes. We create value either by making those processes more effective, doing them better or more efficiently, or doing them more cheaply.[10]

To help businesses identify such value-creating opportunities the stages of a customer relationship can be considered under the three broad headings of: 'pre-sale', or acquisition; 'sale' or consolidation; and 'post-sale' or enhancement, as shown in Figure 8.7.[11]

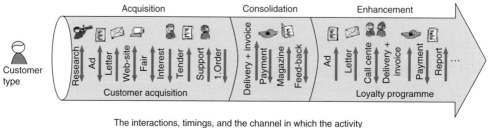

The interactions, timings, and the channel in which the activity takes place need to be closely integrated

Figure 8.7 Understanding the nature of customer encounters.
Source: Based on Storbacka (2001)

These stages can be broken down into more specific elements which will vary depending on the business being considered. For example, a computer manufacturer selling to business customers identified the following key elements:

- marketing communications,
- prospecting and lead generation,
- sales qualification,
- proposal generation,
- pre-sales activity,
- selling,
- installation,
- post-sales service,
- ongoing account management.

A similar approach has been suggested by Sandra Vandermerwe, a former Professor at Imperial College, who proposes mapping the 'customer activity cycle'.[12] The objective of this activity is to gain a deep understanding of what customers 'do' (including activities before and after the 'doing') through a detailed mapping of the stages in these customer processes. When these activity cycles are mapped, the next step is to understand where the opportunities lie to create further value. For example, it may involve identifying which elements of that activity cycle are the most complex, uncertain, frustrating or time consuming, or those elements with which the customer is most dissatisfied.

Within these typical stages, a great number of interactions occur between the customer and the organisation across different channels. Understanding the nature of different customer encounters within a multi-channel environment is essential if the organisation's CRM activities are to be fully effective. Also, there needs to be a clear understanding of the costs associated with each stage of the relationship life-cycle, as well as the likely margins delivered by customers at each stage of the life-cycle. Further, customers' needs during the customer relationship life-cycle phases will vary according to the segment to which they belong and the product or service involved. Thus, determining the most appropriate forms of channel options for specific customer segments is also critical. The channel approach adopted by a supplier should be developed in a way that enables the company to meet different customer segments' needs over the life-cycle and to maximise the value it creates for them.

Social media and 'points of non-contact' or 'points of indirect contact'

The rise of customer communities and social media has led to a much greater incidence of customers influencing other customers and being influenced by them. Much of present CRM activity is designed around encounters, or points of contact, over the customer life-cycle. Enterprises are now starting to monitor more closely what we term 'points of non-contact'.

Up until fairly recently, organisations have predominately had the opportunity to access user sentiment and react to it, when 'touched' by the user. Most customers who are dissatisfied with an organisation's value proposition, commercial terms, products, product features, services, customer services, etc., just break off contact. Rarely do customers let the organisation know what their views are. Only when companies use expensive market research do they capture some of this additional information.

By monitoring social media, organisations can, to a much greater extent, capture 'use sentiment'. Such data give organisations the opportunity to react in a much more positive and timely manner. Not only can organisations determine use sentiment they can also identify the key influencers – including the 'terrorists' as well as the 'advocates'. By properly understanding true user sentiments in the community, rather than the potentially skewed view offered through actual points of contact, organisations are offered a substantial opportunity to dramatically improve their CRM activities in a holistic way across the organisation and marketing channels.

The non-contact points for the enterprise represent occasions where the enterprise does not have direct contact with customers or potential customers, but the enterprise is affected in some way by consumers' activities. This is occurring increasingly frequently with the continued rise of social media. We discussed the need to monitor and respond to social media activity in Chapter 4.

Maamar and his colleagues emphasise the weaving of social networks into e-business and mobile commerce. They point out that embracing e-commerce and then m-commerce is typically done at the expense of the development of the social interactions that characterise traditional commerce, such as bargaining with sellers, shopping with friends, obtaining recommendations from friends and making purchase comparisons:

With the emergence of Web 2.0 we witness a major change in software applications development by putting emphasis on the social dimension of end-users' behaviours. Applications like Facebook, LinkedIn, and Myspace capitalise on the ability and willingness of users to interact, share, collaborate, and recommend. Social networking sites, blogs, Wikis, and folksonomies exemplify social applications and, at the same time, reinforce the role of the Internet as a solid and inevitable platform for group collaboration.[13]

Robin Goad, the Research Director at Experian Hitwise, further emphasises the role of social media: 'Search engines are still the key driver of traffic to transactional sites. However, a clear opportunity for retailers lies in increasing traffic from social media sites. A handful of retailers are ahead of the curve with this, particularly in the fashion and entertainment sectors, but many others are missing a trick and therefore potential untapped revenue.' Experian Hitwise found that both Music e-tailers as well as Video and Games e-tailers currently receive 8.9 per cent, and Apparel and Accessories e-tailers currently receive 8 per cent, of their traffic from social networks.[14] These figures will increase substantially in the future.

Understanding the customer experience

Faced with the necessity of offering customers different channel types to meet their changing needs during the sales cycle (pre-sale, sale and post-sale), it is increasingly imperative to integrate the activities in those different channels to produce the most positive customer experience and to create the maximum value. Competitive advantage today is not just about selling products and services to customers; it is about delivering world-class service and building long-term and profitable relationships with customers, which are founded on mutual benefit and trust. To succeed, therefore, the company must consistently seek to offer an individualised relationship, where economically feasible, in every customer interaction through whatever channel is being used.

With the accelerating pace of technology, it is increasingly impossible to maintain competitive advantage merely through the attributes of individual products. Product life-cycles are now so short that soon after launch a company is likely to find competitors or new entrants imitating any new innovation – hence the logic for CRM. Rather than merely producing discrete products for a mass market, the company pursues ongoing relationships with its most profitable existing and potential customers. The value to the customers resides not in any single product but in the reassurance that the company will continue to offer them a stream of products tailored to their particular needs. In a sense, the company becomes the trusted supplier for the customer. By continually offering superior customer value to the customer in an extended relationship, the financial or psychological cost to the customer of switching to another supplier rises dramatically. The result is increased levels of customer retention and profitability and a potential decrease in customer sensitivity to price.

The customer experience and emotional goodwill

However, if a company is to succeed in this endeavour, it needs to ensure that it continues to offer the customer the same individualised relationship over time and across all points of contact, whether direct or indirect. This includes the points of 'non-contact' discussed above. In other words, the structure and flow of activity in the different channels through which the company and customer interact must be integrated so that the channels, both individually and collectively, consistently deliver the value proposition in the eyes of the customer. The provision of a 'seamless and consistent customer experience' at every juncture will engender trust, which in turn will reinforce the relationship and perhaps propel it towards a higher level of opportunity and return.

The collective experiences a customer has developed towards the supplier form 'an emotional reservoir of goodwill'. This reservoir of goodwill is shown in Figure 8.8. High-quality experiences increase emotional goodwill and the likelihood of the customer giving their supplier further custom. In contrast, failure to deliver on the individualised relationship value proposition can leave the customer disappointed and frustrated, leading to dissonance in the relationship and, worse, to the ultimate defection of the customer to a competitor.

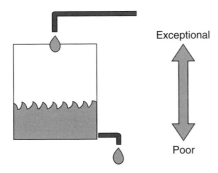

Figure 8.8 The emotional reservoir of goodwill

Evaluating the customer experience

In evaluating the customer experience a five-point customer satisfaction scale is often used. Assume the satisfaction labels attached to the scores on this scale are as follows:

5 – perfect/outstanding

4 – satisfied

3 – average/mediocre

2 – poor

1 – terrible

Findings in a number of studies have confirmed the importance of seeking high levels of satisfaction. For example, the study by Jones and Sasser discussed in Chapters 2 and 3 reached two major conclusions.[15] First, only highly delighted customers (e.g., a '5' on the 5-point scale) can be considered truly loyal. Second, customers who are just satisfied (e.g., a '4' on the 5-point scale) are only slightly more loyal than customers who are thoroughly dissatisfied (e.g., a '1' on a 5-point scale).

Because of the great importance of a 5/5 customer experience, the channel strategy should seek to ensure such an experience occurs within channel *and* across multiple channels. The channel experience needs to be considered, in the context of a company's industry sector and its important customer segments, by asking three questions:

- What is the typical and outstanding/perfect customer experience *within* channel?
- What is the typical and outstanding/perfect customer experience *across* channels?
- How do we sustain and *improve the customer experience* within channel and across channels and how do we substitute an existing channel for a better one?

The customer experience within channel

We investigated over 1,000 customers' views of their experiences within channel including the Internet and call centres and asked the following questions:

- What percentage of telephone calls you have made to a call centre over the past two months have resulted in a perfect/outstanding customer experience? Contrast these with those where you have experienced delays, poor interactive voice response, multiple hand-offs, etc.
- What percentage of the visits to websites you have made over the past two months have resulted in a perfect/outstanding customer experience? Contrast these with those where you have not been able to complete the registration process or experienced unreasonable requests for information at registration, poor layout, broken linkages, poor navigation structures, computer lock-up (apparently due to the website) or unnecessarily long delays in moving around the site.

Over 70 per cent of respondents indicated that only one in ten experiences in contacting a call centre were perfect or outstanding, and more than 60 per cent said that only one in ten experiences in visiting websites were perfect or outstanding. Many complained about the poor customer experience within these channels. Given such poor results, companies need to understand, within their industry, what constitutes an outstanding and what constitutes a typical customer experience among their key customer segments and how they can improve it.

However, improved customer experience must be achieved at an affordable cost. The concept of segmented service strategy is important here. Improvement should be based on the profit potential of different customer segments and service strategies and investment decisions should be made with the knowledge of this profit potential. Where a customer interacts with multiple channels, which is increasingly the case, the customer experience needs to be considered cumulatively across all channel interactions.

The customer experience across channels

The customer experience commences with the communications activities undertaken as part of the company's acquisition programme and continues through all subsequent forms of customer interaction. In communicating with the customer, a company is likely to use a combination of different channel options or media, such as advertising, direct mail, sales promotions, public relations, and so on. If the company is to be successful in forming a particular perception of itself in the mind of the customer and in building a relationship with them on that foundation across channels, it must ensure consistency in the messages conveyed by these different means. Any incoherence or conflict in the messages in different channels will confuse the customer, who may then misinterpret or 'draw a blank' about what the company stands for and what it is offering. This confusion across channels can seriously diminish the customer's view of the company and possibly instigate negative word-of-mouth.

The 'touch points' where the customer interacts with the supplier in multiple channels represent the most crucial opportunities to leverage advantage. It is here that the planned marketing communications meet the reality of what customers actually experience when they interact with the company. The customer's 'experience' of the company will probably be a composite formed through using different types of channel. It will be based, for instance, on how the customer's call is handled when she phoned the company, how efficiently the customer's orders are processed, how professionally the customer's complaints or service queries are dealt with and whether the visiting sales representative listens to the customer and responds appropriately.

If the customer's experience of the company falls short of what she has been led to expect, the customer's disappointment will probably show as frustration or a withdrawal of trust in the company. Unless the resultant quality gap or damage to the relationship can be quickly and fully redressed and the customer reassured, the company's espoused position will be undermined. The danger is not just that the company will lose a customer, but that it will effectively hand the customer to a competitor. At the other extreme, if the customer's experience of dealing with the company meets or indeed surpasses that customer's expectations such that her experiences are outstanding (or better), then the company's reputation will be given a boost and the relationship will be strengthened.

Improving the customer experience – the role of technology

Technology can make a major contribution to achieving a perfect or outstanding customer experience. For example, within a call centre, CLI can identify the caller and rules-based systems can accelerate important customers up a large queue of calls; interactive voice response (IVR) can assist a customer to find the most appropriate person to speak to without multiple hand-offs; CTI tools, in conjunction with CLI, can enable a customer's computer records to be called up instantaneously and shown on the call centre operator's screen. Together with an empathetic and well-trained company representative, these technologies can dramatically improve the customer experience, in this case in the contact centre environment. Further, social media analytics can identify both opportunities and problems and can use the information derived from sources such as Facebook and Twitter to feed back into marketing activities.

However, inappropriate use or overuse of technology can have a negative impact on customers. Many companies are now using contact centre software that is used to predict when a call centre agent is free, initiating an outbound call to a customer. However, if the call centre agent is still occupied on the call, this results in 'phantom' phone calls to customer, with no-one on the telephone line when the customer answers the phone. A further problem can occur where call centres use rules-based prioritisation favouring new customers over existing customers, or, as noted above, where they use the socio-demographics of the area from which the call originates to prioritise calls. However, in the latter case customers may sometimes call from their home in an affluent area and sometimes call from their office, which may be in a depressed area – resulting in varying service levels.

A study undertaken by ATG, showed that by 2011 around 50 per cent of US consumers were using their mobile devices to research and browse products and service. Further, almost one-third of the consumers that were polled had made at least one purchase on a mobile device.[16] 'We are doing almost everything on a mobile device' states Michael Fauscette, Group Vice President of software business solutions for analyst firm IDC. 'We are always connected. We have evolved into having the constant interactivity of the Internet, so it's just natural that I want to take the next step and want to do some type of commerce, or I want some customer experience tied into the mobile device as well as other things.'[17]

The advent of increasingly sophisticated database technologies has greatly enhanced the ability of companies to target and differentiate their products, customers and customer communications. Special search, analysis and tracking features also enable companies to monitor the effectiveness and efficiency of marketing activity and thus to maximise the return on marketing expenditure. By recording the customer's responses to different messages sent through different communication channels, the company can learn progressively more about its individual customers and how they (and others like them) are likely to respond to certain communications. Based on this information, the company can develop models to use in predicting the customer response behaviour of different segments to various types of communication. These educated projections can then be employed to help marketers evaluate alternative communications programmes and the probable return on investment these might achieve. As a result more informed multi-channel strategies can be developed.

However, ironically those companies that achieve high ratings in terms of the customer experience, both within a channel and across channels, often do not have superior or proprietary technology. Rather they typically achieve their superiority by *how* they utilise the technology solution and through the quality of staff at the customer interface.

The 'perfect' customer experience

All enterprises need to consider how they should 'engineer' their customer experience. The objective for most businesses should be to offer an outstanding or 'perfect' customer experience at an affordable cost, especially to their most important customers and customer segments. We define outstanding or 'perfect' in this context as achieving a 5/5 score on customer satisfaction. Note the word perfect is in quotes, for it needs to be considered in the context of the nature of customer expectations relating to that offer. To achieve a 5/5 score on a first class flight with Singapore Airlines or British Airways costing say $8,000, expectations are likely to be very high. However, a similar 5/5 score in customer experience may be achieved with a low-cost airline such as Southwest Airlines or easyJet with a fare of, say, $80. Here, expectations are that the staff members are pleasant, the plane is clean and it departs and arrives on time – even though the seats are cramped and the food minimal or non-existent.

There are many aspects to achieving an outstanding or perfect customer experience. Perhaps the most important one is a deep knowledge of customer needs and the criticality of ensuring CRM operates across the business in a cross-functional manner. However, this cross-functional working is the exception rather than the rule. For example, Evert Gummesson, a professor at Stockholm University, describes Lee Iacoccas' first impressions when he took over Chrysler Corporation three decades ago:

Nobody at Chrysler seemed to understand that interaction among different enterprise functions in a company is absolutely critical. People in engineering and manufacturing almost have to be sleeping together. These guys were not even flirting ... The manufacturing guys would build cars without even checking with the sales guys. They just built them, stuck them in a yard, and then hoped that somebody would take them out of there. We ended up with a huge inventory and a financial nightmare.[18]

We consider the use of the term 'perfect' can help engage all staff, across all departments and business functions, in delivering an outstanding product or service. Two case studies at the end of this chapter, on TNT Express Services and Guinness, provide examples of companies seeking to develop a 'perfect' customer experience. These companies provide examples from both the B2B and B2C sectors.

The first case study on TNT Express Services is a good example of an organisation in the B2B sector that uses the concept of the 'perfect' customer experience to ensure all employees: have a deep knowledge of customer needs; operate in an aligned manner across functions and in all customer encounters; and deliver superior customer service. The second case study shows the concept of the 'perfect' customer experience is equally relevant to the B2C sector. The Guinness case study highlights the importance of cross-functional involvement and the need for customer education to ensure the ultimate consumer has an outstanding experience. While the first case study deals with a direct channel, the second case study deals with an intermediated market.

Building a multi-channel strategy

Building a multi-channel strategy involves a channel design that offers the greatest value for the customer and the company. This involves assessing the value created for the end consumer by different channels structures, understanding the economics of different channel structures and determining the channel strategy that will create the maximum value for consumers and the greatest profit for the company.

Developing a multi-channel strategy that delivers an appropriate customer experience for a company's main customer segments includes a number of key activities:

- develop strategic multi-channel objectives;
- understand the needs and concerns of key customer segments;
- undertake a strategic review of industry structure and channel options;
- understand shifts in channel usage patterns;
- review channel economics;
- develop an integrated channel management strategy.

Drawing on earlier discussions, each of these activities is now reviewed.

Develop strategic multi-channel objectives

The starting point for formulating a multi-channel strategy is to determine the key strategic objectives. The overall objective of multi-channel integration is to provide a significantly enhanced customer experience resulting in higher customer satisfaction and increased sales, profits and share of wallet. Ideally, this should be accompanied by a lower cost to serve, through alternative channels, for example, from direct sales force to desk-based account management, or from desk-based account management to the adoption or an increase in the use of electronic solutions.

Specific strategic objectives should be developed by a company to reflect the earlier CRM strategy development and value creation processes.

For example, the broad objectives set for a new multi-channel strategy by a leading company for its major business clients include:

- improve the customer experience,
- increase account coverage,
- improve revenue growth,
- decrease operating expenses,
- utilise the full skills and resources of our business and its employees.

These objectives were then translated into more specific quantified objectives. Companies undertaking this task will typically need to undertake a benchmarking exercise in order to understand the experiences of similar companies or undertake a pilot project to quantify potential targets. The objectives are likely to be further refined as a result of the further steps outlined below.

Understand the needs and concerns of key customer segments

It is crucial that a *market-driven approach* should determine channel choice. This choice, of course, has to be mediated by the relative economics of different channel options from both the customer's and the organisation's perspectives. This step will also involve reviewing the value propositions (discussed in Chapter 3) at the market segment level as well as researching customers' channel preferences. The needs, wants and concerns of customers should be a primary force in considering the design of marketing channels. Central to understanding these needs and concerns is a detailed segmentation analysis that is typically undertaken as part of the CRM strategy development process.

However, as mentioned previously, consumers will have different needs at different stages of the relationship life-cycle. Thus, channels need to be considered in the context of the whole interaction with the customer over the whole of this cycle, not just at the point of sale. It is a company's activities in this wider context that determines the value it creates for customers and the relationship it develops with them, both over a single sale and over the series of subsequent activities that make up the customer relationship.

The customer activity cycle can be divided into three phases: pre-sale, sale and post-sale. The initial pre-sale stage may be characterised by consumers initially gathering information to learn about the product area and to identify and evaluate possible alternatives. They may have specific questions they wish to find answers to; some of these may be routine and some complex. They may require help to determine what version of a product would best meet their needs. They may seek information from social media. Then there follows the sales phase. Here the process needs to be easy from the customer's point of view with accurate and reliable information meeting the customer's needs. Following the sale comes the post-sale phase. For example, the customer may require support in using the product. This may be in the form of general advice on how to use the product or assistance if it develops a defect or needs servicing. In some cases, the customer may need physically to return the product either for repair or to receive a replacement.

Naturally, the needs customers will have over the sales cycle will vary according to the type of product and the customer's experience with it. Thus, for some products, all the consumer may require is that it is readily available when desired. For example, the channel strategy of Coca-Cola is simply based upon ensuring that a can is always within 'an arm's reach of desire'. For other products, customers may have far more complex needs. For example, when buying a computer, a customer requires a great deal more in the pre-sale, sale and post-sale phases. Similarly, the needs may differ by customer segment. UK bank First Direct's cash-rich, time-poor consumers need to be able to perform transactions at any place, at any time of the day, on any day of the year. By contrast an old-age pensioner may value the social interaction and exercise involved in a visit to the bank branch between 9 a.m. and 4 p.m. Having 24-hour telephone or Internet access would offer these customers little additional value.

This activity of understanding the needs and concerns of key segments should result in an understanding of the needs and concerns of the company's different customer segments at different stages of the life-cycle. In addition, as customers are likely to have several needs at any given stage of the cycle, it is also necessary to determine the relative importance customers attach to those needs. This can be established through standard research techniques such as observing customer behaviour, questionnaire research or using focus groups of segment members, and it can be augmented by social media research.

Undertake a strategic review of industry structure and channel options

The review of the industry structure will involve the identification of the channel particip-ants described earlier. This will require a review of the channel alternatives currently being used by the company as well as those used by its competitors and, in addition, the potential for structural change by means of disintermediation or reintermediation. This task can be assisted using a tool called *channel chain analysis*, which considers how a combination of channels is used at different stages of the customer interaction with the supplier and how it may change in the future.

Figure 8.9 provides an example of channel chain analysis with an illustration from the B2B personal computer market of channels offered by competitors at different points in time. In this case, the traditional key account management structure on the left is now mainly used only for large computers or large accounts, as other channel chains now offer better channel economics. The direct model in the middle was introduced in the mid-1990s and was pioneered by Dell, with press advertising being the major promotional activity, additional information being supplied by product brochures and call centre employees. The order could be placed by a variety of means – often through a traditional means such as a fax or mail order sent to the accounts department. Lastly, the Internet was added to the channel mix, as shown on the right of Figure 8.9.[19]

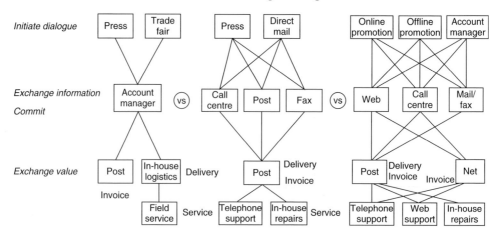

Figure 8.9 Channel chain analysis for personal computers.
Source: Based on Wilson and McDonald (2001)

Having understood past and present models, future channel chain diagrams can be constructed and experimented with to consider other options. As academics Hugh Wilson and Malcolm McDonald, note:

[T]he next step is to consider possible future channel chains. This requires experimentation with channel chain diagrams to think through not just how the sale is to be made, but also how every other aspect of the customer's needs will be satisfied. Will a mobile phone purchaser buying over the Web be able to return a faulty phone to a nearby store? Will an e-hub be able to handle not just price negotiations, but also information flows on stock levels, complaints, returns and product development – and if not, what additional channels will be needed? . . . There is a timing issue to be considered as well. Even if a channel chain offers a theoretically better proposition to customers, they may not yet be ready for it. A channel chain innovation, like a product innovation, is likely to proceed along the lines of the diffusion of the innovation curve.[20]

This analytical framework should be used creatively, getting input from different groups of company executives. It is also of value to seek the views of analysts, consultants and industry experts as well as benchmarking experiences in analogous industry sectors. In their book on multi-channel marketing, Wilson and his colleagues provide further examples of the use of channel chain analysis in an export consultancy and a department store.[21]

Understand shifts in channel usage patterns

The consideration of possible channel options can be assisted by an understanding of how shifts will occur in channel usage patterns. From the start of the 2000s there has been a continued rapid growth in Web-based, e-mail-based and social media channels. An exploration of past trends and future forecasts in channel usage should be considered with respect to the company's main customer segments. Also, the relative importance of different channels during different transactions and at different customer relationship life-cycle stages for the product or proposition needs to be considered. Usage of different channels by different customer segments may vary considerably and, if this is the case, the potential adoption for different key segments should be estimated.

Figure 8.10 shows the analysis of a high cost to serve, low value customer segment, based on the work by Forte Consulting Group. It illustrates the annual frequency of contact by specific channel segments including: dealer, call centre, e-mail, Twitter, interactive voice response and self-care. Interactions marked in bold represent the greatest opportunity to migrate to another channel. The boxes highlighted in grey shading represent the ideal destination for each of these transaction types.

High Cost of Serve, Lower Value # 3–472,000 Customers–Migration Opportunities Analysis						
	Annual Frequency of Contact (Total), by Channel					
Transaction Type	Dealer	Call Centre	Email	Twitter	IVR	Self-Care
Complaint	422,102	**918,391**	4,281	1,910	0	0
Service Activation	879,201	**3,291,091**	1,203	0	0	542,191
Product Purchase	**871,201**	391,201	0	0	291,391	1,201,029
Service Cancellation	284,911	**4,910,102**	0	0	0	598,102
Bill Payment	**4,542,102**	343,910	0	0	642,039	291,101
General Inquiry	442,102	**2,102,938**	20,817	31,091	0	0
Other	102,381	**210,128**	4,421	2,102	219,201	0

Highest Cost Transaction ... Lowest Cost Transaction

Highest Cost to Serve Channel → Lowest Cost to Serve Channel

Interactions marked bold represent the largest opportunities for migration tactics, with boxes marked in 'gray' representing the ideal migration destination for the given transaction.

Figure 8.10 Interactions shift to new channels.
Source: Forte Consulting Group (2011), Channel Migration Strategies – Matching Customers to the Optimum Channels

Review channel economics

The next step is to review channel economics. In some industries marketing channel costs represent a substantial proportion of the price paid by the customer, so these often represent a prime opportunity for cost reduction. Alternative channel structures and channel options have widely differing economics in terms of transaction costs, infra-structural costs and relative usage.

Transaction costs across different channels vary so markedly that they are frequently the primary area of focus in discussions on channel adoption. Figure 8.11 provides an illustration of relative transaction costs for a $5,000 to $7,000 industrial product across the Internet, telesales, volume distributors, value-added partners and field sales force channels, based on work by high-tech expert Kamran Qamar.

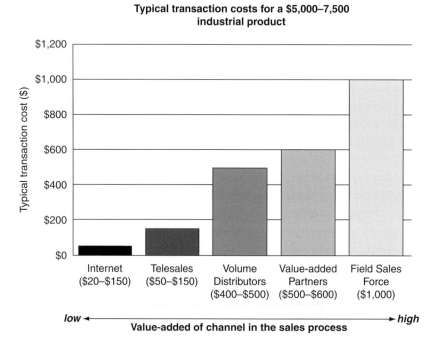

Figure 8.11 Transaction costs per sales channel.
Source: Qamar (2011)

As Figure 8.11 illustrates, for the same transaction, the sales force costs equal $1,000 (about 20 per cent of the deal), value-added partners cost $500 to $600 (10 per cent of the deal), and volume distributors cost 8 per cent. Other direct channels such as telesales cost only 3 per cent of the deal, and the Internet costs less than 1 per cent of the deal. Thus, low-cost channels should be utilised wherever possible.

Figure 8.12 shows the relative strength of sales and marketing channels across the various activities of awareness, investigation, consideration, selection, purchase, satisfaction, loyalty and advocacy. These activities represent an expansion of the broader customer life-cycle categories of acquisition, consolidation and enhancement shown earlier in

	Awareness (Branding)	Investigation (Lead Generation)	Consideration (Prospecting)	Selection (Negotiation/Close)	Purchase (Fulfilment)	Satisfaction (Customer Service)	Loyalty (Up/cross-sell)	Advocacy (WOM/Referral)
One way								
TV/Radio/Print	■	◻	◻					
Events/Trade shows	■	■	◻	◻				
Product Placements	◻	◻	■	■				
Two way								
Direct Mail		◻	■		◻		■	
Sales Reps		◻	◻	■	■	■	◻	
Business Partners (Resellers, Distributors)		◻	■	■	◻			
Business Partners (VARs, Service Providers)					■	■		
Telemarketing		■	■	◻	◻	■	◻	
Stores	◻	◻	◻	■	■	◻	◻	
Multi-directional								
Email	◻	◻	■			◻	◻	
Blog	■		◻			◻	◻	◻
Website	■	■	◻	◻		■	◻	■
Demos	■	■	◻				◻	◻
Video	■	◻	◻					
Social Media	■	◻						■
Forums		◻				◻		■
Mobile		◻	◻					

Figure 8.12 Strengths of sales & marketing channels.
Source: Qamar (2011)

Figure 8.7 above. The darkness of the squares in Figure 8.12 represents the relative strength of the different sales channels, which are categorised under headings of one-way, two-way or multidirectional.

Figures 8.11 and 8.12 show that not every channel is appropriate for building strong customer experience across the various activities in the customer life-cycle. As Kamran Qamar points out:

[S]alespeople are very good at relationship building and consultative selling, but they despise generating new leads. Depending upon the complexity of your product, a telesales channel may be very good at providing customer service and generating new leads, but may be unable to close sales and may not be the best way to increase customer loyalty. The Internet may be an excellent source for generating leads or providing self-help customer service but prove to be a difficult channel when it comes to quoting a custom price. Therefore, expecting that a channel should complete sales and deliver the cost savings promised above is an unrealistic expectation that has been hurting many businesses for a long time.[22]

Wherever possible the most appropriate and most cost-effective channel should be utilised with the aim of providing a superior customer experience. The objective is to utilise these multiple channels to ensure integrated channel management. This concept of integrated channel management is illustrated within the multi-channel integration process in the CRM Strategy Framework at the start of this chapter.

However, not surprisingly, many businesses have rushed into the online channels because of its low transaction costs. While channel transaction costs are important, other aspects of channel economics must also be explored. The apparently low transaction costs involved in selling on the Internet need to be considered alongside other considerations such as marketing, website development, fulfilment and other costs.

A study undertaken by McKinsey & Co. and Salomon Smith & Barney found the economics of selling on the Internet varied greatly. Their study focused on sectors within five industries and found that the online retail categories showing the highest customer net present values were, in order: groceries, prescription drugs, specialty apparel, department store apparel, direct mail apparel, pure play books, pure play toys and pure play apparel.[23]

A considerable amount of work needs to be undertaken to fully examine the economics of undertaking business activities on the Internet, or on other channels within a given industry sector. It is common for such studies to be undertaken by leading consulting firms. The McKinsey study, while undertaken over a decade ago, provides a valuable illustration of the thinking that needs to go into an examination of the economic costs of doing business within a given channel, in this case the Internet. We now briefly review the economics of two sectors from this study.

Economics of the online retail toy market

McKinsey's examination of pure play toy retailers illustrates how full economic costs need to be taken into account as well as transaction costs. For this sector, they concluded that even if a contribution to gross income of $11 per order was received (which is extremely ambitious given high fulfilment costs), the company would need more than $1 billion in revenues to support the $130 million cost it would have in warehouse, website, marketing and overhead costs. At the time the study was undertaken, McKinsey concluded that such a company would need to capture an extremely high 5 per cent of the total US toy market to be viable. This highlights the potential difficulties in some sectors for late entrants into the pure play world.

Economics of the online grocery market

In the grocery sector, the McKinsey study found the average online grocery order generated only $9 of gross income. With a typical online customer buying groceries on the website, say, 30 times per year, the overall net present value (NPV) can be calculated. Order frequency drives the NPV of an online grocery customer to $909 dollars over a four year period according to the study data.

For many grocery retailers seeking to create an online business – either new entrants or existing grocery retailers – the building of special dedicated warehouses with low cost of order picking appears attractive. The initial approach adopted by supermarket chains such as Tesco of having their staff pick customers' orders from a normal store was dismissed as too expensive. However, the original approach taken by Tesco Direct – now the largest online grocery store in the world – was vindicated. A number of early online grocery entrants, such as Streamline and Peapod in the US, used dedicated warehouses and failed to develop viable business models. The substantial order volume needed to justify using expensive dedicated warehouses was not achieved by these companies.

The economics of businesses such as those discussed above can shift within a few years and it is essential that thought is given to how the economics of the business will change over time and as volume increases. The examples above are illustrative of the approach that needs to be taken. However, these statistics above apply to a particular point in time, in a given country and in a particular business sector. Analyses from another company, country, product category or at another point in time cannot be relied upon by other companies, especially in the fast changing world of the Internet. Each enterprise needs to do its own analysis of the economics of doing business within and across its own channels.

Develop an integrated channel management strategy

This step involves making decisions regarding how the company's strategic channel objectives will be achieved through a properly integrated channel management strategy. The choice of the appropriate multi-channel strategy will depend upon the desired customer experience for the key target segments, the complexity of the channel interaction and the channel economics. The economics of channels and the relative degree of use of alternative channels by different customer segments will have significantly different profit outcomes. Understanding the different profit contributions of customer segments and successfully exploiting this is a factor of superior channel management.

Developing an integration channel management strategy gives rise to the following issues:

- How to achieve brand consistency in the formal communications programmes of different channels.
- How to achieve consistency in how customers experience the company when they deal with its various channels.
- How to ensure the communications and services a customer receives through different channels are coordinated and coherent, tailored to their particular interests and cognisant of their previous encounters with the company.

As noted earlier, the nature of the total customer experience across different channels needs to be carefully addressed. The concept of customer experience design is a relatively new concept. However, a number of books on experience design and managing customer experiences have made a significant contribution to our thinking in this area.[24]

The relative complexity of the interactions leading to the sale and the costs of serving the channel also need to be fully considered. Companies such as BT and Xerox, working with leading consultants such as Marketbridge,[25] are pioneering new approaches to multi-channel integration. Figure 8.13 provides an illustration of this in a business-to-business sector.

The channel options need to be considered in the context of the channel participants or channel members that are used. Selection of appropriate channel members, discussed earlier in the chapter, can result in different industry structures that may include business partners, value-added resellers and other intermediaries as well as direct sales models. Each channel member should utilise the most appropriate range of channel alternatives. The channel alternatives shown in Figure 8.13 have different advantages and challenges.

Each element of customer interaction needs to be analysed to ensure the appropriate channel is being engaged for that activity. While the face-to-face channel used in much

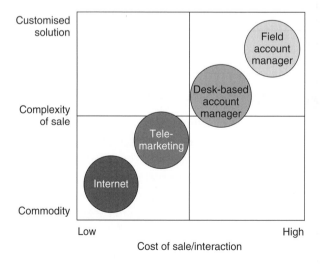

Figure 8.13 Channel alternatives based on cost and the complexity of sale

account management is costly, it is necessary for complex tasks and important customer segments. However, less complex tasks may be handled for the same key customers through other lower-cost channels. Desk-based account management might involve a highly experienced salesperson who can immediately access customer information and use it in a highly interactive and customised manner, while telemarketing may deal with more routine sales, service and queries. The Internet and electronic channels provide the opportunity for high-quality personalised self-service. However, the development of this channel will be dependent on high-quality portals and customer education and acceptance.

Leading companies are now driving considerable cost out of their account management structure by introducing innovations in this area. The creation of a differentiated and superior value proposition hinges on the provision of open and responsive interactions and dialogue with customers. This means actively recognising what are the best channels for reaching individual customers and what channels individual customers prefer to use for different tasks, how they use them at present and how their usage in the future may change.

The benefits of deploying an integrated multi-channel approach are considerable. Marketbridge point out the benefits: 'All activities combined, enabled by CRM processes and technologies, lead to a more complete view of the customer that allows deeper understanding of account buyer behaviour and consistent customer interaction through shared account information. These benefits spawn opportunities to cross-sell and up-sell, and thus increase sales growth and market share.'[26]

Planning channel strategy across stakeholders

The discussion above has focused on multi-channel integration in the context of customers. However, the issues discussed above also apply to other stakeholders including employees, partners and suppliers. Figure 8.14 provides a simplified illustration of how one company might plan to shift their channel mix with customer, employees and partners over a three-year period.

Relationship		Today % employees/partners/customers	Tomorrow % employees/partners/customers
Marketing	Web	15	30
	Phone	30	30
	Face	55	40
Selling	Web	0	55
	Phone	10	15
	Face	90	30
Servicing	Web	10	70
	Phone	70	20
	Face	20	10

Figure 8.14 Channel mix change matrix for customers, employees and partners.
Source: Based on Broad Vision

In the example shown in this figure, for marketing, sales and service there is a high degree of migration to Web-based interactions. This can create not only significant cost savings but also new opportunities to create value through utilisation of Web-based personalisation.

Companies in a wide range of industries have already taken steps to implement new channel strategies that improve both efficiency and effectiveness in their stakeholder relationships. For example, Walmart and Tesco have developed highly integrated electronic channel strategies with their suppliers and Oracle Corporation in the US has saved a huge amount of employee administration costs by migrating these activities to the Web.

SUMMARY

This chapter has examined the role of the multi-channel integration process in customer relationship management. A comprehensive multi-channel integration strategy that has the support of both management and staff is essential for any company that wishes to maintain a first-class level of customer experience within and across its channels.

Providing quality products and services in new as well as traditional channels is important for companies wishing to meet the expectations of today's customers. However, many companies do not seem to recognise the need to maintain equally high standards of service *across all channels*. The quality of a company's service is only as high as the weakest link in its channel offer and the enterprise needs to uphold the same high standard of service and customer experience in all channels. If one of the channels does not function, the customer will be disappointed. For example, if the booking service with a mobile phone does not work properly the customer will be upset and it will make no difference to the displeased customer that the customer service in a face-to-face situation is exemplary and the website is superb.

A review of experience of companies implementing a multi-channel approach involving adding new channels suggests some practical issues that need to be considered by managers. First, in offering a range of channels to customers it is important that the benefits do not seem too one-sided. Some companies emphasise the benefits to themselves of a multi-channel approach as opposed to the benefits to their customers. Second, extensive communication to staff of the reasons why the new multi-channel approach is being adopted is essential. In particular, the sales staff needs to be taken through the economic arguments, as well as an explanation of any likely impact on their work role, including their remuneration. Third, companies should be aware how staff in one channel may seek to sabotage other channels. Finally, companies should use social media, where relevant, as an early detection device of any customer problems within or across channels.

Of critical importance is the technology required to support integration of the offline and online channels. This can only be prescribed once a single clear understanding of the business processes and associated channel 'maps' is determined across marketing, sales and service. Here the information management process, the subject of the next chapter, has a key role to play.

CASE 8.1: TNT – creating the 'perfect' customer transaction

The company

TNT Express Services UK & Ireland (TNT Express) is the UK's leading business-to-business express operator delivering in excess of 100 million items per year. It has the largest individual share of the national market and has an extensive network of 64 strategically located express delivery depots, three sortation hubs and three National Customer Contact Centres. TNT Express was formerly an operating division of TNT NV, an international services company with headquarters in Hoofddorp, The Netherlands. In 2011 TNT Express was demerged from TNT Mail, taking a listing on the Euronext Amsterdam Stock Exchange with the parent company rebranded as TNT Express NV. In 1978 the company employed 500 staff in the UK with sales revenue of around £5 million. By 2012 it has grown to some 9,000 employees with sales revenue of over £700 million.

The challenge

Although TNT Express's growth has been dramatic, senior management recognised that in an increasingly competitive market with a large number of parcel courier companies, simply delivering customer satisfaction was not enough. Over the past decade and a half, TNT Express has been developing an increasingly sophisticated approach to improving customer satisfaction. This initiative commenced with a research project on measurement of customer satisfaction.

This research showed very high levels of customer satisfaction. Some 90 per cent were satisfied, with the balance being neutral or dissatisfied. However, the company concluded that those customers who were merely 'satisfied', as opposed to those that were 'very satisfied' could be in danger of defection, especially if they had some subsequent reason for dissatisfaction. The company recognised that it was imperative to improve the experience of these customers, shifting them to being *highly satisfied* and thereby increasing their loyalty and profitability. Further, as this initiative developed, senior management recognised the need for a strategic roadmap to help focus the organisation on the customer.

The solution

TNT Express undertook further research and found that by asking whether customers had any problems with the service that they received from TNT Express, they obtained a much clearer picture of the customer experience and how it could be improved. TNT Express launched a radical programme aimed at creating the 'Perfect Transaction' for all customers.

The first step was to understand where improvements could be made to the customer experience. TNT Express started by asking customers, in much greater detail than had been done previously, about what they wanted. Then, using this information, a list of areas where the customer experience could be improved was developed. Before any performance enhancements were made, statistical modelling was used to prioritise this list. Costs associated with these improvements were carefully considered. TNT Express senior managers recognised that outstanding customer service had to be delivered at a reasonable cost – in terms of cost both to the customer and to the company. Next, the opportunities for improvement were analysed by weighting the frequency of occurrence with the impact of the problem to pinpoint enhancements that really mattered to the customer. This led to the identification of the key areas which would lead to the perfect transaction.

Customers asked for a dedicated contact when they called into TNT Express in order to avoid excessive call transfers, too many contact points and long telephone holding. TNT Express commits to a dedicated sales contact for every customer account. Also, those accounts who spend over a threshold get a dedicated customer service agent. As a result, the customer services department was strengthened. Instead of multiple points of contact, a customer who calls in now deals with one individual who can handle any enquiry. Employees have greater ability to respond to customer queries through wider knowledge, greater authority and enhanced technology. The result is that the customer gets better and faster service. Implementation is ongoing, with the list of improvements continually being added to and modified. Always service enhancement is driven by feedback from the customers.

TNT Express also focused on employee satisfaction. The company found that employees enjoy giving better service to the customer but become frustrated when they lack the skills and authority to do so. TNT Express provides extensive customer service training. One innovative programme was called 'The Perfect Transaction'. The 'Perfect Transaction' identifies the chain of events from when a customer requests a collection to the time that payment is received for the consignment – as shown in Figure 1. Here employees are trained to understand that they play an important role in delivering the customer experience. Teamwork is essential, with each person sharing in the responsibility of achieving perfection in each step of the transaction. This can only be achieved if employees share a positive attitude – striving to beat their previous best performance.

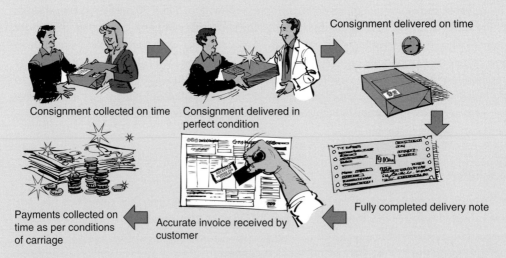

Figure 1 The 'perfect customer transaction' at TNT

In order to help align the whole organisation to the business strategy, in 2008 TNT Express developed a strategy map which focused more specifically on what needed to be done to deliver a superior customer experience and to ensure future profitable growth. This strategy map is shown in Figure 2.

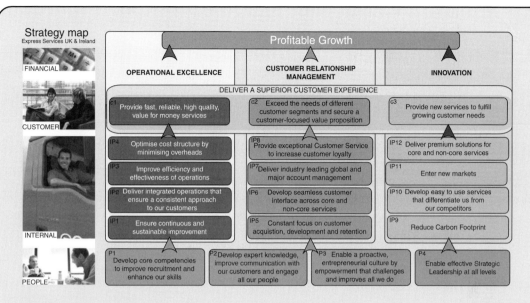

Figure 2 TNT strategy map

This strategy map is based on the service profit chain and Balance Scorecard concepts developed at the Harvard Business School. The strategy map follows the service profit chain sequence of leadership → people → customers → financial results. The four foundational elements in TNT Express's people strategy include: the development of core competencies; the development of expert knowledge and improved communication with customers; encouraging a proactive entrepreneurial culture; and enabling effective strategic leadership at all levels. Measurable internal objectives are outlined in three key areas: operational excellence, CRM, and innovation. Each of these elements has four key objectives, shown in Figure 2, aimed at delivering superior customer experience. These lead to specific outcomes for the customer.

In terms of CRM these objectives include:

- delivering industry leading global and major account management;
- delivering seamless customer interface across core and non-core services;
- having a constant focus on customer acquisition, customer development and customer retention;
- provision of exceptional customer service aimed at increasing customer loyalty.

TNT Express has highly developed customer segmentation and performance measurement systems and the company uses a range of advanced customer satisfaction measurements as part of its strategy to deliver a superior customer experience.

A further related customer-focused initiative, the 'Customer Promise', was introduced in 2010. This initiative aimed at putting in place a commitment to 'win the trust of our customers by delivering on our promises'. TNT Express's Customer Promise is a set of ten pledges which highlight the company's commitment always to strive not only to meet but exceed customer expectations, as shown in Figure 3. Again, TNT Express has been led by customer insight, which demonstrates that in addition to rational performance measures customers are motivated at an emotional level. The promises communicate the culture and mentality of TNT Express which can't be described using empirical measures.

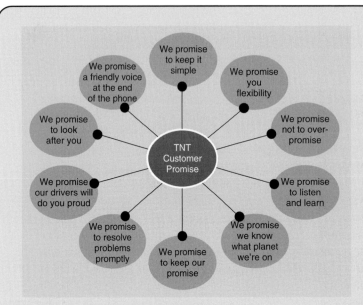

Figure 3 TNT customer promise

These promises are not just high-level platitudes. They are backed up by detailed explanations of what each promise means and what customers can expect, as illustrated by the example of one promise detailed in Figure 4. Full details of all ten promises are made available to customers in a printed brochure and they are also published on the company's website.

We promise to look after you

Whether you send lots or just a little with us, you have a named account manager to look after you. They will get to know you, your business and what you expect from us. They will also talk straight, sort things out and look after your interests with the right solutions at the best value.

What to expect
- Your account representative will proactively contact you at an agreed frequency to ensure our effective management of your account.
- If you wish to see a representative of TNT we will arrange an appointment at an agreed time and date.
- Our representatives will be able to offer a solution for all of your distribution requirements.
- We will provide you with all relevant contact details to ensure that you are able to get the right assistance when using our services.
- We will ensure your requests for our stationery are fulfilled within three working days
- We will keep you informed of our ongoing improvement activities resulting from continuous customer research, via our regular customer communications and our website

---

Figure 4 Specific TNT customer promise: 'We promise to look after you'

TNT Express's Customer Promise initiative underlines the courage of its convictions with regards to customer service. The company views these pledges as 'a set of commitments designed to ensure TNT customers receive the best possible service and the company remains at the pinnacle of the express delivery sector in the UK'.

TNT Express considers their Customer Promise is a key differentiator in the highly competitive express delivery market. As Stuart Stobie, former Divisional Managing Director of TNT Express UK and now Managing Director Special Services at TNT Express Worldwide, points out: 'Our Customer Promise is important for two very good reasons: it sets us apart from our competitors and provides evidence of the true value of our service in an intensely competitive market.' He adds: 'Consisting of a set of clear commitments reflecting what customers expect from TNT as a market leader and innovator, the Customer Promise is peace of mind that we are doing all we can to not only meet, but exceed expectations. We are raising the bar and will do everything we can to ensure we live up to the standards our customers expect, and that we demand of ourselves.'

TNT Express has also invested heavily in CRM and e-solutions in support of its commitment to delivering a superior customer experience. TNT Customer Interface Technology (CIT) utilises an innovative range of dispatch, tracking and tracing systems aimed at making TNT Express services even faster and more accessible to customers. The sophisticated system developed by TNT Express uses data from consignment barcodes so that individual packages can be tracked at any point during transit. This system enables the company to let customers know the status of consignments at any time in the entire process from the collection of parcels to the delivery of parcels. Customers can also track their own shipments via the Internet, mobile phone apps and through an e-mail tracking service. A further range of e-solutions includes e-invoicing facilities and a re-delivery website where customers can select appropriate times to ensure successful delivery. The company offers a range of Internet and PC-based services including myTNT, ExpressShipper and ExpressManager, all of which are designed to make TNT Express simple and quicker to deal with.

The results

The results of this strategy have been enviable. TNT Express is recognised as the UK's leading business-to-business express delivery operator. The company has the largest individual share of the national market and the international market where an export or import has been paid for in the UK by UK customers. TNT Express delivers in excess of 100 million items per year on behalf of UK businesses. In recognition of its achievements, the company has been awarded numerous industry awards for service excellence and customer care. Since the Customer Promise was introduced, TNT Express has seen a marked increase in the numbers of customers who say TNT Express is exceeding their expectations.

Although TNT Express had provided Internet tracking for their customers for more than decade, it has continually enhanced its multi-channel offerings and its extensive set of applications means consignments can be monitored via a wide range of communication devices. This gives customers the ability to check the whereabouts of their goods via mobile phones, handheld computers, e-mail, Web browsers as well as conventional touch-tone phones. TNT Express has continually developed and refined performance targets for key support processes. The company now gathers information on a weekly basis on customer query handling, credit notes, client contacts, complaints received and other key outcomes that provide measures of their ability to satisfy customers.

TNT Express's adoption of European Foundation for Quality Management Business Excellence Model as a way of working throughout the company has provided a framework for all employees to achieve continuous improvement. Ongoing application of the business excellence model has become a way of life within TNT Express and the company has stayed ahead of all other competitor carriers as a result of widespread commitment to the concept of continuous improvement.

Following setting up an Office of Strategy Management and the adoption of the Balance Scorecard methodology in 2007, TNT Express has focused on making strategy execution a core competency. Despite a significant economic downturn, since adopting the Balance Scorecard market share has grown 14 per cent, and customer loyalty 34 per cent. In 2010 TNT Express was inducted into the Palladium Balanced Scorecard Hall of Fame for Executing Strategy. The Palladium Hall of Fame recognises those organisations that are exemplars of strategy management discipline through their application of the Kaplan-Norton Balance Scorecard approach to strategy execution. Each Hall of Fame member has achieved measurable breakthrough financial and non-financial results.

CASE 8.2: Guinness – delivering the 'Perfect Pint'

The company

Guinness was founded in Ireland by Arthur Guinness in 1759. Within a short period of time the dark rich beverage was brewed so well that it ousted all imports from the Irish market, captured a share of the English trade and revolutionised the brewing industry. By 1825 Guinness Stout was available abroad and by 1838 Guinness' Irish Brewery was the largest in Ireland. In 1881 the annual production of Guinness brewed had exceeded one million barrels a year, and, by 1914, St James's Gate was the world's largest brewery.

Guinness is now also brewed in over 35 countries around the world. All of these overseas brews must contain a flavoured extract produced at the St James's Gate brewery in Dublin. Hence the special brewing skills developed at Arthur Guinness' brewery remain at the heart of every one of the ten million glasses of Guinness enjoyed every day across the world.

Today, Guinness, part of Diegio plc, is one of the most well-recognised global brands and has a loyal following of consumers. However, producing a consistently high quality product was one of the key problems facing Guinness.

The challenge

Product quality is recognised as a critical factor in building loyalty among consumers – especially in converting occasional drinkers into loyal consumers. Research suggests that acquiring a taste for thick dark beer requires the product to meet consumer expectations on every occasion. In each brewery, manufacturing processes are carefully controlled. Ingredients are rigorously checked, with every brew containing a special ingredient which is brewed in Dublin.

Each day Guinness' trained tasters do taste tests on dozens of samples of beer. All the company's products are tasted at regular stages throughout their life-cycle to ensure they are in top condition for their consumers. These tasters score the beer for its aroma, flavour and head quality, as well as detecting any problems or deviation in product quality.

However, producing a standard product is not enough to ensure that every customer enjoys the same 'Perfect Pint' every time – anywhere. Research in the UK suggested that consumers often were presented with a less-than-perfect pint at the point of consumption. Guinness Brewing GB recognised this as a major challenge, involving a total management of the supply chain. Hence they needed to address the challenge of ensuring a consistently perfect consumer experience at the point of delivery.

The solution

Achieving this lay beyond the remit of any one department. To ensure a perfect consumer experience at the point of delivery the company formed a special cross-functional process improvement team charged with the job of delivering the 'Perfect Pint'.

The team carefully mapped and measured the entire product delivery process, from brewery to consumer. The team drew up a detailed programme which when implemented would consistently deliver the 'Perfect Pint'. The control of the supply chain, which Guinness calls the 'quality chain', involves four main stages:

- ensuring quality of the raw materials being supplied to Guinness;
- ensuring quality within the brewing and packaging processes;
- ensuring that the publican serves the 'Perfect Pint';
- ensuring that the customer is educated in enjoying the final stages of consumption.

During the first two stages quality control involved rigorous purchasing and checks on manufacturing standards. Dedication to quality at Guinness starts with suppliers and purchasers working together to meet these standards, while manufacturing involves world-class techniques and Total Quality Management. All employees are educated to share the 'quality vision' and are trained to understand how every person plays a vital role in the quality chain. During the brewing process samples are tested at every stage. Even the loading into kegs, cans and bottles is carefully controlled to ensure that beers are more consistent in flavour and appearance in the glass.

However, the 'Perfect Pint' team found that often problems developed once the beer arrived at the licensed premises. Guinness, like other cask beers, is a 'live' product and needs to be handled carefully. Frequently, the beer was not stored and presented correctly and even though this was not directly within the control of Guinness, it was critical to the quality delivered to the consumer.

The team undertook considerable research to ensure consistency of quality in the final stages of the supply chain. Results of their work include guidelines for the publicans on all aspects of the 'pub dispense quality'. These guidelines include advice on the correct gas mixture when pulling the pint, the ideal dispensing temperature, cleaning beer lines, washing glasses and the perfect presentation.

Guinness put considerable research and development effort into the areas of dispensing equipment and methods employed in pulling pints. For example, the current tap used by pubs to dispense Guinness was developed at a cost of over £1 million. The tap has been designed so that it is easy to operate and so it ensures that every pint is perfectly presented. Other developments include the introduction of a new gas-blending programme for pubs selling draught beer. The installation of such initiatives helps ensure consumers experience a 'Perfect Pint' on each occasion.

Training of bar staff has not been neglected. The 'Perfect Pint' team recognised the important role of staff that pull the 'Perfect Pint' and deliver the experience. The famous 'two-part pour' requires practice. Detailed instructions and training were provided by Guinness to ensure the 'Perfect Pint' was pulled properly and drunk correctly by consumers:

> Hold the glass at a 45 degree angle close to the spout to prevent large bubbles from forming in the head. Pull the tap fully open and fill the glass 75 per cent full. Allow the stout to settle completely before filling the rest of the glass. The creamy head will separate from the dark body. To top off the pint push the tap forward slightly until the head rises just proud of the rim. Never allow the stout to overflow or run down the glass.

Every Guinness employee is trained to recognise their responsibility in ensuring that the 'Perfect Pint' is enjoyed everywhere. Employees learn how to execute the two-part pour and are encouraged to check the pouring technique and test the depth of the head and temperature of the pint in licensed premises. Employees can alert the 'Perfect Pint' support team if a problem is encountered, so that the publican can be offered further advice or training.

The results

But achieving the 'Perfect Pint' does not stop there. Research showed Guinness that consumer education was also important if the consumption experience was going to be consistent – every time. Guinness needed to communicate to consumers their part in securing the 'Perfect Pint'. Point-of-sale laminated cards were used which explained, on one side, how to pour the 'Perfect Pint' and on the reverse side, the correct serving temperature and a ruler that allowed consumers to measure the correct thickness of the head on their pint.

Consumers were also targeted with a highly successful advertising campaign that extolled the virtues of waiting for a 'Perfect Pint' – as it takes between 90 and 120 seconds for a 'Perfect Pint' of Guinness to settle. This waiting time has been promoted by Guinness with advertising campaigns such as 'Good things come to those who wait'. Thirsty customers now wait patiently for their Guinness. They have become part of the process and are now convinced that if it's worth having, then it's worth waiting for. Even the core customers have learned to deal with the wait involved. As one pub owner observed: 'The old timers finish their pints in three sips. They re-order right after the second sip; by the time they finish the last sip, a fresh one will arrive. They're hearty men.'

Guinness has developed strong relationships with their highly committed customers. As brand commentator Fred Richards observes:

> The Guinness brand experience drives a visceral, interactive and expressive relationship with its consumers. The visceral relationship manifests itself by the excitement one feels when first encountering this brand; the beer's color, smell, the sound of its pour. The interactive relationship begins with the all-important opening ceremony: The pint arrives and the consumer . . . waits . . . The visceral and interactive relationships comprise a rich, robust brand experience which, when repeated, fosters consumer loyalty and drives an expressive relationship with the brand: If you are loyal to Guinness, you are eager to share the experience with others. In a bar, this relationship becomes obvious when other Guinness consumers subtly acknowledge the ritual first pour and reaffirm their exclusive club membership.

Guinness places strong emphasis on multiple channels and multi-channel integration. These channels include physical facilities, Web, mobile and social media. The flagship 'Guinness Storehouse' premises at St James's Gate in Dublin encourages visitors, with over one million people visiting in 2011. Sales jumped 10 per cent following the 2011 visits of both President Barack Obama and Queen Elizabeth II. The Storehouse is Ireland's number one fee-paying tourist draw.

Guinness have a sophisticated Web, social media and mobile presence; and for the sport- and style-aware 18 to 40 year olds, who are comfortable with technology, they have an advanced website, a range of developing mobile applications and over 250,000 Guinness Ireland Facebook fans. In the mobile area, marketing agency Marvellous has developed a range of Java downloads to deliver cutting edge brand engagement for those who are 'connected'. Much activity is focused around the Irish celebration of St Patrick's day in March each year. Some applications include:

Pubfinder – this enables users to identify nearby pubs via location-based services. The application can also find the nearest St Patrick's party pub, the nearest pub with sports TV, or the nearest pub serving Guinness Red. Because the Pubfinder is a Java download, the data can be dynamically refreshed on the handset, keeping it up-to-date.

Pub Quiz – a selection of four Java-based quizzes where consumers answer as many questions as possible in 119.5 seconds, the time it takes to pour the perfect pint of Guinness. They could then submit their scores to a 'national leaderboard', also accessible via Facebook, with great Irish prizes for the top scorer.

Picture Gallery – St Patrick's party-goers are asked to send in photos of their celebrations to a special shortcode. There they can view their own, their friends' and a random selection of all photos submitted. Also, the photographs can also be viewed on the Guinness Facebook pages.

This customer experience strategy and multi-channel strategy has propelled Guinness to achieving a high share of the total draught market. Guinness recognised that the presentation of beer is critical in terms of ensuring repeat purchase – and this requires a total integration of all aspects of the supply chain – including the consumer. The 'Perfect Pint' project was so successful that the approach has been applied worldwide to improve the presentation and quality of draught Guinness. Today, Guinness is one of a few truly global beer brands and sells over two billion pints every year in over 150 countries.

9 | Information and technology management

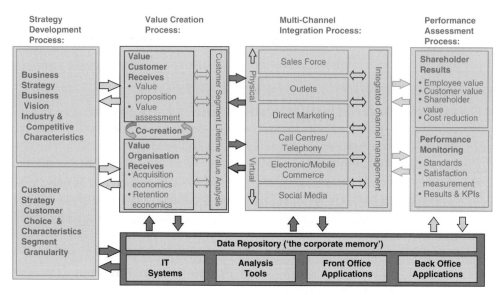

Information Management Process

The CRM Strategy Framework

The information management process, highlighted in the CRM Strategy Framework, is concerned with two key activities: the collection and collation of customer information from all customer contact points and other sources and the utilisation of this information to construct complete and current customer profiles which can be used to enhance the quality of the customer experience, thus contributing to the value creation process. As discussed in Chapter 5, information should be collected not just from the company's own internal sources but all appropriate external sources. As well as traditional market research, the organisation needs to expand its activities to encompass the domain of social media. The sentiments and trends available from the analysis of activity in social media have two key advantages. First, highly current information can be accessed in almost real time. Second, information acquired from social media can be substantially less expensive than that acquired through formal market research methods such as focus groups and customer interviews. Social media may potentially also provide access to a very large number of customers, whereas market research budgets may limit sample sizes.

As companies grow and interact with an increasing number of customers through an increasing diversity of channels, the need for a systematic approach to organising and employing information becomes ever greater. Two questions are of special importance in the information management process:

1. How should we organise information on customers?
2. How can we 'replicate' the mind of customers and use this information to improve our CRM activities?

Where customer information is spread across disparate functions and departments, interactions with the customer can be based on partial or no knowledge of the customer, even though the customer may have been with the organisation for years. This fragmentation of customer knowledge creates two major problems for the company. First, the customer is treated in an impersonal way, which may lead to dissatisfaction and defection. Second, there is no single unified view of the customer upon which to act and to plan.

In an effort to keep pace with escalating volumes of data, the tendency has been for organisations to create more or bigger databases within functions or departments, leading to a wealth of disparate silos of customer information. Companies are thus left with a fragmented and often unwieldy body of information upon which to make crucial management decisions. The elevation of CRM from the level of a specific application such as a call centre, to the level of a pan-company strategy requires the integration of customer interactions across all communication channels, front-office and back-office applications and business functions. What is required to manage this integration on an ongoing basis is a purposefully designed system that brings together data, computers, procedure and people – or what is termed an integrated CRM solution. This is the output of the information management process.

The information management process can usefully be thought of as the engine that drives CRM activities. It consists of several elements that need to work closely together. Information should be used to fuel, formulate and facilitate strategic and tactical CRM actions.

As the figure above shows, the other processes that make up the CRM Strategy Framework all depend on the information management process. The *strategy development process* involves analysing customer data in different ways to provide insights that could yield competitive advantage. The *value creation process* utilises customer information to develop superior value propositions and to determine how more value can be created for the organisation. These first two processes largely involve what, in Chapter 1, we termed *analytical CRM*. They provide information to help the firm make strategic decisions about its activities. The *multi-channel integration process* is highly dependent on the systems that capture, store and disseminate customer information. This is the realm of *operational CRM*. Operational CRM helps manage customer contact and ensures a consistent high quality customer experience. The *performance assessment process* requires financial, sales, customer, operational and other information to be made available to evaluate the success of CRM and identify areas for improvement.

To appreciate fully the significance of the information management process within strategic CRM, it is important first to be clear about the role of information, information technology and information management in CRM.

The role of information, IT and information management

Information

CRM is founded on the premise that relationships with customers can be forged and managed to the mutual advantage of those in the relationship including all relevant stakeholders. However, suppliers and their value chain partners cannot interact and nurture relationships with customers they know nothing or very little about. While having information about customers is therefore essential to relationship building, it is not alone sufficient. Of much greater importance is being informed and making informed decisions. In other words, the real value of information lies in its use, not in its mere existence. This simple truth is evident in the fact that many companies possess vast amounts of information on their customers, but few fully exploit this treasure trove for greatest benefit.

IT

Many equate CRM with IT. For instance, the bigger your database, the more advanced you are in CRM. This notion of a direct correlation between the two is misleading, for CRM is a management approach and IT is a management tool. Further, in the terms in which we define CRM, it is possible to have highly sophisticated CRM without having highly sophisticated IT. The traditional corner shop proprietor built intimate relationships with his regular customers by recognising their individual needs and circumstances and tailoring his service accordingly. Historically, he did not log their buying habits and preferences in an electronic database as no such thing existed, but he referred to his own memory of customers and applied it conscientiously. The shopkeeper knew which customers were most valuable and how to retain them by delivering appropriate value.

Businesses today compete in a much more complex environment and potentially with millions of customers they have never actually met, so IT has become a vital feature of managing customer relationships. However, the corner shop principle still applies, in that a working 'memory' of customers, supported by two-way dialogue, is what enables effective customer relationship management. Thus it is important to keep the technological aspect of CRM in the correct perspective: as the means to an end and not the end itself.

Information management

Information management is about achieving an acceptable balance between operating intelligently and operating idealistically. Consider the following scenario. The heart surgeon may have all the latest equipment, superlative training and a genuine commitment to saving the life of his patient, but if he operates on the basis that he is replacing a valve in a serious but routine procedure, rather than working to rectify the multiple complications he finds once the patient's chest is opened, he will probably fail in his efforts to help and possibly with fatal consequences. So who will be to blame? The surgeon for not knowing enough about his patient's unique needs and condition and not being prepared for the unexpected, or the patient for not forwarding more information about the patterns or progression of her illness? Often we do not know what it is we need to know to address a problem, or by the same token, what we really do not need to know. Clearly, neither the undersupply nor oversupply of information is satisfactory. The quest is therefore to find the right information and at the right time. Learning that the patient has a family history of a rare coronary disease after she has fallen into a coma on the operating table is of little comfort or benefit.

This analogy serves to emphasise the constituent dimensions of information: quality, quantity, relevance, timing, ownership and application. The function of information *management* in the CRM context is to transform information into usable knowledge and to apply this knowledge effectively and ethically in the creation of customer value. The acronym 'DIKW' – *data, information, knowledge* and *wisdom* – is used fairly extensively within the information technology industry to describe this process.

This process, shown in Figure 9.1, is known as the 'wisdom hierarchy', the 'knowledge hierarchy', the 'information hierarchy', or the 'knowledge pyramid'. It refers to models that represent purported structural functional relationships between data, information, knowledge and wisdom. Raw data which sit within, say, the data warehouse need to be analysed and translated into information that provides answers to 'who', 'what', 'where' and 'when' questions relating to customers. The translation of data and information represents knowledge and answers 'how' questions. Finally, wisdom is achieved by interpreting and applying the knowledge to make informed relevant business decisions. Some protagonists suggest the framework should be expanded to include the further step of understanding.

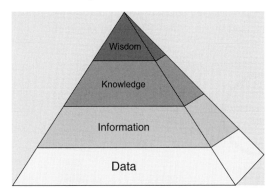

Figure 9.1 The knowledge hierarchy

The right information in the wrong hands or at the wrong time has little constructive value. Further, the 'perishable' quality of information demands that it needs constant updating and replenishing. The management of information therefore encompasses the organisation (capture, storage, and dissemination), utilisation (analysis, interpretation and application) and regulation (monitoring, control and security) of information.

The information management process

The information management process should be considered in two stages. First, the CRM strategy (or the relevant component of it) needs to be reviewed in the context of the organisation's information management needs. Second, the technological options needed to implement the agreed strategy have to be determined. The first stage will involve a strategic review of the current condition, capability and capacity of the information management infrastructure, in relation to the customer, channel and product strategies defined in the preceding CRM processes.

Chapter 6 explained that each organisation, depending on the core business and a number of related strategic issues, needs to consider precisely which CRM strategy is appropriate now and in the future. Figure 9.2 reintroduces the CRM strategy matrix, discussed in that chapter, which identified four broad strategic options facing organisations – *product-based selling*, *customer-based marketing*, *managed service and support* and *individualised CRM* (or what is termed 'one-to-one marketing'[1]). The latter option is the most sophisticated – it requires collection and analysis of extensive information about customers and also the desire and ability to give customers individualised service.

Here the strategic issues to be reviewed will include: Is customer information extracted from each interaction or transaction regardless of the channel the customer uses? Is this information centralised and leveraged and exploited across all functions and channels? Is the information technology platform deemed appropriate for the present and for the future? The results of such a review will highlight the strengths and weaknesses of existing information management provision. Importantly, it will help clarify the completeness of information (how much customer information is held and how sophisticated is the analysis of that information) and the degree of customer individualisation (the extent to which customer information is used to provide customised service).

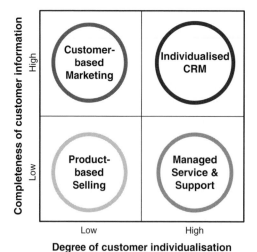

Figure 9.2 The CRM strategy matrix

As the number of channels increases with the development of newer electronic channels such as WebTV and fourth generation mobile technology, the information management process will become even more central to the management of customer relationships and thus to the achievement of customer-centric strategic goals. A key role of the information management process is to ensure the customer centricity and relevancy of the organisation by embedding the customer perspective in all business activity. In effect, the firm must be able to 'replicate the mind of the customer' if it is to provide the kind of individual or customised service that will attract, retain and grow profitable customer relationships. Thus the emphasis in this process needs to be on how we can use information in a proactive way to develop enhanced relationships with the customer, rather than on the elegance and sophistication of the technology. The design of the technological components of CRM should therefore be driven not by IT interests, but by the organisation's strategy for using customer information to improve its competitiveness.

With this in mind, an information management infrastructure that will support and deliver the chosen CRM strategy should be developed. For most companies, this will involve the incorporation of specific technologies. As depicted in the CRM Strategy Framework at the start of this chapter, the main technological components of the information management process comprise the data repository, analytical tools, IT systems, front-office applications and back-office applications. These five components contribute to building better customer relationships by making the organisation 'market intelligent', 'service competent' and 'strategy confident'. Development of the technological framework should take account of the technical barriers in CRM as well as the five technological components of the information management process.

The technical barriers in CRM

The technical barriers in CRM are highlighted by the gap between expectations and results. When our growing expectations of technological tools are not matched by their capacity to meet those expectations, the tools become, in our perception, barriers rather than enablers. In reality, the 'obstacles' are less a matter of tool malfunction than they are our own misalignment of the strategic 'will' with the tactical 'way'. Where once our IT tools were considered adequate, our demands on them have changed, because our requirements and expectations are different. Managing customer relationships effectively at one time meant getting customers' address details correct on mass mailings and ensuring that everyone received a copy. Today it means understanding customers' individual buying habits and contact preferences and strategically targeting communications via a multitude of channels. What is required to overcome these technical barriers is a more accurate understanding of what we wish to achieve and a more appropriate means of achieving it. The experience of the automobile industry is a case in point.

A study of the UK's leading car manufacturers, importers and dealers by Cap Gemini some years ago found that most computerised customer databases had serious gaps or deficiencies. The databases did not support the recording of customer lifestyles or interests and could not record essential demographic information. Even when customer data were captured, they were not always accessible to marketing or other customer-facing functions. The study concluded these defects caused strategic problems in the companies' sales and marketing activities, frequently making them unlikely to be able to track either customers or prospects efficiently, focus advertising programmes accurately or develop effective personalised direct marketing campaigns. Despite improvements over more recent years these problems are still commonplace in the automotive sector and other sectors.

This serves to illustrate how poor customer information can limit the success of CRM and other strategic initiatives. When we encounter such problems, we are forced to ask ourselves some basic questions. Are we really capturing the customer information we need? Is customer information being made available to the people who can use it to increase sales and add customer value? Are we getting the most out of the information we collect, or does our data analysis capability need to be improved?

The data repository

To make an enterprise customer-focused, it is not sufficient simply to collect data about customers, or even to generate management information from individual databases, because they normally provide only a partial view of the customer. To understand and manage customers as complete and unique entities, it is necessary for large organisations to have a powerful corporate memory of customers – an integrated enterprise-wide data store that can provide the data analyses and applications.

The role of the data repository is to collect, hold and integrate customer information and thus enable the company to develop and manage customer relationships effectively. It thus represents 'the corporate memory' of the organisation. We use the term data repository here to refer to all of an organisation's databases, data marts and data warehouses combined. Before exploring the selection and combination of these as technology options for CRM we will first consider the key elements of a data repository.

From an IT architecture perspective, the data repository for a large organisation, dealing with many customers, can comprise two main parts: the *database* and the *data warehouse*. There are two forms of data warehouse: the conventional data warehouse and the operational data store. Databases are computer program software packages for storing data gathered from a source such as a call centre, the sales force, customer and market surveys, electronic points of sale (EPOS) and so on.

Each tactical database usually operates separately and is constructed to be user-specific, storing only that which is relevant to the tasks of its main users. Management and planning information drawn from a single database is therefore limited in value because it provides an incomplete view of customer-related activity. However, the value of databases extends well beyond their function as a collection of data about customers from which we can understand current customer relationships and develop prospective customer relationships. If properly exploited, databases can provide a 'reality check' to help us become more *relevant* to those customers and prospects.

The data warehouse is a collection of related databases that have been brought together so that the maximum value can be extracted from them. A data warehouse is a single data store containing a complete and consistent set of data about an organisation's customer and business activities. In this chapter we will use the term 'data mart' to describe a single subject data warehouse and the term 'data warehouse' to describe an enterprise data warehouse system. Although the principle of the data warehouse is simple, the process of creating one can be quite complex due to the fragmented nature of the databases from which data are copied and the large scale of the task. Thus it is necessary to use a data conversion process to coordinate the conversion task. Technically the data warehouse is structured for query performance.

The operational data store (ODS) is a special form of data warehouse, much smaller than a conventional data warehouse, storing only the information necessary to provide a single identity for all customers, regardless of how many identities they have in different back-office systems. Technically the ODS is structured for transactional performance. This is used mainly by front-office systems and processes to provide a single view of the customer. For example, it enables call centres, sales force automation and e-commerce solutions to have a consistent view of customer activities.

The data conversion process copies data from tactical databases to the data warehouse in such a way that data duplication is minimised and inconsistencies between databases are resolved. The process makes use of an enterprise data model, which describes the contents of each tactical database and includes rules for combining data from different databases after appropriate data cleansing and de-duplication. The main benefit of using an enterprise data model is that the rules for copying and integrating data are all kept together, making them easier to manage than the copy programs that connect individual pairs of databases together for creating decision support systems (DSS) or data marts. These centralised rules make the task of integrating databases easier for IT staff, reducing the cost and effort of providing complex information for tasks such as CRM.

When a successful data warehouse implementation is achieved, analytic tools can be used in conjunction with it to develop opportunities to create value for both the customer and the organisation.

Technology options for CRM

We have pointed out that the CRM technology approach adopted will be highly dependent on the organisation's CRM strategy. There are four broad alternative technology options for facilitating different degrees of development of CRM strategy in terms of data repository. These include:

- a tactical database with decision support systems,
- data marts (or single subject data warehouses),
- an enterprise data warehouse, and
- integrated CRM solutions.

These options, which progressively extend the range of CRM applications available, are outlined in Figure 9.3. However, it should be pointed out that not all organisations have implemented CRM in such a structured manner. Organisations often adopted multiple decision support systems as 'point solutions' throughout the enterprise for reasons of expediency. The time to market imperative sometimes drives businesses to adopt available tactical DSS solutions to meet immediate needs rather than strategic, properly architected solutions which may take considerable time to develop and implement. Competitive activities may result in a window of opportunity being quite short and necessitating a sub-optimum solution.

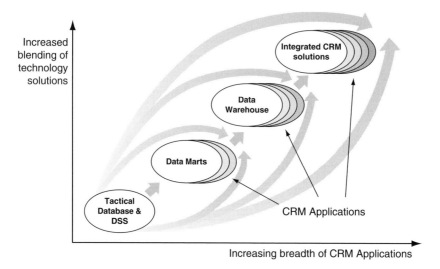

Figure 9.3 Technology levels for CRM

Although point solutions have advantages in terms of time to implement and cost, proliferation of multiple decision support systems can eventually increase costs. This can also result in multiple (and different) views of the same customer. Later, we discuss the use of an enterprise data warehouse to capture a 'single view of the customer'. A single view of the customer means that every department within an organisation will be using the same corporate memory with the aim of providing each and every customer with a consistent high-quality experience.

It is not necessary to choose one of these four technology options to the exclusion of others. On the contrary, most large organisations will need to blend these solutions creatively as they progressively adopt more sophisticated forms of CRM and migrate from product-based selling to individualised relationship marketing on the CRM strategy matrix shown in Figure 9.2. We now describe how these technology options can be used to assist in CRM. As we discuss these options we will refer back to the strategic positions on the CRM strategy matrix.

Tactical database and decision support systems

Most organisations already have some form of 'product-based selling' – i.e. various forms of marketing databases, sales databases and associated decision support systems. At the most basic level they have a marketing database which holds the names and addresses of customers. This may have a basic application package associated with it and the database can usually be extended to include basic segmentation information on, for example, geography, job title and size of organisation. The database and software technology used is often on a personal computer.

It is common to develop a database to support specific needs like mailing lists or for simple but specific analysis and reporting. The database typically can only retain data for a short time and does not have a link back to the customer. It is often built, owned and managed by the marketing department. The structure of a tactical database is shown in Figure 9.4.

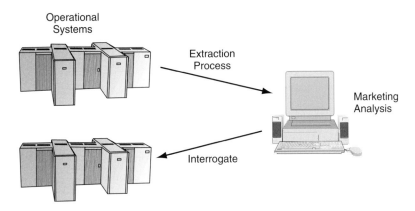

Figure 9.4 Tactical database and decision support systems

In addition to the database used in marketing, different parts of the organisation often build up their own separate databases. For example, the commercial department might have one for general mailings and the sales department might have their own for contact management purposes. In this way, lists can be developed for mass mailings to customers in isolation or through merging of these lists.

Advantages

These systems can be quick to establish and require very little investment in terms of IT. However, even at this level, more in-depth analysis can provide significant benefits, such as better targeting of direct marketing activity or a better understanding of market buying behaviour.

The use of query and reporting tools or more advanced analysis tools (such as data mining tools) can help identify new sales and marketing opportunities. These end-user tools provide multi-dimensional views of the data which better reflect the business and provide advanced user interfaces that allow the users to interact directly with the data.

These analysis tools are important elements of any technology solution used by a marketing organisation for CRM purposes, because they will help it to unearth the 'nuggets of gold' in the data and help analyse customers either as individuals or in product-based segments.

Disadvantages

However, using such simple systems will severely limit the sophistication of the sales and marketing strategies that an organisation can deploy. Tactical marketing databases inevitably require extensive manual work to load and maintain. This diverts resources away from the key role of analysis and often makes the extension of the system prohibitive.

Using query and analysis tools directly on existing operational systems also limits the scope of analysis, i.e., it is impossible to link data which are kept on different operational systems. Significant query and analysis activities can also adversely affect the performance of the operational system themselves and therefore may not prove to be popular with the IT department maintaining them.

However, any analysis is only as good as the quality and breadth of data that are available from the organisation. If only product and financial data are available then this may be useful for reporting sales or identifying products which are selling well. However, it does not help the company build up a consolidated 'single view of the customer' so that every department in the business sees the 'same picture' in terms of data on customers enabling it to identify and execute appropriate relationship marketing strategies.

Data marts

It is the ability of computers to act as an enormous memory and capture all the information on a customer that has been the driving force behind the adoption of CRM IT applications. This ability, coupled with the rapidly decreasing cost but increasing power of computers, has lowered the entry point for many organisations and has made the applications affordable.

Moving from 'product-based selling' to 'customer-based marketing' requires a more advanced CRM system. Users need more complex analysis power and the business needs a much more structured approach to the collection, sorting and storage of data regarding the customer. This typically involves building what is termed a data warehouse. This is separate from the operational systems which currently hold the data and it is built solely to 'warehouse' all the data that need to be collected in order to support a CRM system. The simplest form of data warehousing is usually called a data mart.

A data mart is technically a repository for information about a single source. In other words it is a 'single subject' data warehouse, implying it is not as grand in scope as its big brother, the enterprise data warehouse (discussed below), which is built for the entire organisation. Data marts are a natural extension of the database (enabled by more developed technology). So far as marketing is concerned, the single subject would be typically based around the customer. A simple representation of data marts is shown in Figure 9.5.

Data mart solutions can be purchased as part of a packaged application or as an integral suite of software which allows the extraction of data from operational systems. However, the sorting, organising and design of that data are done in a form which is optimised for analysis of data, not for running business operations. Thus, additional software products may be needed so that data can be presented in simple-to-use graphical forms which enable users to understand them.

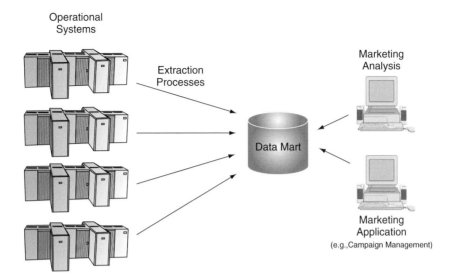

Figure 9.5 Data marts

The data mart package may also include query and analysis tools to enable the analysis of those data. Some tools allow the user to analyse data directly from older legacy systems. However, while this is useful, these tools are often limited in terms of their power of analysis.

Advantages

The data mart will typically run on a departmental server technology rather than on a PC. This permits a vast number of users to connect to it and use information from it. Organisations are now starting to consider moving from the departmental server to the 'Cloud'.

Data marts are proving popular for organisations with departments (or lines of business) that want to respond quickly to a new market or business opportunity. Other organisations may introduce a data mart to get a pilot system up and running quickly and achieve easily identifiable paybacks.

Disadvantages

Organisations must be careful that multiple, unconnected data marts do not spring up in many areas of the company making a 'single customer view' across multiple systems difficult to achieve.

In order to achieve a customer-centric view across the entire organisation, multiple subject data must be held (i.e., financial and transactional data on the customer). This implies that an enterprise data warehouse will ultimately need to be constructed that brings all relative customer information into one consistent store.

Many data warehouse solutions start as data marts forming part of a pilot scheme, with the aim of achieving an initial win within the organisation. However, it is important that, although on the surface they are a data mart, they should from the start be architected as a data warehouse.

Any analysis is only as good as the quality and breadth of data that are available. If only product sales and financial data are available then this may be useful for recognising the best customers and their profitability, but it does not help the company build up a consolidated 'single view of the customer' so every department in the business sees the 'same picture'.

It is the 'single customer view' across an organisation which will help drive the identification of true customer value (including 'share of customer' and 'customer lifetime value') and will also ensure that appropriate customer service is provided. This can only be achieved by the adoption of more 'business-critical' computer solutions and database technology which can grow in size and scope. These business-critical solutions are often classed as data warehouses even though, as far as the common definition of the term is concerned, they may be called data marts, albeit very large ones.

Enterprise data warehouse

As business shifts from product-based selling to more developed forms of customer-based marketing or managed service and support (see Figure 9.2), there is a requirement for more data and greater integration of data, both from the front office (call centres, customer-facing applications) and the back office (general ledger, human resources, operations). As the volume of data expands and the complexity increases, this may result in many databases and data marts. Therefore, it is much more logical and beneficial to have one repository for data. For CRM systems this is an enterprise data warehouse, shown in Figure 9.6.

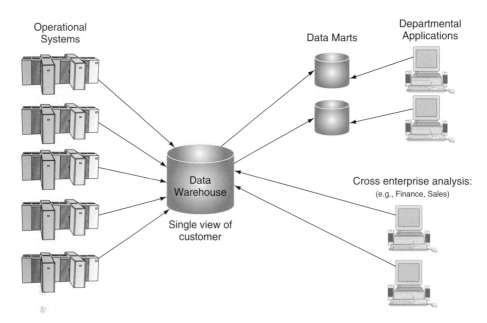

Figure 9.6 Enterprise data warehouse

Once the data warehouse is created with cleansed, 'single version of the truth' data, the appropriate query and analysis tools and data mining software can be applied to start to understand customer behaviour better and the organisation can plan more advanced CRM strategies. The data warehouse can then evolve into a multi-tier structure where parts of the organisation take information from the main data warehouse into their own systems. These may include analysis databases or dependent data marts (single subject repositories which are data-dependent on the central version of the data warehouse).

Until now we have not discussed other customer databases which may also be used to support a call centre or any other customer service application. These relate to the 'managed service and support' strategies in the bottom right-hand corner of the CRM strategy matrix in Figure 9.2. Here, customers' data are typically captured as part of the system running the customer service application. Initially this may continue to run as a stand-alone application. However, as the CRM strategy takes shape within an organisation and a data warehouse is put into operation, data from applications such as a call centre need to be captured and enhanced by the data warehouse.

In the early stages this may involve file transfers of information (e.g., from call centre to data warehouse), a file containing changes to customer details or products purchased (e.g. from data warehouse to call centre), lists of customers being developed for outbound telemarketing offers, or 'flags' being created for credit rating.

As the data warehouse evolves and the organisation gets better at capturing information on all interactions with the customer, so does sophistication of the CRM strategies employed. This is possible because the data warehouse can track customer interactions over the whole of the customer's lifetime.

Advantages
Using a data warehouse has several advantages. First, it stops complex data analysis from interfering with normal business activity by removing a heavy demand on the databases. Second, the data in a data warehouse change only periodically (e.g., every 24 hours), allowing meaningful comparisons to be made on stable sets of data which exist in between updates of the data warehouse. If databases were used for analysis, analyses made at different times would produce different results, making it impossible to compare, for example, the sale of different products or the volume of sales in different regions. The further advantage of the enterprise data warehouse approach is the fact that an organisation can refer to one 'single version of the truth' which can then feed numerous data marts with consistent data.

Disadvantages
Enterprise data warehouses are large and complex IT systems that require significant investment. This may result in lengthy lead times to implementation. As the business may not be able wait for the data warehouse to be implemented, it needs to make decisions today and a cheaper, less appropriate solution may be adopted.

Integrated CRM solutions

In addition to computer and database memory capabilities, Internet technology has become embedded for most organisations. The Internet can potentially connect any individual to any other individual or organisation around the globe. The attraction of using this as a customer relationship management tool is obvious. However, electronic commerce websites are at widely differing levels of sophistication – some of them are relatively simple, some of them are highly sophisticated. The most advanced use their website regularly to collect information from the customer and provide highly individualised information and service back to the customer. This technology-enabled approach to CRM has created greatly increased opportunities to interact with large numbers of customers on a one-to-one basis.

However, in order to use the Internet effectively for sophisticated CRM applications the organisation must have integrated its e-commerce systems with a customer-orientated data warehouse which is able to push and pull customer intelligence from the Internet. An organisation usually cannot conduct sophisticated electronic commerce without first installing some form of data repository.

If an organisation, because of its marketing ambitions to utilise a new channel (e.g., social media) or its desire to be first in attracting a particular customer group, redeploys the Internet as a mechanism to service its customers, a more advanced set of CRM technologies needs to be introduced. Figure 9.7 shows an outline of the final stage of CRM development – integrated CRM solutions.

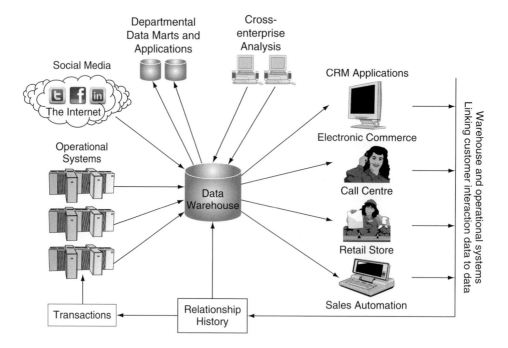

Figure 9.7 Integrated CRM solutions

Traditionally, successful marketing organisations have built their CRM systems around their transactional relationship history with customers. They run customer-facing CRM applications that provide a consistent brand and image to the marketplace. But however good these CRM systems are, they still have their limitations. First, they can only provide information on what business a customer has done with their own organisation. No insight into share of wallet is possible. Second, customer perceptions of value proposition and quality of service can only be measured when the customer is in contact with the organisation. Now organisations can add to their understanding of individual customers and the sentiment of the marketplace by analysing what is being said on consumer-oriented social media portals such as Twitter and Facebook. For business-to-business (B2B) organisations it may also be possible to understand customer sentiment by analysing postings on LinkedIn (the leading business network).

An integrated CRM solution utilising data from social media can enrich the data warehouse with 'opinion' and 'sentiment' concerning all aspects of an organisation's marketing. Everything from brand awareness and image through value propositions and pricing to competitive positioning can be analysed. Even simple analysis of what is 'hot' and what is 'trending' can provide an organisation with appropriate keywords that can be used to optimise their corporate website(s) to maximise search engine hits. This is commonly referred to as Search Engine Optimisation (SEO). This type of analysis is vital when organisations are paying for targeted advertising on search engines. As most of these paid advertising schemes are charged per click, normally referred to as pay per click (PPC), it makes sense to maximise the relevance of each click.

To implement such a solution, the organisation does not need to add further data marts or data warehousing technology. In fact, the business may have all the data and sophisticated architecture that are needed, but it has to deal with these in a more intelligent way. However, the organisation does need to add a range of integrated CRM applications to the top of the existing data marts and data warehousing architecture. This can mean using an interactive electronic commerce application, allowing the customer to interact with the company's website and make purchases in real time.

The backbone to this approach is the enterprise data warehouse, which serves both as a capture device and as the memory for the system, enabling the customer to be given a totally individualised and coordinated service across all CRM interfaces. Several components are needed. These include a specially designed Web front-end for interacting with the customer; sophisticated application software for the capture, navigation, processing and matching of customers to products and services; a link to other customer systems such as the call centre and field sales support systems and links to the main operational systems.

To achieve total integration means linking the enterprise data warehouse tightly into both the front- and back-office applications. Complete systems that provide this high level of integration are now improving in capability. They provide organisations with the potential for a quick implementation path for the adoption of CRM and significantly reduce the potential development risks.

Advantages

An integrated CRM solution will enable an organisation to move towards the top right-hand corner of the CRM strategy matrix, in other words towards 'Individualised CRM' in Figure 9.2. A range of sophisticated CRM strategies can be adopted which are appropriate for the organisation without being handicapped by existing IT. The business opportunities are significant for those who can get to this position first.

Disadvantages

Like the enterprise data warehouses, integrated CRM systems are complex and require significant investment in both the warehouse and operational systems. Organisations need to reduce the risk and cost of these systems by buying packages where available and working with established and proven technology suppliers.

There are now numerous examples of successful organisations that have adopted electronic commerce mainstream solutions including Amazon.com, lastminute.com, Expedia.com, cdUniverse.com, RS Components and all major airlines, to name but a few.

Electronic commerce websites are at widely differing levels of sophistication. The most advanced collect information from the customer and provide highly individualised service back to the customer. This advanced technology-enabled approach to CRM has created greatly increased opportunities to interact with large numbers of customers on a one-to-one basis.

The choice of technology options

In considering the choice of these technology solutions, managers who are currently using a tactical database typically ask questions such as: When do we need simple query and analysis tools and when do we need a data mart? Why do I need a data warehouse when I have a satisfactory query and reporting tool on my data base?

If all an organisation needs to do is query its existing database (and it is getting the ease of use and the answers that it wants from the query and reporting tools that it has), then it does not need a data mart or a data warehouse. It clearly has the technology solution that it currently needs. If, however, it needs to access information from more than one system, or if the end users question their capability to correct a query which goes across two different proprietary systems (e.g., data on an individual customer's name may be stored in different ways in different data sources) then a simple database may not be suitable. Also, if the organisation wants to look at additional information, such as historical data, then a data mart is needed.

A data mart may be the appropriate solution if an organisation has a requirement for only one data mart. However if the sales, finance and marketing functions in an organisation all require a data mart, then problems can develop. The data mart solution for these multiple business functions may not be easy to manage technically and nor does it scale easily (any changes on the operational or the business side need much work to be done on them in terms of transformation and extraction routines). In this situation a data warehouse will provide a more satisfactory solution.

From a practical perspective it will be appropriate, especially in large organisations, to combine the above technologies creatively. For example, a more complex CRM may include a strategic application with dependent data marts on a data warehouse, together with a tactical application which allows staff to build independent data marts for more tactical solutions. A tactical data mart may be needed quickly for a particular business activity – one that does not need integrating with the rest of the organisation.

In choosing technology solutions, 'scalability' is an important consideration. The business needs to create flexible technology architecture suitable for both present and future needs. It needs to take account of the building blocks in place at present as well as requirements which may exist in two years' time. Managers may not yet know what will be needed and perhaps the technology does not exist at present. It is also necessary to create an architecture which will be responsive to the increasingly sophisticated requirements of CRM in the future.

One key to success will be the ability to 'think big and start small'. The organisation needs to have a vision of what it wishes to achieve and what will be required in the future and then break this down into appropriate components. By undertaking a scoping study the organisation can ensure that the solutions decided on are extendable, scalable and manageable. The best approach is to plan ahead for the integration of the future business-based solutions that will be needed. This may involve evolutionary deployment of one or more dependent data marts with the type of architecture outlined above, with the aim of maximising the benefits and minimising the risks to the organisation.

The topic of data warehousing is a vast one. Author and consultant Ron Swift provides a good description of data warehousing in the context of CRM.[2] Further books by Laberge,[3] Golfarelli and Rizzi,[4] Ponniah[5] and Kimball and his colleagues[6] deal with this topic in much greater detail.

Analytical tools

The analytical tools that enable effective use of the data warehouse or other elements of the data repository can be found in both general data mining packages and in specific software application packages. Data mining is a discovery method applied to vast collections of data, which works by classifying and clustering data, often from a variety of different and even mutually incompatible databases and then searching for associations. It is primarily a form of statistical analysis but may also include artificial intelligence. Data mining can be used to reveal meaningful patterns about customer buying habits, lifestyle, demographics and so on, which would otherwise remain hidden and thus provides indications of how customer relationships can be improved. More specific software application packages include analytical tools that focus on such tasks as campaign management analysis, credit scoring and customer profiling. These task-specific software packages combine several of the general functions of data mining with support for the task that will not be found in standard data mining software.

While data mining technologies are extremely powerful and can lead to some profound insights into customer behaviour, some of them have historically been difficult to use and require considerable experience to be of real benefit. However, this drawback is beginning to disappear as analytical tools are incorporated into task-specific packages that make them easier to use.

Standard data mining packages will typically include some, or all, of the following techniques:

- visualisation: histograms, bar charts, line graphs, scatter plots, box plots and other types of visual representation;
- clustering/segmentation, prediction, deviation detection and link analysis;
- neural networks and decision trees.

Task-specific software packages combine these general types of data analysis with specific marketing support, resulting in analytical tools such as:

- market segmentation analysis,
- affinity grouping,
- churn management,
- customer profiling,
- profitability analysis,
- sentiment analysis (when analysing social media).

Real-time analytical processing tools are data reporting rather than data mining tools, but they can also be used to analyse data held in a data warehouse.

It is worth considering each of these analytical techniques briefly to gain an appreciation of the scope and scale of technology available.

Standard data mining

Visualisation tools
Visualisation tools enable complex data analyses to be represented in simple form. This not only enhances understanding by providing a manageable view of data, but also aids the accurate interpretation of various aspects of the data. For example, a column graph emphasises the values of items as they vary at precise intervals over a period of time, while a pie graph emphasises the relative contribution of each data item to the whole. Such presentation graphics make group discussion of data analyses easier by ensuring everyone is working from the same 'picture'.

Segmentation, prediction, deviation detection and other analyses
Segmentation involves dividing data on the basis that some database entries have similar characteristics (e.g., some customers buy similar items at the supermarket). Segmentation analysis using data mining can be controlled by the user to test how well defined existing clusters really are, or it can be done automatically in order to identify new clusters.

Prediction involves developing a model (e.g., of customer behaviour) and applying it to historic customer data to estimate the impact of a change, such as an advertising campaign or the introduction of a new product. A predictive model might be built using responses to a customer survey. If, for example, a survey provides data on gender, age, occupation; PC/smartphone/tablet ownership; home and work Internet usage; and newspaper and magazine subscriptions, blogs, Twitter feeds and social network membership, a model could be derived to estimate the likely uptake of an online service and to target advertising to the appropriate media channel.

Deviation detection tools extend segmentation tools by analysing data that fall outside of well-defined clusters. These tools can be used for a variety of tasks, ranging from identifying unusual questionnaire responses to spotting unusual transaction patterns for fraud prevention. Neural networks can be used for some types of deviation detection and statistical analysis can be applied to determine the significance of deviations once they have been identified.

Network analysis tools are a fairly recent development that involve identification and quantification of the influencers and the influenced. They enable marketers to listen for mentions of their brand and their competitors' brands, involving identifying such things as: who is talking about the brand; what people are saying about the brand; and where they are talking about the brand.

Sentiment analysis is a new technology that enables marketers to capture trends and opinions in social media. A number of specialist companies are now offering sentiment analysis services. This form of analysis is not restricted to customers' opinions regarding companies. For example, there has been extensive coverage of sentiment analysis relating to President Obama's performance in office. A key feature of sentiment analysis is making sense of written and spoken language and analysing attitudinal information.

Link analysis finds relationships between sets of data entries in a database. It can be used to discover relationships between the purchases that customers make over time and, in a form known as *market basket analysis*, can be used to work out which products shoppers buy in combination, so that the products can be positioned together in supermarket aisles.

Link analysis is based on the idea that events relate people, places and other things together. When you fly from London to New York, for example, the plane links the two cities together and 'being a passenger' links you to the plane. Similarly, when you make a telephone call, you are linking together two (or more) telephones. Most data analysis techniques ignore link information, focusing instead on single objects (e.g., customers), rather than the relationships between them. Understanding these links can, however, provide important insights into the nature of customer interactions, making link analysis a valuable tool.

Neural networks

Neural networks are computer models that are based on some processes in the brain. They are essentially statistical processes that have built-in feedback mechanisms so that they can 'learn'. These tools are readily available in off-the-shelf software packages and have been used for quite a wide range of business processes. Neural networks are capable of identifying different types of relationships, including the detection of clusters. As the internal mechanism of the network adapts automatically, however, neural networks do not explain relationships. This is one of their weaknesses, which can be overcome by using the neural network to identify relationships and then applying other data mining techniques to explain why they exist.

A neural network is trained by providing it with a range of different examples, all described in terms of inputs and outputs. We could, for example, describe customers in terms of their age, gender, income and other factors and describe their outputs in terms of the banking services they use. We then provide the neural network with 'inputs' from existing customer data. The neural network predicts the banking services for each customer. If it predicts wrongly, the neural network adjusts itself. Over time, it becomes more accurate at making predictions. When a neural network has been trained, it can be used on new customer information to make predictions that marketers and other decision makers can act upon.

Neural networks are very powerful tools for making predictions about customer behaviour. They must be used with some caution, however, as they only predict based on the data inputs that are provided. If, for example, 'number of children' were an important variable in the use of financial services, the neural network would only be effective if it was programmed to include number of children as an input. Another limitation is that neural networks work best when the relationships between the inputs and outputs are stable. On occasion, customer behaviour can change quite significantly. Neural networks will adapt to a limited degree but do not change radically once programmed. If business conditions change dramatically, neural networks will be less effective and should be replaced by other more appropriate analytical tools.

Decision trees

Decision trees structure data according to well-defined rules. They are popular because, unlike neural networks, they explain why a particular outcome is recommended. Decision analysis tools classify existing data in order to identify rules that lead to valid recommendations. These rules can then be used to support business decision making.

Automated tools for constructing decision trees work by splitting data in a way that spreads all items (products, customers, transactions, etc.) most evenly. If, for example, a group of customers is 90 per cent male and 50 per cent single, then marital status would be used first to classify the data. The aim of forming the tree is to split the items into groups with similar characteristics. When an effective decision tree structure has been formed which classifies individual cases accurately, the tree can be converted into decision rules and used to support decision making. For a more detailed discussion of data mining see the books by experts such as Han, Kamber and Pei[7] and Tsiptsis and Chorianopoulos.[8]

Task-specific analysis tools

Market segmentation analysis

Market segmentation was discussed in some detail in Chapter 6.[9] Customers can be segmented according to their basic characteristics, such as geography and job title, without using any special analysis. We simply specify the postcodes or job titles of interest and extract the relevant customers from the database. This kind of segmentation is very limited and does not help us gain insights into the preferences and buying habits of customers. To do this we must analyse detailed historical information about sales. If we succeed in identifying a meaningful cluster of customers, we can target this cluster with a particular offer that is likely to attract their attention. This can help stimulate extra sales and gain customer loyalty by developing products and services that better suit their requirements. Two types of analysis tool can help in identifying new segments using customer data in the data repository.

The first option is visual analysis, as described above. By plotting graphs using different dimensions, we can sometimes see groupings of customers with similar characteristics. If we plotted customer age against purchases of coffee, for example, we might find that certain age groups consume more filter coffee, while another age group consumes most decaffeinated coffee. Unfortunately, visualisation is only useful for analysing two or three dimensions. On many occasions, we will need to identify clusters using many different pieces of customer data. In these cases, the second approach of using automatic cluster detection is the preferred option.

There are several different types of automatic cluster detection. One of the most common forms splits the database into a number of segments specified by the user. This method is best suited to working with numerical data, although it can be used with other data in a limited way. An alternative approach, known as agglomeration, begins by treating each entry in a database as a cluster (of one record) and combines similar clusters until only a small number of clusters remain. Alternative techniques can be used for dealing with non-numerical data, such as counting the number of data fields that match in a set of customer records. Clusters can also be identified using some kinds of decision tree and neural network methods.

Affinity grouping

Affinity grouping is used to identify individual data items that tend to be associated with one another. A typical application is analysing supermarket purchases to discover items that are bought together so that store layouts can be improved (it is for this reason that affinity grouping is sometimes called *market basket analysis*). The data mining technique underlying affinity grouping is the generation of *association rules* using link analysis procedures (described above). An association rule takes a form such as, 'People who buy nappies on Friday also tend to buy beer or wine'. This suggests two possible courses of action: displaying nappies near the alcohol section (on Fridays) and putting snacks, such as crisps and nuts, near to the nappies to 'remind' customers to buy their wine or beer. These techniques can be used on entire data sets to find general relationships or on small data sets to find more localised rules (e.g., to identify sales trends specific to stores in urban and suburban areas).

Churn management

In highly competitive industries where customers are able to change suppliers at little cost, companies will be continually losing some customers to competitors and gaining others. This is known as churn in industries such as telecommunications, or attrition in industries such as banking. In some industries, churn is a serious problem. Some estimate that in the mobile telephone market in Europe, churn rates are over 25 per cent, while attracting a new customer costs an average of $400. Improving customer retention (or reducing churn) by even a small amount can clearly lead to substantial cost savings. Customer retention is examined in some detail in Chapter 7.

The first stage in churn management is to measure existing churn and to understand churn in the context of the entire distribution network, which may include a number of channels. The aim should be to identify particular trouble spots that can be targeted for direct action. The use of powerful analytical tools to create performance indicators is usually sufficient and is supported by many dedicated churn management packages. These tools enable churn rates to be correlated with geographic areas, dealers, service plans and so on. High correlations will indicate, for example, that some dealers have much higher churn rates than others. These tools also support the identification of customer segments that have both high churn rates and high potential value. These segments can then be targeted with customer retention campaigns. Some tools use neural networks and decision trees to identify customers likely to churn and to explain why.

With churn analysis data, two approaches to churn management can be used: reactive and proactive. The reactive approach involves providing churn analysis data to customer service representatives so that they can offer appropriate incentives to customers who are threatening to switch to a competitor. The proactive approach involves identifying problem customer segments and targeting them with appropriate services, direct mail, e-mail, text messaging or telephone calls.

Customer profiling

Customer profiling uses predictive analysis tools to model customer activity so that in future, value propositions can be tailored more closely to customers. Rather than using internal databases, a more complete profile can be obtained by also analysing social media. Models can be created that are based on customer needs, behaviours and profitability; by drawing upon a large volume of data about customer segments, such models can be used to predict how customers will react to new situations. Marketing campaigns, for example, can be enhanced by using predictive customer profiles to estimate the likely responses of different customer segments.

Profitability analysis

Traditionally, companies have focused on the profitability of their products and services. Recently, improved understanding of the costs of customer acquisition versus customer retention have suggested that measuring and managing the profitability of individual customers can be a more effective strategy. Hence, organisations are now increasingly estimating customer segment lifetime value (discussed in Chapter 7).

Effective customer management is now expressed in terms of satisfying profitable customers so that they will not switch suppliers and migrating unprofitable customers to a profitable position.

Profitability analysis involves improving data integration and data capture at a number of points. First, integrating customer databases is essential for determining the total number of products and services that a customer has bought. This requires integration of departmental databases, usually by data warehousing. Second, data must be captured on the cost of servicing each customer. This may involve using CRM tools that capture the amount of time spent by operators who answer the customer's calls and reply to letters and e-mails.

Without such specific data, the costs of providing customer service are simply averaged over all customers, disguising the fact that some, seemingly valuable, customers are actually unprofitable because they use up disproportionate amounts of customer service time. Once such data are collected, profitability of individual customers can be determined and customers segmented according to a combination of their profitability and other characteristics. These segments can be used as the basis for developing customer migration strategies, as well as for identifying valuable customer segments that need to be protected from competition.

In some industries, online marketplaces (or 'market spaces') have greatly reduced profit margins. Adapting profitability analysis tools to this problem has made it possible for suppliers to determine which requests for quotes (RFQs) are likely to be profitable and at what level bids in online auctions no longer promise a profit.

Analytical processing

Analytical processing is a data reporting tool, which provides more sophisticated facilities than the query tools described earlier. It is not a data mining tool because it provides summary data rather than identifying patterns in data. Analytical processing tools are powerful and quite easy to use. They can make a significant contribution to extracting value from customer databases, adding to the value of data mining applications rather than replacing them.

Analytical processing tools have advanced graphical interfaces that make it possible for users with little statistical knowledge to explore large volumes of data. Underlying this interface is a multi-dimensional database structure (sometimes called a 'cube'). This makes 'slicing and dicing' of data quicker and easier. Whereas conventional reporting tools can take hours to gather data, analytical processing tools can provide reports in only a few seconds. It should be noted, however, that achieving this fast response comes at the expense of losing some precision in the storage of certain types of data. This is because to maximise speed, data is pre-aggregated into the 'cube'. In conventional query tools, data are aggregated in real time while processing a query, which takes more time to execute.

The key differences between data mining and analytical processing tools are best summarised by considering the kinds of management issues they each address. Data mining is more forward looking, providing insights into the best ways to manage different groups of customers. It is intended to support decision making. Reports from analytical processing tools have a more historical focus, summarising the data on, for example, recent sales performance and highlighting trends. Analysis of past sales, for instance, may show that some products sell best on a particular day. It does not, however, tell us why this is the case. A data mining technique, such as affinity grouping, may provide some insights to explain this trend. Another use of analytical processing is for visualising the results of data mining analysis. Perhaps one of the more important contributions of analytical processing, however, is that its ease of use makes data analysis accessible to a much wider range of people within the organisation.

Analytical tools are instrumental in sorting data and extracting meaning to guide the development of management strategies. In identifying customer and market trends, techniques such as data mining can help clarify budget inefficiencies and the most useful allocation of resources. Segmentation and predictive modelling can be used to identify new customer groups to enhance propositions, or to provide an early warning system. Importantly, the ongoing development and utilisation of the data warehouse also facilitates the exchange of information and knowledge between the enterprise and customers.

IT systems

IT systems refer to the computer hardware and the related software used within the organisation. Hardware consists of the pieces of physical equipment (desktop PCs, laptops, database servers, Web servers, mainframe computers and major peripherals) on which software, or computer programs, is run. However, the traditional idea of owning and managing your own hardware and software has changed. After evolving through all forms of 'sourcing' (insourcing, outsourcing, near-shoring, etc.) and 'hosting', we now also have the 'Cloud' and Cloud computing, which we discuss later in this chapter.

For CRM to be effective, IT systems must be able to deliver the information needed on customers both now and in the future and to accomplish an array of other administrative duties such as billing, processing, distribution, stock ordering etc. These tasks represent an enormous dependency and demand on technology. As the number of customers and customer transactions escalate, the organisation's capacity to scale existing systems or plan for the migration to larger systems without disrupting business operations becomes critical. So too is the integration of data from highly contrasting systems, such as structured databases and rich multi-media networks.

Normally, an organisation's IT systems are developed over a period of time and in response to particular departmental needs. Thus, different, and often incompatible, computing systems – both hardware and software – are utilised in different parts of the business. While new IT systems tend to be based around open technical standards, reducing compatibility problems, old legacy systems can be very difficult to integrate. In some cases, replacing the legacy hardware and applications may be a more attractive option. In response to this issue, a large number of CRM vendors are now offering Cloud versions of their products.

Where separate CRM systems are implemented, hardware and systems software integration must take place before databases can be connected to the data warehouse and user access can be provided across the company. The integration of disparate IT systems into a holistic architecture represents a major undertaking, requiring substantial investment. It is therefore crucial that proposals for systems integration be firmly based on a robust CRM strategy (which has taken account of IT infrastructure) and a thorough strategic review of IT systems. The agreed IT architecture should be designed to integrate or replace existing IT systems and to provide flexibility for future changes and expansion.

A constant challenge when planning IT architecture is matching solutions with the demands of users. There are various options available, including internal/external hosting or Cloud-based computing. These options can be 'mixed and matched' to form IT networks that satisfy a range of different needs.

Selecting a hardware platform

When introducing CRM into the organisation, it is likely that at least some users will require new computer hardware. For some users, this will be a desktop PC. For those working in the field, a laptop or other mobile data solution will be required. For call centre workers, some form of computer-telephony integration (CTI) will be used to improve worker productivity. The range of technical options is enormous and continues to increase.

Choosing a hardware platform requires a focus on user needs and consideration of how users work and under what conditions. The appropriate solution for a user or analyst could be physical hardware, such as a PC, or could be 'virtual' hardware, such as a remote desktop running on local host hardware that may include a PC or a 'thin client' Net PC (a standard for diskless PCs).

For business analysts and users performing complex data mining, more powerful machines are likely to be needed. The specification depends upon the volume of statistical analysis and the use of visualisation tools. These machines will have larger high resolution displays than normal. The choice of hardware platform will depend upon the infrastructure and technical support available in the organisation.

The choice of mobile equipment for users in the field is important as both the interaction with the customer and the security of the remote connection must be taken into account. Considering interaction between, for example, the salesperson and customer is particularly important when selecting hardware. Smaller 'smart' devices such as smartphones and tablets are much lighter and less obtrusive but use different versions of software from a laptop computer. With continuing advances in high-speed mobile access to the Internet, workers in the field can more easily and cheaply connect directly to the company's data repository. This makes it possible to change customer details, place orders, check stock availability and so on.

For call centres and help desks, CRM solutions are now using advanced CTI. CTI solutions permit the caller's number to be used to help identify the caller. This makes it possible to retrieve the customer's details automatically from a customer database ready for the operator to answer the call. Similar technologies can also be used for providing interactive voice response services, where customers press numbers on their keypad or use voice response systems to select options offered to them by a computerised voice. In addition to telephony, many companies are now using online interactive tools such as e-mail, 'chat' and 'call me back' as further channels.

Front-office and back-office applications

Front-office applications are the technologies used to support all those activities that involve direct interface with customers, including the website, call centre and sales force automation (SFA). These applications can be used to make sales and improve customer retention. *Back-office applications* support internal administration activities and supplier relationships, involving human resources, procurement, warehouse management, logistics software and some financial processes.

The growth of enterprise-wide systems and e-business is blurring the distinction between front office and back office and challenging the structure and operation of existing information management processes. Goods tracking, for example, has traditionally been a back-office system used by employees who do not have any interaction with the customers. However, corporate requirements for transparency through 'end-to-end processing' and 'straight-through-processing' is causing a more holistic view to be taken. In response to this, many companies are now providing customers with direct access to goods tracking software via the Internet so that they can track their own orders. In this case, goods tracking must be regarded as a front-office system because its performance affects the customer's perceptions of the organisation.

The overriding concern in CRM about front- and back-office systems is that they are sufficiently connected and coordinated to optimise customer relations and workflow. It is essential that they combine to support all stages of interaction between the customer and the organisation. This can be difficult to ensure because there can be dozens of applications spread throughout the organisation which have evolved over time to meet departmental needs. Often departments have been organised around products/services or business functions, rather than being designed to support the customer relationship. For this reason, it is useful to review existing applications from the perspective of customer interaction so that the adequacy of applications can be assessed. By identifying the organisation's key activities and mapping IT to support them, it is possible to identify areas where new applications are required or where existing applications need to be connected together or integrated to provide seamless customer service. Performing such an analysis ensures that customer needs drive technology solutions, rather than the other way around.

Attention is increasingly being focused on the implications of e-business self-service strategies that put customers and business partners into direct contact with corporate systems. This increased access to operational data creates new challenges for CRM, which may demand changes in the approach to data warehousing and the organisation of front-office and back-office applications. One such challenge is the pressure e-business creates for a 'real-time' marketing response, which requires all customer interactions to be conducted with an enterprise-wide view, rather than just the marketing planning activities.

In some cases, this change may lead to pressure for data analysis to use real-time data, rather than a data warehouse that is only updated periodically.

The two case studies at the end of this chapter address these issues. The first case study, Royal Bank of Canada focuses on building client service commitment by increasing the productivity and improving the efficiency of the bank's enquiry management processes. The second case study is on the UK's DVLA – the Driver and Vehicle Licensing Agency. This provides an example of an innovative CRM initiative in the public sector where the agency developed business self-service strategies.

Front-office applications

Front-office applications can be used to improve the value created for customers and the value delivered by customers. They provide a means for increasing sales closure rates, improving customer service and enhancing cross- and up-selling. Thus they are key to raising levels of customer retention and customer profitability. The most common front-office applications are:

- sales force automation (SFA),
- call centre and help desk management,
- campaign management.

Sales force automation

SFA refers to sales and marketing applications which can be accessed from the field. SFA enables rapid order processing and order status reporting. The incorporation of forecasting and reporting tools ensures that customer information is accurate and up-to-date, which enhances sales forecasting. Most of the leading CRM vendors offer products in this area, often as part of their CRM packages. These vendors typically often also offer a Cloud-based version of their SFA solution. This has a key advantage in that sales force, customer service and marketing activities are viewed and updated with the same set of integrated customer information.

SFA tools offer most benefit when they are applied to inefficient sales processes, particularly administrative tasks, where time and resources are consumed consolidating sales information which has been stored and reported in different ways. Many organisations have now embraced SFA as an opportunity to change their sales approach altogether.

When introducing SFA software, it is important to focus on the management of customer information flows. Primary consideration should be given to deciding what information needs to be captured and where, and who is responsible for examining, processing and updating the data. Particular attention should be paid to locating and resolving any duplicated activities or areas where information falls down a 'black hole'.

Call centre and help desk management

Call centres have become increasingly important as many companies have reduced their physical presence on the high street. Although communication and transactions can be conducted via electronic channels, customers still often prefer to speak with a human representative for assistance. The telephone is both a channel in its own right and an important form of support for other channels. As telephone and data technologies converge, the role of the call centre will continue to expand, both as a customer interface and as an internal information resource.

Call centres (or contact centres) may be 'inbound' (mainly concerned with customer support), 'outbound' (mainly concerned with sales) or 'blended' a combination of both outbound and inbound. The ability to deliver effective customer service from a call centre depends on the availability of full and accurate customer information, as well as product and service information. This requires the integration of customer data across the organisation, so that call centre workers are able to deal with inbound enquiries or outbound calls by themselves, only redirecting the customer to another employee when particular expertise is required. The integration of customer data is also required to support multi-channel integration, which focuses on the call centre.

Increasingly, call centre operatives are interacting with customers via shared Web pages and Internet telephony. To maintain the quality of service provided, the organisation will need to retain a single view of the customer regardless of what channels the customer uses. Integrated IT systems will also need to ensure that customer communications are prioritised according to need, rather than according to the channel used. Software to support call centres is continually improving in quality and functionality. Multi-channel and multi-media features (e.g., video conferencing with VOIP and 'whiteboarding' (where computer screens are shared between customer and call centre operatives, etc.) are increasingly being used.

Incident management software is used by IT departments for tracking problems within the organisation. For call centres, this software has been extended to help customer service representatives handle problems raised by customers. These packages also typically support the tracking of orders, accounting and billing and the calculation of the customer's cost of ownership. Some of them also support the identification and sharing of best practice in dealing with customer problems. For those organisations that provide on-site customer support, specialised field service software is available. These systems manage the dispatch of field service personnel, spare parts inventory and repair depots. Perhaps the most important feature of these systems, however, is that they help bring together customer data from multiple legacy systems so that customer service and sales staff have access to a complete customer history.

By extensively analysing social media, organisations can now get early warning regarding issues or problems with their products or service. This information can be proactively used by the call centre to contact customers and minimise both negative word-of-mouth and potential damage to the brand of the enterprise.

Campaign management

Growing profitable customer relationships involves developing customised value propositions and delivering them to the customer. (We discuss value proposition development in Chapter 7.) Marketers must have ready access to up-to-date information in greater volumes and in more diverse formats than ever before. Campaign management involves, wherever possible, taking manual marketing processes and automating them through the use of defined business rules and executing them electronically. For example, many aspects of the following marketing processes can be automated: lead generation, prospect qualification, customer segmentation, contact management, customer value measurement and the development of behavioural models for testing planned marketing campaigns.

Most campaign management tools enable the marketer to specify the steps involved in the marketing campaign and to calculate costs and commercial returns. They also support 'what-if' analyses on customer segments. These tools help the organisation to target its marketing at customers who are valuable to the company and likely to respond to campaign offers. By automating some tasks, they can also make communications with the customer more effective.

Campaign management typically begins with market segmentation analysis and extends this by using the segmentation information to help develop personalised marketing messages. Customer profiles/models are created and used to feed information into campaign management software. This software is then used to design a campaign designed to gain responses from each of the target segments and to communicate details of the campaign to all employees (and business partners) who will come into contact with the targeted customers. This ensures that interaction with the customers is consistent across channels during the campaign. The campaign management software is then used to direct the marketing campaign and to assess its impact. Where campaigns use social media and the Internet as a communications channel, e-mail messages and websites can be personalised for customers in the target segments. Some of the tools for developing personalised websites learn customer preferences by analysing the customer's use of the website. As more preference data are collected from the website, the personalised pages are improved in real time.

A key part of campaign management is assessing the response to the campaign. Support for response assessment is typically offered in the form of tools for monitoring customer engagement. Some tools monitor customer responses through all channels, making it possible to identify changes in customer behaviour with particular marketing efforts on specific channels. This is an increasingly important facility as companies adopt a multi-channel approach to CRM (see Chapter 8). Taking response assessment further, some campaign management packages use neural networks or other forms of analysis to build models of customer behaviour using the new response data and other data sources. Further, sentiment analysis and network analysis of affinity groups and customer brand communities can be used to analyse campaigns utilising social media.

Back-office applications

Back-office applications streamline internal business processes and include general accounting and financial systems, inventory management and human resources. In many cases, they are legacy systems or software packages using specific databases. Some companies are using enterprise resource planning (ERP) systems to provide integrated back-office systems, also adding the benefits of data warehousing and providing additional management and control tools. Difficulties in implementing e-business strategies have shown that there is also a strong need for integration between back-office and front-office systems. For this reason, many ERP vendors have extended their systems to include front-office CRM applications.

Another area of back-office technology is the use of mass customisation technologies. These are increasingly seen as the key to competitiveness in manufacturing and service industries. These technologies give the customer direct input into the value creation process. All motor car manufacturers offer mass customisation that enables customers to choose which accessories they want to be fitted to their new car.

For mass customisation technologies to operate efficiently, it is essential to achieve a high level of integration between back-end systems (such as production scheduling) and front-end systems (such as an order information system). In manufacturing, integration may also be required with suppliers to ensure that stocks of components are replenished in line with fluctuations in demand. By connecting production scheduling to customer service systems via the Internet, it is also possible to provide the customer with delivery dates and order-tracking facilities. For example, for many years Apple and Dell Computers have expanded their mass customisation activities by permitting customers to configure their PCs online.

Integrating analytical and operational CRM

Developing a customer-focused information management process requires both an enterprise-wide data warehouse and the integration of the software applications supporting all channels including social media. The combination of these involves integrating analytical CRM and operational CRM as shown in Figure 9.8.

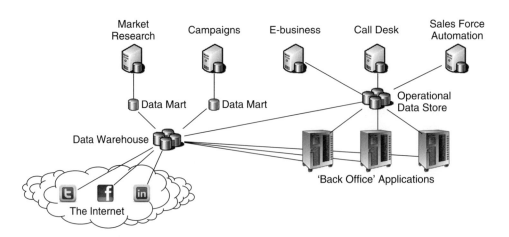

Figure 9.8 Integrating analytical and operational CRM

Market research and campaign management, on the top left of Figure 9.8 are examples of analytical CRM. The data warehouse, used as the data source for analytical CRM, can be enriched by the addition of data from social media. This use of data from social media can create a 'community sales funnel'. This involves exploiting word-of-mouth and more clearly identifying the percentage of customers: that are interested in buying, that might be interested in buying and those that are definitely not interested in buying. This aims at obtaining better brand awareness, higher conversion rates, higher cross-sell/up-sell ratios, 'outside looking in' customer-driven product improvement, higher quality leads, shorter sales cycles, lower acquisition costs and lower churn rates.

E-business, call centres, sales force automation applications and the operational data store on the top right of Figure 9.8 form part of operational CRM. We have already discussed the role of these earlier in this chapter. The back-office applications for an organisation such as a bank might include applications for credit cards, cheque accounts and mortgages. The operational data store is used to provide each operational CRM application with a single view of the customer across these back-office applications. In order to provide this single view of the customer, the operational data store needs to be able to resolve any discrepancies in data held on each and every customer within each of the back-office applications. Any changes to data in the back-office applications that is already held in the analytical CRM data warehouse needs to be refreshed in the data warehouse. Likewise, any changes to data in one of the operational CRM applications needs to be refreshed in other operational CRM applications, back-office applications and the analytical CRM data warehouse. This is all managed by the operational data store.

All the elements in Figure 9.8 may be run internally by the organisation, hosted externally, outsourced or moved to the Cloud. The choice of these options is determined by the specific corporate requirements of a given organisation. The requirements of confidentiality, integrity and availability for analytical and operational CRM are vastly different. Operational CRM is mission critical requiring 100 per cent availability during business hours. Operational CRM also has significant high requirements for confidentiality and the integrity of information. Conversely, analytical CRM is not so mission critical and does not have such stringent requirements for confidentiality and the integrity of information. The specific circumstances for a given company regarding confidentiality, integrity and availability issues will dictate what possibilities there are for alternative hosting, outsourcing or moving to the Cloud. In the next section, the nature of Cloud computing services is reviewed.

Cloud computing services

Cloud computing refers to technologies that provide hardware, software, data access, and storage services that involve remote location and configuration of the system that delivers the services. Many 'analytical' CRM applications and data can easily be pushed to a Cloud environment (e.g., all lead generation and campaign management activities).

However, the case for utilising Cloud services for 'operational' CRM applications is not so clear cut. While in theory the concept of the Cloud is highly attractive, for reasons of privacy and certain legislative aspects the physical location of the data may need to be known or specified. Many European companies are subject to overwhelming legislation controlling the possible location of corporate data. Marketers need to be aware of the relevant requirements in the jurisdictions in which their enterprise operates and tailor the Cloud environment (public, private, internal and external) to comply with corporate and legislative requirements.

Cloud computing providers deliver Internet-based applications which are accessed from Web browsers and desktop or mobile applications with data and software being stored on remotely located servers. Cloud computing offers new ways of obtaining computational resources. Instead of having to buy and maintain your own computers and purchase, install and maintain software, it is now possible to utilise hardware and software paying only for its usage. This 'pay for what you use' model is very attractive to many enterprises. Generally Cloud computing services are categorised into three levels:

1. *Cloud application services*, referred to as 'Software-as-a-Service' (SaaS). These provide software as a service over the Internet. This eliminates the need for enterprises to install, run and maintain the application.
2. *Cloud platform services*, referred to as 'Platform-as-a-Service' (PaaS). These provide a computing platform as a service, delivering a complete environment of everything required to run a specific application (such as campaign management or sales force automation).
3. *Cloud infrastructure services*, referred to as 'Infrastructure-as-a-Service' (IaaS). These provide a virtual infrastructure to enable multiple PaaS platforms to run. The functionality provided includes storage, networking, Internet access, printing, etc. These are typically billed on a utility computing basis, i.e., based on the amount of resources consumed.

Organisations require some way of measuring the 'fitness-for-purpose' of these three levels of Cloud computing services. As already discussed, some CRM applications are easy to move to a Cloud environment. However, CRM applications that store and/or access personal customer information are not so easy to move to 'the Cloud'.

Nevertheless, if 'fitness-for-purpose' is used to differentiate requirements for Cloud computing services then it should be much easier for most CRM applications to be deployed in the Cloud. The Open Group Jericho Forum has identified four criteria to differentiate Cloud formations. These are shown in Figure 9.9 and discussed below.[10]

The four criteria defined by the Jericho Forum are:

Internal/External
This is the dimension that defines the physical location of the data.

- If the physical location of the data is within your own physical boundary then it is classed as 'Internal'.
- If the data are not within your own physical boundary then it is classed as 'External'.

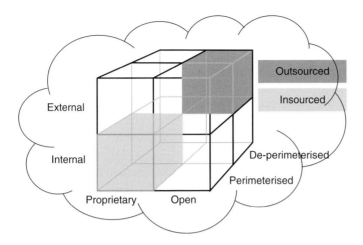

Figure 9.9 The Cloud cube model.
Source: Based on The Open Group's Jericho Forum

Most organisations only think of the Cloud as 'public' and therefore only 'External'. By exploiting the possibility of deploying data internally, most of the issues concerning 'privacy' are minimised.

Propriety/Open

This is the dimension that defines the state of ownership of the Cloud computing services interface.

- If the organisation providing the Cloud computing services is keeping the means of provision under their ownership then these are classed as 'Propriety'.
- If the organisation providing the Cloud computing services is offering services that are not Propriety then these are classed as 'Open' (for example e-mail services using standard SMTP servers for sending mail).

As with any form of computing there are standard advantages and disadvantages for choosing either option. The choice effectively comes down to exploiting leading edge technology innovation for business advantage against lower costs by utilising commodity services.

Perimeterised/De-perimeterised

This third dimension represents a virtual IT view of the first physical dimension of 'Internal' and 'External'.

- 'Perimeterised' implies continuing to operate within the traditional IT perimeter (often taken as being 'inside' the corporate firewalls). It is similar to 'Internal' in the first dimension.
- 'De-perimeterised' implies operating outside the traditional IT perimeter. It is similar to 'External' in the first dimension.

Choosing 'External' but 'Perimeterised' Cloud computing services offers a wide scope for deployment of most CRM applications to the Cloud.

Choosing 'De-perimeterised' Cloud computing services will require a paradigm shift in rethinking CRM applications that require access to privacy or company sensitive information.

Insourced/Outsourced

This fourth dimension defines who actually provides the Cloud computing services.

- 'Insourced' implies Cloud computing services are provided by your own staff, totally under your own control.
- 'Outsourced' implies Cloud computing services are provided by an external third-party.

Companies need to take a view as to what benefit Cloud computing services could offer to some or all of their CRM activities. In practice, most organisations are finding that some analytical CRM activities need to be deployed using Cloud computing services, for example, campaign management contact management and lead generation. As operational CRM has stringent requirements regarding confidentiality, integrity and availability it may be necessary to consider the use of 'private' Cloud computing services rather than 'public' Cloud computing services. Some CRM vendor companies such as salesforce.com have been very successful offering Cloud-based CRM services.[11] For a detailed discussion of Cloud architectures see books by Reese[12] and Rhoton.[13]

Selecting a CRM solution

As the previous discussion demonstrates, the technology aspects of CRM are complex. CRM solutions can be costly and are continually evolving. An enterprise needs to consider carefully all the stages of development in creating an integrated CRM solution. These include the early stages of identifying the key CRM needs of the enterprise, through vendor selection to training users to get the most out of the new systems. In general, selection of a CRM solution should be based on purely meeting the business requirements and independent of the IT deployment (i.e., hosting, outsourcing and competing services). However, some product choices automatically imply a Cloud computing service solution as they are only offered as Software-as-a-Service.

In terms of selecting CRM software, there are integration and best practice issues which emphasise the importance of careful selection. Regarding the choice of CRM software, it is important to note that most CRM products initially focused on specific tasks, such as sales force automation or mass e-mail promotions. Consequently, they have some core strengths but they may have weaknesses in other areas. For this reason, it is important when selecting a CRM vendor to have a clear understanding of CRM needs and where a company requires particularly strong CRM support. If no single vendor has key strengths in all the company's key areas, it may need to select more than one vendor and integrate components of the CRM products.

As the range of available CRM software applications illustrates, many organisations now have a multitude of complex databases and software applications. These applications provide valuable support for a range of business activities. They can make life difficult, however, by creating islands of information that cannot be readily accessed by other CRM solutions. Certain CRM tools use proprietary data formats, within a database, which make it difficult for this data source to be accessed by other vendors' CRM tools. The ideal situation, if using different CRM tools, is for the CRM solutions to use the same data source.

In order to make informed decisions about hosting, sourcing or Cloud computing services for CRM solutions, the company should evaluate potential vendors and implementation partners against specific criteria.[14]

Some fundamental questions relating to *vendor selection* include:

- Does the firm possess the requisite core technology competence and have a successful track record to prove it?
- Does the firm have experience of working similarly in partnership with other organisations and have those relationships been trouble-free/extended/deepened?
- Does the firm offer compatibility in terms of technology, philosophy, practice (i.e., can it demonstrate the ability to fully support the planned CRM activities and processes)?
- Does the firm demonstrate assurance and necessary maturity in terms of quality, reliability, integrity (i.e., does it have the internal control and capacity to deliver)?
- Does the firm compete in a populated market or does it represent a niche market (i.e., is the choice of vendor limited by number of vendors operating in the problem areas)?
- If the firm is to be one of several vendors engaged, is it willing and able to work collaboratively in the best interests of the employing organisation?
- Does the firm represent a justifiably cost-effective option (i.e., does it have and will it provide the scalability and flexibility to accommodate change)?
- Does the firm have proof of delivery on time, to specification, and within budget for similar projects?

Some fundamental questions relating to *implementation partner selection* are very similar to those for vendor selection. We return to vendor and partner selection again in Chapter 11.

Timing of technology introduction

One of the key aspects of managing information effectively using integrated technologies is adopting the right technology at the right time. Clearly, software technologies provide a tremendous aid in automating common processes and in identifying, prioritising and managing customer relationships.

All IT projects, including the introduction of CRM solutions, need to consider the business window of opportunity that defines the delivery requirements for the project. Figure 9.10 illustrates how a substantial amount of time, people and money may be required before any business benefit can be realised from the implementation of a CRM solution. It is only after this effort is expended that a tipping point is reached where a small increment achieves a significant increase in business benefit. It is important for the marketing team to specify when the project needs to be delivered. If a CRM solution is delivered late a substantial amount of business may be forgone.

Decisions relating to technology upgrades or installations should take account of what degree of technological intervention is required to create and deliver customer value. Is

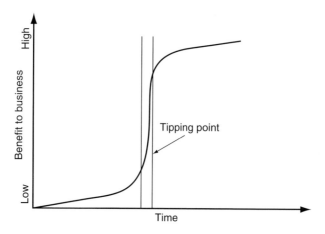

Figure 9.10 Timing of technology delivery

the technology appropriate to the customers and the requirements of the business? Additionally, is the technology capable of delivering what its vendors promise and when? Technology is continually advancing. At present, the self-service tools offered by CRM vendors make it possible to provide customers with access to their personal information and to view order status information and service requests. However, relatively few companies have so far succeeded in using this functionality fully to support online customer self-service.

Data protection, privacy and codes of practice

The final topic we consider in this chapter is that of data protection. Issues of data protection, privacy and security should be a major item on the corporate agenda. As the technological interface between customer and company grows, the issues of privacy and security become increasingly important. Marketers need to achieve the appropriate balance between privacy legislation, the company's ethical requirements of doing business and the moral requirements of customers.

As greater amounts of intimate business or personal details are collected, this information is potentially more widely accessible internally (within the company) and externally (within partners and agents in the supply chain). Each company needs to ensure that the levels of confidentiality, integrity and availability are aligned with the organisation's code of conduct regarding privacy.

For example, posting company information on the Web or buying a product electronically over the Internet runs the risk of personal information ending up in inappropriate hands. Controlling access to information such as names, addresses and credit card details forms a major part of the information management process. There is increasing focus on data protection of personal information throughout the world. Different countries have taken different approaches, so there is no uniform standard procedure. However, there is growing pressure to work together to protect the rights of consumers as personal information crosses international borders.

Drawing on CMAT data (see Chapter 11), Findlay and her colleagues compiled an overview of trends in data protection at the start of the 2000s. They concluded that only:

- 15 per cent of companies have clear and published data standards for imported data;
- 26 per cent comply fully with the terms of list rental agreements;
- 30 per cent consistently store the source of their customer data on the custom database, for each new record added;
- 17 per cent could demonstrate complete understanding of data protection legislation;
- 7 per cent have comprehensive and clear customer information quality standards;
- 7 per cent give proper incentives to relevant staff concerning customer information quality;
- 10 per cent document core customer information in such a way that relevant non-systems people can understand it;
- 7 per cent formally validate customer records once a year or more often;
- 20 per cent have a clear policy for archiving customer information.[15]

This represented an extremely poor picture of data use and archiving at this time. These researchers concluded that most companies' problems with compliance with data protection laws arise from not paying close enough attention to their data infrastructure, including the processes by which customer data are gathered, maintained and supplemented and the systems on which data are held.[16]

Since then, data protection has increasingly hit the headlines and public awareness of the importance of protecting personal information has escalated to a high level.[17] Data protection is no longer viewed as a bureaucratic inconvenience but rather an important protection of individuals' rights. However, as Edwards points out, in a review of data protection in the UK, the European Union (EU), the Asia-Pacific Economic Cooperation Countries (APEC) and the US, there remain many infringements and breaches of data protection. Some of these involve a substantial number of individuals. For example, in 2008 the UK Ministry of Defence lost a disk containing the personal details of some 1.7 million people. This included information such as passport and National Insurance numbers, driving licences and bank details. A year before this, a UK Government department lost personal details relating to 25 million people on their child benefit database.[18]

Edwards notes a number of problems, issues and inconsistencies across different jurisdictions with respect to data protection:

- Local regulators throughout the EU member states take different approaches to enforcement of data protection legislation.
- There are differences in local regulators' attitudes to transferring personal data and records outside the EU.

- The US data protection law has developed in a piecemeal manner mainly through industry-specific or data-specific laws at state level. The US does not have a comprehensive national or federal law covering the processing of personal information.
- There are extreme difficulties for US headquartered multinationals in simultaneously complying with applicable EU data protection legislation and the requirements of the Sarbanes-Oxley Act in the US.
- There is no harmonised data protection approach amongst APEC countries.
- In Japan, despite the existence of the Personal Information Protection Act, the Japanese Cabinet office does not have power to implement the Act.
- There is no comprehensive data protection law in many countries, including India and China.[19]

Edwards's review of data protection makes it clear that multinational organisations have an exceptionally difficult task in achieving global compliance with data protection regimes in different countries.

The rise of social networking sites such as Facebook and LinkedIn raises further issues for data protection and the need for codes of practice. While social networking sites have privacy settings that permit users to protect their privacy, a substantial number of users do not alter the default privacy settings. This means that the privacy of users is to a large extent in the hands of the providers of these social networking services.[20]

Kosta and her colleagues have pointed out the dangers of social networking in the context of data protection. They described an experiment conducted by the information security company Sophos, which wished to increase user awareness on the dangers of social networking:

Sophos created a Facebook account for 'Freddi Staur' (an anagram of 'ID Fraudster'). The account was represented by a small green plastic frog who divulged minimal personal information about himself. A total of 200 friend requests were sent out in order to collect information regarding the response of the users and the degree of personal information they were willing to divulge. A total of 87 of the 200 Facebook users contacted responded to Freddi, with 82 leaking personal information (41 per cent of those approached), while 72 per cent of respondents divulged one or more e-mail address and 78 per cent of respondents listed their current address or location.[21]

Kosta and her colleagues conclude that the ease with which users reveal personal information in social networking services, as well as the lack of awareness and understanding regarding the threats and dangers inherent in such disclosure of personal information, have alarmed data protection bodies and the public alike. Initiatives aimed at data protection for social network users will be an important ongoing area for regulatory bodies to monitor throughout the second decade of the 2000s.

EU data protection law, despite some shortcomings, continues to be the most advanced and will create a model for many other countries. A comprehensive work by Carey and Carey provides a detailed exposition of EU data protection law.[22]

SUMMARY

The information management process plays an increasingly critical role in CRM, in supporting the collection, analysis and use of enormous volumes of complex customer data. Since customer data have a limited shelf life, it is crucial that data are accumulated, updated and deployed in an organised and integrated manner to provide a current and comprehensive view of customers. The ability to 'replicate' the mind of the customer and use it to improve the customer experience is a central tenet of CRM.

Selecting the appropriate IT hardware, software and systems to achieve this can be a challenging task, given the constraints of legacy systems, the enormous range of technology options and the uniqueness of every business situation. The variety of CRM tools and services on offer from IT vendors further complicates the questions of what constitutes the best CRM solution and how to implement and where to host the technology. Whatever option, or combination of options, is pursued, the underlying principle is that the IT infrastructure should create a 'nerve centre', integrating disparate customer data into customer interactions that create superior customer experiences.

Through the effective use of analytical tools, such as data mining and market segmentation analysis, the data warehouse can be used to help identify the most promising customers and to assist in developing strategies to retain them and enhance their value. Data warehouses are particularly valuable to organisations whose sheer scale of operation may mean they are losing touch with individual customers. More importantly, once created, the data warehouse can support the monitoring of customers and provide a mechanism for testing and refining customer strategy. This capability is increasingly significant as markets become ever more dynamic and personalised services and one-to-one marketing become more commonplace.

Organisations should, however, also be aware of the potential drawbacks of data warehousing. Data warehouse functionality is limited by the quality and comprehensiveness of the data it contains. The marketing team needs to consider all appropriate means of enhancing the comprehensiveness of data in the data warehouse from external sources. For example, social media can be used as a source of data enrichment.

To ensure that technology solutions support CRM, it is important to undertake IT planning from a perspective of providing a seamless customer service across channels, rather than planning activities from a departmental or functional perspective. Such a customer-centric approach to IT planning will ensure that customer information is used effectively to maximise customer value and profitability. Furthermore, enterprises need to be diligent in protecting customers' data, addressing privacy concerns and making sure that they have solid codes of operating practice to guide employees. Finally, data analysis tools, such as those outlined above, make it possible to *measure* business activities to determine whether new ways of managing customer relationships will be advantageous in increasing shareholder value. This measurement provides the basis for the performance assessment process, the subject of the next chapter.

CASE 9.1: Royal Bank of Canada – building client service commitment

The company

The Royal Bank of Canada (RBC) is one of Canada's largest banks as measured by assets and market capitalisation, and is among the largest 20 banks globally by market capitalisation. RBC provides personal and commercial banking, wealth management services, insurance, corporate, investment banking and transaction processing services on a global basis. The bank currently employs some 74,000 full- and part-time employees who serve more than 15 million personal, business, public sector and institutional clients through offices in Canada, the US and 56 other countries. RBC holds strong market positions in the following business segments: Canadian Banking, Wealth Management, International Banking, Capital Markets and Insurance. RBC has long been regarded as a leading pioneer and best-practice exemplar in CRM. The bank is an excellent example of what can be achieved when strategic information technologies are leveraged with a strong customer focus.

The challenge

RBC's business philosophy focuses on always earning the right to be its clients' first choice. In the competitive world of financial services, RBC knew that it needed to have a vision and methodology to drive its customer first mission and meet the ever-changing business needs of its customers. When it was looking at methods for improving customer experience, RBC focused on making it easier for clients to get rapid and predictable responses to their inquiries and requests.

This initiative focused on increasing the productivity and improving the efficiency of RBC's inquiry management processes. Client requests arrive in RBC's service centres through multiple channels, including phone, branch, fax, e-mail and mail. Within RBC's Canadian Operations, requests are sent in from staff in eight different geographic regions to 14 different service fulfilment groups. Each group uses different systems and processes to manage its work, which raises the question of 'which operations team do I need to contact to help resolve this issue and how do I best engage them for a quick turnaround?' With such a complex web of fulfilment options, customer service representatives were challenged to find the right path for specific client inquiries, how to accurately set client expectations on response times, and provide updates on existing requests.

A key business issue for RBC was that its large, diverse customer support staff, distributed over diverse geographies, had to address the high service experience demands of its customers. This needed to be achieved while reducing operational costs, increasing organisational transparency and complying with regulatory mandates

The solution

RBC's client service team executed several studies across RBC's customer base that supported the theory that loyalty is a key driver of growth. Through these proprietary studies, the team was able to quantify the hard dollar benefit of an improved customer experience. This became one of the key business benefits of the business case required to turn this project from a pure operational productivity and IT effectiveness proposal into one that supported the 'Client First' vision.

RBC identified Pegasystems SmartBPM® as the key technology to deliver an end-to-end rebuild of their client inquiry and problem resolution process, creating a single system across channels and lines of business. SmartBPM would serve as the backbone for their 'new client action and request tool' (CART). A key requirement of CART was the need to deliver a value-added solution to the front-office service staff. The bank needed a simple way to capture a client's request and ensure all requirements were met to guarantee proper and timely resolution.

Through the use of easily navigated screens, coaching tips, and step-by-step prompts, RBC was able to guide field service staff through the complexities of documenting the problem and in many cases resolving it right there at the point of service. This was delivered so successfully that when the system was first rolled out there was no need for any formalised end-user training. The field service staff were able to click on the 'create a new client request' button and successfully drive the process through to resolution.

Additionally, the supportive coaching tips actually helped determine that many cases were requests that could be resolved right at the point of contact through scripting. Real-time duplicate checking also avoided doubling efforts, as any potential duplicates, such as a spouse who initiated the same request or a duplicate request initiated from a different channel, were identified immediately and resolved by the field team. Once requests were captured into the system, the process automation capabilities of the Pegasystems SmartBPM servicing backbone drove higher rates of straight-through-processing. This involved:

- automatically looking up supporting customer information to enrich the request with required data to help resolve it;
- automatically determining the correct support group, location and even individual for routing and presentation;
- automatically generating supporting forms and correspondence as well as receiving inbound materials supplied by the customer or other support groups.

These steps were manual before this initiative began and prone to error. With the automated processes in place, the support staff were able to focus their time on just the steps that required their skills and judgment, not the menial tasks that added little value to the process. The result was that RBC realised a reduction in total elapsed time to resolve core processes. In some cases, requests that previously took up to five days could be processed in just 30 minutes. The excess capacity enabled RBC to reduce headcount in the support organisation by 20 per cent. This was accomplished mostly through non-hiring of replacement positions and redeployment of staff to other, more value-added, tasks and groups.

The results

In the prior environment, client service agents had little knowledge of how soon a resolution or response to the problem would take. RBC saw that delivering a strong client service commitment at the point of service would create a strong loyalty bond. Because the CART system now had enforceable service level agreements (SLAs) that were tuned for each request type, customer segment and fulfilment group, it could present the service agent with a client service commitment that had a high likelihood of being met. This enabled customer service representatives to confidently and accurately manage the client's expectations, which led to better customer service and achieved RBC's corporate mission of putting their customers first.

The benefits included: significant reduction in time to resolution of basic inquiries – in some cases from five days to 30 minutes; predictable, accurate and consistent client service commitments at point of service and reduction in user training time. As Martin Venema, Director of Sales & Service Automation at RBC, states: 'We were able to improve the ability for front-line staff to handle more inquiries during their first interaction with our customers and set credible client service commitments, driving higher overall customer satisfaction and per-client profitability.'

RBC's achievement with its overall approach to CRM is demonstrated by customer survey results which show strong growth of 26 per cent between 2003 and 2012 in the Net Promoter Score. Today, RBC is ranked number one or number two in market share in all consumer and business product categories in Canada, and the bank leads all Canadian banks in overall volume growth. Further, the bank's CRM strategies have borne fruit in terms of cross-selling success. A 2011 survey undertaken by *Ipsos-Reid* showed 18 per cent of RBC's customer households have transaction accounts, investments and borrowing products compared to an industry average of 10 per cent. In 2011 revenues were CAN\$ 27.4 billion and earnings from continuing operations were CAN\$6.65 billion, up 16 per cent on the prior year, demonstrating the strength of RBC's strategy. RBC's success has also been recognised though the many industry awards it has received. In 2011 RBC was named 'Bank of the Year' for Canada by *The Banker* magazine. RBC was recognised for maintaining its strong leadership position, having a strong international presence and being resilient throughout the global financial crisis. It was also listed as one of the 2011 Best Workplaces in Canada. In 2012 *Global Finance* magazine named RBC the safest bank in North America and the tenth safest bank globally.

CASE 9.2: The DVLA – innovating with CRM in the public sector

The organisation

The Driver and Vehicle Licensing Agency (DVLA) is an agency within the UK Government's Department for Transport. The agency is responsible for a range of activities that include issuing driving licences, collecting excise duty on vehicles and selling private number plates. It maintains some 44 million drivers' records and 36 million vehicle records. Operating from its headquarters near Swansea in South Wales and 39 local offices, it currently employs over 7,000 staff. A large call centre is located in its own purpose-built premises close to the main office.

Up until the mid-1960s, vehicle registrations were managed by local authorities. However, as the number of vehicles and drivers increased dramatically, these local authorities were unable to cope with the volumes of records. In 1965 the government commenced plans to centralise record keeping. By 1974 a network consisting of the DVLA and the Local Driver and Vehicle Licensing

Offices (LVLOs) began operations. The DVLA was responsible for activities such as maintaining the central vehicle record, issuing driving licences and registration documents and licence reminders. The LVLOs were responsible for registration of new imported vehicles and the issue of vehicle licences. At this time, the UK post offices took on the task of routine vehicle licensing. Over the next three decades many new innovations were introduced including more efficient new vehicle computer systems, automated first registration and licensing, which enabled car dealers to issue a licence disc when selling a new vehicle, introduction of photocard driving licences and a pilot scheme so drivers could relicense their vehicles by telephone. By 2004 the DVLA was exploring a multi-channel CRM system to enable customers to be able to license vehicles by the Internet as well as by telephone or in person.

The challenge

The DVLA's strategy had historically been orientated towards coping with predicted growth. Planning was focused on increasing resources to deal with the steady forecast growth in telephone calls and mail items, in line with the growth in the number of vehicles and drivers. For example, the 19 million inbound calls in 2005 were forecast to rise to around 22 million over the next two years. Customers were encouraged to phone or write if they needed to contact DVLA. Business processes were developed to handle vast quantities of paper. However, the traditional processes were prone to human error rates, misinterpretation and losses of documentation. The costs of operating the DVLA were substantial, with the agency dependent on high cost face-to-face channels and paper-based systems to transact with its customers. Also, from a customer perspective, the renewal of licences created a considerable degree of inconvenience. This process involved customers joining in end-of-the-month queues at the nearest post office providing the services, visiting one of the few licensing centres or using the postal service. Presentation of a correctly validated insurance certificate and MOT test certificate (an annual test of roadworthiness) was required. However, many customers presented incorrect documentation, resulting in a wasted trip to a licensing centre or post office. With the government setting tough new targets to reduce the overall public service budget, the challenge was to reduce costs and improve customer service in the DVLA.

The solution

The increasing availability of Internet access and secure automated telephone systems provided new opportunities to reduce the operating costs of the DVLA's services. Resource planning needed to move away from being growth-based to considering strategies that would reduce levels of activity and associated costs, for example, reducing the levels of inbound calls by removing the need for customers to call in the first place. To realise the benefits that could be achieved from enabling services to be transacted over the Internet or through automated telephony, DVLA also required real-time electronic access to other databases of information within both the public and private sectors. IBM Global Business Services were selected by DVLA as a 'transform and operate' partner in developing and implementing the new strategy. A key initial stage in IBM's approach to projects of this scale is to undertake a very detailed analysis and assessment of current processes. A partnership agreement was put in place with IBM. Labelled 'Partners Achieving Change Together', it was aimed at extracting the skills and thinking from an IT expert in order to drive change in a government organisation.

Market research played a crucial role in identifying whether to invest in the Internet channel. Unless sufficient numbers of the population were prepared to use this channel to undertake transactions with DVLA, then this might not be a cost efficient option. Through research, undertaken in 2004, the agency ascertained that Internet access and familiarity with using this channel had reached the threshold levels that would make this a highly attractive lower-cost channel for delivering DVLA services. The research confirmed that between a third and a half of those who were business online users would be interested in accessing a range of DVLA services, covering informational updates via e-mail, renewing/amending operator licences, accessing confidential information on drivers or vehicle fleets, amending a vehicle logbook, buying road tax, and booking and paying for a vehicle test.

To help plan for the needs of different customer groups, DVLA undertook a market segmentation study. The purpose of the study was to identify common needs, attitudes and behaviours and maximise the benefits for both customers and the DVLA. Six segments were identified as shown in Figure 1. The segments were given names, based on the characters in the movie *Star Wars*, to reflect customers' nature, likely channel usage and communication preferences.

Segment name	Proportion of market	Profile and impact of online channel	Implications for DVLA communications strategy
Luke Skywalker	8%	Young & go-getting, Luke types enjoy being different. Use the internet for nearly everything. Expect 24 hrs access and to save time by transacting online	• Communicate through online advertising • Use PR to raise awareness • Likely to become frequent user • Establish email reminder system
Qui Gon Jinn	10%	Independent thinkers who care little for the opinion of others. Quite disorganised/busy; leave it late to renew. Potential convenience of ELV is offset by low awareness	• Strong call to action on V11 envelopes etc. • Use PR to raise awareness • Use national quality press to raise awareness
R2 D2	18%	Busy working; looking for time saving related benefits; pay 12mths possibly by DD. Have internet access but concerned about Internet security; prefer to use phone	• Highlight phone & Web in V11 material • Use specific PR to allay security concerns • Ensure communications address online security concerns
C-3PO	26%	Minimal Internet access; can't be bothered with online transacting. Prefer phone & will tolerate simple IVR	• Highlight phone channel in V11 material • Use PR to raise awareness
Master Yoda	38%	Prefer face-to-face, like social interaction of post office, no time constraints. Would consider DD instalment payment (with no additional charge), but unlikely to consider other options	• Ensure V11 instructions for post office are rewritten in plainer language • Communicate when DD option available
Darth E-Vader	mimimal	Passives Respectables	• Use examples to educate • Use PR to raise awareness • Publicise DD & EVL in CREC outgoing mail • Establish email reminder system

Figure 1 DVLA customer segmentation

The plan for implementing the online channel for electronic vehicle licensing (EVL) did not just depend on the willingness of the public to use the Internet. Historically, physical sight of the necessary supporting documents for a vehicle certificate was required, whether the application was in person or via the post. However, the success of this channel depended on being able to electronically access other sources of information. Access to MOT and other vehicle records in real time was essential in order to confirm that an application to renew a vehicle licence for a vehicle over three years old had a valid MOT certificate. This required access to the Vehicle and Operator Services Agency database. Associated with this, 20,000 MOT agents (authorised vehicle workshops, testing garages and car dealerships) needed to have new technology installed that enabled MOT details to be entered directly into the database. Additionally, all vehicle licence applications require evidence of valid insurance cover. This required real-time access to the motor insurance industry's database (the Motor Insurance Database) of policy holders, with confirmation of the vehicle and policy holder's details. A further link was also necessary to the Department for Work and Pensions to facilitate applications from disabled vehicle keepers who are not required to pay to re-license their vehicles. Finally, the capability for secure credit and debit card payments was also essential to delivering the service. The integrating system of this CRM initiative is shown in Figure 2. A further important initiative followed the vehicle licensing initiative – the issuing of driving licences. This latter initiative involved an electronic link to the UK Passport Office database which provided the necessary digitised signature and photograph that could be printed onto new driving licences without the need for applicants to provide them.

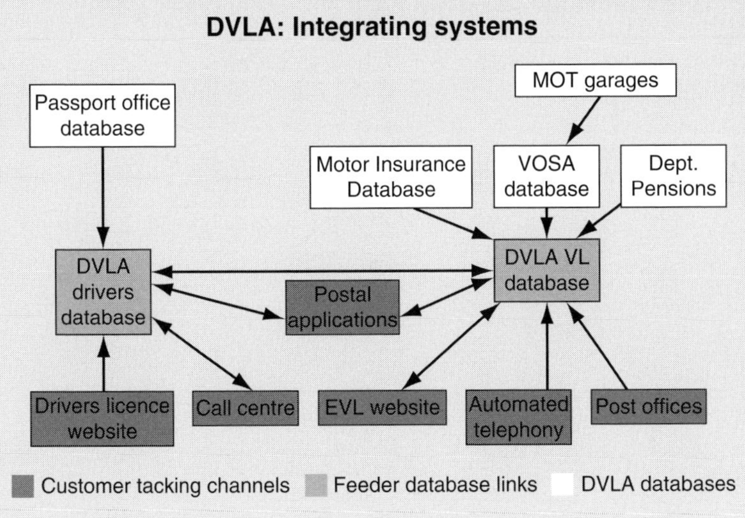

Figure 2 DVLA databases and CRM system

The results

The electronic vehicle licensing initiative has been a great success for the DVLA. Within two years, over 25 per cent of eligible vehicle owners were using the electronic service. Customers were quick to see the benefits which include: convenient, simple, 24/7 access without leaving home or joining a queue; documentation within five days; an increased variety of channels and payment methods; no need to produce supporting documentation (i.e., insurance and MOT certificates) and an electronic vehicle enquiry service. Market research showed a very positive response to the new services, with 91 per cent of those using this channel stating they would be likely or very likely to use it again. Over the next five years use of the service doubled. In 2011, over 26 million transactions were carried out using the digital service. This represents 52 per cent of all transactions, including vehicle dealers registering vehicles for the first time. The DVLA's digital service has now been used more than 100 million times.

The project has been acclaimed as a major step forward for CRM in the public sector in the UK. The DVLA's Electronic Vehicle Licensing system has won two awards for the creative and innovative use of new technology: the Modernising Government category of the New Statesman New Media Awards and the Central e-Government Excellence Strategy & Leadership Award for delivering and implementing e-government strategies. The DVLA's CRM journey from a 'paper factory' to a secure online and telephone service for high volume transactions has been an impressive accomplishment and the agency is now poised to reap further benefits through further operational consolidation and economies of scale.

This case study is based on an earlier case study written by Peter Mouncey for the Cranfield Customer Management Forum and is used with kind permission of Peter Mouncey and Professor Hugh Wilson. It draws on a presentation made by Noel Shanahan, formerly Customer Service Director and now Chief Executive of the DVLA, at a Cranfield Customer Management Forum workshop and publicly available documents. It was updated in 2012 by Professor Adrian Payne and A/Professor Pennie Frow.

10 | Performance assessment

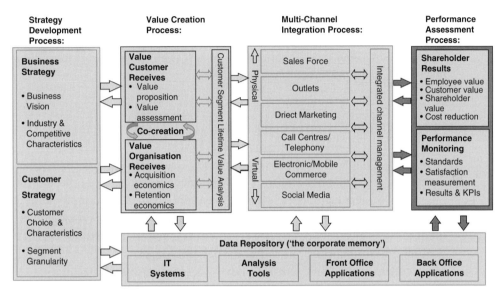

The CRM Strategy Framework

The *performance assessment process* is the final process in the Strategy Framework for CRM. The purpose of this process is to ensure that the organisation's strategic aims in terms of CRM are being delivered to an appropriate and acceptable standard and that a basis for future improvement is firmly established. As shown in the above figure the process has a dual focus on *shareholder results*, which provides a 'macro-view' of the key drivers of CRM performance, and on *performance monitoring*, which involves a more detailed 'micro-view' of the key descriptors of CRM performance. This process involves focusing on two key issues:

1. How can we create increased profits and shareholder value?
2. How should we set standards, develop metrics, measure our results and improve our performance?

Together these issues provide an understanding of how CRM delivers shareholder results and how CRM performance can be measured and thus further enhanced.

As emphasised earlier, CRM breaks with traditional management practice in that it involves the whole organisation and emphasises avoiding functional divides. In so doing CRM embraces a new logic for commercial relevance: business success ultimately derives from the creation of customer value, which is achieved through the skilful management and development of customer relationships involving all key stakeholders. Market leaders will be those who can demonstrate an unfailing ability continually and consistently to deliver products and services that fulfil customers' needs and expectations and can do so in a manner that highlights organisational competencies and cost-effectiveness. This is a tall order and demands the coordinated effort of all company members and partners throughout the supply chain.

Likewise, the evaluation and enhancement of performance needs all the required information to be supplied in a timely and accessible manner by the information management process. This requires the adoption of a more inclusive and comprehensive perspective. We believe that concerns about the effectiveness of CRM solutions are a key factor driving companies to consider CRM in this broader context of business strategy and to monitor CRM performance more carefully against specially selected criteria.

The need for a systematic approach

As noted in Chapter 2, firms have historically tended to organise themselves in terms of functional responsibility and thus performance measures have reflected the individual objectives of departments or strategic business units. For example, Finance has been driven by profit, Sales by volume and Marketing by customer acquisition. The movement towards greater convergence and consolidation in many industries has blurred the distinctions among the aims of traditional allocations of organisational responsibility. More collaborative work practices have necessitated more consultative measurement and monitoring systems. In short, a redefinition of the business model requires a recalibration of business performance. Because CRM is a cross-functional activity, CRM performance measurement must use a range of metrics that span the gamut of processes and channels used to deliver CRM.

As yet, there is no universally recognised system for measuring the success of CRM. This is partly due to the fact that every CRM programme is unique and cannot be judged identically and partly because formalised CRM is still a relatively new discipline. Although customer relationship management is usually considered the remit of marketing as it builds on the tenets of relationship marketing (although sometimes it is inappropriately the remit of the IT department), in practice it touches the job of every employee in every department. This sharing of customer responsibility compounds the difficulty of agreeing specific measures that will accurately reflect CRM performance and strategic progress.

Early attempts to measure marketing performance were largely directed at monitoring financial outputs. These included profit, sales and cash flow. In the 1980s, there was a realisation that non-financial measures also played a part in delivering the overall performance of marketing. Organisations began to recognise that variables such as brand equity, customer satisfaction and customer loyalty were very important in transforming marketing inputs to organisational outputs.

During the 1990s, the emphasis switched to the use of multiple measures that would together provide a more complete picture of marketing performance. However, this method raises difficult issues for managers, including which measures should be included in performance monitoring models and how to account for the interrelationships between measures.

There is now recognition of the need for a more definitive framework identifying the principal measures of CRM performance and how these measures organise into a system that can be used continually to monitor, track and improve performance in support of the CRM vision. The performance assessment process, highlighted in the CRM Strategy Framework above, provides a structure for developing such a system based on the following key actions:

1. Understand the *key drivers of shareholder results* and the significance of the linkages between them.
2. Identify the *appropriate standards, metrics and Key Performance Indicators (KPIs)* against which the various CRM activities can be measured.
3. Establish an *effective CRM performance monitoring system* to apply these measures on an ongoing basis.

Each of these key actions is now examined in turn.

Understanding the key drivers of shareholder results

To achieve the ultimate objective of CRM – the delivery of excellent shareholder results through an increase in shareholder value – an organisation must maximise the main sources of revenue, profit and growth within the context of both business and customer strategy. The four main elements are:

- building employee value,
- building customer value,
- building shareholder value,
- reducing costs.

The first three elements impact key stakeholder groups, while the latter is a potentially significant means of directly improving profits. The development of the 'linkage model' or 'service profit chain'[1] shown in Figure 10.1, confirms the relationship correlation between value creation and profitability, as well as the linkage between employee value, customer value and shareholder value.

The linkage model suggests that an improvement in leadership and management behaviour has a positive impact on employee attitudes and employee satisfaction. The more satisfied and motivated an employee, the longer he is likely to stay with an organisation and

Figure 10.1 The linkage model

the better he will do in his job. This will have a positive effect on customer satisfaction, so customers will stay longer and generate higher sales for the company. The result is stronger profitability and increased shareholder value. This model provides a key logic to the broader perspective of CRM. We will return to the model later in this chapter.

Employee value, customer value, shareholder value and cost reduction

Many organisations now recognise the importance of improving their performance by managing the value input and impact of each major stakeholder group. It is obvious that certain stakeholder groups are more important than others. While this importance will vary to some extent from organisation to organisation, three stakeholder groups – shareholders, customers and employees – have emerged as the core focus for most organisations in terms of value management and performance improvement. Frederick Reichheld of consulting firm Bain & Co. points out that these three key stakeholders – the 'forces of loyalty' – are pivotal in achieving commercial success.[2] These key drivers of shareholder results are shown in Figure 10.2. This figure emphasises the need to consider each of these stakeholders from the perspective of the value of the stakeholder group to the organisation *and* the value of the organisation to that stakeholder group.

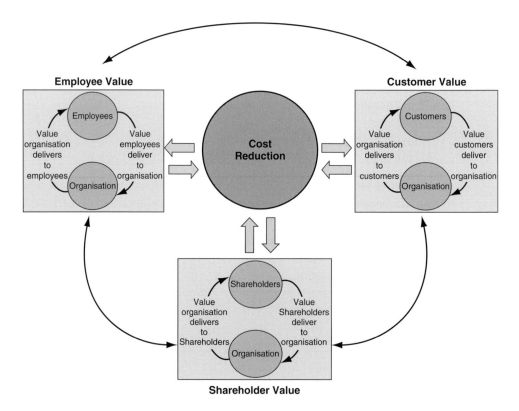

Figure 10.2 Key drivers of shareholder results

It is useful to make a distinction between building shareholder value and achieving shareholder results. In the context of this book, *shareholder value* creation is viewed in a more narrow sense as being concerned with identifiable value in terms of returns on capital that stem from initiatives such as improved customer satisfaction and increasing customer retention, excluding stock market measures. *Shareholder results* include how shareholders and the stock market respond to these improvements in shareholder value: that is, they reflect the stock market perspective. Research shows that shareholders take a range of non-financial measures into account when valuing companies. For example, one study suggests that on average 35 per cent of an investment decision is driven by non-financial data.[3] Hence, issues such as communicating a coherent and well-planned CRM strategy may have a significant part to play in achieving improved shareholder results.

Cost reduction is an obvious source of potential increase in profits and shareholder results. Improving efficiency and the use of lower cost channels are common means of achieving cost reduction. However, as we will discuss shortly, it is important that this is not done at the expense of lower levels of customer satisfaction and customer value.

Employee value

In addressing CRM performance it is tempting to focus immediately on standards for CRM, metrics and KPIs. However, the need first to focus on the drivers of shareholder results should be emphasised.

John McKean in his book *Information Masters* made a critical observation that typically 92 per cent of the historical investment in CRM expenditure goes into data and technology, but these aspects only represent 25 per cent of the competency determinants for success.[4] Organisations also need to make sure the other most critical elements that represent 75 per cent of the competency determinants for success, such as people, processes, organisation, culture and leadership, actively support CRM activities in a relevant manner. McKean's research indicates that a total of 60 per cent of the competency determinants for success involve people, organisation, culture and leadership. Thus the people element is absolutely critical in making CRM work. These issues are discussed in more detail in Chapter 11.

Employee value needs to be considered from two perspectives – the value employees deliver to the organisation and the value the organisation delivers to employees. Further, a motivated employee can add value to the customer.

The value employees deliver to the organisation is usually measured against a number of performance objectives. Often these represent short-term goals, where employee performance is appraised against performance targets. Employee value of this form is closely linked to employee retention, for long-tenured employees are more likely to know their jobs and the goals of the organisation and are thus able to be more productive.

The value the organisation delivers to its employees comprises the benefits the work force receives in exchange for the opportunity cost, time and labour expended in performing their jobs. This bundle of benefits includes the internal service quality created by management practices, encompassing reward and appraisal policies, training and development opportunities and the motivation and empowerment of employees.

Linking employee remuneration to specific customer objectives, such as customer satisfaction and customer retention, supports the creation of value for both the employees and the organisation.

How the company's leadership, human resources and culture are organised are therefore key factors in determining employee value, which, in turn, has a significant bearing on customer and shareholder value. This is evident in the types of measures used to monitor the value delivered by employees, for example, product quality measures, employee turnover, recruitment costs and employee satisfaction.

Customer value

Customer value is concerned with both *the value the organisation receives from the customer* and *the value the customer receives from the organisation*. As the topic of customer value has already been discussed in Chapter 3 and Chapter 7, only a short recapitulation is given here.

The value the organisation receives from customers is determined by the profits obtained from customers over the lifetime of their relationship with the organisation, or their 'customer lifetime value' and the economics of customer acquisition and retention.

The value the customer receives from the organisation is defined by the perceived benefits of the offer made to the customer, which extend beyond the core product or service. These higher-level benefits, or 'added values', emanate not from basic product features but from intangible factors, such as the provision of better customer service or association with a quality brand image. A number of measures are used to monitor this aspect of customer value including customer retention, customer acquisition costs, customer satisfaction and customer profitability.

The key issues relating to customer value, discussed in Chapter 3, include the following:

The nature of 'the offer' a company makes to its customer

Customer value is an inherent part of the product or service offer which the company can actively manage to benefit the customer. Customers do not buy goods or services, but rather a bundle of benefits in the form of product features and added value. This total offering – or 'the offer', as it is commonly called – represents the value that customers co-create when they buy goods or services.

The use of relationships and branding to increase customer value

Building better relationships with customers through offering superior customer service is one way of securing competitive advantage. The use of customer service as a more important competitive weapon derives from increasingly sophisticated customer requirements and the demand for ever-higher standards of service. Developing greater customer involvement with the company's products is a good way to use the brand to enhance customer value. The Harley-Davidson Owners Group, discussed in Chapter 3, provides a good illustration of this.

The value proposition

The value proposition comprises three key steps: choose the value, provide the value and communicate the value. Success rests on the thoroughness and innovation that goes into developing the value proposition and communicating it throughout the supplying organisation.

The value of customers to the company

To calculate a customer's real worth, the company must look at the expected profit flow from the customer over the customer's lifetime, rather than the results this year: the longer the customer relationship, the greater the profit per customer.

Shareholder value

The growing power and influence of financial analysts has driven many company Boards to regard the creation of shareholder value as their primary business objective. However, the emphasis is frequently placed on quarterly results rather than the longer term. Balancing long-term and short-term returns and communicating this balance to shareholders, is, therefore, becoming a priority.

Shareholder value is created by achieving a favourable rate of return on capital invested. This can be accomplished in a number of ways. Cornelius and Davies have summarised the five principal strategies that can lead to the creation of shareholder value.[5] These are:

1. Increasing the return generated on existing capital invested;
2. Investing more capital where the rate of return exceeds that required;
3. Divesting assets which generate a return lower than that required, thus releasing capital for more productive use;
4. Extending the period over which returns above the required rate are generated;
5. Reducing the cost of capital.

These strategies require a 'value-based management' approach that emphasises creating and maximising the wealth of shareholders in every aspect of the business. Such an approach involves measuring and managing the following key financial variables, or 'value drivers':

- the opening amount of capital invested,
- the rate of return generated on capital,
- the rate of return that investors require,
- the growth in the value of capital invested,
- the time horizon over which returns are expected to exceed those required by shareholders.

Most of what has been written on shareholder value focuses on the *value the organisation delivers to shareholders*. Over the last decade there has been particular emphasis on tools that measure shareholder value creation and shareholder results, including economic value added (EVA), shareholder value added (SVA), market value added (MVA) and cash flow return on investment (CFROI). A summary of key measures of shareholder value is shown in Figure 10.3.[6]

Company	Shareholder Value Product
LEK/Alcar Consulting Group	Shareholder Value Added (SVA)
Stern Stewart & Co	Market Value Added (MVA) Economic Value Added (EVA™)
McKinsey & Co	Various methods
Marakon Associates	Various Methods
Braxton Associates	Cash Flow Return on Investment (CFROI)
The Boston Consulting Group	Cash Flow Return on Investment (CFROI) Cash Value Added (CVA)
Holt Value Associates	Cash Flow Return on Investment (CFROI)

Figure 10.3 Shareholder value measures.
Source: Based on Myers (1996)

Although there is an ongoing debate as to which technique most accurately measures shareholder value, what is important is to consider shareholder value in the context of the whole business and, in particular, in relation to customer value. The specific measurement of shareholder value is complex and beyond the scope of this book. The interested reader should consult the detailed report by Cornelius and Davies,[7] recent work by Venanzi[8] and a more detailed discussion of corporate valuation by Monks and Lajoux.[9]

Although the issue of the *value the shareholders deliver to the organisation* is emphasised much less, the loyalty of shareholders and other investors is an issue of considerable importance. Frederick Reichheld, of Bain & Co., points out that shareholder churn in the average public company in the US is more than 50 per cent per annum and argues that managers find it very difficult to pursue long-term value creation strategies without the support of loyal and knowledgeable shareholders. He notes that many of the world's leading companies (in terms of high customer loyalty and high customer retention) are either privately owned, 'mutual' or public companies, where there is a high shareholder loyalty and thus a high value delivered by shareholders to the organisation.[10]

Delivering value to shareholders is an increasing concern of CEOs. However, an obsession with maximising shareholder value has sometimes led to the neglect of other stakeholder groups, causing high employee turnover, poor quality products and services and ultimately reduced shareholder value. It is therefore crucial that shareholder value be viewed as a balance between immediate financial return and longer-term sustainability. This will be discussed further in the following chapter.

Cost reduction

Cost reduction can represent a good source of increase in profits and shareholder results. Opportunities for cost reduction lie in:

- Exploiting economies of scale;
- Benchmarking best practice within and outside the industry;
- Outsourcing non-core activities;
- Leveraging shared activities across the organisation;
- Improving CRM efficiency and effectiveness.

Better information management can be a primary source of cost reduction in CRM. For example, one large US investment bank found they could redeploy 45 per cent of their staff in marketing, sales and service because the time required to undertake these activities was significantly reduced through gaining a higher level of information competency.[11]

Deploying electronic systems, such as automated telephony services, which lower costs by enabling reductions in staff and overheads, is an attractive potential source of cost reduction. However, an over concentration on cost reduction as a means of delivering shareholder results can be counterproductive if it *decreases customer value*. For example, the creation of a central call centre in a bank will help reduce costs but may disenfranchise customers who prefer to interact with bank employees whom they know. Dealing with bank representatives who are unfamiliar with their individual circumstances and banking habits can be regarded as an affront to their long-standing status as loyal customers. Some years ago, a large UK bank had to reverse its new policy of customers only being able to speak to a central call centre, rather than directly to their branch, as a result of many complaints from angry customers. Thus, any cost reduction strategy needs to be considered in the context of its effect on customer value.

The utilisation of new electronic channels, such as online self-service facilities on the Internet – that lower the costs of customer acquisition, customer transactions and customer service – offers a further opportunity for cost reduction. With its innovative website Dell places much of the buying process in its customers' hands. Using the benefits of Web self-service, customers can configure their own product and place their own orders. This dramatically speeds up the buying process, improves accuracy, decreases costs of correction and problem resolution and is considerably less labour intensive for Dell. Further, storage and distribution costs are cut because of more timely and efficient stock management and delivery.

Achieving a sensible balance between cost reduction and customer satisfaction means understanding that value is created or sacrificed in the management of customer relationships. The value process constitutes a central element of CRM, for it is that which drives success in the organisation. A well-managed value process will lead to a better quality of workforce in terms of the organisation's ability to attract and retain highly motivated, committed and appropriately skilled employees. Such a dedicated workforce is more likely to deliver a better customer experience, which in turn will deliver better shareholder value through increased sales, repeat orders and customer referrals.

The importance of an appropriate value exchange is clear: concentrating on how much value (in the form of profits) an organisation can extract from its customers, without understanding what customers value from the organisation in order to provide it satisfactorily, is not a sustainable strategy in today's competitive environment. Nor is a strategy of profit improvement through cost reduction where cost savings are made at the expense of customer value. Thus, an integrated approach is needed to optimise the contribution of each stakeholder group and the opportunities for cost reduction, as well as to exploit the *linkages* between them.

Linking shareholder value, employee value, customer value and cost reduction

In addition to the profit-enhancing potential of each group's value contribution, there is potential contained in the linkages between them. There is also an obvious connection between cost reduction and the three key stakeholders discussed above. As Figure 10.2 suggests, cost savings can be used to increase employee value (e.g., through investing in staff training or job incentives); increase customer value (e.g., through augmenting the value proposition) or increase shareholder value (e.g., through improving 'the bottom line').

Conversely, improvement in these value areas can result in substantial cost reductions. For example, an improvement in customer value may drive increased customer satisfaction, resulting in high levels of advocacy among the customer base and consequent savings in marketing costs. This knock-on effect is evident in organisations such as First Direct, the UK bank which acquires a third or more of its customers through customer referrals rather than through traditional marketing activities. Thus its average acquisition costs for each customer are significantly reduced.

We have noted above the linkage between three areas: employee value, customer value and shareholder value – but how are they related? The linkage model shown in Figure 10.1 gives insight into the logic but not the specific relationships between variables within these areas. It is not clear for most organisations how much one variable needs to improve to achieve a given level of improvement in another variable. For example, if employee attitudes and satisfaction increase by a measurable amount, what specific impact will this have on customer satisfaction and resulting profitability?

As discussed shortly, some leading companies are using advanced modelling approaches to verify the exact nature of the linkages between these sources of added value in their businesses and to use them to improve shareholder results. As the search for new and improved ways of measuring the performance of key variables *across* these critical linkages continues, organisations are recognising the importance of addressing these higher-level drivers before determining CRM standards, metrics and KPIs.

Developing appropriate standards, metrics and KPIs

Despite the increasing focus in businesses on customer-facing activities, there is growing concern that the standards and metrics generally used by companies for assessing CRM performance are not as advanced as they should be. In particular, more detailed standards, measures and KPIs are needed to ensure CRM activities are planned and performed effectively and that a feedback loop exists to maximise organisational learning and improvement.

As shown in the CRM Strategy Framework, assessing CRM performance involves a consideration of the contribution and interaction of multiple processes. The five inter-related and cross-functional processes common to all commercial organisations are:

- the strategic development process,
- the enterprise value creation process,
- the multi-channel integration process,
- the information management process, and
- the performance assessment process.

These processes centre on how the organisation delivers value to the customer while enhancing the value received by the company in terms of shareholder results. While these processes have universal application, the extent to which they are emphasised will vary according to the situation of the organisation concerned.

Companies need simultaneously to consider what standards and metrics should be used by them and what their CRM priorities are, given their specific circumstances. Organisations can benefit from first learning about existing standards and metrics used by other organisations before reinventing what others have already done.

Standards

The lack of an internationally recognised set of standards for CRM has hindered efforts to measure and benchmark best practice – a prerequisite to achieving improved performance in CRM. As yet, few companies have developed their own integrated and detailed processes for measuring CRM performance. The complexity of measuring the many processes contributing to the success of CRM makes this a potentially daunting task.

However, the increasing importance of CRM measurement has resulted in a number of organisations developing CRM standards for more general external use. These standards typically relate to either a complete view of CRM activity or a specific part of it. Two such initiatives are the QCi Customer Management Assessment Tool used as a general CRM review and the Customer Outsourcing Performance Centre (COPC) standards for customer service centres.

The QCi Customer Management Assessment Tool (CMAT)

CMAT™ is a proprietary assessment tool for understanding how well an organisation manages its customers. It is carried out by trained assessors who are experienced CRM practitioners within 'The Customer Framework',[12] a specialist CRM consultancy or one of its partner organisations.

The model is based on the following elements:

1. Analysis and planning
2. The proposition
3. People and organisation
4. Information technology
5. Process management
6. Customer management activity
7. Measuring the effect
8. The customer experience.

Each of these elements is further subdivided into component parts. For example, 'people and organisation' covers:

- organisational structure
- role identification
- competencies definition and gap analysis
- training requirements and resources
- objective setting and monitoring
- supplier selection and management.

CMAT uses over 250 questions to assess the organisation's performance. Each question in the assessment is based on known and demonstrable good practices from the clients of QCi and from accepted industry benchmark organisations. A 'scoring based on evidence' approach is taken to answering each question and a broad range of people, from senior directors to operational level practitioners, are interviewed. The approach is specifically designed to identify *clear plans*, *real delivery* and an *identifiable effect* of each of the practices questioned. In this way the all too common gap between senior management perception of the situation and the 'front line' reality is often identified.

Figure 10.4 provides data for 'United Bank' in term of its overall performance and eight component measures of the CMAT model. The figure also compares the bank with the overall average across all industry sectors and also, more interestingly, within more direct competitors in banking, insurance and other finance businesses. Thus, United Bank can compare itself with its competitors and also best practice across all industries.

The output of the assessment is a report and Board-level presentation that positions the organisation against a relevant benchmark of other organisations. It also provides a quartile positioning for each of 27 CRM areas into which the sections of the customer management model are divided. The assessment has been carried out in over 100 organisations worldwide so provides a rich set of data against which a company can benchmark its performance.

The objective of the CMAT tool is to provide an objective and quantitative assessment of how well the organisation currently manages its customers with a score that correlates to business performance and benchmarks the organisation against a relevant set of other organisations. This is especially beneficial when the company can compare itself against competitors in its own vertical industry sector, such as those shown in Figure 10.4. It also

	Overall AV	United Bank	Insurance	Other Finance	Retail Banking
Overall scores	32	40	28	30	41
Analysis & planning	28	28	27	19	37
The proposition	30	26	26	24	36
People & organisation	38	54	31	40	49
Information & technology	37	36	32	38	46
Process management	29	36	27	36	35
Customer management activity	31	37	26	30	37
Measuring the effect	35	60	29	36	49
The customer experience	28	40	20	16	42

Figure 10.4 CMAT performance benchmarking for 'United Bank'.
Source: © QCi Assessment Ltd., used with permission

forms a clear 'baseline' against which improvements delivered by a CRM programme can be measured and provides a broad-based check that all the necessary CRM foundations are in place before investing in specific programmes or technology.

Customer Operations Performance Centre (COPC) standard

Other standards focus on particular aspects of CRM in more detail. One such approach is the *COPC standard* developed by users of customer service centres, call centres and fulfilment services in the US. It was initiated by representatives of a number of leading companies – including American Express, Dell Computer Corp., Microsoft, Novell and L. L. Bean – in response to their concerns about the performance of call centre providers.

The developers of this standard believed that improvement standards could help augment service quality within a service environment, just as had been seen in manufacturing industries that employed similar quality measures. Although some service providers used existing standards such as ISO 9000, these were orientated towards manufacturing industries and failed to give the operational benefits that were needed in service businesses.

The COPC-2000 standard[13] is awarded to companies successfully completing a formal audit measuring the effectiveness of their internal customer-facing operations. Among its aims is to distinguish between excellent service providers and those that are mediocre, enabling companies who are outsourcing call or service centres to use this information before they make their purchasing decision. The standard includes developing process specifications based on customer requirements, so service delivery processes are customer and not operationally driven.

The COPC standard is based on a number of well-recognised criteria used in the Malcolm Baldridge Quality Award. There are four key areas used within these standards.

- *Performance standards*, includes customer satisfaction, product and service quality, employee satisfaction and supplier performance;
- *Processes*, includes process control, supplier management, internal quality audits and product development;
- *People*, includes recruitment and development, compensation, recognition and the work environment of employees;
- *Planning and leadership*, includes leadership, planning and performance review.

Although COPC does not set specific performance objectives that every call centre must meet, it does require that all performance metrics are tracked by linking them to customer satisfaction drivers. This information is then used to improve overall call centre performance.

The aim of the COPC standard is to improve performance of all outsourced call centres through widespread adoption of the standards. The measures have been widely accepted and, although call centres have often chosen not to pursue accreditation; many employ the performance metrics. By 2012, COPC Inc. had assisted more than 1,300 organisations in 60 countries to improve customer service by using the COPC Family of Standards.

While the COPC standards are designed for specific types of organisations with a strong emphasis on customer service delivery, they are useful as an example of an integrated approach to measuring effectiveness within a key area of CRM.

Metrics

The identification of appropriate metrics is another challenge for companies seeking to evaluate and enhance their CRM performance. The main problem lies in determining the critical measures of CRM-related activity that are most appropriate to the organisation and managing them effectively.

It is important at this stage to note the distinction between metrics and KPIs. *Metrics* involve all those CRM-related activities that should be measured. *Key performance indicators* are the high-level measures that are critical to the success of the business and that should be monitored closely by the Board and top management.

We consider five main categories of CRM metrics are especially important – customer metrics, operational (employee and process) metrics, strategic metrics, output and comparative metrics, and specialised metrics. These key metrics represent the 'vital statistics' of healthy CRM, signalling the strength or weakness of the underlying CRM processes. The specialised metrics will also be needed to meet specific company requirements such as those relating to e-commerce and social media. Relevant CRM metrics should be applied regularly to provide an overall appraisal and monitoring of CRM effectiveness.

Customer metrics

Customer metrics measure both the value delivered by the organisation to the customer and the value delivered by the customer to the organisation. They are focused around measures of customer attitude and behaviour.

Customer metrics are used to measure:

- Customer acquisition and customer retention rates
- Customer satisfaction measures
- Customer lifetime value
- Customer experience within channel and across multi-channels
- Customer complaints and the seriousness of them
- Segment and micro-segment profitability
- Share of wallet
- Product density (number of products and services used by a customer)
- Customer recommendation and advocacy measures
- Increase in customer value through cross-sell and up-sell.

People and process metrics

People and process metrics focus on how well the organisation's resources are managed to optimise CRM at an operational level. People metrics are concerned with standards used to monitor the skills and motivation of employees in delivering the customer experience. Process metrics reflect the efficiency of the organisation in delivering CRM, including cost savings secured through process enhancement.

People metrics are used to measure:

- Employee performance against customer service standards
- Employee satisfaction
- Employee attitudes and motivation
- Employee productivity
- Staff absenteeism
- Employee retention and employee tenure
- Recruitment costs.

Process metrics are used to measure:

- Customer service levels
- Order fulfilment
- Supplier performance targets
- Variation within key customer processes
- New product/service development targets
- Time to market
- Process improvement targets.

Strategic metrics

Strategic metrics measure the organisation's success in achieving its business objectives within the strategic approach to CRM that has been adopted. They measure, for example, the extent to which the business strategies meet the required shareholder value targets and strengthen the organisation's position in the marketplace.

Strategic metrics are used to measure:

- Shareholder value added/market value added
- Profitability and cash flow
- Returns on net assets, sales, CRM investments, etc.
- Growth rates
- Expense ratios
- Market positioning
- Innovation
- Brand equity
- Specific targets for other stakeholders.

Output and comparative metrics

Output and comparative metrics measure the output of the organisation's CRM strategy, especially in relation to competitor activity and recognised best practice. These comparative measures are frequently more important than absolute measures. Sole reliance on internal metrics can be dangerous, for they provide an isolated and insular view of the situation. For example, a market share of 20 per cent may be advantageous if the largest competitor has a market share of 10 per cent; however, it may be risky if the two largest competitors have market shares of 30 per cent each. Similarly, high levels of service quality and customer satisfaction are generally only beneficial if they are higher than those of the competition.

Output and comparative metrics are used to measure:

- Relative profitability
- Relative market share
- Relative customer satisfaction
- Relative customer retention
- Relative employee retention and satisfaction
- Relative product or service quality
- Cost reduction
- Improvements in employee value (in terms of employee retention and satisfaction)
- Increased competitive differentiation.

Special metrics

Special metrics can be used as stand-alone metrics or they can be used in conjunction with the other four main categories of metrics outlined above. For example, companies with intermediaries may need to implement customer performance measures at different channel levels. Businesses with a strong e-commerce component may need to address the different characteristics of an Internet channel by developing specific e-metrics. Interestingly, despite the availability of data from Web channels, relatively few companies use these data to measure and monitor the effectiveness of their e-CRM activities. The rise of social media has led to the need for metrics that relate to social influence marketing.

Special e-metrics

Special e-metrics can be used to measure:

- Stickiness (the website's ability to hold visitors' attention and to get them to become repeat users of the site);
- Focus (the scope and intensity of site visitor behaviour);
- Personalisation index (how well the e-business uses personal customer data captured during site visits);
- Lifetime value (the contribution to company profits over the duration of the customer relationship. Measuring lifetime value is particularly important as less valuable customers using other channels can be moved to improved levels of profitability through using the Web channel);
- Loyalty value (this includes visitor frequency, visit duration, number of pages viewed per visit, time elapsed between the user's first visit and most recent visit);
- Freshness factor (how often content on a website is reviewed and renewed versus how frequently users visit the site).[14]

Special metrics for social influence marketing

A 2009 study by Mzinga and Babson Executive Education found that 84 per cent of professionals, representing a variety of industries, do not measure return on investment (ROI) for their company's social media programmes.[15] However, more recently top management is putting greater emphasis on the measurement of ROI for their social media activities. Companies are also shifting emphasis from simple measures, such as visitors to sites and numbers of followers, fans and members, to a broader range of measures with an emphasis on estimating the ROI of social media. While each company will have particular needs, Ranson Consulting (2011) has identified the following important social media metrics:

- Social media leads (tracking Web traffic from all social media sources, including referrals);
- Engagement duration (for some enterprises, engagement duration is more important than page views. Tracking of pages visited should also be undertaken);
- Bounce rate (if visitors are coming to a company's website from social media sites, but quickly leaving, this suggests the company's landing page needs better, more relevant, copy or better product offerings);
- Membership increase and active network size (the portion of the company's social networks, e.g., Twitter and Facebook, that actively engages with its social media content);
- Activity ratio (level of activity in the company's collective social network);
- Conversions (conversions into subscriptions, sales, Facebook application use, or other offerings that can be directly or indirectly monetised);
- Brand mentions in social media (measurement and tracking of amount of both positive and negative sentiment);
- Loyalty (the extent to which social members interact in the network repeatedly, sharing content and links, mentioning a brand and acting as an advocate for a brand);

- Virality (social members might be sharing Twitter tweets and Facebook updates relevant to a company, but is this information being reshared by their networks? How many FofFs (Friends of Friends) are resharing a company's links and content?);
- Blog interaction (encouraging responses either directly in the comments section of blog posts, or via social media such as Twitter).[16]

A detailed review of social media metrics and ROI measurement is beyond the scope of this book. Readers wishing to explore this area in more detail should see Sterne,[17] Novak and Hoffman,[18] Lovett,[19] Sponder[20] and Blanchard.[21]

Key performance indicators

As noted above, it is necessary to make a distinction among the metrics outlined above. Some of them will be relevant at an operational level and some important at a strategic level. The latter metrics are the key performance indicators that are critical to the success of the business and need to be monitored regularly at Board level.

Tim Ambler, a leading researcher on performance metrics at London Business School, concluded that large companies have far too many KPI measures. He suggests that 10 to 20 external metrics, plus 2 to 5 for the internal market (employees), are enough for the main Board of a large company. Ambler's research into the most commonly used marketplace KPIs is summarised in Figure 10.5.[22]

This research is of particular interest because it not only measures companies' use of these KPIs but also the percentage of companies where these KPIs reach the main Board of Directors. The research findings raise concern as key aspects of CRM, such as customer satisfaction and customer retention, only reach the Board in 36 per cent and 51 per cent of companies, respectively.

Decisions regarding which CRM metrics and high-level KPIs should be adopted for measuring the effectiveness of CRM processes and activities should not be taken casually. Using the wrong measures or measuring the wrong things is clearly self-defeating. Many

Metric	% of firms using measure	% that reach the top Board
Awareness	78.0	28.0
Market share (volume or value)	78.0	33.5
Relative price (market share value/volume)	70.0	34.5
Number of complaints (level of dissatisfaction)	69.0	30.0
Consumer satisfaction	68.0	36.0
Distribution/availability	66.0	11.5
Total number of customers	65.5	37.4
Perceived quality/esteem	64.0	32.0
Loyalty/retention	64.0	50.7
Relative perceived quality	62.5	52.8

Figure 10.5 Commonly used key marketplace metrics.
Source: Based on Ambler (2004)

companies will therefore need to establish a formalised system for monitoring CRM performance in order to ensure that the right metrics are used to manage activities at operational level and the right KPIs drive strategic decisions at Board level.

Multiple measures and linkage models

A relatively new development in measurement and metrics is the use of multiple metrics involving cross-functional measures and the identification of relationships between them. There has been a growing recognition of the importance of considering multiple measures in this way as traditional financial accounting measures are prone to giving misleading results. Proposals for a more balanced presentation of both financial and operational measures have begun to proliferate.

A range of models has been proposed for measuring different aspects of enterprise-wide performance in a more systematic manner. These include the Malcolm Baldridge Award, the EFQM Award and the balanced scorecard. These models represent measurement systems for monitoring and controlling enterprise performance; additionally they act as communication devices. In particular, they emphasise the importance of measuring employee satisfaction, customer satisfaction and business results in monitoring business performance in a more integrated way.

However, there are drawbacks with some of these models. For example, although the Baldridge and EFQM quality models encouraged organisations to measure their performance in terms of employee satisfaction, customer satisfaction and financial results, the measures are not systematically linked together so as to identify the *relationships* between them.

The balanced scorecard

One of the most popular attempts to provide cross-functional measures is the balanced scorecard approach developed by Robert Kaplan and David Norton.[23] Their approach advocates the combination of four different perspectives of performance:

1. *the customer perspective*, which focuses on how the customer sees the organisation;
2. *the internal perspective*, which identifies what an organisation must excel at;
3. *the innovation and learning perspective*, which focuses on how an organisation can improve and create value; and
4. *the financial perspective*, which considers how an organisation appears to its shareholders.

The 'balanced scorecard' has become an important part of many organisations' CRM activities as it contains a customer outcome dimension. However, the mixed focus of the scorecard approach can lead to inadequate levels of customer responsiveness and lethargic change management initiatives. The developers of this model also point out that companies need to create their own unique scorecards which reflect the nature of their own businesses and key priorities. In the same way, CRM performance measurement needs to be approached in an appropriately tailored way. Later in this chapter we show how the balanced scorecard criteria can be used to create a tailored 'success map' for a specific organisation.

Linkage models and the service profit chain

Linkage models illustrate the relationships between employees, customers and organisational performance. The service profit chain model shown in Figure 10.6, the best-known version of the linkage model, establishes the relationships between profitability, customer loyalty and employee satisfaction, loyalty and productivity. The researchers have described their model, as follows:

The links in the chain, which should be regarded as propositions, are as follows: Profit and growth are stimulated primarily by customer loyalty. Loyalty is a direct result of customer satisfaction. Satisfaction is largely influenced by the value of services provided to customers. Value is created by satisfied, loyal and productive employees. Employee satisfaction, in turn, results primarily from high-quality support services and policies that enable employees to deliver results to customers.[24]

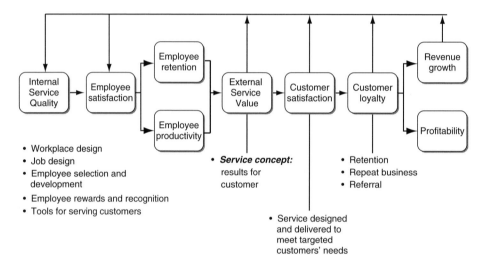

Figure 10.6 The service profit chain.
Source: Based on Heskett et al. (1997)

The service profit chain model shows how the linkages between these metrics are related and how KPIs can be leveraged to secure improved results. Advances in economic and statistical modelling can now enable companies to identify the various relationships with greater accuracy and determine where improvements can most profitably be made. This work has been pioneered by the international consultancy CFI Group, founded by University of Michigan econometrician Claes Fornell.

However, although the concept of using a linkage model is potentially very attractive, there are still relatively few examples of companies that could be described as 'advanced' in terms of adoption of such an approach. This finding may not be surprising as very few of the companies involved in the original service profit chain research had explored *all* the linkages across the model, let alone used causal techniques of measurement. The case study at the end of this chapter on Sears, the leading US department store, is considered one of the best exemplars of this approach. Sears uses a modified version of the service profit chain to predict and manage performance and shareholder results.

Although the underlying ideas behind the service profit chain reflect the practices of many leading service organisations, very few companies have sought to develop detailed metrics to understand the linkages between employee value, customer value and shareholder value and how they contribute to corporate success.

Establishing a CRM performance monitoring system

As a company gains a good understanding of existing CRM standards, as well as CRM metrics and models in general use, it should also be considering its own requirements. This involves determining the key CRM standards, metrics and KPIs needed for its own specific business and putting a CRM performance monitoring system in place.

CRM starts with the strategy development process. A key aspect in this process is agreement on the high-level goals and strategy of the business. This can then lead to the development of a strategy map or a success map that captures the performance model underlying the business strategy.

Developing strategy maps and success maps

Experts in performance measurement have identified a significant barrier to improved measurement: the need for senior management to agree on the business performance model for their firm *before* a comprehensive system of performance measurement can be developed.

A number of authors have pointed out the benefits of developing 'strategy maps' or 'success maps'. A success map provides a graphic outline of the highest-level goals the organisation is striving to achieve and the current progress status. By juxtaposing the proposed end goal and the existing position, it is possible to identify the metrics necessary to ensure that the goal is achieved successfully. This process can be used to distil a wide range of measures down to those that matter most.

Kaplan and Norton have developed one of the best-known versions. Their *strategy map* involves identifying a chain of 'cause and effect' logic that connects the company's strategy with the drivers that lead to commercial success. It incorporates each of the four perspectives of the balanced scorecard.[25] Andy Neely and his colleagues have developed an extension of the strategy map, the *success map*, to emphasise the need for a broader perspective on stakeholders and a resolute emphasis on end goals.[26]

These mapping techniques can be extremely helpful in determining the most appropriate metrics and KPIs for monitoring CRM performance at any given time. Success maps may be complex or relatively simple.

Sears developed their initial performance model utilising data from over 800 stores.[27] It used 20 customer measures, 25 employee measures and 19 financial performance indicators by store (these included measures of productivity, revenues, margins, payroll costs, number of transactions, etc.). Although the approach to measurement used by Sears involves many individual customer, employee and financial measures, these can be summarised in a relatively simple success map based on Sears' three key strategic objectives – to become:

- a compelling place to shop at,
- a compelling place to work at,
- a compelling place to invest in.

Sears attached to each of these strategic imperatives (aimed at the three main stakeholder groups: customers, employees and shareholders) a set of high-level metrics which, when agreed, became the KPIs (see Case 10.1). A simplified summary of the Sears' success map is shown in Figure 10.7.

Strategic Imperatives:	Metrics:
▸ Compelling place to shop	• meeting customer needs • creating customer satisfaction • retaining customers
▸ Compelling place to work	• achieving personal growth and development • empowered teams
▸ Compelling place to invest	• return on assets • sales growth • sales per square foot • operating income margin • inventory turnover

Figure 10.7 Simplified success map for Sears, Roebuck

A further example of a success map is shown in Figure 10.8.[28] In this case, it is based on insights from the balanced scorecard and uses the financial, customer, internal and learning perspectives.

This approach provides the business logic for understanding the explicit levers that top executives need to manage and monitor for success.

Development of metrics, KPIs and dashboards for the business

From an examination of the success map and the lists of metrics above, the most relevant KPIs for the business can be identified and used to develop a monitoring system. Wherever feasible, metrics and KPIs should be consistent across the functions, business units and territories of the business. While existing measures may be available in many areas of the business, it is essential that these are complemented by new KPIs and standards that thoroughly assess the relationship with the enterprise's customers and other relevant stakeholders, and which enable benchmarking of operational efficiency against competitors and other appropriate organisations. Self-assessment, benchmarking and comparisons with external standards such as QCi and COPC are useful to gain this broader perspective.

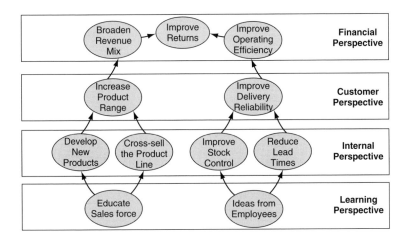

Figure 10.8 Success map based on the balanced scorecard.
Source: Based on Neely (2002)

One approach to metrics endorsed by a number of CRM senior executives is to get a broad picture of overall CRM activity but then to focus down in a much more detailed way on the most critical areas for the company. As one financial services executive said: 'I want to have a micro view of how we are doing compared to our competition across the full gamut of CRM; but I also need a summary dashboard of the really important KPIs that I need to focus on.' This is a pragmatic solution as it addresses the need to have an enterprise-wide view of CRM and to focus on the key performance areas to achieve targets in terms of profits and shareholder value. Once the relevant metrics have been identified, it is important that these are communicated clearly and in a visually engaging manner to management.

The example of a CRM scorecard visualisation, or dashboard, shown in Figure 10.9 demonstrates how a graphic depiction of CRM status can be a powerful tool in communicating progress against goals on the basis of those CRM KPIs considered most important. In this example, key higher-level CRM metrics for a telecommunications and cable TV company are reported, including customer acquisition, customer retention and customer value. Further 'drill-down' facilities into more detailed subsidiary metrics are available, as indicated by the magnifying glass symbol.

Other formats can also be used. One performance monitoring system used by companies such as GE involves developing a strategic 'route map', which gives the overall direction to be followed, together with a metrics 'dashboard' that reports the key performance measures, often using a 'traffic-light' colour scheme of green, yellow and red to indicate whether each key metric is on target or otherwise.

Several CRM vendors and consulting firms have developed sophisticated dashboards. Salesforce.com, a global enterprise software company headquartered in San Francisco, has developed one of the most advanced set of interrelated dashboards. These include:

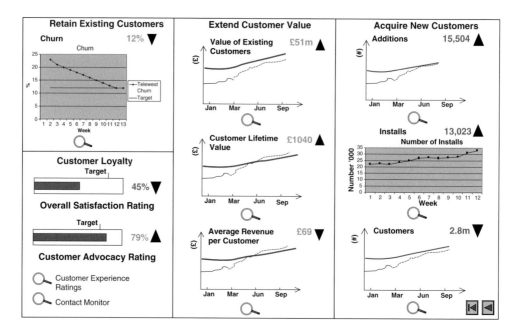

Figure 10.9 Example of a CRM dashboard.
Source: Based on Neely et al. (2002)

Sales & marketing dashboards

- Marketing Executive Dashboard
- Sales Executive Dashboard
- Sales Manager Dashboard
- Sales Representative/Salesperson Dashboard

Customer service dashboards

- Agent Supervisor Overview Dashboard
- Service Executive Overview Dashboard
- Service KPIs Dashboard.

Figure 10.10 shows an example of a Marketing Executive Dashboard. Some of the bottom sections of this and the following dashboard are truncated slightly in the interests of readability.

The *Marketing Executive Dashboard* is for marketing executives, such as marketing directors and marketing vice presidents. Their aim is to get a high-level understanding of how effective the enterprise's marketing activities are. Such executives can use this dashboard for assessing overall performance and developing specific activities such as creating efficient campaigns and generating and converting leads.

The *Sales Executive Dashboard* provides information on how the organisation is performing in terms of its total sales activities. Thus, this form of dashboard aims at providing a picture of performance for executives such as sales director or vice president of sales.

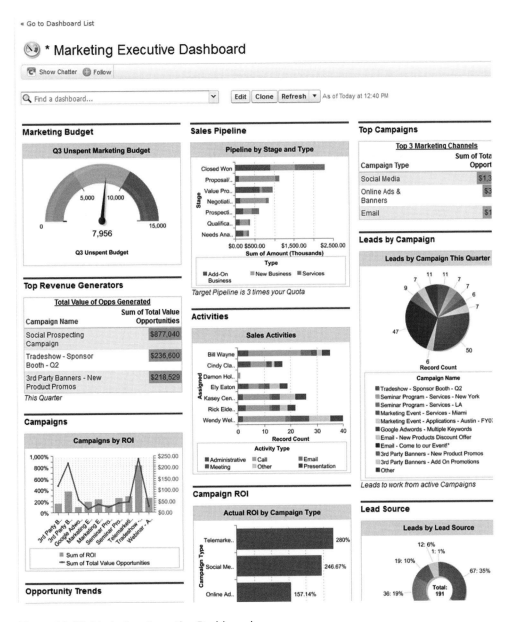

Figure 10.10 Marketing Executive Dashboard.
Source: © salesforce.com, inc., used with permission

At the level below this, the *Sales Manager Dashboard* provides information for sales managers to identify how their team is performing each month. An example of this form of dashboard is given in Figure 10.11.

At the level below the sales manager's dashboard, is the *Sales Representative's Dashboard*. This dashboard enables the sales manager to keep track of his or her sales pipeline and have an up-to-date opportunity analysis immediately available. Details of sales quotas

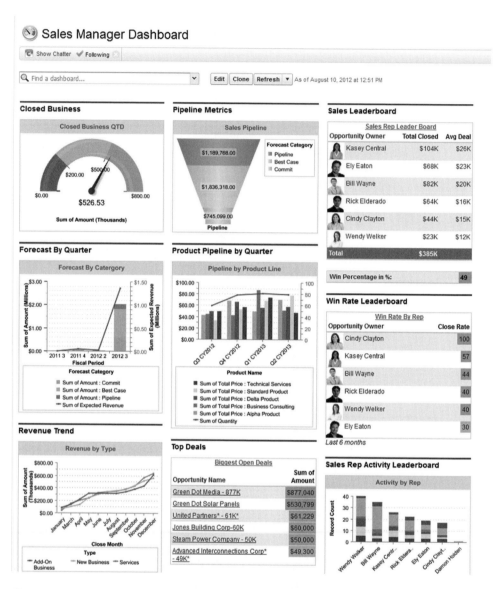

Figure 10.11 Sales Manager Dashboard.
Source: © salesforce.com, inc., used with permission

versus performance to date are visually portrayed. An example of this form of dashboard is given in Figure 10.12.

Salesforce.com's other dashboards include Customer Service Dashboards, which make it easy for people in different service and support roles to keep track of customer cases for their organisation and for their agents, and enable trends and key performance indicators to be measured. Such dashboards enable service executives to gain visibility into their day-to-day operations, including identifying areas that need attention and the extent to which the enterprise is meeting its service goals. Importantly, they also provide

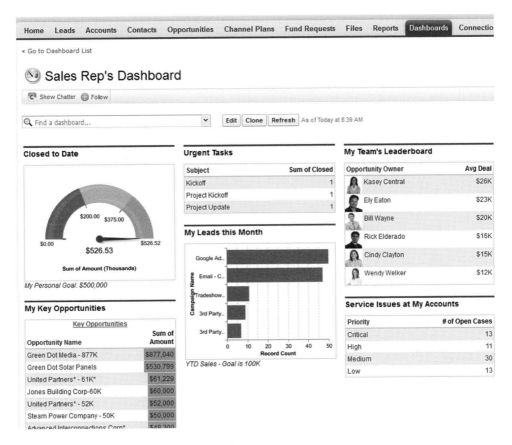

Figure 10.12 Sales Representative's Dashboard.
Source: © salesforce.com, inc., used with permission

information on potential 'at risk' accounts which can be forwarded to the appropriate members of the marketing and sales teams.

It is said that a picture counts more than a thousand words. The representation of the key marketing, sales and CRM data in a highly visible form in dashboards substantially assists executives' understanding of detailed and potentially complex data. The topic of CRM and marketing dashboards is receiving substantial interest from both practitioners and academics, as recent books by Eckerson[29] and Kerzner[30] and a Marketing Science Institute paper by Pauwels and his colleagues[31] demonstrate. The Multinational Software Company case study at the end of this chapter provides a description of how a large multinational developed a marketing dashboard.

Evaluating and communicating CRM return on investment

In addition to defining and applying the right standards, metrics and KPIs, an effective CRM performance monitoring system must be capable of measuring and communicating the return on investment (ROI). Because CRM places considerable emphasis on the use of

IT in managing customer relationships, it is a potentially costly management option, in terms of both required IT expenditure and inherent adjustments to internal infrastructure and existing systems. Given the number of reported CRM failures, the business case for investing in CRM should therefore address the following questions:

- Is an investment in improving CRM likely to lead to improved business performance?
- How can investments in CRM be measured?

Relating CRM performance to business performance

Although common sense would suggest that successful CRM performance should lead to improved business results, decisions to invest in CRM must be soundly justified. Companies that have used success maps to link a range of key CRM metrics to financial and shareholder results, such as those used by Sears, support the view that well-based CRM initiatives are worth the often considerable investment that is involved.

A QCi study showed that CRM performance (as measured by CMAT) correlates strongly with business performance. This study examined data from 21 companies (12 of these were from financial services, two from utilities, two from distribution, three from manufacturing and two from other sectors). A panel of independent experts assessed the business performance of each organisation against a broad range of measures such as sales growth, profitability and asset growth. The assessors did not know how well each organisation had performed in its CMAT assessment. The ranking of the organisation's business performance was then compared to its ranking in terms of CMAT score. Figure 10.13 shows the results of the study in terms of CRM performance (measured by the CMAT score) and business performance.[32]

This research supports the view that CRM performance is related to overall business performance and concludes that the most important factors are:

- people and leadership;
- measurement and deployment processes to achieve results; and
- implementing appropriate CRM practices such as targeting high lifetime value customers.

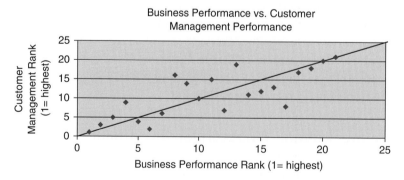

Figure 10.13 Comparison of CRM performance to business performance.
Source: © QCi Assessment Ltd., used with permission

Despite a relatively small sample, these findings are encouraging and reinforce what experienced practitioners and knowledgeable consultants already know: attention to the 'people' element, implementation of customer-oriented practices, and proper measurement systems constitute the critical success factors (CSFs) for CRM. However, given the incidence of CRM problems, further research is needed in this area.

Measuring CRM return on investment and links between CRM and performance

A further issue of concern is measuring the return on CRM initiatives. A Cranfield University Research Report[33] examined how companies measure the payback on their investment in CRM projects and found that the following four criteria are typically used when evaluating the success of investments in CRM activities. These criteria carry advantages and disadvantages.

1. *Improvements in customer service, satisfaction and retention:* These metrics are of greatest value when specifically linked to approaches that show their impact on profit and shareholder value. We have noted earlier that retention of the best customers has a critical impact on profitability.
2. *Return on investment on the CRM systems adopted:* Measuring ROI on CRM systems is beneficial where there are specific investments in certain CRM applications, such as sales force automation (SFA) or campaign management systems which can be directly linked to customer metrics, or where there are identifiable efficiencies or cost reductions. However, it is important to ensure customer satisfaction is not adversely affected as a result of introducing such systems.
3. *Changes in overall company performance:* Changes in overall company performance as a result of investment in CRM may be difficult to evaluate as it can often be hard to tell what would have happened without the CRM investment. Performance improvements, for example, could be the result of many factors such as decreased promotional activities by competitors.
4. *Increases in customer and segment profitability:* Measuring increases in the profitability of customers and customer segments and understanding how this ultimately impacts on shareholder value is an area of growing interest. It involves a consideration of both current and future profit impact potential. Hence, estimates of potential customer lifetime value need to be calculated alongside existing customer lifetime value.

ROI measurement is an important element of CRM. As stressed throughout this chapter, CRM performance assessment should be viewed in the context of a strategic approach to CRM. The typical criteria for measuring CRM ROI listed above clearly embrace this company-wide view of CRM.

However, as noted earlier, introduction of CRM to an enterprise does not automatically result in improved performance. Academic research confirms that studies of the relationship between CRM and corporate performance are mixed. A review undertaken in 2010 by Reimann and his colleagues[34] identified that several prior studies report positive relationships, others do not identify any significant links and two studies report negative relationships. These authors found, however, that business strategies of differentiation and cost leadership (discussed previously in Chapter 6), positively mediate the performance effect of CRM. In other words, while CRM does not affect performance outcomes directly, its indirect effect through the business strategies of differentiation and cost leadership are significant.

A further study by Holger and his colleagues in 2011[35] showed that CRM has primarily been investigated only in the context of existing product portfolios. These authors stress the importance of viewing CRM as a dynamic concept in which the understanding and management of value creation *in the future* is critical for achieving long-term market success. Following an empirical study of 200 German companies, they concluded that linking CRM to new product development is crucial in improving an enterprise's performance. They concluded that firms failing to make this linkage may end up satisfying existing customers, but are likely to miss future business opportunities. Earlier work by Boulding and his colleagues[36] discuss how Xerox, an award-winning CRM pioneer, was consistently ranked high in terms of customer satisfaction. Its CRM activities were focused on its existing products and the company failed to recognise the importance of developing new technologies and products. This ultimately led to poor market performance. Thus, new product performance also has a mediating role in improving enterprise performance.

SUMMARY

The performance measurement systems adopted by organisations in the past have tended to be functionally driven. Thus, financial measures were mainly the concern of the Board and the finance department, marketing measures the domain of the marketing department and people measures the responsibility of the HR department. Such a functional separation of performance measures is inappropriate for CRM, which, as we have constantly stressed throughout this book, involves a cross-functional and holistic management approach.

The performance assessment process in the CRM Strategy Framework involves an evaluation of the success of CRM activities in order that gaps in performance can be identified and improvements made. It is this process which ensures that the organisation's strategic aims in terms of customer relationship management are being delivered to an appropriate and acceptable standard. The key actions involve understanding the drivers of shareholder value, identifying the appropriate metrics and standards against which the various CRM activities can be measured, establishing an effective monitoring system to apply these measures on an ongoing basis and communicating and acting on resultant learning.

A number of approaches are open to organisations seeking to establish CRM metrics and KPIs for measuring, monitoring and benchmarking their CRM performance. They include use of external benchmarks such as the QCi and COPC standards and measuring and monitoring performance using tools such as the balanced scorecard and linkage models. However, in order to improve the performance of its CRM activities, a company must develop its own composite set of measures based on its own success maps. Such efforts to develop individually tailored and relevant performance assessment processes are critical, given the high incidence of reported CRM failure and the impressive returns for those who achieve CRM success.

This chapter concludes Part III of the book, which covers each of the key processes in the CRM Strategy Framework. However, developing an effective customer management strategy does not conclude with the performance assessment process – the last of these processes. In the final chapter that forms Part IV of this book, we address implementation. We review the readiness of the organisation to engage in strategic activities and also key issues of change management, project management and employee engagement that play such a crucial role in achieving relationship marketing and CRM success.

CASE 10.1: Sears – the service profit chain and the Kmart merger

The company

Sears, Roebuck and Company has been a leading US retailer for over 100 years. A household name, Americans associate it with value and quality. When Sears was founded in the late 1800s, there were only 38 states in the US and most of its product deliveries were horse drawn. In the ensuing decades, the company progressively refined its business processes and systems. However, during the last 20 years Sears has had to fight hard to overcome the difficulties inherent in a mature market, to combat adverse trading conditions and to compete with Walmart, a much larger competitor. Sears realised that its familiar ways of doing business were no longer enough to keep ahead of competitors

The challenge

In 1992 Sears, Roebuck and Company reported massive losses of $3.9 billion on sales of $52.3 billion. This was the worst trading year in the company's history. This resulted from various trends, most of them directly related to the company's lack of focus. During the 1980s, Sears had diversified into other markets such as insurance, financial services, brokerage and real estate. At the same time other retailers, such as Walmart, were focusing on the retail consumer and were taking market share away from Sears.

Sears needed to refocus on its core business and to develop a performance model that would help drive a return to profitability. This ultimately led to it merging with Kmart in 2004 to form Sears Holdings. This case focuses on one of the best illustrations of the application of the service profit chain concept to improve corporate performance. Following a discussion of this initiative, the case traces the fortunes of Sears to the present time.

The solution

A new CEO, Arthur Martinez, was appointed in 1992 to head the merchandise group and he undertook a streamlining of the business. He closed 113 stores and terminated the 101 year old Sears catalogue, which was a household institution within the US. He also set about changing the service strategy, focusing on women, who were the most important buying decision makers.

Martinez set up four task forces (customers, employees, financial performance and innovation) to define world-class status in each specific area, identify obstacles and define metrics for measuring progress. The task forces spent months listening to customers and employees, observing best practice in other organisations and establishing measures against objectives. Gradually it became apparent that what was needed was a model to show *direct causation* from employee attitudes, through customer satisfaction to profits. The company needed to know how management actions, such as investment in sales force training, would directly translate into improved customer satisfaction, retention and higher revenues. What was needed was an operationalisation of what they termed *the employee-customer-profit chain*. The revised model of this is shown in Figure 1 below.

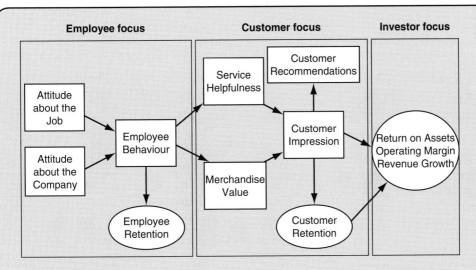

Figure 1 The revised employee-customer-profit chain at Sears.
Source: based on data from Sears, Roebuck and Co.

Sears defined a set of measures based on its key objectives. These were broken down into three objectives which focused on making Sears – 'a compelling place to *work* at, to *shop* at and to *invest* in'. This represented a focus on three value domains: employees, customers and shareholders. Relationships between changes in key metrics were identified using causal pathway modelling. The econometric modelling of the relationships was undertaken by CFI Group.

Sears' enterprise performance model was built using data from over 800 stores. It used 20 customer measures, 25 employee measures and 19 financial performance indicators by store (these included measures of productivity, revenues, margins, payroll costs, number of transactions, etc.).

The results

The results of this performance work were impressive. Direct causal links were identified between employee measures, customer measures and revenues, so total profit indicators for the company could be established. Employee attitudes towards the job and company were found to be critical to employee loyalty and behaviour towards customers, while customer impression directly affected customer retention and the likelihood of recommendations. After further refinement, the model was used as a predictor of revenue growth: a 5 unit increase in employee attitude drives a 1.3 unit increase in customer impression, a 0.5 increase in revenue growth and a quantifiable increase in store profitability.

To implement the service profit chain model successfully it was necessary for Sears to change the behaviour of its senior managers and encourage them to take responsibility for the company's culture and understand how this impacted on revenues. In addition, employee rewards needed to be aligned to the model for financial and non-financial measures.

Later, a further change was made by streamlining Sears' CRM systems. Some 18 separate legacy databases were transformed into an integrated data warehouse, as shown in Figure 2 below.

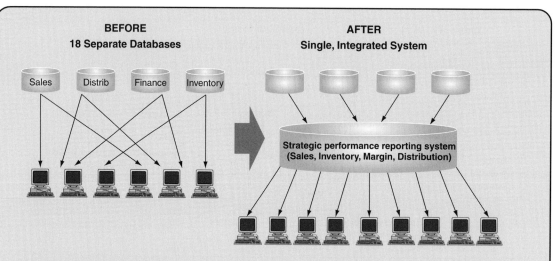

Figure 2 The IT transformation at Sears.
Source: Ron Swift, formerly of Teradata

As a result, in 1993 the company reported a net income of $752 million – a dramatic reversal of fortunes for a mature company such as Sears. In the period following the implementation of the enterprise performance model, employee satisfaction at Sears rose by 4 per cent and customer satisfaction by almost 4 per cent. More than $200 million additional revenues were achieved through this value creation process.

Figure 3 shows the relative performance improvement on selected measures including profitability, customer satisfaction and associate (their term for employees) attitudes between 1992 and 1998.

Confidence in the data was such that Sears computed 30 per cent to 70 per cent of its executive compensation from these measures. Sears delivered earnings of $1.3 billion in 1997. In terms of shareholder value, the total return to investors between September 1992 and April 1997 was 298 per cent. This was a remarkable improvement for a firm in such a mature business. Sears now uses this measurement system to improve future revenues and profits.

Ongoing performance

By 1998 a new challenge had emerged, the lack of sales momentum. Sears was in a difficult and highly competitive sector. To address these challenges, the company needed a fresh approach to managing its relationships with customers. In 1999 President and CEO Arthur Martinez said: 'Now, what we need is renewed energy. We need what I'm calling a Second Revolution – a second revolution and our marketing communications to our customer to send a stronger message about who we are and what our value proposition is.' Sears responded with a new reorganisation, a major new marketing campaign and other initiatives. Martinez was also a driving force behind e-commerce activities at Sears. These began in 1996 with the launch of Sears.com, and by 1999 it was rated by Nielsen as the fourth fastest growing shopping site. In 2000 it was relaunched with enhanced capabilities.

Alan J. Lacy, the former president of services, took over as CEO in late 2000. His appointment followed him taking the ailing Sears credit card operation in the late 1990s and turning it into a money

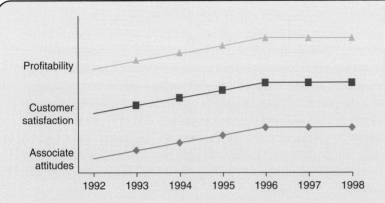

Figure 3 Sears, Roebuck – selected performance measures, 1992–1998.
Source: Based on data from Sears, Roebuck and Co.

machine that accounted for 55 per cent of the retailer's profits. Financial analysts agreed that the retail giant needed to continue focusing on a growth strategy to overcome the difficulties of this troubled sector. This led to the purchase of Lands' End in 2002 through a $1.86 billion cash transaction. With Lands' End being the largest mail order and Internet specialty apparel retailer, Sears gained a successful leading clothing brand, which it had previously lacked.

In late 2004, Kmart announced it would buy Sears for $11 billion to form Sears Holdings Corporation. This united the two retailers in an effort to survive against giant rivals like Walmart, which passed both companies in the 1990s on its way to becoming the nation's largest retailer. The takeover was initially considered a success for Kmart's largest shareholder, Edward S. Lampert, a billionaire investor who pushed Kmart to emerge from bankruptcy, shut many stores and sold dozens of others to Sears as he presided over a run-up in Kmart's value on Wall Street.

The global financial crisis which commenced in 2008 led to lots of empty retail space. Lack of consumer demand resulted in funds not being invested in updating stores to lure shoppers back. By 2009, five years after the merger, Sears Holdings' sales were markedly worse than its competitors'. In a response to engage customers, Sears emphasised online shopping, mobile apps and an Amazon.com-like marketplace with other vendors, along with heavy promotions in stores. They have been involved in using social media since 2009. Its online community now boasts more than 300,000 users. They have developed online customer communities that include MySears.com, MyKmart.com, and MyVoice.com for the MyGopher concept – a trial online service that offers a range of quality products including supermarket food, prescriptions, health and beauty products and electronics. Sears is also using social media extensively in its fitness division, 'Fitstudio'. A small number of initial fans on Facebook have grown to a community of over 75,000 members.

In 2011 Lampert announced the appointment of Lou D'Ambrosio, a former IBM executive and CEO of telecom equipment company Avaya, as the company's new CEO. D'Ambrosio's lack of experience with retail operations makes it seem like Lampert is looking to reconsider the retailer's business model. That model is likely to focus on further cutting down the cost of doing business and, whenever possible, subleasing unprofitable stores to other retailers. Later in 2011, Sears announced that it was going to open up its 3,800 retail properties to other retailers. This could include smaller outlets on the property, in-store kiosks and a retail presence next to a Sears or Kmart store.

The wisdom of having a hedge fund manager in charge of Sears and then having the company run by a CEO without deep retail experience has been questioned by analysts. However, despite its recent poor performance, the Sears chain has several strong assets, including a well-known brand name and several highly respected consumer brands, including Craftsman tools, Kenmore appliances and the Lands' End clothing line. Sears has been around for some 125 years and has seen many transitions.

Sears is still investing a lot of money into becoming a leading online retailer, but many observers believe that monetising their properties and building their brands outside of their retail stores is their best hope. Real estate transactions may help Sears with cash generation to buy back outstanding shares and become a private company. Regardless of the future ownership structure, central to Sears' success as a business will be performance measuring and management of critical relationships with employees, customer and shareholders.

CASE 10.2: The Multinational Software Company – driving results with a metrics dashboard

The company

A $5-billion US-based multinational software company had experienced rapid growth through a series of software innovations and several large acquisitions. Business units serving the enterprise, small and medium business and consumer markets became all part of a single company. Product lines had expanded from a few to several dozen. Acquisitions had brought a mélange of marketing processes and cultural pre-dispositions. Geographic expansion had complicated the situation with language barriers and significant channel complexities.

The challenge

The marketing organisation was spending significant amounts of money just meeting the many demands for support on a strategic business unit (SBU)/product/regional level. But they too had been cobbled together from a variety of cultures and experiential backgrounds, with no common understanding of resource allocation process and no definitions or targets for marketing effectiveness or efficiency. The Chief Marketing Officer (CMO) was increasingly frustrated trying to define opportunities and threats from the hundreds of ad hoc reports and dozens of 'metrics' being tossed about in Excel and PowerPoint files by factional silos within the marketing organisation. More importantly, the CMO couldn't adequately answer the questions of the CEO and Chief Finance Officer (CFO) about the value of maintaining or increasing the present rate of marketing expenditures. This was creating significant conflicts between marketing and sales for access to discretionary dollars. The conflicts were fuelled by altruistic but highly subjective interpretations of what would be best for the business.

The solution

A common marketing dashboard was proposed to unify the marketing organisation behind a select set of prioritised metrics and a disciplined process for producing and interpreting them.

The process began with in-depth discussions with key executive stakeholders in marketing, sales, finance, and the SBUs, regarding their perceptions of the role of marketing in helping the organisation achieve its stated business goals. Differences in perspectives were rationalised through a series of facilitated sessions, ultimately arriving at a clear definition of the specific and prioritised roles marketing was being assigned. A number of highly specific roles were identified, including: generation of qualified sales leads; development of the brand asset to assure pricing power; identification of market trends and possible product/service innovation opportunities; and increases in customer value amongst key market segments. These marketing roles were incorporated into a strategy map (based on Kaplan and Norton's balanced scorecard concept) alongside those of sales, R&D and the SBUs. The strategy map was then debated, modified and approved by the Executive Committee.

Working from the consensus on the role of marketing, a broader group of senior and middle managers from the four functional areas was interviewed to identify a superset of the possible metrics for measuring the performance of marketing vis-à-vis its responsibilities. This superset of 100+ possible metrics was evaluated by a cross-functional steering committee and an outside consultant against the criteria of comprehensiveness, reliability of data streams, diagnostic insight, predictive insight and credibility. Importantly, ease of implementation was deliberately *not* a factor considered at this stage so as to avoid a tendency towards an availability bias in metric selection.

With an objective of ultimately limiting the critical metrics to approximately ten, the steering committee realised that it could not reduce the number below 25 at the present time due to lack of clarity and understanding of which metrics would offer the most valuable insights. So the 25 metrics were arranged in logical groups, one group to a 'page', and the dashboard was designed to be a collection of seven pages, each telling part of the story of marketing effectiveness/efficiency. One page, for example, tracked the flow of qualified leads in relationship to marketing expenditures by product and by region. Another evaluated the changes in the size and effectiveness of the distribution partner channels. And a third focused on the changes to customer value by segment and geography. The screens in this dashboard were similar to the screenshot shown in Figure 1.

Once the steering committee (a cross-functional group including marketing, sales and finance) agreed on the final dashboard structure, a work team was assembled to build the necessary data collection, validation and transformation processes. A Web-based dashboard management platform was licensed to provide a simple point-and-click means of comparing metrics side-by-side and moving fluidly between products, segments and geographies. Implementation was staged in quarterly 'releases' where additional metrics were added until the full 25 metrics were deployed. Data were refreshed monthly.

The CMO then structured monthly conference calls and quarterly marketing resource reviews around the information flowing through the dashboard. Each marketing manager requesting re-sources was required to support their request using facts derived from the dashboard. In addition, the CMO met regularly with the CFO and Executive Vice President Sales to review dashboard summaries, discuss the implications, and agree on appropriate action steps.

The first iteration of the dashboard quickly morphed into a second, and subsequently a third. Each successive version was tuned to modify some of the metrics for increased relevancy, while dropping

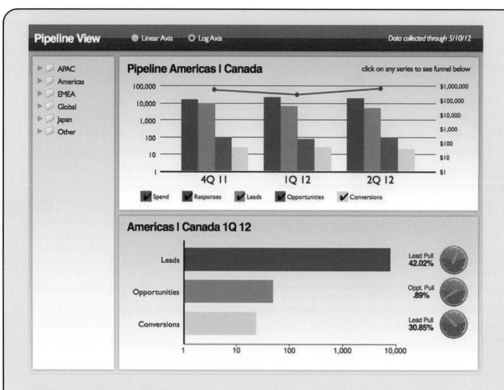

Figure 1 Dashboard illustration.
Source: Dashboard image courtesy of www.MarketingNPV.com

some completely as they were found to be of little value. For every three dropped, two were added (often completely new ideas not included in the original superset) in a continual search for the most insightful set of metrics. The process was controlled by the steering committee.

The results

The entire global marketing organisation has now developed:

- A common lexicon for marketing performance measurement and resource allocation;
- A shared definition of what is important and how it relates to their individual responsibilities;
- A framework for resolving differences of subjective interpretation; and
- A clearer understanding of what effective and efficient resource allocation means.

Overall, the dashboard was the tangible manifestation of a significant effort to align expectations and definitions both across and within functions. It has become the centrepiece of a continuous improvement process for improving the effective and efficient allocation of marketing resources.

This case study was written by Pat LaPointe, Managing Partner of consulting firm MarketingNPV. It is reproduced with his kind permission.

Part IV

Strategic customer management implementation

11 | Organising for implementation

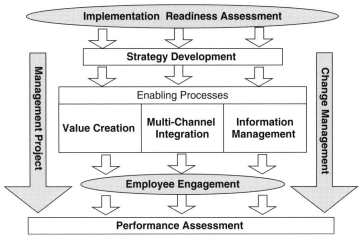

Key elements in organising for implementation

In the previous chapters we examined relationship marketing and CRM in some detail. Chapter 1 provides an overview of the book, Chapters 2 to 5 explain the key concepts in relationship marketing and Chapters 6 to 10 review the key processes in CRM. In this final chapter we examine the key issues involved in organising for implementation of a strategic approach to customer management. As the previous discussion and case studies throughout the book illustrate, the effective management of customer relationships involves many different and interlinked aspects. Understanding these factors and their implications is critical to the success of any initiative. However, simply thinking through the processes of CRM is not enough to ensure an initiative is successfully implemented. The enterprise has to *organise* to deliver results from their customer management initiatives.

Relationship marketing and CRM in context

At the start of this book we highlighted the confusion in both academic literature and managerial practice regarding the terms used to describe the management of customers. In particular, the terms relationship marketing and CRM are often used interchangeably.[1] In Chapter 1 we discussed the conceptual differences between the terms CRM, relationship marketing and customer management, defined these terms and highlighted the key differences between them – proposing that these three terms collectively represent the domain of *strategic customer management*.[2]

Shukla illustrates there are several fundamental principles that are common to both relationship marketing and CRM:

The first is an emphasis on customer retention and extending the 'customer lifetime value' . . . of customers through strategies that focused on retaining targeted customers. The second is a recognition that companies need to develop relationships with a number of stakeholders, or 'market domains', if they are to achieve long-term success in the marketplace. The third common feature is that both are seen as a pan-company or cross-functional responsibility and not solely the concern of the marketing department. The fourth is that both relationship marketing and CRM strive for value maximisation . . . Furthermore, both CRM and relationship marketing focus on the marketing interaction of multiple players in the markets . . . From the above discussion it can be observed that relationship marketing theories and concepts aid the CRM effort and, in turn, CRM provides empirical validity and reliability to relationship marketing.[3]

As Egan points out, relationship marketing should be regarded 'as a general "umbrella philosophy" with numerous relational variations, rather than a wholly unified concept with strongly developed objectives and strategies'.[4] Mitussis, O'Malley and Patterson suggest: 'It is therefore time to truly re-engage with the fundamental axioms of relationship marketing and to reassess the ability of CRM technologies to operationalise relational ideals.' They point to the necessity for CRM to focus on 'the processes of engagement, which are themselves the desired outcomes of relationships' and point out that CRM implementation may result in failure, if the holistic vision that is at the core of relationship marketing is not embraced.[5]

This book addresses these latter authors' concerns that CRM literature and practice do not properly engage with the philosophy of relationship marketing. The lack of clarity and definition of CRM has created confusion and its association with technology, rather than customer relationships, has had a negative impact – as evidenced by the high failure rates of CRM. Our approach to CRM embraces the relationship marketing philosophy and takes into account the impact of the full extent of relational exchanges in which enterprises are involved. Thus, CRM represents a renewed perspective on managing customer relationships, based on relationship marketing principles, in an era of unprecedented technological innovation, market transformation and social interaction.

Gummesson observes that CRM emphasises the values and strategies of relationship marketing – 'with a particular emphasis on the relationship between a customer and supplier – turned into practical application and dependent on both human action and information technology'.[6] He pithily points out that 'RM [relationship marketing] is an attitude and CRM is a tool.'[7] This chapter focuses on organising for implementation with a particular emphasis on CRM. It emphasises the philosophy of relationship marketing within the context of CRM implementation activities. CRM is seen by many practitioners and academics as the solution to the implementation of relational strategies.[8]

In this chapter we focus on the customer market domain. Elsewhere in the book we address relationships with the other market domains. In Chapter 2 we introduced the concept of the relationship management chain, a planning framework that takes into account both customer and non-customer market domains, and we also discussed how attention needs to be selectively directed at non-customer market domains through the development of well-documented marketing planning procedures. In Chapter 4 we provided a framework for identifying the appropriate emphasis to be directed at the broader set of stakeholder relationships within relationship marketing.

CRM implementation

Use of CRM by enterprises is now substantial. Bain & Co.'s 2011 survey of 1,230 executives identifies a projected usage rate of CRM by 82 per cent of respondent enterprises.[9] However, despite the heavy investment in CRM, there is a concern regarding the likelihood of success in CRM implementation. On the one hand, Krigsman identifies eight studies of CRM undertaken between 2001 and 2009 that report failure rates of between 18 and 69 per cent.[10] On the other hand, corporate websites abound with case studies of successful CRM[11] and those CRM implementations that are successful provide strong evidence of the benefits that can be delivered by CRM.[12] This raises the question of what research has been conducted on CRM implementation.[13] We address this question before we turn to the topic of organising for implementation.

Some substantive studies relating to CRM implementation have recently started to appear in the academic literature.[14] However, the majority of the literature on CRM implementation is practitioner-oriented. These practitioner publications suffer from several problems: CRM is usually not rigorously defined; there is inconsistency in what constitutes CRM success; and much of the discussion appears to be based on anecdotal evidence or consultant experience, rather than being based on rigorous empirical research. A recent review of the academic literature on the impact of CRM on firm performance by Reimann and his colleagues[15] reviewed eight earlier studies and found inconclusive results. While several studies found positive relationships, others identified insignificant links and two studies reported negative relationships between CRM and firm performance. The disparate findings on CRM success suggest a critical need for future work to be undertaken in this area.

We now provide an overview of some key findings from academic research on CRM implementation that support the approach taken in this book. At the outset of adopting CRM, the strategic goals for CRM need to be determined and linked to the business strategy.[16] CRM involves continuous learning where information about individual customers is transformed into a customer relationship.[17] All key functional managers should understand the requirements and benefits of CRM, not just marketing managers who may be more involved with CRM implementation.[18] The belief that CRM affects only customer-facing processes often makes executives overlook the need for changing the internal structures and systems before investing in CRM technology. Finnegan and Currie point to the importance of developing an appropriate culture for CRM which is both customer-centric and willing to learn and change as a result of experience with CRM.[19] King and Burgess found that CRM implementation involved complex changes to interrelated processes. For example, unwillingness to share data between departments led to problems with systems integration and weakened front-line employees' ability to deliver customer service.[20] Eid found that top management should be personally knowledgeable about the business case for CRM and involved in leading the internal marketing effort to support organisational change.[21] Leaders need to understand the role of CRM in enhancing the strategic capability of an organisation.[22] Changing an organisation and the people within it can be essential to the success of CRM but it is probably the most difficult issue to resolve.[23] Change is often necessary as the majority of organisations are structured around products, not customer needs. This brief summary points to the necessity of organisations carefully organising for the implementation of their strategic customer management initiatives.

Organising for implementation

The navigation diagram at the start of this chapter shows the key CRM processes, which are addressed in the preceding five chapters, in the context of organising for implementation. In this diagram, these processes are positioned relative to four critical elements for successful implementation: implementation readiness assessment; change management; project management and employee engagement. This figure provides an organising framework and illustrates the broad stages of progression in implementation. However, the framework is recursive, rather than linear, in that its many activities need to be managed concurrently and some elements will need to be revisited as a consequence of later activities. Organising for implementation involves systematically and interactively addressing each of these four elements as they relate to the five key CRM processes.[24]

Before a CRM strategy is developed, it is important to first assess whether the organisation is really ready and willing to implement customer-focused strategies and initiatives. CRM is not an appropriate strategy for a company to adopt if it does not have the leadership of the enterprise engaged in supporting CRM and a Board-level sponsor – ideally the CEO – committed to its success. Thus, the cultural and leadership implications of implementation must be fully understood if CRM is to have a chance of contributing to business improvement. We now consider how the elements of implementation readiness assessment, change management, project management and employee engagement come together to support the enterprise's implementation of its CRM strategy. We start by considering the implementation readiness assessment which helps the business leaders and CRM sponsors assess the enterprise's overall position in terms of readiness to progress with CRM initiatives, and to identify how well developed their organisation is relative to other companies.

Implementation readiness assessment

In an assessment of implementation readiness two tasks should be undertaken. First, an assessment should be made of the enterprise's overall CRM maturity relative to other companies that have embarked on the CRM journey. Also, any barriers to success should be identified. This will provide managers with a perspective on the enterprise's current situation and help it benchmark where they are placed relative to other organisations. This is important as it provides the opportunity to assess relative competitive advantage.

Second, a CRM readiness audit will determine both how advanced your company is in its overall readiness to adopt or further develop CRM, and on which of the five processes in the CRM Strategy Framework the enterprise needs to place greatest emphasis. This audit will help the enterprise identify the key areas of importance in terms of CRM performance. Thus, a decision to adopt or enhance an enterprise's CRM activities should be based on understanding:

- its current stage of development and potential barriers to success,
- its overall readiness to adopt CRM, and
- the specific CRM activities that need to be addressed.

An assessment of these elements through a CRM maturity assessment and a CRM readiness audit will assist the organisation in deciding how to organise its activities.

CRM maturity assessment

The emphasis an organisation places on using data to help design and implement customer management strategies is reflected in the organisation's stage of CRM maturity. In Chapter 6 we discussed how each organisation should adopt a level of CRM sophistication appropriate to their competitive environment and their current and future needs. We identified four broad strategic options: product-based selling, customer-based marketing, managed service and support and 'individualised' CRM – the latter requiring collection and analysis of extensive information about customers and the desire and ability to give customers highly individualised service. These options, addressed as part of the strategy development process, now need to be considered in the context of implementation requirements. In particular, the extent of CRM development in other organisations provides a useful benchmark for the enterprise.

Our research has shown that there are identifiable stages of CRM maturity. Each stage represents a level of maturity characterised by the extent to which customer information is used to enhance the customer experience and customer-generated cash flows. However, each stage encompasses issues beyond choice of strategic options. More often than not CRM requires wide-ranging adjustments within the firm, especially where marketing activity needs to shift from a transactional focus to a relationship focus. The kinds of organisational changes needed to embrace CRM can range from a revolution in mindset to a realignment of systems and processes. Special change management, project management and customer engagement activities are usually necessary to minimise disruption and maximise performance. Enterprises that do not take these considerations on board are unlikely to succeed with their implementation initiatives.

To identify an enterprise's experiences and use of CRM, Ryals and Payne undertook a study to investigate the development of CRM in organisations.[25] As their research identified that CRM is generally more advanced in the retail financial services sector than in most other industry sectors, their study focused on this sector. They identified five levels of maturity in CRM development:

1. Pre-CRM planning,
2. Building a data repository,
3. Moderately developed CRM,
4. Well-developed CRM,
5. Highly advanced CRM.

Stage 1: Pre-CRM planning

The first stage involves planning for the introduction of CRM. This is the point at which organisations recognise the importance of CRM; however, they have not yet progressed to a stage where the CRM project has been fully scoped. Enterprises at this stage should particularly consider the implications for their organisation of the four broad strategic options discussed earlier: product-based selling, customer-based marketing, managed service and support and 'individualised' CRM. Companies planning to introduce CRM should undertake a CRM readiness audit – the structure of which is outlined shortly.

Stage 2: Building a data repository

The second stage of CRM is concerned with building an appropriate data repository – often in the form of a data warehouse. As discussed in Chapter 9, building a main data repository involves collecting and reviewing existing data and cleaning and de-duplicating customer records. If the data repository is to be used predominantly for analytical CRM, a data warehouse needs to be built to support the required analytical tasks. If the data repository is to be used primarily to support operational CRM then an operational data store is required. This topic was also discussed in Chapter 9. Where companies need to address analytical and operational CRM, it is likely both forms of data warehouse may be required. Plans for the organisation's data infrastructure are based on the data warehouse. Pilot data warehouses, or smaller data marts, may be built as a preliminary step prior to full implementation.

The key task associated with building a data warehouse is improving customer information and data capture. Because of the data quality issues that emerge as companies begin to collect and centralise their customer data, organisations in the early stages of CRM development may find they have to focus heavily on identifying *who* their customers are. Multiple records for a single customer and missing or out-of-date addresses are common problems. Managers may find gaps, ambiguities and omissions in data that they had previously assumed were complete and accurate. Often, enormous amounts of effort have to be expended in compiling accurate customer information. This typically involves collecting and integrating information from many separate databases and legacy systems. Data integrity needs to be checked carefully. In one bank, a manager described how his organisation was proud of the fact it had date of birth information for most of its customers. However, when the bank reviewed this information it found out that a significant number of customers in the customer database appeared to have been born on 11 November 1911, or 11/11/11. It was later discovered that some of the bank's data entry operators were too embarrassed to ask certain customers their date of birth and, pressured to fill the required data field, they found they could enter any number and the system would accept it. A series of '1's was the most popular choice. Such data integrity problems may require considerable efforts to rectify.

Stage 3: Moderately developed CRM

Organisations which are moderately developed in terms of CRM are those which have typically progressed to a full data warehouse, although it may still be limited to a single business unit rather than being enterprise-wide. They begin to use tools such as sales force automation, call centres and computer-telephony integration and campaign management – what we term tactical customer management in Chapter 1. At this stage, the CRM focus shifts towards data mining and identifying the value that can be extracted from the organisation's existing customer information.

Having gathered and cleaned their data, organisations at this stage turn their attention to the task of customer profitability analysis and segmentation and recognise the need to identify their most profitable customers, to profile them and to find more customers like them. However, few companies at this stage are able to generate fully satisfactory customer profitability analyses. In some cases initial customer profitability analyses challenged received wisdom. For example, one bank found that the most profitable 10 per cent and the least profitable 10 per cent of its customers had purchased almost identical numbers of the bank's products. Clearly, for this bank, their existing strategy of 'sell more products, make more money', was not always appropriate.

Some organisations at this stage change their approach to segmentation as a result of the development of their data warehouse. Previously, segmentation was viewed by them as a way to divide up the total customer base into more or less homogeneous groups. However, it may be difficult to determine which individual customers should go into which segment. After a data warehouse becomes operational, managers are better able to identify their most profitable customers. They can then profile these individuals and focus efforts on acquiring more customers like them. In such cases, the segmentation approach shifts from one using a set of general customer characteristics to one incorporating the level of customer profitability or customer value. Companies at this stage of development may add information gathered from social media sources. Customer brand communities and affinity groups can be more clearly identified through analysis of social media engagement and information from these sources can be used to enhance marketing activity.

Stage 4: Well-developed CRM

'Well-developed' suggests an organisation that is moving towards an enterprise-wide data warehouse, widening its user base and increasing the number of users and further developing front-office tools such as sales force automation and contact centres. Such organisations will be more advanced in e-commerce applications. At this stage the organisation should also consider significantly enriching the contents of the data warehouse with information from social media and other external data sources. In addition to using social media to collect information, the organisation may start to use social media in a more proactive way to engage with customers in whichever social media platforms (e.g., Facebook, Twitter, LinkedIn, etc.) are appropriate.

A key task at this stage is customer prioritisation. Gaining a deeper understanding of profitable customers becomes an important part of CRM activities. Use of increasingly sophisticated segmentation and profiling to do this becomes common. Customer prioritisation also leads to strategies for reducing the cost of serving less profitable customers. Enterprises in this group are more effective at utilising campaign management and fully exploiting the potential of their data warehouses. One insurance company, at this stage of development, contrasted their current highly targeted approach with their previous practice of mailing one-twelfth of their database each month, irrespective of whether the products they were prioritising were relevant to the customers they were mailing.

Stage 5: Highly advanced CRM

Organisations that have reached the highly advanced or 'best-in-class' status are fully integrated, offering extensive data warehouse access within the company across departmental functions. They may use advanced techniques such as neural networks and genetic algorithms to generate more refined data and continually learn from their customer information. They are highly advanced in terms of their market segmentation strategies and understanding of the required level of segment granularity. They routinely use predictive modelling. Because these organisations typically have a wide user base using their data warehouse, they also employ data visualisation tools to present data in an easier-to-use chart format. Relatively few organisations have reached this level of CRM sophistication. American Express, USAA (the US insurance company) and MBNA (the credit card company now owned by the Bank of America) are examples of companies that have reached this stage of development.

A task associated with such advanced usage of CRM is more active customer management in which organisations use tools for campaign management to engage in an ongoing dialogue with a customer and to reap the maximum profit potential throughout the customer's lifetime. Where it is relevant, companies at this stage become sophisticated users of social media. They use it both to enrich their customer data and to derive business advantage from social media campaigns.

Reviewing your stage of CRM maturity

Organisations should use these guidelines on CRM maturity to review their own stage of development. Generally managers characterise their stage of development fairly accurately. However, we have found IT managers tend to rank their own organisations at a higher stage than do their marketing colleagues. This is possibly because the IT managers have not understood how data are used by the marketing department and what their data requirements are.

Experienced CRM managers and consultants should already know which stage of CRM development a company is at. However, we have found several large corporations and many mid-sized companies with a surprising lack of knowledge as to how far they had progressed with their CRM, when compared with their competitors. A view should also be taken on the stage of development of key competitors. This will require research. Competitors' customers, industry reports, multi-client research studies and vendors who have provided solutions to a range of companies in that sector are good sources of this information. Submissions for industry awards and websites of CRM vendors are also often good sources of competitive information.

Organisations in earlier stages of CRM development can also benefit greatly by benchmarking CRM activities of leading non-competitors who are at an advanced stage of CRM. We have led a number of benchmarking programmes in 'CRM best practice' and found companies in non-competing industries can be extremely generous in sharing their knowledge. CRM best practice workshops of around three days' duration typically involve a review of CRM maturity, a CRM readiness audit, visits to leading exemplars of relevant CRM practices and action planning. Such workshops are usually directed at senior management including the operation's Board and senior CRM managers. Our experience is that in-company workshops can be very powerful in emphasising the business benefits of CRM and in providing senior executives with strong motivation to provide the leadership necessary to ensure successful implementation of CRM activities.

Identifying barriers to CRM success

When reviewing CRM readiness it is useful for companies to consider the barriers typically faced by other organisations in developing CRM programmes. Our research has identified a number of common barriers to success. Interestingly, the problems of existing legacy systems, which executives might expect to be a main source of difficulties and delays, appear to be less common than problems associated with internal attitudes and organisational structure.

Lack of skills

Lack of skills in building and using a new IT-based CRM system are a major barrier to the implementation of CRM. One CRM manager referred to a 'chronic technological skill shortage'. The organisation for which he works was unable to recruit enough technically skilled people for a large-scale CRM implementation project. Other executives also high-lighted the need for skills in operating the new system and several said that they relied on vendor training to meet this need, which was not always available quickly and was not of a uniform standard.

Inadequate investment

Gaining adequate funding for CRM requirements is an important issue for organisations, particularly as many of the projects expand dramatically in cost and in scope. Some organisations have overcome the problem of funding by adopting what was referred to as a 'quick wins' approach. By structuring their CRM implementation projects to deliver quick wins and visible benefits at incremental stages, such as improvements in customer service or higher response rates to campaigns, they were able to demonstrate immediate progress and returns. This helped to improve internal buy-in and motivate other parts of the business to extend CRM systems within their own areas.

Poor data quality and quantity

Organisations at different stages of development experience different issues with respect to data quality and data quantity. For companies at an early stage of CRM development data quality is a key issue. The extent of data quality problems and the amount of work necessary to remedy them surprise many managers. More advanced companies tend to have undertaken data cleansing and de-duplicating; for these organisations data quantity is a greater problem than data quality.

Failure to understand the business benefits

Low initial awareness among senior management of the full benefits of a data warehouse is also a barrier for companies less advanced in CRM. This problem tends to be overcome as the data warehouse goes live and begins to deliver results. Managers point out that the data warehouse is perceived as a high cost and senior management often fail to under-stand the potential financial benefits in the earlier stages of the CRM project.

Functional boundaries

Managers at a functional or business unit level may be reluctant to cooperate at the early stages of the CRM project. It may require considerable organisational effort to make functional and business unit managers aware of the benefits of greater company-wide operations and cross-functional working. This is a change management issue – which we consider later in this chapter.

Lack of leadership and top management involvement

A lack of top management involvement and leadership of CRM activities is a further barrier to CRM success. Enlightened CEOs should also view themselves as 'chief customer officer'. Their role is to ensure a high-level executive, ideally at Board level, acts as a sponsor and champion for the company's CRM activities and that the importance of transforming the company's relationships with customers through CRM is understood and shared by the Board and senior management. Leadership represents one of the key issues in change management.

Inadequate measurement systems

CRM managers often point out how poor or inappropriate measurement and reward systems can hinder the initiation and fulfilment of CRM projects. Measures used to determine the success of CRM performance are often considered inadequate. Sometimes, the problem is that the organisation is not clear about its goals or does not communicate its goals to its people. Issues relating to CRM performance measurement were discussed in Chapter 10.

CRM readiness audit

Once the stage of development and the potential barriers to CRM have been considered, the enterprise should then proceed with a more detailed assessment of CRM readiness. The CRM Strategy Framework, explored in detail in Chapters 6 to 10, can be used by enterprises to assess their CRM readiness and to identify and address priorities.

As noted earlier, although these five processes have universal application, the emphasis on them will vary according to each organisation's unique situation. Large customer-facing businesses are likely to review all these CRM processes and the key questions underpinning them in considerable detail. In such cases, key issues will include: leadership and sponsorship; how your company compares with other organisations; how satisfied your customers are with the products and services offered by your organisation; and whether your enterprise has the skilled and motivated people and appropriate IT systems to deliver an outstanding customer experience. However, smaller companies will have more limited resources and they may need to focus on a smaller number of more specific priorities.

We now consider two forms of readiness assessment – *the overview CRM audit* and *the comprehensive CRM audit*. If an organisation is in the early stages of CRM development, it may be useful to start with an overview audit to help get senior management understanding and buy-in at an early stage.

The overview CRM audit

The overview form of readiness audit can be used quickly to form an initial view on the key priorities, to define the relative importance of these priorities and to determine where effort needs to be applied. The 'overview CRM audit' involves examining each of the five processes in the CRM Strategy Framework and determining the key areas of importance that need to be addressed.

First, the company's existing capabilities on the five key CRM processes should be considered. Second, the proposed change in emphasis should be determined. To gain insight into an enterprise's progress with CRM, it is valuable to have a cross-section of managers independently score their organisation's performance across the five processes outlined above in terms of the existing and proposed future emphasis.

This follows a detailed consideration of these key processes. Managers can then compare their individual assessments and can then reach agreement for an overall score on each process. The results of such an exercise for a major retail bank are shown in Figure 11.1.

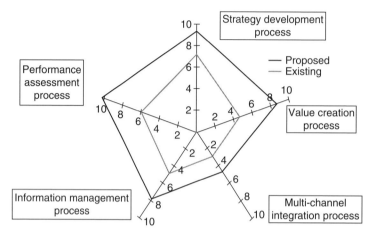

Figure 11.1 Present and proposed emphasis on CRM processes in a retail bank

Initiatives can then be developed to address each of the priority gaps that are identified. We have used this overview audit approach with many organisations and often found significant differences between the current position and the desired position on each process. In the case of the retail bank highlighted in Figure 11.1, changes were considered to be necessary in all processes, with the greatest improvement needed in the value creation and performance assessment processes. A number of important new CRM initiatives were identified and project teams were formed to implement them.

In one of Europe's largest service businesses we used this overview audit with 150 of its most senior staff, including three divisional managing directors. Working in teams of six, each group identified current progress and the considerable challenges confronting their organisation. There was a remarkably high degree of agreement from the 25 separate groups that undertook this exercise regarding existing poor performance and the areas that needed improvement. This overview audit was instrumental in highlighting a number of key problems that had not been addressed previously. The high level of consensus amongst this senior management group motivated the Group CEO to agree a plan of rapid focus on the CRM priorities identified as performance gaps.

Although simple in concept, the completion of this overview audit – and a structured discussion with the enterprise's managers around the scorings – has been found to be extremely valuable in highlighting the areas on which an organisation should concentrate in order to improve its CRM performance. To extend the response rate it is possible to develop a simple Web-based program to collect and aggregate the information from around the enterprise, as can be done with a more comprehensive audit.

The comprehensive CRM audit

As with any organisational initiative, the success of a CRM programme depends very much on the existence of a sufficient level of preparedness within the organisation. While the overview audit is a useful device to highlight opportunities and challenges and build consensus on the way forward, a more thorough insight into an enterprise's existing and potential use of CRM is usually needed. This involves a detailed review of the five key CRM processes as well as a consideration of cultural, leadership and sponsorship issues. These latter factors are of particular relevance in preparing for a CRM programme and generating enthusiasm for it.

Each company will have different business priorities and market objectives. For this reason it is recommended that a tailored set of questions be developed for each of the major CRM processes. In the Annex to this chapter we provide details of a 'comprehensive CRM audit'. This audit includes a total of 100 questions, including 20 questions on each of the five CRM processes. Although this is a generic audit that can be used as it stands, we recommend it is adapted to suit the size and nature of the enterprise concerned. The questions in this generic comprehensive CRM audit can form the basis of an audit which is modified to suit the needs and circumstances of a particular enterprise.

In the comprehensive audit in the Annex the five CRM processes are broken down into two sub-sections, each comprising ten questions. For example, the strategy development process is divided into business strategy (including leadership and sponsorship) and customer strategy; the value creation process is divided into the value the customer receives and the value the organisation receives and so on. There are three elements to score on a scale 0 to 5. These elements are: (1) importance to our organisation (5 = very important; 0 = no importance); (2) existing performance rating for our organisation – how the enterprise is currently performing (5 = very well; 0 = very poorly); and (3) desired performance for our organisation – how we wish the enterprise to perform within a given time period – say, two years (5 = very well; 0 = very poorly).

An enterprise can use the comprehensive CRM audit provided in the Annex to this chapter (or tailor its own audit, based on the generic list of questions in this audit) or it can use other standardised CRM assessment tools. If a tailored audit is required, we recommend a cross-functional team of executives is deployed to develop an audit to suit the special circumstances of the particular enterprise. When completed and pilot-tested, a cross-section of managers can then be asked to complete the audit. The data from this audit can be usefully presented in a series of graphs or matrices that show the rating for the organisation and the importance to the organisation. This will quickly help flag key CRM issues, problems and priorities.

A number of other CRM assessment tools have also been developed, mainly by consulting firms. These audits vary greatly in detail and quality. Some are little more than a quiz and others show little evidence of thinking through the wide range of strategic issues relevant to CRM. Some audits, like the CMAT assessment tool developed by QCi Ltd., are more robust. We discussed the CMAT assessment tool in Chapter 10 in terms of using it to understand how well the company is managing its customers. It can also be used to consider CRM readiness more broadly. This form of CRM audit is carried out by experienced CRM assessors who work with The Customer Framework, a specialised CRM consultancy.[26] This consulting firm has accumulated a substantial amount of data from many businesses in different industries, which permits comparisons to be made not only across industries, but also within relevant industry sectors. Because it is a proprietary tool, a company cannot use it themselves for a detailed self-audit; however, the overall cost of undertaking a CMAT assessment for large enterprises is affordable.

Determining key CRM priorities

Regardless of the form of CRM readiness assessment audit used, the output of it should be the identification of the specific CRM activities and priorities that need to be addressed. Companies' individual circumstances will dictate how they wish to consider their key CRM priorities.

In one bank we worked with, 12 groups of employees identified an initial list of over 100 activities and tasks that were considered worthy of more detailed examination. Several senior managers then assessed these activities and categorised them using the matrix shown in Figure 11.2. Each activity was then considered in more detail. On closer inspection some of the activities were related to each other so they were reclassified. A significant number were rejected as being of minor importance. As a result of this exercise, the number of activities was reduced. Issues that were considered to have a high impact on the business and were also easy to implement were addressed immediately. A total of six projects that were difficult to implement, but that potentially had a high impact on the business, were assigned to six project teams. Those that were hard to implement and had little expected payback were to be monitored, over time, to see if their importance changed. A number of the activities that were classified as low impact, but

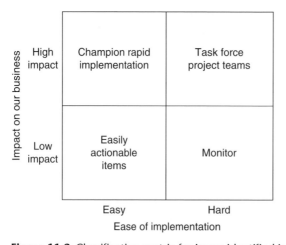

Figure 11.2 Classification matrix for issues identified in CRM audit

easy and inexpensive to implement, were proceeded with – as they were considered likely to have a positive impact on employee morale.

A classification matrix such as the one shown in Figure 11.2 helps the enterprise form a clear view on its key priorities. Every organisation starting a substantive new CRM programme needs to consider its overall readiness for implementation and what needs to be done to prepare the enterprise for CRM.

Once a readiness assessment has been undertaken and a decision has been made to proceed with new or expanded initiatives, the key CRM processes need to be addressed in a structured and integrated manner. The critical synergies generated by careful management of these five processes and the accompanying engagement of all employees, are highlighted by two activities which run in parallel with these processes – change management and project management.

Change management

As the enterprise addresses each of the key CRM processes – strategy development, value creation, multi-channel integration, information management and performance assessment – it needs to consider the change management implications of them. For a large-scale and complex CRM initiative, companies will typically have to undergo substantial organisational and cultural change in order to implement the initiative. A critical dimension of any large CRM programme, therefore, is an effective change management programme within the organisation.

Change management is primarily concerned with people, systems and organisational change. We make a distinction here between change management, which is concerned with strategic organisational change, and employee engagement, which we see as a more operationally oriented set of activities. They are, of course, closely entwined and activities relating to employee engagement, discussed later in this chapter, need to be carefully integrated with a change management initiative.

First, we review a framework that will assist in identifying the broad change management activities that need to be addressed. Because CRM is potentially so wide-ranging in terms of the organisational ramifications, we need a robust analytical framework to help assist business leaders in identifying all the organisational change management issues in relation to a particular CRM programme. Second, we review three important and recurrent issues in CRM change management and implementation.

A framework for change management

The 'Seven S' framework, developed by strategy consulting firm McKinsey & Co., provides a powerful device for planning CRM change management initiatives. The framework, shown in Figure 11.3, consists of seven elements: strategy, structure, systems, staff, style, skills and shared values. Each of these is briefly described in this figure.[27]

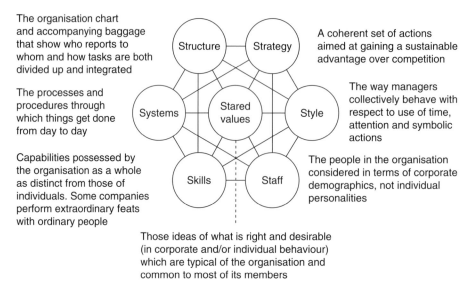

The organisation chart and accompanying baggage that show who reports to whom and how tasks are both divided up and integrated

A coherent set of actions aimed at gaining a sustainable advantage over competition

The processes and procedures through which things get done from day to day

The way managers collectively behave with respect to use of time, attention and symbolic actions

Capabilities possessed by the organisation as a whole as distinct from those of individuals. Some companies perform extraordinary feats with ordinary people

The people in the organisation considered in terms of corporate demographics, not individual personalities

Those ideas of what is right and desirable (in corporate and/or individual behaviour) which are typical of the organisation and common to most of its members

Figure 11.3 The McKinsey 'Seven S' framework.
Source: Adapted from Waterman Peters and Phillips (1980)

In addition to more traditional aspects of change – strategy, structure and systems – this framework highlights the need for an enterprise to consider four other elements: style, staff, skills and shared values, if they are to be successful with a change management initiative. This framework can help organisations become more effective at CRM change management by carefully managing and orchestrating the relevant component parts of each element. Each of the seven elements should be aligned, like compass needles pointing in the same direction, so that they support each other. The types of skills and breadth of knowledge required to make CRM succeed are quite different from those inherent in the traditional functional management model. For example, cross-functional process management, leadership skills and management development will be important.

The 'Seven S' summary shown in Figure 11.4 shows many dimensions of change management that are involved in changing the organisation to process-oriented CRM.[28] This is not intended to be a comprehensive list, but it is illustrative of the issues that emerge when using the 'Seven S' framework. This suggests that a strategy to develop CRM must be supported by selected staff with appropriate skills along with a set of shared values, systems, management style and organisational structure.

This framework provides a means of viewing organisations as packages of key skills, or skill gaps. Hence, it can be used as a tool for analysing organisational deficiencies, building on positive skills and identifying new skills needed. An analysis can be undertaken by determining – for each of the seven elements – the key enablers to CRM, the key barriers to CRM and the new capabilities that need to be built.

The changes involved in making the transition to CRM are clearly substantial. There are a number of potential obstacles to this transition, not least the entrenched interest in

	From	To
Strategy	Market to major customer segments	Add value to individual customer relationships through tailored interactions
Shared values	Serve customers well	Service customers differently; serve best customers really well
Structure	Product orientation with focus on current period economics	Customer-segment orientation with focus on lifetime customer value
Skills	Analytical orientation with focus on current period economics	Ability to gather, analyse and interpret data and design systems to exploit a large, constantly evolving customer information base; ability to react at individual customer (or at least micro-segment) level
Staff	Marketing analysis managed statistically, information technology acts as support, but not as an active partner	Integration of marketing creativity with systems competencies to create capability that is both ideas-driven and analytically intense
Systems	Detailed, segmented, but relatively static decision support tools	Extensive, dynamic and flexible marketing support tools, programme management and execution systems, and operating links to support front-line actions
Style	Marketing plan orientation with emphasis on programmes for major segments delivered within standard period; mass media focus	Analytical approach and experimental attitude with emphasis on continuous learning (do, test, measure, fix) and value of data
Leading measures of success	Market share Current period profits	Share of most attractive customers (based on lifetime profit potential) Continuous learning/tailored marketing Large impact on a small set of customers

Figure 11.4 CRM change management issues.
Source: Adapted from Child et al. (1995)

preserving the status quo. Understanding and acting on change management requirements is therefore a prerequisite to successful CRM implementation.

Key issues in CRM change management

Given the great diversity of potential CRM initiatives, a general framework such as the 'Seven S' framework is a powerful tool to help an organisation identify those issues relevant to its particular context. These issues will typically vary from one organisation to another. However, we have found three specific CRM issues that regularly need to be addressed in CRM programmes regardless of their nature some of which were raised in the earlier discussion in this chapter on barriers to CRM success. These include the need to establish a senior sponsor for CRM, to ensure an appropriate CRM vision and underlying set of values is in place and to have a supportive culture that facilitates improved cross-functional working within the organisation.

Ensure senior CRM sponsorship

As noted earlier, lack of leadership for CRM is a barrier to success. The attitude of the chief executive and senior management can be the determining factor in the success or failure of a CRM programme. The chief executive should appoint a Board-level sponsor for CRM. The development of an organisation totally focused on building profitable customer relationships usually requires intense effort on the part of senior management to shift existing employee attitudes towards developing a more customer-driven approach and involving use of new technological tools. This requires the appointment of a strong leader and champion to oversee the organisation's CRM activities – someone with vision, imagination, energy and persistence.

Without this person, the CRM programme can fail or degenerate into a situation where a limited number of employees are committed to the initiative. Bain & Co., the US strategy consulting firm, has examined why CRM initiatives fail so often. Their research draws on examples from more than 200 companies across a wide range of industries. They conclude that one major reason that CRM fails is that most senior executives 'don't understand what they are implementing, let alone how much it costs or how long it will take'.[29]

The general skills of the CRM leader will include the following:

- in-depth understanding of business environment, markets and market segments;
- credibility at all levels within business;
- knowledge of data management/data mining tools;
- experience in dealing with complex IT issues;
- financial skills;
- comfortable operating at Board level;
- strategic thinker and planner;
- excellent communication and leadership skills and ability to coordinate projects across functional departments;
- familiarity with all operational areas of business.

The specific skills required in the leader will vary from company to company according to the circumstances of the CRM project and the availability of internal human resources. The commitment of senior managers and other employees to the CRM initiative will be heavily influenced by the visible behaviour of this leader and champion, including the ways in which he or she communicates the worthiness of the goals and the results obtained from CRM initiatives. CRM managers point out the difficulties of obtaining 'buy-in' to what are often very expensive projects. Having a Board-level sponsor is vital, not only for initiating projects but also for overcoming delays caused by passive resistance to change.

Establish a CRM vision

With a CRM leader in place, an early change management issue that needs to be addressed is the organisation's shared values. In a sense, these shared values are the 'glue' that holds the organisation together. A clear and well-communicated CRM vision is an important means of building shared values. In Chapter 6 we explained that a business vision and its associated values form an important element of a company's strategy and we reviewed the research undertaken by Hugh Davidson into making vision and values work in organisations.

A specific CRM vision is a powerful means of helping create shared values and a customer focus. Orange, the UK mobile service provider, is an example of a company with a strong customer focus. A number of years ago, following an appraisal of its operations, Orange developed a clear vision, shown in Figure 11.5, that highlights the importance of an increased customer focus. We especially like this CRM vision as it is one that is memorable and motivating to employees.

'Our mission is to build strong enduring relationships with our customers, thereby increasing customer lifetime value and company profitability and building sustainable competitive advantage. We will achieve this through the application of CRM strategies.'

'CRM is about building relationships to turn customers into advocates, so that their decision to stay with you becomes more "automatic"; they buy more and spend more, and they tell their friends and colleagues about your products and services too.'

Figure 11.5 Orange's CRM vision

Many companies score poorly on the development of a clear and strong vision because their visions are neither memorable nor motivating. Davidson has suggested the key issues an organisation should address in order to overtake other companies in terms of vision management:

- establish candidly who you are and what you stand for;
- develop a future vision that excites and challenges;
- involve all your people in developing vision and values;
- communicate by action, signals and repetition;
- embed vision and values into all practices, behaviours, processes and systems;
- develop a distinctive brand proposition for your organisation, which honestly reflects its substance and sets it apart;
- regularly measure how well you are managing vision and values.[30]

Successful CRM implementation involves developing strong support for a customer orientation. A well-accepted vision will help build commitment to CRM throughout the organisation, but it needs to be carefully and explicitly linked to the CRM project. CRM consultant Nick Siragher has emphasised how the CRM processes should be defined so that end users and non-technical personnel understand what needs to occur from an operational point of view to achieve the CRM vision:

The process mapping must ensure a close and continuing relationship between strategic vision and the implementation of 'the solution'. Without this close relationship, CRM is nothing more than the implementation of a few software tools and operational changes to achieve some process efficiencies. Consequently, the vision is lost ... To realize the CRM vision, users must see the impact on how they work on a daily basis, and what achieving the vision means to them. The vision therefore needs to be explicit and understandable ... The link between CRM vision and CRM solution is the very essence of the CRM project challenge.[31]

Supportive culture and improved cross-functional working

We emphasise that CRM requires cross-functional working and a major transition from the classic 'silo' mentality to a more 'customer-centric' view of the world. Successful CRM demands that members of different functions such as marketing, information technology and human resource management work together.

In many organisations there are inter-functional tensions that inhibit a positive customer-oriented organisational culture and climate and that prevent effective cross-functional collaboration. Conflict and anxiety between departments can arise for a number of reasons, including differences in cultural or professional background, work perspectives, job tenure, age, and level of understanding of the jobs performed by others.

One approach that is especially useful for surfacing the different perspectives and attitudes held by employees in different functions is the cultural web developed by Johnson.[32] This provides a structure for auditing an organisation's culture. The cultural web includes a number of interdependent subsystems, including organisation structures, power structures, control systems, symbols, stories and myths, and routines and rituals, all of which are interconnected with the 'mindset', or paradigm – this is the set of common organisational assumptions and views held by most members of the organisation or a department, function or unit within it.

Our experience suggests considerable divergence in organisational values and perspectives often exists between the IT function and the marketing function – the two groups most typically concerned with CRM implementation. Figure 11.6 shows the views of a group of IT managers in a large company with regard to their marketing colleagues, based on research by colleagues at the Cranfield School of Management. This figure shows how IT managers ascribe a considerable number of negative sentiments with respect to the marketing managers in their organisation. These include a general lack of respect – 'over-sexed, overpaid, overrated, underworked and mystical' – and a belief that they do not contribute as much as they should to the organisation.

Marketing managers also tend to have clear stereotypical views of their colleagues in IT. In the same organisation, as shown in Figure 11.7, marketing managers viewed their IT colleagues as 'inflexible aliens' who spent vast sums and were rewarded on qualifications and skills rather than their contribution to organisational performance.

These views are clearly unhealthy. While such strong negative views of colleagues are not held in all organisations, such highly charged perspectives are by no means uncommon. Other strong differences often exist between marketing (and IT) and other functional departments such as finance, human resources and general management. One

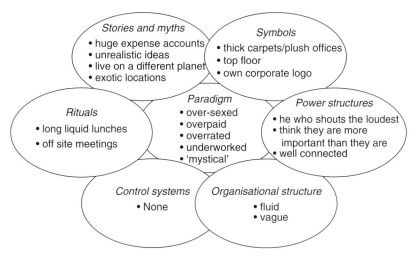

Figure 11.6 IT's view of marketing

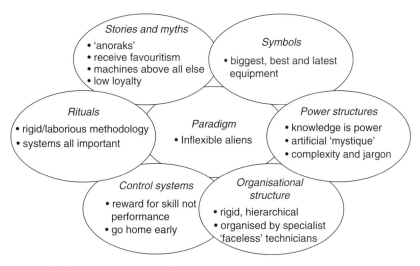

Figure 11.7 Marketing's view of IT

study in a Fortune 500 electronics giant elicited the following opinions from groups of non-marketing staff: marketers are '... naïve, conceited, insensitive, inexperienced and wrong; concerned only with advertising, promotion and enjoying themselves with customers; overpaid; largely unnecessary; lacking in business understanding; ignorant of financial matters; unnecessarily demanding; too often trying to change the company; uncontrollable; failing to achieve the wild goals they set; unwilling to learn from their mistakes; and a waste of funds needed by more important departments'.[33]

A good starting point in achieving better cross-functional integration is to surface the different views of functional departments held within the organisation using a tool such as the cultural web and then to identify what needs to be done to reconcile any negative aspects so that the functions can work together in a more joined up way. Researchers suggest that change is likely to fail if it only focuses on one or two elements within the cultural web. Instead, all the elements need to be considered together to form coherent change structures and systems, including the softer aspects such as symbolism and communication.

Addressing these three key elements of change management should help companies in all stages of CRM adoption, but especially those in the earlier stages. Successful change management almost always needs a champion, a clear vision (including clearly linking it to CRM business objectives and processes) and a culture that facilitates cross-functional working. Use of tools such as the 'Seven S' framework and the cultural web will help surface other key elements that need to be addressed in a company-specific change management programme.

Project management

While change management is needed for virtually all CRM initiatives regardless of the scale of the CRM initiative, project management has increasing relevance as the size and complexity of CRM initiatives increase. In this section we briefly review the principles of project management before addressing specific issues relating to CRM projects.

CRM project management comprises two types of project. First, where a team of specialists is brought together on a temporary basis to address a particular project with a finite completion date. Second, where a cross-functional team is assembled with a remit of ongoing management of the enterprise's CRM initiative. (Some may argue that strictly speaking the latter is not a 'project' as it does not have a defined completion date.)

Projects are specific sets of activities designed to deliver specific outputs usually within defined timeframes. Successful CRM projects deliver against the CRM objectives derived from the corporate objectives and should be supportive of and complementary to the overall business strategy. Effective CRM project management is essential as experience has shown that CRM projects that overrun budgets and timescales can do considerable harm.

It is imperative for those devising and managing CRM projects to understand fully the particular role that IT plays in their specific CRM implementation. There are several reasons for using IT in CRM: to provide efficiencies, to create more customer value through improved customer knowledge and to improve the customer experience or to reduce cost. If a proposed IT investment in CRM cannot be justified on the benefits it brings it should be carefully re-examined.

A framework for project management

Projects are becoming increasingly widespread in every industry sector. This reflects not only an environment of greater complexity and rapid change but also the move throughout industry and government towards defined, goal-orientated, work activities.[34] In most projects these activities cross the functional boundaries of the organisation. As a result there has been a greatly increased need for the cross-functional working discussed in the previous section on change management.

The reason for the upsurge in popularity of the cross-functional project team approach to management is that it provides the flexibility necessary for organisations to adapt amid constant change. Although project management is often thought of as comprising techniques aimed at the control of time and cost, it uses and enhances many of the common practices of general management including teamworking, cross-functional perspectives, process orientation and leadership. Today, project management has extended into sophisticated methods for the management and control of time, cost, resources, quality and performance.

Projects can be considered to be the vehicles for the delivery of one or more elements of a CRM or business strategy. The management of groups of projects is often known as either programme management or multi-project management. There is a framework or hierarchy of programmes, projects and activities, shown in Figure 11.8, which helps identify the different levels of project management activity.

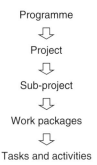

Programme
⇩
Project
⇩
Sub-project
⇩
Work packages
⇩
Tasks and activities

Figure 11.8 Framework for project management

CRM 'projects' can fall within all of these levels depending on whether an enterprise-wide strategic initiative is involved or a much more tactically focused activity such as planning a particular campaign management activity.

A further dimension also needs to be considered – the benefits to the organisation. It is likely that there will be a series of trade-offs and values, cost and quality (or specification) that deliver different CRM benefits to the organisation. It is important to understand the relationship between project resources and the business benefits. We now examine an approach for considering this relationship.

Delivering business benefits

Large-scale CRM projects need to be managed so as to deliver benefits to the business, not just to deliver a CRM system on time and budget. The Benefits Dependency Network (BDN) is a project management tool that has been developed to help deliver business benefits. The BDN works backwards from the project's objectives to ensure that all necessary business changes are made, as well as CRM technology solutions implemented. The BDN approach has the following steps:[35]

1. *Define business drivers*: The drivers of the project are defined, based on the nature of the opportunity in relation to the strategy from the application portfolio. A driver is a view by top managers as to what is important for the business, such that the business needs to change in response to that driver; for example, the need to achieve a greater return on shareholder funds.

2. *Determine investment objectives*: The investment objectives are a statement of how the project will contribute to achieving changes in relation to one or more of the drivers. Investment objectives may include increase in sales turnover, increase in market share, better targeting of most profitable customers, etc.

3. *Establish business benefits*: In order to achieve the investment objectives, some benefits will need to be delivered to the enterprise and/or its customers. These business benefits need to be explicitly identified and quantified. They may include increasing stock turnover, better response from campaign management, improving customer service, etc.

4. *Identify business changes*: In order to achieve the benefits, it is necessary for the enterprise and its employees to work in different and more effective ways. These changes are identified at this stage in the BDN. Business changes may include online provision of sales and stock information to the field sales force, changes in channel structure, using the data warehouse to improve customer targeting, etc.

5. *Identify enabling changes*: These are other one-off changes that may also be needed before the technology can be implemented, for example to define new processes which are needed and to establish new skill requirements, such as refining customer segmentation, designing new customer service processes and introducing a new account management process.

6. *Determine CRM technology requirements and enablers*: It is only when this analysis of the objectives and benefits has been undertaken and the necessary changes to realise them have been identified, that the specific role that the CRM technology will play in the project's objectives can be defined in detail. These technology changes represent information systems and information technology (IS/IT) enablers that will lead to the realisation of the business benefits. They include items such as extensions to the company's data repository, a new or improved website, a sales force automation system or new mobile devices for the field sales force, etc.

The BDN represents a useful tool for identifying the business changes that are needed to make the new use of CRM technology effective. Managers wishing to use this tool may find it useful to examine worked examples from other industries. Such examples are documented in the research relating to the BDN.[36] A BDN framework can usually be agreed within two to three half-day workshops; however, detailed scoping of the CRM technology requirements may not be achieved within this timescale for more complex projects.

Key issues in CRM project management

In a study of 23 European companies, Henneberg identified two CRM implementation approaches taken by organisations: a dominant 'hard' implementation of CRM (focusing on IT, analytics, centralisation and campaign management) and a 'soft' implementation of CRM (focusing on decentralised customer experience management and customer relationships). Of 23 companies Henneberg examined, 16 of them adopted the 'hard' approach, four adopted the 'soft' approach and three of them utilised a combination of approaches.[37] IT-based CRM project management will clearly be of greatest importance in 'hard' CRM implementations.

The 'hard' or analytical dimension typically emphasised: integrating the customer database with marketing data marts; a shared data model; marketing analysis and data mining tools (such as propensity models for targeting and triggering activities); centralised CRM and campaign management functions; the integration of all touch points/channels with feedback loops to the centralised database; and a standardisation of customer interaction and service processes via treatment strategies. The main implementation activities here are software adaptation and integration, process redefinition, organisational integration, sales force automation and campaign management.[38]

Henneberg found that the 'soft' or customer experience dimension encompasses aspects of direct customer interaction management. It is more decentralised and focuses on customer interaction skills and strategies; a deep understanding of customer or customer segment relationship needs; the development of new customer-centric touch points and the ability to use the customer information to build relationships. The main implementation activities are skill advancement, process definition, organisational learning and the development of ways to capture customer information as part of the interaction routine.[39] This equates more to developing a customer-centric approach through change management as opposed to an IT-based approach.

Given the difference between these different CRM implementation approaches, the key issues that will need to be addressed under the heading of CRM project management will vary greatly across different projects. However, three issues will be of importance to most organisations: determining if a CRM technology solution is likely to be of benefit; deciding if a pilot project should be undertaken; and planning for the CRM project's implementation. Considering these issues will also help the organisation determine the relevant emphasis that needs to be placed on both project management and change management for its own CRM implementation.

Utilising a CRM technology solution

Henneberg found that companies using the 'hard' CRM implementation approach often had only a vague strategic understanding of the CRM project in place before they defined the process and technical requirements. This suggests that standard IT processes may often be used to derive strategic CRM guidelines, a reversal of a best-practice approach where IT processes are developed from strategic and customer-based considerations.[40] The CRM Strategy Framework outlined in this book emphasises that strategic considerations must be addressed first – before the IT solutions. Tools such as the BDN described above will then help identify the general CRM technology requirements in the context of business strategy and drivers.

Adopting a CRM solution

Around the start of the millennium, two-thirds of all US telecom operators and half or more of all US financial services, pharmaceutical and transportation companies were either implementing or had already operating such solutions. Across the US and Europe, approximately 40 per cent of the companies in the high technology, aerospace, retailing and utilities sectors had invested in CRM systems.[41] Today, most major enterprises have now adopted some form of CRM.

Most large organisations dealing with a substantial number of customers have adopted or will adopt one or more IT-based CRM solutions. Medium-sized and smaller organisations need to consider their existing and potential scale in relationship to the technology requirements. Management consultant Michael Gentle has written extensively on CRM project management. Drawing on a range of sources he outlines a number of organisational conditions that make a company an ideal candidate for adopting an IT-based CRM solution:

- Do you have a large number of people in sales and service in direct contact with customers, say more than 30?
- Are you in a highly collaborative environment, with customer interaction requiring input from multiple players within each function (sales and service)?
- Do you sell complex products that require a high degree of configuration and customisation?
- Do you have a large number of customers, say more than 10,000?
- Is a typical customer relationship worth a lot to you from a profit standpoint, i.e. will it cost you to lose one?
- Can your customers interact with you across multiple channels?
- Do you have frequent contact with large groups of customers, or all customers, across multiple channels?
- Is there a need to customise what you are saying to each customer through these channels?[42]

Companies which respond 'yes' to most of these conditions should certainly consider adopting a CRM solution, if they have not already done so. For other companies, a consideration of the CRM strategy matrix (see Figure 6.11 in Chapter 6 and Figure 9.2 in Chapter 9) will help determine the relevance and timing of new CRM solution adoption. Having identified the need for adoption of a CRM technology solution, attention then needs to be turned to vendor selection, determining if a pilot project is required and detailed project planning.

Selecting a CRM vendor

The CRM software marketplace is extremely complex, with over 1,000 products offered by a cluttered and dynamic community of more than 350 vendors worldwide.[43] As many as

50 CRM vendors may be present at major CRM conferences. Faced with such a plethora of vendors, choosing the appropriate vendor or vendors can be daunting.

The starting point in understanding different vendors is to consider the broad categories of vendors within the CRM market and determine what types of categories are relevant to the company's needs. In Chapter 1 we presented a classification of vendors for CRM applications and CRM service providers, based on a classification by Gartner, together with some illustrative examples of companies in each category. This listing is restated below.

The key segments for CRM applications architecture types include:

- CRM Suite (e.g., Microsoft, salesforce.com, Siebel – owned by Oracle)
- Enterprise Suite (e.g., Oracle, Sage, SAP)
- CRM Best of Breed (e.g., SAS, Teradata)
- Model-driven Application (e.g., Oracle, SAP/Netweaver)
- Model-driven Framework (e.g., Pegasystems).

The wide variety of CRM service providers and consultants that offer implementation support include:

- Corporate strategy (e.g., McKinsey & Co., Bain & Co.)
- CRM strategy (e.g., Peppers & Rogers)
- Change management, organisation design, training, HR, etc. (e.g., Accenture)
- Business transformation (e.g., IBM, PwC)
- Infrastructure build, systems integrators (e.g., Logica, Unisys)
- Infrastructure outsourcing (e.g., EDS, CSC)
- Business insight, analytics, research, etc. (e.g., SAS, Dunnhumby)
- Business process outsourcing (e.g., Acxiom).

The complexity of the vendor marketplace is compounded by a considerable ongoing consolidation within the CRM vendor marketplace, a constant stream of new entrants to the market, with some companies having a poor reputation for support and implementation and some established companies being very good at applications or implementation skills that they are generally not known for in the CRM marketplace.

Any list of vendors can become outdated quickly, given the rapid change and consolidation that is occurring within the CRM industry. It is beyond the scope of this book to review the huge list of CRM vendors. However, CRM vendors are regularly reviewed by analyst firms such as Gartner and Forrester.

Subscribers to Gartner's services are able to obtain up-to-date and comprehensive overviews of many of the main CRM vendors. Such overviews provide vendor functionality ratings across a range of front-office applications including:

- field sales
- telesales
- e-commerce
- channel management

- PRM (partner relationship marketing) sales and marketing
- analytics – business intelligence
- analytics – predictive
- field service
- call centre management
- e-service, etc.

Further, Gartner evaluates the major vendors, ranking them on their CRM applications, their vertical industry expertise and their business stability. This includes positioning each of these vendors on a matrix display based on their ability to execute specific CRM applications and the completeness of their CRM vision. This firm also ranks vendors' expertise in specific vertical markets such as retailing, banking/brokerage, automotive, pharmaceutical, insurance/healthcare, manufacturing and hi-tech and telecoms.

Consultants Detica, now BA Systems Detica, use six evaluation criteria for vendor selection. These criteria are functionality, technical complexity and integration, track record, implementation and timescales, risk and total cost of ownership. Figure 11.9 outlines a profile for two vendors based on these criteria. This figure shows that the factors that contribute to whether the project succeeds are much broader than just functionality. Each of the factors relevant to the CRM implementation concerned needs to be carefully evaluated. The risk dimension is one that often does not receive sufficient attention. Gentle provides a comprehensive risk analysis questionnaire for CRM projects that enables managers to form a detailed view on the relative risk of the CRM project.[44] Where appropriate, the criteria should be weighted according to their relative importance.

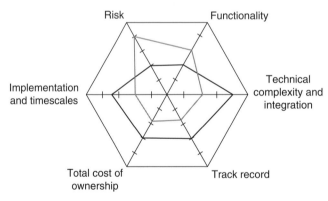

Figure 11.9 CRM vendors' profiles on evaluation criteria.
Source: Based on Detica Ltd.

We advocate developing your own criteria for CRM vendor selection. Checklists of criteria such as that provided above can be supplemented with issues and sub-issues relating to the particular circumstances of the company including its in-house capabilities and the nature of the CRM project. Such issues may include asking questions such as:

- Does the vendor have a well-integrated internal implementation or professional services team?
- What is the size of this group and how committed is it to existing projects?

- To what extent does it rely on third-party partners for implementation?
- Does it have significant relevant experience in your vertical market or one that is directly analogous?
- How forthcoming is the vendor with respect to introducing you to reference sites for similar projects?
- Can you get access to a range of users and managers from different functions within these sites?
- What is its on-time and on-budget performance with projects of similar size and complexity?

Finally, vendor stability is very important. In selecting vendors to help the business design and build the appropriate CRM architecture it also pays to take into account whether the vendor has a sufficiently strong and stable position in the market. An article in *The McKinsey Quarterly* quoted the example of one company that was developing a data warehouse and which had rejected a market-leading vendor in favour of one whose product was marginally faster. Unfortunately, within three years the latter vendor had fallen behind its more prominent competitors and its system had proven unreliable and costly to maintain. The company was then faced with high costs in moving to another supplier.[45]

Piloting CRM projects

Some organisations consider that a large-scale and very comprehensive approach to CRM improvement, covering many CRM initiatives more or less simultaneously, is necessary. Certainly, some companies need such a total, comprehensive and large-scale approach. However, we have found that more often an incremental and modular approach to CRM development or enhancement is appropriate. Such an approach involves a series of smaller individual CRM projects, undertaken in an appropriate sequence, each with clearly defined objectives and return on investment outcomes. These projects will help determine whether the immediate emphasis needs to be placed on analytical CRM, operational CRM or collaborative CRM. The project might involve a specific task within a CRM process, such as upgrading a call centre operation or introducing sales force automation, or a complete CRM process, such as improving multi-channel integration. Further, many of these projects will best be initiated by means of a 'pilot' project.

There are various reasons for a pilot project to be considered. Pilots can be used to: prove a CRM concept at a much lower cost; to trial an approach with high business or political risk; to avoid incurring large-scale licence fees before the application is proven; to overcome potential staff buy-in to a CRM initiative; and so on. Buy-in is an important issue and it can be an important issue at many organisational levels including individual, departmental, regional, national or international.

Interdepartmental conflict and disagreements, highlighted in the earlier section on change management, are also a frequent cause for lack of buy-in. It is easier to launch a pilot project when faced with some organisational or cultural resistance to change than it is to 'hit the wall' head on. Without top-level support, innovators can only stretch the 'cultural elastic' so far and it may be counterproductive and politically misguided to attempt to challenge and overturn the company's system of beliefs and assumptions without piloting the project first. International CRM projects face particular problems that are amplified by geographic and cultural differences. For a review of critical success factors (CSFs) in international CRM projects, see Gentle.[46]

There are two types of CRM pilot: the 'conference-room' pilot and the 'operational' pilot or 'live' pilot. Siragher outlines the differences between them.[47] The conference-room pilot takes place in a conference room, rather than in the working environment. It tests processes without the risk of any adverse impact on either customer relations or the reputation of the CRM solution within the business and paves the way for a more general pilot in the live environment. It can also be used for piloting CRM training concepts and it should replicate a complete period of use for the user – perhaps three months. This can be done in a fraction of the elapsed time and can provide extensive use of the solution in a short timescale. Live pilots, by contrast, are typically more resource intensive and require similar resources to when the project goes live. In a live pilot, the same hardware and ideally the same version of the software as planned for the roll-out should be utilised. Siragher's work outlines the resources required for a pilot and an illustrative plan for a roadmap for a pilot CRM project including training. In practical terms, running pilot project training provides an opportunity to identify how easy or how difficult it will be for users to learn the solution and also to identify any issues relating to cultural change.

Planning for CRM project implementation

The CRM project plan must be developed into specific actions that result in the project being implemented and the business objectives achieved. The CRM Strategy Framework outlines a set of clearly defined processes that should be addressed in the plan. The format of a CRM plan will vary considerably from one organisation to another and it must be carefully crafted to meet the needs of the organisation.

The CRM plan must be produced in a manner that stands the tests of completeness, consistency, ease of understanding and succinctness. Project plans are best communicated and managed if they are presented visually. Further, areas of potential risk should be considered. Here contingency planning has an important role to play. In practice, plans are not always developed in a linear manner. It should be recognised that the early stages of planning may be 'messy' and that planning is an interactive and iterative process. Further, as consultant Jill Dyche has observed, whatever its scope, planning a CRM programme is rarely as straightforward as it first seems.[48]

Establishing project priorities and their direction

In the planning phase of CRM projects it is necessary to develop an integrated plan covering projects, the project goals, metrics for measuring success and the project priorities and then develop a roadmap for implementing them. Determining priorities is especially important.

In one large financial services organisation, a uniform approach to the management of projects was adopted, including:

- a Board member assigned to each major project;
- each project has an assigned project manager who;
  – suggests and assigns task force members to specific tasks as appropriate (with senior management team agreement),
  – proposes a work plan, detailed action plans and timetable to follow through with implementation;
- a nominated director to have overall CRM programme responsibility.

Duration of projects varies considerably depending on their nature. A project involving setting up direct marketing activities can be completed within three months, while other projects such as sales force automation across different countries may take several years. Projects should be broken up into discrete steps with deliverables being defined at appropriate points in time. Experience suggests that with longer projects there is a high risk that the project may be discontinued, if the project duration is more than three years or some tangible benefit to the business is not achieved within 18 months.

The CRM project plan

The activities in a CRM project plan will vary according to the timescale, the complexity and other issues such as whether a pilot has been undertaken. For a longer project lasting, say, three years, the typical activities involved in planning the project may include the following:

First Year:

- *Define project goal and critical success factors;*
- *Develop a roadmap;*
- *Discrete steps of no more than three months*:
  – identify low risk, quick wins;
- *Sell plan internally*:
  – find corporate sponsor,
  – get corporate commitment,
  – get buy-in from key decision makers,
  – get buy-in from other stakeholders,
  – get resources (people, money, time);
- *Initiate project*:
  – start monitoring and reporting,
  – employee engagement,
  – start preparation for roll-out,
  – start delivery.

Second Year:

- *Review project goal and critical success factors, modify if necessary;*
- *Review roadmap*:
  – continue with discrete steps of no more than three months,
  – continue looking for low risk, quick wins;

- *Manage ongoing project*:
  – continue delivery,
  – continue monitoring and reporting;
- *Continue internal marketing*.

Third Year:

- *Further review of project goal and critical success factors, modify if necessary;*
- *Further review roadmap*:
  – continue with discrete steps of no more than three months,
  – continue looking for low risk, quick wins;
- *Manage ongoing project*:
  – continue delivery,
  – continue monitoring and reporting,
  – continue internal marketing;
- *Planning for project completion*:
  – politics,
  – shareholders and stakeholders,
  – business,
  – customers,
  – alliances.

As the CRM project plan is implemented, two issues should be considered: creep in project scope and understanding the implications of scale. McKinsey & Co. point out that as a project grows in scope, the system's development can take on a life of its own, incorporating new features that do not support business objectives but add considerable complexity and cost. IT professionals have learned that the bigger a project, the harder it is to integrate and the more likely it is to miss deadlines or be scrapped altogether.[49] The business objectives that the CRM system was intended to achieve must be kept under constant scrutiny and any efforts to increase the scope of the project must be evaluated very carefully.

As a project is planned, it is critical that the implications of scale increases are understood. Point estimates of future demand are not very helpful. Instead, estimates should be based on three levels of potential future demand: optimistic, most likely and pessimistic. As the numbers of users and customers grow, the system must be robust enough to accept the changes in volume. Also, having sufficient capacity to provide high levels of customer satisfaction needs to be considered in the plan. The main features of CRM implementation can be summarised under three very broad headings: people, systems and processes. An organisation cannot develop and operate appropriately customer-focused systems and processes without appropriately motivated and trained employees. Staffing resources need to be planned not only on the basis of most likely demand, but also potential peak demand. Ensuring the delivery of a superior customer experience during times of unexpectedly high demand requires the active engagement and commitment of all customer-facing staff and is a hallmark of a well-planned CRM implementation. The case study of

Nationwide Building Society's use of a CRM at the end of this chapter provides an excellent example of the key issues that need to be addressed in CRM implementation including the importance of employee engagement.

Employee engagement

The last of the four elements outlined at the start of this chapter is the engagement of employees to support the various initiatives that comprise the overall CRM programme. Employees have a crucial role to play within each of the CRM processes examined in this book and the change management and project management activities discussed in this chapter are highly dependent on engagement of employees for their success.

Organisations now recognise the significant value that their employees contribute to the business – which extends well beyond the basic fulfilment of core duties. Employees are instrumental in implementing customer service policy, improving process efficiencies and nurturing consumer confidence and custom. The importance of employee engagement is in the ascendant as companies focus more on creating an outstanding customer experience.

Employee engagement requires commitment from the company's personnel. However, across the world, research indicates that employees show a general inability to commit. A landmark global study was conducted by Walker Information Global Network and the Hudson Institute. More than 9,700 full- and part-time employees representing business, non-profit and government organisations in 32 countries participated in the study.[50] The researchers found 34 per cent of employees are 'truly loyal', 8 per cent are 'accessible', 31 per cent are 'trapped' and 27 per cent are 'high risk'. Only slightly more than half feel a strong personal attachment to their employer and only six in ten employees believe their organisation deserves their loyalty. This unwillingness to commit breeds an even weaker sense of loyalty.

'Truly loyal' employees are the most desirable employees as they feel a deep attachment to their organisations, want to be there and plan to stay for at least another two years. In turn, these truly loyal workers are prepared to go the extra mile to get the job done and often serve as role models for their peers. 'Accessible' employees are satisfied with their employers; however, they might not stay with the organisation. A much lower level of commitment is found among employees identified as trapped or high risk. Although trapped employees do not want to remain in the organisation, they intend to stay because they do not have other options or may be unable or unwilling to make the effort to pursue other employment. An amazing 31 per cent of workers worldwide are 'trapped' – these workers are typically poorer performers, at least in part because they are not likely to go 'beyond the call of duty'. The 27 per cent of high risk employees do not want to stay and plan to leave.

Among the most significant findings of this study is verification that an employee's job performance is directly tied to their level of commitment to the organisation. Therefore, how all the company's human resources are engaged, but especially those who have any form of customer contact, is a key factor in determining CRM success. There is a wide body of research to support the claim that the surest way to enhance competitive performance is through recruiting and selecting the best employees, training and motivating them and providing effective leadership. This will maximise the likelihood of employees effectively engaging with both customers and their colleagues.

John McKean, a veteran CRM expert, has recently identified eight major areas the enterprise needs to focus on to achieve strong customer relationships:

1. *Leading the human firm* – leading the human firm is about selecting, developing and fulfilling your employees so they can impact most effectively on the key needs of the customer.
2. *Acknowledging customers* – understanding and acknowledging the customer's existence, importance, feelings and special requirements.
3. *Treating customers with respect* – understanding how best to treat the customer and respecting factors such as their time, privacy, personal space and diversity.
4. *Building trust* – customers should always be treated honestly and ethically. Responding rapidly to problems or queries helps develop trust.
5. *Communicating humanly* – involves understanding and developing the skills to create the most effective communication between employee and customer.
6. *Implementing the human touch consistently* – is concerned with making the customer feel that they are being treated by a caring fellow human being.
7. *Understanding and applying the human touch as a process* – each human touch can be viewed as one of a series of steps to make up the total customer experience. Businesses should recognise the need to deliver a consistent experience regardless of the channel used by the customer.
8. *Implementing technology to humanise* – CRM technology dehumanises as much as it humanises. Efforts must be made to create a similar level of outstanding customer experience to that of a personal experience with an employee.[51]

McKean's research supports the need to select, develop and empower employees to bring about their full engagement and their commitment to delivering an outstanding customer experience. We now address selection, development and empowerment of employees.

Selecting employees

Employee engagement starts with the recruitment process – ensuring that the best employees are selected in the first place. The high cost of recruitment means that it is important for employers to find recruits with both the necessary skills and the willingness to be trained and retained by the company. Success rates can be greatly enhanced by providing potential employees with full and accurate information about job requirements and expectations and the work environment. Failure to do so can result in disillusioned employees, low employee retention rates and negative word-of-mouth as employees warn other potential recruits not to apply for positions within the company.[52]

Companies should exercise special care in selecting employees who not only demonstrate appropriate skills and experience, but whose values and motivations match those of the corporate ethos. More often than not technical or task-based aptitudes can be taught and developed once the person is in the post. The individual's work ethic and psychological characteristics are likely to be less malleable. Companies should adopt an approach of 'recruit for attitude, train for skills'.

Techniques such as psychometric testing are frequently used as a means of identifying the personality profile of people who are likely to be successful in delivering service quality and developing relationships with customers. Traditionally, such testing techniques were more likely to be used for management and graduate positions than for customer contact, or administrative or secretarial jobs. However, the high costs associated with employee turnover and the general trend towards greater job mobility have caused many organisations to hone their selection practices. Increasingly companies are using techniques such as psychometric testing and assessment centres for a wider range of employment positions. This underlines the importance that companies are now placing on the 'emotional content' of front-line roles.

Customer-facing employees can only function effectively with support from others in the company who, though they do not come into direct contact with the customer, nevertheless play a very important role and directly influence the service ultimately provided for customers. By viewing employees as a value-adding element, companies can direct the appropriate level of attention towards maximising the impact of employee activities and motivating and rewarding employees to make the desired contribution.

Developing employees

Research has shown that employees who are unclear about the role they are supposed to perform become demotivated, which in turn can lead to customer dissatisfaction and defection. So new employees must be carefully prepared for the work ahead of them, as their early days in a company colour their attitudes and perceptions towards it. Those organisations lacking a strong service ethos may need to introduce a major change management programme aimed at all employees. Internal marketing programmes aimed at instilling customer consciousness and service orientation are increasingly being adopted by organisations.

The basic premise behind internal marketing involves getting employees to recognise the impact of their behaviour and attitudes on customers. This is especially important for employees who are as close – or closer – psychologically and physically to customers as they are to each other. Their skills and customer orientation are critical to the way the customer views the organisation and, therefore, help determine their future loyalty.

Some of the best examples of employee engagement programmes come from the airline industry. Companies such as Virgin Atlantic, Singapore Airlines and Southwest Airlines are good examples of sustained positive employee engagement. The Disney Corporation is also a good example of a company with a strong employee engagement programme. Development of employees plays a major role in Disney's success.

Engaging and empowering employees

Employees need to be motivated to use their discretion in order to deliver a better quality service to customers. Engaging employees involves creating the right culture and climate for employees to operate in, hence the close linkage with change management. Employees need the knowledge that allows them to understand and contribute to organisational performance and the power to take decisions that influence organisational direction and performance.

Au Bon Pain, a chain of bakery cafés on the east coast of the US, has focused on employee engagement as a means of creating increased employee value in its bakery café chain. Managers are empowered to make significant alterations to processes, procedures, store layout and other policies, in order to develop service quality and marketing activities designed to build stronger relationships with frequent customers. These changes led to a significant performance improvement. Staff turnover in one of the Boston stores dropped to 10 per cent per annum for entry-level jobs versus an industry norm of about 200 per cent. Absenteeism plummeted and sales soared as customers developed a relationship with counter staff. Productivity levels have increased despite the reduction in employee numbers. Under the Partner-Manager Program at Au Bon Pain, employees can earn double the industry-average wage. With this approach the quality of employees changed radically and word-of-mouth created a strong demand for jobs at all levels within the chain.

One of the barriers to employee engagement is middle managers feeling threatened when they have to delegate power and authority to subordinates. Equally, some staff are reluctant to take on such responsibility and believe that making decisions is a manager's responsibility. Engaged and empowered employees provide a faster and more flexible response to customers' needs. The benefits of employee engagement need to be balanced with potentially increased labour, recruitment and training costs. Hence the costs have to be seen as a long-term investment in CRM.

Training and development

CRM initiatives should usually include both employee training and executive development activities. Depending on their scope and scale these activities could be considered as part of change management or employee engagement. Training and development activity starts with a needs analysis. This will involve a thorough review to identify the requisite mix of knowledge, skills or attitudes that need to be developed for effective CRM to take place. It should be based on interviews with appropriate executives and employees within the firm and needs to be undertaken by someone with a good understanding of the organisation and the particular training requirements of any CRM technology being adopted.

The focus of executive development will be on ensuring managers understand the full extent of the enterprise's CRM initiative including its opportunities and potential problems. As noted earlier, research suggests that executives are often not fully aware of what they are implementing, or the costs and timing of the CRM programmes. We have found a number of instances where detailed employee training is in place but there is no supporting executive briefing or executive development.

Executive development activities programmes typically comprise a series of workshops or events involving managers drawn from all functions within the organisation. These should precede employee training and should make management fully aware of the nature and objectives of the company's CRM initiatives. The objectives and scope of these programmes will vary considerably across different organisations. Figure 11.10 shows a selection of programmes that we have developed for different companies.

CRM Implementers Programme

Industry: Insurance *Objective:* A senior executive programme of workshops to create a common understanding and vocabulary of CRM; to review findings of a CRM readiness audit and to determine key CRM actions to be implemented. *Scope*: Top and senior management. A series of three two-day workshops involving a total of 50 executives.

CRM Promoters Programme

Industry: Postal services and logistics *Objective:* A senior executive programme aimed at developing a full appreciation of the current and future role of CRM in a major postal administration. This executive group's role was proactively to promote CRM to its customers and internal staff. *Scope:* One-day workshops for 150 top executives including business unit chief executives.

Customer Management Programme

Industry: Banking *Objective:* A change management programme aimed at major improvement in external and internal customer service. *Scope:* All employees in a major division of a North American bank. A series of one-day workshops for a target audience of 500 employees from Board of Directors to all managers, administrative and secretarial staff.

CRM Account Directors Programme

Industry: Telecommunications *Objective:* A series of CRM workshops aimed at developing a common framework for CRM throughout the organisation; sharing examples of customer successes and successful internal CRM applications; introduction and use of a new customer diagnostic tool. *Scope:* A series of fifteen one-day workshops for account directors, senior sales staff and executives. Part of an integrated CRM initiative involving more specialised training, production of white papers, etc.

Customer and Strategy 'Focus' Programme

Industry: Telecommunications *Objective:* A series of three-day workshops for top executives and one-day workshops for next level of management involving a detailed review of customer and business strategy. *Scope:* A series of cascade programmes for 400 top managers. The first, 'Focus 100', aimed at 100 top executives reporting to divisional chief executives; The second, 'Focus 300', aimed at 300 managers reporting to these executives.

Figure 11.10 Examples of CRM executive development programmes

Employee training may focus on developing particular skills or on changing attitudes. A skills-oriented approach may be appropriate for introduction of a new call centre system. An approach emphasising attitude change may be used to address issues such as improving customer service or building a customer-oriented culture. Where a CRM technology solution is adopted in the organisation, the training should include sessions designed immediately to practise and apply the newly acquired knowledge.

Where implementation problems are being experienced they should be discussed frankly with employees, together with an explanation as to what is being done to address them. Lack of this awareness can cause CRM initiatives to falter or fail. For example, in a major sales force automation project in a large pharmaceutical company, the failure to communicate problems and resulting resistance by the sales force to using the system almost caused failure of the project.

In many instances a CRM employee training and executive development programme needs to be cascaded throughout the organisation so that all levels of employees are informed and engaged. A large-scale CRM programme will typically have different component parts aimed at different levels within the organisation. The case study on implementing CRM at Mercedes-Benz at the end of this chapter is a good example of an integrated CRM development programme that has a set of tailored developmental, experiential and executive development activities that cascade from the Board of Directors to all customer-facing employees.

The CRM budget

Many CRM budgets are underfunded in terms of what is required for successful implementation. In this chapter we have examined four critical elements of a successful CRM programme that support the five key CRM processes examined in detail in the previous chapters – readiness assessment, change management, project management and employee engagement. Of these, the last three represent line items that may be seriously underfunded or even neglected as line items in the budget. Only the implementation readiness assessment represents an item that is generally modest in cost and which can be readily identified in terms of its cost.

If we examine the budget items that are typically associated with CRM, when viewed from an IT perspective, the total is likely to be a very large amount. However, even that may not be enough as costs associated with change management, project management and employee engagement may not have been taken into account. Lack of company experience about the real total costs of a major CRM initiative is the usual major reason for this.

In Chapter 6 we discussed the critical observation that most of the historical investment in CRM goes into data and technology, but these aspects represent only 25 per cent of the competency determinants for CRM success. It is the areas that involve people, organisation, culture and change where the funding levels may be neglected or not adequately provided for in the CRM budget. However, these areas are critical to the success of companies' CRM initiatives.

The IT department is frequently responsible for planning the CRM budget, as the most obvious and visible expenditure will be the software licences, hardware, systems integration and consulting. However, as Gentle points out, the IT department is often less experienced with regard to CRM projects. As a result, it omits non-obvious costs in the budget and may make budgetary mistakes on both the hard and soft elements of CRM projects by:

- seriously underestimating the number of data sources that need to be migrated over and the corresponding quality;
- seriously underestimating how consulting costs can spiral out of control when there is no cross-functional agreement on business processes. This may result in a lot of additional work, as consultants and the business work to define things that the system integrator's methodology assumed were already known;
- being unaware, or underestimating, certain business-related line items that are not present in other types of IT projects, which consequently fall through cracks. These include: user training on a far greater scale than what the company is used to; resources for change management to drive process change and ensure data quality; and resources for data operations, to manage the importing and exporting of data;
- seeing the budget as a means to drive a project through to implementation only, after which time the project is assumed to be either self-sufficient or able to wait till the next budget cycle for subsequent funding.[53]

This provides a good argument for input in the development of the CRM budget from a cross-functional CRM team with representatives from marketing, human resources, procurement and finance, as well as IT. A consideration of the full implications of change management, project management and employee engagement by these groups will help ensure a more accurate and balanced budget. Also, the benefit of a pilot will help identify budget costs more accurately.

For international projects, there is frequently the expectation that everything should be centrally funded. While this may be the case for software licences, consulting, implementation and IT costs, it is rarely so for in-country change management resources. With no central funding for the CRM project, countries may be unable or unwilling to provide the resources for this critical function.[54] As a result, the success of CRM initiatives in other countries may be under threat.

CRM budgets are difficult to determine and their preparation will benefit from early involvement with business-oriented internal finance staff and experienced CRM managers or consultants. Our experience in reviewing CRM budgets for large organisations points to several other problems such as:

- significantly underestimating change management, training and employee engagement costs;
- significantly overestimating licence costs and not understanding the discounts that could be achieved from vendors in a 'soft' market;
- not understanding the items that could be capitalised as capital expenditure (capex) and the items that needed to be expensed as operating expenditure (opex);
- not understanding the internal financial approval system for large opex and capex expenditures by senior finance committees and the Board;

- using business case modelling that was superficial and based on point estimates (rather than looking at a range of estimates including pessimistic and optimistic scenarios);
- not properly considering the political issues associated with international business units and their agreement to sign up to potentially large local budget commitments;
- key elements of a CRM programme not being time and money 'boxed' to force the 80:20 rule of delivering quick wins;
- not having some contingency funding sources available.

In summary, CRM budgets are frequently inaccurate, underfunded and poorly constructed. This is usually because of a lack of company experience in developing CRM budgets, a failure to consider non-IT related elements of CRM, not taking into account capex and opex considerations and not seeking independent expert advice in vendor assessment and licence negotiations. There is also a lack of published material on this topic.[55] Considerable efforts should therefore be directed at constructing thorough and well-argued budgets to implement the CRM project. Having progressed to the stage of developing a comprehensive and detailed plan for a strategic approach to a new CRM initiative, it would be highly disappointing to have the budget for it delayed or under-resourced because of reductions in budgeted items, or budgeted items not being approved.

SUMMARY

This final chapter examines the topic of organising for implementation with reference to four elements that are critical to a successful CRM programme: implementation readiness assessment, change management, project management and employee engagement. Implementing CRM represents a considerable challenge in most enterprises. Any successful CRM implementation should be preceded by the development of a clear, relevant and well-communicated CRM strategy. Organisations need to adopt a strategic definition of CRM that focuses on business issues rather than emphasising IT issues.

This is especially important if the IT-based CRM failures of the past are to be avoided. The frequently quoted examples of CRM failure usually refer not to failure of CRM as a concept (unless very narrowly and inappropriately defined), but to the failure of a CRM technology project or CRM solution. In the early 2000s, when CRM was still a relatively new approach, few people had experience of the new leading edge CRM solutions. As with pioneers in any area, managers who broke new ground with CRM solutions made mistakes. Today, there is no excuse for not learning from past experience and taking a thorough, well-planned approach to implementation.

We have now learned a number of important lessons in implementing CRM. Short-term wins have more chance of securing enterprise-wide commitment than do drawn out CRM projects with over-ambitious goals. A CRM strategy designed to deliver incremental returns provides the flexibility and scope for progressive improvement. We have also learned the benefits of benchmarking best practice in CRM. Among leading corporations around the world, benchmarking CRM has now become a more prevalent practice. Most of all, we have learned that an effectively implemented strategic approach to CRM is an important source of competitive advantage.

Successful CRM demands coordination and collaboration and, most of all, integration: integration of information and information systems to provide business intelligence; integration of channels to enable the development and delivery of a single unified view of the customer; and integration of resources, functions and processes to ensure a productive, customer-oriented working environment and competitive organisational performance.

We have now completed our exploration of what we term *strategic customer management*. Strategic customer management encompasses relationship marketing and CRM as well as the more tactically oriented customer management activities such as campaign management. Although these terms are widely used within the business and academic communities, there remains today considerable confusion regarding their meaning, focus and coverage.

In this book we have called for a clear distinction to be made between relationship marketing and CRM and, in particular, for their integration. Relationship marketing represents an overarching philosophy that recognises the importance of building relationships with multiple stakeholders, or market domains, with the objective of creating successful customer relationships which lead to shareholder value creation.

Strategic customer management starts with a focus on the broader stakeholder ecosystem that is inherent within the contemporary view of relationship marketing. As an overarching concept, relationship marketing encompasses many aspects, which we have examined in Chapters 2 to 5. The emphasis placed on different stakeholders or market domains will vary substantially according to the industry sector in which the enterprise operates. In the business-to-business sector a whole range of infrastructural government and regulatory stakeholders need to be considered in concert with customer relationship considerations. In the business-to-consumer sector, enterprises also need to sharpen their focus on relationship-oriented issues, such as customer communities, social media, co-creation and an increasingly empowered and engaged customer base.

We contend that a focus on the broader set of stakeholder relationships inherent in relationship marketing is more likely to deliver superior financial and business benefits. Research in this latter area is embryonic. However, recent evidence from 1,716 firms over a four-year period found that, in general, placing more emphasis on a broad set of stakeholders (including customers, employees, suppliers, shareholders, communities and regulators) when developing marketing strategy is more important in achieving superior market performance than engaging in more traditional market-driven or sustainability-centred efforts.[56]

It is from this background of a broader range of relationships that the enterprise should formulate and implement its CRM initiatives. Management of relationships is admittedly a complex task but, by adopting an integrated approach to relationship marketing and CRM, enterprises will be better placed to realise the huge benefits of having superior relationships with customers and other stakeholders and make progress on the journey towards achieving excellence in strategic customer management.

Annex

The comprehensive CRM audit: Part 1

The strategy development process

Score each statement on a scale 0 to 5

Rating for the organisation – existing and desired performance (5 = very well; 0 = very poorly)
Importance to the organisation (5 = very important; 0 = no importance)

1. The strategy development process	Importance to the organisation	Existing performance for the organisation	Desired performance for the organisation
Business strategy (including leadership and sponsorship)			
1. Senior management in the organisation has demonstrated strong leadership in introducing and supporting CRM initiatives.			
2. There is a strong and well-supported Board-level executive who is a committed sponsor of the organisation's CRM initiatives.			
3. Senior management work together in a united manner and resolve cross-functional conflicts.			
4. The organisation has a vision, mission, purpose, or statement of direction that clarifies its commitment to quality and customer focus and that is clearly understood by staff. The organisation has a clear set of values that support the vision and these are shared by most of our staff.			
5. The organisation develops and reviews strategic and annual business plans that incorporate an analysis of market trends, customer characteristics, industry evolution, the competitive landscape and technology impacts in electronic and social media.			
6. The organisation has a clear view on the value discipline on which it competes: customer intimacy, operational excellence or product leadership disciplines and their relative emphasis.			
7. The likely future changes and impacts in electronic commerce and social media, as well as shifts in role of channels and intermediaries are considered on a regular basis by senior management.			

8. The overall strategic plan serves as the basis for the annual business plans of the organisation and its functional departments.

9. Managers and supervisors understand their specific responsibilities in carrying out the actions in the strategic plan.

10. The organisation comprehensively reviews and improves its management systems at least annually to an international, industry-specific or internally developed standard.

Customer strategy

11. The organisation has a clear view on which customers it wishes to serve and which ones it does not wish to serve.

12. The organisation considers not only its immediate customers but also its customer's customer in making its marketing decisions.

13. The organisation has done a thorough and recent segmentation of its customer base.

14. The organisation has selected the appropriate level of segmentation of its customer base, i.e., macro-segments, micro-segments or one-to-one.

15. We consider customer segments in terms of value preferences of benefits sought, in addition to more general customer characteristics.

16. The organisation customises its product or service offer to different segments where appropriate.

17. At least annually the organisation seeks new customer opportunities beyond its existing offer to customers.

18. Our business strategy and customer strategy are closely aligned.

19. We have considered the appropriate degree of customer individualisation given our position in the market and the nature of our competition.

20. The organisation has plans for future customer individualisation and customer information requirements.

The comprehensive CRM audit: Part 2

The value creation process

Score each statement on a scale 0 to 5

Rating for the organisation – existing and desired performance (5 = very well; 0 = very poorly)
Importance to the organisation (5 = very important; 0 = no importance)

2. The value creation process *The value the customer receives*	Importance to the organisation	Existing performance for the organisation	Desired performance for the organisation
1. The value the customer receives gets as much attention with senior management as the value they receive by way of revenue and profits.			
2. We have a clear view throughout the organisation regarding the nature of the 'core' and 'augmented' offer made to our customers.			
3. At least annually we review whether further supplementary services should be added to our offer to increase the value received by our customers.			
4. Customer relationships and the impact of the brand are fully understood and managed within the organisation.			
5. The organisation recognises the importance of maximising the number of customer 'advocates' and taking action to minimise customer 'terrorists' and we have established listening posts to monitor consumer sentiment.			
6. The organisation has developed a written value proposition identifying the value offered to customers.			
7. Our value proposition is tailored to different customer segments.			
8. The organisation assesses customer value and end-user customer satisfaction and quantifies overall satisfaction with specific attributes such as responsiveness, accuracy and timeliness.			
9. We set targets using comparative data drawn from high-performing organisations.			
10. We measure complaints and other key indicators of customer (end user) dissatisfaction (e.g. returns, warranty claims), record these indicators by cause and act on them.			

The value the organisation receives

11. We utilise an appropriate level of segmentation based on satisfaction measures, sales, profits and other relevant historical information.

12. The organisation has identified how acquisition costs and annual profit earned per customer vary at the segment level. We have identified our most profitable customers and calculated our share of their wallet.

13. We measure customer retention rates at the segment level and have quantified the profit impact of improvement in retention rates.

14. The organisation has identified profitable and non-profitable segments and adjusts the style and cost of campaigns, win-back strategies, customer service and support accordingly.

15. We have identified the amounts we spend on both customer acquisition and customer retention at the aggregate and segment levels and have confirmed these expenditures are appropriately balanced.

16. We have identified targets for customer retention improvement at the segment level and have developed plans to achieve them.

17. The organisation understands the value that each customer segment brings to the company in terms of their lifetime value.

18. We have calculated the relative potential profit improvement from: acquisition, cross-selling, up-selling, retention and advocacy at the segment level and have plans to realise this potential.

19. We use a comprehensive set of metrics to measure customer acquisition, retention, profitability and lifetime value at the segment level and these are reported to senior management at least quarterly.

20. We regularly review competitive activity and quantify how this activity may impact on our customer value metrics; any significant changes are always communicated to senior management.

The comprehensive CRM audit: Part 3

The multi-channel integration process

Score each statement on a scale 0 to 5

Rating for the organisation – existing and desired performance (5 = very well; 0 = very poorly)
Importance to the organisation (5 = very important; 0 = no importance)

3. The multi-channel integration process: 'the customer contact zone'

Channel options and strategies

	Importance to the organisation	Existing performance for the organisation	Desired performance for the organisation
1. Our senior management has considered the future role of both existing and potential channel participants in our industry.			
2. We have a clear view on the future impact of all electronic channels, including social media, in our industry.			
3. Possible structural changes in our industry (disintermediation or reintermediation) have been fully considered.			
4. We fully understand the advantages and disadvantages of the major channel categories (sales force, outlets, telephony, direct, e-commerce, mobile, social media, etc.) when developing our channel strategies.			
5. The organisation formally reviews the range of channel strategy options every year.			
6. The organisation understands the channels our customers wish to use at different stages of their relationship with us; e.g. pre-sales, sales and post-sales.			
7. We know how customer channel preference varies at the segment level across different products or services sold by our company.			
8. We utilise appropriate analytical tools such as market structure maps to identify the value and volume of goods and services passing through different channels for our company and for our competitors.			
9. Changes in our customers' channel usage and preferences and general trends in channel usage are reviewed regularly.			
10. The organisation has an agreed set of metrics for measuring channel performance.			

Customer experience and multi-channel integration

11. The organisation has a strategy for integrated channel management.

12. We monitor the customer experience within channel and across channels and compare our performance with that of our competitors.

13. The organisation has identified what constitutes an outstanding (or 'perfect') customer experience and strives to deliver it.

14. The customer experiences consistency in 'look, touch and feel' across channels and this experience is in keeping with our brand image.

15. The organisation collects information on all relevant types of customer interactions (e.g., calls, faxes, mail, e-mail, Web, social media and EDI transactions) to ensure that customer requirements and targets are met.

16. The economics of different channels are thoroughly understood.

17. The organisation is effective in adding new channels to complement existing channels.

18. New channels are integrated with existing channels so that an individual is recognised as the customer regardless of the channels used.

19. Customer-affecting applications, such as order handling, work across all our channels. Products purchased in one channel (e.g., the Internet) can be returned through other channels (e.g. a retail outlet).

20. We consider channel integration issues for our employees and partners as well as our customers.

The comprehensive CRM audit: Part 4

The information management process

Score each statement on a scale 0 to 5

Rating for the organisation – existing and desired performance (5 = very well; 0 = very poorly)

Importance to the organisation (5 = very important; 0 = no importance)

	Importance to the organisation	Existing performance for the organisation	Desired performance for the organisation
4. The information management process *The data repository and CRM architecture*			
1. Where data on customers resides in different data bases we know its location, accuracy and completeness.			
2. We have created a central data warehouse and have a single view of the customer. Information in the warehouse is accurate and complete.			
3. The organisation has an appropriate structure for its data repository (data warehouse, data marts, etc.) given our present and planned customer data requirements.			
4. Our data structure reflects our business and customer strategies in terms of segment granularity and personalisation requirements.			
5. Our customer information links with the company's existing systems such as fulfilment, service and finance.			
6. We have an appropriate strategy for our IT systems including hardware and software. We have taken account of potential of developments such as outsourcing/'the Cloud', Web services and social commerce.			
7. We effectively utilise general data-mining tools for customer insight and task-specific analysis tools for market segmentation, customer profiling, profitability analysis, predictive modelling, social analytics, etc.			
8. We have identified and utilised appropriate front-office systems for CRM and considered integration issues with back-office systems.			
9. We realistically appraise and address significant: systems integration, people, processes and training tasks associated with introduction of any new CRM system, e.g., sales force automation.			

10. We fully investigate and budget for change management, project management and employee engagement issues associated with any proposed new CRM systems we plan to introduce.

Information and customer knowledge management

11. The organisation has introduced processes to provide relevant data and information to all appropriate staff.

12. The organisation ensures the integrity of the data it collects in terms of relevancy, accuracy, currency and objectivity.

13. We ensure security of all sensitive customer data (e.g., credit card numbers and personal information).

14. We verify that all individuals who have access to sensitive and proprietary data understand the security requirements and protocols.

15. The organisation has implemented processes to prevent the unauthorised use or alteration of sensitive and proprietary data.

16. We regularly consider opportunities to introduce new e-commerce applications to improve customer service or to reduce costs.

17. There is an integrated plan agreed across all channels and functional departments for the collection and use of customer information.

18. The customer information system allows information about individual customers to be recognised and used to produce summary information about the customer for use in customer applications and campaign management.

19. The company uses customer analysis techniques to provide proactive customer information for cross-selling and up-selling purposes.

20. The company makes effective use of analytical techniques, such as predictive modelling, that use customer information to develop greater customer profitability and increased lifetime value.

The comprehensive CRM audit: Part 5

The performance assessment process

Score each statement on a scale 0 to 5

Rating for the organisation – existing and desired performance (5 = very well; 0 = very poorly)
Importance to the organisation (5 = very important; 0 = no importance)

5. The performance assessment process *Shareholder results*	Importance to the organisation	Existing performance for the organisation	Desired performance for the organisation
1. Our top management recognises the importance of leadership in creating employee, customer and shareholder value.			
2. The key drivers of shareholder results – employee value, customer value, shareholder value and cost reduction – are fully understood.			
3. We place sufficient emphasis in the organisation on employee value.			
4. We rank ourselves highly in terms of recruiting, selecting, developing and empowering our employees.			
5. We place sufficient emphasis in the organisation on customer value.			
6. We rank ourselves highly in terms of delivering superior customer value opportunities in every attractive customer segment.			
7. We place sufficient emphasis in the organisation on shareholder value.			
8. We rank ourselves highly in terms of creating shareholder value compared with our major competitors.			
9. We take full advantage of all opportunities for cost reduction. Cost reduction strategies do not negatively impact customer satisfaction.			
10. We have developed, or are developing, a balanced scorecard or linkage model in the organisation that addresses the relationship between employee satisfaction, customer satisfaction and business results.			

Standards, metrics and key performance indicators

11. We have developed our own standards across all the areas of CRM that are important to us.

12. We have adopted standards developed by others (e.g., CMAT or COPC standards) and used these to benchmark our performance against relevant external comparators.

13. We have identified and put in place appropriate customer metrics.

14. We have identified and put in place appropriate people and process metrics.

15. We have identified and put in place appropriate strategic metrics.

16. We have identified and put in place appropriate output and comparative metrics and special metrics for e-commerce and social influence marketing.

17. A strategy map (or success map) has been developed that identifies the chain of 'cause and effect' logic that connects our company's strategy with the drivers that lead to commercial success.

18. The organisation has identified the most important KPIs and these are reported to senior management on a regular basis.

19. Frameworks such as the balanced scorecard are utilised to ensure there is a focus on all relevant areas of performance, not just financial ones.

20. A CRM performance monitoring process is in place and attention has been given to making sure KPIs are communicated in a visually engaging manner to management and other relevant employees, e.g., by using dashboards.

CASE 11.1: Nationwide Building Society – fulfilling a CRM vision

The company

Nationwide is one of the UK's leading financial services providers. It has 15 million customers and over £193 billion in assets. Its origins lie in Northampton and within the cooperative movement in London in the 1800s. Over one hundred mergers later – most notably the merger between the Nationwide and the Anglia Building Societies in 1987 – it is now the UK's third largest mortgage lender and second largest savings provider. More significantly, it is the largest building society in the world.

Nationwide is a mutually owned organisation; it belongs to its members and is run for their benefit. It is this mutual status that makes Nationwide different from traditional banks and it is committed to staying mutual. Its business strategy is very straightforward. It aims to be the UK's leading financial services provider, offering a meaningful and unique alternative to the publicly listed banks, demonstrated through long-term superior products and customer service.

Nationwide maintains an extensive branch network. This is complemented by services available by phone, post and by using PCs, mobile phones and tablet devices for Internet banking. Nationwide was the first to launch an Internet banking service in the UK, first to have an Internet banking service available through TV and offered Europe's first Pocket PC PDA mobile banking service. This case study examines Nationwide's continuous innovation in CRM over the ten years from 2002 to 2012.

The challenge

At the start of the 2000s, Nationwide needed a CRM solution so it could access customer data and update data in real time across all customer touch points. It also realised that any solution would be part of an ongoing CRM journey. The CRM system needed to handle over two million transactions per month, including new data being recorded or updated, and employees interacting with the customer files. Any solution needed to be available and reliable to meet customers' growing expectations in the competitive financial services space. At this time, Nationwide had over 12,000 employees at call centres or in the branches throughout the UK, who required fast accurate access to customer data.

The CRM initiative needed ongoing consultancy, project management, testing and development to provide a continually evolving CRM system for Nationwide, one which would provide outstanding customer service for Nationwide's members. Nationwide needed strong technology partnerships for such a large and highly complex CRM project, in a market where many other projects have failed. Nationwide also recognised that, for successful CRM, project management needs to be supported by an enduring change management programme that ensures employee engagement and commitment.

The solution

As a mutual, Nationwide has long been recognised as a highly customer-centric organisation. Nationwide's ongoing CRM development programme commenced in the early 2000s. Unisys, the global IT services company, was chosen to undertake the first phase project because of its intimate understanding of Nationwide's business and in-depth experience in the financial services market. The first project went 'live' in late 2002.

Nationwide's goal was to enhance the quality of interactions with its customers. This was achieved by deploying Pitney Bowes Portrait software to all users in the branches, call centres and central operations teams. The CRM system provides a single customer view of a member's profile and accounts so Nationwide's employees can identify a customer's needs in a timely and accurate manner. The database also details previous conversations, which reduces time spent assisting the customer and ensures the customer feels more attention is being paid to their personal needs. A significant budget was set aside for training and change management so that Nationwide's employees would be able to embrace its vision and the associated changes needed in process and behaviour. This initiative won the CRM magazine award for the best customer interaction management led CRM project, was a finalist in the Gartner CRM Excellence Awards and won the Institute of Financial Services CRM Financial Innovation Award.

The CRM system enabled Nationwide's call centre agents to maximise the value of inbound communications from customers by using inbound opportunities to collect and correct missing or inaccurate data, allowing the agents to create more meaningful and valuable future dialogues. Predictive analytics can even put a value on each item of missing data, helping the balance between selling, service and data quality. Between 2002 and 2007, Nationwide doubled its annual profits and achieved its aim of increasing customer loyalty, with half of its customers regarding the society as a 'customer advocate' that puts their interests ahead of its profits.

Since the initial implementation, further initiatives went live, each one incrementally improving the scope and functionality of the system. The second phase in 2003 introduced personalised sales and service messages to branch and call centre employees, enabling employees to maximise new business opportunities. This system enhances the service to members and helps identify potential business. For example, if a fixed rate mortgage is approaching maturity, the system provides an automatic prompt to employees, who can then remind the customer when there is contact through any channel – retail, phone or mail, with the Internet being added in 2005.

Nationwide developed new and better ways to transform the way it interacts with its customers so that it delivers the right experience, but at the right cost. With the CRM system, employees can now easily view and assess members' profiles and their specific needs at a glance, which means employees are more informed and members have enhanced interactions with the society. Focused initially on event-based marketing, the integrated system provides a comprehensive view of each customer relationship. It presents Nationwide's customer advisers with relevant offers based on campaigns built using Unica's campaign management software. The marketing analytics system allows Nationwide to deliver more personalised marketing offers, based on customer behaviours and engagement with the building society. For example, if a customer rings the call centre, the agent is alerted to relevant products that he or she can speak to the customer about. Unica automatically generates these relevant offers based on the customer's account and transaction data, helping Nationwide's marketing team determine the best follow-up offers to provide via the Web, direct mail or during the customer's next interaction with the branch or call centre.

Having achieved CRM integration into all its main business operations, in 2006 the focus at Nationwide turned to how to exploit the embedded CRM capability to support an increasing rate of business change and challenge. A new 'service request' feature was added that allowed employees to record free text interactions with a customer that would help tailor the future service offered. The ability to 'hand-off' service processes from front to back office was added, while showing progress of activities such as charge refund requests in the contact history to help manage customer queries. Many different solutions were found to solve new business problems quickly, and at low cost, by using the joined up CRM system. A notable success was the implementation of a new employee rewards system that relies on Portrait to capture all lead referral and sales recording interactions.

Customer interactions recorded in Portrait are sampled and used for independently managed customer service research through the Society's 'Service Tracker' initiative. This provides fast customer feedback on recent interactions at a business unit level, be they at branch or call centre level, to help identify good and bad service experience issues and drive improvements in service levels.

By 2010, recognising the growing need to share more customer insight with front-line employees, and wanting to increase focus on relationship building through cross-selling activities, work started on the latest milestone in the CRM journey. In 18 months, over ten key new features were added including a unique interactive visualisation of the customer's financial relationship known as the 'Scoping Wheel', a new customer needs analysis electronic form, a new lead distribution capability to pass centrally produced leads out to the channels, new consumer risk credit acceptance insight alerts shown in the Scoping Wheel and streamlined data capture screens.

In 2011 Nationwide redeveloped its Internet banking platform to improve usability and provide a flexible architecture for the future. Developed in partnership with IBM, the new platform integrates with over 30 line-of-business applications and took nearly three years to develop. The Internet banking platform integrates with Nationwide's multi-channel CRM system using Pitney Bowes Interaction Optimiser to deliver customer offers and service messages into the new Internet bank. The CRM system enables Nationwide to cross-sell products more effectively. At its peak, 196 people were involved in the project, together with 50 subject-matter experts. The new platform works with iPad and Android tablets, with other smaller devices, such as smartphones, being evaluated.

The results

This ongoing CRM programme has been judged highly successful and has resulted in increased sales, customer satisfaction and profitability. There has been a wide range of further benefits realised by using the CRM system. For example, Nationwide has substantially reduced the number of mailings, saving money and time. The building society is highly successful in encouraging members to use the Internet for their financial needs, be it banking, mortgage advice, investment or insurance.

Nationwide places strong emphasis on collecting, analysing and acting on customer and employee feedback. Its efforts have been recognised for many years through a large number of external industry awards including the Management Today/Unisys Service Excellence Award for the Financial Services sector, as well as being the overall winner of the award for all the categories. In 2011 Nationwide won over ten major awards for its products and services, including best building society and online lender.

Nationwide reported a strong performance for the second half year in 2011. There was a 4 per cent increase in gross lending and an underlying growth in mortgage assets funded by new savings deposits of £1.4 billion, up 250 per cent, and a growth in balances of £2.4 billion, up 167 per cent. Nationwide has continued to progress its strategy of expanding its market share in other areas, most notably banking products.

In the future, Nationwide's CRM system and data will become more and more comprehensive with increasing access to more customers' needs, preferences and interactions, widely relied upon to build relationships at a local level, support a genuinely multi-channel distribution strategy and provide the right insight to underpin the customer strategy and effective decision making.

CASE 11.2: Mercedes-Benz – building strategic customer management capability

The company

Mercedes-Benz is one of the world's most successful premium brands. Its technical perfection, innovative design features and numerous car legends have made the Mercedes star one the world's best-known trademarks today.

By 2000 major changes in the competitive structure of the European car market were under way. After a long history of reigning over a sellers' market, Mercedes-Benz experienced increased competition. Other premium brands such as BMW, Lexus, Audi and Jaguar were competing fiercely in the luxury car market where Mercedes was traditionally very strong. Also, many of these brands were expanding into new market segments. For example, the Mercedes 'A Class' focused on a new market segment that was more price sensitive than those in which the brand traditionally competed.

Historically, Mercedes-Benz cars had been sold in the UK through a franchised network of some 138 dealerships. Each of these was autonomous, with the exception of three dealerships owned by the distributor DaimlerChrysler UK (DCUK) – later to become Daimler UK, following the sale of the Chrysler brand in 2007. Mercedes-Benz UK (M-B UK) had relatively little control over relationships between these dealers and their customers. Dealers managed their own relationships, including customer research, data base management, acquisition and retention processes.

The challenge

With these major changes in the competitive structure of the car market, M-B UK was faced with a challenge. Research suggested that some Mercedes-Benz customers were less than happy with the service they received. Although the technical quality of the product was highly regarded, customers complained that the service that they received was not of the same high standard. This translated into declining customer satisfaction and increased defection. M-B UK recognised that the entire chain of relationships between manufacturer, dealers and customers needed a new approach.

Customers reported that there was an inconsistency between the communication that they received and the service that was delivered. Communication to the customer included both national product marketing along with some local dealer marketing initiatives. Enquiries from the customer went directly to the dealerships and were handled through their internal processes. These were sometimes inadequate. So, for example, request for test drives may not have been followed up by complacent salesmen, resulting in poor sales conversion rates. At this time, a uniform problem across dealerships of most car marques in the UK was that each dealership operated its own database. The information in this database could be out of date, inaccurate and missing important information. Critically, sales-people did not always appreciate that it was essential to record correct and complete customer information if effective contact was going to be sustained. In the past, like most distributors, M-B UK had focused primarily on the relationship with its dealer franchise network. In the future, the company needed to have a greater input into how the end customer relationship was managed. This entailed a new strategic approach to the distribution of cars.

This case study reviews M-B UK's sustained strategic customer management programme over a 12 year period aimed at addressing the challenge of continually improving CRM activities and customer relationships.

The solution

As a first step, in 2000 M-B UK decided to adopt a new distribution model for Mercedes-Benz passenger cars. They re-organised the market into 35 new, larger geographical areas and invited a number of existing dealerships to enter into new retailer agreements. This entailed these dealerships taking over responsibility for the retail sales and service of Mercedes in specific geographic territories or 'market areas' (MAs). For most franchises, these new MAs included up to six dealer outlets and required a substantial additional investment in new premises and facilities. M-B UK also decided to become much more heavily involved in retail operations through direct ownership of the MAs in London, Manchester and Birmingham. However, changes in the distribution were only the starting point for building improved relationships with customers.

Within M-B UK, a project management team was established, drawn from managers in marketing and operations. The project management team set about identifying the key CRM processes and determining how each process would be implemented throughout the new retail structure. Every aspect of the customer relationship needed to be carefully examined, to ensure value was created at every opportunity: for the customer, the MAs and M-B UK. The next step was to benchmark Mercedes-Benz against other leading marques as well as other best-in-class organisations. The research suggested that there were several areas where greater value could be delivered to the customer during both the sales process as well as during the ownership experience.

Under the new retail agreements entered into by the MAs, M-B UK gained closer control of the Mercedes brand, while providing greater support and guidance to the MAs on delivering the best experience to the customer. A new retail concept was devised, which required dealers to improve their showrooms and service areas. A new approach to the marketing structure within each MA was set out, which involved a CRM and marketing team for each MA. Each team was given the responsibility of database management, customer support and regional marketing.

M-B UK, working closely with one MA on a pilot programme, mapped out each of the critical customer processes. These included prospect management (enquiry through to sale); customer contact (communications throughout the period of customer ownership) and complaint management (acknowledging that complaints are an opportunity for improvement and also for forging deeper understanding with customers). Salespeople would continue to be the main contact with the customer during the sales process, but now they would have the backing of a dedicated CRM team to generate and qualify leads, ensure follow-up during the sales process and maintain regular communication with customers during the customer ownership experience.

With the new, carefully set out CRM processes, every aspect of the customer relationship from prospect through ownership was set out along with a channel strategy for each stage. Instead of salesmen owning a customer, each relationship was carefully managed centrally through the new CRM marketing team set up within each MA. For example, the customer support team managed telephone enquiries and passed them to a salesperson. Follow-up was done by the customer support team, which ensured consistency of the customer contact and accurate data gathering. Then the customer support team continued building each customer relationship through a mix of mail, telephone, face-to-face and e-mail – each contact carefully timed to fit with the typical ownership cycle.

Each communication channel was carefully integrated so that the customer received relevant messages by an appropriate channel at various critical points during the ownership cycle. So, for example, direct mail of a high-quality magazine was sent to customers reinforcing the brand and improving the ownership experience. This was coupled with direct mail and follow-up telephone calls for service bookings. Figure 1 outlines the process of integrating the relationship between the customer, the retailer and the distributor (M-B UK).

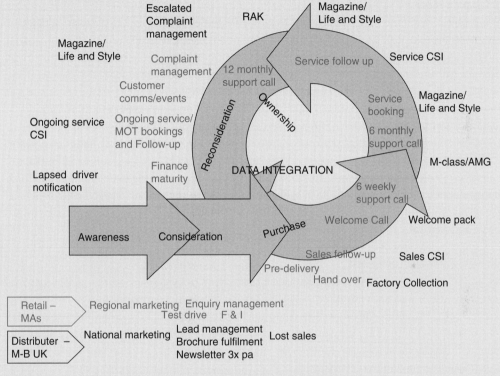

Figure 1 Integrating customer, retailer and distributor relationships

M-B UK recognised that managing data was critical to the success of CRM at Mercedes-Benz. Central to the whole new approach was building a total picture of the customer. First, instead of multiple databases operated by each dealership and M-B UK, a single database was set up. This was implemented across all MAs and M-B UK. Using IT, every customer contact would now be recorded and acted upon using an organised approach. Second, the sales process was carefully set out to support data capture. Customer support and sales personnel were trained in how to accurately record important customer information, improving the quality of data. Salespeople were encouraged to obtain as much customer information as possible, while dedicated data capture agents were responsible for all data entry. Importantly, the imperative of building a complete profile of a customer was made clear to all staff and especially salespeople. M-B UK set targets for the MAs covering every aspect of the customer experience – including retail and after-sale. For example: the prospect follow-up target was increased to 100 per cent; the number of prospects converted to test drive and subsequent sale was increased and CSI (customer satisfaction index) on pre-delivery was increased.

At the outset of the CRM initiative, a business case was set out to win the support of dealers for CRM and to determine the benefits and returns that would be delivered to the customer, to each MA organisation and to M-B UK. It was critical that measures were put in place to prove that CRM delivered the anticipated results and justified the massive expenditure within the businesses. M-B UK and the dealers agreed a range of measures and these were used in two ways. First, these measures enabled monitoring the success of all aspects of CRM, including customer satisfaction, customer retention, sales performance and profitability. Second, the measures would be used within the CRM margin, a critical portion of the reward structure for MAs ensuring that there was a total focus within the business on CRM processes.

One problem facing the CRM initiative was that the new dealer network included dealers at different stages along the road to CRM. Some MAs had undergone massive structural reorganisation, including buying and selling of dealerships as well as many changes in staffing and roles. Other MAs had less experience with applying technology to understand their customers. At the other end of the spectrum, some MAs had undergone little reorganisation and were relatively unsophisticated in their use of the customer data base to build customer relationships. An immediate task was to determine the state of readiness to adopt CRM within each MA, so that CRM processes could be implemented smoothly.

The CRM team recognised that processes alone would not deliver enhanced customer service; the success of CRM would depend on engaging the hearts and minds of both the leaders and employees throughout the distribution network. An examination of MAs pointed to the need for comprehensive training designed to educate employees at every level in CRM as well as to gain their commitment to it. The training programme was devised with four individual modules, designed for various groups within the MAs and M-B UK.

CRM Best Practice Workshops

These workshops were designed specifically for the senior management teams within each MA, as well as directors within M-B UK with direct responsibility for the MAs. Each workshop aimed to build awareness of the benefits of CRM as well as to educate how to implement successful CRM through case studies of best practice in CRM. The workshops included visits to companies where successful CRM was evident and development of a plan for each MA aimed at changing the mindset within the MAs and successfully implementing the CRM strategy.

CRM Uncovered

This module was designed primarily for customer-facing staff, both within the MAs and DCUK. The one-day course aimed at building enthusiasm for CRM as well as creating understanding of the benefits of CRM for the MA, the customer and for the customer-facing staff themselves. The training programme was highly interactive so that participants could easily transfer the skills they learned to their work situation.

Systems and Processes

The CRM project team recognised that it was imperative that all staff within each MA, as well as many within M-B UK, received comprehensive training on the new Kerridge CRM software. Training involved two steps: first, a basic training on the system, its benefits and capabilities; second, specific training within the MA, to provide practical experience of operating the system.

Soft Skills

The fourth module of training involved specific soft skills training. An analysis of training needs would identify specific requirements and then groups of staff would attend appropriate courses. These skills related to building relationships with customers, including telephone skills, communication skills, customer complaint handling and customer service.

Implementing these programmes across a large dealership base represented a very substantial undertaking. The programmes were progressively implemented throughout the MAs between 2001 and 2006. From 2007, other initiatives were added to this programme. These included a more sophisticated programme of outbound calls in dealerships and greater emphasis on website content. A customer experience centre, Mercedes-Benz World, based at Brooklands, Britain's first motor race track, was also opened. The multi-million pound brand experience centre enabled visitors to view every model in the Mercedes range, book a driving experience on the circuits, which included a wet skid circle and a ten acre off-road course, and 'travel' on a simulated ride through the Mercedes-Benz factory.

In 2009 M-B UK's internal CRM capability was substantially increased with the Retail Marketing and CRM function being restructured to include a new role of Marketing Intelligence and CRM manager. The team included data specialists, customer satisfaction specialists and customer insight analysts. These activities were supplemented by a new enquiry management system linked with the retail database. A new series of training programmes were then initiated to further develop marketing and CRM capability. These included: a Customer Development Improvement Programme; a Business Development through CRM programme and a CRM Managers Programme.

M-B UK then started investing in digital marketing and, by 2010, it was allocating 50 per cent of its UK marketing budget to digital. The key to the company's success in online marketing was the creation of specialist expertise within the company. As Anders Sundt Jensen, Vice President for Brand Communications at parent company Daimler AG, notes: 'We don't have normal marketers just doing online ads, or just putting our TV ads online. We have a whole department, for example, at our headquarters in Germany just doing digital marketing.' By 2012 further digital and social media initiatives had been implemented by M-B UK. These included a focus on the younger market. One initiative included a virtual reality racing initiative at Mercedes-Benz World, offering fans the chance to race F1 driver David Coulthard. Another was an online marketing campaign incorporating print, online, broadcast and YouTube, where consumers could win a Mercedes C 350 Coupé.

The results

At the start of this CRM initiative it was critical to win the hearts and minds of leaders and employees within M-B UK and the retail outlets. Quickly, the financial benefits to the MAs were established, as well as steady improvements in the key measures of customer satisfaction and customer loyalty. Cross-selling and up-selling opportunities were used to advantage and the MAs reported that relationships with customers were extended and deepened. The MAs could justify the significant expenditure on CRM because of the financial returns and the improvements in critical customer measures. For example, additional volume of business was generated by CRM activities in the following areas: services booked, extra work booked, sales leads, test drives, finance deals and annual safety checks booked. Importantly, customers reported that they liked the new consistent approach in the way their relationship was handled. Communicating these results to other MAs reinforced the business case for adopting CRM. Despite widespread acceptance of the benefits of CRM, continual efforts needed to be made to support this new approach to the customer.

The results of this strategic customer management initiative, which has now extended over a decade, have been extremely worthwhile. There is now strong recognition within the MAs and M-B UK of the importance of the ongoing efforts to improving the customer experience and building closer relationships with customers. It has been a long but rewarding journey. Between 2003 and 2011, President and CEO of M-B UK Wilfried Steffen presided over an all-time record increase in market share to 3.7 per cent. The brand and its retail network now rate consistently high in its customer service ratings and Mercedes-Benz took the number one place in the 2011 Superbrands Consumer Survey in the UK. Importantly, there is now full recognition that the future of the Mercedes-Benz brand lies in a continuing journey of matching the highly acclaimed product with an outstanding customer experience.

NOTES

Chapter 1 Strategic customer management

1. J. N. Sheth and A. Parvatiyar (2001), Evolving Relationship Marketing into a Discipline, *Journal of Relationship Marketing*, Vol. 1, No. 1, pp. 3–16.
2. A. R. Zablah, D. N. Bellenger and W. J. Johnston (2004), An Evaluation of Divergent Perspectives on Customer Relationship Management: Towards a Common Understanding of an Emerging Phenomenon, *Industrial Marketing Management*, Vol. 33, pp. 475–489.
3. P. Frow and A. Payne (2009), Customer Relationship Management: A Strategic Perspective, *Journal of Business Market Management*, Vol. 3, No. 1, pp. 7–28.
4. M. Christopher, A. Payne and D. Ballantyne (1991), *Relationship Marketing: Bringing Quality, Customer Service and Marketing Together*, Oxford: Butterworth-Heinemann.
5. P. Doyle (1995), Marketing in the New Millennium, *European Journal of Marketing*, Vol. 29, No. 3, pp. 23–41.
6. E. Gummesson (1995), *Relationship Marketing: From 4Ps to 30Rs*, Malmö: Liber-Hermods.
7. R. K. Srivastava, T. A. Shervani and L. Fahey (1999), Marketing, Business Processes, and Shareholder Value: An Organisationally Embedded View of Marketing Activities and the Discipline of Marketing, *Journal of Marketing*, Vol. 63 (Special Issue), pp. 168–179.
8. W. Boulding, R. Staelin, M. Ehret and W. J. Johnston (2005), A Customer Relationship Management Roadmap: What is Known, Potential Pitfalls and Where to Go, *Journal of Marketing*, Vol. 69, No. 4, pp. 155–166.
9. L. L. Berry (1983), Relationship Marketing, in Berry, L. L., Shostack, G. L. and Gregory, D. U. (eds.), *Emerging Perspective on Services Marketing*, Chicago, IL: American Marketing Association, pp. 25–28.
10. T. Levitt (1983), After the Sale is Over, *Harvard Business Review*, September–October, pp. 87–93.
11. B. B. Jackson (1985), *Winning and Keeping Industrial Customers: The Dynamics of Customer Relationships*, Lexington, MA: D.C. Heath & Co.
12. Christopher, Payne and Ballantyne (1991).
13. Central Intelligence Agency (2011), The World Factbook, Central Intelligence Agency. Available at: www.cia.gov/library/publications/the-world-factbook/fields/2012.html.
14. C. Lovelock, P. G. Patterson and J. Wirz (2011), *Services Marketing: An Asia-Pacific and Australasian Perspective*, Frenchs Forest, NSW: Pearson Australia.
15. T. Levitt (1974), *Marketing for Business Growth*, New York, NY: McGraw-Hill, p. 5.
16. E. Gummesson (2010), The New Service Marketing, in Baker, M. J. and Saren, M. (eds.), *Marketing Theory: A Student Text*, 2nd edn., London: Sage, pp. 399–421.
17. S. L. Vargo and R. F. Lusch (2004), Evolving to a New Dominant Logic for Marketing, *Journal of Marketing*, Vol. 68, January, pp. 1–17. Also see: S. L. Vargo and R. F. Lusch

(2008), Service-dominant Logic: Continuing the Evolution, *Journal of the Academy of Marketing Science*, Vol. 36, No. 1, pp. 1–10.

18. This table is based on Vargo and Lusch (2008).

19. N. Borden (1965), The Concept of the Marketing Mix, in Schwartz G. (ed.), *Science in Marketing*, New York, NY: Wiley.

20. E. J. McCarthy (1960), *Basic Marketing*, Homewood, IL: Irwin.

21. B. H. Booms and M. J. Bitner (1981), Marketing Strategies and Organisation Structures for Service Firms, in Donelly, J. H. and George, W. R. (eds.), *Marketing of Services*, Chicago, IL: American Marketing Association.

22. E. Gummesson (1997), Relationship Marketing as a Paradigm Shift: Some Conclusions from the 30R Approach, *Management Decision*, Vol. 35, No. 4, pp. 267–272.

23. E. Gummesson (2002), *Total Relationship Marketing*, 2nd edn., Oxford: Butterworth-Heinemann.

24. B. Shapiro (1985), Rejuvenating the Marketing Mix, *Harvard Business Review*, September–October, pp. 28–33.

25. P. Kotler (1992), It's Time for Total Marketing, *Business Week Advance Executive Brief*, p. 2.

26. See: Christopher, Payne and Ballantyne (1991); M. Christopher, A. Payne and D. Ballantyne (2002), *Relationship Marketing: Creating Stakeholder Value*, Oxford: Butterworth-Heinemann; and A. Payne, D. Ballantyne and M. Christopher (2005), Relationship Marketing: A Stakeholder Approach, *European Journal of Marketing*, Vol. 39, Nos. 7/8, pp. 855–871.

27. Payne, Ballantyne and Christopher (2005).

28. D. Peppers and M. Rogers (1993), *The One-to-One Future; Building Relationships One Customer at a Time*, New York, NY: Currency Doubleday.

29. Berry (1983).

30. J. Egan (2008), *Relationship Marketing: Exploring Relational Strategies in Marketing*, 3rd edn., Harlow: FT/Prentice Hall.

31. M. J. Harker (1999), Relationship Marketing Defined? An Examination of Current Relationship Marketing Definitions, *Marketing Intelligence & Planning*, Vol. 17, Issue 1, pp. 13–20.

32. S. J. Dann and S. M. Dann (2001), *Strategic Internet Marketing*, Milton, Queensland: Wiley.

33. A. K. Agariya and D. Singh (2011), What Really Defines Relationship Marketing? A Review of Definitions and General and Sector-Specific Defining Constructs, *Journal of Relationship Marketing*, Vol. 10, Issue 4, pp. 203–237.

34. R. Kotorov (2003), Customer Relationship Management: Strategic Lessons and Future Directions, *Business Process Management Journal*, Vol. 9, No. 5, pp. 566–571.

35. G. Dowling (2002), Customer Relationship Management in B2C Markets, Often Less is More, *California Management Review*, Vol. 44, No. 3, pp. 87–104.

36. A. Parvatiyar and J. N. Sheth (2001), Conceptual Framework of Customer Relationship Management, in Sheth, J. N., Parvatiyar, A. and Shainesh, G. (eds.), *Customer Relationship Management – Emerging Concepts, Tools and Applications*, New Delhi: McGraw-Hill, pp. 3–25.

37. Parvatiyar and Sheth (2001).

38. Zablah, Bellenger and Johnston (2003) suggest that CRM is 'a philosophically-related offspring to relationship marketing which is for the most part neglected in the literature'. The use of the term CRM is further complicated with some organisations, such as the consulting firm Accenture, adopting the term *customer management* in place of CRM in a response to many companies' incorrect association of CRM with technology solutions. See: A. R. Zablah, D. N. Bellenger, and W. J. Johnston (2003), Customer Relationship Management: An Explication of Its Domain and Avenues for Further Inquiry, in Kleinaltenkamp, M. and Ehret, M. (eds.), *Relationship Marketing, Customer Relationship Management and Marketing Management: Co-operation–Competition–Co-evolution*, Berlin: Freie Universität Berlin, pp. 115–124.

39. S. Grabner-Kraeuter and M. Gernot (2002), Alternative Approaches Toward Measuring CRM Performance, *6th Research Conference on Relationship Marketing and Customer Relationship Management*, Atlanta, 9–12 June, pp. 1–16.

40. A. Payne and P. Frow (2005), A Strategic Framework for CRM, *Journal of Marketing*, Vol. 69, No. 4, pp. 167–176.

41. Gummesson (2002).

42. Payne and Frow (2005).

43. E. Thompson (2012), The Top Five Technology Trends to Disrupt CRM Architectures and Technology, Gartner Inc. Available at: www.gartner.com/it/content/1322300/1322319/april_7_top_5_technology_trends_to_disrupt_crm_ethompson.pdf.

44. Payne and Frow (2005).

Chapter 2: Relationship marketing: Development and concepts

1. L. L. Berry (1995), Relationship Marketing of Services – Growing Interest, Emerging Perspectives, *Journal of the Academy of Marketing Science*, Vol. 23, pp. 236–245.

2. See: C. Grönroos (1994), From Marketing Mix to Relationship Marketing: Towards a Paradigm Shift in Marketing, *Management Decision*, Vol. 32, No. 2, pp. 4–20; and C. Grönroos (1996), Relationship Marketing: Strategic and Tactical Implications, *Management Decision*, Vol. 34, No. 3, p. 5.

3. See: Berry (1995); and J. N. Sheth and A. Parvatiyar (1995), The Evolution of Relationship Marketing, *International Business Review*, Vol. 4, pp. 397–418.

4. K. Moller and A. Halinen (2000), Relationship Marketing Theory: Its Roots and Direction, *Journal of Marketing Management*, Vol. 16, pp. 29–54.

5. T. Levitt (1983), After the Sale is Over, *Harvard Business Review*, September–October, pp. 87–93.

6. B. B. Jackson (1985), *Winning and Keeping Industrial Customers: The Dynamics of Customer Relationships*, Lexington, MA: D. C. Heath.

7. L. L. Berry (1983), Relationship Marketing, in Berry, L. L., Shostack, G. L. and Upah, G. D. (eds.), *Emerging Perspectives on Service Marketing*, Chicago, IL: American Marketing Association, pp. 25–38.

8. Berry (1995).

9. L. Coote (1994), Implementation of Relationship Marketing in an Accounting Practice, in Sheth, J. N. and Parvatiyar, A. (eds.), *Relationship Marketing: Theory, Methods and Applications*, Atlanta, GA: Emory University, Center for Relationship Marketing.

10. M. Christopher, A. Payne and D. Ballantyne (1991), *Relationship Marketing: Bringing Quality, Customer Service and Marketing Together*, Oxford: Butterworth-Heinemann.

11. See: C. Grönroos (1990), Marketing Redefined, *Management Decision*, Vol. 27, No. 1, pp. 5–9; and C. Grönroos (1991), The Marketing Strategy Continuum: A Marketing Concept for the 1990s, *Management Decision*, Vol. 29, No. 1, pp. 7–13.

12. See: E. Gummesson (1987), The New Marketing: Developing Long-Term Interactive Relationships, *Long Range Planning*, Vol. 20, No. 4, pp. 10–20; and E. Gummesson (1994), Making Relationship Marketing Operational, *International Journal of Service Industry Management*, Vol. 5, No. 5, pp. 5–20.

13. Berry (1995).

14. Levitt (1983).

15. J. Perrien, P. Filiatrault and L. Ricard (1993), The Implementation of Relationship Marketing in Commercial Banking, *Industrial Marketing Management*, Vol. 22, pp. 141–148.

16. Sheth and Parvatiyar (1995).

17. For example, see: P. W. Turnbull and M. T. Cunningham (1981), *International Marketing and Purchasing*, London: Macmillan; and H. Hakansson (1982), *International Marketing and Purchasing of Industrial Goods: An Interaction Approach*, New York, NY: Wiley; and D. Ford, L-E. Gadde, H. Hakansson, A. Lundgren, I. Snehota, P. Turnbull and D. Wilson (1997), *Managing Business Relationships*, Chichester: Wiley.

18. J. Egan (2008), *Relationship Marketing: Exploring Relational Strategies in Marketing*, 3rd edn., Harlow: FT/Prentice Hall.

19. Christopher, Payne and Ballantyne (1991).

20. Christopher, Payne and Ballantyne (1991).

21. J. N. Sheth and A. Parvatiyar (2000), *The Handbook of Relationship Marketing*, Thousand Oaks, CA: Sage.

22. L. L. Berry (2000), Relationship Marketing of Services, in Sheth, J. N. and Parvatiyar, A. (eds.), *The Handbook of Relationship Marketing*, Thousand Oaks, CA: Sage, pp. 149–170.

23. J. Egan and M. J. Harker (eds.) (2008), *Relationship Marketing: Exploring Relational Strategies in Marketing*, Volumes 1–3, London: Sage.

24. R. W. Palmatier (2008), *Relationship Marketing*, Cambridge, MA: Marketing Science Institute.

25. J. N. Sheth (1996), Paradigm Shift or Shaft?, paper presented at the annual meeting of the Academy of Marketing Science, Miami, FL.

26. R. K. Srivastava, T. A. Shervani and L. Fahey (1999), Marketing, Business Processes, and Shareholder Value: An Organisationally Embedded View of Marketing Activities and the Discipline of Marketing, *Journal of Marketing*, Vol. 63 (Special Issue), pp. 168–179.

27. See: N. Piercy (2010), Improving Marketing-Operations Cross Functional Relationships, *Journal of Strategic Marketing*, Vol. 18, Issue 4, pp. 337–356; and C. Kim and L. Minho (2010), The Effects of Collaboration between Marketing and Production on Internal and External Performance, *California Journal of Operations Management*, Vol. 8, pp. 11–20.

28. P. M. Madhani (2011), Value Creation through Cross Functional Collaboration: Making a Case for SCM and Marketing Integration, *DHAROHAR International Management Journal*, Vol. 1, No. 1, pp. 36–48.

29. M. Brettel, F. Heinemann, A. Engelen and S. Neubauer (2011), Cross Functional Integration of R&D, Marketing, and Manufacturing in Radical and Incremental Product Innovations and Its Effects on Project Effectiveness and Efficiency, *Journal of Product Innovation Management*, Vol. 28, No. 2, pp. 251–269.

30. Christopher, Payne and Ballantyne (1991).

31. A. Parasuraman, V. A. Zeithaml and L. L. Berry (1985), A Conceptual Model of Service Quality and Its Implications for Future Research, *Journal of Marketing*, Vol. 49, Fall, pp. 41–50. Also see: N. Seth, S. G. Deshmukh and P. Vrat (2005), Service Quality Models: A Review, *International Journal of Quality & Reliability Management*, Vol. 22, No. 9, pp. 913–949.

32. R. D. Buzzell (2004), The PIMS Program of Strategy Research: A Retrospective Appraisal, *Journal of Business Research*, Vol. 57, pp. 478–483. This article provides a review of the overall research programme. The results of much of the earlier work are described in: R. D. Buzzell and B. T. Gale (1987), *The PIMS Principles: Linking Strategy to Performance*, New York, NY: The Free Press.

33. Christopher, Payne and Ballantyne (1991).

34. R. Morgan (2000), Relationship Marketing and Marketing Strategy: The Evolution of Relationship Marketing within the Organisation, in Sheth, J., and Parvatiyar, A. (eds.), *Handbook of Relationship Marketing*, Thousand Oaks, CA, Sage, pp. 480–505.

35. J. Cumby and J. Barnes (1998), How Customers Are Made to Feel: The Role of Affective Reactions in Driving Customer Satisfaction, *Journal of Customer Relationship Management*, Vol. 1, No. 1, pp. 54–63.

36. L. Crosby, K. Evans and D. Cowles (1990), Relationship Quality in Services Selling: An Interpersonal Influence Perspective, *Journal of Marketing*, Vol. 54, No. 3, pp. 68–81.

37. R. Palmatier (2008), Interfirm Relational Drivers of Customer Value, *Journal of Marketing*, Vol. 72, July, pp. 76–89.

38. S. Vargo and R. Lusch (2004), Evolving to a New Dominant Logic for Marketing, *Journal of Marketing*, Vol. 68, No. 1, pp. 1–18.

39. F. R. Dwyer, P. H. Schurr and S. Oh (1987), Developing Buyer-Seller Relationships, *Journal of Marketing*, Vol. 51, No. 2, pp. 11–27.

40. J. P. Meyer and N. J. Allen (1991), A Three-Component Conceptualisation of Organisational Commitment, *Human Resource Management Review*, Vol. 1, pp. 61–89.

41. E. R. Andersen and R. Weitz (1998), Commitment and its Consequences in the American Agency System of Selling Insurance, INSEAD Working Papers, 94/42, MKT.

42. R. Morgan and S. Hunt (1994), The Commitment Trust Theory of Relationship Marketing, *Journal of Marketing*, Vol. 58, pp. 20–38.

43. P. W. Farris, N. T. Bendle, P. E. Pfeifer and D. J. Reibstein (2010), *Marketing Metrics: The Definitive Guide to Measuring Marketing Performance*, Upper Saddle River, NJ: Pearson Education.

44. L. J. Gitman and C. D. McDaniel (2005), *The Future of Business: The Essentials*, Mason, OH: South-Western.

45. T. Jones and W. E. Sasser (1995), Why Satisfied Customers Defect, *Harvard Business Review*, November/December, pp. 88–99.

46. B. Mittal and W. M. Lassar (1998), Why Do Customers Switch? The Dynamics of Satisfaction Versus Loyalty, *Journal of Services Marketing*, Vol. 12, No. 3, pp. 177–194.

47. For a detailed discussion of this work, see: L. L. Berry and A. Parasuraman (1991), *Marketing Services: Competing Through Quality*, New York, NY: The Free Press; and J. J. Cronin and S. A. Taylor (1992), Measuring Service Quality: A Re-Examination and Extension, *Journal of Marketing*, Vol. 56, No. 3, pp. 55–68.

48. Egan (2008).

49. Mittal and Lassar (1998).

50. F. F. Reichheld (1988), Loyalty and the Renaissance of Marketing, *Marketing Management*, Vol. 2, No. 4, pp. 10–21.

51. R. L. Oliver (1997), *Satisfaction: A Behavioural Perspective on the Consumer*, Singapore: McGraw-Hill.

52. G. R. Dowling and M. Uncles (1997), Do Customer Loyalty Programs Really Work?, *Sloan Management Review*, Vol. 38, No. 4, pp. 71–82.

53. A. Dick and K. Basu (1994), Customer Loyalty: Towards an Integrated Framework, *Journal of the Academy of Marketing Science*, Vol. 22, No. 2, pp. 99–113.

54. Rowley, J. (2005), The Four Cs of Customer Loyalty, *Marketing Intelligence & Planning*, Vol. 23, No. 6, pp. 574–581.

55. S. Baron, T. Conway and G. Warnaby (2010), *Relationship Marketing: A Consumer Experience Approach*, London: Sage Publications.

56. R. Palmatier, R. Dant and K. Evans (2006), Factors Influencing the Effectiveness of Relationship Marketing: A Meta-Analysis, *Journal of Marketing*, Vol. 70, July, pp. 136–153.

57. D. Peppers and M. Rogers (1995), A New Marketing Paradigm, *Planning Review*, Vol. 23, No. 2, pp. 14–18.

58. E. Gummesson (2000), Return on Relationships (ROR): Building the Future with Intellectual Capital, *2nd WWW Conference on Relationship Marketing*, 15th November. Also see: C. Grönroos and P. Helle (2012), Return on Relationships: Conceptual Understanding and Measurement of Mutual Gains from Relational Business Engagements, *Journal of Business & Industrial Marketing*, Vol. 27, Issue 5, pp. 344–359.

59. S. Fournier and J. Avery (2011), Putting the 'Relationship' Back into CRM, *MIT Sloan Management Review*, Vol. 52, No. 3, pp. 63–72.

60. S. Fournier (1998), Consumers and their Brands: Developing Relationship Theory in Consumer Research, *Journal of Consumer Research*, Vol. 24, March, pp. 343–373.

61. J. Andersen and J. Narus (1990), A Model of Distributor Firm and Manufacturer Firm Working Partnerships, *Journal of Marketing*, Vol. 54, January, pp. 42–45.

62. For example, see: Dwyer, Schurr and Oh (1987); and T. Levitt (1986), *The Marketing Imagination*, New York, NY: The Free Press.

63. See: A. C. Tynan (2008), Metaphors and Marketing: Some Uses and Abuses, in Kitchen, P. J. (ed.), *Marketing Metaphors and Metamorphosis*, Basingstoke: Macmillan; and A. C. Tynan (1999), Metaphor, Marketing and Marriage, *Irish Marketing Review*, Vol. 12, No. 1, pp. 17–26.

64. See: I. F. Wilkinson and L. Young (1994), Business Dancing: An Alternative Paradigm for Relationship Marketing, *Asia-Australia Marketing Journal*, Vol. 2, No. 1, pp. 67–80; and I. F. Wilkinson, L. Young and P. V. Freytag (2005), Business Mating: Who Chooses and Who Gets Chosen? *Industrial Marketing Management*, Vol. 34, pp. 669–680.

65. Fournier and Avery (2011).

66. M. McDonald and D. Woodburn (1999), *Key Account Management: Building on Supplier and Buyer Perspectives*, Cranfield School of Management Research Report, London: FT/Prentice Hall.

67. See: E. Gummesson (1995), *Relationship Marketing: From 4Ps to 30Rs*, Malmö: Liber-Hermods. Grönroos' work during this period focused principally on the relationships between firms and their customers; however, he explicitly noted the importance of relationships with 'other parties as well'. (See: C. Grönroos (1994), From Marketing Mix to Relationship Marketing: Towards a Paradigm Shift in Marketing, *Management Decision*, Vol. 32, No. 2, pp. 4–20.) Grönroos also emphasised the importance of the internal market domain. (See: C. Grönroos (1990), Relationship Approach to Marketing in Service Contexts: the Marketing and Organisational Behaviour Interface, *Journal of Business Research*, Vol. 20, No. 1, pp. 3–11.)

68. For a discussion see: R. E. Freeman and M. Hitt (2010), *Strategic Management: A Stakeholder Approach*, Cambridge: Cambridge University Press.

69. M. Polonsky, L. Carlson and M. Fry (2003), The Harm Chain, *Marketing Theory*, Vol. 3, pp. 345–364.

70. P. Kotler (1972), A Generic Concept of Marketing, *Journal of Marketing*, Vol. 36, No. 2, pp. 46–54.

71. Christopher, Payne and Ballantyne (1991).

72. P. Kotler (1992), It's Time for Total Marketing, *Business Week Advance, Executive Brief*, p. 2.

73. R. Morgan and S. Hunt (1994), The Commitment Trust Theory of Relationship Marketing, *Journal of Marketing*, Vol. 58, July, pp. 20–38.

74. Gummesson (1995).

75. P. Doyle (1995), Marketing in the New Millennium, *European Journal of Marketing*, Vol. 29, No. 13, pp. 23–41.

76. F. Buttle (1999), The S.C.O.P.E. of Customer Relationship Management, *International Journal of Customer Relationship Management*, Vol. 1, No. 4, pp. 327–336.

77. G. R. Laczniak and P. E. Murphy (2006), Normative Perspectives for Ethical and Socially Responsible Marketing, *Journal of Micromarketing*, Vol. 26, No. 2, pp. 154–177.

78. W. Ross and D. Robertson (2007), Compound Relationships between Firms, *Journal of Marketing*, Vol. 71, No. 4, pp. 108–123.

79. C. B. Bhattacharya and D. Korschun (2008), Stakeholder Marketing: Beyond the 4 Ps and the Customer, *Journal of Public Policy and Marketing*, Vol. 27, No. 1, pp. 113–116.

80. Gummesson (1995).

81. A. Payne, D. Ballantyne and M. Christopher (2005), Relationship Marketing: A Stakeholder Approach, *European Journal of Marketing*, Vol. 39, Nos. 7/8, pp. 855–871.

82. Payne, Ballantyne and Christopher (2005).

83. E. Gummesson (2002), *Total Relationship Marketing*, 2nd edn., Oxford: Butterworth-Heinemann.

84. M. Christopher, A. Payne and D. Ballantyne (2002), *Relationship Marketing: Creating Stakeholder Value*, Oxford: Butterworth-Heinemann.

85. B. Hedberg, G. Dahlgren, J. Hansson and N. Olve (1997), *Virtual Organisations and Beyond*, Chichester: Wiley.

86. M. Bjork (2008), *Gant: The Story*, Stockholm: Ekerlids.

87. M. Godson (2009), *Relationship Marketing*, Oxford: Oxford University Press.

88. C. Grönroos (1996), The Rise and Fall of Modern Marketing and Its Rebirth, in Shaw, S. A. and Hood, N. (eds.), *Marketing in Evolution: Essays in Honour of Michael J. Baker*, London: Macmillan, pp. 14–35.

89. Fournier and Avery (2011).

90. C. Grönroos (1999), Relationship Marketing: Challenges for the Organisation, *Journal of Business Research*, Vol. 46, pp. 327–335.

91. M. McDonald, P. Frow and A. Payne (2011), *Marketing Plans for Services*, Chichester: Wiley.

92. Christopher, Payne and Ballantyne (1991).

93. M. McDonald and H. Wilson (2011), *Marketing Plans: How to Prepare Them, How to Use Them*, Chichester: Wiley.

94. C. Webster (1990), Toward the Measurement of the Marketing Culture of a Service Firm, *Journal of Business Research*, Vol. 21, pp. 345–362.

Chapter 3: Customer value creation

1. T. Levitt (1983), *The Marketing Imagination*, New York, NY: The Free Press, ch. 4.

2. Levitt (1983).

3. B. Collins (1995), Marketing for Engineers, in Sampson, D. (ed.), *Management for Engineers*, Melbourne: Longman Cheshire.

4. See: C. H. Lovelock, J. Wirtz and P. Chew (2008), *Essentials of Services Marketing*, Englewood Cliffs, NJ: Prentice Hall, pp. 88–107; and C. Lovelock (1995), Competing on Service: Technology and Teamwork in Supplementary Services, *Planning Review*, July/August, pp. 32–39.

5. M. J. Bitner, A. L. Ostrom and F. N. Morgan (2008), Service Blueprinting: A Practical Technique for Service Innovation, *California Management Review*, Vol. 50, No. 3, pp. 66–94.

6. H. Davidow (1986), *Marketing High Technology*, New York, NY: The Free Press, p. 172.

7. R. E. Wayland and P. M. Cole (1997), *Customer Connections: New Strategies for Growth*, Boston, MA: Harvard Business School Press.

8. T. Jones and W. E. Sasser (1995), Why Satisfied Customers Defect, *Harvard Business Review*, November/December, pp. 88–99.

9. Jones and Sasser (1995)

10. D. A. Aaker (1991), *Managing Brand Equity: Capitalizing on the Value of a Brand Name*, New York, NY: The Free Press.

11. K. L. Keller (2008), *Strategic Brand Management: Building, Measuring, and Managing Brand Equity*, 3rd edn., New York, NY: Prentice Hall.

12. M. Lindstrom and T. Andersen (1999), *Brand Building on the Internet*, London: Kogan Page.

13. Lindstrom and Andersen (1999).

14. J. Neff (2011), Ad Age Digital A-List: P&G, *Advertising Age*, 27 February 2011. Available at: http://adage.com/article/special-report-digital-alist/ad-age-digital-a-list-p-g/149083.

15. See: M. Bower and R. A. Garda (1985), The Role of Marketing in Management, *McKinsey Quarterly*, Autumn, pp. 34–46; and M. Bower and R. A. Garda (1998), The Role of Marketing

in Management, in Buell, V. P. (ed.), *Handbook of Modern Marketing*, 2nd edn., New York, NY: McGraw-Hill, pp. 1–10.

16. See: M. Lanning and L. Phillips (1991), Building Market Focused Organisations, Gemini Consulting White Paper.

17. A. Kambil, A. Ginsberg and M. Bloch (1996), Reinventing Value Propositions, NYU Centre for Research on Information Systems Working Paper IS-96-21, New York University.

18. Kambil, Ginsberg and Bloch (1996).

19. For example see: M. McDonald and H. Wilson (2011), *Marketing Plans: How to Prepare Them, How to Use Them*, Chichester: Wiley.

20. Lanning and Phillips (1991).

21. For example, see: D. A. Aaker, V. Kumar, G. S. Day and R. P. Leone (2010), *Marketing Research*, 10th edn., New York, NY: Wiley.

22. Aaker, Kumar, Day and Leone (2010).

Chapter 4: Building relationships with multiple stakeholders

1. IBM (2010), *Capitalising on Complexity: Insights from the Global Chief Executive Officer (CEO) Study*, IBM Institute for Business Value.

2. E. Gummesson (2008), *Total Relationship Marketing*, 3rd edn., Oxford: Butterworth-Heinemann.

3. For the most recent version see: A. Payne, D. Ballantyne and M. Christopher (2005), Relationship Marketing: A Stakeholder Approach, *European Journal of Marketing*, Vol. 39, Nos. 7/8, pp. 855–871.

4. N. K. Malhotra and J. Agarwal (2002), A Stakeholder Perspective on Relationship Marketing: Framework and Propositions, *Journal of Relationship Marketing*, Vol. 1, No. 2, pp. 3–37.

5. N. Tzokas and M. Saren (2004), Competitive Advantage, Knowledge and Relationship Marketing, *Journal of Business and Industrial Marketing*, Vol. 19, No. 2, pp. 124–135.

6. Payne, Ballantyne and Christopher (2005).

7. H. Peck (2001), Towards a Framework of Relationship Marketing: a Case Study Approach, PhD thesis, School of Management, Cranfield University.

8. L. Brennan and E. Brady (1999), Relating to Marketing? Why Relationship Marketing Works for Not-For-Profit Organisations, *International Journal of Nonprofit and Voluntary Sector Marketing*, Vol. 4, No. 4, pp. 327–337.

9. M. Christopher, A. Payne and D. Ballantyne (1991), *Relationship Marketing: Bringing Quality, Customer Service and Marketing Together*, Oxford: Butterworth-Heinemann.

10. M. Bulearca and S. Bulearca (2011), Romania Branding Campaign – An IMC Perspective, *International Journal of Business, Management and Social Sciences*, Vol. 2, No. 3, pp. 35–58.

11. The following material in this chapter draws on: A. Payne (1991), Relationship Marketing: The Six Markets Model, Working Paper, Cranfield School of Management [and revised version, 1998]; as well as materials from the Relationship Marketing Research Seminar Series, Cranfield School of Management; H. Peck, A. Payne, M. Christopher and M. Clark (1999), *Relationship Marketing – Strategy and Implementation: Text and Cases*, Oxford: Butterworth-Heinemann; M. Christopher, A. Payne and D. Ballantyne (2002), *Relationship Marketing: Creating Stakeholder Value*, Oxford: Butterworth-Heinemann; and

A. Payne, D. Ballantyne and M. Christopher (2005), Relationship Marketing: A Stakeholder Approach, *European Journal of Marketing*, Vol. 39, Nos. 7/8, pp. 855–871.

12. H. M. File, B. B. Judd and C. A. Prince (1992), Interactive Marketing: The Influence of Participation on Positive Word-Of-Mouth and Referrals, *Journal of Services Marketing*, Vol. 6, No. 4, pp. 5–14.

13. F. F. Reichheld (1996), *The Loyalty Effect*, Boston, MA: Harvard Business School Press.

14. C. Kolb (2010), The Building Blocks of Corporate Statesmanship, *Huff Post*, July 23. Available at: www.huffingtonpost.com/charles-kolb/the-building-blocks-of-co_b_657387. html.

15. S. Beechler and I. C. Woodward (2009), The Global War for Talent, *Journal of International Management*, Vol. 15, pp. 273–285.

16. This brief discussion is based in part on an interview on a video made by Harvard Business School.

17. R. Pascale (1999), *Nordstrom*, in, Peck, Payne, Christopher and Clark (1999), pp. 375–401.

18. V. C. Judd (1987), Differentiate with the 5th P: People, *Industrial Marketing Management*, Vol. 16, pp. 241–247.

19. See: D. Nikbin (2010), *Internal Marketing and Strategy Implementation: The Impact of Internal Marketing Practices on Employees Satisfaction and Commitment in Implementing Firms' Strategic Orientations*, Saarbrücken, Germany: Lambert Academic Publishing; S. M. Drake, M. J. Gulman and S. M. Roberts (2005), *Light Their Fire: Using Internal Marketing to Ignite Employee Performance and Wow Your Customers*, Chicago, IL: Dearborn Publishing; K. A. Pervaiz and M. Rafiq (2002), *Internal Marketing: Tools and Concepts for Customer-Focused Management*, Oxford: Elsevier; and B. Lewis and R. J. Varey (2000), *Internal Marketing*, London: Routledge.

20. A full discussion of marketing planning is beyond the scope of this book. For a detailed review, see: M. McDonald and H. Wilson (2011), *Marketing Plans: How to Prepare Them, How to Use Them*, Chichester: Wiley; and M. McDonald, P. Frow and A. Payne (2011), *Marketing Plans for Services*, Chichester: Wiley.

Chapter 5: Relationships and technology: Digital marketing and social media

1. S. VanBoskirk (2011), *US Interactive Marketing Forecast, 2011 To 2016*, Forrester Research Inc. updated: 7 September.

2. These definitions draw on: V. Beal (2011), The Difference between the Internet and World Wide Web, Webopedia. Available at: www.webopedia.com/DidYouKnow/internet/2002/web_vs_internet.asp.

3. J. Volpe (2012), BBC News Online Adapts Mobile Site to Smartphone Demands, Doesn't Discriminate against Specs. Available at: http://androidtablet-shop.com/android-tablet-news/1-latest-news/2917-bbc-news-online-adapts-mobile-site-to-smartphone-demands-doesn-t-discriminate-against-specs.

4. C. Finnamore (2012), Lenovo's Cloud Service Part of 'Four Screen Strategy'. Available at: www.expertreviews.co.uk/general/1289500/lenovos-cloud-service-part-of-four-screen-strategy.

5. e.marketer.com (2011), US Tablet User Penetration by Race/Ethnicity 2010–2014, November, 134319.

6. P-E. Gobry (2012), Tablet Sales Will Blow Past PC Sales to Nearly 500 Million Units a Year by 2015. Available at: http://articles.businessinsider.com/2012-02-14/tech/31057828_1_tablet-sales-post-pc-era-lower-prices#ixzz1yq6QeR2i.

7. The Boston Consulting Group (2012), *The Internet Economy in the G-20: The $42 Trillion Growth Opportunity*, Boston, MA: The Boston Consulting Group.

8. N. Spivak (2007), Web 3.0: The Third Generation Web Is Coming. Available at: http://lifeboat.com/ex/web.3.0.

9. Spivak (2007).

10. Myspace.com (2011), Digital Lifestyle Information Survey 2011. Available at: www.myspace.com/pressroom/2011/04/digital-lifestyle-information-survey-2011/.

11. Some of these definitions draw on: G. Beekman and B. Beekman (2012), *Digital Planet: Tomorrow's Technology and You, Complete*, 10th edn., Upper Saddle River, NJ: Pearson/Prentice Hall.

12. Razorfish (2009), *Digital Outlook Report 2009*, Razorfish LLC.

13. S. Hollensen (2003), *Marketing Management: A Relationship Approach*, Harlow: Pearson Education.

14. The Boston Consulting Group (2012).

15. The Boston Consulting Group (2012).

16. Oracle (2012), 2012 B2B E-Commerce Trends – Insight into Key Trends and Areas of Investment for Building a Stronger Online Presence, *Oracle Daily*, March. Available at: www.unitask.com/oracledaily/2012/03/01/2012-b2b-e-commerce-trends-insight-into-key-trends-and-areas-of-investment-for-building-a-stronger-online-presence-3/.

17. These definitions are based on: Wikipedia (2012), Digital Marketing. Available at: http://en.wikipedia.org/wiki/Digital_marketing.

18. B. Thompson (2012), Social CRM is Dead, Long Live the Social Customer Experience, *Customer Think*, June. Available at: www.customerthink.com/blog/social_crm_is_dead_long_live_social_customer_experience.

19. D. Schultz (2007), Snackbyte: a View of the Ecosystem. Available at: www.deborahschultz.com/deblog/2007/11/snackbyte-a-vie.html.

20. F. Cavazza (2012), An Overview of the Social Media Ecosystem, *Forbes*. Available at: www.forbes.com/sites/fredcavazza/2012/03/12/an-overview-of-the-social-media-ecosystem/.

21. Cavazza (2012).

22. D. M. Boyd and N. B. Ellison (2007), Social Network Sites: Definition, History, and Scholarship, *Journal of Computer-Mediated Communication*, Vol. 13, No. 1, article 11. Available at: http://jcmc.indiana.edu/vol13/issue1/boyd.ellison.html.

23. Twitter (2012), Twitter, in your Language, *Twitter Blog*, January 6.

24. Twitter (2011), One Million Registered Twitter Apps, *Twitter Blog*, 9 January, 2.

25. A. M. Kaplan and M. Haenlein (2010), Users of the World Unite! The Challenges and Opportunities of Social Media, *Business Horizons*, Vol. 53, No. 1, pp. 59–68.

26. Source: www.industrygamers.com/news/social-games-market-to-hit-864-billion-in-2014/.

27. P. Marsden (2009), *Social Commerce: Monetising Social Media*, Unique Digital and Syzergy Report.

28. Marsden (2009).

29. C. Barry, R. Markey, E. Almquist and C. Brahm (2011), *Putting Social Media to Work*, Boston, MA: Bain & Co.

30. A. M. Muniz and H. J. Schau (2011), How to Inspire Value Laden Collaborative Consumer Generated Content, *Business Horizons*, Vol. 54, No. 3, pp. 209–217.

31. B. Solis (2010), Behaviorgraphics Humanize the Social Web, March. Available at: www.briansolis.com/2010/03/behaviorgraphics-humanize-the-social-web/.

32 G. Sverdlov (2012), Global Social Technographics Update 2011: US and EU Mature, Emerging Markets Show Lots Of Activity. Available at: http://blogs.forrester.com/gina_sverdlov/12-01-04-global_social_technographics_update_2011_us_and_eu_mature_emerging_markets_show_lots_of_activity

33. Sverdlov (2012).

34. Solis (2010).

35. Sverdlov (2012).

36. Sverdlov (2012).

37. P. O'Neill, P. Burris and S. Vargas (2011), *BT Social Technographics 2011: Age Matters*, Forrester Research Inc., August.

38. R. Divol, D. Edelman and H. Sazrrazin (2012), Demystifying Social Media, *McKinsey Quarterly*, April. Available at: www.mckinseyquarterly.com/Demystifying_social_media_2958.

39. C. Benson (2010), The Five Steps of an Integrated Social Media Campaign, Alterian White Paper. This is one of a series of excellent white paper produced by Alterian. This discussion draws directly on key elements of Benson's steps. For a fuller discussion, see this White Paper which is available on the Alterian website.

40. Benson (2010).

41. Tata Consulting Services (quoting Gartner) (2011), Social Analytics, White Paper, Tata Consulting Services Ltd.

42. Tata Consulting Services (2011).

43. J. Owyang and J. Lovett (2010), Social Media Analytics: A New Framework of Measuring Results in Social Media, Altimeter Group and Web Analytics Demystified.

44. A. Ostrow (2011), Inside Gatorade Social Media Command Center. Available at: http://mashable.com/2010/06/15/gatorade-social-media-mission-control/.

45. Barry, Markey, Almquist and Brahm (2011).

46. These descriptions are based on: H. Albrecht (2011), Strategic Digital Marketing, November, presentation at School of Marketing, University of New South Wales.

47. For a more detailed discussion on social media ROI, see: O. Blanchard (2011), *Social Media ROI: Managing and Measuring Social Media Efforts in Your Organisation*, Indianapolis, Ind.: QUE Corporation/Pearson; A. Kaushik (2010), *Web Analytics 2.0: The Art of Online Accountability and Science of Customer Centricity*, Indianapolis, Ind.: Wiley; K. D. Paine (2011), *Measure What Matters: Online Tools for Understanding Customers, Social Media, Engagement, and Key Relationships*, Hoboken, NJ: Wiley; and J. Sterne (2010), *Social Media Metrics: How to Measure and Optimize Your Marketing Investment*, Hoboken, NJ: Wiley.

48. S. Corcoran (2009), Defining Owned, Earned, and Paid Media. Available at: http://blogs.forrester.com/interactive_marketing/2009/.

49. G. Shove (2012), The New PEO (Paid, Earned, Owned) Media Model. Available at: www.imediaconnection.com/content/29345.asp.

Chapter 6: Strategy development

1. E. Gummesson (2008), *Total Relationship Marketing*, 3rd edn., Oxford: Butterworth-Heinemann.
2. P. Sue and P. Morin (2001), A Strategic Framework for CRM. Available at: www.crm-forum.com.
3. R.S. Winer (2001), A Framework for Customer Relationship Management, *California Management Review*, Vol. 43, Summer, pp. 89–105.
4. See: D. Peppers and M. Rogers (2004), *Managing Customer Relationships: A Strategic Framework*, Hoboken, NJ: Wiley; and D. Peppers, M. Rogers and B. Dorf (1999), *The One to One Fieldbook: The Complete Guide for Implementing a 1 to 1 Marketing Program*, New York, NY: Doubleday.
5. F. A. Buttle (2001), The CRM Value Chain, *Marketing Business*, February, pp. 52–55.
6. M. Porter (1985), *Competitive Advantage*, New York, NY: The Free Press.
7. J. Radcliffe, J. Kirkby and E. Thompson (2001), The Eight Building Blocks of CRM, Decision Framework Research Note, DF-14–2111, Gartner Inc., 17 August.
8. N. Woodcock, M. Stone and B. Foss (2003), *The Customer Management Scorecard: Managing CRM for Profit*, London: Kogan Page.
9. R.K. Srivastava, T.A. Shervani and L. Fahey (1999), Marketing, Business Processes, and Shareholder Value: An Organisationally Embedded View of Marketing Activities and the Discipline of Marketing, *Journal of Marketing*, Vol. 63 (Special Issue), pp. 168–179.
10. E. Gummesson (2002), Practical Value of Adequate Marketing Management Theory, *European Journal of Marketing*, Vol. 36, March, pp. 325–49.
11. A. Payne and P. Frow (2005), A Strategic Framework for CRM, *Journal of Marketing*, Vol. 69, No. 4, pp. 167–176. The 32 companies referred to below include organisations from B2B manufacturing (5), B2B services (5), retailing (4), financial services (3), FMCG (3), telecommunications (2), professional services (2), pharmaceuticals (2), travel and tourism services (2), airlines (1), an industry association (1), a global charity (1) and a performing arts company (1).
12. R. Norman and R. Ramirez (1993), From Value Chain to Value Constellation: Designing Interactive Strategy, *Harvard Business Review*, July/August, pp. 65–77.
13. I. McDonald Wood (2011), What is Strategic Capability? FutureValue Strategic Value Research Programme. Available at: www.futurevalue.co.uk/future-value-about-us-team.html.
14. M. McDonald, P. Frow and A. Payne (2011), *Marketing Plans for Service Businesses*, Chichester: Wiley.
15. H. Davidson (2002), *The Committed Enterprise*, Oxford: Butterworth-Heinemann. The following discussion on vision and values is based on his work.
16. M. E. Porter (2002), Strategy and the Internet, *Harvard Business Review*, March, pp. 63–78.
17. M. E. Porter (1980), *Competitive Strategy*, New York, NY: The Free Press. Also see an updated description of his framework: M. E. Porter (2008), The Five Competitive Forces that Shape Strategy, *Harvard Business Review*, January, pp. 78–93.
18. S. F. Slater and E. M. Olson (2002), A Fresh Look at Industry and Market Analysis, *Business Horizons*, January–February, pp. 15–22.
19. G. Stonehouse and B. Snowdon (2007), Competitive Advantage Revisited: Michael Porter on Strategy and Competitiveness, *Journal of Management Inquiry*, Vol. 16, No. 3, pp. 256–273.
20. C. M. Christensen, J. H. Grossman and J. Hwang (2008), *The Innovator's Prescription: A Disruptive Solution for Health Care*, New York, NY: McGraw-Hill.

21. C. M. Christensen, M. B. Horn and C. Johnson (2008), *Disrupting Class: How Disruptive Innovation Will Change the Way the World Learns*, New York, NY: McGraw-Hill.

22. A. M. Brandenburger and B. J. Nalebuff (1997), *Co-opetition: A Revolution Mindset that Combines Competition and Game Theory Strategy that's Changing the Game of Business*, New York, NY: Doubleday.

23. Porter (1985).

24. E. Kim and D. Nam and J. L. Stimpert (2004), The Applicability of Porter's Generic Strategies in the Digital Age: Assumptions, Conjectures, and Suggestions, *Journal of Management*, Vol. 30, No. 5, pp. 569–589.

25. J. A. Parnell (2006), Generic Strategies after 2 Decades: A Reconceptualisation of Competitive Strategy, *Management Decision*, Vol. 44, No. 8, pp. 1139–1154.

26. M. Treacy and F. Wiersema (1995), *The Discipline of Market Leaders*, London: Harper Collins.

27. Treacy and Wiersema (1995).

28. C. Bowman (2008), Generic Strategies: A Substitute for Thinking?, *360–The Ashridge Journal*, Spring, pp. 6–11.

29. W. C. Kim and R. Mauborgne (2000), *Blue Ocean Strategy: How to Create Uncontested Market Space and Make the Competition Irrelevant*, Boston, MA: Harvard Business School Press.

30. This discussion and diagram are based on M. Rubin (1997), Creating Customer Oriented Companies, *Prism*, Fourth Quarter, pp. 5–28.

31. See: D. Peppers and M. Rogers (1993), *The One-to-One Future; Building Relationships One Customer at a Time*, New York, NY: Currency Doubleday; and D. Peppers and M. Rogers (2008), *Rules to Break and Laws to Follow*, Hoboken, NJ: Wiley.

32. S. Godin (1999), *Permission Marketing: Turning Strangers into Friends, and Friends into Customers*, New York, NY: Simon & Schuster.

33. S. Godin (2009), Ten Years of Permission Marketing. Available at: http://sethgodin.typepad.com/seths_blog/2009/05/ten-years-of-permission-marketing.html.

34. B. J. Pine (1992), *Mass Customization: The New Frontier in Business Competition*, Boston, MA: Harvard Business School Press. Also see: F. Salvador, P. M. de Holan and F. T. Piller (2009), Cracking the Code of Mass Customisation, *MIT Sloan Management Review*, Vol. 50, No. 3, pp. 71–78.

35. A. M. Kaplan and M. Haenlein (2006), Toward a Parsimonious Definition of Traditional and Electronic Mass Customisation, *Journal of Product Innovation Management*, Vol. 23, pp. 168–182.

36. B. J. Pine, D. Peppers and M. Rogers (1995), Do You Want to Keep Your Customers Forever?, *Harvard Business Review*, March/April, pp. 103–114.

37. M. McDonald and I. Dunbar (2010), *Market Segmentation*, Oxford: Goodfellow Publishing. Also see: C. Bailey, P. R. Baines, H. Wilson and M. Clark (2009), Segmentation and Customer Insight in Contemporary Services Marketing Practice: Why Grouping Customers is no Longer Enough, *Journal of Marketing Management*, Vol. 25, Issue 3/4, pp. 219–396.

38. J. Abbott, M. Stone and F. Buttle (2001), Customer Relationship Management in Practice – A Qualitative Study, *Journal of Database Management*, Vol. 9, No. 1, pp. 24–34.

39. S. Deck (2001), Learning Curve. Previously available at: www.darwinmag.com/learn/curve/column.html?ArticleID=104.

40. See: P. Frow and A. Payne (2009), Customer Relationship Management: A Strategic Perspective, *Journal of Business Market Management*, Vol. 3, No. 1, pp. 7–28.

41. H. Wilson, R. Street and L. Bruce (2008), *The Multichannel Challenge: Integrating Customer Experiences for Profit*, Oxford: Butterworth-Heinemann.

Chapter 7: Enterprise value creation

1. This chapter draws on: A. Payne and P. Frow (2013), The Value Creation Process in Customer Relationship Management, draft working paper, Australian School of Business, University of New South Wales.

2. This section draws on M. Christopher and H. Peck (2003), *Marketing Logistics*, 2nd edn., Oxford: Butterworth-Heinemann.

3. D. Peppers and M. Rogers (2004), *Managing Customer Relationships: A Strategic Framework*, Hoboken, NJ: Wiley, pp. 113–135.

4. A. Al-Sunaidy and R. Green (2006), Electricity Deregulation in OECD (Organisation for Economic Cooperation and Development) Countries, *Energy*, Vol. 31, Issue 6/7, pp. 769–787.

5. This example is from A. Payne (2006), *The Handbook of CRM: Achieving Excellence in Customer Management*, Oxford: Elsevier Butterworth-Heinemann.

6. This diagram is based on data from Bain & Co.

7. F. F. Reichheld and W. E. Sasser (1990), Zero Defections: Quality Comes to Services, *Harvard Business Review*, September/October, pp. 105–111.

8. For discussion see: M. Christopher, A. Payne and D. Ballantyne (2002), *Relationship Marketing: Creating Stakeholder Value*, Oxford: Butterworth-Heinemann, pp. 56–57.

9. See: Payne (2006); and M. Clark and A. Payne (1997), Achieving Long-Term Customer Loyalty: A Strategic Approach, in Payne, A. (ed.), *Advances in Relationship Marketing*, London: Kogan Page, pp. 53–65.

10. R. W. T. Buchanan and C. D. Howell (1989), *Improving Performance by Using Best Demonstrated Practices*, London: Fellowship of Engineering.

11. M. Christopher (1994), Customer Service and Logistics Strategy, in Baker, M. (ed.), *The Marketing Book*, Oxford: Butterworth-Heinemann.

12. This section is based on A. Payne and P. Frow (2013), ACURA: A Framework for Value Creation, draft working paper, School of Marketing, University of New South Wales.

13. See: F. Reichheld (2006), *The Ultimate Question: Driving Good Profits and True Growth*, Boston, MA: Harvard Business School Press; and F. Reichheld (2003), The One Number You Need to Grow, *Harvard Business Review*, December, pp. 46–54.

14. T. L. Keiningham, B. Coill, T. W. Andreasssen and L. Aksoy (2007), A Longitudinal Examination of Net Promoter and Financial Revenue Growth, *Journal of Marketing*, Vol. 71, July, pp. 39–51.

15. L. Ryals (2008), *Managing Customers Profitably*, Chichester: Wiley.

16. D. Peppers and M. Rogers (1993), *The One-to-One Future; Building Relationships One Customer at a Time*, London: Piatkus, pp. 41–42.

17. R. C. Blattberg, G. Getz and J. S. Thomas (2001), *Customer Equity*, Boston, MA: Harvard Business School Press, ch. 2. Also see: M. Page, L. Pitt, P. Berthon and A. Money (1996), Analysing Customer Defections and their Effects on Corporate Performance: The Case of Indco, *Journal of Marketing Management*, Vol. 12, pp. 617–627.
18. Ryals (2008).
19. S. L. Vargo and R. F. Lusch (2006), Service-Dominant Logic: What It Is, What It Is Not, What It Might Be, in Lusch R. F. and Vargo S. L. (eds.), *The Service Dominant Logic of Marketing: Dialog, Debate and Directions*, Armonk, NY: M.E. Sharpe, pp. 43–56.
20. Vargo and Lusch (2006).
21. This section draws on: A. Payne, K. Storbacka and P. Frow (2008), Managing the Co-Creation of Value, *Journal of the Academy of Marketing Science*, Vol. 36, No. 1, pp. 83–96.
22. K. Storbacka and J. R. Lehtinen (2001), *Customer Relationship Management: Creating Competitive Advantage through Win-Win Relationship Strategies*, Singapore: McGraw-Hill.
23. J. Langhout, R. Brinkhorst and I. Thijssen (2010), *Co-creation Beyond the Hype: Results of the Global Co-creation Survey 2010*, Utrecht, Netherlands: Cap Gemini.

Chapter 8: Multi-channel integration

1. P. Kotler (1997), *Marketing Management: Analysing, Planning, Implementation and Control*, Englewood Cliffs, NJ: Prentice Hall, 1997, p. 45.
2. A. M. Chircu and R. J. Kauffman (1999), Strategies for Internet Middlemen in the Intermediation / Disintermediation / Reintermediation Cycle, *Electronic Markets – The International Journal of Electronic Commerce and Business Media*, Vol. 9, No. 2, pp. 109–117.
3. B. A. Johnson (2000), Fault Lines in CRM: New E-Commerce Business Models and Channel Integration Issues, in *Defying the Limits*, Andersen Consulting.
4. M. McDonald and I. Dunbar (2010), *Market Segmentation: How to Do It, How to Profit from It*, Oxford: Goodfellow Publishing.
5. A. Payne and P. Frow (2005), A Strategic Framework for CRM, *Journal of Marketing*, Vol. 69, No. 4, pp. 167–176.
6. This table and sections of this chapter draw on: A. Payne and P. Frow (2012), The Multi-channel Integration Process in CRM, draft working paper, University of New South Wales, Sydney.
7. See, as just one of very many examples: C. Kermond (2011), Vodafone Faces Fines after Formal Complaints, *Sydney Morning Herald*, 21 December.
8. B. Rosenbloom (2012), *Marketing Channels: A Management View*, 8th edn., Mason, OH: South-Western.
9. McKinsey & Co. and Salomon Smith Barney Study (2002), Summary reported in press release on McKinsey website: www.mckinsey.com.
10. M. Christopher, A. Payne and D. Ballantyne (2002), *Relationship Marketing: Creating Stakeholder Value*, Oxford: Butterworth-Heinemann.
11. K. Storbacka (2001), Customer Relationships as Assets: Evaluating the Impact of CRM on your Organisation's Profitability and Shareholder Value, in *Profitable Customer Relationship Management Strategies*, ICBI Management Report, pp. 23–32.
12. S. Vandermerwe (2000), How Increasing Value to Customers Improves Business Results, *Sloan Management Review*, Vol. 42, pp. 27–37.

13. Z. Maamar, N. Faci, S. K. Mostéfaoui and F. Akhter (2011), Towards a Framework for Weaving Social Networks into Mobile Commerce, *International Journal of Systems and Service-Oriented Engineering*, Vol. 2, Issue 3, pp. 26–31.

14. Webloyalty (2010), Driving Sales from Social Networks and mCommerce is the 2010 Challenge, *Webloyalty etail Strategy Summit 2010 Event*. Available at: www.webloyalty.co.uk/news-a-research/2-press-releases-2010/14-webloyalty-etail-strategy-summit-2010-event-summary.

15. T. Jones and W. E. Sasser (1995), Why Satisfied Customers Defect, *Harvard Business Review*, November/December, pp. 88–99.

16. B. Farb (2011), Mobile Commerce: The New Retail Therapy, *CRM Magazine*, Vol. 15, No. 7, p. 1.

17. Farb (2011).

18. E. Gummesson (2002), Relationship Marketing in the New Economy, *Journal of Relationship Marketing*, Vol. 1, No. 1, pp. 37–57.

19. H. Wilson and M. McDonald (2001), Serving Customers through Multiple Channels, in Rock, S. (ed.), *Unlocking Customer Value*, London: CBI Business Guide/Caspian Publishing, pp. 19–25.

20. Wilson and McDonald (2001).

21. H. Wilson, R. Street and L. Bruce (2008), *The Multichannel Challenge: Integrating Customer Experiences for Profit*, Oxford: Butterworth-Heinemann.

22. K. Qamar (2011), From Multiple Channels to Integrated Multichannel Selling, *Red Queen Effect*. Available at: http://kamraan.com/marketing-srategies/cracking-the-code/from-multiple-channels-to-integrated-multichannel-selling.

23. McKinsey & Co. and Salomon Smith & Barney (2000), Amid E-tail Shakeout, New Study Highlights Viable E-tail Business Model, 22 August, www.atmckinsey.com.

24. See for example: R. Soudagar, V. Iyer and V. Hildebrand (2011), *The Customer Experience Edge: Technology and Techniques for Delivering an Enduring, Profitable and Positive Experience to Your Customers*, New York, NY: McGraw-Hill; C. Shaw, Q. Dibeehi and S. Walden (2010), *Customer Experience: Future Trends and Insights*, Basingstoke: Macmillan; M. Wilburn (2007), *Managing the Customer Experience: A Measurement-Based Approach*, Milwaukee, Wis.: ASQ Quality Press; and B. H. Schmitt (2003), *Customer Experience Management: A Revolutionary Approach to Connecting with Your Customers*, Hoboken, NJ: Wiley.

25. See: www.market-bridge.com.

26. See: www.market-bridge.com.

Chapter 9: Information and technology management

1. For a succinct review, see: N. Arora, X. Dreze, A. Ghose, J. D. Hess, R. Iyengar, B. Jing and Y. Joshi (2008), Putting One-To-One Marketing to Work: Personalisation, Customisation, and Choice, *Marketing Letters*, Vol. 19, pp. 305–321.

2. R. S. Swift (2001), *Accelerating Customer Relationships: Using CRM and Relationship Technologies*, Upper Saddle River, NJ: Prentice Hall.

3. R. Laberge (2011), *The Data Warehouse Mentor: Practical Data Warehouse and Business Intelligence Insights*, New York, NY: McGraw-Hill.

4. M. Golfarelli and S. Rizzi (2009), *Data Warehouse Design: Modern Principles and Methodologies*, New York, NY: McGraw-Hill.

5. P. Ponniah (2010), *Data Warehousing Fundamentals for IT Professionals*, Hoboken, NJ: Wiley.

6. R. Kimball, M. Ross, W. Thornthwaite, J. Mundy and B. Becker (2008), *The Data Warehouse Lifecycle Toolkit*, 2nd edn., Indianapolis, Ind.: Wiley. Available at: http://en.wikipedia.org/wiki/Special:BookSources/0471200247.

7. J. Han, M. Kamber and J. Pei (2012), *Data Mining: Concepts and Techniques*, 3rd edn., Waltham, MA: Morgan Kaufmann Publishers.

8. K. Tsiptsis and A. Chorianopoulos (2010), *Data Mining Techniques in CRM: Inside Customer Segmentation*, Chichester: Wiley.

9. For a more detailed discussion see: M. McDonald and I. Dunbar (2010), *Market Segmentation*, Oxford: Goodfellow Publishing; and S. Dibb and L. Simkin (2008), *Market Segmentation Success*, London: Routledge.

10. This discussion is based on: Jericho Forum (2009), *Cloud Cube Model: Selecting Cloud Formations for Secure Collaboration*, The Open Group, April.

11. M. Benion and C. Adler (2009), *Behind the Cloud: The Untold Story of How Salesforce.com Went from Idea to Billion-Dollar Company and Revolutionized an Industry*, San Francisco, CA: Jossey Bass.

12. G. Reese (2009), *Cloud Application Architectures: Building Applications and Infrastructure in the Cloud*, Sebastopol, CA: O'Reilly Media.

13. J. Rhoton (2011), *Cloud Computing Architected: Solution Design Handbook*, Tunbridge Wells: Recursive Press.

14. See: M. Gentle (2002), *The CRM Project Management Handbook*. London: Kogan Page; and J. Dyche (2002), *The CRM Handbook – A Business Guide to Customer Relationship Management*, Upper Saddle River, NJ: Addison-Wesley.

15. G. Findlay, M. Stone, M. Leonard, M. Evans and B. McEnroe (2002), Data Protection, in Foss, B. and Stone, M. (eds.), *CRM in Financial Services – A Practical Guide to Making Customer Relationship Management Work*, London: Kogan Page.

16. Findlay, Stone, Leonard, Evans and McEnroe (2002).

17. J. C. Edwards (2008), Data Protection: Where Are We Now? *Database Marketing & Customer Strategy Management*, Vol. 15, No. 4, pp. 285–292.

18. Edwards (2008).

19. Edwards (2008).

20. E. Kosta and C. Kalloniati (2010), Data Protection Issues Pertaining to Social Networking under EU Law, *Transforming Government: People, Process and Policy*, Vol. 4, No. 2, pp. 193–201.

21. Kosta and Kalloniati (2010).

22. P. Carey and P. Carey (2009), *Data Protection: a Practical Guide to UK and EU Law*, Oxford: Oxford University Press.

Chapter 10: Performance assessment

1. See: J. L. Heskett and W. E. Sasser Jr. (2010), The Service Profit Chain: From Satisfaction to Ownership, in Maglio, P., Kieliszewski, C. and Spohrer, J. (eds.), *Handbook of Service Science, Service Science: Research and Innovations in the Service Economy*, New York, NY: Springer, part 1, pp. 19–29.

2. F. F. Reichheld (1996), *The Loyalty Effect*, Boston, MA: Harvard Business School Press.

3. P. Bierbusse and T. Siesfeld (1997), Measures that Matter, *Journal of Strategic Performance Management*, Vol. 1, No. 2, pp. 6–11.

4. J. McKean (1999), *Information Masters – Secrets of the Customer Race*, New York, NY: Wiley.

5. See: I. Cornelius and M. Davies (1997), *Shareholder Value*, London: FT Financial Publishing; and M. Davies, G. Arnold, I. Cornelius and S. Walmsley (2002), *Strategic Focus on Managing for Shareholder Value: A Comprehensive Guide to Creating Value for Shareholders*, London: LLP Professional Publishing. Also see: P. W. Kontes (2010), *The CEO, Strategy, and Shareholder Value: Making the Choices that Maximize Company Performance*, Hoboken, NJ: Wiley.

6. R. Myers (1996), Metric wars, *CFO*, Vol. 12, No. 10, pp. 44–50.

7. Cornelius and Davies (1997).

8. D. Venanzi (2012), *Financial Performance Measures and Value Creation: the State of the Art*, Berlin: Springer (see chapter, 'The Metric War', pp. 33–60).

9. R. Monks and A. Lajoux (2011), *Corporate Valuation for Portfolio Investment: Analyzing Assets, Earnings, Cash Flow, Stock Price, Governance, and Special Situations*, Hoboken, NJ: Wiley.

10. Reichheld (1996).

11. McKean (1999), p. 31.

12. See: www.thecustomerframework.com.

13. See: www.copc.com.

14. M. Cutler and J. Sterne (2000), *E-Metrics: Business Metrics for the New Economy*. NetGenesis and Target Marketing. Also see: A. Kaushik (2010), *Web Analytics 2.0: The Art of Online Accountability and Science of Customer Centricity*, Indianapolis, Ind.: Wiley.

15. Mzinga, Inc. (2009), Survey: Social Software in Business, Waltham, MA: Mzinga, Inc. Available at: www.mzinga.com/communities/resources.asp?pagen=1.

16. Ranson Consulting (2011), The 10 Social Media Metrics Your Company Should Monitor. Available at: http://ranson.co/blog/social-media/the-10-social-media-metrics-your-company-should-monitor.

17. J. Sterne (2010), *Social Media Metrics: How to Measure and Optimize Your Marketing Investment*, Hoboken, NJ: Wiley.

18. T. P. Novak and D. L. Hoffman (1997), New Metrics for New Media: Toward the Development of Web Measurement Standards, *World Wide Web Journal*, Vol. 2, No. 1, pp. 213–246.

19. J. Lovett (2011), *Social Media Metrics Secrets*, Indianapolis, Ind.: Wiley.

20. M. Sponder (2012), *Social Media Analytics: Effective Tools for Building, Interpreting, and Using Metrics*, New York, NY: McGraw-Hill.

21. O. Blanchard (2011), *Social Media ROI: Managing and Measuring Social Media Efforts in Your Organisation*, Indianapolis, Ind.: QUE Corporation/Pearson.

22. T. Ambler (2004), *Marketing and the Bottom Line*, 2nd edn., London: FT/Prentice Hall.

23. R. S. Kaplan and D. P. Norton (1996), *The Balanced Scorecard: Translating Strategy into Action*, Boston, MA: Harvard Business School Press. Also see: J. Creelman and N. Makhijani, (2011), *Creating a Balanced Scorecard for a Financial Services Organisation*, Singapore: Wiley and G. Cokins (2010), The Promise and Perils of the Balanced

Scorecard, *Journal of Corporate Accounting & Finance*, Vol. 21, Issue 3, pp. 19–28. Most discussion of the balanced scorecard relates to commercial enterprises. For a review of the application of the balanced scorecard concept in the non-profit sector, see: P. R. Niven (2008), *Balanced Scorecard: Step-by-Step for Government and Nonprofit Agencies*, Hoboken, NJ: Wiley.

24. J. L. Heskett, W. E. Sasser Jr. and L. A. Schlesinger (1997), *The Service Profit Chain*, New York, NY: The Free Press. Also see: J. L. Heskett, W. E. Sasser Jr. and J. Wheeler (2008), *The Ownership Quotient: Putting the Service Profit Chain to Work for Unbeatable Competitive Advantage*, New York, NY: The Free Press.

25. R. S. Kaplan and D. P. Norton (2004), *Strategy Maps: Converting Intangible Assets into Tangible Outcomes*, Boston, MA: Harvard Business School Press.

26. A. Neely, C. Adams and M. Kennerley (2002), *The Performance Prism: The Scorecard for Stakeholder Relationship Management*, London: FT/Prentice Hall. Also see: E. Barrows and A. Neely (2011), *Managing Performance in Turbulent Times: Analytics and Insight*, Hoboken, NJ: Wiley.

27. A. J. Rucci, S. P. Kirn and R. T. Quinn (1998), The Employee Customer Profit Chain at Sears, *Harvard Business Review*, January/February, pp. 83–97.

28. A. Neely (2002), Measuring Business Performance, presentation at Cranfield University, April.

29. W. W. Eckerson (2010), *Performance Dashboards: Measuring, Monitoring, and Managing Your Business*, Hoboken, NJ: Wiley.

30. H. Kerzner (2011), *Project Management Metrics, KPIs, and Dashboards: A Guide to Measuring and Monitoring Project Performance*, Hoboken, NJ: Wiley.

31. K. Pauwels, T. Ambler, B. Clark, P. LaPointe, D. J. Reibstein, B. Skiera, B. Wierenga and W. T. Thorsten (2008), *Dashboards & Marketing: Why, What, How and Which Research is Needed?*, Cambridge, MA: Marketing Science Institute. Also see: J. A. Petersen, L. McAlister, D. J. Reibstein, R. S. Winer, V. Kumar and G. Atkinson (2009), Choosing the Right Metrics to Maximise Profitability and Shareholder Value, *Journal of Retailing*, Vol. 85, No. 1, pp. 95–111.

32. N. Woodcock (2000), Does How Customers are Managed Impact on Business Performance? *Interactive Marketing*, Vol. 1, No. 4, pp. 375–389.

33. L. J. Ryals, S. D. Knox and S. Maklan (2000), *Customer Relationship Management: The Business Case for CRM*, London: FT/Prentice Hall.

34. M. Reimann, O. Schilke and J. S. Thomas (2010), Customer Relationship Management and Firm Performance: The Mediating Role of Business Strategy, *Journal of the Academy of Marketing Science*, Vol. 38, pp. 326–346.

35. E. Holger, W. D. Hoyer, M. Krafft and K. Krieger (2011), Customer Relationship Management and Company Performance: The Mediating Role of New Product Performance, *Journal of the Academy of Marketing Science*, Vol. 39, No. 2, pp. 290–306.

36. W. Boulding, R. Staelin, M. Ehret and W. Johnston (2005), A Customer Relationship Management Roadmap: What is Known, Potential Pitfalls, and Where to Go, *Journal of Marketing*, Vol. 69, No. 4, pp. 155–167.

Chapter 11: Organising for implementation

1. J. N. Sheth and A. Parvatiyar (2001), Evolving Relationship Marketing into a Discipline, *Journal of Relationship Marketing*, Vol. 1, No. 1, pp. 3–16.

2. P. Frow and A. Payne (2009), Customer Relationship Management: A Strategic Perspective, *Journal of Business Market Management*, Vol. 3, No. 1, pp. 7–28.

3. P. Shukla (2010), Relationship Marketing and CRM, in Bidgoli, H. (ed.), *The Handbook of Technology Management, Volume 2: Supply Chain Management, Marketing and Advertising, and Global Management*, Hoboken, NJ: Wiley, pp. 462–472.

4. J. Egan (2008), *Relationship Marketing: Exploring Relational Strategies in Marketing*, 3rd edn., Harlow: FT/Prentice Hall.

5. D. Mitussis, L. O'Malley and M. Patterson (2005), Mapping the Reengagement of CRM with Relationship Marketing, *European Journal of Marketing*, Vol. 40, Nos. 5/6, pp. 572–589.

6. E. Gummesson (2008), *Total Relationship Marketing*, 3rd edn., Oxford: Butterworth-Heinemann, p. 7.

7. Gummesson (2008), p. 339.

8. M. J. Harker and J. Egan (2006), The Past, Present and Future of Relationship Marketing, *Journal of Marketing Management*, Vol. 2, No. 1–2, pp. 215–242.

9. D. K. Rigby and B. Bilodeau (2011), *Management Tools and Trends 2011*, Boston, MA: Bain & Co.

10. M. Krigsman (2009), CRM Failure Rates: 2001–2009, *IT Project Failures*. Accessed at: www.zdnet.com/blog/projectfailures/crm-failure-rates-2001-2009/4967.

11. For example, see: R. Levitt (2009), IT Managers and Executives Share CRM Success Stories, Oracle Corporation, 13 October 2009. Accessed at: http://blogs.oracle.com/oraclopenworld/entry/executive_customer_panel_explo; and J. Van Der Linden (2010), Three Top Success Stories for Microsoft Dynamics CRM, InterDyn Artis. Accessed at: www.crmsoftwareblog.com/2010/09/three-top-success-stories-for-microsoft-dynamics-crm.

12. For example, see: L. Ryals (2005), Making Customer Relationship Management Work: The Measurement and Profitable Management of Customer Relationships, *Journal of Marketing*, Vol. 69, pp. 252–261; and F. Piskar and A. Faganel (2009), A Successful CRM Implementation Project in a Service Company: Case Study, *Organizacija*, Vol. 42, No. 5, pp. 199–208.

13. This section draws on P. Frow, A. Payne and A. Luong (2012), A Systematic Review of Correlates of Success in CRM Implementation, Working Paper, University of New South Wales.

14. For example, see: T. Bohling , D. Bowman, S. LaValle, V. Mittal, D. Narayandas, G. Ramani and R. Varadarajan (2006), CRM Effectiveness Issues and Insights, *Journal of Service Research*, Vol. 9, No. 2, pp. 184–194; B. Ramaseshan, D. Bejou, S. Jain, C. Mason and J. Pancras (2006), Issues and Perspectives in Global Customer Relationship Management, *Journal of Service Research*, Vol. 9, No. 2, pp. 195–207; S. F. King and T. F. Burgess (2008), Understanding Success and Failure in Customer Relationship Management, *Industrial Marketing Management*, Vol. 37, pp. 421–431; M. Reimann, O. Schilke and J. S. Thomas (2010), Customer Relationship Management and Firm Performance: The Mediating Role of Business Strategy, *Journal of the Academy of Marketing Science*, Vol. 38, No. 3, pp. 326–346;

and H. Ernst, W. Hoyer, M. Krafft and K. Krieger (2011), Customer Relationship Management and Company Performance – The Mediating Role of New Product Performance, *Journal of the Academy of Marketing Science*, Vol. 39, pp. 290–236.

15. Reimann, Schilke and Thomas (2010).

16. R. Eid (2007), Towards a Successful CRM Implementation in Banks: An Integrated Model, *Service Industries Journal*, Vol. 27, No. 8, pp. 1021–1039.

17. A. Osarenkhoe (2007), An Exploratory Study of Implementation of Customer Relationship Management Strategy, *Business Process Management Journal*, Vol. 13, No. 1, pp. 139–164.

18. D. Elmuti, H. Jia and D. Gray (2009), Customer Relationship Management Strategic Application and Organisational Effectiveness: An Empirical Investigation, *Journal of Strategic Marketing*, Vol. 17, No. 1, pp. 75–96.

19. D. J. Finnegan and W. L. Currie (2010), A Multi-Layered Approach to CRM Implementation: An Integration Perspective, *European Management Journal*, Vol. 28, No. 2, pp. 153–167.

20. King and Burgess (2008).

21. Eid (2007).

22. Elmuti, Jia and Gray (2009).

23. L. E. Mendoza, A. Marius, M. Pérez and A. C. Grimán (2007), Critical Success Factors for a Customer Relationship Management Strategy, *Information and Software Technology*, Vol. 49, pp. 913–945.

24. This discussion is partly based on A. Payne and P. Frow (2006), Customer Relationship Management: From Strategy to Implementation, *Journal of Marketing Management*, Vol. 22, Nos. 1/2, pp. 135–168.

25. L. Ryals and A. Payne (2001), Information Empowered Relationship Marketing: Leveraging Customer Information in Financial Services, *Journal of Strategic Marketing*, Vol. 9, pp. 1–25.

26. See: www.thecustomerframework.com.

27. See: R. H. Waterman, T. J. Peters and J. R. Phillips (1980), Structure is not Organisation, *Business Horizons*, June, pp. 14–16; and, T. Peters (2011), A Brief History of the 7-S ('McKinsey 7-S') Model. Accessed at: www.tompeters.com/dispatches/012016.php.

28. P. Child, R. S. Dennis, T. C. Gokey, T. McGuire, M. Sherman and M. Singer (1995), Can Marketing Regain the Personal Touch? *McKinsey Quarterly*, No. 3, pp. 112–125.

29. D. K. Rigby, F. F. Reichheld and P. Schefter (2002), Avoid the Four Perils of CRM, *Harvard Business Review*, February, pp. 101–109

30. H. Davidson (2002), *The Committed Enterprise*, Oxford: Butterworth-Heinemann.

31. N. Siragher (2001), *Carving Jelly: A Managers Reference to Implementing CRM*, High Wycombe: Chiltern Publishing International Ltd. Also see: D. Finnegan and L. P. Willcocks (2007), *Implementing CRM: From Technology to Knowledge*, Hoboken, NJ: Wiley.

32. G. Johnson (2002), Managing Strategic Change – Strategy, Culture and Action, *Long Range Planning*, Vol. 5, No. 1, pp. 28–36.

33. D. Shipley (1994), Achieving Cross Functional Coordination for Marketing Implementation, *Management Decision*, Vol. 32, No. 8, pp. 17–20.

34. R. J. Levene (2001), Project Management: Context and Processes, Cranfield School of Management, September.

35. See: H. Wilson, E. Daniel, M. McDonald, J. Ward and F. Sutherland (2000), *Profiting from eCRM*, London: FT/Prentice Hall; M. McDonald and H. Wilson (2002), *The New Marketing*, Oxford: Butterworth-Heinemann; and J.M. Ward and P. Murray (2000), Benefits Management Best Practice Guidelines, Cranfield School of Management.

36. Wilson, Daniel, McDonald, Ward and Sutherland (2000).

37. S.C.M. Henneberg (2003), An Exploratory Analysis of CRM Implementation Models, 11th International Colloquium in Relationship Marketing, University of Gloucestershire, September, pp. 1–20.

38. Henneberg (2003).

39. Henneberg (2003).

40. Henneberg (2003).

41. M. Ebner, A. Hu, D. Levitt and J. McCory (2002), How to Rescue CRM, *McKinsey Quarterly* (Special Edition: Technology), pp. 49–57.

42. M. Gentle (2002), *The CRM Project Management Handbook*, London: Kogan Page.

43. Estimate by Ed Thompson, Vice President and Research Director, Gartner.

44. Gentle (2002).

45. J. Dempsey, R. Dvorak, E. Holen, D. Mark and W. Meehan (1997), Escaping the IT Abyss, *The McKinsey Quarterly*, No. 4, pp. 80–91.

46. Gentle (2002).

47. Siragher (2001).

48. J. Dyche (2002), *The CRM Handbook – A Business Guide to Customer Relationship Management*, Upper Saddle River, NJ: Addison-Wesley.

49. Ebner, Hu, Levitt and McCory (2002).

50. K.J. Sweetman (2001), Employee Loyalty around the Globe, *MIT Sloan Management Review*, Winter, p. 16. This is based on: Walker Information Global Network, *Commitment in the Workplace: The 2000 Global Employee Relationship Benchmark Report* (2000).

51. J. McKean (2002), *Customers Are People: The Human Touch*, New York, NY: Wiley.

52. M. Clark (1999), Managing Recruitment and Internal Markets: A Relationship Marketing Perspective, draft working paper, Cranfield School of Management.

53. Gentle (2002).

54. Gentle (2002).

55. For three exceptions: see Siragher (2001), ch. 4; Gentle (2002), ch. 7; and Finnegan and Willcocks (2007).

56. T. Hult and J.A. Mena (2012), Market Orientation, Sustainability and Stakeholders, 41st EMAC Conference, Lisbon, May.

INDEX